Springer Biographies

More information about this series at http://www.springer.com/series/13617

Carl Baudenbacher

Judicial Independence

Memoirs of a European Judge

Springer

Carl Baudenbacher
Urumea AG
St. Gallen, Switzerland

ISSN 2365-0613 ISSN 2365-0621 (electronic)
Springer Biographies
ISBN 978-3-030-02307-2 ISBN 978-3-030-02308-9 (eBook)
https://doi.org/10.1007/978-3-030-02308-9

Library of Congress Control Number: 2018959253

This Springer imprint is published by the registered company Springer Nature Switzerland AG
The registered company address is: Gewerbestrasse 11, 6330 Cham, Switzerland

Preface

The present narrative is the product of the twenty-two and a half years I spent as a Judge on the EFTA Court, fifteen of which as the Court's President. It covers the creation of the EEA Agreement, which extended the EEC Single Market to the participating EFTA States in 1994, a process that has greatly affected millions of lives including my own. While the book is based on my experiences on the EFTA Court bench, much of what is discussed is relevant to international courts in general and to parties and participants appearing before them. I have sought throughout these reflections to make this distinct area of the law accessible to the widest audience possible.

The work's recurring theme is judicial independence and impartiality. According to general belief, independence is part and parcel of the role and function of a judge. International and European judges may, however, be placed in a difficult situation in that regard. Owing to the framework of their engagement, in particular their nomination by a government, the nature of their limited-term appointment and the possibility of reappointment, judicial independence may be at hazard. Certain governments have a record of choosing candidates who they believe may be kept on a leash. And they are not afraid to exert political influence. Private parties are at risk of losing out.

The book addresses how the EFTA Court developed from its foundation in Geneva as a court of five judges before its move to Luxembourg as a court of only three judges. I consider the alliance of today's participating EFTA States: Iceland, Liechtenstein and Norway, and the activities of the EFTA Surveillance Authority in its role as a partial analogue of the European Commission. Among the topics I broach are the most important features of the EEA Agreement, a *sui generis* treaty, which sits on the cusp of classic public international law and supranational EU law. Another particular aspect is that the EEA Agreement is a two-pillar treaty. Each pillar, the EU and the EFTA, is governed by its own, independent institutions, the European Commission and the ECJ on the one hand and the EFTA Surveillance Authority and the EFTA Court on the other. The EFTA Court has faced the task of deciding on crucial issues that were left open by the EEA Contracting Parties. To give a few examples, the Court has not recognised the principles of direct effect and of primacy found in EU law. And the preliminary reference procedure in the EFTA pillar leaves more power to the Member States and their courts than in the EU pillar.

Yet, in view of the principles of homogeneity, reciprocity and loyalty, the Court found State liability and fundamental rights to be part of EEA law. It has, importantly, remained faithful to specific EFTA values such as the belief in free trade and open markets or a modern image of man.

Homogeneity is one of the foremost principles of EEA law; its evolution has gone hand-in-hand with the growing strength of the Court. Homogeneity of the case law in the EEA as a whole can be achieved only through judicial dialogue. The relationship between the EFTA Court and the ECJ constitutes thus another focus of this book. As for the rest, the publication puts special emphasis on the substantive EEA Single Market law, the "beef", as I have come to call it. And since Single Market law is economic law, the importance of economics, often overlooked, will be underlined. Finally, I consider some of the pressing political and economic questions of modern times in Europe. I address Switzerland's complicated relationship with, and Britain's impending departure from, the European Union.

For important input and critical remarks, I am indebted to (in alphabetical order) Dr. Dr. Mads Andenæs, Professor at the University of Oslo and Director of the Centre of Financial and Commercial Law, IALS, at the University of London; my wife, Luxembourg publisher Dr. Doris Baudenbacher-Tandler; our daughter, Brussels attorney Dr. Laura Melusine Baudenbacher; University of Bristol Professor Dr. Dr. Eirik Bjorge; my former Head of Cabinet Michael-James Clifton; my former legal secretary Theresa Haas; the EFTA Court's former Registrar Skúli Magnússon, now a Judge on the Reykjavík District Court; Vaduz attorney Dr. Florian Marxer; my former PA Kerstin Schwiesow; the EFTA Court's Registrar Gunnar Selvik; and the director of legal and executive affairs of the EFTA Surveillance Authority Carsten Zatschler. It goes without saying that I bear sole responsibility for any mistakes this memoir may contain.

London, UK/Luxembourg/St. Gallen, Switzerland Carl Baudenbacher
June 2018

20 Year Anniversary Reception with Doris and Laura Melusine

Prologue

The EEA

From 1995 to 2018 I, a Swiss national, served as the judge nominated by the Principality of Liechtenstein on the Court of Justice of the European Free Trade Association (EFTA) States that are party to the European Economic Area (EEA) Agreement, more commonly referred to as the EFTA Court. I was the Court's President for 15 years, from January 2003 to December 2017. The EFTA States which are part of the EEA are Iceland, Liechtenstein and Norway. The EEA Agreement (also "EEA" or "Agreement") is a multilateral treaty concluded by the European Union (EU) and its Member States on the one hand and the three EFTA States on the other. It is based on a two-pillar structure whereby each pillar, EU and EEA/EFTA, is governed by its own institutions. In the EU pillar, there are the Commission and the Court of Justice of the European Union (ECJ); their counterparts in the EFTA pillar are the EFTA Surveillance Authority (ESA) and the EFTA Court. The EFTA Court is, thus, closely linked to its sister court, the ECJ. It is part of an exceptional legal framework that was unprecedented at the time of its creation and has since developed into a unique form of integration. The purpose of the EEA is to integrate Iceland, Liechtenstein and Norway in the Single Market, but not in the EU customs union. The three EEA/EFTA States have thus retained their sovereignty with regard to foreign trade.

For centuries, international treaty law was not enforced by the courts. In later times, the application of treaties was left in the hands of the national tribunals of the contracting parties. Under most agreements, this is still the case. Nevertheless, in the twentieth century an evolution began which came to be called the "proliferation of international courts and tribunals". After the three big revolutions—the collapse of the old world order in 1918 at the end of World War I, the victory of the Allies in 1945 in World War II and the end of the Cold War in 1989—a number of international courts were established. The EFTA Court is, like the World Trade Organization (WTO) Appellate Body, a child of the post-Cold War period.

The Definition of Independence—Being off Leash

According to the Encyclopedia Britannica, judicial independence is

> "the ability of courts and judges to perform their duties free of influence or control by other actors, whether governmental or private".

Similar definitions can be found in other reference works. The opposite term of judicial independence is judicial dependence. A dependent judge is not free, he/she is kept on a leash. According to the Cambridge Dictionary, a leash is

> "a piece of rope, chain, etc. tied to an animal, especially to a dog at its collar when taking it for a walk".

Merriam-Webster defines a leash as

> "a line for leading or restraining an animal" and as "something that restrains" or "the state of being restrained".

There are, however, also leashes for humans. The Romans used to lead captives like dogs on a leash. Toddlers are sometimes restrained by similar devices, although their use is controversial. Other examples include electronic systems that allow the surveillance of children or the elderly in the home. The expression that somebody or something is kept on a leash is also frequently used figuratively. In certain political systems, the media are kept on a leash. Political parties may be restrained by strict regulations. Adolescents are said to be kept on a tight or short leash by parents and educators, meaning that they are watched closely and often subject to curfews. The same may apply to students, soldiers, spouses, employees or bureaucrats, just to give a few examples. It seems that human coexistence almost always implies the dependence of one group on another such that the former are controlled by the latter.

However, one category of humans that should never be leashed by anybody are the judges. This was, in principle, guaranteed in the English Act of Settlement in 1701, which British lawyers proudly count as a first. The judges' appointments were valid as long as they exhibited good behaviour ("*quamdiu se bene gesserint*"). If they did not behave, they could be removed only by resolutions of both Houses of Parliament. But they could not be sacked at the pleasure of the appointing authority ("*durante bene placito*"). That was a powerful guarantee for the rule of law. Today, the independence of judges is deemed to be an indispensable element of the judicial system in Western democracies. And yet, the question arises as to whether this principle also applies to European judges. Or are they in reality kept on the leash of the government to which they owe their nomination? The present book describes my own experiences in this field.

The Independence of the European Judiciary

Candidates for European judgeships (as for judgeships of international courts in general) are nominated by the individual governments and appointed by common accord of those governments. This is also the case in the EFTA Court. The relevant provisions[1] underline the need for independence. However, since appointment is for a 6-year term with the possibility of reappointment or non-reappointment, the judges are vulnerable. The EFTA governments are regular ("repeat") players in cases before the court, whose judges they themselves pick. They have vested interests in most of the proceedings. The same goes for the governments of the EU States as regards the Court of Justice of the EU. Those who choose the candidates for judgeship may thus be tempted to opt for a safe pair of hands. I have frequently witnessed governments in both EEA pillars nominating candidates that they thought they could keep on a rather short leash. Such judges are sometimes referred to as political appointees. They are expected to look to their capital at least in cases in which their government has a major legal or economic stake. Whether they do so or not is another matter. If a government decides not to appoint a candidate or not to reappoint a sitting judge, it doesn't need to give reasons.

My independence was respected by the Liechtenstein Government. I was renominated and reappointed three times. In fact, I was in a one-off situation when it came to independence. First, I am the only judge in the history of the Union courts and of the EFTA Court who wasn't a national of the Member State that nominated him or her to the bench. I did not grow up in Liechtenstein; I did not go to school there and am not part of its day-to-day life. I have never lived in Liechtenstein and did not spend my weekends and holidays there with childhood friends or former colleagues. I maintained a safe distance from politicians and senior civil servants and I did not meet with domestic Liechtenstein judges any more often than with their colleagues from Norway and Iceland. Second, I was an academic with an international background and a national judge when I was first appointed to the EFTA Court bench. I did not have a past as a civil servant. From 1990 to 1994, I was the lead consultant for the Liechtenstein Government on EEA matters, however the Government itself never employed me. I performed my work as an independent expert on the basis of a mandate. Third, I made it a condition when accepting the nomination to become an EFTA Court judge that I could keep my chair and my position as a Director of the Institute of European and International Law at the University of St. Gallen (HSG) in Switzerland, albeit with a reduced teaching load. This turned out to be an advantage in more than one respect. HSG enjoys quite a reputation. There was and is no institution of higher education on the same level in the three EEA/EFTA States. Most importantly, my St. Gallen position was my fall back option should I not be reappointed after my first 6 years

[1] In the case of the EFTA Court, the first paragraph of Article 30 of the Agreement between the EFTA States on the establishment of a surveillance authority and a Court of Justice (Surveillance and Court Agreement, SCA).

as a judge. Thereafter, it continued to be my alternative option, in particular when a foreign government took the unparalleled step of blocking my reappointment in 2007. I never had to worry about what I would do if not reappointed. In other words, I could not be kept on anyone's leash.

This Book's Content

After brief remarks on my life prior to the EFTA Court, this book explains how I became the Liechtenstein Government's leading advisor during the EEA negotiations and then the Liechtenstein judge of the EFTA Court. It recounts my difficult start as a judge in September 1995. The EFTA Court had been planned to comprise seven judges, it took up its functions on 1 January 1994 with five judges and, on 30 June 1995, it was downsized to three judges. The downsizing was a momentous event. From then on, the EFTA pillar was imbalanced by the presence of a superpower, Norway. Another decisive change was the Court's move from Geneva to Luxembourg in 1996. The EFTA Court is probably the only international court in the world whose headquarters are not located in one of its Member States, but on foreign soil. However, the important thing was that, from then on, we were geographically close to our sister court, the ECJ.

A whole Chapter will be dedicated to the most significant characteristic of the EEA Agreement, the two-pillar system. The treaty has created one economic area with two separate legal orders. The law in those two systems is largely identical in substance, but its interpretation and application lies in the hands of two courts that are independent from each other. Special emphasis will be placed on the structure of the EEA courts and the background of their members.

The five-member Court, which was in office from 1 January 1994 until 30 June 1995, had with its case law laid a solid foundation for the future. At the same time, the five-member Court was divided over the very role that the EFTA Court was to play. This division could be felt for a number of years.

The book will also describe the political and economic systems of the three EEA/EFTA States, including their social models. It will then deal with the tasks and the performance of ESA. For obvious reasons, a special focus will be on the composition of ESA and on its presidency. A Chapter will discuss the preliminary reference procedure in the EFTA pillar. As regards methods of interpretation, the book will concentrate less on high theory than on what is going on in reality. A genuine war was fought over the question of whether, and if so to what extent, the so-called constitutional principles of EU law—direct effect, primacy, State liability and the principle of conform interpretation which requires national courts to interpret national law consistently with EU law—should be deemed to be part of EEA law as applied in the EFTA pillar by the EFTA Court. In that context, it is also important to note that the EFTA Court held that EEA law must be interpreted in the light of the European Convention on Human Rights (ECHR) and of the case law of the European Court of Human Rights (ECtHR).

From the very beginning, the EFTA Court faced difficult questions of substantive EEA Single Market law. However, the discourse in academic literature and at conferences was from the outset dominated by fear on the part of EFTA constitutional lawyers, public international law scholars and political scientists that the institutions of the EFTA pillar, ESA and the EFTA Court, would unduly interfere with Members States' sovereignty. This concern was, and still is, particularly widespread in Norway, where the government and large parts of academia have stuck to orthodox dualism. Dualism perceives EEA law and domestic law as two separate bodies of law. EEA law is not seen as being able to produce by itself any effect in the domestic legal order. According to dualist belief, it may be invoked in domestic courts only if it has been implemented into domestic law. The same preoccupation was present in Iceland; but there the situation eased off several years ago. Liechtenstein, being a monist State, took from the beginning a more positive attitude towards the EEA and the institutions of the EFTA pillar. Monism sees international law as part of domestic law.

Until 2011, the Court's case load was small. But from 2011 onwards, the number of incoming cases increased. The main focus of the book will be on the EFTA Court's contribution to the development of substantive Single Market law, "the beef", as I have chosen to call it. In separate Chapters, the economics of EEA Single Market law, the fundamental freedoms, competition law, State aid law and secondary EEA law will be dealt with. The EFTA Court's case law regarding the principle of proportionality and the implementation of this jurisprudence by the courts of the EEA/EFTA States will also be addressed.

In many of the EFTA Court's landmark judgments, I acted as a Judge Rapporteur (JR). It is the task of the JR to marshal the parties' arguments and to draft the judgment. This book will delve into the politically important decisions in specific Chapters. These rulings concern, in particular, the compatibility of essential elements of the Norwegian social model with EEA law and the most important case decided by the EFTA Court in the almost 25 years of its existence: *Icesave I*.

Special attention will be paid to the EFTA Court's dialogue with the ECJ, its Advocates General (AGs) and the General Court of the European Union (GC). The EFTA Court is bound to be homogeneous in its jurisprudence with the ECJ's case law. Unlike most publications dealing with EEA law, the respective considerations will, however, not be limited to the law on the books, but will meticulously analyse the law in action. If there is relevant ECJ case law, the EFTA Court has mostly, but not always followed it. However, the EFTA Court is in the majority of its cases faced with novel legal questions. I have dubbed this the "going first constellation". The EFTA Court has succeeded in upholding specific EFTA values such as the belief in free trade and open markets, efficiency, fair taxation and a modern image of man. Efficiency does not mean that justice and equity are disregarded. The ECJ, its AGs and the GC have frequently followed the EFTA Court. Conflicts must be sorted out over time by way of dialogue. A Chapter will be dedicated to the EFTA Court's working methods and its judicial style. The latter differs markedly from the style of its EEA sister court.

Similar to all other European and international courts, the EFTA Court does not operate in a political vacuum. There are a number of factors that have made it vulnerable to attacks from various quarters. An important role in the Court's life has been played by the European Commission which has participated in virtually every case.

Separate Chapters will concentrate on the Court's and on my own extrajudicial activities. It was always clear to me that a tribunal of the size of the EFTA Court, which necessarily operates in the shadow of its much larger sister court, must show its colours not only in its case law, but also in other areas. In this context, I would mention regular events and activities such as: an annual conference; the commemoration of anniversaries; the maintenance of good relations with the EU judiciary and national courts in Europe and beyond; and publications and the management of contacts with the media. As regards my own activities, two Chapters will specifically deal with my speeches, interviews, publications and talks concerning the EU- and EEA policy of the fourth EFTA State, Switzerland (which as I have already mentioned also happens to be my home country), and with my activities relating to the burning question of whether EFTA and the EEA could guarantee access to the Single Market for market operators in a post-Brexit Britain. When writing about extrajudicial activities, I will also address the fact that achieving homogeneity requires soft factors too. In that respect, the tireless dedication of my wife, Dr. Doris Baudenbacher-Tandler, to enhancing the position and strength of the EFTA Court has been anything but soft as will be demonstrated by a number of anecdotes provided in this book.

Contents

Abbreviations

AB	WTO Appellate Body
AcP	*Archiv für die civilistische Praxis*, Germany
AECLJ	Association of European Competition Law Judges
AG	Advocate General of the ECJ
AM	Assembly Member
AO	Administration Office for Dock Work, Norway
ARENA	Multidisciplinary centre at the University of Oslo studying the evolving European political order
BAZ	*Basler Zeitung*, Switzerland
BDP	Swiss Bourgeois Democratic Party
BEG	England and Wales Bar European Group
CETA	EU-Canada Comprehensive Cooperation and Trade Agreement
CFI	Court of First Instance of the European Union
CiO	OSCE Chairperson-in-Office
CJEU	Court of Justice of the European Union (ECJ, GC and CST)
CMLRev.	Common Market Law Review
COM	European Commission
ComCo	Swiss Competition Commission
CP	Continental Partnership
CR	*Computer und Recht*, Germany
CST	Civil Service Tribunal of the European Union
CVP	Swiss Christian Democratic Party
DExEU	Department for Exiting the EU, United Kingdom
DG	Directorate-General
DN	Dagens Næringsliv, Norway
DNB	De Nederlandsche Bank
DUP	Democratic Unionist Party, United Kingdom
E.B.L.Rev.	European Business Law Review
EBOA	EFTA Board of Auditors

EC	European Community/European Communities
ECFR	European Company and Financial Law Review
ECHR	European Convention on Human Rights
ECJ	Court of Justice of the European Union
ECLN	European Constitutional Law Network
ECSC	European Coal and Steel Community
ECtHR	European Court of Human Rights
Ed.	Editor
Eds.	Editors
EEA	European Economic Area
EEC	European Economic Community
EFDI	European Forum of Deposit Insurers
EFTA	European Free Trade Association
EJIL	European Journal of International Law
ELR	European Law Reporter
ESA	EFTA Surveillance Authority
ETH	*Eidgenössische Technische Hochschule* (Swiss Institute of Technology)
EU	European Union
EWiR	Entscheidungen zum Wirtschaftsrecht
FAZ	Frankfurter Allgemeine Zeitung
FDFA	Swiss Federal Department of Foreign Affairs
FDP	Swiss Free Democratic Party
FIDE	*Fédération International Pour Le Droit Européen* (International Federation for European Law)
FME	Icelandic Financial Supervisory Authority
FSA	Financial Services Authority
FSCS	Financial Services and Compensation Scheme
FT	Financial Times, United Kingdom
FTA	Free Trade Agreement
GC	General Court of the European Union
GDP	Gross domestic product
GRUR Int.	*Gewerblicher Rechtsschutz und Urheberrecht International*, Germany
HFF	Icelandic Housing Financing Fund
HSG	University of St. Gallen
HSH	His Serene Highness
IALS	Institute of Advanced Legal Studies, University of London
IB	Integration Bureau of the Foreign Department/Department of Economic Affairs, Switzerland
ICF	International Competition Law Forum
ICJ	International Court of Justice
ILO	International Labour Organization
IMF	International Monetary Fund

IP	Intellectual property
IT	Information technology
JR	Judge Rapporteur
KS	Norwegian Association of Local and Regional Authorities
LJZ	*Liechtensteinische Juristen-Zeitung*
LLC	Limited Liability Company
LO	Norwegian Federation of Trade Unions
LSE	London School of Economics
MII	Mass Immigration Initiative, Switzerland METI Ministry of Economy, Trade and Industry, Japan
MP	Member of Parliament
MSP	Member of the Scottish Parliament
NHO	Confederation of Norwegian Enterprise
NJW	*Neue Juristische Wochenschrift*, Germany
NZZ	*Neue Zürcher Zeitung*, Switzerland
ÖBl	*Österreichische Blätter für gewerblichen Rechtsschutz und Urheberrecht*
OECD	Organisation for Economic Co-operation and Development
OEEC	Organisation for European Economic Co-operation
ÖJZ	Österreichische Juristen Zeitung
OSCE	Organization for Security and Co-operation in Europe
PA	Personal assistant
PICT	Project on International Courts and Tribunals
PM	Prime Minister
QC	Queen's Counsel, United Kingdom
RIETI	Research Institute of Economy, Trade and Industry, Japan
RoP	Rules of Procedure
SAAP	State Aid Action Plan
SCA	Surveillance and Court Agreement
SMEs	Small and medium-sized enterprises
SP	Swiss Social Democratic Party
SVP	Swiss People's Party
TEU	Treaty on European Union
TFEU	Treaty on the Functioning of the European Union
TIF	Iceland's Depositors' and Investors' Guarantee Fund
TILJ	Texas International Law Journal
TRIPS	WTO Agreement on Trade-Related Aspects of Intellectual Property Rights
UCL	University College London
UDI	Norwegian Directorate of Immigration
UK	United Kingdom
UKIP	UK Independence Party
UNAM	Universidad Nacional Autónoma de México
UNCTAD	United Nations Conference on Trade and Development

US	United States
UT	University of Texas
VAT	Value added tax
VersR	*Versicherungsrecht*, Germany
WTO	World Trade Organization
WTO AB	WTO Appellate Body
ZSR	*Zeitschrift für Schweizerisches Recht*

List of Cases

EFTA Court

Norwegian Public Works Concession (*ESA v Norway*) (E-4/17)
Icelandic Veterinary Checks (*ESA* v *Iceland*) (Joined Cases E-2/17 and E-3/17)
Konkurrenten v ESA II (E-1/17)
Nobile (E-21/16)
Thue (E-19/16)
Fosen-Linjen (E-16/16)
Yara (E-15/16)
Marine Harvest v ESA (E-12/16)
Netfonds (E-8/16)
Gustav Vigeland (E-5/16)
Failure to comply with an infringement judgment (*ESA* v *Norway*) (E-4/16)
Ski Taxi (E-3/16)
Synnøve Finden (E-1/16)
Sorpa (E-29/15)
Jabbi (E-28/15)
Icelandic Investment Incentive Scheme (*ESA v Iceland*) (E-25/15)
Walter Waller (E-24/15)
Liechtenstein Prior Authorisation Scheme (*ESA* v *Liechtenstein*) (E-19/15)
Ferskar kjötvörur (E-17/15)
Vienna Life and *Swiss Life* (Joined Cases E-15/15 and E-16/15)
Holship (E-14/15)
Abuelo Insua Juan Bautista (E-13/15)
Icesave III—E-9/15
Icesave II—E-8/15
Matja Kumba (E-5/15)
Liechtensteinische Gesellschaft für Umweltschutz (E-3/15)
Kimek Offshore v ESA (E-23/14)

Failure to comply with an infringement judgment (ESA v *Norway)* (E-19/14) (E-19/14)
Wow Air (E-18/14)
Liechtenstein Dentist (*ESA* v *Liechtenstein*, E-17/14)
Deveci v SAS (E-10/14)
Otto Kaufmann AG (E-9/14)
Sævar Jón Gunnarsson (E-27/13)
Atli Gunnarsson (E-26/13)
Engilbertsson (E-25/13)
Hellenic Capital Market Commission (E-23/13)
FIFA v ESA (E-21/13)
Abelia v ESA (E-8/13)
Creditinfo Lánstraust (E-7/13)
DB Schenker V (E-5/13)
Norwegian Merger Taxation (*ESA* v *Norway*), E-14/13
Olsen (Joined Cases E-3/13 and E-20/13)
Míla v ESA (E-1/13)
Hells Angels (E-15/12)
Beatrix Koch (E-11/12)
KADECO (*Iceland v ESA*) E-9/12
DB Schenker v ESA II (E-7/12)
Social Security for Migrant Workers (*ESA v Norway*) (E-6/12)
Jonsson (E-3/12)
HOB-vín ehf. (E-2/12)
Den norske forleggerforening v *ESA* (E-1/12)
Irish Bank (E-18/11)
Icesave I (*ESA v Iceland*) (E-16/11)
DB Schenker v ESA I (E-14/11)
Asker Brygge v ESA (E-12/11)
Regulated Markets (ESA v Norway) (E-9/11)
Clauder (E-4/11)
Sigmarsson (E-3/11)
STX (E-2/11)
Norwegian Appeal Board for Health Personnel (E-1/11)
Liechtenstein and VTM Fund Management v ESA (Joined Cases E-17/10 and E-6/11)
Philip Morris (E-16/10)
Norway Post v ESA (E-15/10)
Konkurrenten v ESA I (E-14/10)
Posting of Workers in Iceland (*ESA* v *Iceland*) (E-12/10)
Liechtenstein, REASSUR and Swisscom v ESA (Joined Cases E-4/10, E-6/10 and E-7/10)
Dr Kottke (E-5/10)

Kolbeinsson (E-2/10)
Periscopus (E-1/10)
Magasin- og Ukepresseforeningen v *ESA* (E-6/09)
Inconsult (E-4/09)
Residence requirements for attorneys, patent attorneys, auditors and trustees and for members of the Board of Directors and the Executive Board of banks (*ESA* v *Liechtenstein*) (E-1/09)
Rindal and *Slinning* (Joined Cases E-11/07 and E-1/08)
L'Oréal (Joined Cases E-9/07 and 10/07)
Nguyen (E-8/07)
Private Barnehagers Landsforbund v ESA (E-5/07)
Golden Widows (ESA v Norway) (E-2/07)
Criminal proceedings against A (E-1/07)
Liechtenstein Helplessness Allowance (*ESA v Liechtenstein*) (E-5/06)
Norwegian Waterfalls (*ESA v Norway*) (E-2/06)
Gaming Machines (*ESA v Norway*) (E-1/06)
HOB Vín I (E-4/05)
Finnmark Supplement (ESA v Norway) (E-3/05)
Icelandic Trading Companies (*ESA v Iceland*) (E-2/05)
Norwegian Life Assurance (*ESA v Norway*) (E-1/05)
Piazza (E-10/04)
Bankers' and Securities Dealers' Association of Iceland v ESA (E-9/04)
Residence requirements for bankers (*ESA* v *Liechtenstein*) (E-8/04)
Pedicel (E-4/04)
Fokus Bank (E-1/04)
Ásgeirsson (E-2/03)
Icelandic Air Passenger Tax (ESA v Iceland) (E-1/03)
Paranova v *Merck* (E-3/02)
Bellona v ESA (E-2/02)
University of Oslo (*ESA v Norway*) (E-1/02)
Karlsson (E-4/01)
Dr Pucher (E-2/01)
Einarsson (E-1/01)
CIBA (E-6/01)
Alcopops (*ESA v Norway*) (E-9/00)
LO (E-8/00)
Dr Tschannett (E-6/00)
Dr Mangold (E-5/00)
Dr Brändle (E-4/00)
Kellogg's (*ESA v Norway*) (E-3/00)
Allied Colloids (E-2/00)
Íslandsbanki (E-1/00)
Finanger (E-1/99)

Norwegian Social Security Act (*Norway v ESA*) (E-6/98)
Fagtún (E-5/98)
Rainford-Towning (E-3/98)
Astra Norge (E-1/98)
Sveinbjörnsdóttir (E-9/97)
TV 1000 (E-8/97)
European Navigation Inc. v *Star Forsikring AS* (E-5/97)
Husbanken v ESA II (E-4/97)
Maglite (E-2/97)
Wilhelmsen (E-6/96)
Ullensaker Kommune (E-5/96)
Ask v *ABB and Aker* (E-3/96)
Ulstein and Røiseng (E-2/96)
Icelandic Commodity Tax (*ESA v Iceland*) (E-1/96)
Langeland (E-3/95)
Eidesund (E-2/95)
Samuelsson (E-1/95)
Mattel and Lego (Joined Cases E-8/94 and E-9/94)
Data Delecta (E-4/94)
Scottish Salmon Growers v ESA (E-2/94)
Restamark (E-1/94)

Icelandic Courts

(1) Supreme Court *Matvælastofnun* v *þrotabú Beis ehf.* 2016, 66
(2) Supreme Court *Icelandic Medicines Control Agency*, 2004, 3097
(3) Supreme Court *Blaðamannafélag Íslands gegn Frétt ehf.*, 2004, 375
(4) Supreme Court *Fagtún,* 1999, 4916
(5) Supreme Court *Sveinbjörnsdóttir*, 1999, 263
(6) Supreme Court *Björgun ehf. v íslenska ríkinu*, 182/2007

Liechtenstein Courts

State Court *Spitzer* v *Landesbank*, 2013/172 (2014)
Supreme Court *Tschannett V*, CO.2004.2-46 (2010)
State Court *Tschannett IV*, 2008/87
Supreme Court *Tschannett III*, CO.2004.2-38 (2008)
State Court *Tschannett II*, 2007/15 (2007)
Supreme Court *Tschannett I*, CO.2004.2-25 (2007)

Norwegian Courts

Supreme Court *Holship*, HR-2016-2554-P
Supreme Court *STX*, Rt. 2012, 1447
Supreme Court *KLM Royal Dutch Airlines*, Rt. 2008, 738
Supreme Court *Finanger II*, Rt. 2005, 1365
Supreme Court *Nucleus*, Rt. 2001, 1062
Supreme Court *Finanger I*, Rt. 2000, 1811
Supreme Court *Port of Sola*, Rt. 1997, 334
Supreme Court *Concession Act*, Rt. 1918 I, 403
Oslo District Court *Ladbrokes*, 04-091873TVIR-04 of 3 October 2008

Swiss Courts

Federal Supreme Court *Publigroupe* ATF 139 I 72 (2012)
Federal Supreme Court *Helplessness allowance* ATF 132 V 423 (2006)
Federal Supreme Court *Nintendo* ATF 124 III 321 (1998)
Federal Supreme Court *Chanel* ATF 122 III 469 (1996)
Federal Supreme Court *Omo* ATF 105 OO 49 (1979)
Federal Supreme Court *Stanley Adams* ATF 104 IV 175 (1978)
Federal Administrative Tribunal *BMW*, B-3332/2012 (2015)
Federal Administrative Tribunal *GABA*, B-506/12 (2013)
Federal Administrative Tribunal *Gebro*, B-463/2010 (2013)

European Union Courts

ECJ

Carrefour Hypermarchés (C-510/16)
Congregación de Escuelas Pías Provincia Betania (C-74/16)
Panayi (C-646/15)
BAWAG (C-375/15)
Dowling (C-41/15)
Andrejs Surmačs (C-127/14)
Gauweiler (C-62/14)
Fonnship (C-83/13)
CB v *Commission* (C-67/13 P)
Opinion 2/13
Kone and Others (C-557/12)
MasterCard (C-382/12 P)
Bouanich (C-375/12)

ECJ *Energie Baden-Württemberg* (C-365/12 P)
Telefonica (C-295/12 P)
Schindler (C-501/11 P)
Alemo-Herron (C-426/11)
British Social Security Systems (*UK* v *Council*) (C-431/11)
Prezes and Republic of Poland v *Commission* (Joined Cases C-422/11 P and C-423/11 P)
Folien Fischer and Fofitec (C-133/11)
Marques Almeida (C-300/10)
Solvay (C-109/10 P)
ECJ *Content Services* (C-49/11)
Commission v *Netherlands* (C-542/09)
Commission v *Portugal* (C-493/09)
Ferreira Manuel (C-484/09)
Strabag (C-314/09)
KME v Commission (C-272/09 P)
Kronoply and *Kronotex* (C-83/09 P)
Rimbaud (C-72/09)
Combinatie Spijker (C-568/08)
Commission v *Spain* (C-487/08)
Akzo Nobel (C-550/07 P)
Commission v *Italy* (C-540/07)
Commission v *Netherlands* (C-521/07)
Menarini and Others (C-352/07)
Markus Stoß (C-316/07)
Liga Portuguesa (C-42/07)
Parliament and Denmark v *Commission* (Joined Cases C-14/06 and C-295/06)
ELISA (C-451/05)
Viking Line (C-438/05)
Laval (C-341/05)
Denkavit (C-170/05)
Fidium Finanz (C-452/04)
Test Claimants in Class IV (C-374/04)
Boehringer Ingelheim II (C-384/04)
Candolin (C-537/03)
Bellio Fratelli (C-286/02)
Ospelt (C-452/01)
Monsanto Agricoltura (C-236/01)
Köbler (C-224/01)
Danish Vitamins (*Commission* v *Denmark*) (C-192/01)
Greenham and Abel (C-95/01)
Altmark (C-280/00)
UPA (C-50/00 P)
Gourmet (C-405/98)
Netherlands v *Parliament and Council* (C-377/98)

Ferreira Vitor (C-348/98)
Andersson (C-321/97)
Rechberger (C-140/97)
Silhouette (C-355/96)
Albany (C-67/96)
Franzén (C-189/95)
Data Delecta (C-43/95)
De Agostini and TV Shop I Sverige (C-34/95-36/95)
Süzen (C-13/95)
Flemish Television (*Commission* v *UK*) (C-222/94)
Bassano del Grappa (C-140/94, C-141/94 and C-142/94)
Kalanke (C-450/93)
Leclerc-Siplec (C-412/93)
Brasserie du Pêcheur (Joined Cases C-46/93 and C-48/93)
Vanacker (C-37/92)
Hubbard (C-20/92)
Opinion 1/92
Keck (C-267/91 and C-268/91)
Cook (C-198/91)
Opinion 1/91
Francovich (Joined Cases C-6/90 and C-9/90)
Marleasing (C-106/89)
Hermann Schräder (265/87)
Spijkers (C-24/85)
Cofaz (169/84)
Sandoz (174/82)
Schloh v *Council*, (85/82)
CILFIT (C-283/81)
Kupferberg (104/81)
Polydor (270/80)
Philip Morris v *Commission* (C-730/79)
Cassis de Dijon (120/78)
Dassonville (8/74)
Costa v *ENEL* (6/64)
van Gend en Loos (26/62)
Plaumann (25/62)

GC

FV v *Council* (T-639/16 P)
Akzo Nobel v Commission (T-345/12)
Evonik Degussa v Commission (T-341/12)
Microsoft v *Commission* (T-201/04)
Schneider Electric v *Commission* (T-77/02)
Jegó-Queré v Commission (T-177/01)

Salzgitter AG v Commission (T-308/00)
Alpharma v Council (T-70/99)
Pfizer Animal Health v Council (T-13/99)
Opel Austria v Council (T-115/94)

Austrian Courts

Supreme Court *Austro-Mechana* ÖBl 1980, 25

German Courts

Constitutional Court, *Gauweiler*, 2 BvR 2728/13 (2016)
Federal Supreme Court *Life Assurance*, IV ZR 271/10 (2012)
Federal Supreme Court *Holzhocker*, I ZR 66/08 (2010)
Federal Supreme Court *STILNOX*, I ZR 173/04 (2007); *Micardis*, I ZR 89/05 (2007); *Lefax/Lefaxin*, I ZR 30/05 (2008)
Federal Patent Court *Mona Lisa*, 24 W (pat) 188/96 (1997)
Imperial Court *Benrath Petrol Station*, RGZ 134, 342 (1931)

Swedish Courts

Supreme Court *Andersson*, Nytt Juridiskt Arkiv (NJA) 2004, 662 ff. (2004)
Patent and Market Court, Mål nr PMT 17299-14 (2016)

UK Courts

Supreme Court *Nuclear Decommissioning Authority* v *EnergySolutions EU Ltd*, [2017] UKSC 34
House of Lords *Fairchild v Glenhaven Funeral Services* Ltd, [2002] UKHL 22
England and Wales Court of Appeal, *Boehringer Ingelheim KG v Swingward Ltd [2004] EWCA Civ 129*
England and Wales Court of Appeal, *Adams* v. *Lancashire CC & BET Catering Serv. Ltd.* [1997] ICR, 834
UK Employment Appeal Tribunal *Frankling*v. *BPS Public Sector Ltd.*, [1999] IRLR 212 EAT
Lord Justice Greer in *Hall* v *Brooklands Auto-Racing Club* [1933] 1 KB 205
Lord Blackburn in *River Wear Commissioners v Adamson* [1877] 2 App Cas 743.

ECTHR

Nišić (60642/08) (2014)
St. Paul Luxembourg (5493/72) (2013)
Menarini (43509/08) (2011)
Ullens de Schooten and ntRezabek v. Belgium (3989/07) and (38353/07) (2011)
Sørensen and Rasmussen v *Denmark*, (52562/99) and (52620/99) (2006)
Pafitis (20323/92) (1998)
Tyrer v *the UK* (5856/72) (1978)
Handyside (5493/72) (1976)

US Courts

Impression Products v. Lexmark International (581 U.S. ___ 2017)
National Federation of Independent Business v. Sebelius ("Obamacare") (567 U.S. 519, 2012)
Golan v. Holder (565 U.S. 302, 2012)
Eldred v *Ashcroft* (537 U.S. 186, 2003)
Planned Parenthood of Southeastern Pennsylvania v. Casey (595 U.S. 833, 1992)
Quality King Distributors v. L'anza Research Int'l, Inc. (523 *U.S.* 135, 1998)
Payne v. Tennessee (501 U.S. 808, 1991)

ILO Administrative Tribunal

Bustani v. Org. for the Prohibition of Chemical Weapons, Judgment No. 2232 of 16 July 2003

Chapter 1
My Pre-court Life

Contents

1 General

In different parts of the world, judges have different careers. The American website www.study.com states:

> Most judges work as attorneys prior to acquiring their judgeship.

This may be true of US judges. In Great Britain too, as in common law countries in general, the majority of judges have extensive experience as private legal practitioners before becoming part of the bench. It seems that in Britain lawyers join the judiciary on average at the age of 55. In the civil law systems of the European continent, this is, however, different. In Germany or in Switzerland, being a judge is a career in itself. Lawyers become judges at a young age and spend their professional life in this function. They generally start in a first instance court and may over the course of time be promoted to the higher courts. Countless books and articles have been written on the issue of whether common law judges or civil law judges are more independent. I will refrain from making such an assessment at this stage. But I want to emphasise that judges in European courts (as in all international courts) are selected according to different criteria than their colleagues in national courts. Whereas both domestic common law and civil law judges have a background as legal professionals—the former mostly in private and the latter mainly in judicial practice—this is not necessarily the case for the judges appointed to European and international courts. European and international judges will have

C. Baudenbacher, *Judicial Independence*, Springer Biographies,
https://doi.org/10.1007/978-3-030-02308-9_1

studied law and obtained a degree in law, but thereafter, many of them will have worked as bureaucrats, diplomats or even politicians. Combined with the specific conditions under which such courts operate—judicial candidates nominated by governments, appointment on a temporary basis, usually with the possibility of reappointment—this lack of a background as a legal professional can pose problems. Certainly, there are also judges of international and European courts with a different record. Some of them were university professors in the past and others were practising attorneys. But the proportion of former government people is high. The question arises as to whether judges who have been trained and socialised as senior civil servants, diplomats or politicians are sufficiently independent or whether they are prone to being kept on a leash.

2 My Socialisation as a Lawyer

2.1 Studies and First Work Experiences

I studied law from 1967 to 1971 at the faculty of law and economics of the University of Berne. After graduation, I worked as a scientific assistant to the leading economic law mind in Switzerland, Walter R. Schluep. In 1978, I obtained my doctoral degree and in May of that year I married Doris Tandler, a German business economist. My thesis entitled "Suggestive advertising and the law of unfair competition" ("*Suggestivwerbung und Lauterkeitsrecht*") was given the highest mark. My work in this field stimulated my interest in economic law. According to German, Swiss and Austrian doctrine, the objective of unfair competition law is not solely to protect competitors from unfair practices such as misleading advertising or creating a risk of confusion or disparagement through false statements, but also to secure the existence and the good functioning of the competitive process.

From 1979 to 1981, I was a guest researcher at the Max Planck-Institute for Intellectual Property Law in Munich where I wrote my habilitation thesis. In the universities of German-speaking Switzerland, habilitation is like in Germany, Austria and some East European countries a requirement to obtain a chair. It is the highest university examination. During my time in Munich, I deepened my knowledge of economic law and of the different schools of thought in the field of competition economics. In 1982, the law faculty of the University Zurich accepted my habilitation thesis which was entitled "Basic economic law, contract law and procedural law problems of general terms and conditions of contract" ("*Wirtschafts-, schuld- und verfahrensrechtliche Grundprobleme der Allgemeinen Geschäftsbedingungen*"). Once again, I placed particular emphasis on economic law, in particular on the fact that a contract is an instrument for optimal risk allocation. In addition to working on my habilitation thesis, I acted as an arbitrator and a secretary for arbitration tribunals. Last, but not least, during this period I wrote a number of legal opinions for private businesses and law firms. From 1982 to 1984, I worked as a legal secretary for the Bülach District Court in the Canton of Zurich.

2.2 My German Journeyman Travels

As regards my academic career, I had been promised a chair in economic law at the University of Zurich once the law faculty accepted my habilitation treatise and my trial presentation. My habilitation procedure formally ended in 1983 and both my examiners, Walter R. Schluep and Arthur Meier-Hayoz, were prominent members of the faculty. When I asked about the promised chair, I was told that I was certainly considered to be a very gifted lawyer, but the faculty had come to the conclusion that before awarding me a chair "I first had to pull in my horns". By this the Zurich law faculty meant that I was too independent and thus unpredictable and that, just like everyone else in Switzerland, I needed to adapt to the system. Here it was again, the desire to put other people on a leash. I was offered an assistant professorship with the prospect of being promoted to associate ("extraordinary") professor after a certain time and eventually—which probably meant by the ripe old age of 50—to full professor, provided that "everything went well".

Thus at the age of 36 I left the University of Zurich. Under normal circumstances, I would have started to work in a law firm, but I received an invitation from the Ruhr University in Bochum to serve as an acting full professor for a semester. I therefore decided to become one of the few of my generation of law graduates who would try their luck in the German academic world. For the next two and a half years, I battled my way through several German universities, *inter alia*, the Free University of Berlin and the universities of Tübingen and Marburg. We lived in Berlin at that time and I commuted to my workplaces by plane. During the Cold War, only airlines owned by the Allies were allowed to fly from Berlin to the Federal Republic of Germany and back. I generally took a Pan Am flight, either to Frankfurt am Main or to Stuttgart. On 19 November 1985, our only child Laura Melusine Charlotte Alice was born in Berlin. Hopping from one German university to the other was undoubtedly the toughest phase of my professional life. Each semester, I was in a new place and had to teach whatever subjects were assigned to me, from German contract and tort law or commercial law, labour law, antitrust law, unfair competition law, company law to the law of sureties and the law of the (German) judicial constitution. At times I had the feeling that I was being given the classes that nobody else wanted to teach. I was never asked how I, who had been educated in Swiss law, would cope with the challenge of teaching these German law subjects. My hosts seemed to assume that Swiss law was an offspring of German law and that a Swiss lawyer could teach German law without major difficulties. This is not untypical of how many German lawyers proceed when faced with the legal system of a small country. They address the issues with the presumption that everything is at least similar to the solution under German law ("*praesumptio similitatis*") and if it is not similar, they deem the foreign solution to be inferior. Many of them also tended to have a know-it-all attitude. After World War II, German academic publications would frequently refer to foreign sources, however, forty years later, the discourse had returned to a more self-centred focus.

German law professors are a special type of human being. It may be that things have changed in the meantime, but I am not convinced that this is so. There were some quirky figures, who called to mind the famous Biedermeier painter Carl Spitzweg. For example, in Marburg, Doris and I met an elderly Professor who liked to talk full-length about his pet topic, the various methods of execution in legal history. In his opinion, being executed was generally painless, provided the executioner knew his trade.

Many German academics continue to be influenced by conceptualism ("*Begriffsjurisprudenz*"). According to the definition of the *Universal-Lexikon*, conceptualism is

> *eine im 19. Jahrhundert entwickelte Methodenlehre, die die Rechtsordnung als lückenloses, in sich geschlossenes System von Rechtssätzen begreift. Ihr liegt die Vorstellung zugrunde, aus den einzelnen Rechtsbegriffen lasse sich im Wege rein logischer Konstruktion ohne Rücksicht auf außerjuristische Gegebenheiten eine juristische ‚Begriffspyramide' gewinnen, die dann für jeden denkbaren Rechtsfall die richtige Entscheidung allein durch formallogisch-begriffliches Deduzieren gewährleiste.*
>
> (a methodology developed in the 19th century that understands the legal order as a complete, self-contained system of legal rules. It is based on the idea that the individual legal terms can be used in a purely logical construction, irrespective of extrajuridical circumstances, to create a legal 'concept pyramid', which then guarantees the right decision for every conceivable legal case solely through formal-logical-conceptual deduction.)

As a rule, German academics take a keen interest in tricky dogmatic questions. Although it is clear that not even the German Civil Code is comprehensive and without gaps, many of them are on an everlasting quest for the "objectively right solution" to a legal problem, and they find this not only a very demanding, but also an extremely exciting task. So exciting, in fact, that even their leisure time is often filled with discussions about legal finesses. During my time in Germany—and I found myself among the private law people—some of the most thrilling issues concerned, for example, the owner-possessor relationship, certain types of mortgage or the right to put forward another person's defence. That German lawyers felt that they were able to resolve such important questions gave them a sense of superiority. On the other hand, there were a number of German professors who clearly played in a different league than most of their Swiss colleagues. It seems that the pressures of the large market they operated in led them to develop ideas and concepts that in a small market were barely tackled. Furthermore, German courts tend to argue in a more sophisticated way than Swiss courts, in particular in crucial fields of economic law such as antitrust law, contract law, tort law or company law. It is no coincidence that both the Swiss legislature and the Swiss courts have always looked, and continue to look to Germany when it comes to coping with novel legal problems. If a legal issue exceeds a certain degree of complexity, Swiss lawyers often have difficulties in unravelling it. On the other hand, they keep their feet firmly on the ground and (mostly) refrain from entering into highly theoretical debates. They prefer to muddle through, which in the end can lead to a perfectly reasonable outcome and with far less effort.

In 1986, I was offered a newly-created professorship in law at the Technical University of Kaiserslautern. Since I was the only lawyer in a faculty that mainly consisted of business people, economists and engineers, the three semesters I spent there were good times without the usual university bickering. I was also contacted by the University of Cologne, where I seemed to have a group of aficionados, and was determined to stay in Germany.

Looking back, I would not have missed my German journeyman travels. In the course of my years of wandering, or *Wanderjahre,* I had learned a lot about the law of one of the most important jurisdictions of the world and about the legal, political, economic, social and cultural differences between Germany and Switzerland. Differences such as the lack of a Hegelian model of State in Switzerland, the system of Rhenish capitalism with the strong role of the labour unions and the more paternalistic image of man in Germany were, at the end of the day, more important than differences in the written law. I had also gained an invaluable insight into the law of the European Community. But that was not all. Life was tougher in Germany than in Switzerland, its pace was faster. There was also more open competition and not just for jobs. Changing work place every semester was also challenging because of the dealings with the public authorities that it required. Generally speaking, German civil servants were more bureaucratic than Swiss. At least in my time they saw themselves as the embodiment of the State, and not as people whose livelihood depended on the taxes paid by the citizens. Importantly, Doris and I had made a lot of friends during our time in Germany and built up a network on which we would later draw. This included not only people from the German legal community, but also from many other countries.

3 University of St. Gallen

In 1986, one of the masterminds of the law faculty of St. Gallen University ("HSG"), Arnold Koller who belonged to the same school of thought as I, was elected Federal Councillor in Switzerland. I applied for his chair and in 1987, I was hired. For one year, I commuted between Berlin and St. Gallen, but then the University insisted that I moved there. In the summer of 1988, we took up residence in St. Gallen. Returning to Switzerland was not easy. My countrymen and women were not used to the open way of speaking I had adopted in Berlin, something I retain to this day. In Switzerland, it is more common to seem to be hand in glove with someone and then to speak behind that person's back.

Life at HSG was pleasant, the law faculty was clearly oriented towards economic law and the university had a peculiar governance structure with a strong President ("Rector"). If you had an idea, it was essentially sufficient to convince this man (there has never been a female rector in the history of HSG) of the merits of the idea. It was even possible to go one level higher and to talk to the President of the University Council, a member of the Cantonal Government, at least on important matters. The biggest advantage St. Gallen offered when compared with other universities was the institute structure. Entrepreneurial professors were given the opportunity to be the director of an institute, which was designed as a profit-making organisation. The pecuniary incentive was modest, but to have an own institute with an own infrastructure was of considerable value. In 1990, I was appointed director of the Institute of European and International law.

In 1994, I was offered the Chair of Private, Commercial and Economic Law at the Ruhr-University in Bochum, Germany, where people still remembered me fondly from my time as an acting professor. Under the German university system, negotiations are (or were at the time) mainly conducted by the competent Ministry of the Land concerned, in my case North Rhine-Westphalia. I was told that in times of limited public means the Ruhr-University was interested in implementing the St. Gallen institute model and the plan was to make me the director of a new institute of energy law. The negotiations failed because the Germans said that under their law it was not possible to grant such an institute the freedom of independent financial management. That would have meant that even for the purchase of pencils and notepads the agreement of a civil servant would have been required, not to mention a flight to the US or a dinner invitation for foreign guests at a decent restaurant. The wages German universities offered were not high. However, professors apparently felt that this was offset by good facilities ("*Ausstattung*"). The facilities consisted of both human and material resources including offices and computers. Depending on the circumstances, a candidate could also bargain for a special credit to expand the library in his/her field. But the biggest achievement in the latter respect was the provision of "reference works" ("*Handapparat*"). These were books that professors would have at their exclusive disposal in their offices. To have a large stock of reference works greatly contributed to the prestige of a German professor. When I said that I was not impressed by the package of benefits that was on offer, the competent civil servant observed that this was all that could be provided if things were done strictly by the book, but that he could offer me new curtains in my personal office and a closet with a washbasin and running water. Experience showed, he added, that after writing on the blackboard with chalk for long periods, professors appreciated having the opportunity to wash their hands. After two rounds of negotiations, I told my counterparts that I would not accept their offer.

I did keep one foot in the German legal world by participating in conferences and giving lectures in Germany and on occasion acting as an arbitrator or as an expert witness. Most of my assistants at HSG came from Germany. It was a win-win situation for both sides. The German lawyers were very well educated, with broad knowledge that they could call upon at all times. Initially, some of them were a bit out of touch with reality, but they were quick learners. A final sweetener was the fact that the salaries in Switzerland were much more attractive than in Germany.

4 University of Texas

In the summer of 1990, HSG granted me seven months of sabbatical leave. Doris and I were determined to spend that time in the United States, but we wanted to avoid the Ivy League universities on the east coast and in California where we would supposedly meet a lot of other Europeans. After some reflection, I contacted the University of Texas ("UT") in Austin and was invited to spend half a year there as a visiting scholar. UT has one of the leading public law schools in the country. In March 1990, we flew across the pond to America. Laura Melusine was four and a half years old and we were able to place her in a good private pre-school. I did research at UT law library and tried to improve my rusty English. In subsequent years, we spent every summer in Austin and sent our daughter to summer camps. From 1993 onwards, I taught European and International law in UT's summer school.

5 EEA Negotiations

In 1990, I became a consultant for the Government of the Principality of Liechtenstein in the negotiations concerning the establishment of a European Economic Area. Working from Texas was a challenge and I fully relied on fax machines. In 1994, I was appointed as an ad hoc judge to the Liechtenstein Supreme Court.

Chapter 2
EFTA Court Judge by Chance

Contents

1 Liechtenstein's Choice of a Judge

On 1 May 1995, the Principality of Liechtenstein became an EEA Member State in the EFTA pillar. The Government thus had the right (and the duty) to nominate a member of the ESA College and a judge of the EFTA Court. The appointment was by common accord of Iceland, Liechtenstein and Norway. The EFTA Court started functioning on 1 January 1994 with five judges from the EFTA States party to the EEA Agreement, namely Austria, Finland, Iceland, Norway, and Sweden. Switzerland signed the EEA Agreement on 2 May 1992, but was unable to ratify it after a negative referendum on 6 December 1992. Liechtenstein, which was part of a customs union with Switzerland, then postponed its ratification of the Agreement. On 1 January 1994, ESA had also started operating with five College Members from the States mentioned. On 1 January 1995, Austria, Finland and Sweden left EFTA and joined the EU. This did not mean that they gave up their EEA membership, they simply switched from one pillar to the other. I emphasise this because in the ECJ's 2003 landmark judgment in the *Ospelt* case, the Austrian Government argued that Austria had on 1 January 1995, when it joined the EU, left the EEA. The five-member ESA ceased to exist on 1 January 1995, but not the EFTA Court. Under a special agreement between the five EEA/EFTA States, the EFTA Court of five judges was to conclude all pending cases in the first half of 1995. On 30 June

C. Baudenbacher, *Judicial Independence*, Springer Biographies,
https://doi.org/10.1007/978-3-030-02308-9_2

1995, the judges nominated by Austria, Finland and Sweden had to resign. Thereafter the Court comprised just two judges from Iceland and Norway. With the appointment of a Liechtenstein judge, the number of judges rose to three, the minimum number required to run a European court.

In Liechtenstein, the cabinet, consisting of five ministers, was competent to decide on who should be nominated as their ESA College Member and their EFTA Court judge. The post of a judge was publicly advertised, but I did not apply. I was the Chair of Private, Commercial and Economic Law at the HSG and the director of the university's Institute of European and International Law. In that capacity, I had been the Liechtenstein Government's most important advisor during the EEA negotiations. In the summer of 1995, St. Gallen granted me another sabbatical semester and I accepted an offer from UT to teach European and International law both in the summer school and in the fall semester. As I have said before, I had already spent considerable time at UT in previous years. In 1995, Doris and I enrolled Laura Melusine, as a fifth grader, in one of Austin's most prestigious private schools, St. Andrews Episcopal School. We were looking forward to living again in the "Great State of Texas".

A few weeks before my family's scheduled departure for the US, I received an invitation from Dr. Michael Ritter, the Deputy Prime Minister of Liechtenstein, to the opening of his own law firm in Vaduz. With the exception of the Prime Minister, the Members of the Liechtenstein Government held part-time positions. I knew Michael because he had been a member of the team that negotiated Liechtenstein's EEA membership on the side of EFTA from 1990 to 1992. He had also been my student in a post-graduate European law course at the HSG. Doris and I gladly accepted his invitation. After the ceremony, we were invited to dinner in a Bavarian restaurant in Vaduz. Michael showed me a list with five names and told me that these were the candidates for the EFTA judgeship. He wanted to have my view on them. I answered, in all innocence, that in my view none of them was convincing. He shared my concerns and finally asked me whether I would consider becoming Liechtenstein's EFTA Court judge. There was no nationality requirement, and as I said before, I had been appointed an ad hoc judge of the Liechtenstein Supreme Court in 1994. The government therefore took the view that I was one of theirs. I told Michael that in a few days, I would fly to Texas with my family where I had accepted a visiting professorship for the fall semester. I was given 48 h to reflect. The EFTA Court had just been downsized from five to three judges and the governments had decided that its seat should be moved from Geneva to Luxembourg. What tipped the scale for me was the opportunity of actively helping to shape the development of both European law and European integration. I would never have chosen a judge's career in Switzerland where, as in most continental European systems, you had to start in a first instance court and then climb up the greasy pole. If you make yourself conspicuous by criticising the higher courts' decisions, you spoil your chances of promotion. In my country, I had gained the reputation of being a restless mind and I am quite sure that for this reason alone I would not have stood a chance of being chosen as the Swiss candidate for any judgeship on a European court. The Liechtensteiners, on the other hand, seemed to like me; I had the advantage of being a "*homo novus*" in the sense that I was not really known. And I liked them.

I informed the Government in Vaduz that I was honoured by their offer, which I would gladly accept. I realised that the nomination was *ad personam*. Unlike certain Swiss judges who served on the ECtHR on behalf of Liechtenstein, there was no Vaduz-Berne political element involved. Many years later, when the Swiss Government started to downgrade the EEA Agreement and the institutions of the EFTA pillar with absurd contentions, my independence from the Berne administration proved to be an asset.[1] As I have said, in view of the Court's limited case load, the fact that appointment was limited in time and the uncertain future of the EEA, I wanted to keep my chair at St. Gallen with a reduced teaching obligation. Most people thought at the time that the EEA did not have a long life expectancy. The Princely Government agreed.

We flew to Texas and I started teaching in the summer school of UT law. In August 1995, the news reached us that the three governments of the EFTA pillar had appointed me as a judge of the EFTA Court as of 6 September 1995. Behind my back, some of my St. Gallen colleagues said that to defeat the few Liechtenstein candidates must have been rather easy. The truth is that I had been in competition with Liechtensteiners, Austrians, Germans and Swiss. Others cracked jokes about a court without cases. At the time, they had a point. There were also some who wondered how the Liechtenstein Government could have chosen a private law guy instead of a constitutional or public international law scholar. However, the icing on the cake was provided by a journalist from the local newspaper, the "*St. Galler Tagblatt*", who asked me whether I felt that it was appropriate for me as a Swiss citizen to serve an organisation in which the Swiss people had refused to participate. It had never crossed my mind that direct democracy could go that far.

The above description of my education and career up to 1995 demonstrates that I was essentially an academic type of judge when I was appointed to the EFTA Court bench in September 1995. I felt that I was well prepared for the job for a number of reasons. First, as I have mentioned, I had been the Liechtenstein Government's principal legal advisor during the EEA negotiations. I therefore knew the agreement inside out. Second, as one of the few Swiss of my generation, I had for a number of years carried out research and taught at academic institutions and universities in Germany where I was confronted with European law. Third, I had always taken a keen interest in legal methodology. My fourth asset, I thought, was my record in what in Germany, Austria and Switzerland is called "*Wirtschaftsrecht*" (economic law). Fifth, I had substantial practical experience as a legal secretary, a legal expert, an arbitrator and a judge.

It is clear that every government somehow has the expectation that its judge will have a positive attitude towards their interests. However, no such remarks were made in my case. The Liechtensteiners only told me that they were looking forward to having an EEA law specialist on the EFTA Court bench. This attitude prevailed

[1] See for details Chapter 30.

throughout my time at the EFTA Court. I never heard a word of criticism concerning our case law from them, no matter whether they prevailed or lost. The same cannot be said of all the EEA/EFTA Governments.

2 Between Austin and Geneva

On 4 September 1995, I boarded a Swissair plane in New York for Geneva. My swearing in as a judge of the EFTA Court was scheduled to take place on 6 September 1995. I had no exact idea of what was expected of me, but I knew that the institution I was about to join did not have any pending cases. In view of this, I did not anticipate any difficulties to arise from the fact that I would mostly be physically absent from the Court until the end of the year. In any case, I could always fly over, even at short notice, if my presence was required.

The ceremony was rather formal and stiff. After my swearing in, there was a lunch in a very fancy Geneva restaurant, *Le Domaine de Châteauvieux*. The food and wines were great, but the conversation reminded me of a graveyard; it was all about the old (glorious) days. Afterwards, I called Doris and told her that I was already considering stepping down from my new position.

Since there were no cases, I finally agreed with the governments that I would be physically present in Geneva from 1 January 1996. Unlike my colleagues, I was not paid a salary during these four months, the difference between them and me being that they were living the good life in Geneva whereas I was working hard in Texas. After seeing in the New Year, I flew from Austin to Geneva. I rented an apartment in Versoix, a bit outside of the city, directly on the lake. I then started commuting between Geneva, St. Gallen, where we still kept a house, and Texas, where my family was living.

3 Flashback: EEA Negotiations

3.1 Start in Hotel Löwen in Vaduz

My EEA life had started almost six years before, to be exact on Wednesday, 10 January 1990. In my capacity as a full professor and director of the Institute for European and International Economic Law at HSG, I was invited by the office of the Liechtenstein Head of Government, Hans Brunhart, to give a speech about the planned EEA before the, supposedly, most critical circles of the Liechtenstein economy—bankers, lawyers and trustees—on the possible consequences of EEA membership on the EFTA side for them. The event was to take place in the hall of Hotel Löwen in Vaduz. Normally, it takes an hour to get from St. Gallen to Vaduz, but that morning there was black ice and fog on the Rhine Valley motorway, and I arrived late at the Löwen. When I entered the hall, the Prime Minister was about to finish his speech, and then it was my turn. I knew no one, but the audience listened attentively. During the discussion, people asked important and probing questions. The professional groups in question (rightly) feared losing many privileges should their country accede to the EEA. Each time, the Prime Minister asked me whether I could take a certain question; many questions he answered himself. We had never met before and it may be that in retrospect things look more glorious than they were, but in my recollection, we were a formidable double act. I should add that after his political career, Hans Brunhart and his wife Bernadette became close friends of Doris and mine. For a number of years, Hans was my partner in the organisation of an annual conference, the Liechtenstein Europe Symposium.[2] Moreover, he gave me valuable advice on many issues. Hans Brunhart, a historian by education, has a better understanding of the functioning of a Single Market than most lawyers. Looking back on the way he led his country into the EEA, I have to say that Hans is one of the few politicians of our time who deserves to be called a statesman. In the government of my home country, Switzerland, there was and is nobody of his calibre when it comes to European politics.

3.2 Advisor to the Princely Government

My performance in Vaduz had left quite an impression with the Liechtenstein Government. In the years to come, I was asked to write numerous legal opinions on the free movement of doctors and lawyers, industrial law, company law, land transfer law, tax law, to name just a few areas. In my institute at HSG, a team of five specialists from Germany and Austria essentially worked for the Liechtenstein Government. We acted under high pressure—in the back-office so to speak—while the negotiators under the leadership of His Serene Highness (HSH) Prince Nikolaus of Liechtenstein, the brother of the Head of State, HSH Prince Hans Adam II, operated on the Brussels front. Prince Nikolaus was assisted by a team coordinated by the Head of the Office of Economic Affairs, the late Ambassador Dr. Benno Beck. It included, among others, the future Prime Minister Markus Büchel, the future Minister for Foreign Affairs Dr. Andrea Willi, the future Deputy Prime Minister Dr. Michael Ritter, and the future ambassador to Switzerland Dr. Hubert Büchel.

The Princely Government also employed other experts. However, after one year, they decided that I was their man. I was not only assessing legal questions and making predictions on future developments. They also asked me to sell the EEA Agreement to well-known opponents such as the lawyers association, the trustees and the bankers. I accepted this task with joy.

[2]See for details Chapter 13.

3.3 The "Shoals" of the EEA

Shortly before the conclusion of the EEA negotiations, the Brunhart Government asked me to draw up a comparative survey of the special regulatory advantages of other low-tax countries. After a thorough study of the application of the State aid rules of the European Community, which were to be incorporated into the EEA Agreement, I concluded that significant "shoals" could open up because of Liechtenstein's offshore companies' tax regime. In this context, the term "shoals" refers to hidden sandbanks under the surface of the water, which could cause the Liechtenstein EEA boat to run aground. These offshore privileges, I wrote, could be classified as unlawful State aid under a future EEA Agreement. Of course, this attracted the EEA opponents' attention, and Prime Minister Brunhart was not amused that "his" expert had highlighted this (alleged) weak point to EEA accession. In a newspaper article, former Prime Minister Alfred Hilbe resorted to the word "shoals" when warning of an EEA accession. Had there been a prize for the non-word of the year at the time, "shoals" would probably have been nominated and chosen in Liechtenstein. In this difficult situation, the government organised an event in the historic rectory of Bendern, where I was the keynote speaker. The hall was full to bursting. I presented my thesis and then the future University of Hamburg Professor Thomas Bruha, who had also done some work for the government on EEA matters, presented his counter position. Being a public international law man, he argued that the fiscal sovereignty of an EFTA State should not be undermined by a broad interpretation of the EEA State aid rules. I stuck to my economic law motivated standpoint.

3.4 The First Liechtenstein EEA Referendum

On 13 December 1992, approximately 56% of the people of Liechtenstein voted in favour of the country joining the EEA. I was always convinced that besides the obvious advantages of EEA membership for industry, banks and insurance companies and the government's well-made pro-EEA campaign, the hangover ("*Katzenjammer*"), which had begun to spread in Switzerland after their rejection of the EEA one week before, played an important part. Allegedly, Liechtenstein women who were married to Swiss men and therefore had dual nationality voted no in Switzerland on 6 December and yes in Liechtenstein on 13 December 1992. The Head of State, HSH Prince Hans Adam II, had on 12 September 1970, as the Hereditary Prince, delivered a famous speech in which he bemoaned the fact that Liechtenstein was barely pursuing its own foreign policy and that it had to get out of Switzerland's rucksack. Thereafter, the speech was dubbed his "rucksack speech". After the Liechtenstein vote, I said on Swiss national radio, perhaps a bit provocatively, that after the two referenda, Switzerland would now find itself in Liechtenstein's rucksack when it came to European policy.

3.5 The Second Liechtenstein EEA Referendum

Due to Switzerland's pulling out, the EEA Agreement needed to be amended. The Liechtenstein Government started negotiations with the Swiss to bring the 1923 Customs Union Treaty into an EEA–compatible form. Both the Swiss Government and the EC organs showed the utmost understanding during this process. After the successful conclusion of these negotiations, the government of Mario Frick, a bright former student of mine, scheduled a referendum for 9 April 1995. The voters perceived this as "a second EEA referendum". My work for the Government had ended with the first EEA referendum. However, in the autumn of 1994, a group of entrepreneurs asked me to write a book for the pro-EEA campaign. The study "The Principality of Liechtenstein before the vote on joining the European Economic Area" was published some months before the second vote. Both newspapers, the "red" *Liechtensteiner Vaterland* and the "black" *Liechtensteiner Volksblatt* quoted from the book for several weeks. With regard to the "shoals" controversy, I defended my economic law approach and pointed out that the special company taxes could also fall foul of Article 23(1)(iii) of the 1972 EC Switzerland Free Trade Agreement to which Liechtenstein participated via a protocol. According to that provision

> any public aid which distorts or threatens to distort competition by favouring certain undertakings or the production of certain goods

is incompatible with the proper functioning of the agreement in so far as it may affect trade between the Community and Switzerland. The amended EEA Agreement was accepted by 56% of the vote.

3.6 Afterword on the "Shoals"

On 10 May 2011, the EFTA Court held that the ESA had rightly qualified Liechtenstein's special offshore tax system as unlawful State aid in a series of cases involving the Liechtenstein subsidiaries of Swiss companies. The aid had to be recovered from the beneficiaries. My prediction from 1992 had become reality. However, that was not all. On 13 February 2007, the European Commission declared in a decision that the tax systems of certain Swiss cantons were incompatible with the EC Switzerland Free Trade Agreement and reserved the adoption of protective measures. Switzerland protested against this unilateral action and refused to negotiate, but it could not avoid entering into a "dialogue" with the EU. In 2015, Switzerland agreed to abolish these tax regimes. Liechtenstein did the same.

Chapter 3
The EEA—One Area with Two Courts

Contents

1 Introduction

There are three types of institutions under the EEA Agreement:

- EU institutions, notably the Commission and the ECJ;
- EFTA institutions: ESA; the EFTA Court; the Standing Committee of the EFTA States; the ESA/Court Committee; and the EFTA Board of Auditors;
- EEA institutions: the EEA Council; the EEA Joint Committee; the EEA Joint Parliamentary Committee; and the EEA Consultative Committee.

Formally speaking, the highest political EEA decision-making body is the EEA Council which comprises representatives of the Commission, the EU Member States and the EEA/EFTA States. It is the main political forum for the EEA.

C. Baudenbacher, *Judicial Independence*, Springer Biographies,
https://doi.org/10.1007/978-3-030-02308-9_3

Meeting at the ministerial level, it has overall political responsibility for the Agreement. Decisions are taken by unanimity. Another forum of political dialogue in the EEA is the Joint Parliamentary Committee. It may express its views in the form of reports and resolutions. Lastly, the EEA Consultative Committee is an advisory body representing the social partners in the EEA States.

When new EU legislation with EEA relevance is launched, the EEA/EFTA States don't have a co-decision right, but they enjoy a co-determination right at the expert level. In other words, they are put on an equal footing with the EU Member States at the preparatory stage ("decision shaping" as opposed to "decision making"). Once new legislation has been passed by the competent EU institutions, it is incorporated into the EEA Agreement by the EEA Joint Committee. The EEA Joint Committee is therefore a "quasi-legislative" link between the Union and the EEA legal order. It is made up of representatives of the Contracting Parties, i.e. the EEA/EFTA States, the EU Member States and the European Commission. Depending on whether the subject at issue concerns a competence of the Union or of the Member States within the EU, either the Commission or the EU Member States will speak for the Union. In most cases the ambassadors of the EEA/EFTA States to the Union and representatives of the Commission meet, as most issues relate to the EU as such.

Decisions to incorporate new Community legislation into the EEA Agreement are taken by agreement between the Community side, on the one hand, and the EFTA States speaking with one voice, on the other. The EFTA States coordinate their positions in the Standing Committee of the EFTA States. The decisions of the Standing Committee are made by unanimous vote. Thus, in all relevant cases each EEA/EFTA State has a veto right as it may prevent the EFTA side from taking a common position, and thus inhibit the Community and the EFTA side to make a decision "by agreement". The Court held in *CIBA* that such a decision

> may constitute a simplified form of an international agreement between the Community and its Member States on the one hand, and the EFTA States party to the EEA Agreement on the other [....].

We added that

> the competence of the EEA Joint Committee is not unlimited. It must, in particular, be exercised within the boundaries of the EEA Agreement and with due respect for essential procedural requirements.

The EFTA Court had already interpreted two Joint Statements of the EEA Joint Committee in *Allied Colloids*. It is remarkable that the Court has the competence to interpret decisions of the EEA Joint Committee since the latter consists not only of the representatives of the EEA/EFTA States, but also of those of the Community and of the EU Member States. The EEA Joint Committee has no competence to change the main part of the EEA Agreement regardless of whether the Treaty on the Functioning of the European Union (TFEU), the text of reference for the EEA Agreement, has been amended. The only institutions which may—by way of rendering judgment and thereby establishing case law—"amend" the main part of the EEA Agreement are the EEA Courts: The EFTA Court, the ECJ, and the GC.

The ESA/Court Committee is the body within which the EEA/EFTA States exercise their functions under the SCA. It consists of the EU ambassadors of the three EEA/EFTA States. The Committee has no legal basis in the SCA. It fulfils the tasks assigned to the governments under the SCA, and its members act upon instructions from the Member States. The Committee is in particular responsible for the approval of the budget and the financial statement of ESA and of the Court. It also deals, e.g., with amendments to the Court's Staff rules and regulations, to the Court's Statute and to its Rules of Procedure in so far as the EEA States have a say. The chair of the Committee rotates every six months. I have attended numerous ESA/Court Committee meetings and it has rarely been a pleasure.

When it comes to surveillance and judicial control, the two pillar structure underlying the EEA Agreement is of particular relevance. When Britain sought EEC membership in 1961 and NATO members Denmark and Norway wanted to do the same, the three neutral EFTA States Austria, Sweden and Switzerland started association negotiations with the European Communities. These talks lasted from 1961 to 1963. Switzerland had the illusion that disputes could be settled by an arbitration tribunal with equal representation. On 24 September 1961, Switzerland in a declaration addressed to the EEC Council of Ministers stated:

> *Les divergences éventuelles touchant à l'exécution des obligations du traité d'association pourraient, en cas de besoin, être portées devant un organe arbitral statuant à la majorité, qui se prononcerait, selon les cas, soit sur le fond du problème soit sur d'éventuelles mesures de compensation.*

> (Any divergences concerning the fulfilment of the obligations under the Association Treaty could, if necessary, be referred to an arbitration body ruling by majority, which would decide, depending on the case, either on the substance of the problem or on possible compensation measures.)

The negotiations were terminated in 1963 because French President de Gaulle vetoed British EEC accession. They therefore never reached a stage where the issue of conflict resolution was discussed. But one thing is clear: The EEC would not have accepted an arbitral tribunal which would have been competent to rule on substantive questions. Had an association agreement been concluded at that time, the three States would have been put under the jurisdiction of the ECJ. It is an irony of history that the Swiss, who made the case for an independent EFTA Court during the EEA negotiations, finally withdrew from the EEA project in 1992. Looking back, it is clear that the establishment of their own court is probably the biggest accomplishment of the EFTA States under the EEA Agreement.

2 The EFTA Court's Difficult Birth

2.1 The ECJ's First EEA Opinion

The first version of the EEA Agreement foresaw the establishment of a combined EEA Court, which would consist of judges from the ECJ and from the EFTA States. The EEA Court was assigned the task of settling disputes between the Contracting Parties and of controlling ESA. The negotiations were concluded on 21 and 22 October 1991 in Luxembourg. Initialisation was, however, postponed since the President of the ECJ on 15 November 1991 informed the EC Member States, the Commission and the Council, that the draft raised serious legal questions. A hearing took place on 26 November 1991. In its famous, some might even say infamous, Opinion 1/91 of 14 December 1991, the ECJ, using rather harsh language, declared the proposed system of judicial control to be incompatible with the EC Treaty. The ECJ held that the divergences that existed between the aims and context of the draft EEA Agreement and those of Community law would stand in the way of the achievement of the objective of homogeneity in the interpretation and application of EEA law. It further stated that an international agreement to which the Community was a party and which provided for the establishment of a court system was in principle compatible with Community law. However, since the EEA Agreement would take over an essential part of the rules which govern economic and trading relations within the Community and which constitute fundamental provisions of the Community legal order, the machinery of courts provided for in the Agreement would conflict with Community law. Moreover, the ECJ found that depending on whether the judges of the ECJ, which were also members of the EEA Court, were sitting on one court or the other, they would have to apply the same provisions but use different approaches, methods and concepts in order to take account of the nature of each treaty and of its particular objectives. It would be very difficult, if not impossible, for those judges, to tackle questions with completely open minds when sitting in the ECJ. The ECJ finally observed that it was unacceptable that the answers it would give to the courts and tribunals in the EFTA States on the interpretation of rules would be purely advisory, as was stated in the draft. Contrary to what might be assumed by its designation, an Opinion of the ECJ is binding legal act. If is is adverse,

> the agreement envisaged may not enter into force unless it is amended or the Treaties are revised.[1]

With hindsight, I think that the ECJ had a valid point when it rejected the idea of a combined court. Nevertheless, other parts of the opinion overshot the mark. This holds true, in particular, for the sections on the alleged impossibility of a homogeneous development of case law in the EEA and on the methods of interpretation. Furthermore, the apparent unwillingness of the ECJ to enter into a dialogue with the

---

[1]Article 218(11) TFEU.

planned EEA Court was disappointing. At the time, nobody could foresee that on this latter point the dialogue between the ECJ and the EFTA Court would develop into an almost partner-like relationship.[2]

2.2 *The ECJ's Second EEA Opinion*

Following the ECJ's first EEA opinion of 14 December 1991, the idea of establishing a joint judicial mechanism was abandoned. It was decided that the EFTA States would set up their own court of law consisting of only EFTA judges with similar competences in the EFTA pillar as the ECJ had in the EU pillar. The EFTA Court was to be structurally independent from the ECJ. On 10 April 1992 the ECJ issued a second Opinion, 1/92, in which it gave its consent to the new solution. On 2 May 1992, the EEA Agreement as well as the SCA were signed in Oporto and on 1 January 1994, the two treaties entered into force.

3 The EEA Judiciary

3.1 *ECJ*

The ECJ was established in 1952 as the Court of the European Coal and Steel Community (ECSC). Its spirit was shaped at a time when it was not truly "European" in the geographical sense of the word. The legal historian Ditlev Tamm, from the University of Copenhagen, wrote on the occasion of the ECJ's 60th anniversary:

> The history of the Court cannot be correctly understood without constantly having in mind how the Court has conceived itself as a part of a political project on the shaping of Europe and has defined its position by broadly interpreting the provisions of the treaties that brought it into being. Those provisions were sufficiently open to enable the Court to develop new principles of law which, in order for European law to fulfil its task, must have direct effect and supremacy in relation to national law.

Today, the ECJ consists of 28 judges; after Brexit, the number of judges will be 27. Every Member State has the right to nominate one judge, no matter how big or small it is. The appointment is made by common accord of the governments of the Member States for a term of six years. In addition, there are 11 AGs whose task it is to render a reasoned opinion in important cases; after Brexit there will be 10 AGs.

The Court of the ECSC was essentially modelled on the French *Conseil d'État*. The *Conseil d'État* is both a legal advisor to the government (since 2008 also to the parliament) and the court of last resort for administrative justice. A central role was

[2]See, for details, Chapter 21.

played by Maurice Lagrange, an assistant to Jean Monnet, Monnet being one of the Founding Fathers of European integration. Lagrange, a former member of the *Conseil d'État*, is considered one of the brains behind the French idea of making AGs independent advisers to the judges. Nevertheless, the AG remains a member of the court. Lagrange himself served as the first French AG from 1952 to 1958 at the Court of the ECSC and from 1958 to 1964 at the ECJ. The ECJ continues to honour Maurice Lagrange's memory. His portrait is displayed alongside those of his colleagues. In his CV on the Court's website there is, however, a gap covering the years 1934–1945. This is clearly due to the fact that he was a partisan of Philippe Pétain's Vichy regime. In his capacity as *Chargé de Mission au Secrétariat Général de la Présidence du Conseil* ("Chargé de Mission at the General Secretariat of the Presidency of the Council"), Lagrange was very actively involved in drafting anti-Jewish legislation; he is even considered the author of the Statute on Jews (*statut des juifs*). On 3 October 1940, the Jews with French nationality lost, by decree of the Vichy regime, their status as full citizens, which they had obtained during the French Revolution on 21 September 1791. Raul Marc Jennar writes of Lagrange:

> *Il fut sans conteste un des principaux rédacteurs du droit antisémite du régime de Vichy.* (He was undoubtedly one of the principal drafters of the anti-Semitic law of the Vichy regime.)

Based on this legislation, over 70,000 Jews were deported to death camps. Jean Monnet was apparently not bothered by that.

In 1958, the Court of the ECSC became the Court of Justice of the European Communities, following the creation of the European Economic Community (EEC) and the European Atomic Energy Community. While the jurisdiction was broadened, the composition remained essentially the same. With each successive enlargement of the Community, the number of members of the Court has risen. With the entry into force of the Treaty of Lisbon on 1 December 2009, the court was renamed the Court of Justice of the European Union (CJEU).

As I have said, the ECJ is strongly influenced by French law and legal culture. Even though a case will "leave" the ECJ in the same language as when it entered the ECJ, deliberations are usually held in French, oral pleadings and any written legal submissions are translated into French and, depending on the circumstances, various other languages. French is thus the ECJ's main working language. Of course, I have never taken part in a deliberation before our sister court. However, I imagine that the language regime is advantageous for the Francophone judges and anyone whose first foreign language is French such as, for example, the Italians. The AGs may work and draft their opinions in a variety of languages, even though they usually choose their mother tongue. The opinions are then translated into French, but also into the majority of the other EU languages. I am told that AGs may work hard on the French translations provided by the ECJ's translation service before these are made available to the other members of the court. The judgment is also drafted in French. The authentic version of the judgment remains the language of the case when it entered the court. Finally, at the end of the process, the judgment is also translated into the other official EU languages.

Even though this appears to be a jungle of languages and translations, it is clear that the prevailing language is French. In this context, the influence of legal secretaries ("*référendaires*") on the case law should not be overlooked. In December 2015, 30.84% of all the legal secretaries in the then three EU Courts (ECJ, GC and Civil Service Tribunal [CST]) were French. At the GC, the figure was 39.78%. 13.22% were Belgian whereas only 10.13% were German, 2.64% British and 2.20% Irish. 40.09% were Francophone, 12.78% Germanophone and only 4.85% Anglophone. Two remarks must be made in this regard. First, the high percentage of French speakers is more than a simple consequence of the fact that French is the working language of the Union courts; many judges, in particular those from the so-called "new Member States", have only a limited knowledge of the language of Molière. For them it is a necessity to hire at least one Francophone legal secretary. Second, this high percentage of French educated lawyers obviously also affects the ECJ's direction. After all, language has an impact on the way we think and thus also influences content and outcome. As Austrian author Karl Kraus famously noted:

> *Die Sprache ist die Mutter, nicht die Magd des Gedankens* (Language is the mother of thought, not its handmaiden).

A former GC Judge said to me on many occasions that French was the appropriate language for the Union courts because it best corresponded to the structure of Union law. A judge from the German Supreme Court told me once that he preferred French as the ECJ's working language over English because it was a continental language and that this was still better than English which was also the language of the Americans.

Whether these contentions are true remains open. Speaking about the important role of legal secretaries, I may add that there is a revolving door between the Commission and the Union courts. Given the Commission's role in proceedings before the ECJ, this is not without its problems. Moreover, there are quite a few EU judges who have started their European careers as legal secretaries. It is therefore sometimes felt that there is a certain amount of inbreeding.

Not only the ECJ's working language follows continental tradition, but also the structural choice against dissenting opinions in judgments. When the drafters of the ECSC Treaty were faced with the question of whether to allow the opinions of minority judges to be made public, they knew that such a system had been implemented at the International Court of Justice (ICJ). However, none of the six founding Member States of what is now the EU had a system of dissenting and concurring opinions in their national legal orders. After discussion, the view prevailed that the independence of the judges and the authority of the court would be better protected without such a system. At the end of the day, the desire to give the impression that the court's decision has been unanimous or—at least—the desire to show a united front to the outside world must have played a role. According to Montesquieu's famous pronouncement, a judge is only the mouth that pronounces the words of the law ("*la bouche qui prononce les paroles de la loi*"). From this perspective, the judge does not add anything to the written law when interpreting it. Therefore, every judge who acts *lege artis* will reach the same result.

Maurice Lagrange stated in 1964 that one reason for creating the function of AG was to create:

> *une sorte de contre-partie à l'interdiction du droit pour les juges de publier éventuellement leur opinion dissidente* (A sort of counterpart to the prohibition on judges' right to eventually publish their dissenting opinion).

This contention is, however, incorrect. In certain cases, the AG may indeed act as a dissenter, for example if there are two ways of answering a legal question and the AG opts for one way whereas the ECJ chooses the other. But as a matter of principle, the difference between AGs and dissenting judges is that the latter give their diverging views knowing what the majority has decided.

French administrative law has played a decisive role in the drafting of the grounds on which an act of a European organ may be declared null: lack of competence, infringement of an essential procedural requirement, infringement of the Treaties or of any rule of law relating to their application, misuse of powers. Finally, French administrative law has had and continues to have an impact on the ECJ's judicial style.[3]

3.2 General Court

In 1989, a Court of First Instance (CFI) was established, which now bears the name General Court (GC). Until recently it consisted of 28 judges, one per Member State, but in December 2015 it was decided to gradually double the number of Judges to 56.

After having come to Luxembourg, I soon realised that there was a considerable power gap between the ECJ and the GC. The difference between the ECJ and the GC is also signalled to the general public. During official sittings and so-called solemn undertakings, events that are mostly held if a member of the EU judiciary leaves office and their successor is being sworn in, the members of the ECJ are enthroned two metres above the ground whereas the members of the GC sit at the same level as the ordinary people.

3.3 EFTA Court

The EFTA Court, which was initially supposed to have seven judges, was launched on 1 January 1994 with five judges and has since September 1995 consisted of three

[3]See for details Chapter 27.

judges. It was in many, but not in all respects, modelled on the ECJ's template. The rules on nomination and appointment of judges were basically taken over from EU law. This was also done as regards the oppression of dissenting opinions and the grounds justifying the annulment of ESA decisions.

However, the French model was not taken over wholesale by any means. For one thing, the EFTA Court's working language is English. In addition, it is significant that the EFTA Court does not have an AG. The drafters of the SCA may have thought that due to the written homogeneity rules which are based on the assumption that the ECJ will decide a legal question first and the EFTA Court will follow, there was no need for this function which didn't exist in any of the EFTA States. The EFTA Court's first President and former EEA and SCA negotiator, the Finn Leif Sevón, gave an additional explanation: the EFTA States were not prepared to spend the money that would have been needed to create the post of AG. In 2011, the Court proposed to the three EEA/EFTA Governments that an AG post should be created in the EFTA pillar. When I spoke about this motion at the University of Oslo in 2011, a practising lawyer put forward a valuable argument: he said that since our preliminary rulings are strictly speaking not legally binding, a national court could, if the EFTA Court did not follow the AG, conclude that the latter's view was more convincing. At the current juncture, it does not seem that there will be an AG at the EFTA Court in the foreseeable future. Together with other factors, the lack of an AG has had an impact on the EFTA Court's judicial style.[4]

The EFTA Court's most important types of procedure are: the infringement procedure, the preliminary reference procedure and the nullity procedure. The respective provisions are essentially taken from EU law, but there are certain differences. In infringement proceedings, ESA is suing an EEA/EFTA State alleging that the latter is in breach of its obligations under the EEA Agreement. With an action for nullity, a private operator or an EEA/EFTA State is challenging the validity of an ESA decision. Infringement and nullity actions are direct actions. In preliminary reference proceedings, a national court of an EEA/EFTA State requests the EFTA Court to interpret EEA law.

When I joined the bench in September 1995, the ECJ was sometimes referred to as "big brother" in EFTA Court circles. This was to a certain extent understandable because we had just been downsized from five to three Member States and accordingly from five to three judges. And yet I disliked this jargon for several reasons, in particular because it bespoke a lack of self-confidence. In the meantime, the ECJ has come to be known as our sister court. The EFTA Court may be the smaller sister, but it has its own voice.

[4]See for details Chapter 27.

4 Judges' Background and Independence

4.1 General

When I speak about a court case with students, my initial question is always "what do you look at first when you start to read a judgment?" The answer I want to hear is "the composition of the court or of the chamber that has decided the case". People and therefore also judges have very diverse views on fundamental issues of life, society, religion, politics, culture, the economy, and, indeed, law. And although legal rules are meant to ensure that the outcome of a court case is predictable, the attitude and the preunderstanding of the decision-makers may be of relevance, in particular when important issues are at stake.

There is research scrutinising the professional background of European judges and political scientists have looked into the question of whether there is a correlation between this background and the judges' voting behaviour. Nevertheless, there are limits to such research because EU and EFTA judges work under a regime of secrecy of deliberations and of vote.

As in any international or supranational court, the EU and EFTA judges owe their jobs to the same governments that are subject to the jurisdiction of their court. Referring to the ECJ, Ditlev Tamm has stated with disarming openness that the important question:

> is that of loyalty of the judges towards their own country and to the Union.

The same applies obviously to the judges of the EFTA Court. To put it bluntly, one could ask: "Do European judges find themselves in the position of Carlo Goldoni's Truffaldino who was 'The Servant of Two Masters' and whose main desire was to fill his stomach no matter from which master the food was coming? Or, to take up the general theme of this book: are European judges on the leash of their countries' governments?"

In this context it is useful to recall the more general controversy concerning international courts between the American Professors Eric Posner and John Yoo, on the one hand, and Laurence R. Helfer and Anne-Marie Slaughter, on the other. According to Posner and Yoo, only dependent tribunals are effective international tribunals, which means ad hoc tribunals staffed by judges who are closely controlled by governments through the power of reappointment or the threat of retaliation. By contrast, independent tribunals, i.e. tribunals whose judges are appointed on terms similar to their colleagues in domestic courts, are said to pose a danger to international cooperation. They are likely to take into account moral ideals, ideological imperatives or the interests of other states. Helfer and Slaughter reject this approach and state that international tribunals must be independent. Otherwise the States are bound to lose credibility. The potential for judicial excess is in Helfer's and Slaughter's view limited by structural, political, and discursive mechanism.

4.2 *Official Commitment to Independence and Impartiality*

Officially, the statutes of European and international courts accentuate the impartiality and independence of judges by using florid formulations. The emphasis is thus put on the judicial function. The first paragraph of Article 30 SCA states that the judges:

> shall be chosen from persons whose independence is beyond doubt and who possess the qualifications required for appointment to the highest judicial offices in their respective countries or who are jurisconsults of recognised competence.

The provision has been taken over from EU law.

Under Article 2 of the Statute of the ICJ, the judges are elected:

> regardless of their nationality from among persons of high moral character, who possess the qualifications required in their respective countries for appointment to the highest judicial offices, or are jurisconsults of recognized competence in international law.

In a similar vein, Article 21 of the ECHR states under the heading "criteria for office" that the judges must be:

> of high moral character and must either possess the qualifications required for appointment to high judicial office or be jurisconsults of recognised competence.

4.3 *Threat to Independence and Impartiality in Practice*

University of Oslo international law Professor Dr. Mads Andenæs argued in his contribution to the farewell symposium of the President of the Higher Regional Court in Dusseldorf (*Oberlandesgericht Düsseldorf*), Anne-José Paulsen, on 1 February 2018, that the position of international and European judges is different from judicial positions as we know them under domestic law. Whereas, under domestic law, the judicial function is predominant, there may be judicial, civil service and diplomatic elements at the international and European level. In fact, different governments have different records when it comes to the question of which of these elements they wish to emphasise. Only if a government puts the emphasis on the judicial criterion, impartiality and independence come to the fore. In many cases, however, governments focus on the civil service and diplomatic aspects which means that the sovereignty of the respective State and the representation of its interests are in the foreground. And thus these sovereign States maintain a considerable degree of control over their judges. Some treat international judges in a way that would not be possible vis-à-vis domestic judges. This may result in a general attitude of state-friendliness on the part of the judges and put private operators who under European law should enjoy the same rights in court procedures as the States, at a disadvantage. According to common parlance, the judges "represent" the States that have nominated them.

If a government focuses on the civil service aspects, a lot depends on whether the judge concerned is willing and actually has the strength of character to retain his/her independence, even at the risk of not being renominated. At this point personal traits come into play. A courageous judge will be less inclined to vote against his/her better judgment than a fainthearted judge. Judges with excellent reputations will not easily be scared because it would be difficult to fire them. At a large court such as the ECJ, judges may be removed from the line of fire by assigning cases concerning their country to another chamber. Alternatively, politically sensitive cases may be assigned to a Judge Rapporteur who will not seek reappointment. However, at the EFTA Court with its three judges, such measures can only be taken to a limited extent.

At the ECJ and the EFTA Court, judges are appointed for six years and may be reappointed an unlimited number of times. In practice, the proposals of the individual governments for appointment and reappointment are not challenged by the other governments. That a candidate has the qualification to become a judge on the highest court of their country is an objective criterion. The same goes for the alternative requirement that a candidate is a jurisconsult of recognised competence. It is commonly understood that this implies holders of a university chair in law, in other words full professors. Whether a judge will act in an independent way can, however, not be determined in advance. If the respective prognosis is made, one may nevertheless base oneself on certain principles derived from experience. Based on what I have seen, it can be assumed that a candidate who has over a long period of time (in particular during his formative years) been socialised as a bureaucrat or as a diplomat is less likely to act in an independent manner than a candidate who comes from the national judiciary, academia or the practising bar.

If you look at the CV's of the members of the ECJ, you will discover that there is in fact a significant percentage of former senior bureaucrats. The policy of a model EU Member State may serve as an example in this respect. Since 1996, Luxembourg, which was once famous for nominating candidates such as Pierre Pescatore or Fernand Schockweiler, has only delegated government officials. Romain Schintgen was a senior bureaucrat when he became a judge of the Court of First Instance (CFI) in 1989 before being promoted to the ECJ in 1996. His successor Jean-Jacques Kasel came directly from government service. After having pursued a fully-fledged career as a Luxembourg and European bureaucrat, which included ambassadorships and the position of Permanent Representative of Luxembourg to the Council of the European Communities respectively the EU as well as the position of Chamberlain to HRH the Grand Duke of Luxembourg, he became an ECJ judge in 2008. In 2013, he was succeeded by François Biltgen, a former Minister for Justice, Minister for Communications and the Media, Minister for Religious Affairs, Minister for the Civil Service and Administrative Reform, and Minister for Higher Education and Research in the Luxembourg Government. The case of Mr. Kasel is particularly puzzling because his career as a European bureaucrat had already been the subject of an ECJ judgment 23 years prior to his appointmentin the *Schloh v Council* case. On 30 June 1983, a panel of three judges annulled a decision of the Secretary General of the Council to appoint Mr. Kasel to the newly created post of Director of the Budget and Staff Regulations of the Council. The so-called "parachute procedure" had been applied whereby the Luxembourg Government and the appointing authority had reached agreement in advance on the appointment of a specific person to a post before the appointing authority had even initiated the recruitment procedure.

As regards their legal experience, the representatives of constitutional and public international law are in a dominant position. Few EU or EFTA judges have a background in fields such as antitrust law, intellectual property law, corporate law, contract law, tort law or private law in general when they are appointed. Judges with a tax law background have rarely been active in corporate tax law, it was more usual for them to have been tax collectors. The high proportion of former civil servants may have an impact on a court's attitude. Unlike other members of the legal profession such as judges, private practitioners or university professors, bureaucrats are during their employment by a government subject to instructions from their superiors. Although they may be very powerful in certain cases, they lack experience as regards what it means to be independent. If such people are appointed to a court of law after having been socialised over years or decades to follow orders, they may in effect be used to taking a favourable stand vis-à-vis government interest and they may have little idea of how to arrive at their own solutions to complex legal issues. Such reliance may take many forms. In extreme cases—and I have experienced this first-hand—a judge may pick up the phone and ask for information on the background of proceedings from a source in his/her home country. Or he/she may discuss the matter on the occasion of a visit at home. Vice versa, government officials may approach judges in order to let them know what their expectations are regarding the outcome of a case. A smoother way for governments to exert undue influence on the outcome of a case is for judges to internalise the respective position. They will then automatically act accordingly.

Since experience has shown that in practice, the commitment to independence and impartiality in the written law was not sufficient to exclude the nomination and appointment of dependent individuals, a panel was established in the EU in 2007 by Article 255 TFEU. The panel's task is to

> give an opinion on candidates' suitability to perform the duties of Judge and Advocate-General of the Court of Justice and the General Court before the governments of the Member States make the appointments.

A number of candidates proposed by individual governments have been rejected by the panel. However, no such mechanism exists in the EFTA pillar of the EEA. In 2011, the Court proposed that the governments establish such a mechanism with the task of scrutinising the candidates for judgeship put forward by the governments and making a non-binding assessment. The governments did not react.[5]

[5]See for details Chapter 28.

Since the hope of being reappointed for an additional term of office may affect the independence of a judge, the system was changed at the ECtHR in 2010. The term of office was prolonged from six to nine years and the possibility of reappointment was abolished. At the ICJ judges may be reappointed for one term.

4.4 The EFTA Court's Record

Four Norwegians, three Icelanders and one judge nominated by Liechtenstein have served on the EFTA Court between its downsizing to three judges in the summer of 1995 and April 2018 when I stepped down. The first two Norwegian judges, Bjørn Haug and Per Tresselt, joined the bench in their sixties after fully-fledged government careers. The third one, Henrik Bull, was an academic who had also worked in the Ministry of Justice. The current judge, Per Christiansen, was an employee of the Norwegian Central Bank, a lawyer, an academic and a bureaucrat in the Ministry of Finance. He had also served as the EFTA Court's registrar from 1995 to 1998. On balance, the Norwegian Government has shown a clear tendency to nominate candidates whose behaviour on the bench is, from the perspective of the State's interest, predictable, in other words people the administration thinks can be kept on a leash. In this context, we must also look at the names and careers of applicants who were not nominated because they were considered too independent. It is finally important not to overlook the fact that the domestic courts in Norway also to a large extent consist of judges who are close to the State.

The Icelandic Government has pursued a different policy. The first Icelandic judge, Thór Vilhjálmsson, had a career as a university professor and a Supreme Court Judge. He was appointed to the EFTA Court from his position as Chief Justice of Iceland. The second appointee, Thorgeir Örlygsson had been a judge and full professor before serving for three years as a senior civil servant. Finally, the current judge Páll Hreinsson had been a full professor and a Justice of the Icelandic Supreme Court.

With my nomination in the summer of 1995, the Liechtenstein Government basically allied itself with the judicial paradigm. I was a full professor and a member of the Liechtenstein Supreme Court before being appointed to the EFTA Court. My teaching and research experience extended to Switzerland, Germany and the U.S.

There is a major difference between the EU pillar and the EFTA pillar which in my view poses problems from the perspective of reciprocity and homogeneity: As I will explain, there is no supranational panel looking into the nominations in the EFTA pillar.[6]

---

[6]See for details Chapter 28.

5 The Backbone of the EEA Agreement

5.1 *Introduction*

The backbone of the EEA Agreement consists of two principles: Homogeneity and reciprocity. According to Recital 4 of the preamble, the Contracting Parties were, when they concluded the EEA Agreement, considering

> the objective of establishing a dynamic and homogeneous European Economic Area, based on common rules and equal conditions of competition and providing for the adequate means of enforcement including at the judicial level, and achieved on the basis of equality and reciprocity and of an overall balance of benefits, rights and obligations for the Contracting Parties.

Homogeneity is referred to in many other provisions, whereas reciprocity is not. But that doesn't mean that reciprocity is not equally important. In fact, the two principles are twin maxims and there are certain overlaps between them.

5.2 *Reciprocity*

The EEA Agreement is a market access treaty and reciprocity is a trade law concept. It means that the EEA States in both pillars must grant citizens and economic operators the same rights to do business. Likewise, the EFTA States cannot support their own operators by granting State aid which distorts competition. In other words, reciprocity boils down to give and take. For the sake of good order, I would add that reciprocity is also an old religious principle. Luke 6:31 reads:

> And as you wish that others would do to you, do so to them.

One could, moreover, invoke Confucius, Egyptian ethics, the Golden Rule—it is always the same. However, in EEA law, the principle goes further than that. It gives citizens and economic operators rights which can be enforced in court. These rights are granted to people and businesses from the other EEA States. AG Kokott, one of the EFTA Court's most important dialogue partners, stated in point 42 of her Opinion of 21 March 2013 in the *British Social Security Systems* case that

> not only does a Norwegian national, to name one example, benefit from the coordination of social security systems [....] within the territory of the European Union, but also a Union citizen in Norway.

However, the principle of reciprocity also has a positive effect in that private entities may bring proceedings against their own governments.

The most important accomplishments benefiting citizens and economic operators in the EU pillar are:

- The ECJ has recognised the principles of direct effect, primacy of EU law, State liability and conform interpretation. Citizens and economic operators may this

invoke EUI law in courts and in case of a conflict between EU law and the law of Member States, EU law prevails
- Courts of last resort are, as a matter of principle, obliged to refer cases involving EU law to the ECJ for a preliminary ruling.
- National courts of the EU Member States are legally obliged to follow the ECJ's preliminary rulings.

EFTA citizens and economic operators directly profit from this legal situation when they are active in the EU pillar of the EEA. From the perspective of reciprocity, their EU counterparts must be granted similar rights in the EFTA pillar. In this context, it must be underlined that according to Recital 8 of the preamble to the EEA Agreement, the Contracting Parties are convinced

> of the important role that individuals will play in the European Economic Area through the exercise of the rights conferred on them by this Agreement and through the judicial defence of these rights.

As University of Cambridge Professor Catherine Barnard has written:

> The principle of reciprocity has a substantive and a procedural dimension. The substantive dimension concerns the content of rights. [....] The procedural dimension [....] requires equal treatment in access to the courts, especially in the context of the Article 34 SCA reference procedure (i.e. EU citizens should enjoy the same rights in EEA states in respect of access to justice as EEA citizens enjoy before the courts in EU states).

Nevertheless, from the very beginning certain governments had difficulties in accepting the relevance of reciprocity for the interpretation of Article 34 SCA, the provision that regulates the preliminary reference procedure.[7]

5.3 *Homogeneity*

The law of the EEA Single Market must, as a matter of principle, develop in a homogeneous way. Economic operators and citizens must be able to compete on a level playing field. Two aspects of homogeneity are to be distinguished: legislative and judicial homogeneity.

5.3.1 Legislative Level

EEA law originates from EU law. As I said, when new EU law which will be incorporated into the EEA Agreement is enacted, the EEA/EFTA States have a co-determination right on the expert level (so-called decision shaping), but they don't have a co-decision right (so-called decision making).[8] In Norway, two notions

---

[7]See for details Chapter 25.

[8]See for details this Chapter.

have been created in that respect: It is asserted that democracy has turned into a "faxocracy" because allegedly new law is being sent to the country by telefax from Brussels. And it is said that Norway is not a "rule maker," but a "rule taker."

In my view the lack of a co-decision right has partly been overstated by Norwegian politicians and diplomats. The same goes by the way for their Swiss colleagues.[9] First of all, a lot of EU legislation is based on global regulation. I will just mention the law of the United Nations (UN), the WTO, or the Basel Accords on banking supervision. Global norms exist, for example, on food safety and environmental law, competition law, public procurement law, the regulation of pharmaceutical products, accounting and auditing, and climate change. Second, the course is often set at the expert level and whether the EEA/EFTA States make sufficient use of their co-determination right has always been controversial. Third, the critics are to a certain extent comparing apples and oranges, since the EEA/EFTA States have retained their sovereignty with regard to the common policies, in particular in the areas of foreign trade, agriculture and fisheries. As regards foreign trade, I would like to mention that Norway has initiated WTO dispute settlement proceedings in three cases. Fourth, politicians in the EEA/EFTA States may resent the fact that they cannot participate in the European Summits. In other words, they cannot play with the big hitters.

Over the years, I have regularly addressed these issues in my speeches and lectures. On 10 May 2017, I said in a talk at the Irish Centre for European Law at Trinity College Dublin that the current EEA/EFTA States prefer to complain about the lack of a voting right instead of making sufficient use of their co-determination right.

On 13 May 2017, the Norwegian newspaper "*ABC Nyheter*" reported on my speech under the heading:

> *EFTA-domstolens president håner norske Europa-politikere.* (The President of the EFTA Court is scorning Norwegian politicians.)

Asked by the newspaper whether my accusation was true, the Norwegian Minister of EEA and EU Affairs Frank Bakke-Jensen contended that I must have relied on an old analysis. The current Norwegian Government put special emphasis on this, he said, not least by the creation of a Department for European Affairs. He added that in many cases the results were good, since Norway was present in the EU at the technical level, the civil servant level and the political level. If this is indeed the case, the situation has considerably improved. It was also positive that the Minister said that he was not complaining about a "faxocracy". For the sake of order, I add that the Norwegian Europe Ministry was abolished on 1 January 2018. It seems, however, that the Ministry of Foreign Affairs has become more EEA friendly than in the past.[10]

---

[9]See for details Chapter 30.

[10]See Epilogue.

In a remarkable essay published on 22 February 2018, the 'Economist' described the Norwegian influence on EU (and thus EEA) legislation as raising concerns over the democratic control of Norwegian law, despite the fact that most EU/EEA Single Market decisions are taken by majority vote. The article went on to state that the EEA has created a platform of trust that:

> gives Norway more say than many people realise and has served as a route to fuller co-operation in many non-economic areas. Its diplomatic mission to the EU in Brussels is by far Norway's largest. Its site is the closest of all to the European Commission's Berlaymont headquarters. Norwegian diplomats say they are fully involved in the early stages of drafting regulations in fields like energy, the environment or veterinary standards (veterinary and phytosanitary rules make up 40% of the single-market rules Norway adopts). This influence is more useful than the formal right to vote, which seldom happens on such technical matters. The Commission even employs a few Norwegian officials. And Norway keeps tabs on laws passing through the Council of Ministers and the European Parliament, where it is not represented, by relying in part on Nordic solidarity.

Moreover, in most democracy rankings, Norway ranks first (and Iceland often ranks second).

Since the conclusion of the EEA Agreement, the Union has taken the view that only Member States can fully participate in legislation. This is said to follow imperatively from the need to protect the EU's autonomy. A glance back at history shows, however, that this is not a compelling argument. When the EEA process started, Jacques Delors, the President of the Commission at the time, in a speech before the European Parliament on 17 January 1989 offered the "close EFTA friends"

> a new, more structured partnership with common decision-making and administrative institutions.

Delors took his pledge back one year later, without further ado. One reason for this may have been that the EFTA States were not unanimous in the period that followed and the majority of them wanted to join the Union anyway. Austria, Finland, Norway and Sweden regarded EEA membership on the EFTA as an intermediary step on the path to accession.[11] Nevertheless, the fact that Delors made this pledge at the time shows that it would not be unthinkable today to have a model which also allows for common decision-making in the legislative process. It is interesting that the Brussels based think tank Bruegel proposed on 29 August 2016 that the EU make a concession on this point. The five authors—among them Jean Pisani-Ferry, the Director for Programme and Ideas of Emmanuel Macron's presidential campaign, and Norbert Röttgen, the Chairman of the Foreign Affairs Committee of the German Bundestag—suggested that the EU Member States and the Non-EU States could enter into a so-called Continental Partnership (CP) Agreement. The discussion of Single Market legislation would take place in a "CP Council", which would consist of EU institutions and Non-EU CP States, and the CP States would have a right to propose amendments. The EU would, in the end, be enacting its law under

[11] See also Chapter 30.

its normal legislative procedure, but there would be a political commitment by the EU Member States to take into account the points made in the CP Council. The name "Continental Partnership Agreement" is to a certain degree a misnomer as the United Kingdom (UK), Norway, and Iceland would presumably be party to it, and they are not continental countries. However, in substance, the proposal is nevertheless worth considering. I will come back to it when dealing with Brexit.[12]

5.3.2 Judicial Level

The Deer in the Headlights

According to Article 6 EEA and Article 3(2) SCA, homogeneity appears to be a one-way street. These provisions state that the EFTA Court must follow relevant ECJ case law rendered before the date of signature of the EEA Agreement (2 May 1992) and take into account case law rendered after that date. The EFTA Court held in its first case, *Restamark*, on 16 December 1994, that these rules (obviously *mutatis mutandis*) also apply to the jurisprudence of the GC. No difference was made between old and new ECJ case law. For the sake of good order, I want to mention that homogeneity is also referred to in other provisions.

It is understandable that in the early years the EFTA Court was very careful to be homogenous with its sister court. In particular in its Opinion 1/91, the ECJ had shown a certain distrust towards the idea of there being a second court dealing with issues of European integration. What's more, after the downsizing of the EFTA pillar to three Member States and the rise of Norway to superpower the EFTA Court was under considerable pressure to deviate from the homogeneity goal. Some Norwegian academics were not shy in openly claiming that when interpreting the EEA Agreement, "Norwegian legal culture" had to be taken into account. In 2006, I systematised these forays for the first time in my contribution to the *Festschrift* for Claus Gulmann, the former Danish AG and ECJ judge. Governments argued, first, that provisions of EEA law needed to be interpreted differently from parallel provisions of EU law due to alleged differences in scope between EU and EEA law; second, that the fundamental freedoms were subject in EEA law to a *de minimis* rule meaning that minor restrictions ought to be accepted; and third that special grounds for justifying national restrictions applied under EEA law. Nationalist critics felt prompted to scold the EFTA Court for not giving in to such insistence arguing that the depth of integration under the EEA Agreement was less far-reaching than under EU law. It is true that under the EEA Agreement integration does not go as far as under the EU treaties. But that doesn't mean that the Governments of the EEA/EFTA States should enjoy a substantial leeway.

And yet, the fact remains that in those formative years, the EFTA Court behaved to a certain extent like the proverbial deer in the headlights. For example, when I disliked a certain wording in drafts presented by my colleagues, because it did not convince me

[12]See Chapter 31.

in substance or because I felt that it was bad style, I frequently discovered that these passages were copy/paste from a corresponding ECJ judgment.

For a number of years, homogeneity was also understood as a snapshot in time. The prevailing view was that after every judgment—either of the EFTA Court or of the ECJ—it was necessary (and possible) to assess whether the case law in both EEA pillars was homogeneous. In particular diplomats thought that if there was a trace of inhomogeneity, it would be appropriate to apply the dispute settlement provisions of the EEA Agreement. This was an unworkable idea from the beginning. If you have one economic area and two independent courts, it is *a priori* impossible that these two courts can go hand in hand at every single point in time.

Process-oriented Notion of Homogeneity and Judicial Dialogue

At some stage, every operator must become an adult and gain self-confidence. The EFTA Court has done that. In the last years, a new concept of homogeneity has emerged which is based on realism. According to this approach, the principle of homogeneity is not just a question of who will lead and who will follow; it is rather a dialectic process. Ultimately it is evident that both courts, the ECJ and the EFTA Court, wish to develop an optimal solution through reasoned arguments. In 2014 the then ECJ President Vassilios Skouris first (and foremost) described this concept of homogeneity in his contribution to the *Festschrift* marking the EFTA Court's twentieth anniversary. He declared:

> The long lasting dialogue between the EFTA Court and the CJEU has allowed the flow of information in both directions. 'Ignoring EFTA Court precedents would simply be incompatible with the overriding objective of the EEA Agreement which is homogeneity.' The symbiotic nature of the relationship has contributed to the successful development of the EEA Single Market. Both courts stand as examples for each other thus depicting mutual respect, strengthening the rules of homogeneity and representing a high level of appreciation. Cooperation between the two was built on strong foundations which have stood the test of time.

Homogeneity had thus developed into a process-oriented concept. My former Head of Cabinet Dr. Philipp Speitler, now a judge in Germany, has elaborated on this. He wrote in 2017:

> [A]s such, any assumed divergence between the EFTA Court's and the ECJ's case law must be assessed in a broader context, take into account the specific and concrete circumstances of each case and, last but not least, has to necessarily be seen from a relative perspective [….] [I]n a dynamic EEA, homogeneity cannot demand the permanent identical interpretation of EEA law by both courts. If this were the case, this concept would reach its limits: it should not be overlooked that the courts never decide cases in parallel. Neither do they have to answer the same questions, nor do they have to decide the same cases at the same point in time. Both courts, however, have to take all the circumstances of the question or the case at hand into consideration; and invariably the circumstances differ. Furthermore, it is a necessity for both courts to be able to take account of developments in science, including economic theories, and changes in technology and society. The decisions about the interpretation of the EEA Agreement are often made after long intervals. So over the years the circumstances, and indeed how to interpret the provisions of the EEA Agreement, may change. Consequently, when the courts give different answers to similar questions about

> EEA law, these differences may by no means entail a breach of the principle of homogeneity.

University of Oslo Professor Hans Petter Graver concurred immediately. Practical experience teaches us that process-oriented homogeneity can only be achieved through dialogue. This means that the courts must constantly discourse with each other and may at certain times hold different views on certain issues. In this context, it should be noted that the written rules of the EEA Agreement on the resolution of a conflict between the two EEA courts are hardly operational. Article 105(2) EEA provides that the EEA Joint Committee, a diplomatic body, must keep the development of the case law of the ECJ and the EFTA Court under constant review and must eventually "act so as to preserve the homogeneous interpretation of the Agreement". If the Joint Committee does not succeed in reaching a homogenous interpretation, the Contracting Parties to the dispute may agree to request the ECJ to give a ruling on the interpretation of the relevant (EEA law) rules.[13] If the dispute is not brought before the ECJ or the conflict persists, respectively, a Contracting Party may either take a safeguard measure or declare the provisional suspension of a part of the Agreement. For the sake of good order, I would add that even if the ECJ were to rule under this special procedure, such a ruling could not set aside the EFTA Court's judgment.

These dispute resolution provisions have never been applied in the 24 years of the EFTA Court's existence. That is no coincidence. As I have said before, the Joint Committee is a diplomatic body consisting of representatives of the EU and of the three EEA/EFTA States Iceland, Liechtenstein and Norway. It acts upon instruction and can only decide by consensus. It is unthinkable that such a political institution would interfere with a judgment of an independent European court of law by taking a decision on the merits of a case. This would be a blatant violation of fundamental principles of law, in particular of the principle of judicial independence and possibly even of the concept of *res iudicata*. During the EEA negotiations, the EU insisted that as regards the ECJ, this had to be laid down expressly. Under Protocol 48 to the EEA, decisions of the Joint Committee may not affect the case law of the ECJ. Already in 1997 I wrote that the same must apply to decisions of the EFTA Court. It is difficult to imagine that the EFTA States would agree to put the matter before the ECJ, the court of the other side. It is also unlikely that the EU would take safeguard measures or declare the provisional suspension of parts of the EEA Agreement because of a judicial conflict; such a step could put the existence of the Agreement at risk. There were those who hoped that such a step would be taken after our judgment in the first *Icesave* case. But nothing happened. The EU which from its early years on has prided itself as being a Community of law would simply lose face if it were to act politically against a ruling of an independent court of law

[13]See Article 111 EEA.

which has been recognised by its EU sister court as a partner institution. Obviously this implies that the EFTA Court's judgment is well-reasoned.[14]

In addition, it should not be forgotten that we are now in 2018. Shielding the independence of the judiciary has become a major issue in Europe. It cannot be that on the domestic level, at least in Western Europe, the mechanisms for protecting judges and courts are more and more refined whereas at the European level an independent court of law such as the EFTA Court should be subject to interference from political bodies. On the contrary, it could be assumed that the Copenhagen criteria, which aim to ensure that any country wishing to join the EU guarantees judicial independence, also apply to the EU itself. If the EU expects acceding States to guarantee judicial independence, it cannot afford to disregard the independence of a fellow European court whose reputation in Luxembourg and Brussels is beyond doubt. Speculation regarding what might have been in the minds of certain negotiators in 1991 and 1992 cannot be decisive when it comes to such fundamental questions.

The ECJ and the EFTA Court are therefore condemned to find homogeneous solutions by way of dialogue. The only question which arises in this situation is whether this is a good or a bad thing. Professor Peter Christian Müller-Graff of the University of Heidelberg, a well-versed expert of EEA law, has written with a somewhat salutary undertone that although the two courts work towards homogeneity, there is no guarantee of it. Nevertheless, this is not necessarily a cause for concern. It may also be a chance because this enables a certain degree of regulatory competition ("*Systemwettbewerb*"). Former WTO Appellate Body (WTO AB) Chairman Claus-Dieter Ehlermann has in fact emphasised that the ECJ benefits from the competition with the EFTA Court. Another specialist of international trade law, the late ECJ judge Pierre Pescatore, has made remarks pointing in a similar direction. This competition is not restricted to the content of the judgments. It may also relate to issues such as handling time, judicial style and quality of reasoning, as well as considerations of consumer-friendliness, transparency etc.

[14]Concerning *Icesave I*, see Chapter 25.

Chapter 4
The Legacy of the Five-Member Court

Contents

1 General

The five Judges who took the oath on 4 January 1994 were Leif Sevón from Finland, Bjørn Haug from Norway, Kurt Herndl from Austria, Sven Norberg from Sweden and Thór Vilhjálmsson from Iceland. Sevón was elected as the Court's first President. He had been a senior civil servant in the Finnish administration, a university professor and a judge on the Supreme Court as well as an EEA negotiator. On 1 January 1995, Sevón became an ECJ Judge and later the Chief Justice of Finland. Bjørn Haug had, after a career in an industrial group, been the Attorney General ("*Regjeringsadvokat*") of Norway. The Attorney General is the State's law office in civil matters. Its task is to assist and represent the government in court. It is, however, not a ministerial, but a civil servant post.[1] In his capacity as Norway's Attorney General, Bjørn's biggest accomplishment was the victory in 1993 in the ICJ case *Norway* v *Denmark* on the maritime delimitation in the area between the Danish territory of Greenland and the Norwegian island of Jan Mayen. Kurt Herndl had been a senior civil servant in the Austrian administration and an ambassador as well as an Assistant Secretary-General of the UN Secretariat in Geneva. Sven Norberg had, *inter alia*, served as a judge of the Svea Court of Appeal in Sweden and as the Legal Director of the EFTA Secretariat. Most importantly, Sven had been

[1]See regarding the Norwegian Attorney General also Chapter 8.

C. Baudenbacher, *Judicial Independence*, Springer Biographies,
https://doi.org/10.1007/978-3-030-02308-9_4

a key player in the EEA project being involved in the preparatory works, but also acting as a negotiator and facilitator. Thór Vilhjálmsson had been a professor of law, the Chief Justice of his country and a judge on the ECtHR. On 1 January 1995, when Finland acceded to the EU, President Sevón was replaced as a judge by Gustav Bygglin, a legal secretary in the Finnish cabinet and a former senior judicial secretary of the Finnish Supreme Court. Bjørn Haug was elected as President. On 30 June 1995, judges Bygglin, Herndl, and Norberg had to resign because of their countries' accession to the EU. The five-member Court ceased to exist. There were no celebrations on that occasion. The climate in the five-member Court had been poisoned by disagreement on crucial issues, in particular the nature of the EEA Agreement and its effect as well as the nature of the EFTA Court's preliminary rulings.

In the 18 months of its existence, the five-member EFTA Court addressed important issues. It dealt—in the context of alcoholic beverages—with the material scope of application of the EEA Agreement, namely the rules of origin, which set out the criteria for a product to be considered as originating within the area of the EEA. It also discussed the rules on product coverage, which determine whether a specific product falls within the scope of the Agreement.

The five-member Court emphasised the significance of homogeneity without discussing the question of what the politically important difference between old and new case law of the ECJ meant in practice. Rulings of the ECJ rendered after the signature of the EEA Agreement were not treated differently to judgments rendered prior to that date. After the disaster caused by ECJ Opinion 1/91, homogeneity was —implicitly—understood as a snapshot in time. This concept has meanwhile largely been replaced by a process-oriented view.[2] As far as interpretation is concerned, in *Samuelsson*, a Swedish case concerning the interpretation of the Insolvency Directive,[3] the five-member Court showed a preference for the teleological approach.

2 Important Precedents

2.1 Access to Justice

The five-member Court took a rather liberal stand in interpreting the notion of court or tribunal entitled to make a reference in *Restamark* and in *Mattel and Lego*. It found that the requirement of an *inter-partes* procedure was not absolute for a national body to qualify as such a court. In *Scottish Salmon Growers*, the Court held that an association of salmon growers representing the overwhelming majority of, if not all, salmon growers in a given country and negotiating on their behalf with

[2]See for details Chapters 3 and 21.

[3]80/987/EEC.

the authorities in that country and with the EC Commission or ESA was to be considered as directly and individually concerned under Article 36 SCA. It therefore had standing to challenge an ESA decision not to investigate a complaint concerning alleged State aid granted to the Norwegian salmon industry.

2.2 *Legal Nature of "Advisory Opinions"*

According to the text of the SCA, opinions of the EFTA Court rendered upon request by a national court are not legally binding on that court. However, if they are disregarded, the Member State in question may find itself in a breach of the EEA Agreement. In view of this *sui generis* nature of its preliminary rulings, the five-member Court referred to them as "judgments" in the *rubrum* and "advisory opinions" in the operative part. This was the right thing to do; it was a courageous decision.

2.3 *Free Movement of Goods*

The five-member Court ruled in *Restamark* that an obligation to obtain an authorisation or licence from a statutory State monopoly in order to import alcoholic beverages and to put them into free circulation resulted in an impediment to intra-EEA trade and was capable of giving rise to delay and abuse on the part of the importing State. Such an obligation constituted, even if the authorisation or licence was granted automatically, a measure having an effect equivalent to a quantitative restriction. Given the discriminatory character of the measure in question, justification by any of the mandatory requirements acknowledged by the ECJ (for example consumer protection) was ruled out. Justification on the grounds of the protection of public health was not deemed to be possible. The Finnish Government could not show that exclusive import rights were necessary in order to achieve the goal pursued and thus proportionate.

The EFTA Court shared the view of ESA and the Commission that a State alcohol import monopoly was incompatible with Article 16 EEA, the monopoly provision of the Agreement. By not abolishing the import monopoly by 1 January 1994, the date of entry into force of the EEA Agreement, Finland had infringed its obligations under the Agreement.

2.4 *Limits of the Transmitting State Principle*

After having shown a pro-integration attitude in its first judgments, the five-member Court made it clear in Joined cases *Mattel and Lego* that it was reluctant to interfere with the legitimate preferences of EEA/EFTA States in culturally sensitive areas. Mattel and Lego had broadcast United Kingdom (UK) commercials targeting children in Norway. The Norwegian Consumer Ombudsman (*Forbrukerombudet*), referring to Norwegian legislation, sued Mattel and Lego in the Market Council, which sent the case to the EFTA Court. The Governments of Norway, Greece, and Sweden argued, together with ESA, that the 1989 Television without Frontiers Directive[4] was to be interpreted as not preventing the receiving State from applying national provisions of the type at issue. Mattel and Lego, as well as the Commission, wanted the directive to be construed as not permitting the receiving State to apply such national provisions. The EFTA Court decided that under the transmitting State principle, a receiving State was precluded from taking action against trans-frontier broadcasts, but that it was still entitled to do so under the Misleading and Comparative Advertising Directive.[5]

2.5 *Effect*

The referring body in *Restamark* wanted to know whether Article 16, the monopoly provision of the EEA Agreement, had direct effect, namely whether citizens and economic operators should be able to invoke this Article before a national court and before the EFTA Court. The five-member Court avoided the question by reformulating it to the effect that the national court wished to know,

> whether Article 16 EEA fulfils the implicit criteria of Protocol 35 of being unconditional and sufficiently precise.

Article 16 EEA obliges the Contracting Parties to ensure

> that any State monopoly of a commercial character be adjusted so that no discrimination regarding the conditions under which goods are procured and marketed will exist between nationals of EC Member States and EFTA States.

According to Protocol 35, a homogeneous EEA is to be achieved through national procedures. For cases of possible conflicts between implemented EEA rules and other statutory provisions, the EFTA States must introduce, if necessary, a statutory provision to the effect that EEA rules prevail in these cases. The EFTA Court held that Article 16 EEA was to be interpreted as fulfilling these criteria. This effect follows from EEA law, not from the domestic law of the EFTA States. EEA law demands that such provisions are given direct effect in the legal orders of the EEA/EFTA States. The States cannot deviate from this without facing consequences.

---

[4] 89/552/EEC.

[5] 84/450/EEC.

3 Cooperation Between National Courts and Governments

In the 18 months of its existence, the five-member Court received references from Finnish, Norwegian and Swedish courts. The governments of these countries also participated in some of the cases. Striking was that the Austrians remained on the side-lines. Austria was the only State that made use of the third paragraph of Article 34 SCA. Under that provision, an EEA/EFTA State may

> in its internal legislation limit the right to request [....] an advisory opinion to courts and tribunals against whose decisions there is no judicial remedy under national law.

Article 6 of the Austrian EEA Federal Constitutional Law stated that the Constitutional Court, the Supreme Administrative Court, the Supreme Court, and other courts of last instance were entitled to request an advisory opinion on the interpretation of the EEA Agreement from the EFTA Court. No objective reasons for this limitation were given, but as the Austrian Judge on the Court, Kurt Herndl, wrote a couple of years later, the aim was to delay, complicate, maybe even avert references to the EFTA Court from Austrian courts.

This explanation fits with Austria's behaviour since. In the almost 25 years of the EFTA Court's existence, the Austrian Government never participated in a case, neither during the country's EEA/EFTA membership nor later. In this context, one should not overlook the fact that Austrian citizens residing or working in Liechtenstein were in a number of cases negatively affected by Liechtenstein legislation and administrative practice. But also in other cases, the EFTA Court has—often as the first court in the EEA—regularly addressed questions which had repercussions on the interpretation of EU law and thus on the situation of Austrian citizens and economic operators. Once or twice when visiting Vienna, I came across the bureaucrat who was responsible for preparing the Austrian submissions to the ECJ and I asked him about the reasons behind this policy. The answer was that this was a question of resources. I suspect, however, that there was another motive: Austria is so proud to be a Member State of the EU (and to sit at the table of the powerful) that it does not wish to be reminded of its 35 year EFTA membership.

4 The Policy of the Three-Member Court

The three-member Court at first continued the same line of jurisprudence on homogeneity. In recent times, however, it has gained more self-confidence.[6] The three-member Court has also confirmed and further elaborated on the interpretation of the notion of "court or tribunal" entitled to make a reference.[7] Unsurprisingly,

[6]See, in particular, Chapter 21.

[7]See further details in Chapter 8.

teleological interpretation always played an important part in the three-member Court's case law.[8] The Court did not, however, stick to the liberal approach of the five-member Court regarding the right to sue ("locus standi") in nullity actions.[9]

As regards substantive Single Market law, the three-member Court took over the case law concerning the applicability of the EEA Agreement to alcoholic beverages, the incompatibility of a State import monopoly with the free movement of goods, and the reluctance to interfere with the legitimate preferences of EFTA/EEA States in culturally sensitive areas. The same goes for the five-member Court's approach towards the effect of EEA law in the legal orders of the EEA/EFTA States.

All in all, the three-member Court largely continued building on the ground laid by the five-member Court. There was, however, one, rather unfortunate exception to that continuity: After the downsizing, the three-member Court started to refer to its preliminary rulings as "advisory opinions" both in the *rubrum* and in the operative part. The goal was to weaken the normative strength of these decisions and to send the message to the national courts that they were in no way binding. Following Bjørn Haug's retirement at the end of 1999, the EFTA Court returned to its original practice. Ever since, rulings rendered under Article 34 SCA have been referred to as "judgments" in the rubrum and "advisory opinions" in the operative part. The *sui generis* nature of these decisions was also referred to in *Vienna Life* and *Swiss Life* where the Court held in its fifth answer to the Supreme Court of Liechtenstein:

> Under Article 34 SCA, the Court has jurisdiction to give advisory opinions on the interpretation of the EEA Agreement upon the request of national courts. After the Court has rendered its judgment, it falls to the referring court to interpret national law in light of the factors clarified by the Court.

At the conference marking the Court's tenth anniversary, on 21 October 2004,[10] the decision of the three-member Court to call its preliminary rulings "judgments" again led to a rather embarrassing incident. Bjørn Haug, as all former judges a guest of honour, asked for the floor. Unlike the other discussants, he marched up to the lectern and read out a prepared statement saying with a grim look that

> he had had the mixed pleasure of being a Judge of the EFTA Court for six years, five of them as President of the Court.

He then strongly emphasised that the opinions of the Court were not binding on the national courts. The EFTA Court, he stated

> has no authority to expand its own mandate for instance in the direction that its advisory opinions should take on the character of decisions legally binding on the national level.

[8]See Chapter 9.

[9]See Chapter 18.

[10]See for details Chapter 13.

Chapter 5
Resurrection from the Dead

Contents

1 What to Do if You Have no Cases?

After the downsizing of the EFTA pillar from five to three States, there were barely any cases. That did not seem to bother my colleagues who were in their mid and late sixties. But I was 48 years old and was champing at the bit to make something of the Court, to develop a case law that would not only be relevant for the EFTA pillar, but also have an impact on the EU pillar and thereby on the EEA as a whole. And who knows, I thought, in certain cases we may even render a judgment which would be relevant for non-European jurisdictions. The atmosphere continued to be ghostly.

Serving on a European court with no cases, I consoled myself with the thought that the ECSC Court was in a comparable situation in 1953. President Haug did his best to keep his fellow judges busy anyway by holding administrative meetings which were basically purposeless. The judge from Iceland, Thór Vilhjálmsson, almost always remained stoic. I had a good relationship with him from the beginning because of his friendly character and because we shared a common weakness: our love of good food. He did not specialise in European law, but was an independent mind with long experience both on his country's Supreme Court and on the ECtHR.

C. Baudenbacher, *Judicial Independence*, Springer Biographies,
https://doi.org/10.1007/978-3-030-02308-9_5

2 Succession of Contracts: Part One

On 7 May 1996 the three-member Court held its only oral hearings in Geneva in the *Eidesund* and *Langeland* cases. Under the current rules, the two cases would certainly be joined since the questions were partly identical. But, in view of its almost non-existent case load, the EFTA Court decided not to join them. The oral hearings in the two cases were held consecutively on 7 May 1996 in a room at the EFTA Secretariat. The judgments in the two cases were delivered simultaneously on 25 September 1996. The Court stated in both rulings

> that arguments made in one case may also be considered in the other without the need for repetition.

The cases concerned the interpretation of the Transfer of Undertakings Directive.[1] The operator of an oil drilling platform in the North Sea had terminated a contract for the provision of catering and cleaning services by an independent company. It had then invited tenders, and, based on those tenders, awarded the contract to another company. The main question was whether this amounted to a transfer with the consequence that the second service provider had to take over the employees of the first. The Governments of Norway, Sweden and the UK participated together with ESA and the Commission. The British Government's agent, Eleanor Sharpston, QC, became an AG on the ECJ in 2006 and is an important interlocutor for the EFTA Court. She later described the hearing in the following way:

> The hearing itself was a model of courteous, but very focussed, interaction between Bench and Bar, conducted without wasting time, but with no sense of constraint or pressure to give an approximate one-sentence answer when a delicate position required four sentences of explanation [....] my trip to Geneva left me as a counsel with a considerable and lasting respect for the three judges who had grilled me.

I spent the summer in Texas with my family teaching in the UT summer school. At the end of August 1996, we returned to Europe.

3 Settling in Luxembourg

Since 1 September 1996 the Court has had its seat in Luxembourg, on foreign soil, at a walking distance from its sister court, the ECJ. When Switzerland dropped out of the EEA project, Austria, Finland and Sweden decided to join the EU and Liechtenstein was not yet a member, the Governments of Iceland and Norway decided to move the Court's seat from Geneva to Luxembourg. My colleagues were not enthusiastic, because they enjoyed life on Lake Geneva, far away from the ECJ where there was no direct competition, but there were nice restaurants and a

---

[1] 77/187/EEC.

beautiful landscape. They were happy in Geneva, off the beaten track and out of the limelight. Although I am Swiss, I felt that the move to Luxembourg was the right thing to do. In Geneva, the three-member EFTA Court would soon have been forgotten. Now that we were located at a walking distance from our big sister court, I relished the opportunity of getting closer to the judges and AGs. I didn't know any of them personally, but I was familiar with the names of the most important ones. I knew that the ECJ was one of the most famous and most powerful courts in the world and I wanted to get to know its members, and, if possible, to exercise a certain influence on their case law. After some back and forth, the European School decided to accept EFTA children.

President Haug had single-handedly looked for premises and negotiated a headquarters agreement with the Luxembourg foreign ministry. The premises turned out not to be so great. We were renting one floor in an architecturally interesting building, the Hemicycle, but there was little daylight and the offices were rather shabby. Since we did not have our own courtroom, hearings were initially conducted in a nearby hotel and then at the Luxembourg Chamber of Commerce. Two reasons may have prompted Bjørn to opt for this location: we were not too far from the ECJ and the rent was cheap. When I became president in 2003, I tried to find a detached house which I thought could be identified as the EFTA Court's seat. But since this would have meant doubling the rent, the governments rejected the request. In 2008, we decided to renovate our offices and to build our own courtroom. The registrar at that time Skúli Magnússon deserves all the credit for the renovation. He was advised by his father Magnus, an Icelandic architect. In the final stages, a young woman architect from the Bauhaus in Dessau gave us some tips on how to design our new courtroom. The most important feature of the courtroom is certainly the bench which is almost at ground level. We did not want to outrank the citizens and counsel appearing before us.

ECJ President Gil Carlos Rodriguez Iglesias and his administration gave us a great deal of support. Professor Dr. Christian Kohler, the Director General of the Documentation and Research Department, was also particularly helpful. I had met him at the Free University of Berlin in 1985 where he spent some time working on a scientific project. We immediately became friends. At the time, neither of us could have imagined that one day we would work almost next door to each other. Christian is one of the Germans who actively contributed to restoring his country's reputation in Luxembourg and beyond Luxembourg after World War II. When then German Minister of Finance Peer Steinbrück in 2009 made disparaging remarks about countries with banking secrecy such as Austria, Luxembourg and Switzerland, he was deeply worried. As a specialist in International Procedural Law and in particular of the Brussels and Lugano regime, which contains the rules determining which courts have jurisdiction in civil and commercial disputes between residents of different European States, Christian has from the beginning taken a keen interest in the EEA Agreement. Being a professor at Saarland University, he also helped in setting up HSG's programme for its Executive Master of European and International Business Law. Christian is a convinced and convincing European, but in contrast to many of his generation he is free from fundamentalist EU thinking. He is one of the most open-minded European lawyers I have ever come across.

4 Succession of Contracts: Part Two

On 25 September 1996, the EFTA Court rendered its judgments in the *Eidesund* and *Langeland* cases. The most important question was whether the termination of a catering contract with a first service provider followed by the conclusion of a new contract for the same services with another service provider amounted to a transfer of an undertaking with the consequence that the workers had to be taken over. In that respect, the EFTA Court avoided giving a clear answer. A Norwegian newspaper therefore called the two judgments quite rightly "*tungetale*". This word is difficult to translate. A Norwegian legal secretary at the EFTA Court told me that "*tungetale*" is commonly referred to within Christian evangelical circles as the "language" spoken by a person who is suddenly touched by the Holy Spirit, typically during an evangelical mass. I should add here that there was no relevant ECJ case law on which the EFTA Court could rely. On other issues, the EFTA Court was more courageous. It held in both judgments that the Transfer of Undertakings Directive exempts all the rights and obligations regarding old-age, invalidity, and survivors' benefits. Accrual of pension benefits and the payment of pension premiums were said to be inseparable. It would make no economic sense to transfer the obligation to pay premiums once it is clear that there is no obligation to pay pensions. Again, there was no relevant ECJ jurisprudence so we had to be the first to stick our necks out. This feature had already become apparent in the case law of the five-member Court. The drafters of the EEA Agreement and of the SCA had assumed that a homogeneous development of the case law of the two EEA courts could be secured by the enactment of rules instructing the EFTA Court to follow the ECJ. In practice, however, the EFTA Court has had to tackle novel legal questions in the vast majority of its cases.

To the best of my knowledge, the ECJ has not yet been faced with the question of whether an obligation of the transferor of a business to pay premiums into a supplementary pension scheme is transferred to the purchaser. However, the England and Wales Court of Appeal followed *Eidesund* in *Adams* v. *Lancashire CC & BET Catering Serv. Ltd.* in 1997. Appeal was denied by the House of Lords. Referring to *Eidesund*, the UK Employment Appeal Tribunal came to the same conclusion in 1999 in *Frankling* v. *BPS Public Sector Ltd.*

Succession of contracts was *à la mode* in those years. The main issue we had dodged in *Eidesund* came back, and this time before both EEA courts at the same time. On 18 January 1995, the Bonn Labour Court ("*Arbeitsgericht Bonn*") in Germany asked the ECJ in the *Süzen* case whether the succession of contracts constituted a transfer of an undertaking within the meaning of the respective directive. The case was about the provision of cleaning services for a school. On 29 March 1996, the Inderøy County Court (*Inderøy herredsrett*) in Norway submitted essentially the same question to the EFTA Court in the *Ulstein and Røiseng* case. A contract for the provision of ambulance driver services for a hospital had been awarded to a second provider. In view of the importance and the political sensitivity of the issue, a prominent member of the ECJ gave us the unrequested advice that we should stay our proceedings until they had given judgment. We decided not to do this for a number of reasons. First, to have done so would have relegated us to the position of a second league court, something the EEA Agreement wanted to avoid. Second, we felt that citizens and economic operators appearing before us were entitled to have their case judged as quickly as possible. Third, there was no legal basis for us to delay the case.

AG Antonio La Pergola delivered his Opinion in *Süzen* on 15 October 1996, the day the EFTA Court held the oral hearing in *Ulstein and Røiseng*. Antonio stated in paragraph 7 that he had misgivings in applying the directive in such a case:

> To transfer the facilities (of whatever kind) required by an undertaking to another body is a decision made in competitive circumstances, which ensures a choice between several competing rivals. I fail to see how there can be any justification for the transferee of the service being required to keep on such staff of the undertaking as provided services of that kind in the past, if it has been excluded or, in any event, whose tender, submitted on that occasion, has been unsuccessful.

This was a statement of great economic law significance. On 19 December 1996, the EFTA Court gave its judgment in *Ulstein and Røiseng*. Our bottom line was such that we came to the same conclusion as AG La Pergola in *Süzen* and held

> that a mere succession of two contracts for the provision of the same or similar services will not, as a rule, be sufficient for there to be a transfer of an undertaking, business or part of a business.

No reference was made to AG La Pergola's opinion since it was not usual at the time for the EFTA Court to make such citations.

In January 1997, Bjørn Haug was elected for another three years as the EFTA Court's President.

5 The Beginning of the Dialogue with the EU Courts

Ulstein and Røiseng was a courageous judgment at a time when the EFTA pillar had just suffered the loss of Austria, Finland and Sweden and some at the EFTA Court were anxiously fixated on the ECJ. On 11 March 1997, the ECJ gave its judgment in the parallel *Süzen* case. It followed the approach taken by AG La Pergola and by us; it did not quote AG La Pergola, but it did refer to our *Ulstein and Røiseng* ruling. It was the first time the three-member Court was cited.

Both the ECJ and the then CFI started to refer to the five-member EFTA Court's case law from the outset. Former CFI President Bo Vesterdorf always proudly emphasised that it was his court that had opened this dialogue. In *Opel Austria*, the CFI on 22 January 1997 referenced the five-member Court's judgments in *Restamark* and *Scottish Salmon Growers* when elaborating on the homogeneity goal underlying the EEA Agreement. The ECJ for its part referenced the judgment rendered by the five-member Court in the joined cases *Mattel and Lego* in the *De Agostini* judgment of 9 July 1997 in the context of transfrontier broadcasts. AGs Lenz and Jacobs based themselves on this judgment in the *Flemisch Television* case and in *De Agostini*. In a further ruling of 14 March 1997 in *Ask* v *ABB and Aker*, another oil drilling platform case dealing with the Transfer of Undertakings Directive, the EFTA Court confirmed its ruling in *Ulstein and Røiseng*.[2]

[2]See for details Chapter 21 regarding judicial dialogue.

Chapter 6
The Member States—An Unholy Alliance

Contents

1 Introduction

All three EEA/EFTA States gained sovereignty relatively late in their history. After having lived under Danish rule since the 14th century, Norway was ceded to the King of Sweden in 1814 by the Treaty of Kiel. Denmark, for its part, had taken sides with Napoleon. Nevertheless, Norway declared independence, adopted a constitution and elected its own King. However, after a short war, it was obliged to enter into a personal union with the Swedish Crown. It was not until 1905 that the Union with Sweden was dissolved. Iceland was under Danish rule for centuries and only achieved sovereignty in 1918. As a consequence of the Danish–Icelandic Act

C. Baudenbacher, *Judicial Independence*, Springer Biographies,
https://doi.org/10.1007/978-3-030-02308-9_6

of Union, the Kingdom of Iceland was established as an independent State under the Danish King. However, Denmark continued to represent Iceland on foreign affairs and defence matters. On 17 June 1944, during the occupation of Denmark by the Third Reich, Iceland broke all remaining ties with Denmark and declared itself a Republic. In 1949, both Norway and Iceland were founding members of NATO. Liechtenstein became a sovereign Member State of the Holy Roman Empire in 1719. The Princely House of Liechtenstein had sought to acquire lands that would be classified as being directly subordinate to the Empire ("*reichsunmittelbar*"). This was a privileged status meaning that the land was free from the authority of any local lord and placed under the direct authority of the Emperor. The Lordship ("*Herrschaft*") of Schellenberg and the County ("*Grafschaft*") of Vaduz both enjoyed this status. In 1699 and 1712 respectively, Prince Hans-Adam I of Liechtenstein purchased Schellenberg and Vaduz. On 23 January 1719, the Holy Roman Emperor Charles VI united the two entities and elevated the new territory to the status of a Principality ("*Fürstentum*"). Nevertheless, as a matter of fact, Liechtenstein has in its recent history always been dependent on one of its neighbours, first on the Austrian-Hungarian Empire and following its collapse in 1918 on Switzerland.

From a sovereignty perspective, there is a difference between Norway and Iceland on the one hand and Liechtenstein on the other. Whereas the two Nordic EEA/EFTA States are overly concerned about their recently gained sovereignty, *inter alia* with regard to their EEA membership, the Liechtensteiners gained sovereignty by entering the EEA Agreement. The Principality is the only European State of its size which is fully integrated into a well-functioning supranational structure with its own independent surveillance authority and its own independent court of law. The situation of European States of comparable size such as Andorra, Monaco or San Marino is much more precarious.

When talking about the Member States, the main focus must be on their economic and social models. An economic and social model is an unwritten idea on how a society and its economy ought to be structured. This not only affects legislation and administrative practice, but also the way people approach conflicts, in particular whether they are resolved by negotiation or by litigation. This is bound to have an impact on the case law of the courts. The economic and social model of a given jurisdiction is not predetermined once and for all. It is often the subject of political struggle and may change over time. Except in revolutionary periods, such changes tend to occur slowly. The following remarks are mainly based on my twenty-two and a half years of experience on the EFTA Court bench, but also on contacts, visits, talks, the reading of legal, economic and political science literature and on following the media.

2 Iceland

2.1 Mixed Economy

Iceland with its 337,000 inhabitants was, for centuries, one of the poorest countries in Europe, relying on traditional agriculture and fishing with small boats. Having evolved away from a largely agriculture-based economy in the early 20th century, Iceland's main export became fish, especially cod. The growing importance of the fishing industry resulted in several clashes with European off-shore fishing nations, in particular the UK. The last "cod-war" ended in 1975 with the extension of the Icelandic fishery zone to 200 nautical miles.

Iceland became a member of EFTA in 1970. Extensive free market reforms were undertaken in the 1990s when Iceland joined both the EEA and the WTO. The country could by then be defined as a mixed economy with less government intervention compared to its Nordic neighbours. The labour market was (and is) coordinated by collective bargaining. Together with a growing global commitment to free trade, this led to strong economic growth over a long period of time. The dominating figure in Icelandic politics at the time was Davíð Oddsson, the longest-serving Prime Minister in the country's history. Davíð held the office of Prime Minister from 1991 to 2004, he then became Minister for Foreign Affairs until 2005 and afterwards served as the Chair of the Board of Governors of the Central Bank of Iceland until 2009. Right from the start, Iceland's attitude towards the EEA and the EFTA Court was generally positive. This was also enhanced by the fact that the first Icelandic judge, Thór Vilhjálmsson, was a respected and independent man. Icelandic newspapers were fair when reporting on the EFTA Court.

By the end of the millennium, Iceland had built up an international banking empire that was worth twelve times its gross domestic product (GDP). However, after the bankruptcy of Lehman Brothers, the whole banking system crashed in the autumn of 2008.[1] It was Iceland's biggest humiliation of modern times. The New York Post described what had happened in a nutshell:

> Fearsome Vikings discovered Iceland. Hedge funds knocked it down. It was a humiliating tumble for the former financial powerhouse, which was proud of its status in Europe. A late bloomer, Iceland had been the last country in Europe to be settled, the Nordic nation rapidly caught up with its wealthier relations. It was all fine until October 2008, when the country's banking system collapsed in a week.

Davíð Oddsson was replaced as the Chair of the Board of Governors of the Central Bank of Iceland in March 2009 after the collapse of the banks. However, he remained influential. Since September 2009 he has been the editor of *Morgunblaðið*, one of the country's leading newspapers.

After the breakdown of the financial system in the autumn of 2008, the Icelandic economy went through difficult years and it had to be restructured. But since

[1]See for details Chapter 25.

Iceland—unlike many EU countries—let its banks go bankrupt and introduced strict capital controls, the economy recovered with surprising speed. Due to the devaluation of the Icelandic currency, exports in fish, silicon and aluminium reached new heights and tourism became the country's largest industry. In the spring of 2017, free movement of capital was re-established. On 17 March 2017, the Financial Times wrote:

> Iceland lifted its remaining capital controls this week in a return to financial normality nine years after its biggest banks collapsed during the global financial crisis. But there is little fear that capital will leave now that the restrictions are gone. If anything, the worry is the opposite: an export and tourism-driven recovery has prompted concern that the economy could be overheating once again.

2.2 *National Character*

Iceland is living proof of Montesquieu's theory that geography and climate have an influence on the nature of men and societies. Weather conditions are tough and can change fast, the country is located on an island in the middle of the Atlantic Ocean straddling the American and Eurasian tectonic plates of the earth's crust. Standing on the continental rift in Þingvellir near Reykjavík with one foot in Europe and the other one in America is an emotional moment in one's life. The land masses are dragged further apart by 1 cm every year.

Icelanders are special people. From the very beginning, I had the feeling that they were difficult to control. When Doris and I were in Iceland for the first time in the second half of the 1990s, we visited Skálholt which in the Middle Ages had been an episcopal see; in fact it was a suffragan of the Archdiocese of Hamburg-Bremen. We were told that, after the adoption of Lutheranism in 1550, the last Catholic bishop, Jón Arason of Hólar, was executed in Skálholt along with his two sons, apparently two of several children. The thought ran through my mind that if the Catholic Church had been unable to enforce celibacy, it would not be easy for us to enforce EEA law.

A unique geography and demography is coupled with Viking ancestry. Icelanders know their sagas and are rightly proud of them, even if one must say that they also belong to the Norwegian people. The Icelanders are equally proud of their language, although most of them also speak Danish and English. They are highly educated people with a world class art scene. Many of them have more than one job. In his 2009 book, "Why Iceland?: How One of the World's Smallest Countries Became the Meltdown's Biggest Casualty", Ásgeir Jónsson, the former Chief Economist of Kaupthing Bank, the country's largest bank before the 2008 collapse, gave a colourful description of Iceland. He stated that his country was characterised by:

> a relentless, sometimes crazed assurance today that a nation of 300,000 people can triumph over other nations [....] no matter how large the opponent looms.

Quite naturally, Icelanders have a small nation complex. I don't know how often I have heard phrases like "we are a small nation" or "we are so few". But a small nation complex is not the same as an inferiority complex. In fact, it tends to mean that Icelanders constantly compete with other countries and aim to be the best. They have no reservations about comparing themselves, say, with the US and they even discuss what lessons the Americans could learn from the Icelandic experience.

The "Viking spirit" definitely played a role in the breakdown of the country's financial system. It was instrumental in leading to the irresponsible behaviour which in the end caused the collapse of the banks. At the peak of the bubble's growth, Icelandic investors arrogantly referred to themselves as the "new Vikings." However, this same spirit has also undoubtedly helped them to fight the rest of Europe under the fierce leadership of their President Ólafur Ragnar Grímsson and to prevail at the end of the day. The spirit reached a new peak at the European football championship in June 2016 when the Icelanders ousted England. After this, they even qualified for the final round of the 2018 football world cup. I always felt that the natural pride of Icelanders found its expression not least in the fact that—together with Japan—Iceland is the only country I have ever visited where tips are not expected.

Iceland is also a leading country as regards the protection of human rights and gender equality. Social conservatism barely exists. But Icelanders are not on some kind of crusade; they simply want to get on with their lives. I have also found them to have a good sense of humour.

Nevertheless, Icelanders can occasionally demonstrate a stubbornness which can be hard to understand for people from abroad. One might characterise such behaviour as atavistic or tribal. A good example is the Icelandic legislation banning the import of fresh meat, raw eggs and raw egg products, unpasteurised milk and dairy products processed from unpasteurised milk from other EEA States. Although it was obvious that these regulations were incompatible with the country's obligations under the EEA Agreement, the government refused to cave in and defended its position with the most bizarre arguments. The Court made it crystal clear in two cases *Ferskar kjötvörur ehf.* and *Icelandic Veterinary Checks* that the bans in question could not be upheld.

2.3 Judiciary

Icelandic judges are appointed for life. Until recently, the country had a two-tier court system with eight district courts and the Supreme Court, founded in 1920. From a district court, litigants could appeal directly to the Supreme Court. The District Court of Reykjavik with its 21 judges is by far the largest and the most active district court as regards references to the EFTA Court. There is one special court, the Labour Court, which is in charge of disputes in industrial relations. On 1 January 2018, a newly created intermediate Court of Appeal took up its functions.

Most Icelandic judges have different careers compared with those of their Norwegian colleagues. Only a few have previously worked for the Attorney General—who is far from being considered as powerful as the Norwegian counterpart—or for other government entities. An example to the contrary is the former Supreme Court President Gunnlaugur Claessen who, after having been employed by the Ministry of Finance, became the Attorney General himself. The Attorney General's office is a small body, even by Icelandic standards. The pool of Icelandic judges has quite a mixed background: some are career judges who started out as deputy judges or law clerks, while others have been practising law, prosecuting or teaching. There are also a few who have a background in the administration. Nevertheless, the Attorney General's office or the Ministry of Justice is not considered a breeding ground for judges. As regards the Supreme Court, one finds people with a judicial career, former practising lawyers and university professors and lecturers.

Recently the 15 judges of Iceland's new Appeal Court were appointed, seven women and eight men. Eight were district court judges, four attorneys (including the City Attorney of Reykjavik), three were professors. However, two of the professors also had a judicial background, one from the ECtHR (Davíð Thór Björgvinsson) and the other from a district court. The third professor had been practising as a lawyer.

As regards the question of judicial independence, there are numerous cases where legislation has been found to be unconstitutional by the courts. The same goes for administrative decisions. Icelandic statistics are quite unique in this respect compared to the other Nordic countries. But the reason for this difference is probably not just the lack of independence in the other jurisdictions, but also other factors such as weaker State institutions and a historical scepticism as regards public authorities which, for centuries were largely controlled by a foreign country. Unlike the Norwegians, the Icelanders do not particularly like the State. Rumour has it that one of the reasons for Icelanders to leave Norway in the Viking Age was that they wanted to evade taxes. I have also learnt that during the "struggle for independence", there was never any rhetoric about an "independent Icelandic State"; the demand was to win "independence for the Icelandic People". I have met many Icelandic judges who are—despite their legalist or even positivist education—rather free spirits.

2.4 *Failed Attempt to Join the EU*

As regards the question of whether the Icelandic position on the EEA and the institutions of the EFTA pillar has changed over the years, depending on who is in government, my answer would be the following: despite political discussions about the desirability of EU membership, the Icelanders seemed to be satisfied with the EEA Agreement until their banks collapsed and the Icelandic krona lost almost half of its value. After this, the conservative Independence Party—the dominant political force of the country—lost power and, after a transitional period, a new government was formed by the social democrats and the left-green movement. This government broke with the traditional Icelandic European policy. An application to replace the krona with the euro had been rejected by the EU. After a narrow vote in Parliament, the new government hastily lodged an application for EU membership. The citizens would have the final say. I have learnt in Switzerland that if you want to win a referendum, you must at least have a clear majority in parliament. I therefore suspected that this project would never get off the ground. From the perspective of the EEA, the problem was, however, that the Icelandic Government used its limited resources for the accession negotiations with the EU and neglected its obligations under the EEA Agreement. Implementing legislation, as well as ministerial decrees, were only enacted after long delays. Even today Iceland has still not fully recovered from this backlog in spite of the public policy efforts to rectify the situation. When the social democratic left-green government lost the 2013 elections, it was clear that the EU accession process would come to an end, and in 2015 negotiations were terminated.[2]

3 Liechtenstein

3.1 Mixed Economy

Liechtenstein has 38,000 inhabitants. It is one of the wealthiest countries in the world with a highly qualified workforce and an innovative economy consisting of over 4,000 businesses. The economy is highly diversified with a strong industrial sector, an important financial centre and countless craftsmen. Liechtenstein has essentially the same number of (very well-paid) jobs as inhabitants. Over 50% of the country's workforce are commuters living abroad, mostly in Switzerland and Austria. The labour market is coordinated by collective bargaining, but union power is limited. Income taxes are low. Illustrious names such as the construction technology group Hilti; the automotive component supplier ThyssenKrupp Presta; Ivoclar Vivadent, a leading international dental company; and the industrial conglomerate Oerlikon Balzers are all Liechtenstein companies.

Bank secrecy was abolished after a major tax scandal in 2008. I heard many unflattering comments about Liechtenstein being a tax haven and worse during my years on the EFTA Court bench, in particular from Norwegians. I don't want in any way to cover up the truth. Everything is a matter of time and the Liechtensteiners had not kept pace with the times. When saying that everything is a matter of time, my countryman Henri Dunant comes to my mind. He was the founder of the Red Cross, and the 1864 Geneva Convention was based on his ideas. In his business ventures Dunant was less successful. After the collapse of his company, he was sentenced for bankruptcy fraud by the Geneva Commercial Court and he was removed from the International Committee of the Red Cross. When Henri Dunant, together with French pacifist Frédéric Passy, received the first Nobel Peace Prize,

[2] I will deal with this development in Chapter 25.

Hans Daae, a Norwegian military physician, managed to place Dunant's part of the prize money, 100,000 Swiss Francs, in a Norwegian Bank, thereby preventing his creditors from getting hold of it!

3.2 Customs and Currency Union with Switzerland and EEA Membership

Since 1719, Liechtenstein has been its own State under the rule of the Princely House of Liechtenstein. In 1806 it became a member of Napoleon's Rhenisch Confederation and thus gained full sovereignty. The Liechtensteiners were, according to a historic description, a peaceful, rural people with many similarities with the Swiss and Austrians living in the nearby Rhine valley. After World War I, the country terminated the customs treaty it had entered into with Austria in 1852 and turned to Switzerland. In 1921 Liechtenstein began to use the Swiss Franc as its currency. However, a formal currency treaty was only concluded in 1980. In 1923 the Principality entered into a customs treaty with its Western neighbour. After Switzerland rejected the EEA Agreement on 6 December 1992 and Liechtenstein approved it on 13 December 1992, the Liechtenstein Government expressed the desire to be part of the customs union with Switzerland and of the EEA Agreement at the same time. As mentioned above, the EEA Agreement was amended to take this new situation into account and the customs treaty with Switzerland was renegotiated and brought into an EEA-compatible form. Liechtenstein then held a second referendum and joined the EEA on the EFTA side on 1 May 1995. As I said, Liechtenstein is a pro EEA country. The two Liechtenstein newspapers "*Vaterland*" and "*Volksblatt*" have always reported on the EFTA Court in a positive way.

3.3 National Character

I have experienced the Liechtensteiners as friendly, industrious, reliable people with their feet firmly planted on the ground. The fact that they are a monarchy has an impact on their self-understanding. The same goes for the small size of the country. But I would still say that, with the exception of the Princely House and of a few politicians and entrepreneurs, the Liechtensteiners tend to make themselves smaller than necessary. Joining the EEA without Switzerland was a huge step, which has brought Liechtenstein more sovereignty. Nevertheless, I often had the impression that the government did not fully realise this. In the last years, there has been little strategic thinking, there is hardly a European policy that deserves this name and too much is left in the hands of too few. Although Liechtenstein has a very successful economy, its *classe politique* lacks a sufficient level of self-confidence.

3.4 Judiciary

Liechtenstein has a mixed judiciary consisting of Liechtensteiners, Austrian and Swiss judges. Full-time judges (14 on the Princely Court and 5 on the Court of Appeal) are appointed for life. Part-time judges, i.e. all the judges of the Supreme Court, the Administrative Court and the State Court as well as lay judges, are elected for a renewable five-year term. Before the enactment of the Constitution of 1921, the Higher Regional Court of Innsbruck was the court of last resort in Liechtenstein. Even today a strong Innsbruck influence remains. All the Presidents of the Supreme Court for the last 50 years came from the Tyrolian capital. The current President is Hubertus Schumacher, a university professor and practising attorney. Other Austrian judges stem from nearby Vorarlberg or from Tyrol. Last, but not least, there are some who come from Switzerland. Except for the Supreme Court, all the courts—the Princely Court, the Court of Appeal, the Administrative Court, and the State Court—are presided over by Liechtensteiners. In the upper courts, many prominent Austrians and Swiss have served. Examples are Professor Franz Gschnitzer from the University of Innsbruck, the President of the Higher Regional Court of Innsbruck Karl Kohlegger, the later President of the ECtHR Luzius Wildhaber and Professor Peter Liver, the famous legal historian from Berne University, who was also one of my teachers.

A lot of people said to me over the years that Liechtenstein has all these foreign judges because they don't have enough manpower. But that is only half the truth. The leading heads of the country understood early on that if all the judges were Liechtensteiners, it would, in view of the size of the country, be difficult to guarantee judicial independence. Furthermore, an additional factor that pleads in favour of having judges from Austria and Switzerland is the fact that Liechtenstein law has taken over elements from both Austrian and Swiss law. This non-nationalistic perspective on the judiciary dramatically contrasts with views in Iceland and Norway.

4 Norway

4.1 Mixed Economy with High Public Ownership

Norway, a founding EFTA State, has 5.3 million inhabitants. The country's economy is a developed mixed economy based on markets on the one hand and planning and economic intervention on the other. The labour market is coordinated by collective bargaining and the unions are very powerful. In my experience, there are also strong corporatist beliefs and neo-mercantilist thinking is quite influential in certain fields, for example when it comes to controlling capital movement or natural resources, defending State monopolies, but also in public procurement law.[3]

[3]See Chapters 15, 21 and 24.

Oil and gas have in past decades made Norway one of the wealthiest countries on the globe. But similarly to other oil economies, the country faces the task of promoting diversification. Compared with other European countries, the Norwegian economy is characterised by a large-scale State ownership in industry. Generally speaking, the system is also marked by strong government intervention. The State is considered to be your guardian and, perhaps, even your best friend.

Although Norway is traditionally profoundly Protestant, social conservatism, which in the US focuses on family values and is opposed to abortion and same-sex marriage, is barely present. With a few exceptions, these have become non-issues. You will occasionally find a conservative mind who dares to tell you that he or she has difficulties with recent developments. However, differences do exist between the leftist and middle-leftist and the rightist and middle-rightist parties as regards fiscal policy. But no matter who is in government, social democratic ideas have largely shaped Norwegian political thinking and the Norwegian welfare system has principally been formed by social democratic influences. For decades, the Labour Party has been the most powerful political group. The deceased Labour politician Einar Forde quipped:

> We are all social democrats.

The Labour Party has traditionally been committed to the idea of a strong welfare state funded by high taxes and duties. Since the 1980s, however, it has moved more in the direction of the "Third Way" proclaimed by Bill Clinton and Tony Blair, by adopting a softer stand on income tax progressivity and allowing the privatisation of State-held assets and services.

One significant feature of the Norwegian welfare State, which has led to important litigation before the EFTA Court, is the strong position of the labour unions. The Confederation of Trade Unions (LO) is the largest and most influential workers' organisation in Norway. About 900,000 workers are affiliated to it.[4] LO has always supported Norwegian EEA membership because it guarantees unhindered access to the EU internal market. This support is, however, a conditional one. In its "Programme of Action 2013–2017" LO stated:

> The EEA agreement affects the Norwegian world of work and our society through decisions taken in Brussels. LO demands that the Norwegian government oppose any restriction on the right to use collective means of action, the collective bargaining system and the right to national wage formation. The ILO conventions, Norwegian collective agreements and Norwegian labour legislation must take precedence over community regulations. This precedence needs to be clarified between the signatories to the EEA agreement.
>
> LO demands that Norway have an active policy towards Europe. Norway must exploit the full scope of the EEA agreement to influence the design of new regulations and their transposition into Norwegian law. The political authorities need to ensure that Norwegian interests are safeguarded. An early on approach to political processes is the key to influencing the outcomes. It is vital that the government have a good dialogue with the social partners when transposing EU regulations into Norwegian legislation. The right of

[4]Further information on LO is available at: www.lo.no.

reservation must be exercised against EU directives that restrict national policies to prevent social dumping or encroach on trade union rights and welfare regimes.

All in all, today's Norwegian economic model is based on the ideas of market economy and free trade: but it has certain traits which may conflict, and actually have conflicted, with EEA Single Market rules. State monopolies may be incompatible with the rules on free movement, State aid may fall foul of the basic prohibition in Article 61 EEA, ownership of natural resources has caused difficulties and so has the wish to protect the Norwegian tax base. In a number of cases, a marked paternalism has played a role. Provisions in collective agreements in favour of the unions and certain forms of industrial action have also proven to be incompatible with EEA law.

4.2 National Character

4.2.1 General Remarks

I have had the opportunity of visiting Norway many times. It is fair to say that society is characterised by solidarity, democracy, and equality. The Norwegian national character is usually described as open, tolerant and inclusive. However, the limits of tolerance can easily be reached should ESA or the EFTA Court dare to tell the Norwegian Government (and, as in America, I understand government to have an executive, legislative and judicial branch) that they are not in compliance with their obligations under the EEA Agreement. Norway also considers itself a leading nation when it comes to human rights and equal treatment.

There is, moreover, an emphatic patriotism which is said to have its roots not least in the German occupation during World War II. I was once present at the Oslo Fjord on 17 May, the Norwegian Constitution Day. I am used to the Swiss waving flags on their national holiday, but the excitement of the Norwegians is unparalleled.

It is interesting to watch Norwegians interacting with Danes and Swedes, their former rulers. Danes and Swedes tend to make jokes about their Norwegian friends; their attitude is often condescending. As regards the Norwegians themselves, the fact that their country was Denmark's junior partner from 1523 to 1814 has disappeared from their collective memory. I noticed early on that if the Norwegian administration had a legal problem, their favourite interlocutors were their Danish counterparts. The relationship with the Swedes appears to be more difficult. When you speak to Norwegians about their eastern neighbour on the Scandinavian Peninsula, you can still sense an inferiority complex vis-à-vis their former masters. In the 2010s, thousands of Swedes moved to Norway in order to work in the services sector of the oil and gas rich neighbouring country. I noticed that many Norwegians tremendously enjoyed being served by their former rulers. On the other hand, a lot of Swedes still tend to look down on their western neighbours no matter how wealthy they have become.

4.2.2 Egalitarianism

Norway is an egalitarian society that is characterised by flat hierarchies. Decisions are based on consensus and compromise; the style of leadership in business is said to be informal. The website "ExpatArrivals" defines egalitarianism in the following way:

> Everybody feels like they can interact directly with everybody else [....], and in line with this principle, Norwegians tend to establish direct contact with the person who can get things moving, rather than doing everything through the line.[5]

The Norwegian welfare state has produced something which is called Norway's version of bourgeoisie in late capitalism. Ordinary life in Norway has been dubbed an "A4 life". It is a standardised, safe life including a uniform education, career, marriage, kids, kindergarten, two full-time jobs, home ownership, short working days, generous allocation of holidays, a mountain cabin, one or two cars, year-long parental leave for each child, subsidised childcare from age one, tax-financed health care. The State is its citizens' friend; the system plainly has patronising traits. After decades of social democratic rule, there is no longer any need for egalitarianism to be imposed on people anymore: almost everyone has internalised it. It is probably no coincidence that one of the best known Norwegian inventions is the cheese slicer. It was created by Thor Bjørklund, a carpenter from Lillehammer and a patent was obtained on 27 February 1925. It is said that Bjørklund constructed the slicer because he wanted to overcome the difficulty of cutting nice slices of hard cheese (most probably *brunost*, the hard brown cheese so loved by Norwegians, which was at the centre of one of the Court's landmark decisions, *Kellogg's*),[6] with a normal knife. But an instrument which guarantees that each slice of cheese has the same size is also a symbol of egalitarianism. Nevertheless, as in every society, there are some who are more equal than others: hence the phrase, heard from time to time over the dinner tables of the Norwegian capital, that so and so is from "an old Oslo family".

It seems that in Nordic countries in general, there are still elements of a pattern of group behaviour towards individuals that is called "Jante's Law." The term "*janteloven*" refers to a catalogue of ten rules which are said to shape the life of society. These commandments were described in 1933, in a satirical way by a Danish-Norwegian author, Aksel Sandemose, in the context of small-town Denmark. The people of the fictional micropolis of Jante were described as abiding by these commandments. The Jante social norms are:

1. You shall not believe that you are someone;
2. You shall not believe that you are as good as we are;
3. You shall not believe that you are any wiser than we are;
4. You shall never indulge in the conceit of imagining that you are better than we are;

[5] http://www.expatarrivals.com/norway/doing-business-in-norway.

[6] See Chapter 11.

5. You shall not believe that you know more than we do;
6. You shall not believe that you are more important than we are;
7. You shall not believe that you are going to amount to anything;
8. You shall not laugh at us;
9. You shall not believe that anyone cares about you;
10. You shall not believe that you can teach us anything.

The concept of "*Janteloven*" is said be a characteristic of all Nordic societies. But it seems that it has fallen on particularly fertile ground in Norway. Generally speaking, Norwegians are expected to put the community ahead of the individual and not to boast about individual accomplishments. The latter includes that you do not show your wealth. Political correctness also seems to play an important role in Norway. However, nowadays *janteloven* no longer applies with the same force as in the past, and the oil and gas boom has changed the life of Norwegians. And yet it seems that in one way or the other certain parts of Jante's Law are hardwired into the Norwegian mind. Having said that, I would add that if you have grown up in German speaking Switzerland, Jante's Law is not entirely unfamiliar. I should perhaps add that, even in such closed societies, there are always individuals who liberate themselves and take the risk of acting independently. This, of course, also applies to the legal profession. It is perhaps also no coincidence that there are so many successful individual athletes and endurance athletes in both Norway and Switzerland.

4.2.3 Recent Oil and Gas Wealth

Owing to its oil and gas production, Norway has become so wealthy that is has been able to maintain a welfare system which can hardly be matched by any other European country. If, however, you are invited to dinner in a private home, you sense that the wealth is recently acquired when Norwegians before leaving say "Thank you for the meal" ("*takk for maten*"). You realise that it is not so long since having plenty of food was not something that could be taken for granted. In fact, until the 20th century Norway was quite a poor country and it seems that life has through the times been difficult.

It goes without saying that newly-acquired wealth has an impact on a society and on its patterns of behaviour. I have also seen this in Switzerland, where it was etiquette to not openly show wealth until, say, thirty years ago, when the change set in. When I visited Oslo for the first time in 1996, it was rather modest. Today, there are quite a number of demanding people, even among professors, and the Norwegian capital is rightly considered to be a global city. To that extent, *janteloven* seems to not apply anymore.

What makes the Norwegian case special is that after the accession of Austria, Finland and Sweden to the EU in 1995, Norway became the superpower of the EFTA pillar. For the first time in their younger history, the Norwegians are the top dog in an international institution. In the old EFTA, Sweden and Switzerland ran the show after Britain left in 1973. Norway pays 89% of the Court's (and ESA's) budget. In the early years, it was not uncommon for this to be mentioned in certain situations.

On the subject of money, the three EEA/EFTA states are legally obliged to make contributions to 16 EU Member States in order to reduce social and economic disparities in the EEA as a whole and to strengthen fundamental European values such as democracy, tolerance and the rule of law in those EU Member States. When the EEA Agreement was negotiated, the EU took the view that the wealthy EFTA States had to make such payments as a quid pro quo for the free access of their citizens and economic operators to the Single Market. At the beginning, this was meant to be a onetime contribution, but later the EEA/EFTA States agreed to make it an ongoing thing ("EEA Grants"). In view of its size, it is clear that Norway is by far the largest contributor. It is important to note that the money does not go into the EU budget. The three EEA/EFTA States have their own organisation and their own projects. In January 2010, I spoke at an antitrust conference in Lisbon and afterwards Doris and I spent a couple of days in Oporto. We stayed at a Pousada, formerly a 19th century palace, which, as three signs in the respective national colours indicated, had been restored with funds from Iceland, Liechtenstein, and Norway.

But that is not all. Norway decided in 2004 to double its contribution. The negotiations for the new financial mechanism in connection with the recent Eastern enlargement of the EU (and subsequently also of the EEA) had not yielded the expected amounts. The EU Foreign Relations Commissioner Chris Patten said that more money was needed. It was on this occasion that the financial mechanism, which originally was meant to be a one-off payment, was for the first time labelled a "membership fee" for participation in the internal market. Norway then offered to set up the "Norway Grants" for the same amount as their share in the EEA financial mechanism, as it was at the time. As regards a quid pro quo, the trigger for the Norwegian offer may have been the prospect of obtaining improved fish quotas. Officially, the fishing negotiations had nothing to do with the EEA financial mechanism, but politically they were connected. The Prime Minister at that time, Kjell Magne Bondevik, a Lutheran vicar, sold the "Norway Grants" programme to the people by saying that, as good Christians, the wealthy Norwegians must give to those less privileged in Europe ("love thy neighbour"). Rumour has it that when the Norwegian Government made this gesture, the two other EEA/EFTA countries were not amused. But the fact remains that they are at least indirectly profiting from the Norwegian generosity.

Politically, since 2004 Norwegians have been of the opinion that they are paying an overly large contribution, and have done everything they can to extract greater rights or benefits on this basis. Iceland and Liechtenstein have always stated that this was Norway's problem. At the same time, Iceland and Liechtenstein have also resisted the idea that Norway's additional payments could be applied to all three EEA/EFTA States. But it is clear that the huge payments contribute to the sense of superiority that certain Norwegian bureaucrats exhibit towards their colleagues from Iceland and Liechtenstein. These factors are all combined with a tendency for the Norwegians to regard the EEA Agreement as a de facto bilateral arrangement between Norway and the EU, with Iceland and Liechtenstein as free-riders who are not supposed to interfere. ESA and the EFTA Court should play a symbolic role.

Paying money is a horizontal measure to influence the course of things. It may work on virtually all levels, from paying to occupy influential decision-making positions to obtaining special treatment or at least buying time when it comes to the question of whether you are in compliance with the law. A former Icelandic ambassador to the EU once said to me:

> Our Norwegian friends have a lot of money, and they are trying to pay their way through.

Liechtenstein diplomats have made similar statements. However, in the final analysis, that is how the game is played. The fact that Norway is also buying influence in the recipient countries with its generous payments is obvious. In certain cases, the respective governments appeared in court proceedings in order to support the position of the Norwegian Government. When asked what the motive behind their participation was, they frankly admitted that they had been asked to do so because Norway was financing a project in their country.

4.2.4 Complacency and a Sense of Mission

Many Norwegian politicians and civil servants tend to think that they have not only created the perfect society, but that they are basically good people. Former Prime Minister Gro Harlem Brundtland said bluntly:

> It is typically Norwegian to be good.

Even if she may not have meant with this that Norwegians do good deeds, but that they are clever, this was a remarkable statement. In the spring of 2007, I flew to New Delhi for a couple of days on a private visit. On the plane, I suddenly found myself in the middle of a group of Norwegian diplomats who were on the way to an ambassadors' meeting in Korea. After a while I said to my seat neighbour "You must be Norwegian, I recognise that from your accent". He asked: "How come that you recognise that?" and I answered that I had been working with Norwegians for years. My neighbour exclaimed in all frankness: "Lucky you!"

When I visited Oslo together with the Court's registrar Skúli Magnússon in September 2011, I wanted to see the Secretary General in the Ministry of Foreign Affairs in order to discuss the Court's proposal to create an enlarged chamber and a post of AG as well as to establish a supranational panel which would scrutinise the Member States' nominees for judgeship and ad hoc judgeship.[7] The Secretary General, Bente Angell-Hansen, received us in a suite at Oslo's most elegant hotel, the "Continental". She was accompanied by a woman of lower rank from her Ministry. I was greeted with the title "Your Excellency" and Skúli was addressed as

---

[7]See for details Chapter 28.

"Dear Nordic brother". French champagne was served as an aperitif, the excellent food was accompanied by Meursault and Bordeaux wines. Bente was a perfect host, she had been an Ambassador to the international organizations in Geneva for some years and she was fascinated by the beauty of the city, the lake and the surrounding area. We spoke about everything except our request. Afterwards, I teased Skúli over his new title. Icelanders are sometimes condescendingly treated as little Nordic brothers by Norwegians. On 11 January 2018, Bente Angell-Hansen was sworn in as the new President of ESA.

Perhaps because I am not a Liechtenstein citizen, Norwegian civil servants and judges always spoke quite frankly with me about Liechtenstein. As I have said, those who know the Principality only from hearsay tend to disparage it as being a fiscal paradise and an appendix of Switzerland. Certainly, the accusation of aiding wealthy citizens of countries with high taxes to evade those taxes is also directed against Switzerland. However, since Switzerland is—in the EFTA of four—an economic and political superpower, this criticism was hardly ever voiced openly. Those who know Liechtenstein speak highly of the tiny alpine country, which is in fact a good performer when it comes to compliance with EEA law.[8]

Similar to the (pre-Trump era) Americans, Norwegian politicians, civil servants and diplomats are constantly on a mission to make the world a better place. There are those who think that this is a consequence of the fact that when Norway became independent from Sweden in 1905, in inherited the Peace Nobel Prize.

This huge, self-imposed task shapes the actions of said Norwegian actors in many respects, both for the good and for the bad. The good part is that Norwegian foreign policy has achieved many positive things over the last few decades, particularly in the field of peace negotiations. The problematic aspect is that if you always think that you must be the best in the class, that you are on a mission to improve the world, you tend to become self-righteous, conceited, and uncritical in relation to yourself. Furthermore, if something goes wrong, you have a perfect excuse because your intentions were good. A good example is provided by the following anecdote: In October 2015, the three judges of the EFTA Court participated in the second Tromsø conference on international courts (The first Tromsø conference had taken place in the spring of 2013[9]). The event was (again) chaired by Arild Eidesen, the President of the Hålogaland Court of Appeal. There were some 40 dinner guests and, when we sat down at the table, I noticed that my place card read "Carl Baudenbacher" whereas Doris' card read "Fru (Miss) Baudenbacher". And this was the same for all the couples present. I could not help teasing Arild over this and said that such a faux-pas would not even occur in Switzerland where women only got the right to vote on the federal level in 1971. He put on a serious look and replied that this was indeed a shame,

> in particular because we Norwegians are supposed to lead the pack when it comes to this sort of issue.

---

[8]See for details Chapter 15.

[9]See for details Chapter 26.

I am used to taking a critical stance towards my own country. I know, for instance, that one of the central features of the Swiss system of governance is that brilliant people must not show their superiority; otherwise they will be decapitated. This beheading principle applies in politics, in the judiciary and in universities, at least in disciplines such as law which do not generate measurable results. Supreme Court candidates are not subject to a deep scrutiny of their abilities; the most important precondition for becoming a Supreme Court judge is that a contender has not attracted too much attention and they are close to a political party which, according to the principle of proportional representation, has the right to claim a seat on the Supreme Court. Judges are proposed by the political parties and elected by the Federal Parliament for a term of six years; re-election is possible. I have always taken the view that due to these framework conditions the Federal Supreme Court is too close to politics. And yet it enjoys a good reputation in particular in the field of private law, but also with regard to its practice in international law.

When I spoke with Norwegian judges or bureaucrats about the Norwegian Supreme Court ("*Høyesterett*"), the general opinion was that here was a court with a perfect or near-perfect selection process. If the Justices refused to refer an issue of unclear EEA law to the EFTA Court, it was because they came, after careful consideration, to the conclusion that a reference was unnecessary. They might also have had other noble motives, such as the need to save time and money. If the Supreme Court deviated from the Court's preliminary ruling, it was not because it wanted to avoid a result which it disliked for political or economic reasons, but because it had in all conscience reached a different conclusion. Obviously, there were always free spirits in Norway who saw things differently, but since in my capacity as a judge and President I had in the first instance to deal with people in official functions, it took me a while to get to know them.

4.2.5 Everything Is Political

I could give countless examples of representatives of the Norwegian Government and of people close to it having a tendency to see almost everything from a political perspective. In my view this is a consequence of the widespread normative positivism that prevails in Norway. When we hired an Icelandic registrar—Skúli Magnússon—the Norwegian faction at the EFTA Court was unamused. However, they reconciled themselves to the decision by saying that people in Norway will say that this was a political decision, and therefore they will understand it. With this, the issue was off the table. The truth of the matter was that Skúli had excellent credentials and in fact his performance exceeded my original expectations by far. Apart from taking care of procedural issues, human resources and finances, he visited national courts in all three Member States, gave numerous speeches on the EEA and the Court's case law, he responded to the Court's opponents in academia and battled valiantly with certain people in the embassies of the EEA/EFTA States. Another example is the manner in which certain Norwegian lawyers, who have not even bothered reading our judgment, speak about the first *Icesave* case. Many of those who spoke to me, also friends, intimated that Iceland had been acquitted for political reasons.

Norwegian bureaucrats and diplomats do not always comprehend what an independent supranational court of law is. Some of them tend to think that the EFTA Court is some sort of an outpost of the Norwegian Government in Luxembourg. From 2006–2007, the EFTA Court and I were personally engaged in a fierce dispute with the EFTA Board of Auditors (EBOA).[10] When the fight was approaching its peak, the desire to control the Court was quite unashamedly voiced. Norway's Ambassador to the EU at that time, Oda Helen Sletnes, claimed that the Court's judges should be subject to the rules applied by the Norwegian court administration ("*domstoladministrasjon*") to Norwegian judges.[11] A similarly remarkable idea was mooted in early 2015 by a senior bureaucrat in the Norwegian Ministry of Foreign Affairs. She called the Court's registrar Gunnar Selvik and told him that she was aware that the EFTA Court had added four additional offices to its premises. Since Luxembourg would hold the EU Presidency in the second half of the year, Norwegian diplomats would have to stay in Luxembourg on a regular basis. It would be nice, she said, if the government could use one of our new offices for that purpose. Gunnar, who is perfect at handling such situations, politely but firmly rejected the proposal.

4.2.6 Result: Norwegian Exceptionalism

All these factors have contributed to the emergence of what one might call "Norwegian exceptionalism" or even "Norwegian supremacy thinking". A high proportion of Norwegian public actors behave, in many respects, in a manner that might make you think that they feel superior to other people. They are convinced that they have the best economic, social and legal model in the world and thus *a fortiori* in the EEA. Consequently, any criticism of Norway that is voiced from the perspective of EEA law is met at first with suspicion. Certain Norwegian civil servants and professors (not all) don't see the harm in harshly criticising others, for example the EFTA Court or even individual judges. However, if you strike back, they act the offended. A good example is the opening speech of University by Oslo Professor Finn Arnesen at the EFTA Court's Spring Conference of 23 June 2013 on the subject "Parallelism and persuasion—on the argumentative force of the EFTA Court's decisions". Finn lambasted the Court for having criticised the Norwegian Supreme Court's *STX* judgment in *Jonsson*, exclaiming that parts of our judgment were one single "outburst". *STX* was a case in which the Supreme Court refused to follow the EFTA Court.[12] Finn also found it necessary to state that if the EFTA Court did not refrain from using *obiter dicta* in the future, Norwegian courts would

---

[10]See for details Chapter 23.

[11]See with regard to Oda Helen Sletnes, Chapter 7.

[12]See for details Chapter 26.

be unwilling to cooperate. However, he didn't say a single word on the unusual, at times even hostile, language in the Supreme Court's *STX* judgment. Nevertheless, resistance to the EEA and the institutions of the EFTA pillar is not equally strong throughout the country. In my experience, Norway is quite divided between the East (Oslo) and the West/North. The EFTA Court and I personally have dealt mainly with Oslo where the nationalist mood is most pronounced. In other parts of the country, people tend to be more relaxed when it comes to issues such as preserving sovereignty.

Norway's attitude towards the EFTA Court has also been reflected in the press coverage. The big Oslo newspapers have not always reported in a fair and unbiased fashion. Certain star journalists have sometimes disregarded the rule that news and opinion must be separated. The same goes for the rule that your (alleged) statements should only be quoted if you were first given an opportunity to comment on them. Generally speaking, we received our best press coverage from the Farmers' newspaper "*Nationen*", from the radical left-wing newspaper "*Klassekampen*" (the Class Struggle) and from the tabloid "*Verdens Gang*".

4.3 Judiciary

Norway has a unitary judiciary but quasi-judicial bodies function in some areas as courts of first instance. Judges are appointed for life. The application of EEA law lies essentially in the hands of the 83 district courts ("*tingrett*"), the six courts of appeal ("*lagmannsrett*"), the labour court ("*arbeidsretten*") and the Supreme Court ("*Høyesterett*"). If Norwegian courts have to decide on a conflict between the State and a private party, they not infrequently tend to favour the State. This is something I noticed from the beginning. A high percentage of judges have been socialised while working for the Attorney General or for State ministries, especially the Ministry of Justice. Lawyers and political scientists have looked into the question of whether there is a correlation between this phenomenon and the voting habits of judges. There is specific research on the Supreme Court's alleged State-friendliness.

Gunnar Grendstad, William R. Shaffer and Eric N. Waltenburg found that the decisions of the Supreme Court justices are influenced by their preferences. The authors carried out a quantitative analysis of the composition of the courts and of their rulings. The voting behaviour was examined from the perspective of economics, gender, and, most importantly, government relations. The analysis showed that judges who had previously worked in the State government were friendlier towards their former employer. Non-State parties were said to have little chance of winning the case.

Ola Tellesbø has even openly asked the question

> *Hvorfor Høyesterett er statsvennlig?* (Why is the Supreme Court State-friendly?)

In his own English summary, he asserts that statistically, the Norwegian Supreme Court adjudicates in favour of the State against private parties. Although private parties rarely prevail, dissenting opinions are mostly rendered in favour of the State. In the author's view, the biases appear to not be limited to the Supreme Court but are probably a trait of the judicial system in general. Based on empirical data provided by two other scholars, Jan Skåre and Asbjørn Kjønstad, the author concludes that the biases are explained by social identification.

As always, such findings are controversial. That certain justices were not pleased with these results is no surprise. But that does not mean that the authors aren't making a valid point. In my experience, the issue is a very real one. To give a recent example: In *Holship*, a landmark case on the relationship between collective bargaining and industrial action, on the one hand, and competition law and fundamental freedoms, on the other, 10 of the 17 justices of the Supreme Court followed our ruling. Of the majority nine held doctorates in law, including the university professors on the panel; one justice in the majority was a former EFTA Court judge. The majority also included four of the five with the longest period as lawyers in private practice. The seven minority justices had all worked for part of their careers in the Ministry of Justice and for the Attorney General, and on average for a much longer period than the ten in the majority.[13] They wished for the unions to win the case.

[13]See concerning *Holship* Chapters 15 and 16.

Chapter 7
ESA—The Great Negotiator

Contents

1 General

In history, mainly politicians have been given the title "great negotiator", for example US President Lyndon B. Johnson for his masterful way of dealing with Congress, former US Senator George Mitchell, who chaired the Northern Ireland peace negotiations that led to the 1998 "Good Friday Agreement", or the South African leader Nelson Mandela who brokered the end of apartheid. In the EEA context, this title belongs to ESA, as I will explain in this Chapter.

ESA plays a crucial role in ensuring the proper functioning of the EEA Agreement and in the Court's life. According to Article 108(2) EEA and Article 31 SCA, it may bring lawsuits against EEA/EFTA States for non-compliance with their obligations under the EEA Agreement (so-called infringement actions). ESA has the task of monitoring the compliance of the EEA/EFTA States with their obligations under the EEA Agreement, but also of controlling State aid, which includes the competence to order the recovery of funds from the beneficiary of illegal aid. Furthermore, it has important competences in the field of competition

C. Baudenbacher, *Judicial Independence*, Springer Biographies,
https://doi.org/10.1007/978-3-030-02308-9_7

law. ESA may be a defendant in nullity actions brought by EEA/EFTA States as well as by natural or legal persons against its decisions under Article 108(2) EEA and Article 36 SCA. Its resources are limited, which implies that it has to set priorities.

The ESA College consists of three members. It takes its decisions by simple majority. A decision to open infringement proceedings against an EEA/EFTA State is either based on one or several complaints or is taken on ESA's own initiative. The focal point of interest is ESA's policy in bringing such infringement cases and in handling competition and State aid cases. Nevertheless, the Authority's role in preliminary reference cases should not be overlooked; it submits written observations and takes part in the oral hearing. Infringement proceedings and preliminary reference proceedings are closely linked: citizens and economic operators may challenge an alleged violation of their rights under EEA law by lodging a complaint with ESA or by instigating proceedings before a national court and asking that court to refer questions to the EFTA Court. They may also proceed via one channel without abandoning the option of having recourse to the other. It should be noted, however, that whereas complaining to ESA is free of charge, court proceedings may be expensive.

Unlike most members of the European Commission, the ESA College's Members are not former government ministers. The College has always consisted of a majority of former civil servants and diplomats from the EEA/EFTA States. This was not always the case for Liechtenstein, however, the Icelandic and the Norwegian College Members all came from their national administrations. And many of them returned to their national administrations after their time in Brussels.

2 ESA as a Prosecutor—A Promising Start

When ESA took up its functions on 1 January 1994, it consisted of the five College Members Knut Almestad from Norway as President, Nie Grönvall from Sweden, Björn Friðfinnsson from Iceland, Pekka Säilä from Finland, and Heinz Zourek from Austria. Knut Almestad is one of the greatest experts of EEA law. Unlike most of his successors, he understood that the treaty is a market agreement and that it cannot function properly without true reciprocity. Knut is not only a diplomat; he is also a brilliant lawyer. He increased ESA's standing and reputation by giving speeches and by publishing articles.

In its first year, ESA opened 115 competition law cases; 103 as a result of a notification/application, eight on the basis of a formal complaint, and four ex officio. One inspection was carried out and in another case the Commission performed an inspection at ESA's request. Roughly two-thirds of these cases had to be transmitted to the European Commission at the end of 1994 because on 1 January 1995 Austria, Finland and Sweden joined the EU. ESA received information about some 400 existing and 67 new State aid schemes in 1994. In November and December of that year, it took 17 decisions relating to 50 existing aid schemes, requesting the EFTA States concerned to discontinue the schemes or to modify them. With regard to the rest of the existing schemes, ESA found no reason to take further action. Of the 67 notifications on new State aid submitted during the year, ESA assessed 46 planned aid measures. Six cases were registered in which aid had been granted without prior approval. As a rule, the new State aid schemes complied with the EEA Agreement. Following the accession of Austria, Finland and Sweden to the EU, all pending cases regarding new aid in those States were transferred to the European Commission. On 28 April 1994, the first action for nullity against ESA was brought by the *Scottish Salmon Growers Association*. The association lodged a complaint with ESA in which it alleged that the Norwegian salmon industry had been granted State aid contrary to the EEA Agreement. In this complaint, the association requested an appropriate investigation. In its judgment of 21 March 1995, the EFTA Court annulled ESA's decision to close the case on the grounds that the decision lacked sufficient reasoning. In 1996, ESA closed the case for lack of competence. At the end of 1994, President Almestad wrote in ESA's first Annual Report that the major aspects of the EEA Agreement had been implemented in the legal systems of the EFTA States and that several hundred new acts had been incorporated in the EEA Agreement in the course of the year. However, the Report also pointed to problems in the process of implementation, to imperfections of a technical or legal nature, to examples of delays in the legislative processes, to cases of "nonchalant tardiness", and "finally a very restricted number of instances where disagreement on substance has prevailed".

On 1 January 1995, the College was reduced from 5 to 3 members. For a transitional period of four months, it consisted of Knut Almestad, Björn Friðfinnsson and the Finn Pekka Säilä. The problem was that there were now only two EEA/EFTA States, Iceland and Norway. The third (prospective) State, Liechtenstein, was on the point of holding its second EEA referendum. On 1 May 1995, when Liechtenstein joined the EEA on the EFTA side, Pekka Säilä was replaced by the Liechtensteiner Bernd Hammermann, a lawyer from the in-house legal department of a major industrial firm. It is clear that a College of five is structurally more independent from the governments than a College of three. Moreover, the EFTA pillar became rather inhomogeneous after the downsizing.

It is understandable that in infringement cases a new authority exercises a certain caution and tries to resolve conflicts by way of negotiation. However, negotiations always presuppose that both sides act in good faith. ESA brought its first infringement action on 19 January 1996 against Iceland in a case concerning commodity tax. When the Icelandic Parliament abolished the disputed provisions, the proceedings were discontinued. At the time, it was not clear whether State liability would be part of EEA law.[1] From 1997 to 1999, no substantive infringement cases were brought before the Court. ESA's infringement actions in those years concerned the uncontested non-implementation of directives. In 2000, two substantial cases were brought before the Court, *Kellogg's* and *Alcopops*.

[1]See for details Chapter 10.

On 31 December 2001, when Knut Almestad's presidency ended, ESA was well-positioned. Knut had been a strong leader who left his mark on his Authority during those eight years. He benefited from his deep knowledge and understanding of international and European law in general and of the EEA Agreement in particular. He also knew that at the end of his time at ESA, he would retire from the administration. This made him independent. In fact, Knut subsequently started a successful third career in private practice, which somehow irritated the Norwegian administration. I remember that when he spoke up against the government in one case, a minister felt the need to publicly remind him that as a former civil servant he would receive a pension from the Norwegian State.

3 After 2002: High Fluctuation and Low Action

3.1 The Course of Things

Knut Almestad left big shoes to fill. No ESA President after him has been able to participate in a similar way in a sophisticated discussion on EEA law. The speeches his successors have given have generally been of a political nature. A fundamental problem of the ESA College is the lack of cabinets. The individual College Members are essentially on their own. This may make them dependent on their old networks in the capitals. The first paragraph of Article 8 SCA states, *inter alia*, that the members of ESA must neither seek nor take instructions and that

> [e]ach EFTA State undertakes to respect this principle and not to seek to influence the members of the EFTA Surveillance Authority in the performance of their tasks.

In the light of my experience, I would qualify the latter provision as soft law. That being said, I should add that certain College Members did not even need instructions; they seemed to know what their government expected them to do and not to do. In other words, they found themselves on a leash. This attitude is certainly one explanation for ESA's reluctance to bring infringement actions before the EFTA Court. Another case in point is the strict application of the so-called "six years" rule by the ESA College. This rule states that the initial appointment of a staff member will normally be for 2–3 years and that it may normally be renewed only once, for a period of up to 3 years, if this is in the interests of the institution. This text provides a certain flexibility, however, at ESA, the rule is enforced without the circumstances of the case being taken into account. The only plausible explanation is that this corresponds to the wishes of certain governments. This policy contributes to systematically weakening ESA. ESA staff have less self-assurance than their counterparts at the Commission. This has become apparent on many different occasions. Unlike the Court, ESA held no commemorative events for its tenth or twentieth anniversaries. The Authority has no regular annual symposium where it can blow its own trumpet. The College Members almost never see a Commissioner face-to-face. They must content themselves with meeting Commission heads of unit. The following is a true story: An ESA President was once received by a Commissioner for a brief conversation. At the end, the Commissioner wished the President a safe flight back to Oslo.

ESA's determination not to offend the governments reached a low point in the oral hearing of 26 September 2017 in the *Marine Harvest* hearing (*Marine Harvest* v *ESA*). The case involved the question of whether ESA had any competences to assess aid which distorts competition granted by Iceland and (in particular) Norway to their fisheries sector. The Court dismissed the action of Marine Harvest on the grounds that under the so-called fish protocol (Protocol 9 to the EEA Agreement), it is for the Contracting Parties (i.e. the States) to take the necessary measures. The Commission nevertheless suggested that ESA's general competence to adopt recommendations or resolutions should also apply to State aid to fisheries. However, in response to a question from the bench, ESA's agent stated that since ESA had no decision-making power, it also lacked the competence to make recommendations. I had always thought that it would be somewhat natural for a surveillance institution to try to expand its power.

On the other hand, ESA deserves praise for its openness in hiring staff from outside the EFTA pillar. All of ESA's legal directors have come from EU countries and I recall listening to many brilliant pleadings from British, French, German and Greek agents. This does not imply that there were no excellent pleaders from EEA/EFTA countries, but clearly combining people with knowledge concerning the EEA/EFTA States with others who were socialised in an EU State was beneficial. This is all the more true because education in European law doesn't seem to be a high priority in all EEA/EFTA universities. Too often, European law is dealt with as part of public international law, and this from the perspective of its (undesired) impact on domestic law. ESA itself states in its rules on recruitment:

> The dissemination of knowledge into the EEA States and the EU Institutions ensures increased awareness and understanding of the EEA Agreement. ESA must also remain connected to and up to date on relevant developments in the EEA States and the EU Institutions. ESA therefore aims to ensure a balance between the development and retention of internal expertise and the introduction of new approaches and experience into the organisation. At the same time, ESA recognises the organisational impact and costs of limited-term employment and staff turnover as well as the limiting effect this has on opportunities for professional development, which all have to be balanced.

I add that it would be in the spirit of the EEA if the EU institutions were also to employ people from the EEA/EFTA countries.

Between 2002 and 2017, ESA had no less than 6 presidents and the fluctuation of College Members was high. On 1 January 2002, the Norwegian Einar M. Bull succeeded Knut Almestad as ESA President. The other College Members were Hannes Hafstein from Iceland and Bernd Hammermann from Liechtenstein. In that year, ESA brought an infringement action against Norway in the *University of Oslo* case. In its 2003 Annual Report, ESA wrote under the heading "Prospects for 2004":

> The Authority seeks to develop a more pro-active approach to the detection and prosecution of infringements of the EEA competition rules in anticipation of the forthcoming modified competition regime.

This announcement remained, however, a vain aspiration. It had no visible consequences. ESA stuck to its negotiating approach. Most of the cases concerned the non-implementation of directives and were uncontested.

In 2004, there was a change in the presidency. For the first (and only) time, an Icelander, Hannes Hafstein, was appointed to the top post. Einar M. Bull continued to serve as a College Member, together with Bernd Hammermann. The negotiating policy was expressly confirmed. The 2004 Report stated:

> Most infringement cases are resolved following a letter of formal notice. Only a fraction of cases are referred to the EFTA Court.

On 7 August 2005, President Hafstein died. Einar M. Bull once again became President. Bernd Hammermann left office on 30 June 2005 and was succeeded by Kurt Jäger. The new Icelandic College Member, Kristján Andri Stefánsson, took office on 1 November 2005. This meant that there was no regular College Member from Iceland from August 2005 until the end of October 2005. In this period, in addition to a number of uncontested non-implementation cases, ESA brought the *Finnmark supplement* case and the Norwegian *Life Assurance* case against Norway, as well as the *Icelandic Trading Companies* case against Iceland. ESA had from the start pursued a policy of only proceeding with what they deemed to be watertight cases, i.e. cases which they were virtually certain to win. *Finnmark supplement* was the first infringement case that ESA lost. The circumstances were somewhat unusual. ESA's action was based on a complaint lodged with the Commission which forwarded it to ESA.

Given ESA's caution in bringing cases, the *Gaming Machines* case was a tour de force. In its 2005 Annual Report, ESA described the events leading up to the bringing of the infringement action in November of that year. In the summer of 2003, the Norwegian Parliament adopted new legislation granting a monopoly for the State owned company Norsk Tipping AS to operate gaming machines offering money prizes. After having received complaints from private operators who had previously been allowed to operate gaming machines, ESA in October 2004 delivered a reasoned opinion to Norway concluding that the legislation constituted an infringement of the right of establishment and the freedom to provide services. In parallel with ESA's infringement proceedings, the new legislation was also challenged before the Norwegian Courts. Concurring with ESA's reasoned opinion, the Oslo District Court (*Oslo Tingrett*) held the new law to be contrary to the EEA Agreement in October 2004. On 26 August 2005, the Court of Appeal (*Borgarting Lagmannsrett*) overturned that decision. The Court of Appeal's ruling was appealed to the Supreme Court who decided to hear the case in plenum in January 2006. On 17 October 2005, a request to refer the case to the EFTA Court was rejected. ESA's Annual Report went on to state that:

> As the case raised important questions of EEA law that ought to be assessed on a European level by the EFTA Court, the Authority decided on 17 November 2005 to bring the case before the EFTA Court. Subsequently, on 5 December 2005, the Norwegian Supreme Court decided to postpone its further proceedings and await the EFTA Court's decision.

On 1 January 2006, Bjørn T. Grydeland from Norway succeeded Einar M. Bull as ESA President. Kurt Jäger and Kristján Andri Stefánsson continued to be College Members. On 26 April 2006, ESA brought the *Norwegian Waterfalls* case before the Court. Pre-litigation proceedings had started in March 2001. On 14 November 2006, the *Liechtenstein Helplessness Allowance* case was brought. ESA's 2006 Annual Report contained a bold statement regarding its willingness to act before the Commission has taken up a parallel case in the EU pillar. The cases *Gaming Machines* and *Norwegian Waterfalls*, ESA claimed, illustrated that it was "prepared to take on difficult cases of this kind" and that the homogeneity objective had not prevented it

> from pursuing a case against an EEA/EFTA State on the basis of an alleged breach of EEA law, just because a similar case has not been brought before the European Court of Justice.

Following Grydeland's departure on 12 August 2007, his Norwegian countryman Per Sanderud was appointed ESA President with effect from 20 August 2007.[2] Kurt Jäger and Kristján Andri Stefánsson remained College Members. Only two cases were brought before the Court in 2007 by ESA. One of them was the so-called *Golden Widows* case, in which the pre-litigation procedure had already started in July 2001. I criticised ESA's passivity in a number of speeches and publications, and this lead to a rather embarrassing incident. When the Court opened its restored premises in November of 2008, the ESA College, together with many judges and AGs from the Union courts and ambassadors accredited to Luxembourg, participated in the celebration. I gave a short speech and then President Sanderud asked for the floor. He mentioned my ongoing complaint regarding ESA dragging its feet when dealing with infringement cases. Per then pulled a roll of deeds out of a bag and handed it to me with the remark:

> As a gift on the occasion of the opening of your own courtroom, we have brought you a case.

I saw the looks on faces of my friends from the EU judiciary and was relieved that we could move on to the aperitif. 2009 was a rather uneventful year. Of the six infringement cases ESA brought to the Court in that year, only one, a Liechtenstein residence requirement case, was contested. It was, however, a case in which the legal issues were clear.

At the beginning of 2010, the Icelander Kristján Andri Stefánsson returned to his home country. He was replaced by Sverrir Haukur Gunnlaugsson. The Liechtensteiner Kurt Jäger resigned on 14 June 2010 and was succeeded by Sabine Monauni-Tömördy. In its 2011 Annual Report, ESA proudly wrote:

---

[2]See for details Chapter 23.

> The EEA legal world is becoming more litigious. As the Authority brings more substantive infringement cases, more cases before the EFTA Court are likely. Likewise, as the Authority investigates more state aid and competition matters, the likelihood of legal challenges to its decisions increases.

Nevertheless, six out of the seven cases brought by ESA in 2010 were uncontested. The one contested case concerned the posting of workers in Iceland. A novelty was, however, ESA's lawsuit against Norway for its failure to comply with the EFTA Court's judgment in the *Golden Widows* case. There, the Court had held that certain provisions relating to survivor's pensions in the Norwegian Public Service Pension Act breached EEA rules on equal treatment for men and women. Three years had passed since that judgment had been rendered. We sentenced Norway for a second time. Unlike the situation under the EU pillar, no penalty payment can be imposed on a State in such a situation in the EFTA pillar. After this case, ESA brought two more actions for non-compliance with an infringement judgment and the Court sentenced Norway accordingly.

In 2010, two challenges to ESA's decisions stand out: namely the nullity actions in the *Norway Post* case and the *REASSUR* cases. *Norway Post* will be dealt with in Chap. 16 of this book. The *REASSUR* case was directed against ESA's decision that the Liechtenstein Tax Act concerning the taxation of captive insurance companies was incompatible with EEA State aid rules. It was brought by the Liechtenstein Government and two companies which had benefited from the taxation rules at issue. The Court ultimately dismissed the action and upheld ESA's decision. The Liechtenstein Government also unsuccessfully challenged ESA's negative decision on the taxation of investment undertakings in two other cases in 2010 and 2011, *Liechtenstein* v *ESA* and *VTM Fund Management*.

On 30 June 2011, Per Sanderud resigned and was succeeded on 1 July 2011 by his Norwegian countrywoman Oda Helen Sletnes both as College Member and President. The other two College Members continued to be Sverrir Haukur Gunnlaugsson and Sabine Monauni-Tömördy. The main focus remained, and in fact compared to the previous year increasingly became, the implementation of new secondary law. It is no coincidence that ESA's 2011 Annual Report reiterated the old mantra that

> problems can often be resolved through exchange of information and discussions between the Authority and the EFTA State concerned without a need to resort to formal proceedings.

In May 2011, the action against Norway in the *Regulated Markets* case was brought and in December 2011 the action in the first *Icesave* case followed. In 2012, ESA brought two cases before the Court regarding the uncontested non-implementation of secondary legal acts in addition to one substantive infringement case concerning benefits for the children of migrant workers. The 2013 Annual Report stated in the foreword:

> During the last two years, the EFTA Surveillance Authority has brought a record number of cases before the EFTA Court on the basis that Iceland and Norway have failed to incorporate new rules in a timely manner, or to correctly apply such rules. In the same period the Authority has opened hundreds of formal infringement procedures. Fortunately, in most of

> these cases a solution can be found. However, the deadlines for incorporation may be breached by as much as one year or more. On top of this, the Authority notes that there is a backlog of about 500 legal acts that have not yet been incorporated into the EEA Agreement, even though they are already in force in the EU. While the EU Member States continue to improve their ability to implement new, common rules into their national legislations, the situation in the EFTA States is more critical.

This record number consisted of ten cases, eight against Iceland and two against Norway. Nine concerned the uncontested non-implementation of acts of secondary EEA law and one concerned an uncontested action based on the fundamental freedoms (different taxation of domestic and cross-border mergers).

On 1 January 2014, Sverrir Haukur Gunnlaugsson was succeeded by Helga Jónsdóttir. At the same time, Frank Büchel replaced Sabine Monauni-Tömördi. In 2014, ESA lodged a record number of 17 infringement cases with the Court. However, once again, only two of them were contested. The first was a follow-up to the *Regulated markets* case, in which ESA claimed that Norway had not complied with the Court's judgment of 2011. The second was the Liechtenstein *Dentisten* case, a rather symbolic exercise. On 31 March 2015, the Court held that Liechtenstein had violated the freedom of establishment by maintaining in force a provision of the Health Act, which required that a person holding the qualification referred to in German as "*Dentist*" must work under the direct supervision of a dental practitioner. The only "*Dentist*" in Liechtenstein retired in 2017.

Oda Helen Sletnes resigned at the end of June 2015 from her position as ESA's President. On 1 September 2015, she was succeeded by Sven Erik Svedman from Norway. ESA brought 20 infringement cases in 2015 because, as stated in the Annual Report of that year, the EEA/EFTA States "delivered too little too late". Only one of those cases was a substantive one. It concerned the prior authorisation scheme for establishment and cross-border services in Liechtenstein law. In 2016 and in 2017 ESA continued to bring quite a number of uncontested non-implementation cases, but very few substantive actions.

Since 2002 ESA has brought on average one substantial infringement case per year. It should not be assumed that all the other cases were resolved *à l'amiable*. The only plausible explanation is that this was based on a political decision not to be too tough on governments. In many cases, ESA continued to negotiate for many years, even though it should have realised that it was being strung along.

Unlike the European Commission, ESA is not a political hybrid with legislative, administrative, domestic and foreign policy functions, but a simple surveillance and enforcement agency. ESA was thus predestined to act as a truly independent watchdog. This makes it all the more disappointing that, following the EFTA Governments first defeats before the Court, ESA has let itself be driven by political considerations and the College has acted as a filtering mechanism. Some individual College Members, like Kurt Jäger who served at ESA from 2005 to 2010, have occasionally attempted to act more proactively.

3.2 Musical Chairs

In politics, the expression "playing musical chairs" describes a pattern of behaviour whereby people move from one office to another, regardless of whether the change is compatible with the challenges of that office and whether the people occupying the chair fulfil the respective requirements. This metaphor can be aptly used to describe the systematic shuffling of people from the EEA/EFTA States' national administrations to the ESA College and from there back to the administrations again. In particular, some College Presidents have performed this jump. In the period between the downsizing of the EFTA pillar in 1995 and the end of 2017, 15 people served as ESA College Members. Most, but not all of them, came from their national administration where they had been employed for many years or even decades. What is of even greater concern is that, with the exception of Knut Almestad, Hannes Hafstein, Sverrir Haukur Gunnlaugsson, Helga Jónsdóttir and Sven Erik Svedman, they all returned to government posts after their time in Brussels. Two former Norwegian ESA Presidents were appointed as ambassador to Italy. A well-known Oslo business lawyer mockingly stated that the Norwegian embassy in Rome had become the reward for good behaviour at ESA's helm.

3.3 Oda's Double U-Turn

On 6 January 2006, the Norwegian newspaper "*webavisen*" reported that Sletnes was to become Norway's EU ambassador ("*Sletnes blir Norges EU-ambassadør*"). It was added that Sletnes would take over the ambassador's post from Bjørn Grydeland who would become President of ESA. In mid-2007, Grydeland stepped down from the position as ESA President. In mid-August of that year, he was replaced by Per Sanderud. In the spring of 2011, Sanderud resigned from the ESA presidency. On 17 June 2011, the Norwegian newspaper "*ABC Nyheter*" reported that Oda Sletnes was to become the new ESA president ("*Oda Sletnes blir ny ESA-president*"). Barely four years later, on 7 May 2015, the EFTA Court's old friend Alf Ole Ask reported in *Aftenposten*, a leading Norwegian newspaper, that Oda Sletnes was to become the new EU ambassador ("*Oda Sletnes blir ny EU-ambassadør*"). As I will explain, Mr Ask had expressed deep concern about the independence of the judges in the Engeseth affair.[3] As regards Oda's double U-turn, he was less worried.

Oda was not the first Norwegian ambassador to the EU who as an intermediary career step became ESA president and after a few years hopped on to the next post in the Ministry of Foreign Affairs. However, her progression through the ranks went beyond anything that could have been anticipated. The almost four years during which Oda was at the head of the ESA College could have been a decisive period

[3]See Chapter 23.

for the functioning of the EEA. However, as regards infringement actions, nothing changed. We at the Court heard about numerous cases that had been prepared by ESA's services, which were never brought before the Court, in particular, but not exclusively, in the field of labour law. Knut Almestad had announced as early as 1995 that

> the activities of the Authority will bring more into focus the problems which will stem from the *application* of the Agreement and the national legislation emanating from it at the various administrative levels in the EFTA States [...] [which] will require new approaches and new techniques as compared with those employed during the implementation phase.

Fifteen years after Knut's remark, Oda was still speaking of implementing secondary law as such. Governments simply went on doing business as usual. Let me quote the farsighted Knut Almestad once again. In 2012, long after his time at the helm of ESA, he wrote:

> I have over the years become increasingly worried that the EFTA side has built a rather inflated self-image of being at the top of the class with regard to compliance with the Agreement. Occasionally this has indeed been so when it comes to the implementation of directives. Yet, there exists no similar scoreboard with regard to regulations, and there are no recorded data as regards the quality and consistency of the national rules by which the main part of the Agreement and the secondary legislation are implemented.

Whenever ESA's passivity in bringing cases was criticised, the response was that the negotiating approach was superior to litigating. This is not convincing. First, it is in the interests of legal security that major questions of EEA law are clarified in open court and not behind closed doors. The EFTA Court must have the opportunity to render guideline rulings, which factually have an *erga omnes* precedential effect. It certainly seems to be the case that in the EU pillar the Commission also increasingly relies on the negotiating track; as evidenced by the fact that the number of infringement actions has declined in recent years. There are, however, differences between the EU pillar and the EFTA pillar when it comes to the system of remedies. In the EU pillar, private enforcement functions much better. And the sheer size of the EU pillar makes it more likely that important questions will be brought to court than in the small EFTA pillar.

There is one fundamental EEA law problem which has never been broached by ESA. Under Article 3 of the Icelandic EEA Act,

> [s]tatutes and regulations shall be interpreted, in so far as appropriate, to accord with the EEA Agreement and the rules based thereon.

Whether this rule is compatible with Protocol 35 to the EEA Agreement, has been a moot issue from the very beginning. This protocol obliges Iceland to give EEA rules primacy in the event of conflict between implemented EEA rules and other statutory provisions.[4] It is, to put it mildly, astonishing that in 24 years ESA has not been brave enough to have this question clarified by taking Iceland to the EFTA Court. Having said this, I should add that the Court also hasn't exactly been heroic

---

[4]See with regard to Protocol 35, Chapter 4.

regarding this issue. In paragraph 50 of its *Einarsson* judgment, it held "*a bassa voce*" that the main part of the EEA Agreement had been made part of Icelandic law, which under Sect. 3 of the Icelandic EEA Act statutes and regulations, must be interpreted, in so far as appropriate, to accord with the EEA Agreement and the rules based thereon, and that in presenting the Bill for this Act to Parliament, the Government stated

> that this was intended as a special rule of interpretation, and that it would be limited by the provisions of the Icelandic Constitution.

Second, the negotiating approach can lead to long, drawn-out discussions. We noticed that in a number of high profile cases, ESA had been involved in negotiations with governments which lasted up to ten years. In our *Regulated markets* judgment of 16 July 2012, we felt that this problem had to be addressed. Paragraph 68 of that judgment reads:

> When ESA, whether upon a complaint or on its own motion, considers that an EFTA State has failed to fulfil an obligation under the EEA Agreement, it is in the interest of the proper functioning of the EEA Agreement that ESA proceeds within an appropriate time when assessing whether to bring a Contracting Party before the Court. The Court recalls that the aim of the Agreement is, in particular, to promote a continuous and balanced strengthening of trade and economic relations between the Contracting Parties with equal conditions of competition for citizens and economic operators, and the respect of the same rules. In the matter brought before the Court in the present case, i.e. the proceedings that result from the letter of formal notice issued on 16 December 2009, ESA has acted without undue delay.

In the judgment itself, we did not mention that before the proceedings in question took place, ESA had conducted other fruitless negotiations. The review of the legal framework for the Norwegian financial market had in fact started in 2001. After much to-ing and fro-ing between ESA and the Norwegian authorities, the case was closed in 2010, but a new case was immediately opened. I was hopeful that ESA would appreciate our statement because it was meant to provide support vis-à-vis the governments. But my hopes were in vain. The book commemorating the Court's twentieth anniversary contains a contribution from President Sletnes. The article contends that with its statement in *Regulated Markets*, the EFTA Court departed from the well-established case law of the ECJ which allowed the Commission almost unlimited discretion in deciding when to bring an infringement action. The Court, she continued, seemed to be willing

> to examine *of its own motion* the speed with which the Authority brings infringement cases whereas the Court of Justice requires that the defendant State claims and proves that any delay impaired its ability to defend itself and [...] [the Court] may seem intent *to reduce the margin of discretion* of the Authority to start infringement proceedings when it considers it appropriate to do so.

In view of ESA's record, this was not only sophistry, it amounted to comparing apples and oranges. It culminated in the preposterous assertion that the EFTA Court's approach could have the paradoxical effect of reducing the Authority's possibility to achieve compliance in the case of long-lasting infringements by the Contracting States.

3.4 *Competition Law in Particular*

As regards competition law, ESA's 2012 Annual Report proudly stated that

> [o]n the basis of our earlier decisions in cases concerning Norway Post and Color Line the Authority collected approximately 30 million euros in fines in 2012.

In reality, these two decisions were the only ones in which ESA imposed fines in a period of 24 years. ESA's inactivity in this important field led to several interventions in the European Parliament, all to no avail. The fine of EUR 11,112 million which was imposed on Norway Post by the Court was distributed among the three EFTA States Norway, Iceland and Liechtenstein at the end of 2012 according to the following formula: Norway got 89%, Iceland 9%, and Liechtenstein 2%. Since Norway Post is owned by the Norwegian State, almost 10 of the 11,112 million were in the end paid back to the wrongdoer. The speed with which this repayment was made contrasts in an unfavourable way with the fact that ESA had been dragging its feet for such a long time. The Court held in paragraph 88 of its judgment that

> penalties such as the one at issue pursue aims of both repressive and preventive character. They are intended to act, in the interest of society in general and the good functioning of the EEA single market in particular, as a deterrent against future breaches of the competition rules both for the perpetrator and for all other undertakings that enjoy a dominant position on the market.

Whether these goals were achieved in Norway Post is doubtful.

ESA's passivity in this field is also demonstrated by the fact that it closed what could have become its biggest competition law case without imposing any sanctions. The Authority had in a decision of July 2010 identified concerns that the discount system applied by Norway Post in the field of B-to-C parcel services might constitute an abuse of a dominant position. The decision pointed, *inter alia*, to: the possible loyalty-inducing effects of retroactive rebates used by Norway Post; the granting of discounts that were dependent on whether customers reached certain annual targets; indications that targets were equivalent or close to the total requirement of customers thereby discouraging customers from buying from competitors; the use of rebate criteria with seemingly little or no relation to cost savings made by Norway Post; indications that Norway Post discriminated between customers depending on whether there was competition for the customers or not; indications that volume rebates did not apply equally to all customers; a lack of transparency regarding the rebate criteria giving Norway Post more flexibility to grant differentiated discounts for the same volumes; and clauses in Norway Post's standard contracts that might induce buyers not to buy from competitors.

In 2001, Norway Post presented a revised discount system. ESA still had some objections and a third discount model was presented in 2006. In 2008, after Norway Post had submitted information to ESA on recent market developments, which indicated that competing distributors of B-to-C parcels had been able to conclude distribution agreements with leading daily consumer goods retail groups and were expanding their activities in Norway, ESA closed the case without imposing a sanction. DB Schenker sought access to ESA's documents, but on 17 July 2015, the undertaking made an application to discontinue proceedings after reaching a settlement agreement with Norway Post in proceedings before the Oslo District Court. In my Presidential Order to remove the case from the register, I stated in paragraph 42:

> During the hearing in particular, the applicants discussed at length the actions in this case of the former President of ESA during his time in office, and hence of ESA as a whole. The former President of ESA was, before being appointed to ESA, a high official in the Ministry of Transport and Communications which owns Norway Post. However, no concrete charge of serious misconduct or 'abandoning responsibility or impartiality of his office' was made. The President therefore limits himself to note, for the sake of order, that Articles 7 to 9 of the Agreement between the EFTA States on the Establishment of a Surveillance Authority and a Court of Justice lay down detailed rules on the independence and impartiality of ESA College Members who, incorporate, form the EFTA Surveillance Authority.

3.5 National Supreme Courts Disregarding EEA Law

There are only two cases in which ESA has opened infringement proceedings against an EEA/EFTA State after a ruling of that State's Supreme Court. In 2009, it did so against Iceland asserting that the Icelandic Supreme Court had given the Icelandic rules concerning the transfer of undertakings an interpretation that was incompatible with the relevant directive.[5] The Supreme Court had on 25 February 2005 in "*Blaðamannafélag Íslands gegn Frétt ehf.*" found that a claim for unpaid wages which fell due before the transfer could not be based on the national rules implementing the directive. The new employer was thus not liable to pay the wages owed to a worker. The Icelandic Parliament amended the law and on 15 June 2010, ESA closed the case. The other case which prompted ESA to become active is *STX* in which the Supreme Court of Norway threw down the gauntlet to the EFTA Court. At the time of writing, the case is still pending before ESA.[6]

---

[5]77/187/EEC.

[6]See Chapter 26.

4 Persistent Norwegian Dominance

4.1 The Facts

Unlike the President of the Court who is elected by the judges, the President of ESA is appointed by the EEA/EFTA States' governments. Except for a short period of 19 months (from January 2004 to 7 August 2005) when Hannes Hafstein from Iceland served as President, ESA was always presided over by its Norwegian member. As I will further elaborate in Chap. 17 of this book, the President has almost always been in charge of the State aid dossier.

4.2 An Odd Attempt to Justify

The Sejersted Committee observed in its 2012 report on Norway's relations with the EU, that Norway as the EFTA pillar's super-power always aspired to exercise a certain control over ESA by claiming the presidency for one of its own nationals.[7] It was added that this policy was the subject of criticism from other EFTA countries which argued that there should be some rotation, but that Norway brushed such challenges aside. The study also mentioned the criticism by the weekly newspaper European Voice, as referred to in my 2010 book "The EFTA Court in Action. Five Lectures",[8] concerning the career related background of the Norwegian College Members, which may explain ESA's reluctance in bringing cases to the Court. The study offered two explanations for this Norwegian policy. One was that Norway possibly wanted to control ESA in order to safeguard Norwegian interests rather than the interests of the Agreement. The other, somewhat more sympathetic, interpretation was that Norway's approach was a way of giving priority to ESA and ensuring that it has competent people with good knowledge of the EU and the EEA, and of the various aspects of Norwegian society. This assertion is untenable. ESA is the institution which decides whether cases are being brought before the Court or not. It is obvious that by claiming the presidency as a "right", Norway is trying to supervise ESA. The remark that this policy aims to ensure that ESA has competent people is also insulting, since it implies that College Members from the two other EEA/EFTA States are less competent.

[7]See for details Chapter 24.

[8]See for details Chapter 7.

4.3 New Rhetoric

On 2 July 2015, the Norwegian Prime Minister Erna Solberg, who after the general election of September 2013 built a coalition government of the Conservative Party and the Progress Party with the support of the Liberal Party and the Christian Democratic Party, paid an official visit to the Court. It was the first visit by a Norwegian Head of Government. In the early years, Mario Frick, Head of the Liechtenstein Government at the time, had visited us and Iceland's Prime Minister Sigmundur Davíð Gunnlaugsson attended our twentieth anniversary conference. After my introductory lecture, Ms Solberg participated, together with her delegation, in a working session with the Court's judges and the registrar. For the first time during my tenure, I heard a high-level Norwegian protagonist speaking unreservedly of the importance of a properly functioning market economy, open borders and free trade.

On 1 September 2015, Sven Erik Svedman was appointed ESA President. He had been one of the most prominent representatives of Norwegian foreign policy in his previous life. Sven said in a speech delivered on 15 December 2015 in Brussels on the occasion of the launch of my "Handbook of EEA Law":

> [I]t is a worthy task to monitor the EFTA States to ensure the effective implementation of Internal Market rules into their domestic law. Keeping markets fair, level and open is good for our economies and societies. It establishes a good environment for business in Europe where companies can generate wealth, create jobs, and invest in the future.

In a talk at the EFTA Court on 19 October 2016, Sven used similar words. It was a new tone, marked by optimism. For the first time since Knut Almestad, ESA was again led by a communicator. Being an economist, Sven didn't see the EEA Agreement as a threat, but as an opportunity. Sven Svedman's litmus test came when the EEA/EFTA Governments decided to reappoint the incumbent Norwegian judge for an abridged second term of only three years. That this decision violated Article 30 SCA should have been as clear as a glass of moonshine to any halfway decently educated EEA lawyer. ESA was at first reluctant to regard the matter as an infringement case. However, when seven Norwegian scholars lodged an initial complaint and two of them followed up with a further one, the Authority acted swiftly.[9]

However, the hope that ESA would change its general policy as regards bringing infringement actions was premature. At the Svalbard EFTA Ministerial meeting on 26 June 2017, Helga Jonsdóttir who represented ESA once more praised the negotiating approach.

[9]See for details Chapter 28.

5 Input in Preliminary Reference Proceedings

If it is not a party to the proceedings, ESA participates in the Court's cases by submitting written and oral observations.[10] The respective provisions concern the preliminary reference procedure. Often, when governments have a strong interest in the outcome of a case, ESA may, together with the Commission, provide a counterbalance. Generally speaking, ESA's agents see eye to eye with the representatives of the Commission. On the one hand, it seems that College Members tend to interfere less with what ESA's position should be in preliminary ruling proceedings. On the other hand, ESA's staff has over the years acquired considerable experience. This is all the more remarkable as the six-year rule means that ESA loses its best people, just as they have acquired sufficient experience. The rule, which applies to employees of all three EFTA institutions, that after six years they must leave, should be replaced by a more sophisticated system. The EFTA Secretariat and ESA decided to enforce the rule strictly, something I refused to do at the Court. The six-year rule's effect is twofold: it weakens ESA and it provides national administrations with a workforce that has been trained in EEA law. Having said that, I must add the situation at the Court isn't perfect either. Those who are in good standing with their superiors have the chance to be extended indefinitely, while others who openly express their opinions may have to leave.

Of ESA's many important pleadings, I want to highlight four: In 1999 ESA, concurring with the Commission, submitted convincing observations in the *Finanger* case. The question was raised as to whether an EEA/EFTA State could lawfully exclude insurance coverage for a person who had taken a ride with the intoxicated driver of a motor vehicle.[11] In 2001, ESA, unlike the Commission, argued in *LO* that national courts had to apply a fully-fledged proportionality test when assessing whether clauses of a collective agreement were compatible with the EEA competition rules.[12] In the *Irish Bank* case, ESA in 2012 took a courageous position on the difficulties caused by the Icelandic appeal system for preliminary rulings. It submitted that if the Supreme Court had amended the questions formulated by the District Court upon appeal, the EFTA Court should answer the questions as formulated by the District Court.[13] ESA's finest hour came in the 1998 *Sveinbjörnsdóttir* case where it was the only participant arguing in favour of EEA State liability. The Governments of Iceland, Norway and Sweden were opposed, and so was the European Commission.[14] I will refrain myself here, but the list of cases could be far longer.

[10]See Article 20 of the Court's Statute and Article 97(1) RoP.

[11]See for details Chapter 11.

[12]See for details Chapter 16.

[13]See for details Chapter 8.

[14]See for details Chapter 10.

6 Contribution to ECJ Case Law

ESA has also made significant contributions to the case law of the ECJ in a number of preliminary ruling cases involving EU law provisions that have been incorporated into EEA law. This is obviously valuable from the perspective of homogeneity. Of equal importance is the fact that ESA has defended the Court‘s case law in proceedings before the ECJ that involved similar issues.[15] It is, however, regrettable that ESA has not been able to develop a coherent policy in this regard. In order to build up its standing as a key player, the Authority should appear before the ECJ on a regular basis, not just in cases directly related to pressing EEA problems.

As regards direct actions, in 2011 ECJ President Vassilios Skouris denied ESA the right to intervene in direct actions before his court in *Commission* v *Portugal.*[16] In *Commission* v *Netherlands*, he also refused Norway that right. This practice is not only incompatible with the Declaration by the European Community on the rights for EFTA States before the EC Court of Justice of 3 January 1994, which states that legal homogeneity within the EEA should be reinforced by “opening of intervention possibilities for EFTA States and the EFTA Surveillance Authority before the EC Court of Justice”. It also contradicts the precedents of Skouris’ predecessor Gil Carlos Rodriguez Iglesias who in the *Parliament and Denmark* v *Commission* case and in the *Netherlands* v *Parliament and Council* case had allowed Norway to intervene. I can’t shake the impression that Vassilios would have thought twice before making this change if ESA had built a stronger reputation for itself from the outset.

[15]See for details Chapter 8.

[16]See for details Chapter 25.

Chapter 8
Preliminary References: All Options Open?

Contents

1 Starting Point: The EU Model

As a two-level legal order, EU law is particularly vulnerable. Member States may violate their obligations under the Treaties, in particular the fundamental freedoms, they may also either not implement or incorrectly implement acts of secondary law or fail to comply with State aid rules. The uniqueness of the EU manifests itself in the system of remedies that aim to ensure compliance with and thereby the effectiveness of EU law. Not only does the European Commission act as a law enforcer, but citizens and economic operators may also take on this role. By defending their rights under EU law, they also protect the public interest. Broadly interpreted, they can even be seen as private attorneys general. The number of EU law enforcers

C. Baudenbacher, *Judicial Independence*, Springer Biographies,
https://doi.org/10.1007/978-3-030-02308-9_8

thereby becomes almost immeasurable. EU law is in fact the most judicialised body of international law and the ECJ is one of the most important international (supranational) courts in the world. Consequently, access to justice for individuals and economic operators is pretty broad. They may lodge a complaint with the Commission, in the hope that it will either: (i) open infringement proceedings; (ii) negotiate a solution; or, finally, (iii) bring an infringement action against the Member State concerned under Article 258 TFEU. Or they may bring a lawsuit in a national court and if necessary ask the judge to make a reference to the ECJ under the preliminary ruling procedure (Article 267 TFEU). Obviously, they may also combine these two options. Whether a Member State adheres to a dualist or a monist approach in its internal law is, from the perspective of the Union, irrelevant. In practice, it depends, however, on the Member States and their courts whether and to what extent provisions of European law are enforced. Unlike in the US, where the federal courts are located in the States and are often close to the State courts, there is no EU judiciary in the EU Member States. National courts must act at the same time as both domestic and European courts, and they are expected to act accordingly.

According to the third paragraph of Article 267 TFEU, courts of last resort are legally obliged to make a reference to the ECJ. However, in paragraph 21 of its 1982 *CILFIT* judgment, the ECJ held that a national court of last resort must make a reference when a question of interpretation of EU law arises, unless the answer is

> so obvious as to leave no scope for any reasonable doubt.

2 Complex Situation in the EFTA Pillar

2.1 History

The legal situation in the EFTA pillar can only be understood in the light of historic development. In the first version of the EEA Agreement, the drafters provided that the combined EEA Court, which was planned at that time, would not have jurisdiction to give preliminary rulings on the interpretation of the agreement. However, the EFTA States could allow their courts to ask the ECJ "to express itself" on the interpretation. The ECJ struck this down in its Opinion 1/91. The ECJ held that nothing would prevent an international agreement from conferring on it jurisdiction to interpret the provisions of such an agreement for the purposes of its application in non-Member States.[1] It also stated that the freedom of the EFTA States to authorise or not to authorise their courts and tribunals to refer questions to the ECJ, placing no obligation on those courts and tribunals to make such references, could not questioned. However, the ECJ added that:

[1]See for details Chapter 3.

> In contrast, it is unacceptable that the answers which the Court of Justice gives to the courts and tribunals in the EFTA States are to be purely advisory and without any binding effects. Such a situation would change the nature of the function of the Court of Justice as it is conceived by the EEC Treaty, namely that of a court whose judgments are binding [....].

In Opinion 1/91, the ECJ also rejected the proposed combined EEA Court, which would have consisted of judges from the ECJ and from the EFTA States and would have been functionally integrated within the ECJ. The negotiators subsequently established a structurally independent EFTA Court and the EFTA States decided to create their own preliminary reference procedure. There is nevertheless a remnant of the original version of the EEA Agreement. Article 107 EEA states:

> Provisions on the possibility for an EFTA State to allow a court or tribunal to ask the Court of Justice of the European Communities to decide on the interpretation of an EEA rule are laid down in Protocol 34.

The wording "to decide" should make it clear that the ECJ's rulings would be legally binding on the referring court. Article 107 EEA was apparently maintained in order to placate the ECJ which, as the negotiators knew, would give a second opinion on the new version of the Agreement. It was, however, for reasons of sovereignty, very unlikely from the outset that an EFTA State would make use of this option. Article 107 EEA is a classic example of what in the sociology of the law is referred to as "symbolic legislation".

2.2 *Written Law*

Article 34 SCA states:

> (1) The EFTA Court shall have jurisdiction to give advisory opinions on the interpretation of the EEA Agreement.
>
> (2) Where such a question is raised before any court or tribunal in an EFTA State, that court or tribunal may, if it considers it necessary to enable it to give judgment, request the EFTA Court to give such an opinion.
>
> (3) An EFTA State may in its internal legislation limit the right to request such an advisory opinion to courts and tribunals against whose decisions there is no judicial remedy under national law.

There is no doubt that this text was based on a deliberate choice by the EFTA States, and it seems that it was the Swiss who insisted on it. That means that there is no written provision in the SCA that would oblige national courts, against whose decision there is no judicial remedy under national law, to make a reference to the EFTA Court. There are currently five courts in the EFTA pillar against whose decision there is no legal remedy in national law: The Supreme Court of Iceland; the State Court of Liechtenstein; the Supreme Court of Liechtenstein (competent for civil and criminal affairs); the Administrative Court of Liechtenstein; and the Supreme Court of Norway. The wording of the relevant provision indicates, moreover, that the rulings rendered in the respective procedure are not meant to be legally binding on the national court.

Article 34 SCA can not, however, be read in isolation. The EEA Agreement is clearly based on the principle of reciprocity, as well as on the duty of loyalty, which also binds national courts. Furthermore, national courts must comply with the principle of homogeneity. Finally, there are certain rights enshrined in the ECHR, which could be relevant in this regard. In order for the EEA Agreement to function properly, important cases involving unclear questions ought to come to the EFTA Court's table.

3 To Refer or Not to Refer

3.1 The Early Years

Hamlet's question "to be or not to be" is one of the most frequently quoted lines in English literature. Whereas Hamlet had to decide whether he should continue to bear the pain of life or commit suicide and thereby face the uncertainty of death, courts of last resort of the EEA/EFTA States had to answer the question of whether they should refer cases involving EEA law issues to the EFTA Court or whether they should continue to handle them at national level.

In view of the wording and the history of Article 34 SCA, it is fair to say that things started off fairly smoothly. The number of cases was pretty low in the first few years, even though there was an expectation that the number of cases would gradually increase. Nonetheless, it should be noted that the first case to ever be registered at the Court, *Restamark*, was a request for a preliminary ruling. In 1994, the first year of the Court's existence, six out of the nine cases which were registered at the court were preliminary references. Already in the early days some of the requests were made by the highest courts in the EFTA pillar. On 22 September 1994, the Swedish Supreme Court referred the *Data Delecta* case to the Court concerning a provision of Swedish law, which obliged foreign plaintiffs to provide security for costs for court proceedings. After Sweden's accession to the EU, the case was withdrawn and brought before the ECJ which decided it on 26 September 1996. On 12 May 1998, the Liechtenstein Administrative Court referred questions concerning the residence requirement of the managing director of a company in the *Rainford-Towning* case. On 26 June 1998, the Supreme Court of Iceland asked the Court questions concerning public procurement law in the *Fagtún* case. On 13 and 15 June 2000, the Liechtenstein Administrative Court posed questions concerning the compatibility of the Liechtenstein single practice rule for medical doctors with the right of establishment, in three cases, *Dr. Brändle*, *Dr. Mangold* and *Dr. Tschannett*. The Norwegian Supreme Court referred a case on security for costs (*European Navigation Inc.* v *Star Forsikring AS* on 16 September 1997. After the appellant in the national proceedings withdrew his appeal, the reference was withdrawn. On 23 June 1999, the Norwegian Supreme Court referred the *Finanger* case, which involved the issue of whether it was compatible with EEA law to exclude a person from insurance coverage if she got into a car driven by an intoxicated driver and knew or must have known about the intoxication. On 17 December 2002, the Supreme Court of Norway posed questions concerning certain modalities of the re-packaging of pharmaceuticals by a parallel importer in the *Paranova* v *Merck* case.

3.2 Gradual Progress in Iceland and Liechtenstein

Iceland is the only EEA/EFTA Member State that has introduced a system of appeal as regards the decision of a first instance court to request a preliminary ruling from the EFTA Court. Decisions of first instance courts to make a reference to the EFTA Court may be challenged before the Supreme Court. Since the third paragraph of Article 34 SCA gives the EEA/EFTA States the possibility to limit the right to make a reference to the EFTA Court to courts of last resort, the system of appeal established in Iceland must be deemed to be lawful under the maxim *a majore ad minus*. With one exception, all of the references from Icelandic first instance courts have been made by judges of the Reykjavík District Court. As I have stated above, on 1 January 2018 a new intermediate Court of Appeal was established.[2]

From the beginning, the Attorney General of Iceland challenged certain (but not all) of the reference decisions by district courts before the Supreme Court. The latter acted as a filter, throwing out cases, deleting questions or modifying them. The Supreme Court's refusal to confirm the reference decision of the Reykjavík District Court in the *Icelandic Medicine Control Agency* case met with particularly harsh criticism. The lower court's decision was reversed on the following grounds:

> [I]t is the role of the EFTA Court to interpret the EEA Agreement and the acts referred to in the Annexes thereto. The assessment of evidence and the factual circumstances of the case, as well as interpretation of domestic legislation and acts referred to in the annexes to the EEA Agreement that have been made part of domestic legislation, fall upon the Icelandic courts. On this basis and in line with the factual circumstances of this case, it is the view of the Court that it is not likely to be relevant for the outcome of this case to request an advisory opinion from the EFTA Court concerning interpretation of the aforementioned provisions of the Directive (sc. Directive 65/65/EEC) which are substantially the same as the provisions of Administrative Regulation No. 462/2000, and which are in dispute.

Professor Davíd Thór Björgvinsson, at the time the Icelandic Judge on the ECtHR, rightly observed that if this reasoning was correct,

> there would almost never be an occasion to request an advisory opinion except in circumstances where the relevant EEA rules have *not* been made part of the domestic legislation even though the State is under such an obligation.

---

[2]See for details section II.3 of Chapter 6.

Other influential authors concurred. In fact, this case law conflicted directly with the principle of homogeneity. A bit later, the Supreme Court dropped the respective policy. As I sensed during my regular visits to Iceland, the relationship between the EFTA Court and the Supreme Court was gradually improving. An important step was the appointment of Thorgeir Örlygsson as a Justice of the Supreme Court of Iceland in September 2011. He greatly contributed to improving the mutual understanding between our two institutions. In the years thereafter, the Supreme Court changed its strategy of filtering cases that had been referred by district courts. On a number of occasions, the Supreme Court ordered a district court to refer a given case. And the Supreme Court made a number of references on its own initiative. On 1 January 2017, Thorgeir Örlygsson was elected Supreme Court President.

In Liechtenstein, the Administrative Court under the leadership of its President Andreas Batliner continued its EEA friendly policy. However, the other two Supreme Courts were dragging their feet. The State Court made its first reference only in November 2013. For years, the State Court had upheld the traditional Liechtenstein rule on security for costs before national courts, even though it was common knowledge that it was incompatible with EEA law. An application to have the case referred to the EFTA Court was rejected. Finally, in December 2004, a single judge from the Princely Court ("*Landgericht*"), Dr. Wilhelm Ungerank referred a case, which touched upon this politically sensitive question. The situation at the Supreme Court was similar. When I gave a lecture at the University of Innsbruck in the early 2000s, I invited Hansjörg Rück, President of the Supreme Court at that time, who was living in the Tyrolian capital, to dinner. He told me that he would love to make a reference, but that unfortunately they didn't have any cases involving EEA law. It may well be that Hansjörg was acting in good faith when he made that statement, but I knew that they had such cases.

In the light of the fact that the main goal of the EEA Agreement is to protect the rights of individuals and not the sovereignty of the States, I continued to put pressure on the courts by giving speeches and interviews in the Liechtenstein newspapers. In 2010, Dr. Gert Delle Karth, another Tyrolian, took over as President of the Supreme Court. Nothing changed and when I gave a lecture at the University of Liechtenstein in November 2011, I criticised the Supreme Court's unwillingness to make use of the preliminary reference procedure. Dr. Delle Karth who was sitting in the first row reacted rather harshly, claiming that there was hardly any reason for making references because the most important questions of European law had been resolved by the ECJ. I didn't share his view, and I said so. The Court of Appeal made its first reference in May 2010 in the *Dr. Kottke* case, which concerned security for costs before national courts. However, the driving force in the Liechtenstein judiciary was Wilhelm Ungerank, who not only made numerous references, but also spoke with other judges in order to convince them to become active themselves. Willi is a very effective operator with a great sense of humour. I was once invited to participate in the traditional New Year's dinner of the Liechtenstein judiciary. In a witty speech, he lavished praise on colleagues who had referred a case and made fun of those who had remained passive.

In 2013, I was appointed to the Judicial Selection Committee by the Liechtenstein Acting Head of State, HSH Hereditary Prince Alois. Dr. Delle Karth appeared before the Committee at certain intervals and had to answer questions concerning the administration of justice. He promised on several occasions that before leaving office, he would refer a case to the EFTA Court—as if this were simply a question of making me happy. However, nothing changed. And yet he was—both inadvertently and indirectly—the reason for a major, even revolutionary, policy shift in the case law of the State Court. When he retired in 2013, Dr. Delle Karth was given a *Festschrift* to which I contributed an essay on the preliminary ruling procedure in the EFTA pillar of the EEA ("*Das Vorabentscheidungsverfahren im EFTA-Pfeiler des EWR*"). In the introductory remarks, I wrote that my essay was dedicated to the President of a Supreme Court of an EEA/EFTA State which had not so far made use of the preliminary reference procedure. That I was critical of this was natural, but that did not affect my personal and professional esteem for the jubilee. And then, I set out my view that if unclear questions of EEA law are not referred to the Court, there is a risk of fragmentation and re-nationalisation of EEA law. On 7 April 2014, the State Court, basing itself on my extrajudicial contribution, held in *Spitzer* v *Landesbank* that it considers itself bound to ask the Court for a preliminary ruling if EEA law is relevant to the solution of a case and the legal situation is unclear. The State Court held that if these two requirements are met the application of a party to refer the case and to stay the national proceedings must be upheld ("*ist dem Antrag [....] stattzugeben*"). It can only be assumed that this principle also applies to the other two Liechtenstein courts of last resort.

In the summer of 2015, the Supreme Court referred two important cases, *Vienna Life* and *Swiss Life* in quick succession.[3] As is so often the case, this change in attitude was prompted by a change of leadership. On 1 January 2015, Dr. Hubertus Schumacher, a Tyrolian attorney and professor at the University of Innsbruck, had become President of the Supreme Court.

3.3 *Reluctance in Norway*

Measured in terms of the country's population and economic strength, the number of preliminary references by Norwegian courts has remained low. As I will explain elsewhere in this book,[4] the Supreme Court did not make a single preliminary reference between 2002 and 2015. This boycott only ended after an unusually open clash between the *Høyesterett* and the EFTA Court.[5]

---

[3]See for details Chapter 18.

[4]See for details Chapter 26.

[5]See for details Chapter 26.

4 Legal Nature of the Court's Rulings

In the abovementioned *Finanger* case, the Norwegian Supreme Court felt prompted to elaborate on the nature of the EFTA Court's ruling. Since such an opinion was advisory, the Supreme Court stated that it was both competent and obliged to assess independently to what extent it should be decisive for its own judgment. At the same time, the Supreme Court pledged that it would give preeminent weight ("*vesentlig vekt*") to the EFTA Court's ruling. It went on to state that the EFTA States had deemed it necessary to create a separate court of justice for the EFTA pillar, it further referred to the EFTA Court's expert knowledge of EEA law, to the fact that legal methodology in EEA law may deviate from domestic law, and to the Rules of Procedure allowing input from the European Commission, the ESA and the EEA Member States. This wording might have been intended to be no more than symbolic, in order to show that they had not formally handed over power to the EFTA Court. The Supreme Court then went on to state that the Norwegian Parliament had also assumed that the EFTA Court's opinion should be given significant weight. If you read the relevant parliamentary materials, there is no mention that the Supreme Court must independently assess whether it's going to follow the opinion of the Court. Be that as it may, the Supreme Court followed our *Finanger* judgment, although both the defendant in the national proceedings and the Norwegian Government urged it not to do so.[6]

The Icelandic Supreme Court made a similar statement in *Fagtún*. In its judgment of 18 November 1999, it followed the EFTA Court's ruling stating:

> The advisory opinions of the EFTA Court are not binding for the Icelandic courts [....]. However, the Icelandic courts are empowered to request such an advisory opinion in order to facilitate coherence and homogeneity in the interpretation of the provisions of the EEA Agreement and thus a homogeneous application of these rules within the whole European Economic Area, which is one of the aims of the Agreement [....]. From this it follows that Icelandic courts must take account of advisory opinions of the EFTA Court when interpreting the provisions of the EEA Agreement. No specific reasons have been advanced which would lead the Court to deviate from the aforementioned advisory opinion of the EFTA Court.

This has become the standard formula used by the Supreme Court. Icelandic courts have, nonetheless, followed the EFTA Court's rulings in essence. It is noteworthy that the Supreme Court also upheld the Reykjavík District Court's *Sveinbjörnsdóttir* judgment on State liability, which had implemented the EFTA Court's landmark decision.[7]

In Liechtenstein, it has never been questioned that the Court's rulings rendered under Article 34 SCA must be followed.

---

[6]See for details Chapter 11.

[7]See for details Chapter 10.

5 The Role of the Governments

5.1 Iceland

I have already mentioned that in the early years, the Icelandic Attorney General challenged district courts' decisions to refer a case to us before the Supreme Court. This policy was based on an instruction from the Davíð Oddsson government. The goal was to keep the EFTA Court out of politically sensitive cases where the Icelandic Government feared that we might reach a decision that would have negative consequences for the Icelandic State, even if it would be positive for private operators. However, the Attorney General did not pursue the policy in question in an obsessive way. The references of the Reykjavík District Court in the cases concerning State liability and the primacy of EEA law remained unchallenged.[8] It should be noted in this context that no Norwegian court has ever taken the risk of making a reference concerning the possible EEA law relevance of these general principles.

Icelandic judges are, generally speaking, less state-friendly than their Norwegian colleagues. As I have said before, most of them are career judges or have worked as academics or as practising attorneys before joining the judiciary.[9]

Icelandic authors have always emphasised that national supreme courts are free to refer to the Court and that the Court's answers under the Article 34 SCA procedure are advisory. They reached this conclusion from a textual interpretation of the provision. The tide started to turn when Skúli Magnússon, the Court's registrar from April 2007 to September 2012, opined in several well-reasoned publications that Article 34 SCA had to be interpreted to the effect that courts of last resort were not free to make a reference, and that the Court's rulings are factually binding. A number of younger scholars took this up in their writings. When I participated in a panel at the private University of Reykjavík in April 2013, I noted this new attitude with satisfaction.

Let me add one more thing here: I am a functionalist. It is in my view not so important that a supreme court openly pledges that it will not refrain from sending politically sensitive cases to the EFTA Court and will, generally speaking, follow the latter's ruling. What counts is a supreme court's demeanour. As a well-known proverb says:

> The proof of the pudding is in the eating.

Whenever I was in Iceland, I argued in speeches and interviews that the Icelandic legislature should abolish the appeal system, to no avail. Nevertheless, my efforts were not completely in vain. The Supreme Court has gradually abandoned its policy of blocking disagreeable reference decisions from district courts.

---

[8]See for details Chapter 10.

[9]See Chapter 6.

5.2 Liechtenstein

In liberal Liechtenstein, there is no Attorney General. I am not aware of any attempts by bureaucrats to dissuade, say, the Administrative Court, a court of last resort, from referring cases to us. This was different when Judge Wilhelm Ungerank from the Princely Court made his first references. Some people expressed dismay. When Willi gave a lunchtime talk at the EFTA Court in 2010, he spoke, *inter alia*, about his first reference in the *Piazza* case. He pulled out a letter from the breast pocket of his suit and quoted from it, much to the amusement of the audience. The President of the Liechtenstein Court of Appeal at that time, a Swiss man who was strictly opposed to making references, asked him to withdraw the case because everybody knew what the EFTA Court thought about the Liechtenstein security of costs legislation. Willi reacted both stoically and professionally; he simply put the letter in the case file.

In Liechtenstein legal literature, there were already, at an early stage, voices asking the EFTA Court to acknowledge an obligation for courts of last resort to refer. As regards the nature of our rulings, Administrative Court President Andreas Batliner wrote extrajudicially in 2004 that his court adopted a policy of strictly following them. In 2014, he stated that

> [l]egal certainty and legal peace can be established only when the highest court decides on a contentious issue. In European legal issues it is not the Constitutional Court, however, but the EFTA Court that is the highest competent court for Liechtenstein.

5.3 Norway

In most cases before the EFTA Court, the Norwegian Government is represented by lawyers from the Office of the Attorney General. This entity is a very powerful institution that cherry-picks young lawyers with the highest grades from the universities. These people regard themselves, and are regarded by others in Norway, as a kind of praetorian guard. In the Imperial Roman army, the "*cohortes praetorianae*" were an elite unit whose members served as the Emperor's personal bodyguards. The Attorney General is the legal advisor to the Norwegian Government. Since many Norwegian judges have served with the Attorney General at the start of their professional career, often for a lengthy period, the institution has considerable influence on the outcome of national court proceedings. As regards the role of the State's lawyers in EFTA Court proceedings, I would, based on 22 years of experience, describe the Attorney General's unwritten instruction manual as follows:

(1) *Norwegian courts: Don't refer!*;
(2) *EFTA Court: Throw out cases!;*
(3) *EFTA Court: Beware!;*

(4) *Norwegian courts: Don't follow!;*
(5) *If all else fails and the stars look favourable: Let's try at the ECJ*

I will now address each of these instructions in detail.

(1) *Norwegian courts: Don't refer!*

The first task the Attorney General sets for itself is, and has been for a long time, to dissuade national courts from referring politically sensitive cases to us. This approach has had the support of many sceptical EEA law scholars. In my contribution to the 2012 book "Judicial Protection in the European Economic Area", I, somewhat sarcastically, drew up a list entitled: "The Ten Commandments against making a reference" after having analysed the arguments regularly employed by those who were opposed to using the preliminary reference procedure. The Ten Commandments are:

- The EFTA Court lacks importance because it is small and has only a limited docket;
- The wording of Article 34 SCA makes it clear that supreme courts are free to refer or not;
- Since the Court's rulings are "only" advisory, there is little to gain from them;
- Only the ECJ is entitled to make certain decisions of major importance;
- A national supreme court is in a better position to decide certain sensitive cases than the Court;
- The Court is prepared to embark on judicial activism;
- The Court is "more Catholic than the Pope", meaning that it is tougher on Norway than the ECJ is on the EU Member States;
- Even in groundbreaking cases, the Supreme Court has little to gain from a reference since the EFTA Court's answer will only be provisional. If the ECJ does not follow its ruling, the Court will have to adjust its case law. All the Court does in such cases is to predict what the ECJ will do in a future parallel case. Instead of the Court, national supreme courts can do this themselves;
- If a national supreme court discovers that there is a conflict between the EFTA Court and the ECJ, it may or should follow the ECJ without making a reference to the Court;
- Delay and costs speak against referring cases.

As I wrote at the time, none of these "ten commandments" was convincing. Some are even ludicrous. The goal was simply to provide Norwegian judges, who were unwilling to refer a case, with pseudo-scientific excuses and to persuade those who were in any doubt whether to refer or to keep the cases for themselves. As far as time and costs are concerned, I would add that once a Norwegian court has made up its mind, it can, depending on the complexity of the case, take 6 to 12 months until the questions are formulated. This is a consequence of the fact that Norwegian judges, despite the wording and purpose of the second paragraph of Article 34 SCA, tend to leave the formulation of the questions largely in the hands of the parties.

(2) *EFTA Court: Throw out cases!*

The Norwegian Government also tried to convince the EFTA Court that a narrow definition of the concept of "court or tribunal" entitled to make a reference was warranted. The goal once again was to keep cases out of the Court.

As already mentioned, the five-member Court in its first case *Restamark* had accepted a reference from the Appeals Committee of the Finnish Customs Board ("*Tullilautakunta, Tullnämnden*").[10] This move was rather controversial. The Finnish Government, the Norwegian Government and ESA submitted that the request should be declared inadmissible on the ground that the Appeals Committee could not be regarded as a court or tribunal within the meaning of Article 34 SCA. The Commission stated that the Court should, in the event of there being any doubt, conclude that the requesting body did constitute a court or tribunal. The Court found that although the Appeals Committee appeared to be closely linked to the central customs administration, it was, in fact and law, independent and impartial. Bearing in mind that the goal of the advisory opinion procedure is to provide the national courts with the necessary elements of EEA law to enable them to decide on the cases before them, the request was held admissible. This was before my time, but deciding otherwise would have meant excluding matters of EEA law, which are handled by courts of law in jurisdictions outside Scandinavia, from being referred to the Court. Obviously, the EFTA Court did not want to throw out its first case—and such a beautiful case!—as that would have given the wrong signal from the perspective of protecting the rights of individuals and economic operators. However, the Court also did not want to lose a case that raised questions which needed to be answered. This functional approach laid the ground stone for the further development of the Court's case law. In later cases, both the GC and the ECJ referred to *Restamark*. In Joined Cases *Mattel and Lego* the five-member Court found that the Norwegian Market Council ("*Markedsrådet*") was a court or tribunal for the purposes of Article 34 SCA. This qualification was not contested. The same goes for the decision of the three-member Court to accept the reference from the Market Council in *Pedicel* and from the Liechtenstein Appeals Commission of the Liechtenstein Financial Market Authority in *Inconsult*.

On the other hand, the Norwegian Government made a big fuss over admissibility in the following two cases. In *Norwegian Appeal Board for Health Personnel*, it contested the admissibility of the request arguing that the Board lacked the necessary independence, due to its status as a party in national judicial proceedings and organisational links to other administrative authorities, demonstrated by its power to order other authorities to conduct a further examination of a case. The Government also claimed that the lack of *inter partes* procedure was manifest, in that the private party in question was the sole party in the review proceedings before the Board and that the Board itself handled the investigation of any cases brought before it. The Court rejected all of these contentions and accepted the reference. In the Court's *Olsen* case, one of the referring bodies was the Tax Appeals Board for

[10]See Chapter 4.

the Central Tax Office for Large Enterprises. First, the Norwegian Government claimed that this authority lacked compulsory jurisdiction, since the applicants in the national proceedings could have challenged the tax assessment directly before the national courts and that they were not obliged to exhaust their rights of administrative appeal prior to doing so. The Government also argued that the Board was only the first administrative body of appeal at national law, and its decisions could subsequently be contested before the National Tax Appeals Board. Second, the Government asserted that the proceedings before the Board were not *inter partes*. Third, it contended that the Tax Appeals Board was not sufficiently protected against external intervention or pressure liable to jeopardise the independent judgment of its members. Fourth, the Government submitted that there were no adequate safeguards in place to ensure the impartiality of the Tax Appeals Board's members, since there was no independent secretariat responsible for preparing its cases; it was claimed that this work was done by a case officer at the Central Tax Office for Large Enterprises. The Court rejected all of these submissions.

In *Vigeland*, where the referring body was the Norwegian Board of Appeal for Industrial Property Rights, the Norwegian Government pushed their arguments to their limits. Contrary to all the other participants in the case, it once again pleaded inadmissibility, claiming that the referring body was not independent, that the case would most likely be heard by an ordinary court anyway and that the various administrative appeal boards in Norway generally lacked the requisite skill, knowledge and practice necessary for the concise formulation of a reference, as they did not receive the same training as courts in this regard. This final observation was particularly remarkable. The chairman of the Norwegian Board of Appeal for Industrial Property Rights was University of Oslo Professor Ole-Andreas Rognstad, an internationally recognised intellectual property (IP) law specialist. The EFTA Court first critically observed that in virtually all the cases referred by a body that constituted an administrative entity under Norwegian law, the Norwegian Government argued that the case should be dismissed because those bodies did not constitute a court or tribunal within the meaning of Article 34 SCA. It rejected the arguments put forward by the Government and held that the Board of Appeal constituted a court or tribunal and that the request was thus admissible. As regards the assertion that public bodies do not have the necessary knowledge required for the concise formulation of a reference, the Court noted, that in its own experience, "obstacles of this nature have not caused difficulties". In fact, the decision the Board rendered based on our ruling is of excellent quality.[11]

(3) *EFTA Court: Beware!*

If a reference case nevertheless reached the EFTA Court, the Attorney General's lawyers pulled out all the stops. Some, albeit not all, of these agents have acquired an arrogant and bossy habit when pleading. As the Court's former registrar Skúli Magnússon once wrote, they have a hard time understanding that when appearing

[11]See for details Chapter 18.

in Luxembourg, the situation is quite different to that in a Norwegian court. Notably, in the Court's first years, the Norwegian Government's agents did not hesitate to warn that if the Court did not follow their advice, it would be committing a serious mistake that could impact on the pro-EEA mood in Norway, and more of this ilk. Some lawyers were so obsessed by what they perceived as their mission that they forgot one of the basic teachings of trial advocacy: don't alienate the judge!

(4) *Norwegian courts: Don't follow!*

Once the EFTA Court has decided a case against their government, the Attorney General's lawyers have tried, in major cases, to convince the referring court not to follow the ruling. For obvious reasons, these attempts to sabotage the Court's ruling were camouflaged behind pseudo-legal reasoning. One tried and tested method is to contend that the Court was not aware of all the facts of the case and that therefore the basis of the judgment ceased to exist. This *modus operandi* has proved to be successful in a number of cases, in particular as regards applying the proportionality principle in fundamental freedom cases. State-oriented professors have paved the way by arguing that the proportionality test involves not only legal but also factual issues, meaning that the national court may in good faith reach a different conclusion than the Court. The Attorney General has moreover profited from the fact that Norwegian judges are not used to applying the principle of proportionality as developed in European law.[12]

Another tactic is to try to identify a judicial conflict with the ECJ and to tell the Norwegian court that it must follow the latter if that serves the State's interest. The Attorney General will, for example, argue that the EFTA Court has either not followed relevant ECJ case law, which existed at the relevant time, or that between the pronouncement of the Court's ruling and the resumption of the case by the national court, the ECJ has issued a judgment that conflicts with the Court's approach. The Attorney General can then assert that for reasons of homogeneity the Norwegian court was obliged to follow the ECJ's more recent judgment. A case which stands out in this regard is *STX*.

(5) *If all else fails and the stars look favourable: Let's try at the ECJ*

If the State's lawyers do not succeed because the Norwegian courts do not follow their argument, they may grasp at the last straw and in a subsequent parallel EU law case try to convince the ECJ to come to a different conclusion, in the hope that in a future case the Norwegian court will overrule its EFTA Court-based case law. If successful, this *modus operandi* could also damage the EFTA Court's reputation. This tactic was used, unsuccessfully, for the first time in *Candolin*. The ECJ fell in line with our *Finanger* jurisprudence on accepting a ride in a car driven by an intoxicated chauffeur. Our sister court also concurred with our view on the

[12]See for details Chapter 15.

possibility of reducing the compensation on the grounds of contributory negligence.[13] The late AG Ad Geelhoed cited several parts of our *Finanger* judgment and the ECJ referred to the respective parts of the Opinion.

A second, recent, example is the *Panayi* case. In our *Olsen* judgment of 9 July 2014, we were the first to hold that the fundamental freedoms were applicable to a trust created in Liechtenstein the "participants" in which were taxed in Norway.[14] In *Panayi*, the Norwegian Government, once again, this time with the help of the UK Government, tried to convince the ECJ to go against us. In her Opinion of 21 December 2016, AG Juliane Kokott stated in point 39 that the ECJ had not yet ruled on the question of whether trusts are "other legal persons" within the meaning of the rules on the freedom of establishment. The active management of external assets was an economic activity pursued on a self-employed basis and that:

> Contrary to the Norwegian Government's submission, the principles governing the assumption of the status of taxable person for VAT purposes are not applicable to the assessment, as a condition of enjoyment of the freedom of establishment, of whether an activity is an economic activity pursued on a self-employed basis. This is true not least because the fundamental freedoms, in eliminating obstacles in the internal market, and VAT law, in taxing the end consumer, pursue different objectives. It is true that, according to settled case-law, a simple holding company (known as a financial holding company) is not regarded as a taxable person within the meaning of Article 9 of Council Directive 2006/112/EC of 28 November 2006 on the common system of value added tax. It may nonetheless rely on the freedom of establishment where its profits are taxed on the ground that its registered office has been transferred.

In its judgment of 14 September 2017, the First Chamber of the ECJ followed our *Olsen* ruling. Although the referring British court had cited *Olsen* and both ESA and the Commission had broadly pleaded our judgment, the Chamber did not refer to us, but limited itself to citing the Opinion of AG Kokott. From the perspective of intellectual honesty, this is problematic.[15] Be that as it may, the additional question arises of whether the *modus operandi* of the Norwegian Government is compatible with their duty of loyalty under Article 3 EEA. According to the second paragraph of this provision, the Contracting Parties

> shall abstain from any measure which could jeopardize the attainment of the objectives of this Agreement.

Result

The Attorney General's policy of urging national courts to refrain from making a reference has been successful for many years. I am not talking about arguing against making a reference in one case or another; I am talking about a systematic approach, which aims to keep as many cases out of the EFTA Court as possible.

---

[13]See for details Chapter 11.

[14]See for details Chapter 15.

[15]See for details Chapter 21.

This policy must be seen in a broader context. In 2012, Knut Almestad rightly observed that

> there seems in the course of the last decade to have emerged something resembling procrastination tactics in order to avoid legal clarification of sensitive issues. These tactics appear to be three-pronged: (a) to engage ESA in a protracted dialogue, often by promising solutions once lengthy studies and legislative processes covering broader issues have been completed, but which in the end turn out to be inadequate, (b) to consistently oppose that national courts request Advisory Opinions from the EFTA Court, and (c) when the going gets really tough, to do as ESA demands but declaring that the measure is an autonomous act and not an obligation under the Agreement.

What the former French judge of the ECtHR, Louis-Edmond Pettiti wrote in 1985 in a general international law context largely applies to the functioning of the EFTA pillar:

> The nature of decisions which can be referred by national courts to international jurisdictions are commonly delicate and sensitive ones [...] and thus states may be tempted to put pressure on local national courts to avoid such references. This, in turn, would logically neutralize the effectiveness of international courts by starving them of work.

Over the years, I got into the habit of asking the parties in the oral hearing of preliminary reference cases how the reference had come about and whether the Norwegian Government had opposed it. I also posed similar questions in cases originating from Iceland and Liechtenstein. The Governments had to be made aware of the fact that their actions did not go unnoticed. There are clear indications that a policy of systematically opposing the making of references is barely compatible with the EEA/EFTA States' duty of loyalty. However, also on this crucial matter, ESA remained passive.

In contrast, the Attorney General's policy of asking the Court to declare cases referred from administrative bodies inadmissible, was a total failure. The Court did not throw out a single case based on the finding that the referring entity did not constitute a court or tribunal. However, if the majority of the three judges had been political appointees, things might have gone differently. This demonstrates that a court with only three judges is vulnerable.

A success story from the Norwegian Government's perspective is, however, the Attorney General's stratagem of arguing before the national court that restrictions of fundamental freedoms not only pursued a legitimate goal, but were proportionate. The Norwegian Government won several landmark cases on its home turf that it richly deserved to lose.[16] Ingvald Falch, the company's attorney in the *STX* case and now a Supreme Court Justice, wrote that the Supreme Court

[16]See for details Chapter 15.

> followed the submissions of the State [....] – submissions that had already been made to the EFTA Court.

Falch is right to observe that it

> is inadmissible that a Government whose arguments have not been followed by an international court, that the very same Government has agreed to set up, shall be able to win the case with the very same arguments before its own courts. It is undermining the EEA Agreement.[17]

However, it may be that with the Supreme Court's *Holship* judgment of 16 December 2016, a change for the better has been initiated.[18]

Attempts to undermine the EFTA Court's rulings in preliminary reference cases by submitting observations in subsequent parallel ECJ cases, with the goal of creating a judicial conflict have so far been unsuccessful.

In October 2016, I gave a lecture at the Norwegian Bar Association. A well-known lawyer from the Attorney General's Office asked for the floor and said that it was normal for the Norwegian State to defend its interests using all means available. After the conference, a practising attorney, who had pleaded a number of cases before us for non-State parties, came up to me and said that the way the Norwegian State handled these cases was far from normal. He was right, but it struck me that he did not make this remark publicly.

6 *Irish Bank* and *Jonsson*

6.1 Restriction of the Freedom to Refer

In January 2011, Norwegian researcher Halvard Haukeland Fredriksen, today a professor at the University of Bergen, revealed in a sub-study to the Sejersted report[19] that between 1994 and 2010, the Supreme Court of Norway had dealt with over 50 cases involving EEA law issues. In only three cases had a reference to the EFTA Court been made and since 2002 no case had been sent to the EFTA Court. I had time and again heard that cases were being kept at national level, even if a party had asked the Supreme Court to make a reference. But I had never imagined the true scale of the matter and I felt that this could no longer be tolerated. Such a systematic boycott was incompatible with the foundations on which the EEA Agreements rests, namely homogeneity and reciprocity.

The chance to react came when the *Irish Bank* case was referred to us by the Reykjavík District Court. Judgment was rendered on 28 September 2012. Although

[17]Available at: https://www.nho.no/siteassets/nhos-filer-og-bilder/filer-og-dokumenter/arbeidslivs politikk/brevet-til-esa.pdf.

[18]See for details Chapters 15 and 16.

[19]The report is dealt with in Chapter 24.

no pleadings had been made on this point, the EFTA Court decided to make a few fundamental statements on the preliminary reference procedure in the EFTA pillar. It pointed to the differences between EEA and EU law in this respect and stated that regarding the question of whether a reference should be made, the relationship between the Court and the national courts of last resort was "more partner-like", compared to that in the EU. However, we added in paragraph 58:

> At the same time, courts against whose decisions there is no judicial remedy under national law will take due account of the fact that they are bound to fulfil their duty of loyalty under Article 3 EEA. The Court notes in this context that EFTA citizens and economic operators benefit from the obligation of courts of the EU Member States against whose decision there is no judicial remedy under national law to make a reference to the ECJ [....].

6.2 *Lack of Clarity*

In the judgment in the *Jonsson* case, in which I did not participate, the EFTA Court emphasised the issue once again. It held in paragraph 60 that the reference of unclear EEA law questions was important and added.

> Thereby unnecessary mistakes in the interpretation and application of EEA law are avoided and the coherence and reciprocity in relation to rights of EEA citizens, including EFTA nationals, in the EU are ensured.

The legal situation regarding the freedom of courts of last resort to refer was summarised in an interpretation case, *HOB-vín ehf.* The Court stated in paragraph 11:

> [A] national court or tribunal is entitled to request the Court to give an Advisory Opinion on the interpretation of the Agreement [....]; for the different legal situation concerning courts against whose decisions there is no remedy under national law, see [....] [Irish Bank and Jonsson].

6.3 *Limiting the Effects of the Icelandic Appeal System*

In *Irish Bank*, the EFTA Court also took a position on crucial aspects of the Icelandic appeal system. The Reykjavík District Court had on 8 November 2011 posed two questions concerning the interpretation of a provision in the Directive on the reorganisation and winding up of credit institutions.[20] When the defendant, Kaupthing Bank hf., appealed, the Supreme Court substantially amended these questions, such that the decisive issues in the second question were no longer reflected. On 22 December 2011, the Reykjavík District Court referred the two modified questions to the Court. We held that a reference decision by a lower court may be subject to the remedies normally available under domestic law. Nevertheless, if a court of last resort overruled the decision of a lower court to refer

[20] 2001/24/EC.

a case, or upheld the decision to refer, but amended the questions asked by the lower court, the standards of Article 6(1) ECHR, which guarantees the right to a fair trial, would applied. Such a decision by a court of last resort may fall foul of this provision if it is not reasoned and as a result should be considered arbitrary. In the *Irish Bank* case, we found that there was no substantive difference between the first question in the first ruling of the Reykjavík District Court and the two questions posed by the judgment of the Supreme Court. We therefore decided to answer the amended question posed by the District Court and thereby also responded to the questions as amended by the Supreme Court and the original question from the District Court.

As regards the second question posed by the District Court, we found that the Supreme Court's judgment did not clearly show that it had taken a different view, nor did it give any reasons why the issues raised by the second question had not been addressed. We therefore also answered the District Court's second question. With this, we strengthened the position of the district courts in general without offending the Supreme Court.

6.4 Background: 2011 Spring Conference

The basis for these revolutionary changes was, to a certain extent, laid at the EFTA Court's Spring Conference of 17 June 2011 and in the book containing all the speeches and transcripts of the discussion panels.[21] Prominent participants such as the eminent Irish lawyer Professor Dr. John Temple Lang and the Court's registrar Skúli Magnússon, but also many others, argued that in the light of their duty of loyalty and the principle of reciprocity, the EEA/EFTA States' courts of last resort were not free in their decision as to whether to refer a case to the EFTA Court or not. I had always taken this view. Regardless of whether the EFTA States had clear ideas on this point in 1992, historical and textual interpretation are not the end of the story. The SCA must be construed in the light of the purposes of the higher ranking EEA Agreement, whose main goals are to secure homogeneity and reciprocity, also as regards access to European justice. It is notable that a persistent lack of understanding of the reciprocity principle is what prevented many supposedly important thinkers from realising that a textual approach would not suffice. The Court is the final arbiter in the EFTA pillar and the only way to avoid fragmenting and re-nationalising EEA law is to ensure that major questions of EEA law are dealt with by the EFTA Court. There were also important voices who said that the EFTA Court's respective rulings are *de facto* binding on the referring court. Whether these judgments are in fact enforced depends, however, on the courage of ESA.

[21] See EFTA Court, Ed., Judicial Protection in the European Economic Area, German Law Publishers, 2012.

7 Conclusions

The preliminary reference system in the EFTA pillar of the EEA is more flexible than the one in the EU pillar. The lack of a written obligation on national courts of last resort to make a reference and of a provision that declares that the EFTA Court's rulings are binding has an impact on the Court's judicial style.[22] The EFTA pillar preliminary ruling procedure can only function if the EFTA Court's answers are convincing. Here again, the EEA Agreement's main characteristic—the *sui generis* character, the mixture between binding rules and cooperation—is apparent.

As its sister court ECJ, the EFTA Court has the competence to reformulate the questions referred by the national court in order to give the latter a useful answer. Correcting technical mistakes and misunderstandings is undoubtedly legitimate. Another matter is whether the Court has the right to make sure that it gets the case it wants irrespective of the intention of the referring judge. In special circumstances, such a modus operandi may be necessary. Obviously, good reasons must be given in such a case.

[22] See for details Chapter 27.

Chapter 9
A Matter of Interpretation

Contents

1 Introduction

"A matter of interpretation" is the title of an essay by the late US Supreme Court Justice Antonin Scalia. Scalia considered himself a textualist, i.e. a judge interpreting a legal text as it was written, neither more nor less. The twin concept of textualism is originalism. Originalists claim that the words of the American Constitution must be interpreted as they were understood at the time they were written. Scalia was also the leading advocate of originalism in America. Both textualism and originalism imply a very conservative idea: namely that judges must not approach legal norms in an "activist" way. This is what Scalia considered to be the correct way of interpreting legal norms. However, the words "a matter of

C. Baudenbacher, *Judicial Independence*, Springer Biographies,
https://doi.org/10.1007/978-3-030-02308-9_9

interpretation" do as such not imply a conservative approach. On the contrary, they sound quite neutral. That is why I think they make an appropriate title for the respective Chapter of this book.

The ECJ has from its beginnings in the 1950s, and in particular in the 1960s, felt free to interpret texts dynamically when it regarded this as necessary in a specific case in order to give full effect to a provision of EEC law. This was, and remains, in direct contrast to the conservative public international law rules laid down in the Vienna Convention on the Law of Treaties. In the light of the fact that the EEA Agreement is a multilateral agreement and that securing a level playing field for citizens and economic operators is an indispensable precondition for the functioning of the EEA Single Market, it seemed to be rather clear during the negotiations that the methods used by the ECJ when construing EEC law would also be relevant for the proposed EEA Court. However, in its Opinion 1/91 which was guided by the desire to annihilate that court, the ECJ stated with regard to the EEA Agreement in paragraph 14:

> An international treaty is to be interpreted not only on the basis of its wording, but also in the light of its objectives. Article 31 of the Vienna Convention of 23 May 1969 on the law of treaties stipulates in this respect that a treaty is to be interpreted in good faith in accordance with the ordinary meaning to be given to its terms in their context and in the light of its object and purpose.[1]

Orthodox dualists in our Nordic Member States were very pleased with this statement. They took the view that the EEA Agreement was a classical treaty under public international law, which as a corollary would also produce some benefits for citizens and economic operators. And yet it was clear from the beginning that the Agreement's main goal, the creation of a homogeneous and dynamic EEA, could not be achieved if the EFTA Court were to treat it as a simple international law treaty and to apply the methods of the Vienna Convention. Interestingly, the ECJ did not mention this point in its second—positive—EEA Opinion 1/92. In any case, the EFTA Court never applied the Vienna rules. It developed its own methods of interpretation, methods which resemble those used by the ECJ.

2 Relevant EU Case Law Available

2.1 ECJ Judgments

As I have repeatedly stated, the EFTA Court has taken the written homogeneity rules seriously from the start, and it has, in principle, followed relevant ECJ jurisprudence. However, on some occasions, the EFTA Court decided to go its own

[1] See for details Chapter 3.

way. It needs to be emphasised that the homogeneity rules do not mean that ECJ case law will be taken over in a mechanical manner. This can only happen after careful consideration.

2.2 AGs Opinions

The EFTA Court has always taken into account relevant opinions of the ECJ's AGs. In 2001, we made this visible for the first time by referencing the Opinion of the British AG Francis Jacobs in *Albany* in the *LO* case.[2] Opinions of AGs are sources of inspiration of high quality. They often help in understanding what the ECJ wanted to say in a judgment. Nevertheless, the EFTA Court has occasionally also taken the liberty of following the AG's opinion in cases in which the ECJ did not do so.

2.3 GC Judgments

The EFTA Court decided at an early stage that the written homogeneity rules also apply to the case law of the GC. However, it goes without saying that it should be borne in mind that the GC is not a court of last instance.

3 Extra-Legal Considerations

3.1 General

As I have said before,[3] I was educated at the school of law and economics of Berne University in the late 1960s and early 1970s. Most of my professors were elderly gentlemen who were convinced—or at least claimed to be convinced—that legal interpretation was and should remain an objective business. That the Swiss legislature had in Article 1 of the Civil Code not only recognised the existence of gaps in the written law, but also instructed judges to fill them as if they were the legislature barely concerned them. In fact, Article 1 of the Swiss Civil Code famously states under the heading "Application of the Law":

> [1] The law applies according to its wording or interpretation to all legal questions for which it contains a provision.

---

[2]See for details Chapter 27.

[3]See for details Chapter 1.

[2] In the absence of a provision, the court shall decide in accordance with customary law and, in the absence of customary law, in accordance with the rule that it would make as legislator.

[3] In doing so, the court shall follow established doctrine and case law.

Some think that this provision was inspired by the French (Alsatian) scholar François Gény, a representative of the so-called free law movement. The German free law movement was a reaction to the strictly formalist conceptual jurisprudence. It distanced itself from traditional conceptualism right after the entry into force of the German Civil Code on 1 January 1900. However, my professors argued that the power to correct the law did not follow from Article 1, but from Article 2(2) of the Civil Code. That provision states (in the French tradition) that the "manifest" abuse of a right is not protected by law. My teachers claimed—without the slightest proof, it was a pure and simple *petitio principii*—that rewriting the law was only legitimate if the result of interpretation "lege artis" had led to a "manifestly" unjust result. A *petitio principii* is the logical fallacy in which a premise is assumed to be true without any basis for this assumption. They believed that methodological rules could be a means of preventing judges from interpreting the law in the light of totalitarian ideologies such as national socialism or communism. While writing my doctoral thesis and my habilitation work, and also during my time as a legal secretary at a Swiss first instance court, I discovered that these ideas had little to do with reality.

3.2 Preunderstanding or Attitude

In those days, two books were set for every critical mind: Topics and Law ("*Topik und Jurisprudenz*") by the German legal philosopher Theodor Viehweg and Truth and Method ("*Wahrheit und Methode*") by the German philosopher Hans Georg Gadamer. Viehweg had rediscovered topics, an ancient method used by Aristotle and Cicero. Topics consider a legal question from a problem-oriented perspective rather than by means of logical deduction. Legal thinking is said to take place in such a way that points of view ("*topoi*"), which may be the solution to a problem, are listed and discussed. The *topoi* can be collected in catalogues, but the catalogues must remain open. Gadamer was the leading representative of modern hermeneutics. He argued that it is the judges' preunderstanding or preconception ("*Vorverständnis*") of the law that above all determines the choice of method. Preunderstanding is formed, in particular, by the specific legal knowledge and by the general knowledge of circumstances outside the law, such as aspects of social or economic policy or culture in general. Preunderstanding constitutes the starting point for every interpretation. Like every interpreter, a judge may understand a text only when approaching it with a certain purposeful expectation of the meaning. This provisional meaning is then continuously corrected by the knowledge acquired by the interpreter in the course of the further penetration of the meaning.

Preunderstanding or preconception cannot be equated with prejudice. The influence of preunderstanding cannot, however, be totally eliminated.

The German doctrine of preunderstanding has similarities with the attitudinal model of judicial decision-making as developed by American political scientists. According to this theory, the judge's own ideological, political and other views and beliefs are more important in the decision-making process than the law. A judge's attitude is shaped by experience and surroundings.

In the US, I became familiar with the teachings of legal realism. According to this influential school, adjudication is an inherently subjective system. It produces inconsistent, sometimes incoherent results that are largely based on the political, social, and moral predilections of judges. Oliver Wendell Holmes who later became a Justice of the US Supreme Court wrote that

> [t]he life of the law has not been logic, it has been experience.

Jerome N. Frank stated that

> [a] judge's psychological and personality characteristics also sway the judicial decision-making process.

And US Supreme Court Justice Benjamin N. Cardozo called judges "legislators in robes".

During my stays in America, I also started to see the European precursors of legal realism, the free law movement and the jurisprudence of interests, in a new light. The free law movement's leading figure, Hermann Kantorowicz, claimed that judges must be freed from the straightjacket of conceptualism and that they must take into account life's full spectrum of values, knowledge and experience. Regarding jurisprudence of interests, Roscoe Pound, the chief advocate of "sociological jurisprudence" in the US, noted a shift from

> thinking of the task of the legal order as one of adjusting the exercise of free wills to one of satisfying wants [….]. [W]e must start today from a theory of interests, that is, of the claims or demands or desires which human beings, either individually or in groups or associations or relations, seek to satisfy, of which, therefore, the adjustment of relations and ordering of conduct through the force of politically organized society must take account.

That the American legal realists have built on the ideas of the German free law movement is, *inter alia*, shown by the biography of one of their main protagonists, Karl Llewellyn. Llewellyn was studying in Paris when World War I broke out in 1914 and decided to fight on the German side. He was injured in the first Battle of Ypres and was decorated with the Iron Cross, 2nd class. He then returned to the US and finished his studies at Yale.

The legal realists launched a frontal attack on methodological conservatism in the 1920s and the 1930s. They alleged that, between 1895 and 1937, formalist judges had based their decisions on the assumption that the law was an objective, unchanging phenomenon, immune from social influence and both different from and superior to politics. Their goal was to weaken or even dissolve the dichotomy between law and politics. They wanted to show that judicial decision-making was not a mechanistic, impersonal activity, but that it was necessarily shaped by personal values. In reality, they claimed that judicial discretion was significant.

Legal realism famously distinguishes between the law on the books and the law in action. The focus of law in action includes the institutional and political framework of an international agreement, in particular the governments, and in the case of the European integration treaties the supranational agencies and the supranational courts. Under the EEA Agreement, the ECJ's case law is of paramount importance. At any rate, law in action looks beyond the judgments. From that perspective, it may, for example, take into account whether a judge is a liberal or a leftist or rather a conservative or a right-winger. In European law, it may be important whether judges are favourable vis-à-vis integration or whether they are sovereigntists or Eurosceptics. It may matter whether a European judge has in his previous life been a judge in his country of origin or a practising lawyer or a professor or whether a judge has been a politician or a bureaucrat or a career diplomat. It may make a difference whether a judge is appointed for life or only for a certain term, usually with the possibility of reappointment. And it may make a difference whether a judge believes in free markets and competition or in mercantilism.

In certain cases, mostly but not exclusively related to high profile matters, the judge's attitude or preunderstanding may become so decisive that legal considerations recede to the background. Attitude may also be the result of education, religious, economic or political belief, biography and the like. For example, judges who have been divorced five times will think differently about the indissolubility of marriage than their monogamous colleagues.

In the US Supreme Court, the vote, in politically controversial cases, is often taken along ideological lines. This can also be observed, at least to a certain extent, in Supreme Courts in Europe. At the European level, the critical issue is potential judicial nationalism. Judges who have spent their whole professional life as bureaucrats may have a different attitude with regard to the question of whether third parties should have locus standi to challenge a decision of the Commission or of ESA in State aid matters than somebody who has been socialised as a business lawyer or a professor. As I have explained before, appointment to an international or European court is always for a certain term and whether a judge is prolonged lies in the hands of the government of the nominating country—the same government that may also have a strong interest in winning the case in question. If judges become aware that one of their colleagues is about to vote according to attitude, those judges have a duty to point this out—even if that is not always easy in practice because their colleague may be offended. My experience is that the better judges are educated and the more they are socialised as independent legal minds, the more they will be in a position to question their own (and others') preunderstanding. This was confirmed when I delivered a speech to the judges and lawyers of the Court of Justice of the Andean Community in Quito in May 2015. It had become clear in the discussion following my presentation that some of the judges of that important court were political appointees. An apparently independent judge stated very clearly that in her view, good legal education was essential to prevent judges from engaging in nationalist decision-making. To be sure, even the best legal education is no absolute guarantee in this respect.

3.3 Strategic Considerations

Generally speaking, judges can be regarded as casting their vote in a strategic way if they do not vote according to their convictions, but with a view to achieving an overarching goal. Strategic behaviour may occur if judges vote against their own views in order to secure a certain collective decision, to be part of the majority, to avoid an even worse outcome, to make other judges inclined to vote with them in a future case. Situations may also arise where judges make concessions in a case in order to secure the vote of other judges in a presidential election. Finally, strategic voting may occur in order to enhance the court's standing vis-à-vis the political branches of government. In an international court the latter goal is, as a matter of principle, a worthy goal. This holds true, in particular, for a small court or for a court operating in a difficult political environment. All the other patterns of strategic behaviour may constitute reasons for other judges to tackle the judge in question. Again, this can be a delicate undertaking.

Courts are generally dependent on other branches of government when it comes to enforcing their decisions. They will naturally take this into account. At the European level, these constraints are even stronger because the enforcement of the judgments lies in the hands of national entities. Nevertheless, the ECJ's judgments, regardless of whether they were rendered in infringement or nullity proceedings, are legally binding. That is not the case for the preliminary rulings of the EFTA Court. Given the soft framework conditions of the preliminary reference procedure in the EFTA pillar, the EFTA Court must convince the national court in order to win its approval.[4] It goes without saying that public opinion and the opinion of the legal community play a role in this.

I always felt that US Supreme Court Chief Justice John Roberts' voting with the liberals in the "*Obamacare*" case was at least partly strategically motivated. Roberts is a George W. Bush appointee. Despite his conservative reputation, with his Obamacare vote, he positioned himself as an independent mind. When I met the Chief Justice at a dinner in Luxembourg in February 2014, I asked him whether I was right. He laughed and answered that his vote was strictly based on legal arguments.

Another question is whether, in ground-breaking cases, the EFTA Court is also constrained by the possibility that the ECJ will not come to the same conclusion in a subsequent parallel case under EU law. There is no easy answer to this dilemma. On the one hand, it is clear that the EFTA Court will, in view of its size and the

[4]See for details Chapter 8.

structure of the EEA Agreement, try to avoid a judicial conflict a priori. On the other hand, the EFTA Court has demonstrated in numerous cases that it has the courage and the strength to go for what it is convinced is the right solution. In so doing, it aims to persuade the ECJ to follow on the same path. There may, however, also be cases in which the EFTA Court has such strong feelings about a certain outcome that it will accept the risk that the ECJ might not, or not immediately, follow its reasoning.

3.4 Institutional Loyalty

Political scientists have found that judges may, in the event of doubt, opt for an interpretation of the law which benefits their court, i.e. the institution of which they are part. This is actually a concept which covers some of the most pressing challenges of a small international or European court. If judges are not loyal to the court, but let themselves be driven by the wishes of the Government that nominated them (and that may, or may not, re-nominate them) or by other political considerations, this undermines the standing of their court and the standing of the respective international or European agreement or community. When I spoke on this issue to the judges and lawyers of the Andean Court of Justice in May 2015, their President, Luis José Diez Canseco Núñez, reacted immediately and took up the argument of institutional loyalty ("*lealtad institucional*").

4 Legal Considerations

4.1 General

The discipline analysing the way in which interpreters address law and legal phenomena is called legal methodology. Generally speaking, the term methodology describes a body of practices and rules used by those who are active in a given field. In legal texts and commentaries, the notion of methodology is sometimes confused with judicial style. At the end of the day, this is a matter of definition. According to the language used in this book, methodology and judicial style mean two different things. Whether you take into account a certain element of interpretation such as, for example, the case law of other courts or academic literature, is a methodological question. Whether you make this visible in the judgment by explicitly citing those sources is a matter of judicial style.

Domestic legal norms are usually interpreted on the basis of their text, their history, their purpose ("*telos*") and the scheme of the respective law. The text of a norm is always the starting point for interpretation. Whether it is also the endpoint is, however, a matter that has proved controversial. Conservative lawyers tend to favour history and text over *telos* and scheme. The *telos* must in their view be assessed according to the intentions of the drafters of the law. In Europe, the term historic method is commonly used for this approach, while in the US, the notion of originalism has arisen in the context of constitutional interpretation. Conservatives on both sides of the Atlantic Ocean tend to argue that going beyond the historic ("original") meaning of a norm is incompatible with the separation of powers. Thus, if the historic method does not lead to a just and fair outcome, it is for the legislature and not for the judge to correct the law. In their view, judges lack the democratic legitimacy to make corrections to the law. However, the historic method has not been fully implemented in any European country. The highest courts do, at least in certain cases, take the liberty of correcting the law. The same applies for American courts and probably most of the courts working in free and democratic systems.

Text, history, the scheme and the *telos* are also relevant when it comes to interpreting EEA law. Although the materials relating to the EEA negotiations are not officially available, which virtually excludes historic interpretation, the situation may be different for secondary law.

4.2 *Teleological Interpretation in Particular*

Unsurprisingly, the EFTA Court, as a matter of principle, also opted for teleological interpretation, i.e. interpretation in the light of the purpose a provision aims to achieve. This includes current time teleology. A number of expressions have been developed in this context. People speak of dynamic interpretation, judicial law making, evolutive interpretation or interpretation in the light of today's needs. In the *Tyrer* judgment of 25 April 1978 and in other cases, the ECtHR has famously described the ECHR as "a living instrument, which must be interpreted in the light of present-day conditions". All these notions essentially mean the same, namely that a court will, if it feels that this is appropriate, take the liberty of going beyond what the historic legislature or treaty giver might either have had in mind or have stated in the text. This may even imply that a court will, in certain circumstances, come to the conclusion that the relevant text contains a gap, which must be filled, or that the relevant text contains a rule whose application would lead to an unequitable result. That the former EEC was pursuing a political goal was, to a certain extent, camouflaged by the notion that it was a community of law or a community based on the rule of law. However, there were also occasions when this political agenda was highlighted with pride. It was, for example, commonplace, during the time of the so-called "euro-sclerosis" in the 1960s and 1970s, for the ECJ to openly push the process of integration.

When the EFTA Court has to answer a fresh legal question, teleological considerations are of paramount importance. An early example in the jurisprudence of the five-member Court was *Samuelsson*. The case concerned the question of whether under the 1980 Insolvency Directive,[5] a provision of national law, which precluded an employee from further remuneration if, within two years prior to the bankruptcy decision, that employee had been granted remuneration through the guarantee for a wage claim which arose in mainly the same activity, was lawful. Based on the social objective of the directive, the Court denied the question. The three-member Court used a teleological perspective in the *Fagtún* case holding that it cannot be decisive whether in public procurement proceedings you insert a discriminatory clause into the specifications before the tender takes place or after the tender procedure has been closed. In the *Pedicel* case, the Court found that the exclusion of wine from the products covered by the EEA Agreement meant that the provisions concerning services also did not apply to the advertising of wine, since in the conditions of the case at hand, the service was inseparably linked to the sale of wine. This, too, was teleological reasoning. Dynamic interpretation may be an option for the Court also in ground-breaking cases, i.e. not only when we have to close a gap between EU and EEA law, but also when we decide on a fresh legal question. An important example is the judgment in the *Kellogg's* case.[6]

In EU law, a by-product of teleological interpretation is the principle of effectiveness. This, too, has been taken over by the EFTA Court. In the *Celina Nguyen* case the Court recognised this maxim in paragraph 24, almost between the lines, by stating that national provisions governing compensation for road accidents cannot deprive the EEA Motor Vehicle Insurance Directives[7] of their effectiveness. In this case, the EFTA Court was the first European court to hold that, under those directives, insurers are obliged to pay not only for material damages but also for immaterial damages, which includes pain and suffering. The EFTA Court further elaborated on the principle of effectiveness in the *Clauder* case in the context of family reunification.

4.3 Functional Interpretation in Particular

In German and in Swiss methodology there is a further distinction in the area of teleological interpretation, namely between what some authors call micro-teleology, on the one hand, and macro-teleology, on the other. Micro-teleology would investigate the purpose of the norm for the parties concerned, whereas macro-teleology would scrutinise the norm's consequences for the system as a whole. Macro-teleology is also called functional interpretation. In my view, this approach is a promising one for any legal system. In the EEA context, it means that we have to take into consideration what the consequences of a certain interpretation

[5]80/897 EC.

[6]See with regard to the *Kellogg's* case Chapter 11.

[7]72/166/EEC, 84/5/EEC and 90/232/EEC.

are for the well-functioning of the EEA Single Market are or, as the case may be, for the well-functioning of the competition system in the EEA.

As I have said before, the EFTA Court's three Member States have mixed economies in that part of the economy is left to the free or the regulated market and part is managed by the government. Like the EU economy, the EEA/EFTA economy is based on an internal or Single Market which permits government intervention in certain circumstances. From a functional perspective, this is the reference system that needs to be taken into account. EEA Single Market law is economic law; in the Scandinavian countries, "economic law" is sometimes referred to as "market law". Economic law is defined as the law of the economy. The economy is the subject of economic law, as possessions, both movable and immovable, are the subject of property law. More precisely, economic law is the law that governs the coordination of economic activity. Basically, three coordination mechanisms can be distinguished: competition; State planning; and collective bargaining. The principal theme of economic law is the relationship between regulation and the free market. As a starting point, a market economy must guarantee private autonomy, freedom of property, freedom of contract, freedom of association, freedom to make a will, and party autonomy (the freedom to choose the applicable law). However, to what extent a given legal order will rely on the market mechanism and to what extent on planning, depends on policy decisions. The respective questions, which underpin the concept of regulation, have been answered in different ways in diverse economic systems. In fact, the relationship between the State and the economy is politically contested and has changed over time. Every phase in history has its own economic law. Accordingly, it is possible to distinguish the economic law of mercantilism, liberalism, the welfare state, neo-liberalism, socialism, and neo-mercantilism, to name just a few examples.

4.4 National Case Law and Academic Literature

As EU law, EEA law must be interpreted autonomously. However, that doesn't mean that a European court like the EFTA Court should not know what is going on in the courts of its Member States. It is the duty of each judge to inform his/her colleagues of any relevant developments. Whether a court of the size of the EFTA Court will be able to gather reliable information about the state of justice in important EU Member States is another question. Since the EFTA Court does not have a research and documentation unit, its possibilities are limited and everything depends on the willingness and ability of the judges and legal secretaries to conduct the necessary research.

As regards the question of whether academic literature is to be consulted, the answer must clearly be yes. However, that is easier said than done in a court of the size of the EFTA Court which is operating without a research department. At the end of the day, it again depends on the willingness of the individual judges and legal secretaries, and on their comparative law and linguistic competences, whether relevant texts can be read and understood. English texts do not pose a problem and there is obviously a lot of knowledge of Scandinavian languages. Nevertheless, the difficulty exists. I have always made sure that I hired legal secretaries who were not only outstanding specialists of European law, in the broad sense of the word, but who also had the respective skills in the most important continental languages, in particular in French, German, Italian and Spanish.

5 The Accusation of Judicial Activism

5.1 General

The EFTA Court's methodological toolbox does not really differ from the one used by the ECJ. The question is more one of how the available tools are used in practice. If a court goes for dynamic interpretation in a sensitive case, conservatives will be quick to claim that it is crossing the boundary between legislation and adjudication. Such criticism has been voiced throughout history in all legal systems. As regards the ECJ, my late friend Hjalte Rasmussen stated in 1986 that judicial activism may amount to a usurpation of power. Dieter Grimm, a former Judge of the German Constitutional Court, said that the case law recognising direct effect and primacy (*van Gend en Loos* and *Costa* v *ENEL* had the features of a covert coup d'état ("*Züge eines verdeckten Putsches*").

Today, when Brexit is so much a topic of discussion, I should mention that in the UK there has always been a strong tendency to accuse the ECJ of not respecting the balance between judicature and legislature. However, it cannot be denied that the teleological method is also familiar to British courts. Lord Blackburn stated in 1877 in *River Wear Commissioners v Adamson* that

> it is to be borne in mind that the office of the judge is not to legislate, but to declare the expressed intention of the legislature even if that expressed intention appeared to the court to be injudicious; and I believe that it is not disputed that what Lord Wensleydale used to call the Golden rule is right viz. that we are to take the whole statute together and construe it all together, giving the words their ordinary significance unless when so applied they produce an inconsistency or an absurdity or inconvenience so great as to convince the court that the intention could not have been to use them in their ordinary signification and to justify the court in putting on them some other significance which though less proper is one which the court thinks the words will bear.

In modern times, things have not substantially changed.

Whole libraries have been written on what judges are allowed to do and what not. Such methodological instructions are, however, of limited utility. In the end, it all boils down to whether judges' decisions have a sense of proportion and whether they are sufficiently reasoned and accepted. In 1910, the German legal philosopher Gustav Radbruch, the future Minister of Justice of the Weimar Republic, called sciences that deal with their own methodology "sick sciences". This was during the period of conflict between traditional German conceptualism ("*Begriffsjurisprudenz*") and the free law movement ("*Freirechtsschule*"). As a general rule, Radbruch's statement is certainly an exaggeration. Nevertheless, there is some truth to it.

What is more important than methodological guidelines are the constraints that follow from the fact that EFTA Court judges, like their ECJ colleagues, are chosen by the governments of the Member States and EEA/EFTA States, and that their reappointment depends on those governments. Certain governments have shown a clear tendency to nominate people who they think will not be activists.[8] Further restrictions result from the specific framework conditions for preliminary rulings in the EFTA pillar—lack of a written obligation on courts of last resort to make a reference and non-binding nature of the EFTA Court's answers—and the fact that as a three-member institution with little power, the EFTA Court must give broad reasoning for, and disclose the value judgments underlying, its jurisprudence. If you cannot decree like the mighty ECJ, you are a priori restricted.

Another point must be stressed. Even if the EFTA Court uses the same or similar methods of interpretation as the ECJ, that doesn't necessarily mean that it will go in the same direction because the systems of reference are different. The EEA Agreement does not imply that the participating EFTA States should be heading towards an "ever closer union" or anything similar. This is where EFTA values such as free trade, market-orientation, fair taxation or efficiency may come into play.[9]

In my view, there is no clear line between legitimate interpretation of the law and acting *ultra vires*. What is decisive is whether the rulings are accepted by a court's audiences. If this is the case, dynamic interpretation must be deemed to be justified. Nevertheless, when trying to create acceptance, a court of law walks a fine line. In the case of the EFTA Court, the problem in this respect has always been that these audiences had diverging expectations. Whereas, in the field of fundamental freedoms, the Commission and ESA quite naturally wanted the Court to stick to the case law of the ECJ, some EFTA State Governments occasionally urged it to recognise that minor restrictions were irrelevant or that in EEA law there were special grounds justifying a particular restriction. There is no general formula as to how the Court should act in such cases. At all events, providing good reasons for the conclusions reached is crucial. "The EFTA Court is prepared to embark on judicial activism" is a politically motivated slogan that does not stand up to scrutiny. Depending on where a commentator stands, almost every court, and certainly every international or supranational court, is exposed to such criticism. I will hereafter deal with this accusation depending on whether there is ECJ case law on a certain issue or not.

Interpretation that is based on homogeneity is, as a rule, not judicial activism. An activist position was taken by governments calling upon the EFTA Court to deviate from the homogeneity objective, be it in the name of alleged differences in goal,

---

[8]See for details the Prologue.

[9]See for details Chapter 3.

context or even in scope between the EEA Agreement and the EU Treaties or in the name of an alleged *de minimis rule*, national legal culture, or certain "expectations" the governments had or purportedly had when they negotiated the EEA Agreement. Thus, we heard government agents arguing against homogeneous interpretation of substantive, effect-related and procedural rules. In what was arguably the EFTA Court's biggest case so far, *Icesave I*, both ESA and the Commission wanted us to assume the existence of a gap in the Deposit Guarantee Directive[10] with regard to the liability of States and to fill it in accordance with the wishes of the British and the Dutch Government and at the end of the day of the whole European Union. That was an invitation to become activist. We declined.[11]

5.2 *Bridging the Widening Gap*

The EC Treaty, our model of reference, has been amended no less than four times since the conclusion of the EEA Agreement in 1992, namely in Maastricht, Amsterdam, Nice and Lisbon. At Lisbon the EC Treaty was renamed the "Treaty on the Functioning of the European Union" (TFEU). The question has arisen as to whether the EFTA Court should understand the homogeneity principle in the light of present day conditions and thereby implement elements of EU law into EEA law by way of filling gaps or dynamic interpretation. The EEA Joint Committee is not competent to amend the EEA Main Agreement, and the Contracting Parties have so far refrained from reopening negotiations. The Court may therefore face the task of closing the gap once there has been a further development on the EU side. In a way, the Court laid the methodological ground for this in *Pedicel* where it asserted in paragraph 28 that the objective of creating a dynamic and homogeneous EEA

> may make dynamic interpretation of EEA law necessary.

To my knowledge, the ECJ has never made such a statement. The EFTA Court has made it clear that it is in a special situation if homogeneity of the case law is to be preserved. This is a direct result of the EU side moving faster than the EFTA side. The situation has been described as the EFTA pillar dancing a slow foxtrot while the EU pillar dances rock' n roll. Somebody must ramp up the tempo in the EFTA pillar if homogeneity is to be maintained. The Court deals with this challenge on a case by case basis. I will give three examples.

The first is the *Einarsson* case. Under Icelandic law, books written in Icelandic were subject to a VAT rate of 10%, whereas books in a foreign language where subject to a VAT rate of 24.5%. Hörður Einarsson, an Icelandic attorney, felt that this unequal treatment constituted discriminatory taxation and brought an action in the Reykjavík District Court. That court made a reference to the Court. We held that

---

[10] 94/19/EC.

[11] See with regard to the *Icesave* saga Chapter 25.

the Icelandic rule constituted discriminatory taxation within the meaning of the second paragraph of Article 14 EEA, which states that

> no Contracting Party shall impose on the products of other Contracting Parties any internal taxation of such a nature as to afford indirect protection to other products.

Iceland, supported by Norway, tried to justify its tax regime on the ground of the need to protect cultural heritage. However, the EEA Agreement does not mention such a justification ground, nor was there any ECJ case law to that effect. Nevertheless, the Icelandic Government invoked an article which had been incorporated in EC law by the Treaty of Amsterdam, and asked the Court to apply this provision by analogy. According to this provision, the Community had to take cultural aspects into account in its actions under other provisions of the Treaties, in particular in order to respect and to promote the diversity of its cultures. In other words, the Icelandic Government urged the Court to become a judicial activist. This proves that whether judicial activism is seen in a negative or in a positive way always depends on where an observer stands. The Court's position was that you do not need this sort of discriminatory tax legislation in order to protect your language.

Given this outcome and in the light of the small amount of money involved, it seems fair to say that Mr Einarsson acted as a private attorney general.[12] He brought a lawsuit that was in the public interest, benefiting the general public and not just himself. I met Hörður Einarsson four times in person. Once in 2004 when I spoke at a Constitutional Law Conference in *Þingvellir*, the park of *Þingvellir* being Iceland's national shrine. The second time was in March 2016, when I gave a lecture at the Icelandic Lawyers Association in Reykjavík. I told him that with the case he had instigated he had written legal history. Icelanders have difficulties in showing their emotions, but I think that he appreciated this compliment. The third time, I met Hörður was when he attended my lecture at the University of Iceland on "The Contribution of Icelanders to the Functioning of the EFTA Court" on 11 October 2017. It was my last visit to Iceland in my capacity as the EFTA Court's President. And the forth time was on 1 June 2018 when I was bestowed the Commanders Cross (*Stórriddarakross*) of the Falcon Order by the President of the Republic of Iceland

> for my contribution to the functioning and development of the European Economic Area.

Another example is the *Oslo University* case in which I was Acting President and Judge Rapporteur. In Norway, a law had been enacted stating that a certain number of university posts were earmarked for members of the under-represented gender, i.e. women. ESA sued Norway claiming that the legislation in question was incompatible with the 1976 Equal Rights Directive.[13] The ECJ had interpreted that directive as not recognising the concept of group rights. Women could in theory have group rights, like indigenous people in Canadian law, for example. In 1995,

---

[12]See regarding the notion of a private attorney general, Chapter 16.

[13]76/207/EEC.

the ECJ in *Kalanke* established the principle that every individual case must be assessed on its own merits. The Norwegian Government then declared its intention of ignoring this decision. In our case, the Norwegian Government's agent used two conflicting lines of argument. On the one hand, she said that the EFTA Court should follow the ECJ's case law, which, if correctly understood, allowed the earmarking of the posts. On the other hand, the agent argued that we should distance ourselves from the ECJ. Finally, the government claimed that we should not base ourselves on the old EC Treaty, which was relevant when the EEA Agreement was signed, but on the new Article 141(4) of the EC Treaty.[14] This provision states:

> With a view to ensuring full equality in practice between men and women in working life, the principle of equal treatment shall not prevent any Member State from maintaining or adopting measures providing for specific advantages in order to make it easier for the underrepresented sex to pursue a vocational activity or to prevent or compensate for disadvantages in professional careers.

We did not do that. However, in the subsequent *Golden widows*' case, in a slightly concealed half sentence, we did refer to this new provision of EU law.

University of Oslo was, by the way, the first time that the Court was composed of two men and a woman. The regular Icelandic judge, Thór Vilhjálmsson, had fallen ill and we called on his replacement, Dóra Guðmundsdóttir to sit. No woman has served on the EFTA Court bench as a regular judge to date.

The most obvious case of bridging the gap to date has been *Jabbi*, where the EFTA Court held that although the concept of European citizenship is missing in the EEA Agreement, the Citizenship Directive[15] had to be interpreted in such a way as to give third-country nationals a derived right of residence in an EEA/EFTA State under certain circumstances.[16]

6 Balanced Realism

Since the 1970s, there has been a development in American political science which has been called the rediscovery of the rule of law, of the importance of legal ideas and legal doctrine for court decisions. Even legal realists would today recognise that when it comes to interpretation, legal considerations and legal doctrine are important. In 1969, C. Herman Pritchett, a University of Chicago political scientist who had always emphasised that jurisprudence could not be imaged without politics famously wrote:

---

[14]Now Article 157(4) TFEU.

[15]2004/38/EC.

[16]See for details Chapter 19.

> Political scientists who have done so much to put the 'political' in 'political jurisprudence' need to emphasize that it is still 'jurisprudence'. It is judging in a political context, but it is still judging; and judging is something different from legislating or administering.

Washington University Professor Brian Z. Tamanaha therefore speaks of "balanced realism".

Legal methodology is, however, not an exact science. It is in my view useful, in that it provides a number of points of view ("*topoi*") to be looked into. However, the list of *topoi* it covers is not exhaustive, nor is there a hierarchy between them in the event of a conflict. In fact, the main question is how a court ought to proceed if, for example, the historic meaning of a norm contradicts present day needs or if the norm does not provide any answer. This question cannot be answered once and for all, but needs to be addressed in each given case. In certain cases, attitude may play an important role in judicial decision-making. Judges must be aware of their own beliefs and of their past experiences. Even then, preunderstanding will not disappear entirely. Interpreters must examine their own preconceptions against the text of the norm in the so-called "hermeneutic circle". Thereby, they project an understanding for the whole of the text and understand each part in the light of that projection, revising the interpretation step by step while further penetrating the text. The legal considerations serve to question and possibly to justify the emerging solution. Judges' behaviour is sometimes strategic; this cannot be avoided in every case. Most importantly, in the event of doubt, judges must not overlook the interests of their institution.

7 My Approach

After 22 and a half years on the EFTA Court bench, I would describe my approach to legal interpretation in the following way: when a case comes in and you have become familiar with the facts and the possible legal implications, you quite naturally make a first assessment. You have to be aware of this preunderstanding and must be prepared to question it. This was done, as a rule, through discussions with my legal secretaries, that means within my cabinet. Occasionally I discussed a case with outsiders including members of the EU judiciary, within the framework of what was permitted. Since EEA Single Market law is economic law, I felt that economics were of paramount importance in respective cases. When it comes to the legal considerations, no *topos* should be omitted; text, scheme and *telos* count, as does history, at least insofar as secondary law is concerned. However, there are also other important issues such as precedent, judgments of the ECJ and of the GC, opinions of the ECJ's AGs, judgments of other courts, and academic literature. Under the EEA homogeneity regime, the case law of the ECJ is of particular significance. What counts at the end is whether the solution found makes sense.

It seems that, at least indirectly, the well-known former American judge Richard Posner is on a similar track. In an interview, following his resignation in September 2017, he stated that from a "pragmatic" perspective, the judge had simply to go for a common-sense solution:

> [T]o be pragmatic just means to focus on consequences. What are the likely consequences of each of say two alternative rulings that are within the judge's authority to make? [....] [H]aving found the pragmatic result, the judge asks whether it's blocked by some authoritative ruling, principle, rule - whatever. [....] So who were the great judges who were not pragmatists? Holmes was a pragmatist. Hand, Cardozo, Jackson, Friendly, Traynor, Kozinski, Wilkinson—I could keep going, but tell me who are the judges you admire who were/are not pragmatists? Any current member of the Supreme Court?

Let me end this Chapter with a few personal remarks about how lawyers in general should behave. In our litigious societies, the use of lawyers in many day-to-day situations has become almost indispensable. Unfortunately, they are often far removed from so-called ordinary people. What is needed, above all, in legal methodology is honesty and openness. Lawyers must not misapply the power they have been given; they must not act as if they were cold legal technicians. They have secret codes at their fingertips and have been trained in special techniques of reasoning, which enable them to prevail over others. This supremacy can easily be abused. Lawyers—and this goes in particular for judges and legal secretaries—cannot limit themselves to making abstract deductions and engaging in other types of juridical gymnastics. They must also ask the question of whether a certain outcome that has been found based on the use of methodological tricks is appropriate, which means fair and efficient. Judges must be aware of their preunderstanding and they must be prepared to question it. And the must disclose the real reasons that lie behind a judgment. The Dean of Harvard Law School, Erwin Griswold, who later served as Solicitor General under Presidents Johnson and Nixon, stated in 1955 when writing about attorneys:

> Many lawyers never do seem to understand that they are dealing with people and not solely with the impersonal law.

Regrettably, that is still true, and it doesn't only apply to attorneys.

Chapter 10
War Over Constitutional Principles

Contents

1 Starting Point: A Dilatory Formula Compromise

During the EEA negotiations, the Nordic EFTA States Finland, Iceland, Norway and Sweden took the view that accepting the principles of direct effect and primacy as part of EEA law was out of the question, in the light of their dualistic tradition. The Commission for its part wanted to avoid that the situation that had occurred under the 1972 bilateral free trade agreements (FTAs) would repeat itself in EEA law. In view of the accession of the UK, Denmark and Ireland to the EEC, each of the remaining EFTA States concluded an FTA with the EEC. These FTAs were bilateral in nature, but largely identical in substance. Unlike under the EEA Agreement, there was no common court for the EFTA States. As regards the FTA between the EEC and Switzerland, the Swiss Federal Supreme Court in *Stanley Adams* in 1978 and in *Omo* in 1979—and subsequently the Austrian Supreme Court in 1980 in the *Austro-Mechana* case—denied the direct effect of the provisions of the respective FTAs as regards the free movement of goods. In the dualistic Nordic EFTA countries, direct effect was already excluded because the FTAs had not been implemented into the domestic legal orders. Access to justice in the EEC, on the one hand, and in the EFTA countries, on the other, was therefore unequal. The ECJ sanctioned the EFTA States. It gave a double reply.

C. Baudenbacher, *Judicial Independence*, Springer Biographies,
https://doi.org/10.1007/978-3-030-02308-9_10

In *Polydor*, a parallel import case concerning the FTA between the EEC and Portugal, the ECJ held on 9 February 1982 that the similarity between the terms used in the FTA and in the EEC Treaty was not a sufficient reason for transposing the jurisprudence, which determines, in the context of the Community, the relationship between the protection of IP rights and the rules on free movement of goods on the provisions of the FTA. The ECJ came to this result by comparing the more modest aims and the more modest institutional structure of the FTA with those of the EEC Treaty. Although the ECJ did not refer to the interpretation rules of the Vienna Convention on the Law of Treaties, it could well be that the notion of a difference of goals and context between the EEC Treaty, on the one hand, and international agreements concluded by the Community with third countries, on the other, was inspired by Article 31(1) of that Convention, which states:

> A treaty shall be interpreted in good faith in accordance with the ordinary meaning to be given to the terms of the treaty in their context and in the light of its object and purpose.

In *Kupferberg*, in which judgment was rendered 8 months after *Polydor*, the ECJ made the Swiss Federal Supreme Court somehow look bad by showing generosity with regard to the issue of direct effect.

As far as the modalities of effect and primacy in the EEA context are concerned, the Contracting Parties agreed on what Carl Schmitt in his seminal book on constitutional theory ("*Verfassungslehre*") has referred to as a dilatory formula compromise ("*dilatorischer Formelkompromiss*"). The negotiators were not able to agree on a clear solution and passed the hot potato to the courts. A partial solution was found in Protocol 35[1] on the implementation of EEA rules which states:

> Whereas this Agreement aims at achieving a homogeneous European Economic Area, based on common rules, without requiring any Contracting Party to transfer legislative powers to any institution of the European Economic Area; and
>
> Whereas this consequently will have to be achieved through national procedures;
>
> *Sole Article*
>
> For cases of possible conflicts between implemented EEA rules and other statutory provisions, the EFTA States undertake to introduce, if necessary, a statutory provision to the effect that EEA rules prevail in these cases.

Despite this, in the early days a prominent member of the ECJ, AG Walter van Gerven, wrote that direct effect and primacy should be regarded as part of EEA law because a legal system that did not encompass these principles would not be remotely homogeneous with Community law:

> [S]tripping Community law of its general principles amounts to taking its heart. An EEA legal system that would not encompass such general principles would therefore be a legal system that is not at all homogeneous with Community law.

---

[1] See also Chapter 7.

2 Effect: Deference to State Sovereignty

As I have said before, in *Restamark*, the five-member Court avoided the question of whether Article 16, the monopoly provision of the EEA Agreement, has direct effect.[2] Nonetheless, the judgment was described as being courageous in academic literature. There was a feeling that it would have been politically impossible for the five-member Court to acknowledge the direct effect of EEA primary law in its very first case, but that at least the door was now ajar. In the years that followed, former judges Sven Norberg and Leif Sevón, who sat in *Restamark*, wrote publications urging the EFTA Court to recognise direct effect. However, in *Karlsson* and in *Criminal proceedings against A*, the Court decided not to do this. Only EEA rules that have been implemented in the national legal orders of the EEA/EFTA States can directly be invoked in the courts. University of Oslo Professor Hans Petter Graver called this "quasi direct effect." For the Governments of Iceland and of Norway, this was an important decision. It is doubtful whether the development would have been the same had the EEA Agreement been based on a one pillar approach with the ECJ's jurisdiction also extending to the EFTA States.

3 State Liability: Making or Breaking the EEA Agreement

3.1 Reference of the Sveinbjörnsdóttir *Case*

In November 1997, the Reykjavík District Court referred, *inter alia*, the question to us of whether the EEA Agreement entailed State liability. Erla María Sveinbjörnsdóttir had been employed for a number of years at a machine workshop when she was dismissed from her position by a letter of 29 December 1994 with effect from 1 January 1995. Dismissal was with six months' notice and Erla María was not required to work during this period. She received her wages until 12 March 1995. On 22 March 1995, the machine workshop was declared insolvent. Ms. Sveinbjörnsdóttir filed claims against both the insolvency estate of the machine workshop and the Icelandic Wage Guarantee Fund. The claim against the insolvency estate was rejected on the grounds that it could not be given privileged status because the plaintiff was the sister of the holder of 40% of the shares in the machine workshop. Icelandic law provided that claims for unpaid wages, etc. were, as a general rule, privileged but made an exception for claims by persons "close" to the insolvent entity. Under the Insolvency Act, the expression "close" comprised, *inter alia*, the relationship between a person and a company owned to a considerable extent by another person to whom the first person was "related through direct

[2] See for details Chapter 4.

descent or collateral relation". The claim against the Wage Guarantee Fund was rejected on the grounds that it had not been recognised as a privileged claim in the insolvency estate.

The plaintiff then brought an action for compensation against the Government of Iceland. She submitted that the Government was liable for damages for not having adjusted its national legislation correctly to the EEA Agreement, i.e. for not having adapted the relevant provisions of the Wage Guarantee Fund Act and of the Insolvency Act correctly to the 1980 Insolvency Directive.[3] It was the same directive which had given rise to the ECJ's landmark State liability judgment in *Francovich.*

As I have already explained, the Icelandic Attorney General at the time routinely challenged reference decisions from first instance judges.[4] However, no appeal was lodged in this case, which was apparently an oversight. Erla María's lawyer was Stefán Geir Þórisson, a former ESA collaborator who over the years repeatedly appeared before the EFTA Court. President Bjørn Haug who, as a matter of principle, did not act as a Judge Rapporteur, assigned the case to himself.

3.2 Proceedings and Judgment

A large group of Norwegian judges attended the hearing on 17 September 1998. The Governments of Iceland, Norway and Sweden pleaded that to recognise EEA State liability was out of the question. State liability was said to be part of EU law, it could only be contemplated alongside EU-style direct effect and primacy. Sweden had left the EFTA pillar at the end of 1994, but apparently feared that, due to its protectionist attitude in the field of import of motor vehicles, it had some skeletons in the cupboard. Surprisingly, the European Commission also argued against EEA State liability. The Commission's agent, Pieter-Jan Kuijper, apparently thought that direct effect, primacy and State liability were an EU invention, only available to EU operators. Others were not allowed to play with these sacred toys. One could call this a "Toys R Us" approach. In the hearing, I asked Mr. Kuijper how his pleading related to the argument of his colleague Richard Wainright in *Restamark*, who had proposed that the Court should acknowledge the direct effect of the monopoly provision of Article 16 EEA. Mr. Kuijper, a well-known member of the Commission's Legal Service who later became the Director of the Legal Affairs Division of the Secretariat of the WTO and then a professor at the University of Amsterdam, was unaware of his colleague's previous position. Given his standing in the Commission's Legal Service at the time, I initially thought that he acted on his own initiative. However, on reflection, I now think that the Head of the Commission's Legal Service at the time, Director General Jean-Louis Dewost, who

[3]80/897/EEC.

[4]See for details Chapter 8.

had suffered a crushing defeat when the ECJ handed down its Opinion 1/91, wanted to keep the EEA at distance from the EC and instructed Mr. Kuijper to plead accordingly.[5]

ESA, which was at that time presided over by Knut Almestad, was the only participant in the case pleading in favour of State liability. It argued that State liability was part of EEA law due to the similarities between the EEA Agreement and the EC Treaty, the homogeneity objective of the EEA Agreement, the recognition of the important role that individuals play through the exercise of their rights in judicial proceedings and the intention of ensuring equal treatment of individuals and economic operators.[6]

The EFTA Court found State liability to be part of EEA law, mainly for three reasons. First: homogeneity; second: protection of individuals and economic operators; and third: the duty of loyalty laid down in Article 3 EEA. We concluded from this in paragraph 59

> that the EEA Agreement is an international treaty *sui generis* which contains a distinct legal order of its own. [....] The depth of integration of the EEA Agreement is less far-reaching than under the EC Treaty, but the scope and the objective of the EEA Agreement goes beyond what is usual for an agreement under public international law.

The positivists who believed that a European treaty could only be either supranational or international in nature had lost. Then came the second round, just like in every State liability case: the application of the three conditions established by the ECJ on the question of whether the State in fact has to pay. First condition: does the breached provision confer rights upon individuals? Second condition: is the breach sufficiently serious? Third condition: is there a causal link between the breach and the damage sustained? We dealt with the first question ourselves and answered it in the affirmative, while leaving the answers to the second and third conditions to the national court.

As far as substance is concerned, the issue was who could be excluded from the wage guarantee. Ms. Sveinbjörnsdóttir was the sister of the main shareholder in the bankrupt company. The Court had to answer the question of whether the expression "direct relative" was to be interpreted so as to include the sister of the main shareholder. If that question was answered in the affirmative, Ms. Sveinbjörnsdóttir was excluded from the wage guarantee. In other words, the Court had to decide whether direct relatives were only father and mother and daughter and son *or* also siblings. We started with the text, looked into a number of language versions. The English wording "direct relative" was not clear. The Icelandic version ('*ættingi í beinan legg*') had the clear and limited scope of ascendants and descendants, excluding siblings. But from a teleological perspective we came to the conclusion that the Insolvency Directive aims to protect workers. It was therefore correct to interpret that exclusion as narrowly as possible and to allow siblings to be covered by the wage guarantee.

[5]See regarding Opinion 1/91 Chapter 3.

[6]See for details Chapter 7.

3.3 A Salute from the ECJ

Half a year after *Sveinbjörnsdóttir*, the ECJ was faced with EEA State liability in both the *Rechberger* and *Andersson* cases. The facts had occurred in 1994 in Austria and in Sweden when these two countries were EEA States in the EFTA pillar. The ECJ was asked, in references from an Austrian and a Swedish first instance court, whether State liability was part of EEA law. Austria had not implemented the 1990 Package Tour Directive[7] in good time and travellers had suffered damage as a consequence. Sweden had incorrectly implemented the Insolvency Directive (80/897/EEC), the same directive that had been at stake in *Francovich* and in *Sveinbjörnsdóttir*. Two workers had suffered damages and sued the Swedisch State.

In view of the planned accession of four of them to the EU on 1 January 1995, the five EFTA/EEA States had entered into an Agreement on transitional arrangements for a period afterwards. According to this Agreement, after accession, new preliminary reference proceedings could only be brought before the Court for cases in which the facts occurred before accession and the application was lodged with the Court within three months of accession. The five-member Court was to conclude all pending cases within six months of accession. From the perspective of the protection of citizens and economic operators, the transitional Agreement was actually a scandal. On 1 January 1995, Austria, Finland, and Sweden, but not Norway, joined the EU.

The ECJ held that it had no jurisdiction to answer the questions referred because the facts occurred before Austria and Sweden became Member States of the European Community. But the ECJ added in *Rechberger*, *in dicta*, that the EFTA Court found State liability to be part of EEA law in its *Sveinbjörnsdóttir* judgment. However, in *Andersson*, this statement was not made. Both judgments were rendered on the same day, 15 June 1999. External observers don't know the reason for this difference. If you believe in the teachings of legal realism and of legal hermeneutics, the first thing to do when confronted with such a phenomenon is to look at the names of the judges who were sitting on the bench. In fact, the ECJ sat in slightly different compositions in the two cases. In *Rechberger*, 9 judges participated including the Italian judge, the late Giuseppe Federico Mancini. Mancini was, however, not sitting in *Andersson*. On the other hand, the Swedish judge, the late Hans Ragnemalm participated in *Andersson*, but not in *Rechberger*. The *Andersson* chamber consisted of 11 judges. On 21 June 1999, the renowned Swedish newspaper *Svenska Dagbladet* hazarded a guess that the Swedish judge had seen to it that his government did not have to pay up.

The Common Market Law Review immediately realised what the ECJ's reference to *Sveinbjörnsdóttir* in *Rechberger* meant. In editorial comments, the reputed European journal jointly published by the Europa Institute in Leiden and the British Institute of International and Comparative Law stated that with this, the EC Court

[7] 90/314/EEC.

admitted that the thesis that underpinned Opinion 1/91 according to which the EEA Agreement only creates rights and obligations between governments

> has been too one-sided [....]. This is more than a 'coup de chapeau', a salute to the EFTA Court. With this statement, it is important to note, the EC Court appears to endorse the EFTA Court's judgment.

I have good reason to believe that the author of the editorial was a well-known colleague from the ECJ. In the years that followed, *Sveinbjörnsdóttir* was favourably mentioned by important EU protagonists including judges and AG's in speeches and publications. They understood that while the EFTA Court was not prepared to excessively curtail the sovereignty of its Member States, it was serious about creating a level playing field for operators from the EU. I should add that the GC in substance already distanced itself from the ECJ's Opinion 1/91 in its judgment of 22 January 1997 in *Opel Austria*.[8]

3.4 An Extrajudicial Dissent

President Bjørn Haug made public remarks about the way in which the *Sveinbjörnsdóttir* judgment was reached. At the 1999 Nordic Law Conference in Oslo he indirectly, but clearly distanced himself from *Sveinbjörnsdóttir*. He referred to the case and in this context, he criticised the lack of a dissenting opinion system by saying that he found

> it very difficult to function if we [i.e. the judges], if the occasion arises, are not given the opportunity to give 'a dissenting, or even concurring opinion.' One is bound by the majority, not only with regard to the conclusion, but also with regard to the reasoning leading to the conclusion.[9]

Bjørn added that he did

> not intend to break this rule by saying something which could be interpreted as a further reasoning.[10]

People who were present told me that everyone in the room understood what Bjørn meant and indeed it is clear to every reader of the book. His motive for disregarding his oath to keep the secrecy of the deliberations and of the vote was obvious: he was seeking a second term on the Court and wanted to let his Government know that he was innocent. At the same time, he weakened the judgment because, as one commentator put it, he made it public that the Norwegian judge had been outvoted in this landmark case by his colleagues from the tiny States of Iceland and Liechtenstein. During the 1999 EFTA Ministerial meeting in Lillehammer, on 1

---

[8]See also Chapter 21.

[9]Unofficial translation.

[10]Unofficial translation.

June of that year, Bjørn asked to see the Norwegian Minister for Foreign Affairs, Knut Vollebæk, in order to express his wish to be renominated. He received no answer. He then gave an interview in one of his country's largest newspapers in which he declared that he was ready for a second term. It didn't help. At the end of 1999, Bjørn Haug's time on the EFTA Court bench came to an end.

Thór Vilhjálmsson died on 20 October of 2015. In my obituary in *Morgunblaðið* I wrote regarding his role in *Sveinbjörnsdóttir*:

> The EEA law community held its breath when the Reykjavík District Court submitted the question to us whether the EEA Agreement entailed State liability in the Erla María Sveinbjörnsdóttir case. We answered yes, and Thór Vilhjálmsson later said to me that this was the only way forward; had we said no, the EEA Agreement would never have taken off. He realised that the Court found itself in a make-or-break situation. Obviously his human rights background and his humanity, but also his political instincts had helped him reaching the right decision.

In view of what happened at the 1999 Nordic Law Conference and what was documented in the conference book, I no longer felt bound by my own oath in this case.

3.5 A Failed Attempt to Turn the Clock Back

In *Karlsson*, another reference from the Reykjavík District Court that was not challenged by the Attorney General, the Norwegian Government urged the EFTA Court to overrule its State liability finding in *Sveinbjörnsdóttir*. It was a rather unusual attempt to bring the Court to its knees. Whereas the second Norwegian agent, a former collaborator of the Court, acted politely, the first agent felt that it was appropriate to threaten us by saying that we should not underestimate the importance of the call for a reassessment of *Sveinbjörnsdóttir*. That judgment, he said, exceeded the proper limits of interpretation and presupposed an amendment of the EEA Agreement which, of course, was not within the competence of the Court. He went on to claim that, in fact, the EFTA Court had set aside the clear intention of the Parties to the EEA Agreement. The ECJ's reference to *Sveinbjörnsdóttir* in *Rechberger* was downplayed as being an inconclusive *obiter dictum*, in particular in the light of the *Andersson* judgment. It was even contended that the ECJ's ineffable Opinion 1/91 as well as the good faith principle laid down in Article 31(1) of the Vienna Convention on the Law of Treaties precluded EEA State liability.

As any reasonable observer might have predicted, the Norwegian attempt to have *Sveinbjörnsdóttir* overturned in the *Karlsson* case failed. Had we decided otherwise, we might just as well have shut up shop and gone home. The Icelanders at the Court were perturbed by what they called a Norwegian attempt to highjack "their" case. We held on 30 May 2002 that an EEA State may be liable to a prospective importer of alcoholic beverages for loss or damage incurred as a result of maintaining a State monopoly on the import and wholesale distribution of alcoholic beverages. As far as the conditions of liability are concerned, the Court found that the monopoly provision laid down in Article 16 EEA did confer rights upon individuals and that Iceland's breach of that provision was sufficiently serious to trigger liability. It was clear long before the entry into force of the EEA Agreement that an import monopoly could not be maintained. In other words, the Court answered the first two questions itself. All that was left for the national court to decide was whether there was a causal link between the infringement and the damage sustained.

3.6 Acceptance by National Courts and Governments

Step by step, the Supreme Courts of our Member States courts fell into line with our *Sveinbjörnsdóttir* judgment. The Supreme Court of Iceland did so when the case itself ended up before it in its judgment of 16 December 1999. At least this holds true with regard to the outcome. The Supreme Court of Norway followed suit five years later in the second *Finanger* case—despite opposition from the Norwegian Government.[11]

Somewhat sadly, the Supreme Court of Liechtenstein, the sole monist country in the EFTA pillar, only caved in after a rather inglorious interlude, which lasted several years. In a case involving the Austrian physician Dr. Jürgen Tschannett who had been denied a licence to practice in Liechtenstein,[12] it found twice against the plaintiff. The EFTA Court had held on 14 June 2001 that the so-called single practice rule of Liechtenstein law was incompatible with the right of establishment. Under this rule, a licenced physician could not operate more than one practice, regardless of location.[13] In a judgment of 7 December 2006, the Supreme Court held that the government was not at fault because it had not known in advance that the single practice rule was incompatible with EEA law. Strictly speaking, the Supreme Court did not base its ruling on EEA law, but rather on domestic State liability law where there was a fault requirement. The ruling was severely criticised in academic literature. The State Court quashed it on 3 July 2007 and sent it back to the Supreme Court. This time, Dr. Tschannett asked the Supreme Court to make a reference to the EFTA Court. However, the Supreme Court refused to do that on the basis of the astonishing argument that the State Court had mandated the Supreme Court to reassess the case and not the EFTA Court. The Supreme Court on 5 June 2008 once again found against the doctor, this time on the grounds that the breach was not sufficiently serious. I can't help thinking that the Swiss Supreme Court Judge Reinhold Hotz, who was in charge of the case and had been denied a full professorship at St. Gallen, wanted to show me that he wouldn't take any advice from my Court. There are several references to Swiss materials in the reasoning

---

[11]See for details Chapter 11.

[12]See for details Chapter 15.

[13]See Chapter 15.

which are completely out of context. On 24 June 2009, the State Court also overruled the Supreme Court's second judgment. On 7 May 2010, on its third attempt, the Supreme Court acknowledged that the State was liable.[14] On 1 January 2010, Dr. Gert Delle Karth had succeeded Hansjörg Rück as President of the Supreme Court. The concrete amount of money to be paid to Dr. Tschannett remained to be determined by the parties.

In the end, Dr. Tschannett, who had become seriously ill, was forced to agree to a rather modest sum. Government officials had spread the word that he was greedy whereas, in fact, he had simply been defending his rights under the EEA Agreement. I should add that in the Dr. Tschannett matter ESA has not covered itself with glory either. A complaint by Dr. Tschnnett remained unsuccessful. ESA asserted that it could not be ruled out that the ECJ or the EFTA Court would have considered the single practice rule to be justified before the EFTA Court's judgment of 14 June 2001 clarified the situation.

The Swedish Supreme Court opted for EEA State liability in the *Andersson* case by three against two votes. In doing so, it based itself on the EFTA Court's and the Icelandic Supreme Court's judgments in the *Sveinbjörnsdóttir* case. Professor Ulf Bernitz has argued that the *Andersson* ruling of the Supreme Court had important legal consequences in Sweden. First, the judgment made it clear that

> a monistic view in line with what is Community law has been adopted in Sweden also in relation to the application of EEA law,

and second,

> the Swedish Supreme Court's stance in the *Andersson* case concerning liability for damages according to the EEA Agreement has become an important precedent also in relation to the long disputed issue of the Swedish courts' possibilities to award damages to be paid by the Swedish State for violations of the European Convention connected to flaws in Swedish legislation or practices by Swedish courts or other authorities.

4 Primacy: Deference to State Sovereignty

The same issue as in *Restamark* with respect to direct effect arose some years later with regard to primacy in the *Einarsson* case on the compatibility of the Icelandic VAT rate regime for books with EEA law.[15] The EFTA Court decided the question along the same lines and held that an implemented EEA law rule prevails over a conflicting rule of domestic law.

---

[14]See also Chapter 8.

[15]See for details Chapter 9.

5 Conform Interpretation

The EFTA Court also accepted the principle of an EEA law friendly interpretation of domestic law. This is the same maxim as has been recognised by the ECJ in cases such as, for example, *Marleasing*. ESA President Knut Almestad had, at the 2000 Congress of the International Federation for European Law (Fédération International Pour Le Droit Européen—FIDE) in Helsinki, convincingly taken the view that *Marleasing* was of EEA relevance. In *Karlsson*, the Court stated that national courts will consider EEA law, irrespective of whether the respective provisions have been implemented into the national legal system or not, when EEA law has a bearing on the case. This *dictum* was further developed in *Criminal Proceedings against A* and *Liechtensteinische Gesellschaft für Umweltschutz*. In all of these cases, the EFTA Court linked the recognition of the principles of conform interpretation and State liability to the absence of direct and effect and primacy. Nevertheless, the EFTA Court has not completely shied away from preferring EEA law over other possibly conflicting instruments. For example, in the *Fokus Bank* and *Holship* cases it clearly rejected the assertion that international agreements could be preferred over the EEA Agreement. Furthermore, in *Holship* the Court held that the EEA law applicable in this case must in any event prevail over a potentially conflicting domestic collective agreement.

Chapter 11
Two Early Landmark Cases: Veronika's Struggle and Enriched Cereals

Contents

1 Moonshine and the Consequences

On 11 November 1995 in Nord-Trøndelag, Norway, 17-year-old Veronika Finanger attended a party where moonshine was served. The expression "moonshine" describes a drink with a high-percentage of alcohol that is produced illegally. The term became popular during prohibition in America when distillation was done at night while the moon was shining to avoid discovery. However, its origins are much older. The production of illegal moonshine is typical in countries with any kind of alcohol prohibition. After the party, Veronika got into a car driven by her boyfriend who was drunk. He drove the car off the road, severely injuring Veronika and killing another passenger. As a result of the accident, Veronika was left with a 60% medical disability and a 100% occupational disability. She brought an action against the driver's insurance company, Storebrand. Storebrand was, *inter alia*, advised by University of Oslo Professor Finn Arnesen. Years later, Finn explained to me that it was he who drew Storebrand's attention to a provision in Norwegian

C. Baudenbacher, *Judicial Independence*, Springer Biographies,
https://doi.org/10.1007/978-3-030-02308-9_11

law that traditionally was also echoed in the laws of other Nordic countries.[1] According to that rule,[2] passengers of intoxicated motor vehicle drivers were basically excluded from insurance coverage if they knew, or must have known, that the driver was under the influence of alcohol, unless there were special grounds. On the basis of this provision, many victims had been denied compensation. Certainly, the idea that anyone who willingly takes a risk should lose insurance coverage is not a Nordic invention; it has its foundations in German law. Storebrand invoked this rule.

2 Veronika's First Arrow

2.1 EFTA Court: Norway Is in Breach

When the legendary Swiss national hero William Tell was urged to shoot an apple from his son's head, he hit the target first time. Veronika Finanger missed her first shot. She did score a partial hit, but that didn't help her. On 28 August 1997, a single judge of the Inderøy District Court sentenced Storebrand to indemnify Veronika, but reduced the compensation by 50%. On 1 October 1998, the Frostating Court of Appeal confirmed that judgment and only reduced the compensation by 30%. Storebrand brought the case before the Supreme Court and on 23 June 1999, the latter referred the question to the EFTA Court of whether the provision in question was compatible with EEA law, namely with the so-called "Motor Vehicle Insurance Directives".[3]

Finanger was the first case referred to the EFTA Court by the Norwegian Supreme Court that went to trial. This in itself made it a noteworthy matter. The oral hearing was held on 30 September 1999. A group of Norwegian judges led by Agnes Nygaard Haug, the former President of the Borgarting Court of Appeal, decided to make their trip annual to Luxembourg and Strasbourg in late September so that they could attend the hearing. Agnes is the wife of Bjørn Haug, who was at that time President of the EFTA Court. Supreme Court judges from Iceland and from Liechtenstein joined the group. Björn was understandably proud that he could preside over a case which touched upon the Norwegian social model in the presence of so many judges from his home country, but also from Iceland and from Liechtenstein. It was his last case before he retired. One of the Norwegian judges said to me afterwards that if she had had to decide the case that was pending before the Supreme Court, she would have given § 7 paragraph 3 letter b of the Motor

[1]See regarding Professor Arnesen, Chapters 6, 11, 19, and 28.

[2]§ 7 paragraph 3 letter b of the Motor Vehicle Act.

[3]72/166/EEC, 84/5/EEC and 90/232/EEC.

Vehicle Act an EEA-friendly interpretation by relying on the "special grounds" exception.

Storebrand, the Government of Iceland and the Government of Norway proposed to answer the *Høyesterett's* question in the negative. However, the Government of Liechtenstein argued that the rule at issue was incompatible with EEA law. This was one of the few cases in which the Liechtenstein Government participated without being either a party or the government concerned. It is a pity that the Liechtensteiners do not show up more frequently in Court proceedings. The official reason for this is the lack of resources, but apparently they also don't want to step on other governments' toes. This lack of self-confidence is a loss for the Court.[4]

In our judgment in *Finanger* of 17 November 1999, we found that the provision in question violated both the free movement of goods and of persons and was incompatible with the goal of the Motor Vehicle Insurance Directives to protect consumers. The argument put forward by Storebrand and the Governments of Iceland and Norway that the directives did not deal with rules relating to personal liability but only with insurance law, was rebuffed. The EFTA Court held in paragraph 29 of the judgment:

> Even if the main text of the First Motor Vehicle Insurance Directive focuses on insurance coverage, that Motor Vehicle Insurance Directive has been supplemented by the Second and Third Motor Vehicle Insurance Directives in such a way that the three Motor Vehicle Insurance Directives, taken as a whole, provide for limits on the extent to which insurers may rely on contractual clauses or national statutory provisions on liability for compensation to exclude certain situations from insurance coverage altogether. Consequently, the distinction between provisions on personal liability and insurance cover is not decisive in the case at hand. The arguments submitted by the appellant, the Government of Norway and the Government of Iceland on this point must, therefore, be rejected.

We added that reducing compensation due to contributory negligence must be possible in exceptional circumstances. However, a finding that a passenger who passively rode in a car driven by an intoxicated driver should be denied compensation, or that compensation should be reduced disproportionately to the injured party's contribution to the injury, would be incompatible with the directives.

2.2 Supreme Court: Norway Is in Breach, but Veronika Is Left Out in the Rain

On 21 February 2000, the Supreme Court decided that the matter should be dealt with in plenary. In its judgment of 16 November 2000, the Supreme Court followed our ruling in substance by holding that in fact the State had breached its obligations under the EEA Agreement. However, with regard to the effect of our judgment, the

[4]See for details Chapter 6.

Supreme Court chose a rather narrow approach. By a majority of 10:5, Chief Justice Carsten Smith being in the minority, the Supreme Court found that it could not set aside a clear provision of Norwegian law, notably because of the importance of predictability for private parties, in this instance the insurer Storebrand. This meant that the court denied direct effect of the provision in question. The minority was of the view that Norwegian law could be interpreted in a way which would grant Veronika Finanger compensation. The case was about the application of the provisions of a directive and it concerned the horizontal relationship between the insurer and the victim. University of Oslo professor Hans Petter Graver commented that had the case been about a vertical relationship between a private operator and the State, the Supreme Court would almost certainly have found a way of reaching a different conclusion. In the light of later developments, in particular the *STX* case, I am not sure that he was right on that point.[5] Norwegian law was subsequently amended in conformity with the Court's and the Supreme Court's judgments. But that must have been of little consolation to Veronika Finanger.

2.3 Political Implications

In the *Finanger* case, a pattern surfaced, which was greeted enthusiastically by certain Norwegian professors, a pattern that became a standard argument in the hands of the Attorney General in the years to come. On 14 September 2000, before the hearing took place in the Supreme Court, the Fifth Chamber of the ECJ rendered judgment in *Vitor Ferreira*. It held, without mentioning our *Finanger* judgment, that the Motor Vehicle Insurance Directives did not seek to harmonise the rules of the Member States governing civil liability. Based on this, the ECJ found that a provision of the Portuguese Civil Code, which stated that for transport provided free of charge liability could only be incurred if the passenger proved fault on the part of the driver and that this fault was the cause of the accident, was in line with the directives. *Vitor Ferreira* was not a particularly convincing judgment. However, when the Norwegian Supreme Court heard the *Finanger* case, Storebrand and the Norwegian Government argued that in *Vitor Ferreira* the ECJ had distanced itself from the approach taken by the EFTA Court in *Finanger*. In such a case of judicial conflict, the Norwegian Supreme Court ought to follow the ECJ's judgment. However, the Supreme Court distinguished the two cases and followed our *Finanger* ruling. Scholars were nevertheless quick to point out that the Supreme Court had intimated that if it had not been possible to distinguish the two cases, it would have been inclined to follow the ECJ. As I will explain, this attitude gives Norwegian courts the option of cherry-picking their preferred result. If the Court's solution pleases them, they may adopt it, if not they may opt for the ECJ's solution.

---

[5]See for details Chapter 26.

This is not compatible with the tasks of a court of law. Furthermore, it is based on a mechanical and untenable understanding of the homogeneity principle.[6]

3 Veronika's Second Arrow

Since he hit the apple with his first shot, William Tell didn't need to use the second arrow he had put in his crossbow. Veronika Finanger was handed a second bolt by the EFTA Court when the latter in December 1998 acknowledged the principle of EEA State liability in the Icelandic case *Sveinbjönsdóttir*.[7] And Veronika's second arrow scored a bullseye. But again, she had to fight her way through all the instances.

Veronika Finanger brought an action against the Norwegian State, claiming the same amount of money from the State that she had been unable to obtain from the insurance company Storebrand. On 13 March 2003, the Oslo District Court ruled that the State was liable under EEA rules. Referencing the ECJ judgments in *Francovich* and *Brasserie du Pêcheur* and the EFTA Court's rulings in *Sveinbjörnsdóttir* and *Karlsson*,[8] the single judge found that the relevant directives were clear and precise. They stated that gaps in the protection of potential victims of car accidents, with the exception of the driver, had to be closed and thus there was no room left for discretion of the legislature. Historically, the incompatibility of the controversial paragraph with the directives had been taken up by the Norwegian Ministry of Justice, but then the issue had been dropped due to political pressure from the Ministry of Transport and after talks with the Danish Government. The judge concluded that the breach was sufficiently serious and that the other conditions for the liability of the State were also fulfilled.

On 14 January 2005, the Borgarting Court of Appeal acquitted the Norwegian State by 2 votes to 1. There was agreement that the provision in question gives rights to an individual and that there was a causal link between the violation by the State and the damage. However, the majority was of the view that the breach was not sufficiently serious. Invoking the Court's considerations in *Karlsson*, the two majority judges found that an overall assessment of all the circumstances had to be carried out. The years 1992 and 1993 were regarded as being an extraordinary period for the legislature which had to adapt Norwegian law to make it EEA conform. From the perspective at that time, the Motor Vehicle Insurance Directives were generally considered to be cumbersome and complex, even if individual provisions were clear and precise. In 2002, a new directive on excluding individuals from insurance coverage in the event of knowledge of the driver's intoxication was adopted, which was said to vindicate the majority view that the old rules had not

[6]See for details Chapter 21.

[7]See for details Chapter 10.

[8]See for details Chapter 10.

been clear. Seen as a whole, the Norwegian legislature in many areas went way beyond what the directives prescribe with regard to insurance coverage of injured passengers. From this, it could only be concluded that the legislature loyally tried to implement the directives so that it could not be blamed for committing a sufficiently serious breach of EEA law. The dissenting judge took the view that the breach was indeed sufficiently serious. The rules were clear, the legislature had no discretion, and there was no justification for the State's behaviour. By ruling as I have just described, the Borgarting Court of Appeal bought into the arguments put forward by the Attorney General. It was not the only time that this important court acted in this manner.

The hearing before the Supreme Court took place on 13 September 2005. On 28 October 2005, Veronika Finanger's suffering came to an end; by 9 votes to 4 the Supreme Court ruled in her favour. Following our *Sveinbjörnsdóttir* ruling, it acknowledged State liability as being part of EEA law. Reference was also made to the *Sveinbjörnsdóttir* judgment of the Icelandic Supreme Court. The *Høyesterett* found that the conditions for liability were fulfilled and, most importantly, it rejected the argument of the Norwegian Government that the second condition, according to which the breach must be sufficiently serious, was to be interpreted in a more government-friendly way in EEA law than in EU law. Ten years after the accident that changed her life so tragically, Veronika finally obtained compensation, and the money came from the right pocket, namely the purse of the State that had incorrectly implemented the relevant EEA law. I should add that the compensation was reduced by 30% due to contributory negligence. The parties agreed that this reduction should apply if the State was held liable to pay compensation. A reduction of 30% was also what had been suggested by the Supreme Court's minority in the first *Finanger* case.

Lawyers close to the Norwegian Government have often told me that the EEA Agreement was meant to provide the country's operators access to the EU Single Market "without pain". By "pain" they meant that Norway's sovereignty should not be excessively curtailed. This is a myth that mainly exists in the heads of senior bureaucrats and certain professors. What these people do not realise is that without the EEA Agreement, individuals and economic operators would really suffer. The EFTA Court and the Norwegian Supreme Court have ensured that the victims of patently absurd provisions, such as § 7 paragraph 3 letter b of the Motor Vehicle Act, no longer feel the pain.

4 Cornflakes Fortified with Vitamins and Iron

4.1 A New President

In January 2000, Ambassador Per Tresselt replaced Bjørn Haug on the EFTA Court bench. He was a successful bureaucrat and career diplomat. Per had been Deputy

Under-Secretary of State in the Ministry of Foreign Affairs. From 1898 to 1990, he had served as the Norwegian envoy to East Germany, from 1990 to 1994 as Consul-General in the united Berlin and from 1994 to 1999 as Ambassador to Russia. Per Tresselt had hoped to end his diplomatic career with a post in an important European capital. But things didn't work out quite as he had expected. His friends in the Oslo administration then did a deal so that he got the judgeship in Luxembourg, as a consolation prize, so to speak. I don't think that he was very happy about this state of affairs. I met Per and his wife Marit for the first time in September 1999 when they came to Luxembourg in order to look for a flat. The first thing he told me was that he had carefully read the ECJ's Opinion 1/91 and that with regard to the legal nature of the EEA Agreement and the issues of direct effect and primacy, everything that needed to be said could be found there. During his six years in office he faithfully stuck to this belief. His idea of how a European court of law functions had not least been shaped by his experience as a co-counsel to Bjørn Haug in the *Jan Mayen* case before the ICJ.[9] This was, however, a classical public international law case with governments as the only actors. Citizens and economic operators played no role at all.

In the same month, the Icelander Thór Vilhjálmsson was elected President. His term as a judge of the ECtHR had ended one year before when that court became a full time institution. Thór was an experienced lawyer and judge and an independent mind. He was also a friendly, warm-hearted man, but he was somewhat tired. Doris and I always had an excellent personal relationship with him and his wife Ragnhildur Helgadóttir, a former politician and Icelandic cabinet minister.

The case law remained low during Thór's presidency. However, the atmosphere improved dramatically. As I said, policy-wise, a crucial step was that the Court returned to its old practice of referring to its preliminary rulings as "judgments" in the *rubrum* and "advisory opinions" in the operative part. Important cases were *LO* on collective bargaining and EEA competition law, *Einarsson* on VAT and primacy, and *Karlsson* on State liability. However, the most significant litigation by far was *Kellogg's*, a food law case with a global dimension.

4.2 De gustibus non est disputandum—*There's no Accounting for Taste*

A Norwegian delicacy I had never heard of before April 2000 was at the heart of said landmark EFTA Court case, brown cheese or, as it is known in Norway, *brunost*. On 24 January 2013, Norwegian chef *Signe Johansen* wrote in the British newspaper "The Guardian":

> Brown cheese is quintessentially Norwegian, and imbued with all the romantic notions of national identity in this oil-rich country (think Grieg's Peer Gynt, Ibsen's plays, Amundsen

[9]See Chapter 4.

> beating Scott, traditional Marius jumpers, stunning natural landscapes, trolls). It is really only eaten in Norway [….] and we love it.

What Mr. Johansen did not say was that brown cheese is fortified with iron and vitamins. When visiting Norway, I regularly saw *brunost* on the breakfast buffet in the hotel. I have to admit that I was never brave enough to try it.

4.3 The Kellogg's *Ruling*

Kellogg's concerned the following factual situation: All over Europe Kellogg's cornflakes, fortified with several vitamins and some iron, were freely marketed and sold. However, the Norwegian health authorities banned the sale of such cornflakes produced in Denmark. ESA brought an infringement action claiming that this was an unlawful restriction on the free movement of goods. Norway, supported by the Governments of Denmark (as an intervener), France and the Netherlands, unsuccessfully argued that according to an ECJ precedent from 1984 (*Sandoz BV*), the marketing of fortified goods could be banned if there was no nutritional need for the fortification. In detail, the Norwegian Government claimed first, that there was no nutritional need in the country, because the population's diet contained enough iron. We, the State, the government agents said, ensure that they get the iron they need by giving them a piece of goat's cheese fortified with iron—*brunost*—in school every morning until they are fifteen years old; thereafter they have enough iron in their bodies to last the rest of their lives. We rejected the nutritional need argument. Second, the Norwegian Government invoked the precautionary principle, and the EFTA Court accepted this in essence. According to this maxim, a national government is entitled to take action, even if there is no final proof that a product is dangerous, as long as qualified scientists in the field are of the same view. However, this approach means that the government must have carried out a comprehensive risk assessment. It cannot base itself on purely hypothetical considerations and it may only seek to achieve zero risk in the most exceptional circumstances. Furthermore, the government's measures must be transparent, proportionate, non-discriminatory, and the fortification policy as a whole must be consistent. The Norwegian policy was obviously inconsistent. If you promote fortifying products with iron by giving away cheese fortified with iron to all school children, then you are not acting consistently when you ban a product fortified with iron. It should also be noted that Norway allowed or imposed the fortification of other products with vitamins. Thus, Norway lost the case, however, in a future case it could successfully invoke the precautionary principle.

5 Other Prior Authorisation Cases

Prior authorisation requirements have also been an issue in a number of other cases. An example is *the Norwegian Life Assurance case*. Norwegian law provided that costs which accrue when life assurance contracts are entered into have to be charged and paid no later than the date when the first premium payment is due. The Court was called upon to assess whether such a requirement was in conformity with Article 33 of the 2002 Life Assurance Directive.[10] Under Article 33 the Member State of the commitment must not prevent a policy holder from concluding a contract with an authorised assurance undertaking, as long as that does not conflict with legal provisions protecting the general good in the Member State of the commitment. ESA claimed that this provision prevented consumers in Norway from concluding assurance contracts with providers from other Contracting Parties who did not charge contract completion costs in the contested manner.

The EFTA Court held that the directive aims to complete the internal market in direct life assurance; it is built on the principles of mutual recognition and home State supervision. It is for the Contracting Party of commitment to ensure that there is nothing to prevent the marketing within its territory of all the assurance products offered for sale in the EEA by insurance undertakings authorised in other Contracting Parties, as long as they do not conflict with the legal provisions protecting the general good in force in the State of commitment.

The contested requirement was introduced in order to further consumer protection through increased consumer awareness, in order to lower the price of concluding life assurance contracts and thereby eliminate the so called "tie-in effect" caused by contract completion cost debt. This was regarded as a legitimate aim falling under the concept of general good. The Court noted that, in this regard, it is the average consumer, i.e. a consumer who is reasonably well informed and reasonably observant and circumspect, who should be taken into consideration. It added that the directive aims to protect consumers through choice based on information.

In assessing whether less restrictive means existed, the EFTA Court found that in view of the complexity and value of life assurance contracts in general, clauses whereby the completion costs were distributed over a longer period, did not necessarily have to be particularly complicated and, in general, only entailed a minor part of the financial obligations involved. Consumers could be provided with the necessary information by less restrictive means, i.e. by requesting life assurance providers to supply more specific information. The contested requirement was thus found to be disproportionate to the objective pursued.

University of Bergen Professor Berte-Elen Konow stated that to Norwegian lawyers, "accustomed to a protective and regulative State", the rule in question "appeared as a proportionate interference in the market". The EFTA Court's decision, she wrote, appears

[10] 2002/83/EC.

to be grounded in higher expectations to the average consumer and, implicitly, higher appreciation of the freedom of contract than the one underlying the Nordic partiality (sic!) to consumer protection through prescriptive contract law.

In the *Liechtenstein Prior Authorisation Schemes for Establishment and Cross-border Services* case, the EFTA Court held that Liechtenstein had breached its obligations under the Services Directive[11] and violated the freedom to provide services by maintaining provisions setting up a prior authorisation scheme for undertakings intending to establish themselves in Liechtenstein as well as certain additional requirements.

[11]2006/123/EC.

Chapter 12
Fundamental Rights—The EFTA Court Amends the Law

Contents

1 Norway and Iceland Are Fundamental Rights Societies

As I have already asserted in Chap. 6 on the Member States, both Norway and Iceland are what I would call fundamental or human rights societies. A large number of lawyers deal with human rights law and humanitarian law. In universities, this inclination is particularly strong. There seems to be a general feeling that human rights law is of higher moral quality than economic law. Workers' rights have, according to this school of thought, also become human rights. In Europe, the Nordic countries have been trendsetters in this area for quite some time. After the Norwegian Supreme Court had, by 10 voted to 5, rejected the direct effect of EEA law in the Norwegian legal order in the first *Finanger* case,[1] I had an opportunity to discuss this issue with Justice Trond Dolva, a tall, gentle man. He explained to me that if the Norwegian Supreme Court were ever to acknowledge the direct effect of an international treaty Norway had entered into, it would have to be for a human rights treaty and not a simple market law agreement. In Icelandic legal literature, the same approach was taken. However, more recently we have started to see a similar development also on the European continent.

Attaching greater weight to fundamental rights law than to economic law is unjustifiable, and this for two reasons: First, to have an economy that is able to feed people and to support those in need is as important as protecting fundamental rights. Second, there is no clear dividing line between human rights law and economic law.

[1]See for details Chapter 11.

C. Baudenbacher, *Judicial Independence*, Springer Biographies,
https://doi.org/10.1007/978-3-030-02308-9_12

This becomes clear when you look at the development of the case law of the ECtHR. Although the ECHR originally aimed to protect classical human rights such as the rights to life, to privacy or to freedom of expression, the jurisprudence of the Strasbourg Court has over the past decades attained a high degree of economic relevance. It has not only increasingly influenced the economic law of the ECHR Contracting States, but also the law of the EU and of the EEA. The most important examples can be found in areas such as antitrust law, unfair competition law, property law, the law of collective bargaining and industrial action, IP law, and public procurement law. The ECHR and the case law of its Court are, in other words, highly relevant to economic law. Nobody has described this development in a more colourful way than the former British judge of the ECtHR and founding President of the (meanwhile abolished) EU Civil Service Tribunal, Paul Mahoney. Paul wrote in 2011:

> In the beginning [....] things were clear-cut. The Strasbourg Court, as now, entertained cases raising issues of human rights, democracy and the rule of law in Europe; the Court of Justice of the European Communities, as it was then called, [....] was the commercial and economic court of European integration concerned with the establishment of the common market. There was little traffic between the two Courts. But then things began to change. The journey made by human rights down the short road from Strasbourg to Luxembourg, together with the warm welcome they received there from the Luxembourg judges, is a fascinating story [....]. [H]uman rights took up residence in Luxembourg under the head of 'fundamental rights of the European Communities' and found themselves a second home on the European judicial level, not their main European judicial residence perhaps, but a well-used secondary residence.

Nevertheless, influential Nordic academics as well as courts have stuck to the aforementioned artificial distinction. It is thus harder to attack domestic economic law from an international or supranational perspective than domestic human rights law. This is another example of the protective armour used to maintain a traditional social model.

2 Academic Controversy at the Beginning

The EEA Agreement contains only one nod to fundamental rights. In recital 1 of its preamble, the Contracting Parties declare that they are

> convinced of the contribution that a European Economic Area will bring to the construction of a Europe based on peace, democracy and human rights.

When the Swiss legal community thought that Switzerland would join the EEA on the EFTA side, it was claimed in academic literature that in the event of a judicial conflict between the ECJ and the ECtHR, the EFTA Court would be obliged, under the EEA's homogeneity rules, to follow the case law of the ECJ. On the other hand, Professor Walter Kälin from the University of Berne wrote that

> [....] in the EEA, ECJ case-law on the application of the guarantees of the ECHR as general principles of EC law has the status of part of the acquis communautaire and should be adopted by the EFTA Court. The latter could and should, moreover, go a step further and apply the ECHR directly.

However, after the Swiss "no" to the EEA, Swiss academia largely lost interest in EEA law.

In Norway, Karin Fløistad, at that time a lawyer with the Attorney General's Office, argued in 2004 that:

> The problem with this is the issue of sovereignty. Another side of the procedural problem or challenge is, that by including fundamental rights in the EEA Agreement, the institutions guarding the Agreement, such as the ESA and the EFTA Court will interpret and also make final decisions on human rights questions. The system of protection of human rights will be further complicated and there is a risk of overlap and possible contradictions with the decisions made by the ECtHR. There is also the complex issue of how a decision of the ESA or the EFTA Court could be challenged before the ECtHR. [....] These problems are in many ways parallel to the challenges within the Community to harmonize their system with the Strasbourg system. But within the EEA system there is also and perhaps even more so the dimension of competence and legitimacy of ESA and the EFTA Court to make such decisions.

3 Recognition of EEA Fundamental Rights

The EFTA Court was not convinced by Karin's contentions. Using ECtHR Judge Mahoney's imagery, human rights have—under the heading of EEA fundamental rights—in the meantime found a third home in the European judiciary, again in Luxembourg, in the modest premises of the EFTA Court. Certainly, the EEA homogeneity rules only refer to EEA law that is identical in substance to EU law. However, given the role of fundamental rights in the EU legal order and the consequences for Single Market law, it is inconceivable that the EFTA Court could have taken any other direction.

The EFTA Court's first fundamental rights case was *TV 1000*, decided on 12 June 1998. It concerned the prevention of the transmission of hard core pornographic movies from Sweden into Norway. We made our first reference to the jurisprudence of the ECtHR, by referring to the *Handyside* judgment of 7 December 1976 in which the ECtHR had noted that it was

> not possible to find in the domestic law of the various Contracting States a uniform European conception of morals.

We essentially followed this approach. *TV 1000* thus launched the Court's involvement with fundamental rights law—and in particular with the jurisprudence of the Strasbourg Court.

The second landmark judgment was rendered on 12 December 2003 in *Ásgeirsson*. The case was referred by the Reykjanes District Court, a small tribunal south of Reykjavík. Thorgeir Örlygsson and I had visited this court shortly before and encouraged the judges to refer the case. Vessels not flying the Icelandic flag had been fishing cod in the waters off the coasts of Alaska and Russia. The fish was then processed and, since I acted as the Judge Rapporteur, I now know exactly how that is done. You have to take off the head, remove the skin, fillet the fish, salt it and dry it. Then the cod is ready to be sold, in particular in Portugal, Spain, and Italy. The cod was marketed in these countries as Icelandic cod, even though it had neither been caught by a vessel flying the Icelandic flag nor in Icelandic waters. Criminal proceedings were opened against three managers. During the hearing, I had an interesting discussion with one of the attorneys. If you go to one of the temples of molecular cuisine in the Basque country or in Catalonia and order a portion of *Bacalao* you pay a fortune. The lawyer asserted that by processing the cod, a new product under the EEA rules of origin had been generated. However, as the rules of origin are simple, down-to earth rules, he was unsuccessful with that line of argument. He could have successfully pleaded the "new product" argument if the managers had, for example, taken the skin and made a pair of shoes or a handbag out of it. Be that as it may, the most interesting point was to be found elsewhere. One of the three defendants contended that the reference to the Court would in itself lead to a delay of the proceedings and would violate Article 6(1) of the ECHR where the right to a fair trial within a reasonable time is guaranteed. Relying on the ECtHR's *Pafitis* judgment of 26 February 1998, we held that the preliminary reference procedure was part of granting citizens' fundamental rights and that the delay was minimal. In fact, it only took us five months to decide this case. We used it as a good opportunity to clearly state that EEA law must be interpreted in the light of fundamental rights and that the provisions of the ECHR and the judgments of the ECtHR are important sources for determining the scope of these rights.

Fundamental rights have been invoked by creative lawyers on many more occasions. It is important to note that the Court did not primarily recognise the existence of fundamental rights under the EEA Agreement by reference to the case law of the ECJ, but by citing the ECHR and the jurisprudence of the ECtHR directly. There are, as of today, 27 specific references to Strasbourg jurisprudence in 15 EFTA Court cases. And there are other cases in which fundamental rights were referred to in a general way.

The traffic has not been one way. The ECtHR made several references to our judgment in *Icesave I* in the *Ališić* judgment of 16 July 2014.[2] This case concerned the applicants' inability to recover "old" foreign-currency savings—deposited with banks in what is now Bosnia and Herzegovina—following the dissolution of the former Socialist Federal Republic of Yugoslavia. Although these citations were not decisive for the outcome, the Strasbourg Court made it clear that it was aware of the important function the EFTA Court plays in the enforcement of fundamental (in the Strasbourg language "human") rights in Europe.

[2]See regarding the *Icesave* cases, Chapter 25.

4 Interim Result

When all is said and done, the EFTA Court is more than happy to address relevant questions of fundamental rights law that arise and to refer to the ECHR and to the ECtHR's case law. This appears to be something the EEA/EFTA States have—as usual after some hesitation—embraced. Indeed, as stated in 2014 in paragraph 43 of the *Deveci* case, the Norwegian Government

> fully acknowledge[d] the Court's settled case law that any provision of EEA law is to be interpreted in light of fundamental rights common to the EEA States and that the European Convention of Human Rights and the case law of the European Court of Human Rights are to be considered essential sources for determining the scope of these rights.

5 The EU Charter in Particular

Obviously, the question of whether the EU Charter of fundamental rights has a role to play in EEA law is of particular interest. ECJ AG Nils Wahl wrote extrajudicially that the Court indirectly applied provisions of the Charter when it cited in *Norway Post* the Opinions of AG Sharpston in *KME* and AG Kokott in *Solvay* where those AGs referred to the Charter. I am not sure whether this conclusion is correct. The Icelandic Government relied on the Charter in proceedings brought against it in *Icelandic Posting of Workers Act.* In that case, Iceland argued

> that it would be unacceptable as a matter of both national policy and EEA law that workers be afforded less protection under EEA law than under EU law.

Iceland referred to Article 9 TFEU and Article 31 of the Charter, but also to Article 34 of the Charter. Article 9 TFEU reads:

> In defining and implementing its policies and activities, the Union shall take into account requirements linked to the promotion of a high level of employment, the guarantee of adequate social protection, the fight against social exclusion, and a high level of education, training and protection of human health.

Article 31 states under the heading "Fair and just working conditions" that every worker has the right to working conditions that respect his or her health, safety and dignity and the right to limitation of maximum working hours, to daily and weekly rest periods and to an annual period of paid leave. Article 34 deals with social security benefits and social advantages. Neither Article 31 nor Article 34 of the Charter appear to correspond to comparable provisions of the ECHR.

Norway stated in *Deveci* that

> an automatic application of the Charter, which is not incorporated in the EEA Agreement, would challenge State sovereignty and the principle of consent as the source of international legal obligations [....] [since] the Charter provides, in some respects, for fundamental rights beyond those common to the EEA States.

This would mean, *e contrario*, that a non-automatic application, on a case-by-case basis, is according to the Norwegian Government not excluded. ESA has based itself on ECJ case law that applied the Charter. The Commission for its part noted in *Deveci*, a transfer of undertakings case, that the ECJ had found in the *Alemo-Herron* case that Article 3 of the directive must be interpreted in accordance with Article 16 of the Charter.

The EFTA Court has been cautious as regards the relevance of the Charter. In *Clauder*, it made its first reference to the Charter of Fundamental Rights. This case, which was referred by the Liechtenstein Administrative Court, concerned the interpretation of the Citizenship Directive[3] and in particular the decision by the Liechtenstein Government not to grant the Complainant, who was economically inactive and in receipt of social welfare benefits, a family reunification permit for his spouse. The Court

> recalled that all the EEA States are parties to the ECHR, which enshrines in Article 8(1) the right to respect for private and family life

and cited its well established case law that

> provisions of the EEA Agreement are to be interpreted in the light of fundamental rights.

It went on to note

> that in the European Union the same right is protected by Article 7 of the Charter of Fundamental Rights.

This problem as such is not new. It has, whenever the Treaties of the EU have been amended, been dealt with under the title of "the widening gap." Any problems that have arisen have, unsurprisingly, been addressed on a case-by-case basis.[4] In the light of the experience gained, the following points should be considered:

- The Court may refer to the Charter in *dicta*. That is what it did in *Clauder*;
- The Court may come to the conclusion that it does not matter whether the Charter is taken into account or not because it does not add anything new to EEA law, as it stands. This is the approach that was chosen in *Deveci*. I would add that ESA had taken the same stance;
- Cases would be much more challenging if the Charter were to imply something that had not so far been part of EEA law. A particularly sensitive constellation would exist if our sister court were to give a new and specific interpretation to a legal act, which is also part of EEA law, in the light of the Charter. One answer could be that under homogeneity rules the Court would apply the Charter (by analogy or any other way). Another answer could be to say that such an interpretation falls outside the scope of the EEA Agreement;
- At the EFTA Court's 2015 Spring Conference, the former Icelandic Judge on the ECtHR Davíð Thór Björgvinsson made a pragmatic and yet not

[3]2004/38/EC.

[4]See for details Chapter 19.

unproblematic proposal: the EFTA Court, he said, could follow the Charter without citing it. Pundits may wonder whether the Court has followed that advice when holding in paragraph 72 of its landmark judgment in *Fosen-Linjen* that the Remedies Directive for the public sector[5] must "be interpreted in the light of fundamental rights, in particular the right to an effective judicial remedy".[6]

[5] 89/665/EEC.

[6] See concerning *Fosen-Linjen* Chapter 21.

Chapter 13
Putting the EFTA Court on the Map

Contents

1 My Election as President

At the end of 2002, President Thór Vilhjálmsson did not seek renomination. The competent Icelandic ministry proposed Kristinn F. Árnason, a career diplomat, as his replacement. However, the Icelandic Government started to have second thoughts and at the end of the day Thorgeir Örlygsson was nominated and appointed. He had studied law in Iceland and at Harvard, had been a full professor and Vice-President at the University of Iceland and had served for a few years as the Permanent Secretary in the Ministry of Industry and Trade. In 2012, Kristinn F. Árnason was appointed as Secretary General of EFTA.

Our new colleague arrived in Luxembourg two days before the new President was to be elected. He did not know either of the two incumbent judges and had the thankless task of having to vote for one of us. I was unaware of the fact that in the late 1980s, Per Tresselt had served as Norway's representative on the International

C. Baudenbacher, *Judicial Independence*, Springer Biographies,
https://doi.org/10.1007/978-3-030-02308-9_13

Whaling Commission. The Icelandic member was Halldór Ásgrímsson who in 1995 became the Minister for Foreign Affairs of his country. As on previous occasions, the Court held a public sitting. This time, the ceremony took place on 15 January 2003 in Luxembourg's most beautiful hall, the *Cercle Cité*. First, the Court bid farewell to the outgoing President Thór Vilhjálmsson. As the senior judge, it was my task to give the speech in his honour. I teased him by saying that deep in his heart he was a monist, and I saw from the corner of my eye that he had his characteristic smile. Thór gave a colourful speech with many references to the Icelandic sagas. I had visited Finland with my family the year before and bought an original photo of Finnish Field Marshal Carl Gustaf Mannerheim, one of Thór's heroes. It showed Mannerheim in his Mikkeli headquarters during the 1939–1944 wars. I handed Thór the photo as a farewell gift. Thorgeir Örlygsson took the oath and then the Court retreated to elect the new President. After a few minutes, the Court returned in its new formation. I had been elected and gave a short speech. After the public sitting there was a reception at which not only EFTA people, but also a good number of colleagues from the ECJ and the GC participated. It was the first time so many of them attended such an event. The dinner after the ceremony took place in a rather icy atmosphere. I wasn't overly concerned as I was determined to enhance the Court's visibility and to improve its reputation.

2 Taking Stock

Despite the one-sidedness of the written homogeneity rules, both the ECJ and the GC made it clear from the beginning that in cases in which the Court had tackled a novel legal question they were basically prepared to enter a dialogue. The same went for AGs.[1] Yet, there were also situations where our judgments went unnoticed. After the Court's move to Luxembourg, we held two common dinners a year with delegations from the ECJ and the GC.

Contacts with the judiciary of the EFTA Court's three Member States were limited. Once a year a group of Norwegian judges paid us a visit on their way to the ECtHR in Strasbourg and once judges from the Supreme Courts of the three Member States attended a hearing. Otherwise it was basically left to chance whether we saw a judge from an EEA/EFTA State court. The EFTA Court had not developed a policy of reaching out to the national judiciaries.

At the time, EU legal literature scarcely touched on the EFTA Court. At best, text books and commentaries referred to the EEA as part of a chapter on the EU's third-country agreements. The Court was then usually mentioned in a few sentences. The focus was on the ECJ's two EEA opinions—Opinion 1/91 and Opinion 1/92—and on the written, one-sided homogeneity rules. Authors also pointed to Article 107 EEA, which, as I have said, gives the individual EEA/EFTA States the

[1]See for details Chapter 5.

right to empower their courts or tribunals to ask the ECJ for a preliminary ruling. As I have said, this provision was obviously meant to be symbolic from the beginning and has remained a dead letter (*lettre morte*).[2] Nevertheless, citing Article 107 EEA had a political function; it made the EFTA Court look unimportant. All in all, these textbooks gave the impression that the Court was barely an independent judicial institution, but rather a vicarious agent of the ECJ. With this approach, the respective writers a priori avoided any discussion of the Court's case law, of the fact that in most cases it had to break new ground and that the one-sided homogeneity rules of the EEA Agreement and of the SCA were gradually being replaced by judicial dialogue. It goes without saying that these writers also refrained from dealing with ESA's practice. Other EU law authors even hushed up our case law if the ECJ based itself on it. EFTA legal literature, for its part, dealt principally with sovereignty issues.

The EFTA Court's biggest problem was its low case load. I was convinced that in order to get more work, the case handling time had to be shortened and the Court's reputation had to be improved. My personal standing had been strengthened by two awards that were bestowed on me in 2004: the Cross of Honour for Science and Art First Class of the Republic of Austria and the Small States Prize of the Herbert Batliner Europe Institute in Salzburg. The Small States Prize was over the years also given to the President of Estonia, Lennart Meri; the President of Latvia, Vaira Vike-Freiberga; and the Prime Minister of Luxembourg, and later President of the European Commission, Jean-Claude Juncker.

3 Extrajudicial Activities of the Court

3.1 General

Any court can only be successful if its staff members feel comfortable and have the impression that their performance is appreciated. As far as the work on cases is concerned, it is primarily up to the individual judges to achieve these objectives. In the early years, when the number of incoming cases was low, it was also necessary to ensure that people were kept busy in a meaningful way. Events such as the annual excursion and the Christmas dinner certainly contributed to a positive atmosphere.

For a small court which was located on foreign soil and operated in the shadow of a much larger sister court, it was of the utmost importance to actively engage with the outside world, such as academia, other courts, political circles, practicing lawyers and the public at large. Fortunately, I was able to rely on Doris in this regard, whose networking and social skills are unmatched. Without her, it would not have been possible to position the EFTA Court in Luxembourg and in Brussels,

---

[2]See also Chapter 8.

in other EU Member States, in the EFTA States and beyond Europe. Of my wife's manifold interests, I should highlight that she is an avid collector of contemporary jewellery and fashion. This meant that she always cut a fine figure, no matter the nature of the event.

3.2 *Regular Activities*

Participation in EFTA Ministerial Meetings
The EFTA Ministerial meetings are events involving the four EFTA Member States, including Switzerland. The summer meeting takes place at the end of June each year in the country that holds the chair of the EFTA at four. A second meeting takes place towards the end of the year, usually in Geneva. Originally, the ESA College and the EFTA Court were invited to both gatherings, but at one stage this was changed and the two EFTA pillar institutions were restricted to participating in the summer encounters. The meetings are jointly organised by the EFTA Secretariat in Geneva and the EFTA State holding the chair. The Swiss Government was always proud to invite the delegates to one of the top hotels in a famous tourist spot such as Zurich, Interlaken, Lugano, Berne, Montreux, or Gstaad. The venues in Norway and (in particular) in Iceland, were less glamorous and on occasion even had the character of a boy (or girl) scout camp. The main focus of the talks was on EFTA's third-country relations. Nevertheless, the Presidents of ESA and of the Court were invited to give a short summary of their institutions' activities and challenges. The Swiss for their part reported on their bilateral relationship with the EU. Since my appointment to the Court in 1995, I participated in every meeting, usually accompanied by Doris. With my election as President in 2003, it became my task to speak on behalf of the Court. In my presentations, I placed special emphasis on judicial dialogue and mentioned the references by the EU courts and the AGs to the EFTA Court's case law as well as any further references by other courts. In recent years, these reports have also been uploaded to the Court's website. In addition, I gave regular presentations before the parliamentarians and the social partners of the four EFTA countries. My goal in all these activities was to create a better understanding of the EFTA Court's tasks and challenges.

The meetings lasted a day and usually followed the same ritual with gatherings of the ministers, of the parliamentarians and of the social partners. The EFTA Secretariat and the host EFTA State usually ensured that a new free trade agreement with a country outside Europe was signed. This added a global touch to the meetings. The social highlight was the Ministerial dinner with speeches from both the outgoing and the incoming chairs. The following day, there was normally an outing with some sightseeing and a meal. Everything was well-prepared in advance and in most cases everything went according to plan. However, sometimes this was not the case. The last meeting I attended took place under Norwegian leadership in Longyearbyen, the administrative centre of Svalbard, an archipelago in the Arctic Ocean, on 26 and 27 June 2017. The event was marked by a bitter fight between the

Norwegians and the Icelanders. Svalbard is not part of the EEA territory. The 1920 Svalbard Treaty grants Norway sovereignty over Svalbard, but not all Norwegian law applies. Moreover, the Treaty requires that the archipelago and its territorial waters remain a demilitarised and free economic zone for the 45 signatory parties. It seems that on the invitations, the venue was called "Longyearbyen, Svalbard". However, when the Icelanders arrived, they discovered that the Norwegian hosts used the name "Longyearbyen, Norway." In view of the complex international law status of the archipelago, the Icelanders refused to have the common press release published using this wording. When I entered the room where the Ministerial meeting was to be held, on 26 June at 9 a.m., the Swiss Minister Johann Schneider-Ammann, who couldn't believe what was going on, asked me whether, in my capacity as President of the EFTA Court, I could settle the dispute. I declined due to lack of jurisdiction. The quarrel lasted all day and a compromise was only found at night. The press release was published using the wording "Longyearbyen, Norway", but only internally, the Icelanders deposited a note in which they formally opposed this designation. What struck me, but didn't particularly surprise me, was that the Norwegian Minister didn't seem to have any discretionary powers.

Furthermore, every other year, the summer Ministerial either coincided with the FIFA football world cup or the UEFA European cup. If there was an exciting game to watch the participants left the Ministerial dinner in droves. In 2006 in Hofn, Iceland, the EFTA community watched the Swiss, following a draw against Ukraine after extra time, miss three penalty kicks in the round of 16 encounter at the FIFA World Cup in Germany. It was the tournament the Germans refer to as the "summer fairy tale". Switzerland was thus eliminated without conceding a single goal. In 2012, in Gstaad, we saw Italian striker Mario Balotelli singlehandedly knock Germany out of the UEFA European Championship in the semi-final by scoring two fantastic goals, a header and an unstoppable shot. And in 2016 in Berne, the Icelanders went mad when their team ousted England from the UEFA European Championship in the round of 16, just a few days after the Brexit referendum.

Lunchtime Talks

Following my election as President in 2003, as one of the first steps to enhance the visibility of the EFTA Court, I suggested having regular lunchtime talks. My colleagues agreed. The talks were an immediate success, drawing in people from the Union judiciary, the diplomatic corps based in Luxembourg, Luxembourg public life and the local civil society. Sometimes, participants also came from Brussels and nearby Germany. Speakers in recent years were, for example: the Luxembourg Minister of Finance, Pierre Gramegna; the ESA President, Sven Erik Svedman; the President of the Court of Justice of the Andean Community, Luis José Diez Canseco Nuñez; the President of the International Tribunal for the Law of the Sea, Vladimir Vladimirovich Golitsyn; the Icelandic Judge on the ECtHR, Róbert Spanó; and the Former Austrian Vice-Chancellor, Erhard Busek. A particularly moving talk was given by Humboldt University Professor Christoph Paulus on "The trial of Jesus".

Participation in Official Functions of the Luxembourg Authorities

Once it had established itself in Luxembourg, the EFTA Court was invited to participate in all sorts of official events organised by the Luxembourg Government and the Mayor of Luxembourg City. The most important occasion was certainly the *Te Deum*, which was sung in the cathedral every year on the Grand Duke's birthday on 23 June. Men were expected to appear in morning jacket. The ladies wore hats and Doris followed her own inimitable fashion sense. Rather than adorning the typical Royal Ascot style of hat she opted for more daring contemporary creations, notably by the London-based Irish milliner and designer Philip Treacy. Luxembourg public TV broadcast the event, and Doris and her fashionable attire became well-known throughout the country. Under the reign of Jean-Claude Juncker, the *Te Deum*, celebrated by the Archbishop, was an official State event. In addition to the Grand Duke and his family, the political leaders of the country, the ambassadors accredited in Luxembourg, the national and European judges and the representatives of international organisations took part. Afterwards, the Minister for Foreign Affairs gave a lunch for the invited guests and in the evening a white tie reception was held by the Grand Ducal couple in their *Palais*. The ambassadors based in Brussels used to say that the food in Luxembourg was much better than at comparable events in the Belgian capital.

One year Doris decided not to wear a hat, but a garland of ivy leaves. She bought fake ivy leaves and the costume tailor of the Trier theatre formed them into suitable head attire according to Doris' instructions. It was a gorgeous creation. I used one leaf instead of a pocket square in my morning jacket. Archbishop Fernand Franck who had seen Doris during the celebration was slightly shocked and at the aperitif before the luncheon he said to her something along the lines of:

> But my dear lady, this is no hat.

However, the Pope's Nuncio to Belgium and Luxembourg and Doyen of the diplomatic corps, Karl-Josef Rauber, came to Doris' rescue, stating:

> These are wine leaves. This is an allusion to the vineyard of the Lord.

That settled the matter. I should add that later we got to know Monsignor Franck as a friendly and humorous man. When the Liberal-Red-Green Government took power, the *Te Deum* was abolished and replaced by an act of State. The Archbishop still issues invitations to a *Te Deum*, but this is now strictly an ecclesiastical event.

Fostering Relations with the EU Judiciary

For obvious reasons, maintaining good relations with the judges and AGs of the ECJ, as well as with the judges of the GC, is of the utmost importance for the EFTA Court. Understandably, the EU judiciary was at first reluctant to see a new judicial mechanism surface in Europe. However, once the establishment of the EFTA Court was a *fait accompli*, they gave it important logistical support. After a while, we had become so well acquainted—we met at all sorts of occasions—that the bi-annual formal luncheons were dropped. We participated in the ECJ's and GC's official events and they participated in ours. Doris and I were very active on the social networking front, as I will describe when talking about my personal activities. Given the ECJ's size, it was of particular importance to understand its inner life.

Fostering Relations with National Courts

Another crucial goal was to establish a sound relationship with the courts and in particular the courts of last resort of our three Member States. I started to travel to Iceland, Liechtenstein and Norway on a regular basis to meet with judges, but also with practising lawyers, civil servants, academics and politicians, to give speeches and participate in conferences. Doris often accompanied me, and we combined our trips with meeting influential people at dinners and other social events. If there were no suitable occasions, the Court itself took the initiative and acted as the main organiser, often in cooperation with a local university. As a rule, I did not wait until I received a speaking invitation; I announced that I was coming and that I intended to discuss matters of EEA law. During my visits, I spoke, in particular, about the attitude of the national courts in relation to the preliminary reference procedure. In Norway, I visited Oslo most often. My programme normally included a lecture at the University and a visit to at least one court. But I also spoke in Trondheim, Bergen and Tromsø. In Iceland, I gave talks at all four Universities, Iceland, Reykjavík, Akureyri and Bifröst, but also at gatherings of the Bar Association, the Judges Association and the Lawyers Association. In Liechtenstein, I co-chaired an annual Europe Symposium and after the establishment of the University of Liechtenstein, I gave speeches there.

I often invited members of the EU judiciary to accompany me on my trips to our Member States. I wanted people to become familiar with the EEA/EFTA States and with their legal orders. ECJ Judges Christiaan Timmermans, Allan Rosas and Camelia Toader and AGs Francis Jacobs, Miguel Poiares Maduro and Paolo Mengozzi were among those who came along. Thorgeir Örlygsson and Henrik Bull were particularly pleasant colleagues on such occasions. Another goal of such gatherings was to bring together judges from the three EEA/EFTA countries. The Norwegians and the Icelanders saw each other at all sorts of Nordic conferences, but for the Liechtensteiners it was important to connect with their colleagues from the two other EEA/EFTA States. A particular highlight was the three-day meeting at the Court in May 2017 where the Supreme Courts of Iceland and of Norway each attended *in corpore*, joined by judges from all the three Liechtenstein courts of last resort. We called this event, a bit daringly, the "First Judicial Summit of the EFTA pillar". In July 2017, a delegation from the Swiss Federal Supreme Court led by President Ulrich Meyer came to Luxembourg.

Talking to National Administrations

In Iceland and in Liechtenstein, I was regularly invited to meet government ministers and top civil servants dealing with the EEA Agreement whenever I was in the country. In Norway, this was less the case. For example, in the week of 14 March 2016, I visited Iceland upon the invitation of the Minister for Foreign Affairs, Gunnar Bragi Sveinsson, accompanied by Doris and my Head of Cabinet Philipp Speitler. We first met the Minister for Foreign Affairs and his top civil servants for an exchange of views. The next day, I gave a lecture on "The EEA in Action -

Some Thoughts After 22 Years" at the Icelandic Lawyers Association. The session which was attended by some 90 people was chaired by the Chairman of the Icelandic Judges' Association and former EFTA Court Registrar, Judge Skúli Magnússon. One evening, Prime Minister Sigmundur Davíð Gunnlaugsson, and his spouse, Anna Sigurlaug Pálsdóttir, hosted a dinner for my delegation in the government's guesthouse. I also met Bjarni Benediktsson, Minister of Finance and Economic Affairs, the future Prime Minister, and I was interviewed by Icelandic TV host Þóra Arnórsdóttir. Furthermore, during my stay in Iceland, I visited the Supreme Court of Iceland, the Reykjavík District Court and the District Court of Borgarnes. Last, but not least, on the final day of our stay, Doris and I were received for an exchange of views by the President of Iceland, Ólafur Ragnar Grímsson, in his residence. This visit came about in a way that is only possible in small countries. The day before, at noon, Doris and I went swimming with a group of Icelandic civil servants in the Atlantic. The water temperature was 3.6 °C. One of the ladies in the group was the personal assistant to the President. In the afternoon she called and delivered the invitation. Our talk with President Grímsson lasted almost two hours. We gained important insights into the Icesave affair, although it was clear that our host was anxious to write himself into history. In the evening we attended an impressive production of Mozart's "Don Giovanni". In the interval, we met two Icelandic judges, one from the Supreme Court who I had met before and a young woman who was serving in the Reykjavík District Court. The latter was so upset by Don Giovanni's treatment of women that she seriously advocated banning performances of the opera.

Being Part of Court Networks

Another of my key objectives was to establish contact with other courts and to make the Court part of networks, which extended beyond the EFTA pillar and even the EEA. The EFTA Court paid visits to the ECtHR, which also reciprocated the visit. I was received by the Vice-President of the German Constitutional Court and the President of the German Supreme Court. Delegations from the Swiss Supreme Court and the Swiss Administrative Court came to Luxembourg to see us. I also felt that it was important to establish contacts with the high courts of Luxembourg. The EFTA Court was not invited to participate in the two meetings the ECJ held with the US Supreme Court, but on both occasions Doris and I were welcomed to the official dinner. The EFTA Court attracted the attention of the Project on International Courts and Tribunals (PICT), which was created in 1997 by New York University and the University of London. It was included in the "Manual on International Courts and Tribunals" by Ruth Mackenzie, Cesare P. R. Romano, Yuval Shany and Philippe Sands. I was also interviewed by the authors of the book "The International Judge: An Introduction to the Men and Women Who Decide the World's Cases", and invited to contribute to "The Oxford Handbook of International Adjudication". Occasionally, I participated in the meeting of the Presidents of the European Supreme Courts and in 2012, I was invited to the "*Sechsertreffen*", the meeting of the Constitutional Courts of the six German-speaking countries. In 2002, I was one of the founders of the Association of European Competition Law Judges (AECLJ). The AECLJ's website states in that respect:

> The AECLJ was created in Luxembourg in September 2002 by a founding group of judges representing each of the then fifteen Member States of the European Union, with the participation of judges from the European Court of Justice, the Court of First Instance, and from the EFTA Court.[3]

The purpose of the association is to provide a forum for the exchange of knowledge and experience in Europe. Since 2003, European competition law is to a large extent applied by national judges.[4] The AECLJ' website thus states that

> it is of vital importance that judges dealing with this field of law in the Member States are able to communicate on an informal level, discussing matters of common concern and enquiring about parallel proceedings. The consistent application of European competition law largely depends on the existence of a network to facilitate such an exchange of experience.

I spoke at several annual gatherings of the AECLJ which always took place in different European capitals.

In 2005, I attended the Nordic Law Conference in Reykjavík and made an intervention in English. I was told that this was the first time a speaker was allowed to use a non-Nordic language.

In early 2015 the Court established a relationship with the Court of Justice of the Andean Community. The Andean Community has over 100 million inhabitants and was founded in 1969 on the template of what was then the EEC. The current Member States are Bolivia, Colombia, Ecuador and Peru. The Community's most important institutions are: the Andean Presidential Council, an organ of the Presidents of the Member States that coordinates integration efforts; the Andean Community Commission; the General Secretariat; and the Court of Justice which has its seat in Quito, the capital of Ecuador. The General Secretariat is the executive organ of the Community with a permanent seat in Lima, Peru. It is mainly competent to supervise compliance with Andean Community law by the Member States. The types of procedure before the Andean Court of Justice are similar to the ones before the ECJ and of the EFTA Court. The Andean Court is the third most active international court after the ECJ and the ECtHR. It plays a central role in facilitating the integration of the Andean States. It's most important competences are to decide on actions concerning the infringement of Andean Community law ("*acciones de incumplimiento*"), on actions for nullity ("*acciones de nulidad*") and to render preliminary rulings at the request of the national courts of the Andean States ("*interpretaciones prejudiciales*"). Most of the decisions are preliminary rulings and roughly 90% of all cases concern IP law. Strong protection of IP rights is crucial to the Member States of the Andean Community in order to attract foreign direct investment.

---

[3]Further information available at: http://www.aeclj.com/240/About-the-Association.html.

[4]Regulation (EC) No 1/2003.

In May 2015, I visited Quito and the Court of Justice of the Andean Community. In our discussions, President Luis Diez Canseco Núñez complained of the difficult circumstances in which his institution operated. One problem was that some judges were political appointees. Another problem he faced was the fact that some governments and national courts were unwilling to implement the Court's judgments. He asked about my experience in that regard, and I told him that after the downsizing of my Court to three judges, we had similar problems. I also said to Luis that in addition to upholding the law by making well-reasoned judgments, a small court was particularly dependent on the extra-judicial activities of the judges, and that in particular the President should be active in improving the court's standing.

In Quito, I gave two lectures and participated in round-tables. In one of the lectures, I placed particular emphasis on the importance of judicial independence. The judge from Ecuador took the floor and asked me what I thought about the idea of replacing the Andean Court of Justice with an ad hoc tribunal. I answered that I did not consider this to be a good idea. Later I learned that this judge played a part in Rafael Correa's, then President of Ecuador, sacking of the Justices of the Supreme Court of Ecuador under the pretext that they were not working hard enough. In reality, the action was politically motivated. Correa then packed the Supreme Court with his allies. The only Justice who was reprieved was the very judge who had posed this question about replacing the Andean Court of Justice with an ad hoc tribunal. This Justice first served Correa as a placeholder on the Supreme Court and was then rewarded for his loyalty by being nominated to the Andean Court of Justice. What Correa did was to fill up the Supreme Court with people he thought could be kept on a tight leash.

In early 2016, the EFTA Court established contacts with the International Tribunal for the Law of the Sea. In October 2016, I was one of the speakers of the Symposium held in Hamburg on the occasion of the Tribunal's twentieth anniversary.

Hosting Lawyers' and Students' Groups
Once the EFTA Court moved to Luxembourg, it started to host groups of interested lawyers and of students from our Member States. As our fame spread, such visits became more frequent and we increasingly had groups from EU Member States and from Switzerland.

3.3 *Anniversaries*

Tenth Anniversary Conference
The first celebratory symposium we held was the Court's "tin anniversary". When this date was approaching, I felt that we should organise an event to mark the occasion. A solemn undertaking was out of the question and it was finally decided to hold a conference entitled "The EFTA Court Ten Years On" at the *Cercle Cité*. The evening before, the Court invited delegates to a reception in the cloister of

Abbaye Neumunster, a former monastery, military hospital and prison, which had been transformed into a cultural centre. As a gift to the people of Luxembourg, we displayed a court scene by German textile artist Stefanie Alraune Siebert in the entrance hall of the *Abbaye* for one month. It was a provocative artwork with marvellous artificial judges in black robes and colourful private parties appearing before them. On closer inspection, one could easily distinguish that the ladies in the courtroom belonged to the world's oldest profession. It was probably an allegory that justice was sometimes also for sale. When I saw the scene, I initially had some doubts as to whether my colleagues would approve of it, but nobody wanted to risk being accused of being a philistine. That year, we used the same court scene as the design for our Christmas card.

The event was attended by some 200 people, among them the Presidents and numerous members of the two Union courts, the President of the ECtHR, the ESA College *in corpore*, judges from our three Member States and from Switzerland, politicians, civil servants, academics and practising lawyers. In view of the troubled relationship among the members of the five-member Court, it was a matter of great importance to me that all former judges should be invited and should turn up. After some brouhaha, they all came, with the exception of Gustav Bygglin who had served during the final six months of the five-member Court's existence. Gustav had another obligation.

The programme for the conference reflected the challenges that the Court had faced in its first ten years. Most speakers addressed the issues of direct effect, State liability, fundamental rights and homogeneity. Nevertheless, there were also substantive contributions. University of Heidelberg Professor Peter-Christian Müller-Graff spoke about

> The Impact of Climate, Geography and Other Non-Legal Factors on EC Law and EEA Law,

and University of Leiden Professor Marco Bronckers dealt with the subject of

> Exceptions to Liberal Trade in Foodstuffs: The Precautionary Approach and Collective Preferences.

Most importantly, ECJ President Vassilios Skouris gave an impressive talk on

> The ECJ and the EFTA Court under the EEA Agreement: A Paradigm for International Cooperation between Judicial Institutions.

He suggested that

> the ECJ-EFTA Court model of cooperation can serve as a more general paradigm of institutional dialogue between judicial institutions

and made the often-quoted statement that for the ECJ

> ignoring EFTA Court precedents would simply be incompatible with the overriding objective of the EEA Agreement which is homogeneity.

I gave a talk on the Court's case law, the relevance of the jurisprudence of the Union courts as well as on our dialogue with the courts of our three Member States and with the Union courts. My colleagues Per Tresselt and Thorgeir Örlygsson acted as moderators. In the evening, the Court hosted an official dinner for some 80 guests at *Cercle Munster* with Former President Leif Sevón and GC President Bo Vesterdorf as speakers. We had an Icelandic opera singer and people enjoyed themselves.

Twentieth Anniversary Conference

On the occasion of its twentieth anniversary, the "china anniversary", the EFTA Court held another conference. This time, the content and the impact were totally different. On the one hand, the Court had rendered a number of substantive landmark judgments in the preceding years and the dialogue with the Union courts and with the ECJ's AGs had intensified. I had for quite some time felt that the endless politically motivated talk about whether the Court was interfering with the sovereignty of the Member States in an inappropriate way had to come to an end. On the other hand, there was the unresolved conflict with the Norwegian Supreme Court (*Høyesterett*), which had refrained from referring cases to us for more than ten years and refused to follow us in the *STX* case. At the end of the day we drafted a programme that included, in particular, two top class practising EU lawyers in order to hear what they had to say about the Court's performance from the outside.

The conference took place on 20 June 2014 in the *Cercle Cité*. Just like the symposium ten years before, the celebration started with a reception in the cloister of *Abbaye Neumunster* the night before, however, this time without the presentation of an artwork. The conference itself was attended by over 200 participants from all branches of the legal profession. H.E. Xavier Bettel, Prime Minister of Luxembourg, opened the proceedings with a keynote speech on "European integration". He stated that no EU Member State could have "Europe à la carte". I called the Court an example of the judicialisation of international law and said that the EEA Agreement had worked better than expected, due to the performance of its institutions. University of Luxembourg Professor Alexander Rust, analysed the case law of the Court and of the ECJ on direct taxation. AG Juliane Kokott from the ECJ spoke on "European Courts in Dialogue". Brussels and Paris top lawyers Ian Forrester and Eric Morgan de Rivery complimented the EFTA Court on the clarity of its judgments and welcomed the scope of judicial review. A panel chaired by University of Oslo Professor Giuditta Cordero-Moss, which brought together: the Chief Justice of Norway, Tore Schei; the President of the Supreme Court of Iceland, Markús Sigurbjörnsson; the President of the Liechtenstein Administrative Court, Andreas Batliner; and the President of the Administrative Court of Luxembourg, Georges Ravarani, discussed the Shakespearian question in a slightly different form: "To refer or not to refer". It became clear that the approach prevailing in Iceland and in Liechtenstein was quite different from the one used in Norway.[5]

[5]See for details Chapter 26.

Activities of the Four EFTA Member States
In 2000, all four EFTA Member States celebrated EFTA's fortieth anniversary with the publication of a 50-page book. On the occasion of its fiftieth anniversary and the fifteenth anniversary of the EEA Agreement, the EFTA of four organised a seminar in November 2009 in Geneva entitled "Partners in Progress". A book including material from the seminar, called "EFTA 1960 – 2010: Elements of 50 Years of European History," was presented in May 2010. The EFTA of four also published a brochure entitled "European Economic Area 1994 – 2009". The Court *in corpore* attended the seminar in Geneva. I found it surprising that the EFTA Secretariat, which is not a decision-maker under the EEA Agreement, chose to organise talks about the EEA Agreement without inviting the Presidents of ESA and the Court to make a statement. The official speakers were, as usual at that time, rather negative towards the EEA and the institutions of the EFTA pillar. The Liechtenstein Minister for Foreign Affairs, Ernst Walch, was in the chair and gave me the floor for a short declaration. The focus of my intervention was on our growing influence on the case law of the Union courts. All in all, said activities of the EFTA of four reflected the joint interest of the two superpowers Norway and Switzerland of focussing on trade relations with the rest of the world and saying as little as possible about the EEA Agreement. ESA has never organised an event to celebrate an anniversary. I have always supposed that they refrained from doing so out of fear that the Union-friendly elites in Oslo might take offence.

3.4 *Annual Spring Conference*

In 2012, following the incident at the EFTA Secretariat's EEA seminar,[6] the Court's registrar Skúli Magnússon convinced me that the Court should have its own annual discussion forum. Henceforth we organised a Spring Conference in June of each year. As with every new initiative, we started modestly, but over time the event has become a fixed point in the Court's agenda. To give an example, in 2017, the title of the Conference was: "Thoughts on the Future of Europe." It was attended by over 170 participants, including members of EFTA State supreme courts, ESA, the ECJ, the GC, the European Commission, representatives from governments, business associations and trade unions, practitioners and academics. There were six high-level presentations: Justice Wilhelm Matheson of the Supreme Court of Norway discussed "Fundamental Freedoms and Fundamental Rights – Challenges in Deciding the *Holship* Case on the National Level". Dr. iur. HSG Magnus Schmauch from Sweden's financial supervisory authority, a former legal secretary of the Court and my former doctoral student, elaborated on the innovative architecture of financial regulation in the EEA. Peter Freeman CBE QC (Hon), Chairman of the UK's Competition Appeal Tribunal, opened the afternoon session

---

[6]See for details Chapter 24.

with an in-depth analysis of recent EFTA Court competition law jurisprudence. The day's next two sessions addressed the issues raised by Brexit. Kassie Smith QC of Monckton Chambers examined "Brexit and the EEA", and Professor Dr. Heribert Hirte, a member of the German Bundestag, explained the viewpoint of his institution. The final session of the day was a speech by the fifth President of Iceland, H. E. Ólafur Ragnar Grímsson, now Chairman of the Arctic Circle, on "The Future of Europe – A View from the North". The prominent role Grímsson played in the *Icesave* conflict has made him a figure of European significance.[7]

3.5 Publications

The EFTA Court Ten Years On

The speeches and discussions at the Court's tenth anniversary conference were published in a small volume by the renowned English publisher Hart. The book, which was edited by the three judges of the Court, was presented to the public in a ceremony with ECJ AG Francis Jacobs as the main speaker. It has certainly contributed to making the Court more visible in the EEA as a whole. Oslo political scientist Ulf Sverdrup, a known Court sceptic, in a review for "*European Law Books*", wrote that the genre was more a *Festschrift* than a critical assessment, when in fact systematic and independent research was needed. Our book, Sverdrup inferred, did not provide such a critical analysis, however, it was useful as a basis for anyone who was willing to make such an analysis. The question arises as to whether the reviewer knew what a *Festschrift* actually is and whether he seriously imagined that the three editing judges were in a position to tell authors of the calibre of Vassilios Skouris, Marco Bronckers or Peter-Christian Müller-Graff, just to name a few, what they should write. Later, Ulf Sverdrup became the secretary of the Sejersted Committee which in 2012 published a report on Norway's relations with the EU,[8] and he surfaced again in the course of the Brexit/EEA debate in his capacity as the Director of a think tank called *Nupi* (Norwegian Institute of International Affairs). The think tank is partly funded by the Government and is therefore not really off the leash.[9]

Judicial Protection in the European Economic Area

In 2011, the Court held an international conference at the *Cercle Cité* on the issue of: "Judicial Protection in the European Economic Area". The goal was, in particular, to debate controversial issues concerning access to justice. The results of the conference proved to be crucial for what would follow in the years to come in our jurisprudence concerning ESA's handling of infringement proceedings and the

[7]See for details Chapter 25.

[8]See for details Chapter 24.

[9]See for details Chapter 31.

framework conditions of the preliminary ruling procedure.[10] The speeches and the discussions were published in a book.

The EEA and the EFTA Court—Decentered Integration
On 4 December 2014, a *Festschrift* was presented at a ceremony at the Court on the occasion of its twentieth anniversary. The keynote speaker was the Former Vice-President of the European Commission, Viviane Reding. The book entitled: "The EEA and the EFTA Court. Decentered Integration" was once again published by Hart. It contains 37 essays by prominent EU and EEA lawyers and three articles by Japanese and Swiss professors. The Court's judges were not among the authors. The book is divided into six parts: (I) The EFTA Court's Role in the Judicial Architecture of the EEA; (II) Decentred Integration; (III) General Principles and Fundamental Rights in EEA Law; (IV) EEA Business and Economic Law; (V) Actors in the EEA; and (VI) A Look from the Outside. Professor Allan F. Tatham from San Pablo University in Madrid wrote in his review in the Common Market Law Review:

> The *leitmotiv* threading its way through these various contributions is alluded to by both the EFTA Court President, Baudenbacher, and the former President of the EU Court of Justice (CJEU), Skouris, namely the mutual respect and great appreciation between both courts. This common viewpoint is in fact underlined and reinforced by the principle of homogeneity as required to be maintained under the EEA Agreement and as actively developed by the EFTA Court in its case law in tandem with that of the CJEU. The judges of the CJEU and its advocates general for their part have, in turn, likewise cited to EFTA Court cases in their own judicial work. As former President Skouris observes: "Cooperation between the two was built on strong foundations which have stood the test of time."

3.6 *Media*

Courts are generally not good at dealing with the media. One particular problem is that their press releases are often not written with the layperson in mind, but rather from a lawyer's perspective. The difficulty in stimulating media interest for certain legal topics is compounded by the fact that the media are often more interested in high profile criminal cases than in European or international economic law.

As regards the EFTA Court, newspapers in all three of our Member States have reported on major cases that concerned their respective country. However, in the early years, media coverage outside the EEA/EFTA States was rare. If people had heard of us, they tended to think that we led a shadow existence as some kind of auxiliary force under the auspices of the ECJ. Nevertheless, the majority of journalists didn't even know that there was a third court in Europe alongside the ECJ and the ECtHR. In such a situation, you cannot simply sit back and wait until a reporter calls. You must approach them proactively. That is what I did. I not only wanted to inform the press about our tasks and work, I also wanted to highlight our

[10] See for details Chapters 8 and 27.

special relationship with the ECJ. I already started to write essays and give newspaper, TV, and radio interviews when I was a junior judge.

In the Liechtenstein press, I regularly published articles and gave interviews on the Court's work. Liechtenstein citizens, whose government had nominated me, had to be aware of EEA law as it was happening. I was also frequently interviewed by Norwegian newspapers and I was quite often attacked in the Norwegian press. In Iceland, I spoke to journalists whenever I visited the country and made several appearances on national television. Occasionally, I also managed to place articles in Austrian and German newspapers. Last, I had a vested interest in wanting the Swiss public to be well-informed about the Court, not least because Swiss diplomats had made a contribution towards its establishment in the context of the EEA negotiations.

In the light of our limited case load after the downsizing, it was not easy to convince major newspapers outside our three Member States to write about our activities. In view of the EFTA Court's upcoming tenth anniversary, I approached the leading Swiss newspaper the "*Neue Zürcher Zeitung*" (*NZZ*), and offered them an interview. After some hesitation, they agreed and on 11 February 2004 a one-page article was published. The tone was friendly, but slightly patronising. The title, which in most newspapers is set by the editorial desk, was:

> *Stilles Arbeiten im Schatten des grossen Bruders.* (Quiet work in the shadow of the big brother.)

Citing the *Kellogg's* judgment, I emphasised that from time to time we were faced with important cases and underlined the cultural and geographic specificities of our three Member States. However, the article also highlighted our size, as if that had anything to do with quality, and speculated that the Court's future was uncertain. All in all, the text reflected the way the Swiss elites saw the EEA and the EFTA Court: namely, as a surprisingly well-run experiment, whose transitional nature was clear, even if its expiry date had not yet been fixed. And yet, it was a success that this article was published at all.

As is so often the case, publications came about due to a particular individual's efforts. An excellent economic journalist at the *NZZ* reviewed major EFTA Court cases. When he retired in 2009, the paper lost interest. The German flagship newspaper the "*Frankfurter Allgemeine Zeitung*" (*FAZ*) occasionally reported on one of our cases. For example, when the issue of a ban on the visual display of tobacco products was referred to us in *Philip Morris*, Reinhard Müller, the Head of *FAZ's* State and Law section, wrote about the case on 7 September 2011 and profiled me in an article entitled:

> *Zigaretten als Bückware?* (Cigarettes as under the counter goods?).[11]

For obvious reasons, we got worldwide press coverage when we rendered judgment in the first *Icesave* case on 28 January 2013. The general expectation had been that we would cave into pressure from the EU and hold Iceland liable for the inability of

[11]See concerning Philip Morris Chapter 15.

the deposit guarantee fund set up by its banks to compensate depositors. That the EFTA Court acquitted Iceland captured the headlines around the globe.[12] When the EEA Agreement turned 25 on 2 May 2017, I published two major articles, one in *FAZ* and one in *Bergens Tidende*.

Due to its unpopularity with important parts of the Norwegian Government and of Norwegian academia, the EFTA Court was sometimes exposed to violent attacks in the media. When I raised this issue with my colleagues, I was often told that this was the fate of a court such as ours and that the only way to respond was by continuing to render good judgments. This argument is only partly true. Assaults by the press reach countless people, whereas court rulings are predominantly read by specialists. If my colleagues didn't see the need to speak up, I felt that it was my duty as President to defend our institution. It is always difficult to act as a lawyer on your own behalf. Let me therefore cite what my former brother on the EFTA Court bench and now Chief Justice of Iceland, Thorgeir Örlygsson, said in his farewell speech in September 2011:

> Carl Baudenbacher has of course become almost an integral part of the EFTA Court, being the only judge to have served at the Court since Liechtenstein joined the EEA. In this time, his internal contribution at the Court, the arguments, analysis and comments, have proven invaluable, and will without doubt continue to do so. Furthermore, the significance of his external activities on behalf of the Court should also not be overlooked. As President, Judge Baudenbacher has been a tireless campaigner for the Court and the form of international co-operation embodied in the EEA Agreement. He has also been a fierce protector of the Court's independence, without which no Court can lay an earnest claim to credibility.

4 Personal Extrajudicial Activities

4.1 Building Networks with EU Protagonists

Once the Court moved to Luxembourg, I decided to become acquainted with as many ECJ judges, AGs, and GC (at that time CFI) judges as possible. I started, on the one hand, with the judges from the countries that had recently switched from the EFTA pillar to the EU pillar in 1995, i.e. Austria, Finland, and Sweden. On the other hand, I was able to establish good relations with the Italians. I had friendly contacts with the late Federico Mancini and the late Antonio La Pergola. Both magistrates served first as AGs and then as judges of the ECJ. One summer, Antonio La Pergola and I taught two classes at UT's School of Law, independently from each other. The late Antonio Saggio, first a judge and then President of the CFI and subsequently an AG of the ECJ, was a good friend. Italian was my first foreign language, which I had already learned as a child. My mother, an art and antiques dealer, was bilingual and taught Italian in a commercial school. She often spoke Italian with me and my brother, which proved invaluable in later life. In the early 1960s, my parents became friends with an Italian family in Fano on the

[12] See for details Chapter 25.

Adriatic Sea. I spent a number of summers with them and I still have fond memories of that time. In contrast with Switzerland, I was treated like a young adult, there was no curfew or any other kind of restriction. Arriving in Fano was like entering paradise. I shall never forget the Sundays when the whole family, including the grandparents, brothers and sisters, uncles and aunts, sat together and dined until late afternoon. The wine was delivered by a farmer in large wicker bottles. As a result, I have retained an abiding love for Italy and its elegance, food, history, culture, fashion and passion for life.

Among the AGs, I developed a particularly friendly relationship with Professor Paolo Mengozzi, whose right hand Vincent Kronenberger was a former ESA lawyer. Paolo accompanied me to Oslo in September 2005 and to Reykjavík in March 2006. In September 2010, he hosted a workshop on the role of the Advocate General at the European University Institute in Fiesole. Together with the ECJ President at that time, Vassilios Skouris, and most of the ECJ's AGs, I was invited to give a talk on the dialogue between the EFTA Court and the ECJ's AG's. The event was not only memorable because of its academic standard. It was followed by a trip across the Apennine mountains, where a gorgeous dinner was served in a medieval palace that is owned by Paolo and his wife Rosanna.

Other AGs who took special interest in the EFTA Court's case law, were Francis Jacobs, who has since received a knighthood, Miguel Poiares Maduro, Eleanor Sharpston, Nils Wahl and Juliane Kokott. Juliane has over the years become one of the EFTA Court's most important dialogue partners. I know her well because we had for some years been co-directors of the Institute of European and International Law at the HSG. My Head of Cabinet Philipp Speitler also developed a very good relationship with her lawyers.

There were also a number of judges and their spouses, with whom Doris and I managed to maintain excellent relations. I will limit myself to mentioning Gil Carlos and Teresa Rodriguez-Iglesias, Christiaan and Brunhilde Timmermans, Alan and Tula Rosas, Koen and Chris Lenaerts, Jean-Pierre and Eliane Puissochet, Melchior and Janine Wathelet, Leif Sevón, Vassilios and Vasou Skouris, Günter and Marta Hirsch, Peter and Elisabeth Jann, José Luís da Cruz Vilaça and his spouse Marie-Charlotte Opitz, Pernilla Lindh and Virpi Tilli, and many others.

After the EU enlargements in 2004 and 2007, our relationship with the EU judiciary changed a bit. Firstly, it was more difficult to maintain personal relations with such a high number of judges and AGs. Secondly, whereas protagonists from the old EU Member States knew about the role of EFTA in European integration und a number of them had been EFTA actors in their previous positions, this was not necessarily the case with the people from the new Member States. Sometimes I couldn't help feeling that in individual cases, some colleagues from the new Member States wanted to show us that despite EFTA's wealth they had now overtaken us because they were part of the more powerful EU, whereas we remained on the side-lines, so to speak. Truth be told, who could blame them for such thoughts given that influential players in our own Member States thought the same? Despite these difficulties, we were able to build up friendly relations with a number of people from the new Member States. I should mention Uno Lõhmus from Estonia, Alexander Arbadijev from Bulgaria, Verica Trstenjak from Slovenia, and the Cypriots George Arestis and Savvas Papasavvas and their spouses and partners. The Polish Judge of the GC, the late Irena Wiszniewska, became a close friend. The Czech AG Michael Bobek—a leading European law specialist—took an interest in our case law from the start of his mandate.

4.2 *Positioning the EFTA Court in Luxembourg*

Doris and I went to great lengths to introduce the EFTA Court to Luxembourgish politicians and judges as well as to the diplomatic corps and to the Luxembourgish civil society. As we all know, Luxembourg plays an important role in the EU and given their strong belief in political integration, it was far from self-evident that the Luxembourgers would take an interest in the EFTA Court. As regards the judiciary, I was able to establish regular contacts with the respective Presidents of the *Cour de Cassation* and of the Administrative Court of Luxembourg, the latter having its seat in the same building as the EFTA Court. The legendary President of the Court of Cassation, the late Marc Thill, and his wife Anne-Marie also became personal friends of ours. The same goes for the President of the Luxembourg Administrative Court Georges Ravarani and his wife Jacqueline.

4.3 *Social Life*

Doris and I regularly invited colleagues from the EU judiciary to our house and entertained them. We avoided closed gatherings, which would almost inevitably result in endless talking shop. Doris took great pains to group together guests from different backgrounds, including people from Luxembourgish public life, diplomacy, the business community and civil society. We also invited artists and theatre actors and occasionally people came from Brussels, Paris or nearby Germany. And we started to throw an annual summer night costume party. Each year, we had a different theme: safari, ocean, mountains, the 1920s, the 1950s, the Far West, to name just a few. The house and the garden were decorated accordingly. Once they are disguised, even the most inhibited people become more relaxed. The programme for these parties soon began to follow a pattern: we would start on a Saturday in mid-June at 6 p.m. with an aperitif that lasted an hour, then people were told to look for the partner with whom they should eat a St. Gallen bratwurst. In order to break up couples and to encourage our guests to make new acquaintances, we drafted lists of partners. After this, Doris gave a welcoming speech, the guests were then organised into groups and had to participate in three games: spitting cherry stones, throwing tennis balls at cans, and a quiz related to the theme of the evening. The highlight was the cherry stone spitting contest. After these games, two suckling piglets, which had been roasted on a spit, were served with potato salad and peas. Then the dancing started. We always engaged a five-member band from Nancy. At around 10 p.m. the results of the games were announced and the prizes awarded. Finally, the cheese and dessert buffet was opened. My personal assistant Kerstin Schwiesow was of invaluable help in the organisation, she always did a fabulous job. Our summer night parties were attended by people from the European and national judiciaries, lawyers in private practice, diplomats, European and national politicians, civil servants, entrepreneurs, academics and private friends. The guest came from far and wide: Brussels, Paris, Germany, Switzerland, Austria and Liechtenstein. The former Prime Minister of Liechtenstein Hans Brunhart once called the Baudenbacher summer night party "a small Congress of Vienna". The gatherings and summer night parties that Doris and I organised were not a one way street, very often the guests also invited us back.

Together with the French AG at that time, Philippe Léger, and his wife Ghislaine, Doris and I took the initiative to set up weekend trips with ECJ and GC members to Paris, Alsace, the Champagne, and Berlin. A journey to Belgium was organised by the Belgian ECJ judge Melchior Wathelet and his wife Janine. There was always a cultural and a culinary part, however the most important thing was that we got to know and understand each other well. At the same time, all my legal secretaries developed excellent relationships with their colleagues from the ECJ.

The EU people Doris and I have encountered throughout my career have always been very friendly, most of them have also shown interest in the EFTA Court's work and quite a number were inclined to become our friends. In all of our social contacts the most important thing was that we were able to develop private relationships. Occasionally, Doris and I were even invited to family celebrations. Vice versa, we invited colleagues and their partners from the EU judiciary to our house in Vals in the Graubunden mountains.

At a private dinner, I got to know Sven Norberg, the most important founding father of the EEA and the former Swedish judge on the EFTA Court. We realised that we were thinking along similar lines with regard to the Court and immediately became friends. Following Sweden's accession to the EU, Sven became a Director in DG Competition of the European Commission. To be sure, with his broad knowledge of European law in the widest sense of the word and his experience, he would also have been an excellent judge either on the ECJ or the GC. In Brussels, Sven became an honorary member of the Commission Legal Service's swim team. Through him, I got to know most of the senior members of the Legal Service who were in charge of preparing and pleading the cases before the courts in Luxembourg. Once a year, John Forman, who represented the Commission in a number of cases before the EFTA Court, invited his colleagues to a weekend at his summer house by the Dutch Sea. Doris and I were included more than once and we always had a great time swimming, sailing and biking. Later Sven and I would ski together in the Carinthian alps, swim in Lake Wörth and hike in Vals. Sven gave numerous speeches at HSG conferences and was for many years the head of the Board of the St. Gallen International Competition Law Forum (ICF). He has given me good advice in difficult situations and has put me in contact with important people in Brussels as well as in the current and former EFTA States.

4.4 Teaching

After my election as President, I stopped teaching at UT's School of Law. While, in view of the limited case load, I could have easily managed carrying on with the teaching at UT, I felt that I shouldn't be that far away from the Court for a lengthy period of time. I continued to teach at HSG and in 2009 and 2010 I was a visiting professor at the University of Iceland.

4.5 Speaking

I was active as a speaker on general EEA law in the period between 1990 and 1994, when I was an advisor to the Liechtenstein Government. After being appointed to the EFTA Court bench, I started to focus on the structure and tasks of the Court, on its case law and its relationship with the EU courts. Since the case load was low for a number of years, I had, despite my teaching obligations at HSG and UT, plenty of time. After my election as President, I started to increase my speaking activities. Over the years, I gave talks on the Court and its work at countless universities; the most important ones were probably: Basel, Berne, Bonn, Bucerius, Cambridge, City University London, Cologne, Fudan, Harvard, King's College London, Kyoto, Queen Mary London, Lomonosov, Oxford, Princeton, Texas, Tokyo, University College London (UCL), Pontifical Catholic University of Peru, Universidad Nacional Autónoma de México (UNAM) in Mexico City, Vienna, Waseda and Zurich.

In 2002, 2003, and 2004, I chaired three conferences at the UT, which were held in cooperation with the Texas International Law Journal (TILJ). TILJ is a student-run law journal, as is typical in the US. A team from TILJ that was responsible for the logistics. The conferences were broadly on the topic of "Globalization and the Judiciary" and took place in September each year in the UT School of Law's amazing Eidman Courtroom. Speakers were, *inter alia*, European luminaries such as, for example, ECJ AG Francis Jacobs, the President of the ECtHR Jean-Paul Costa, German Supreme Court Judge and Chamber President Joachim Bornkamm or former WTO AB Chairman Claus-Dieter Ehlermann. In 2003, James Bacchus who had succeeded Claus-Dieter Ehlermann as the Chair of the WTO AB, gave a memorable speech with the title "Lone Star: The Historic Role of the WTO". Texas is often referred to as the "Lone Star State". This is an allusion to the fact that from 1836 to 1846, it was an independent State. The five-pointed lone star can still be found on the Texas flag. Prominent members of the UT School of Law and from other American top universities presented the American approach. Texas Chief Justice Thomas R. Phillips was among the speakers. However, we were also able to invite people from Canada and from Latin America. For each of the conferences an official dinner for speakers and participants was held in the Maximilian Room of the Driskill Hotel on 6th street in Downtown Austin, which is a historic site in Texas. The Maximilian Room is famous because there are eight massive gold leaf mirrors that were made in France for the Mexican Emperor Maximilian, the younger brother of the Austrian Emperor Franz Joseph. They were meant to be a wedding gift from Maximilian to his bride, the Belgian Princess Carlota. However, the mirrors never reached Mexico. In 1867 the Emperor was executed by firing squad and the wedding gift ended up in the Driskill Hotel. The Driskill is also the place where the Travis County Democrats gather on election nights. Austin is the seat of Travis County (and the Capital of Texas). The Congressman Lyndon Baines Johnson and Lady Bird Claudia Alta Taylor had their first date at the Driskill Hotel in 1934 and in 1964, President Johnson watched TV there as elections returns came in on election night. In recent decades the Texas Democrats have had little opportunity to celebrate. However, when Barack Obama was elected as the 56th US President on 4 November 2008, Doris and I were in Austin and attended the party at the Driskill.

A fourth conference entitled: "The Role of International Courts" was held in 2007 in cooperation with my friend Erhard Busek, the Former Vice-Chancellor of Austria, in Salzburg. The list of speakers reads like a who's who of international justice. I will just mention Judge Allan Rosas and AG Miguel Poiares Maduro from the ECJ, the President of the ECtHR, Jean-Paul Costa, as well as the Chairman of the WTO AB, Giorgio Sacerdoti, and the American WTO Appellate Body Member Merit E. Janow. The WTO AB is from a functional perspective a world trade court. For political reasons, the judges are, however, referred to as "members" and the President as a "chairperson." The US Government always had difficulties in accepting the independence of these actors. WTO AB members are appointed by the Dispute Settlement Body, the assembly comprising all the WTO governments, for a term of four years. They may be reappointed once. Merit E. Janow only served one term on the WTO AB, from 2003 to 2007, before returning to academia. The official version was that she did not seek a second term. However, insiders suspected that her government had put pressure on her to leave. That the US Government prefers to have a representative on the WTO AB who can be kept on a leash became clear when the reappointment of Merit's successor, Jennifer Hillmann, was blocked by her own government in 2011. No reasons were given, but it was obvious that the US was displeased with Hillmann's actions on the WTO AB. It was a blatant attack on her judicial independence. It should be noted in this context that according to the written law, WTO AB members must be of recognised authority with demonstrated expertise in law, international trade and the subject matter of the covered agreements generally. In addition, they must be "unaffiliated with any government". The sacking of Jennifer Hillmann was the start of an unprecedented crusade against the WTO AB. In 2013–2014, the appointment of James Gathii was blocked. In 2016, the US impeded the reappointment of the South Korean WTO AB member Seung Wha Chang. It was the first time that the prolongation of a non-US citizen was hindered.

Three other gatherings took place in St. Gallen on the subjects of "Dispute Resolution", "Dialogue Between Courts in Times of Globalization and Regionalization", and "The role of Precedent". All these events are documented in special editions of the Texas International Law Journal and in books.

The conferences served, *inter alia*, the purpose of making the EFTA Court known among international judges, practitioners and academics. In the Winter Semester 2005/2006, I taught a class at HSG together with the former EU Commissioner and future Prime Minister of Italy Mario Monti on "Decision-Making in European Institutions." Whereas Mario focused on the political branches, I spoke about the European judiciary.

As I have said before, I also chaired an annual European symposium together with the former Liechtenstein Prime Minister Hans Brunhart for nine years.[13] Many foreign decision-makers from politics, associations, business and the judiciary came to Liechtenstein, and the Liechtenstein intelligentsia was usually strongly represented. The symposium was always attended by the Head of State, HSH Prince Hans Adam II, who received the speakers and their partners afterwards at the Castle of Vaduz. After his son, HSH Hereditary Prince Alois had become Acting Head of State, he gave us the honour. Another important annual event was the Vienna Globalisation Symposium which I chaired for nine years together with Erhard Busek.

As awareness of the Court grew, I was invited to speak at all sorts of conferences, for example in Brussels, Berlin, Paris, Vienna, Moscow, Shanghai and Tokyo. Following the Court's judgment in the first *Icesave* case, I was asked to join P.R.I.M.E Finance, an institutionalised panel of 130 legal and financial experts. I have been a speaker at their annual conference ever since. Obviously, my position at St. Gallen also played a role in all this.

I advised the Governments of Israel, Switzerland and Austria. Moreover, I actively participated in the United Nations Conference on Trade and Development (UNCTAD) programme for the creation of aid laws in third countries in Geneva, and in the Organisation for Economic Co-operation and Development (OECD) programme for training Asian judges in Seoul. During the Brexit debate in the UK, I was invited to give evidence before the competent committees of both the House of Lords and the House of Commons in Westminster.[14] In none of these cases did a conflict of interest ever arise with my EFTA Court role.

Lastly, I encouraged my legal secretaries to give speeches. Generally speaking, my policy was that those who attended conferences had to show the Court's flag. I didn't approve of what I called "judges' and legal secretaries' conference tourism".

4.6 The International Competition Law Forum (ICF) in Particular

The St. Gallen ICF is an annual event which I founded in 1994. At that time, Switzerland was about to enact a new Cartel Act, which was largely modelled on European competition law, and on 1 January 1994 the EEA Agreement entered into

[13]See for details Chapter 2.

[14]See for details Chapter 31.

force. Since my days as a university assistant competition law has been one of my favourite subjects. I have dealt with competition law issues in the framework of arbitration proceedings and advised the Swiss Parliament and the Government on such questions. The EFTA Court rarely had competition law cases in the early years. However, from 2012 onwards, we had the opportunity of addressing a number of crucial competition law issues.

The two-day ICF has become one of the most important competition law, policy and economics conferences in Europe and beyond. As I said, the Advisory Board was for many years headed by the father of the EA Agreement Sven Norberg. In 2010, Dr. Romina Polley, one of the leading competitition law practicioners in Europe, succeeded Sven. At the ICF, around 200 participants gather in the historic Parliament Hall of the Canton of St. Gallen. The faculty usually consists of the EU Commissioner for Competition or of the Director-General Competition, other EU officials, Presidents of national competition authorities as well as judges and AGs from the EU judiciary and judges from national Supreme Courts, attorneys, in-house counsel and academics. Over the years, we have also welcomed prominent speakers from the US, China and other non-European destinations. EU Competition Commissioners Mario Monti, Neelie Kroes and Joaquín Almunia, US Federal Trade Commissioners Tom Rosch and Bill Kovacic, CFI President Bo Vesterdorf and ECJ AG Nils Wahl have been regular speakers. The EFTA Court has profited from the ICF in two ways: on the one hand, my legal secretaries and my humble self were always made aware of the newest developments in European and international competition law. Obviously, this also applied to related matters such as IP law and economics in general. On the other hand, senior EU officials, including Commissioners, became aware of the EFTA Court. In addition, a number of top speakers who had given presentations at the ICF would later accept invitations to talk at the Court's anniversaries, at the Annual Spring Conference or on other occasions. I was able to build up a large network and was invited to speak at competition law events around the world. To give just a few examples, I became a regular speaker at the German Federal Cartel Office's ("*Bundeskartellamt's*") bi-annual Berlin Conference on competition, I was invited to deliver lectures at the Fordham Antitrust Conference in New York, at the British Competition Commission and at other gatherings of competition lawyers in London and at conferences in Brussels, Paris, Moscow and Bratislava, to name just a few. I also gave many presentations at universities and gatherings of attorneys and in-house lawyers. And I actively participated in IP and energy law conferences.

4.7 Publishing

In December 2012, Susan Bartie and John Gava, two lecturers of the Law Schools of Tasmania and Adelaide, published a frontal attack on judges' extrajudicial writings in an article entitled "live legal issues" in the Sydney Law Review. They claimed that the practice threatens the integrity of the judiciary because it amounts to a prejudging of potential legal questions, and acts as a signal to potential litigants. The solution the authors offered to resolve the problems identified was judicial silence. The disapproval of the two Australians obviously also relates to extrajudicial speaking. It seems to me, however, that their criticism is grossly overstated. That judges speak and write corresponds to a great tradition in the European courts in Luxembourg and in Strasbourg as well as in the respective Member States. There are obviously certain dos and don'ts. For example, in the EEA system, as in the EU system, you are not supposed to dissent from a judgment in which you were overruled. In addition, judges must be careful not to give guidance to any prospective parties. Judges who write, as well as judges who speak publicly, will necessarily reveal something about the way they think. Practising lawyers will read, and listen, and try to draw conclusions as regards the judges' leanings. If a judge is too outspoken, this can result in him or her having to step down from a case. Nevertheless, as a matter of principle, I think that it is not only permitted, but necessary for modern judges to speak and write. The EFTA Court's 20-year Commemorative Book bears witness to this. The same applies to the official publications of our EU sister courts. It is, at the end of the day, all a matter of how you do it. In these times of widespread social media, high court judges have also become public figures in Europe. Unwritten rules according to which judges are allegedly not supposed to take a position on certain issues don't count anymore. Wise sayings along the lines of "a judge should not stick his neck out too far" have no merit. Judges, just like other citizens, enjoy freedom of speech. The only limits to this freedom are actual or potential conflicts of interest. I was prompted to clarify this in the context of my Brexit activities.[15]

In view of the limited case load in the early years, I continued to publish as I had prior to being appointed to the EFTA Court bench. However, I focussed more on the EEA in general and on the Court in particular. I intensified my publication activities not only on the Court, but on the role of international/supranational courts in general. Judicialisation of law and politics became one of my fields of research. I also wrote countless contributions on substantive European and international law in European and American law journals.

Besides publishing essays and newspaper articles, I contributed to *Festschrift*s on the occasion of anniversaries and to *libri amicorum* of prominent ECJ, GC and ECtHR judges, senior EU officials, but also of outstanding scholars and practitioners in EU and EFTA Member States. In a number of cases, I was a member of the editing board. I also contributed to publications of the ECJ and other international courts. In May 2010 I brought out a booklet entitled: "The EFTA Court in Action: Five lectures". It was based on five classes I had taught at the University of Iceland in the autumn of 2009.[16] In his review in European Voice, the Brussels correspondent of Reuters, David Lawsky wrote:

---

[15]See for details Chapter 31.

[16]See for details Chapter 7.

> 'As a small dog you must bark louder than a big dog', declares Carl Baudenbacher, President of the Court of the European Free Trade Association (EFTA), which has jurisdiction over 1% of the European Economic Area. And bark it does, loud enough to attract notice from the European Court of Justice (ECJ) with jurisdiction over the other 99%.

On the occasion of the twentieth anniversary of the signature of the EEA Agreement, I created an event entitled

> 20 Years Signature of the EEA Agreement – A Play in Four Acts with Original Performers (*20 Jahre Unterzeichnung des EWR-Abkommens – Ein Vierakter mit Original-Darstellern*).

On 2 May 2012, former politicians, negotiators, advisors and other actors spoke at a well-attended celebration in the Hotel Löwen in Vaduz. The Löwen was the place where my EEA journey had begun.[17] The four acts bore the titles: "The EEA project kicks off", "The first version of the EEA", "The second version of the EEA", "20 years later". The Liechtenstein Head of Government Klaus Tschütscher and I published a booklet with the contributions.

In late 2015, I edited "The Handbook of EEA Law," an 859-page volume. It aimed to provide the reader with a thorough grounding in the EEA Agreement, by describing how secondary EU law is generated and becomes applicable in the EFTA pillar, as well as the roles played by the ESA and the EFTA Court. Furthermore, the Handbook considers the EEA Agreement from the respective perspectives of the national authorities, the courts, and the legal professions of Iceland, Liechtenstein and Norway. It meticulously examines substantive EEA law, beginning with the general principles and the four freedoms, through competition law and State aid law to fields such as the law of natural resources, social policy, IP law, tax law etc. Emphasis is placed on jurisprudence, in particular that of the EFTA Court. Each Chapter was written by a judge, noted practitioner or eminent academic in their respective fields. I contributed with one Chapter on the structure and tasks of the EFTA Court and with another one on our relationship with the ECJ. On 15 December 2015, the Handbook was launched at an event hosted by the EFTA Secretariat in Brussels. Around one hundred guests attended, including representatives of the leadership of the three EFTA institutions, and listened to speeches from Dag W. Holter, Deputy Secretary-General of EFTA, Sven Erik Svedman, President of the ESA, Ian Forrester, Judge of the GC, Anke Seyfried of Springer, the Handbook's publisher, and by my humble self. The evening continued with a reception catered by Léa Linster, Luxembourg's Food Ambassador. Léa, an old friend who is also a TV star, addressed the crowd before she opened the buffet.

In 2017, I edited another book entitled "Fundamental principles of EEA law. EEA ities." It comprises eleven contributions written by EFTA Court and national judges, senior EFTA officials, private practitioners and scholars on the following maxims: legislative and judicial homogeneity, reciprocity, prosperity, priority, authority, loyalty, proportionality, equality, liability and sovereignty. I contributed

[17] See for details Chapter 2.

the Chapters on reciprocity and on proportionality, the latter together with my legal secretary Theresa Haas. The volume was presented to the public on 13 December 2017 in Brussels. ESA President Svedman, who had written a contribution on "prosperity", had graciously agreed to host the event on ESA's premises. Speeches were given by Sven Svedman, Dag W. Holter, former General Court Judge Sir Nicholas Forwood, QC, and by my humble self. To my surprise, Kjetil Wiedswang, the star journalist who had followed our landmark cases concerning essential elements of the Norwegian social model from a rather patriotic perspective and bestowed on me the title "Kong Carl of the EEA", was also present.[18] I was pleased about that.

It would be an exaggeration to claim that by editing and publishing standard works of this type, I was aiming to gain any kind of "communicative supremacy" in the EEA debate. At the same time, I felt that by editing and contributing to these books, I was able to set a counterpoint to the rather one-sided anti-EEA publications of certain academics.

It goes without saying that I also encouraged my legal secretaries to publish. Unlike our big sister court, we don't have an imprimatur system at the EFTA Court. Our people don't need to submit their articles and books to the President or to the Court and seek approval. They are free to express their views on anything. If a legal secretary substantially contributed to one of my own works, I offered him/her co-authorship.

4.8 Media

In two instances, I became, in my personal capacity, active beyond the EFTA pillar. In 2013, the Swiss Government decided to adopt the rather odd idea of using the ECJ, the court of the other side, as a tie-breaker should a conflict arise under the bilateral agreements Switzerland-EU. In order to exclude an EFTA Court model, the Minister for Foreign Affairs and his Secretary of State started a real crusade against us and spread all sorts of untrue assertions. I could not accept such behaviour. Since no politician from an EEA/EFTA State dared to speak up, I felt that it was my duty to take matters in hand.[19] The same happened when Norwegian politicians out of fear of losing their superpower position in the EFTA pillar went on a pilgrimage to the UK in the Brexit context and badmouthed the EEA.[20] My statements concerning the situations of Switzerland and of Britain were widely reported in both the Swiss and British media.

---

[18]See for details Chapter 23.

[19]See for details Chapter 30.

[20]See for details Chapter 31.

Chapter 14
The Economics of EEA Single Market Law

Contents

1 The EEA Agreement Has Created a Market

According to the third recital of the EEA Agreement's preamble, the Contracting Parties are:

> DETERMINED to contribute, on the basis of market economy, to world-wide trade liberalization and cooperation, in particular in accordance with the provisions of the General Agreement on Tariffs and Trade and the Convention on the Organisation for Economic Cooperation and Development.

In a market economy, economic decisions are, as a matter of principle, made by free enterprises competing with each other. The production of goods and services is directed by the laws of supply and demand. Competition has been defined as the rivalry among sellers trying to get what other sellers are seeking at the same time, which leads to increasing sales volume, market share and profit by offering the best combination of price, quality, and service. The clearest manifestations of the EEA Agreement's market orientation are the fundamental freedoms, the competition rules and the State aid provisions. However, a large part of secondary economic law must also be mentioned here. The EFTA Court has never cited the third recital in the preamble to the EEA Agreement in its case law. However, is has taken market orientation into account. In individual cases, the EFTA Court was prompted to stick to EFTA values. Generally speaking, the Court has been reluctant to favour neo-mercantilist policies which aim at restricting trade and protecting domestic industries.

C. Baudenbacher, *Judicial Independence*, Springer Biographies,
https://doi.org/10.1007/978-3-030-02308-9_14

2 Competition Economics

Similar to every market economy, the EEA system rests on certain theoretical assumptions. They have primarily been discussed in the context of competition law. Some competition economists tend to act as if their science were an objective discipline. It is, however, a well-known fact that there are different schools of thought. In the 1970s and 1980s, these schools were in open conflict. With the advent of the Chicago School and its triumph against what Chicago protagonists called the Harvard School, the doctrinal dispute in the US reached its peak. Harvard for its part was a reaction to the model of perfect competition. It was influenced by John Maurice's Clark's theory of workable competition. This doctrine was based on the so-called structure–conduct–performance ("S-C-P") paradigm. There was the assumption that structure influences conduct—the lower the concentration of firms, the more competitive the behaviour of the firms; the smaller the number of firms, the more likely it is that they will behave in a collusive way—and that conduct leads to good performance such as low prices and innovation. Accordingly, the Harvard School recommended an active competition policy aimed at guaranteeing the presence of a sufficient number of actors on each market. This included the protection of small and medium-sized enterprises (SMEs), in particular of dealers. As regards vertical restraints, the focus was on intra-brand competition, i.e. competition among the distributors of the same branded good. Important protagonists were Edward S. Mason, Joe S. Bain, and Philip E. Areeda.

The Chicago School was suspicious and critical of government intervention in the economy. The only legitimate goal of antitrust rules was said to be efficiency; business efficiencies due to cost reduction were deemed to lead almost automatically to economic efficiencies such as higher growth. This would benefit consumer welfare. In the view of the Chicago School, the intensity of competition did not depend on the number of market actors. Even the presence of a monopoly did not hinder competition if it was not of unlimited duration. The profits of the monopoly would attract competitors in the medium and long term. In the field of vertical restraints, the focus was on inter-brand competition, i.e. competition among manufacturers selling different brands of the same product. Prominent protagonists of the Chicago School were Robert Bork, Richard A. Posner and Frank H. Easterbrook. The Chicago School had commonalities with the theory of Contestable Markets. This approach, which was represented in particular by William J. Baumol, John C. Panzar and Robert D. Wilig, suggests that it is not the internal structure of a market that is decisive. Even if there is only one market actor, he may be forced to act as if there were many more. The threat of potential entry may be enough to keep the industry operating at or close to the competitive price and output. If this is the case, the market is a contestable market. The focus is therefore on barriers to entry.

In Europe, the pendulum did not swing as far as in the US, but there were also competing schools of thought. The theory of workable competition was adapted to European (in particular German) needs by Erhard Kantzenbach who adhered to the S-C-P paradigm. Kantzenbach's approach was an answer to the failure of ordoliberalism to achieve "complete competition" ("*vollständiger Wettbewerb*"). The concept of complete competition as defined by Walter Eucken, the head of the ordoliberal school, must be distinguished from the model of perfect competition. In Kantzenbach's view, the ideal market form, which would create optimal competition intensity, was a wide oligopoly with limited product homogeneity and limited transparency. Friedrich August von Hayek and Erich Hoppmann promoted the idea of a spontaneous economic order and von Hayek famously defined competition as "a discovery procedure". What he meant was that since we cannot know what the results of the competitive process will be, we should exercise the utmost caution in interfering with it. Von Hayek's main concern was not efficiency, but freedom. Even if he cannot be called a representative of *laissez-faire* or of the Chicago School, he shared the latter's long-term orientation.

Simplifying the positions, one can say that one side tended to trust in market forces, warned against short-term interventions, saw the State as the worst distorter of competition, and relied on long-term development. The other side emphasised the need to secure competitive market structures because they would lead to good results, and was prepared to intervene more easily. The most famous criticism of long-term orientation stems from John Maynard Keynes who wrote in his Tract on Monetary Reform that

> [i]n the long run we are all dead.

Finally, it should be borne in mind that unlike US antitrust law, European competition law has traditionally been characterised by a two-goal approach: it not only aims to protect competition, but also to complete the EU and EEA Single Market.

After the sharp controversies of the 1970s and 1980s, Post-Chicago and New Harvard, as well as their slightly different European branches, seemed to converge. University of Oxford economist Simon Wren Lewis wrote in 2012 that in the 1990s, macroeconomics

> appeared to become much more unified. It would be going much too far to suggest that there was a general consensus, but to use a tired cliché, most macroeconomists started talking the same language, even if they were not saying the same thing.

The launch of the so-called "more economic approach" by the European Commission around the turn of the millennium may be seen against this background. However, differences remained, in particular in the fields of vertical restraints, abuse of dominance and merger control.

The Swiss Federal Council's Dispatch for the 1995 Cartel Act contains a good summary of the state of the debate at the time. It explains that modern competition theory agrees that horizontal restrictions with regard to prices, quotas and territories are almost always detrimental. Furthermore, it is no longer in doubt that open markets are the best guarantors of the functioning of the competitive process. In the interests of legal certainty, competition policy should, as far as possible, be based on per se rules. However, in the field of abuse of a dominant position and of merger control, the individual cases will have to be assessed. Competition theory also agrees that certain vertical agreements and exclusionary practices only impair competition if dominant firms are involved. This description has retained an astonishing topicality. Nevertheless, it appears that after the financial and economic crisis of 2007–2008, the discipline has to a certain extent become split again.

Economic findings play an important role in evidence law. For example, in its contribution to the OECD's Global Forum on Competition in December 2017, the US stated that the application of US competition law, apart from cartel cases, usually involves some form of economic analysis. Important elements are typically the delimitation of a relevant market and the question of whether the suspect behaviour has or will have anti-competitive effects. Economic analyses of various kinds are important in order to ensure a meaningful and convincing market definition or competitive impact assessment. On the same occasion, the EU too stressed that economic evidence and assessments play an increasingly important role both in the Commission's enforcement of competition law and in the review by the European courts. In substance, the understanding of the functioning of the relevant markets, the competitive interactions in these markets and the assessment of the likely consequences of the practices studied are all involved.

3 State Aid Economics

State aid is a special form of state intervention in the market economy. It consists of the transfer of state resources to certain beneficiaries. Since the actors are the Member States, State aid control is not only about competition, but about a whole range of goals. That is why it is said that a distinct perspective is needed when it comes to economic analysis. State aid control is a specific characteristic of European competition policy. The former Chairman of the German Monopolies Commission, Justus Haucap, has aptly summarised that the control

> relates to possible distortions of competition through state subsidies to private or public companies that are in active or potential competition with other companies.

There is a general ban of State aid both in EU and in EEA law, but there are broad exceptions to the rule. Under certain conditions, State aid is lawful.

In State aid law, economic analysis is much younger than in business competition law and since State aid control is a European thing, significant input from other parts of the world is rare. Economic analysis basically dates back to the launch of the European Commission's "State Aid Action Plan (SAAP)", which was published in November 2005. The main goal of the reform was the application of a "more economic approach". This motion was greeted with considerable scepticism from traditional lawyers. In reality, economic considerations had underlain the essential principles of State aid law for a long time even though the necessary tools had not been available. A good example is the "market economy investor principle", according to which an investment is not State aid if a public authority invests in an enterprise on terms and under conditions that would be acceptable to a private investor operating under normal market economy conditions. The maxim laid down in *Philip Morris* v *Commission*, namely that compatible aid is not a gratuitous advantage and that there must be a "*quid pro quo*" between the State and the recipient, also predates the SAAP. Such findings invited the use of economic analysis. The same applies, for example, to the treatment of public infrastructure investments, privatisations and risk finance, but also to the concept of selectivity. The selective nature distinguishes aid from general economic support. Finally, it should be noted that in the *Altmark* judgment of 24 July 2003, the ECJ held that that financial support that merely represents compensation for public service obligations imposed by the Member States is not State aid. Following this judgment, the question was discussed of whether the funding of economic inefficiency would constitute aid. This too would call for economic analysis.

4 Economics Beyond the Realm of Competition Law

4.1 General

Many lawyers think that an economic approach to law is limited to competition law (and lately to State aid law). This is erroneous. The very concept of a Single Market is based on liberal economics. As for all economic law, EEA Single Market law is centred on the relationship between economic freedom and regulation.

Especially in the US, but in Europe too, economic theory has in fact also been applied to the analysis of legal problems beyond the realm of competition law, in particular in the law concerning the regulation of sectors of industry, in tort law, property law, contract law, corporate law, IP law and insurance law. This school of thought is referred to as "law and economics" or "economic analysis of law". The starting point for the modern theory is usually seen in two ground breaking articles published independently from each other by Ronald Coase and Guido Calabresi in 1960 and 1961: "The Problem of Social Cost" and "Some Thoughts on Risk Distribution and the Law of Torts". Coase and Calabresi have been called the two intellectual heroes of the law and economics movement. Coase received the Nobel Prize in Economic Sciences in 1991. Calabresi later became a judge of the US Court of Appeals for the Second Circuit. In the US, the economic analysis of law has had an impact not only on legal scholarship, but also on judicial decision-making.

Guido Calabresi was concerned with private law, in particular tort law. Whereas traditional tort lawyers assumed that compensation is the main objective of liability rules, Calabresi saw the minimisation of the costs of accidents as the main goal. These costs must, according to him, be divided into three categories: primary costs that are determined by the number and severity of accidents; secondary costs that arise if optimal risk diversification is not given; and tertiary costs, i.e. the costs incurred by the legal system to establish and enforce liability. Under this approach, both efficiency concerns and concerns of equity or justice (Calabresi speaks of "fairness") are taken into account. I emphasise this because representatives of the law and economics movement have always been suspected of one-sidedly focussing on efficiencies. As an aside, I would remind readers that the man who is considered the father of classical free market economics, Adam Smith, has written two seminal books: prior to publishing "An Inquiry into the Nature and Causes of the Wealth of Nations" in 1776, he brought out a book entitled "The Theory of Moral Sentiments" in 1759.

In tort law, efficiency is increased by preventing harmful activities and thus reducing the primary costs of accidents. Justice finds its place in assessing the goal of reducing secondary costs, which leads to optimal risk diversification. In order to reduce primary and tertiary costs, Calabresi developed the concept of the "cheapest cost avoider". Under this approach, the actor who is best placed to carry out the cost-benefit analysis between accident costs and accident avoidance costs and to take preventive action if the accident costs are cheaper than the avoided costs should bear the responsibility.

In 2003, German economic law professors Hein Kötz and Hans-Bernd Schäfer published a book entitled "*Judex oeconomicus*". It contains an economic analysis of twelve landmark judgments of the highest civil courts in Germany, eleven by the Federal Supreme Court and one—the famous *Benrath Petrol Station* predatory pricing case from 1931—by the Imperial Court. Benrath Petrol Station has been analysed by an old friend of mine, Professor Peter Behrens. According to the authors, modern economics is to be understood as a science that asks how individuals behave in decision-making situations. They concede that judicial decisions are often based on estimation, approximation and intuition or common sense. There is no absolute need, they claim, to carry out a sophisticated cost-benefit analysis in every case. However, those who rely on notions such as reasonableness, appropriateness or practicality often overlook the fact that in reality, their judgment has been guided by an inner economic logic to which it owes its persuasiveness. And yet, Kötz and Schäfer convincingly argue that a judgment gains in rationality and transparency and can more easily be criticised if it is not simply asserted that the final result is in accordance with the principle of good faith or that it is reasonable or practical. What is more important is that the outcome is based on an examination that seeks to demonstrate in concrete and comprehensible steps why the proposed solution is efficient, that is to say why it makes people use scarce resources in an economical way.

4.2 Relevance for the EFTA Court

As I have indicated at the start of this Chapter, the EFTA Court has expressly addressed the fact that the EEA Agreement has created a market in its jurisprudence beyond the realm of competition law. An example is the transfer of undertakings case *Enes Deveci* v *SAS*. The defendant before the national court claimed that the

Transfer of Undertakings Directive[1] was to be interpreted in accordance with Article 16 of the EU Charter of Fundamental Rights. This provision recognises the "freedom to conduct a business in accordance with Union law and national laws and practices". The Charter has not been made part of EEA law by the EEA/EFTA governments.[2] The Court held that

> [t]he EEA Agreement has linked the markets of the EEA/EFTA States to the single market of the European Union. The actors of a market are, inter alia, undertakings. The freedom to conduct a business lies therefore at the heart of the EEA Agreement and must be recognised in accordance with EEA law and national law and practices.

As a result of a number of factors, the EFTA Court's case law is overall quite fragmentary. Nevertheless, a number of rulings were rendered in which economic reasoning has played a role. A one-sided utilitarian approach that is only based on efficiency considerations has thereby been avoided. Both efficiency and equity, respectively justice, are objectives that are being pursued.

The principle of liability has been instrumental in two of the Court's landmark judgments, *Icesave I* and *Fosen-Linjen.* Walter Eucken, the leading figure of the German ordoliberal school, has dealt with this maxim in his ground-breaking book on principles of economic policy ("*Grundsätze der Wirtschaftspolitik*"), which was published in 1952, two years after his death. According to Eucken, the fundamental principle of a competition economy is a workable price system. That means that measures such as state subsidies, the establishment of compulsory state monopolies, general price cuts, import bans, and the like are to be avoided. In addition, Eucken called for an active competition policy that aimed to establish a market form that is as close as possible to the ideal type of complete competition. These claims must obviously be seen against the background of German economic policy of the time, but they are of general significance. Further constitutive and regulatory principles of a competition economy are, in Eucken's view, open markets, private property, freedom of contract, the principle of liability and the consistency of economic policy. Eucken attaches great importance to the principle of liability. Only market players who can also be held liable for their actions will act responsibly.

The question of where the line must be drawn between collective bargaining and industrial action, on the one hand, and competition or fundamental freedoms, on the other hand, has played a role in two landmark judgments, *LO* and *Holship*.

Moreover, the principles of freedom of contract and sanctity of contract have become relevant in the EFTA Court's case law (*Beatrix Koch*; *Vienna Life* and *Swiss Life*; *Engilbertsson*; *Sævar Jón Gunnarsson*; *Matja Kumba*). From an economic perspective, contracts are tools that promote the most efficient allocation of resources. Freedom of contract is essential to the operation of a market economy. Sanctity of contract means that an agreement that has duly been entered into is binding on the parties unless there is an exception recognised by law. The parties must honour their obligations by performing their contractual duties.

---

[1] 2001/23/EC.

[2] See for details Chapter 12.

Another important case in which economic considerations played a decisive role concerned the question of whether a work of art that had fallen into the public domain due to the expiry of copyright could be re-monopolised through trade mark registration (*Vigeland*).

Chapter 15
Fundamental Freedoms and the Cursed Proportionality Test

Contents

1 Are All Four Freedoms Indispensable?

The four fundamental freedoms—free movement of goods, persons, services and capital—have been taken over into the EEA Agreement from what is now the Treaty on the Functioning of the European Union (TFEU). Standard legal literature usually asserts that the implementation of these economic freedoms is indispensable to the realisation of a Single Market and that without them, such a market cannot function. In fact, Article 26(2) TFEU states that the internal market (a synonym for Single Market)

> shall comprise an area without internal frontiers in which the free movement of goods, persons, services and capital is ensured in accordance with the provisions of the Treaties.

In 2015, Pedro Caro de Sousa wrote on page 83 of his doctoral thesis that there is an ongoing debate in academic literature on whether all four fundamental freedoms

C. Baudenbacher, *Judicial Independence*, Springer Biographies,
https://doi.org/10.1007/978-3-030-02308-9_15

should be treated equally or whether a specific approach was appropriate for certain of them. He concluded that, in fact, free movement of people and European citizenship deserved a differentiated treatment. De Sousa stated:

> Underlying this trend lurks a challenge to the centrality of the internal market in the European project that seeks to replace the instrumental nature of the economic freedoms in the creation of the common market with a wider rationale centred on the idea of European citizenship and of a political Union that goes well beyond market integration.

In other words, there are attempts at creating a political Union partly through interpretation. I would also remind readers of the tendency to let (classical) human rights prevail over fundamental freedoms in the event of conflict.[1]

Whether this emphasis on free movement of persons is justified from an economic standpoint, is, however, controversial. To give an example, in its paper "Europe after Brexit: A proposal for a continental partnership" of 29 August 2016, the Brussels-based think tank *Bruegel* wrote:

> From a purely economic viewpoint [....], goods, services and capital can be freely exchanged in a deeply integrated market without free movement of workers, though not entirely without some labour mobility. It is also possible for capital to move freely and for banking services to be provided across borders without free movement. Free movement of workers is, thus, not indispensable for the smooth functioning of *economic* integration in goods, services and capital. On the other hand, some degree of labour mobility is an essential counterpart of the free flow of goods, services and capital.[2]

Other economists, for example from the Kiel Institute for the World Economy, have made similar statements. Politically, free movement of persons has been under pressure for quite some time in certain EU Member States. The situation is the same in Switzerland, which has basically recognised this freedom under a bilateral agreement with the EU. Be that as it may, *de lege lata* free movement of persons is to a large extent part of EEA law.

The fundamental freedoms may be restricted by the Contracting Parties either based on the justification grounds laid down in the EEA Agreement or on the ones recognised by case law. Thereby, the principle of proportionality must be satisfied.

2 The EFTA Court's Approach to Proportionality

2.1 Origin and Key Features

Proportionality is the European law principle par excellence. It is part of the general principles of law and has been recognised both by the ECJ and the EFTA Court. Proportionality means that any measures that affect a fundamental freedom or a fundamental right must pursue a legitimate aim, be suitable to achieve the aim, be

[1]See for details Chapter 12.

[2]See for details Chapter 3.

necessary to achieve the aim, which means that there cannot be any less onerous way of acting, and be reasonable, considering the competing interests of different groups (proportionality *stricto* sensu). The third and fourth criteria are often merged into one. The principle's economic law function lies in the fact that it makes restrictions of the fundamental freedoms difficult and thereby contributes to the realisation of an EEA Single Market.

Beyond its function as a tool of judicial review, the principle of proportionality is expressly laid down in the Treaty on European Union, EU secondary legislation, and the ECHR.

According to Israeli Professors Moshe Cohen-Eliya and Iddo Porat, the proportionality test is an indispensable part of a "culture of justification" where

> every action must be justified in terms of reasonableness, which means that it must be the result of proper balance between conflicting considerations and reflect an appropriate means-ends rationality.

The "culture of justification" is said to be a product of the historic developments following the atrocities of World War II, especially in Germany, as well as a consequence of certain beliefs particular to Europe. Compared with this, the US is said to be characterised not by a culture of justification, but by a culture of authority. The two authors believe that

> [a] culture of authority is one that is based on the authority of government to exercise power. The legitimacy and legality of governmental action is derived from the fact that the actor is authorized to act.

Generally speaking, two tests are employed in the European legal orders, when proportionality is assessed: the EFTA Court, like the ECJ, uses a structured "means-ends" test at the centre of which there is the triad of necessity, suitability and proportionality *stricto* sensu. This is a rather flexible tool of judicial review, which implies that neither a right nor a public interest may outweigh one another as a matter of principle. By employing such an approach, it is possible to find solutions tailored to each case. Most importantly, under the "means-ends" test, the burden of proof shifts to the State or the authority that is invoking a public interest. From the perspective of market operators, there is, moreover, another advantage: to enable the courts to conduct a judicial review, the authorities are obliged to state reasons for their decisions. These reasons must be transparent and comprehensive and arbitrary considerations are not permitted. Lastly, the "means-ends" test ensures that individuals are guaranteed an effective tool to challenge administrative decisions and legislative choices.

The ECtHR uses a looser version of judicial review channelled through a "balancing" of interests. Under this approach, the burden of proof for "unreasonableness" lies with the individual alleging that the authority acted unreasonably. Proving that an authority actually proceeded in such a way may be hard, or even impossible, for individuals, as they are naturally "outsiders" to administrative actions.

2.2 *Areas of Application*

The EFTA Court has primarily used the proportionality test in preliminary reference cases, but also in direct actions. In preliminary reference cases, the work is shared between the EFTA Court and the national court. In infringement proceedings, it is entirely up to the EFTA Court to decide whether the measure at issue complies with the principle of proportionality. On some occasions, similar domestic rules were dealt with in both infringement and preliminary reference cases. As regards substance, proportionality assessment is particularly relevant in fundamental freedom cases because, in the field of harmonised law, the possibilities of derogating in relation to a public interest are limited. Proportionality has also been an issue in fundamental rights cases. Furthermore, it has guided judicial review in competition law cases.

3 Some Landmark Cases

3.1 *Free Movement of Goods*

State Monopolies of a Commercial Character

The EFTA Court was the first court in the EEA to rule on the lawfulness of a State retail alcohol monopoly in *Wilhelmsen*. According to Norwegian legislation, the retail sale of beer containing more than 4.75% alcohol by volume was reserved for the State alcohol trading monopoly *Vinmonopolet*. In its judgment of 27 June 1997, the EFTA Court found that the 4.75% demarcation gave rise to discrimination between foreign and local beer brands. As regards a possible justification, combating alcohol abuse was acknowledged to constitute a public health concern. Article 13 EEA, the relevant provision, would only cease to be applicable if the national court were to find that the measures in question aimed to protect domestic production as opposed to foreign production or to restrict trade between the Member States in a disguised way. As regards Article 16 EEA, on monopolies, we held that granting an exclusive right for the retail sale of beer containing more than 4.75% alcohol by volume to *Vinmonopolet* formed an inherent part of the regulations designing the system. Since these were justified on grounds of public health, it was not necessary to examine them further. However, *Vinmonopolet's* selection of strong beers consisted of ten domestic and seven foreign brands. The Court therefore added that a State retail monopoly retaining an exclusive right to sell products was in practice in a position to discriminate against goods from other countries. It was for the national court to assess whether the selection of products was based only on factors such as higher transport costs for foreign beer and local taste—these were the arguments put forward by the Norwegian Government—or whether it was a result of a discriminatory application of the monopoly. Such discrimination would be unnecessary and disproportionate. In this context, the Court held in paragraph 107 that

> the national court must take into account whether the method of selection is able to replace the market mechanism to the fullest possible extent.

In other words, we relied on the notion of "as if competition" ("*als-ob-Wettbewerb*"), as developed by the German ordoliberals. According to this concept, if a monopoly exists a market outcome must be aimed at as would be the case were competition to exist. I may add that Article 16 EEA, the norm mirroring Article 37 TFEU, is very difficult to work with. Economically speaking it is almost impossible to adjust a State monopoly of a commercial character

> so that no discrimination regarding the conditions under which goods are procured and marketed will exist between nationals of EC Member States and EFTA States.

as Article 16 EEA states.

Wilhelmsen had an interesting sequel. In December of 1997, Doris and I flew to Oslo for the first time in our lives. Since I had no contacts in Norway at the time, I asked Sven Norberg whether he could help. Sven contacted his friend Jonas Myhre, Norway's top lawyer in European law matters. Jonas who was the chairman of the Norwegian FIDE group, extended an invitation. The afternoon before my speech I visited the Centre of European Law which I knew was critical of the Court and its case law. What I did not yet realise at the time was that many of the people working there were determined to defend the Norwegian social model at all cost. The talks at the Centre were somewhat one-dimensional. My discussion partners were mainly interested in how to protect the country's sovereignty. On the other hand, my speech at the FIDE Group was well received and I could feel that those who attended were quite curious to get to know this guy from the Alps. We had dinner with Jonas and his, now deceased, wife Kari. It was one of the funniest dinners during my time at the EFTA Court. We immediately became firm friends with the Myhre's.

The day after my speech, I visited the largest *Vinmonopolet* store in Oslo. It was a belated field trip, so to speak. Without revealing my identity, I asked so see the general manager and put the question "how many beer brands do you carry". He truthfully said "seven foreign and ten domestic". When I further queried him about the reasons for this selection, he answered with a smile "because we think that Norwegians should drink Norwegian beer".

Discriminatory Clause in a Public Works Contract

In the *Fagtún* case, Icelandic legislation required that roof elements made of wood were to be ventilated. A respective clause was not part of the tender procedure, but was inserted into the final contract at the contracting authority's request after the bids had been received and considered. The EFTA Court found that from the perspective of free movement of goods this could not lead to a different assessment, as post-tender negotiations could not be separated from the tender procedure itself. Since the effect of such a provision was to preclude the use of imported roof elements for the work, it was deemed to constitute a restriction on the free movement of goods. Concerning a possible justification, the Court rejected the contention that extraordinary weather conditions required that roof elements be produced in the country so that a purchaser may monitor construction and take the necessary measures to ensure conformity with domestic legislation. The provision in question was also found to be disproportionate.

Marketing Ban on Fortified Food

One of the most important cases the Court had to decide in the first 24 years of its existence was *Kellogg's*. The Court emphasised that an import ban is, from the perspective of proportionality, a particularly sensitive measure. The case is dealt with *in extenso* in Chap. 11 of this book.

Ban on the Visual Display of Tobacco Products

Philip Morris was the first case in the whole EEA involving a ban on the visual display of tobacco products at the point of sale. Respective legislation had been introduced in Norway. The EFTA Court held that such a prohibition constituted a measure having equivalent effect to a quantitative restriction on imports if, in fact, it affected the marketing of products from other EEA States to a greater degree than that of imported products that were, until recently, produced in Norway. It was for the national court to determine whether the application of national law had such an effect or whether such an effect could not be clearly verified and, therefore, was too uncertain or indirect to constitute a hindrance to trade.

The EFTA Court found that an EEA State has the power to determine the degree of protection it wishes to afford to public health and the way in which that protection is to be achieved. As EEA States are allowed a certain margin of discretion in this regard, protection may vary from one State to another. Nevertheless, national rules or practices which restricted an EEA fundamental freedom, such as the free movement of goods, or were capable of doing so, could only be justified if they were appropriate to attain the objective in question and did not go beyond what was necessary in order to attain it. However, in the event of any uncertainty as to the existence or extent of risks to human health, an EEA State may take protective measures without having to wait until the reality of those risks becomes fully apparent. Furthermore, an EEA State may take measures that reduce, as far as possible, a public health risk. It follows that where the EEA State concerned legitimately aims for a very high level of protection, it must be sufficient for the authorities to demonstrate that, even though there may be some scientific uncertainty as regards the suitability and necessity of the disputed measure, it was reasonable to assume that the measure would be able to contribute to the protection of human health.

Furthermore, we held that in the absence of convincing proof to the contrary, a measure of this kind may be considered suitable for the protection of public health. Proportionality had to be assessed by the national court.

3.2 *Free Movement of Goods and Freedom to Provide Services*

In *Pedicel*, the Norwegian Market Council asked the EFTA Court, *inter alia*, whether the Norwegian advertising prohibition on alcoholic beverages was compatible with the free movement of goods and the freedom to provide services. The ban flowed from the Norwegian alcohol policy, it had also existed in other Nordic countries. We found that the ban could only be maintained if it was proportionate. Such a prohibition

> may be justified on grounds of the protection of public health, unless it is apparent that, in the circumstances of law and of fact which characterise the situation in the EEA Contracting Party concerned, the protection of public health against the harmful effects of alcohol can be secured by measures having less effect on intra-EEA trade.

3.3 *Freedom to Provide Services and Right of Establishment*

In *the Icelandic Air Passengers Tax* case, the EFTA Court held such a tax regime to be incompatible with the freedom to provide services. The argument that international and domestic air transport services were not comparable was rejected. The claim that any effect on the free movement of services would not be material was also rebutted. The EFTA Court carried out a thorough proportionality analysis and found the restriction to be disproportionate.

Residence Requirements and Similar Restrictions

When the EEA project started in the late 1980s, Liechtenstein Prime Minister Hans Brunhart realised that the EEA offered his country the chance to emancipate itself from Switzerland without jeopardising the close relations with its western neighbour. As I have said before, I was his closest advisor on EEA law matters at the time.[3] When I asked him why his Government left the residence requirements in Liechtenstein law untouched, he smiled and answered that had they abolished them right away, they would have risked losing the referendum. The job was subsequently done by ESA and the EFTA Court.

The EFTA Court handled a series of cases from Liechtenstein, which concerned a multiplicity of residence requirements for foreigners who wanted to work in the country. *Rainford Towning* concerned such a condition for the managing director of a company and *Dr. Pucher* a residence requirement for at least one board member of a domiciliary company. In two cases *ESA* brought infringement actions against *Liechtenstein* claiming that a residence requirement for one member of the management board and one member of the executive management in banks and regulations that required attorneys, patent attorneys, auditors and trustees to be able to perform their duties effectively and regularly because of their place of residence as well as rules requiring the members of the Board of Directors and the Executive

---

[3]See for details Chapter 3.

Board of banks to be domiciled in such a way that they were able to perform their functions effectively and properly were unlawful. In all these cases, the EFTA Court held that the freedom of establishment had been infringed. The respective regulations were also disproportionate. A non-justifiable violation of the freedom of establishment was also found in *Dr. Brändle*, *Dr. Mangold*, and *Dr. Tschannett*. Liechtenstein law stated that physicians and dentists seeking a licence to practise in the country could not operate more than one practice, regardless of location (the "single practice rule"). Based on this legislation, the application of Austrian nationals with an established medical or dental practice in Austria for a licence to set up and operate a medical or dental practice in Liechtenstein was rejected. The Court found such a prohibition to be neither suitable nor necessary in order to attain the objective of maintaining the high quality of medical services.

State Gambling Monopolies

In *Gaming Machines*, Norway had given a State-owned company the exclusive right to operate gaming machines and thereby removed all other private operators from the market. The Court held that the States were free to set the objectives of their gaming policy and to define the level of protection sought, provided that the measures served legitimate aims and were proportionate. A limitation was said to be acceptable only if it reflected a concern to bring about a genuine diminution in gambling opportunities, and if the financing of social activities constituted only an incidental beneficial consequence. Where a State chose to fight gambling addiction by reducing gambling opportunities and running a State-owned monopoly, it could not endorse or tolerate measures, such as extensive marketing, which could lead to an increase in gambling. A consistent and systematic approach also had to encompass an effective control of the monopoly's activities once legislation entered into force. However, as regards the aim of fighting gambling addiction, it could reasonably be assumed that a monopoly operator subject to effective control would tend to accommodate that concern better than commercial operators. ESA's application was dismissed, but the judgment was an "as long as" judgment. As long as public control and enforcement was effective, the monopoly was lawful.

In *Ladbrokes*, the world's largest bookmaker and gaming company was denied permission to operate and market gaming and betting services in Norway. The EFTA Court accepted the aims of fighting gambling addiction and crime and malpractice as being legitimate. However, in order to be lawfully based on the aim of fighting gambling addiction, legislation had to reflect a concern to bring about a genuine diminution in gambling opportunities. The motive of financing benevolent or public-interest activities could not in itself be an objective justification for restrictions. The goal of preventing gambling from being a source of private profit could serve as a justification only if legislation reflected a moral concern; thus if a monopoly was allowed to offer a range of gambling opportunities, the system did not genuinely pursue this aim. The marketing activities and the development of new games by Norsk Tipping were held to be particularly relevant when assessing the consistent implementation of the anti-gambling policy. The policy pursued would be inconsistent if the State took, facilitated or tolerated other measures that would run counter to the objectives pursued. The national court was told to look into the extent and effect of the marketing and development of new games of chance, *inter alia*, how much Norsk Tipping spent on these activities as well as the form and content of the marketing and the susceptibility of the targeted groups.

Dealing with the *Ladbrokes* case brought back memories of my doctoral thesis on suggestive advertising.[4] One of the issues was whether a State monopoly was proportionate if it was allowed to make huge marketing efforts. The Court did not use the expression "suggestive advertising", but held that the national court had to ascertain whether the advertising of the gambling and betting services was more informative than "evocative" in nature. However, in substance, the same thing was meant.

The national court was finally instructed to examine whether the legislation at issue went beyond what was necessary to meet the aims pursued. Again, the level of protection chosen by the Norwegian authorities was said to be decisive. Where other, less restrictive measures would have the effect of fully achieving the objectives at the level of protection chosen, an exclusive rights system could not be considered necessary simply because it might offer an even higher level of protection.

Posting of Workers

The *Icelandic Posting of Workers* case was based on an infringement action by ESA. The EFTA Court found that by maintaining in force rules requiring foreign undertakings, which posted workers temporarily to Iceland, to pay regular wages for sick leave and imposing an obligation on undertakings to take out accident insurance for such posted workers, Iceland was in breach of its obligations under the 1996 Posted Workers Directive[5] in the framework of the provision of services. The directive sets out an exhaustive list of terms and conditions of employment that host EEA States are entitled to require undertakings established in other EEA States to observe when they post workers to their territory. That list includes "minimum rates of pay, including overtime rates". The Court held that since the sickness pay was not set at a minimum rate, i.e. neither as a flat rate of minimum compensation, nor calculated on the basis of a minimum wage, but corresponded to the regular wage the worker received under his employment contract, the entitlement could not fall within the notion of "the minimum rates of pay". The provision on accident insurance concerned the terms and conditions of employment and, consequently, was a matter to which the directive applied. However, this obligation fell outside the scope of the directive, and was thus contrary to the directive. Finally, the EFTA Court held that the Icelandic rules on sickness pay and accident insurance could not be justified under the public policy exception, as Iceland failed to establish that maintaining them was necessary to counteract a genuine and sufficiently serious threat to a fundamental interest of society.

[4]See for details Chapter 1.

[5]96/71/EC.

In *STX Norway Offshore AS and Others*, workers in the maritime construction industry who were posted to Norwegian territory from another EEA State, were under a universally applicable nationwide collective agreement, that secured certain terms and conditions of employment. Among these were maximum working hours, remuneration in addition to the basic hourly wage for work assignments requiring overnight stays away from home and compensation for travel, board and lodging expenses related to such work assignments. The Borgarting Court of Appeal wanted to know whether the 1996 Posted Workers Directive precluded such terms and conditions of employment.

The EFTA Court found that terms and conditions regarding maximum normal working hours, such as those in question, were covered by the directive's mandatory rules for minimum protection. It further held that provisions concerning remuneration paid in compensation for working outside normal working hours were compatible with the directive, provided these fell within the notion of "minimum rates of pay". However, the entitlement to additional remuneration for work assignments requiring overnight stays away from home was found to be liable to make it less attractive, or more difficult, for undertakings established in other EEA States to perform services in Norway. It therefore constituted a restriction on the freedom to provide services. Such a restriction could be justified only if it pursued a legitimate objective and constituted an overriding reason of public interest. If so, the restriction had to be suitable and could not go beyond what was necessary in order to attain the objective. This was for the national court to determine. As regards compensation for travel, board and lodging expenses, the Court stated that such payments could not fall within the notion of pay within the meaning of Article 3(1) of the directive. An EEA State was therefore not permitted to impose such terms and conditions, unless this could be justified on the basis of public policy considerations.

Importantly, following the ECJ's judgment in *Laval*, we held that the questions referred regarding particular terms and conditions of employment

> will, where necessary, be examined jointly under the provisions of the Directive interpreted in the light of Article 36 EEA, and, where appropriate, under the latter provision itself.

Article 36 EEA guarantees the freedom to provide services. As respects compensation for travel, board and lodging expenses in the event of work assignments that require overnight stays away from home, the EFTA Court held, upon a question from the referring court, that the EEA States are, in principle, free to determine the requirements of public policy, but that the notion of public policy, particularly when cited as a justification for a derogation from the freedom to provide services, must be interpreted strictly. The information submitted to the Court did not indicate that the allowances in question were justified on public policy grounds.

Collective Bargaining and Industrial Action

The case *Holship Norge AS* v *Norsk Transportarbeiderforbund*, which has already been mentioned several times, concerned the notification of a boycott by the Norwegian Transport Workers' Union of Holship Norge AS, a Norwegian forwarding agent. The purpose of the boycott was to procure acceptance of the Framework Agreement on a Fixed Pay Scheme for Dockworkers that applied to thirteen ports in Norway, including the port of Drammen. Under a priority clause, unloading and loading operations of ships had to be carried out by organised dock-workers. Since Holship was not a party to the Framework Agreement, it used its own employees to carry out its unloading and loading operations in Drammen. The case was referred to the EFTA Court by the Supreme Court of Norway which posed two sets of questions: a first concerning the compatibility of the boycott with EEA competition rules and a second set regarding the compatibility with the freedom of establishment.[6] It was the Supreme Court's first reference after more than twelve years. Ironically, the Supreme Court ended its boycott of the EFTA Court by referring a boycott case![7] I assigned the case to myself. Judgment was rendered on 19 April 2016.

As respects the freedom of establishment, the Court found that there was a restriction which might, however, be justified either on the grounds laid down in Article 33 EEA (public policy, public security or public health) or by overriding reasons of general interest, such as the protection of workers. Those justifications were to be interpreted in the light of fundamental rights. A limited group of workers was found to be protected to the detriment of other workers. There was nothing to indicate that the boycott aimed to improve the working conditions of Holship's employees. It was for the referring court to determine, having regard to all the facts and circumstance before it and the guidance provided by the Court, whether the restrictive measure at issue could be justified.

3.4 *Right of Establishment and Free Movement of Capital*

Right of Reversion of Waterfalls

In view of its political and economic significance, the seminal *Norwegian Waterfalls* case will be dealt with elaborately in Chap. 23 of this book. Norwegian law foresaw that public undertakings would be granted concessions for acquiring waterfalls for energy production without time limitation whereas others, including all foreign undertakings, would be granted such concessions with time limitations. Furthermore, the property rights to waterfalls utilised for energy production and related installations would be transferred from private undertakings to the State after a certain time, without compensation (so-called right of reversion). The EFTA Court found this to be incompatible with both the freedom of establishment and the free movement of capital. That ensuring security of energy supply and the protection of the environment were legitimate aims was accepted. However, based on a thorough proportionality analysis, the EFTA Court found the controversial rules to go beyond what was necessary in order to attain the legitimate aims pursued.

[6]The competition law part of the judgment is addressed in Chapter 16.

[7]See Chapter 8.

Ownership Limitations and Voting Rights Restrictions

In *Regulated Markets*, *ESA* had sued Norway. The EFTA Court held that by maintaining in force restrictions on the rights of persons and undertakings established in EEA States to own holdings and exercise voting rights in general meetings of financial services infrastructure institutions, Norway infringed the freedom of establishment and the free movement of capital. The Norwegian Stock Exchange Act and the Central Securities Depositories Act prohibited the holding of more than 20% of the shares in stock exchanges or central securities depositories, or the voting rights of more than 20% of the total voting capital or 30% of the shares represented at a general meeting. The holding of shares in contravention of those rules could lead to a compulsory sale, which was subject to the exercise of discretion by the competent authority. Shareholders that for the most part operated or owned a regulated market or a securities depository were eligible for an exception from that ceiling, subject to a suitability assessment. For other shareholders, exceptions were only possible under exceptional circumstances. The EFTA Court found this "dual track system" to restrict the freedom of establishment and the free movement of capital. The objectives of the contested measures—to promote the well-functioning and efficiency of the financial markets by creating safeguards against conflicts of interest and covert misuse of powers in infrastructure institutions as well as to ensure their independence, neutrality and integrity in the market—reflected overriding reasons in the general interest. The contested measures were also deemed to be suitable to achieve the public interest pursued. However, Norway had not sufficiently demonstrated that other, less restrictive, forms of control, even if administratively more burdensome, might not achieve the relevant public interest objectives in an equally effective way. The system was held to go beyond what was necessary to achieve the objective pursued. Finally, the Court found that the principle of legal certainty was infringed.

In *Netfonds*, the plaintiffs, Netfonds Holding ASA, Netfonds Bank AS and Netfonds Livsforsikring AS, claimed compensation from the Norwegian Government on the basis that the latter issued only limited banking and insurance licences despite their request for full licences. The plaintiffs contested the defendant's requirement that, in order to be granted a full banking and insurance licence, three quarters or more of the share capital had to be dispersed through a capital increase or sale effected without any preferential or pre-emption right for shareholders or others, or that, as an alternative to such a dispersion sale, only a limited licence for banking and insurance activity would be issued. The EFTA Court held that, at the relevant time, the relevant secondary legislation of the EU, which had been incorporated into the EEA Agreement, did not prevent the EEA States from maintaining stricter rules concerning the procedure for the authorisation of banks and insurance companies. Nonetheless, such rules must be compatible with the fundamental freedoms. The legislation and administrative practice in question constituted restrictions that appeared to fall predominantly within the scope of the freedom of establishment. Whether this was indeed the case was for the referring court to assess. The Court found that the objective of reducing excessive risk incentives for the owners of banks or insurance companies reflected an overriding reason in the general interest capable of justifying national measures such as the ones at issue. It was for the referring court to identify which objectives were in fact pursued by the national measures, as well as to determine whether the legitimate aims were pursued in a suitable and consistent manner. Nevertheless, the Court indicated that the national rules in question did not seem suitable to achieve the legitimate objective, whereas the administrative practice appeared suitable to the extent that it applied to applications for authorisation as a bank or an insurance company and not to secondary acquisitions after the granting of authorisation. As regards necessity, the Court found that there appeared to be measures, other than those contested, which were less restrictive while being equally effective in attaining the legitimate objective identified.

Recognition of a Trust
Joined Cases *Olsen* concerned the taxation of the Norwegian beneficiaries of an asset management trust established in Liechtenstein and governed by Liechtenstein law, to hold the interests of the Norwegian Olsen family in certain companies. It seems that one of the fictional Simpson characters featured in the animated television series was inspired by one of the Olsen brothers. The EFTA Court held on 9 July 2014 that such a trust falls within the scope of the freedom of establishment provided that it pursues a real and genuine economic activity somewhere in the EEA for an indefinite period and through a fixed establishment. The view of the Norwegian Government that entities that do not have legal personality and are not an integral part of another company or firm fall outside the scope of the freedom of establishment was rejected. Beneficiaries of capital assets set up in the form of a trust should also be able to invoke the free movement of capital. Restrictions may be justified only where they specifically relate to wholly artificial arrangements that aim to evade national tax and where they do not go beyond what is necessary to achieve that purpose. What is decisive is the fact that the activity, from an objective perspective, has no other reasonable explanation than securing a tax advantage. That the French Government sided with the Norwegian Government in this case came as no surprise. That the UK Government found itself in the same camp was probably less obvious. At the end of the day, trust law is an English invention.

3.5 *Free Movement of Capital*

In 1997 and 1998 the Norwegian *Fokus Bank* paid dividends to its shareholders, *inter alia*, two companies residing in Germany and the UK. It withheld withholding tax, which was not done with regard to shareholders resident in Norway. The assumption was that non-resident shareholders were reimbursed in their respective home state based on bilateral double taxation treaties between Norway and the respective EU Member States. In order to be reimbursed, the German and the British shareholders would have had to make an application. The EFTA Court held this to be incompatible with the free movement of capital. Possible tax advantages in the home State, it said, could not offset restriction and discrimination. A Contracting Party could not shift its obligation to comply with the EEA Agreement to another Contracting Party by relying on the latter to make good discrimination caused by the former's legislation. Resident and non-resident shareholders were deemed be in an objectively comparable situation. The safeguarding of the cohesion of the international tax system was not accepted as a justification, since this would have amounted to preferring bilateral tax agreements over EEA law. The legislative history of the Norwegian Corporate Tax Act showed that the respective provisions were motivated by a desire to protect the Norwegian tax base, a purely economic requirement. Likewise, the principle of legal certainty would require that the granting of an imputed tax credit to non-resident shareholders may not depend on whether a tax credit is granted in their State of residence in respect of dividend payments. *Fokus Bank* is a market-oriented judgment. The attempt to fill the state coffers by way of unjustified taxation was rejected.

3.6 General Prohibition to Discriminate

Dr. Kottke concerned the question of whether the obligation of a foreign plaintiff to pay security for legal costs was compatible with the fundamental freedoms. Liechtenstein law provided at the time that persons without residence in Liechtenstein who acted as plaintiffs or appellants were, on an application by the defendant or respondent, obliged to provide the latter with security for costs unless international treaties stated otherwise. The EFTA Court held that such a provision resulted in indirect discrimination on grounds of nationality, but could be justified on the basis of public interest objectives provided it was necessary and not excessive in attaining those objectives. The latter condition was not met if the State in which the plaintiff resided allowed for the enforcement of a costs award, whether on the basis of treaty obligations or unilaterally. Importantly, the Court further found that it would be disproportionate to require security for an amount that would be out of proportion to the costs likely to be incurred by the defendant or unreasonably high or which must be posted within a very short period of time. Whether the conditions for justification would be satisfied in a particular case was left to the national court to determine. With this, the EFTA Court went against ESA and the Commission who had both argued that the national rule in question was, as a matter of principle, incompatible with the fundamental freedoms.

As regards proportionality, the EFTA Court stated that a national rule that is indirectly discriminatory may be justified on the basis of public interest objectives if it

> is suitable for attaining the public interest objective pursued, is necessary to achieve that objective and not excessive in its discriminatory effects having regard to the objective sought.

4 Does Proportionality Mean Proportionality?

4.1 Liechtenstein Courts

The proportionality test used by the EFTA Court has not been adopted with the same stringency by the judiciaries of all three Member States. In that respect, Liechtenstein has a clear advantage over its two Nordic brother countries. Due to the embeddedness of the country in the German legal family, the Liechtenstein courts have no difficulties in carrying out the test, which has also been adopted by the Swiss courts. The principle of proportionality has been codified in important laws, in particular in the Police Act and the Act applicable to administrative actions.

The Administrative Court held on 19 September 2016 that the principle of proportionality is a general principle of law in Liechtenstein, even if the application itself varies, depending on the case in which it is employed. In some cases, the Administrative Court conducts an assessment based on a balancing of interests, while in others, it employs the criteria of necessity and suitability. In constitutional law, the Liechtenstein State Court has since 1973 consistently referred to the principle and held that an interference with individual rights must be assessed against the background of suitability, necessity and appropriateness (proportionality *stricto* sensu).

Since Liechtenstein courts have never claimed that rulings rendered by the EFTA Court under Article 34 SCA must be assessed independently, considerations on proportionality tend to be short in cases where the EFTA Court has already made such a test. Cases in point are *Dr. Brändle*, *Dr. Mangold* and *Dr. Tschannett*, which concerned the Liechtenstein "single practice rule" for medical doctors, and *Dr Pucher*, all referred by the Administrative Court.

4.2 Icelandic Courts

The Icelandic Constitution expressly provides for individual proportionality clauses in relation to fundamental rights. Article 71 provides that the

> freedom from interference with privacy, home and family life may be otherwise limited by statutory provisions if this is urgently necessary for the protection of the rights of others.

Article 72 provides:

> No one may be obliged to surrender his property unless required by public interests.

The provision on freedom of expression, Article 73, accepts the existence of restrictions

> by law in the interests of public order or the security of the State, for the protection of health or morals, or for the protection of the rights or reputation of others, if such restrictions are deemed necessary and in agreement with democratic traditions.

In view of Iceland's accession to the EEA, the principle of proportionality was incorporated in various statutes. As regards the Administrative Procedures Act, the

Supreme Court held on 15 December 2016 in *Matvælastofnun* v *þrotabú Beis ehf.* that an authority may only reach an adverse decision if it pursues a legitimate aim, the objective cannot be achieved by another, less restrictive, measure, and the measure does not go beyond what is necessary to achieve the objective. The case concerned a restriction on the import of certain goods, which the competent authority adopted by referring to the aim of preventing the consumption of caffeine in an amount that is, or could be, harmful. The Supreme Court rejected the authority's argument, finding that labelling, for example, would be sufficient to achieve the legitimate aim, while also being less onerous on the importer. This judgment could have been rendered by a German court. In *Björgun ehf. v íslenska ríkinu*, the Reykjavík District Court referred to the "constitutional principle of proportionality" when assessing the constitutionality of legislation. In its judgment of 27 September 2007, the Supreme Court, however, did not label proportionality as clearly as the District Court, even though it ultimately conducted a proportionality assessment.

The former EFTA Court legal secretary and former Icelandic judge of the ECtHR Davíð Thór Björgvinsson wrote that Icelandic courts have, in principle, implemented the Court's preliminary rulings.

Within the more specific ambit of proportionality, this statement is supported by the example of the free movement of goods case *Fagtún*, where the Icelandic Supreme Court followed our ruling without conducting a proportionality assessment of its own. In the *Icelandic Air Passenger Tax* case, the EFTA Court held, following a proportionality assessment, that the Icelandic air passenger tax could not be justified. Icelandic law was subsequently amended. The explanatory notes on the proposal to amend the relevant statute expressly refer to the EFTA Court's judgment.

4.3 Norwegian Courts

Norwegian law does not generally acknowledge proportionality. Nevertheless, influenced by the ECtHR's case law, Norwegian courts tend to apply a type of proportionality test when dealing with fundamental rights. However, they are hesitant to review administrative and legislative measures. As Eirik Bjorge, now a full Professor at the University of Bristol, has stated, the legislature, not the judiciary, is considered the "guardian" of the Constitution. Professor Tor-Inge Harbo noted in this regard that, according to

> Norwegian/Scandinavian legal realism and Norwegian Constitutional law, the judicial branch should exhibit considerable deference *vis-à-vis* both the legislative and the executive (administrative) branches.

All in all, Norwegian courts employ a cautious approach towards proportionality also in the context of fundamental rights, and tend to favour the public interest as defined by the administration. This is even more the case when they apply the fundamental freedoms. In several preliminary ruling cases, Norwegian courts used a proportionality test that led them to find in favour of the State although our judgment was to the contrary.

Pedicel: An Unsuccessful Start The *Pedicel* case, which involved the issue of the compatibility of the Norwegian advertising ban for alcoholic beverages with the free movement of goods and the freedom to provide services, was destined to fail from the beginning because of an appalling translation error. The EFTA Court's English phrasing of answer 3 that such a prohibition may be justified on the grounds of the protection of public health, "unless it is apparent" that this can be secured by measures having less effect on intra-EEA trade was translated into Norwegian as "med mindre det er åpenbart," which means "unless it is obvious".[8] The Supreme Court seemingly attached great weight to the term "obvious" in its decision.

Beyond this, the Supreme Court assessed both the suitability and the necessity of the advertising ban. However, it only briefly discussed alternative means, finding very generally that less comprehensive measures—such as allowing advertising in specialist journals only—could weaken the effect of the ban. To the Supreme Court, it was a natural presumption ("*naturlig formodning*") that advertisement and consumption were linked. The State was thus not required to provide any evidence beyond this. In doing so, the Supreme Court set a very low threshold for the State to discharge its burden to demonstrate that there were no other less restrictive but equally effective means. Alternative measures were not exhaustively addressed. It fits the picture that the Supreme Court gladly accepted the precautionary principle, contrary to the EFTA Court's finding in paragraph 60 that in

> a situation such as that at issue, the precautionary principle as recognized by the Court does not apply.

Tor-Inge Harbo rightly observed that in departing from the EFTA Court's judgment, the Supreme Court granted the State a greater margin of appreciation. This is not compatible with the proportionality principle.

Philip Morris: The Curse of the Evil Deed As Friedrich Schiller wrote in *Wallenstein's Death*,

> *Das eben ist der Fluch der bösen Tat, Dass sie fortzeugend immer Böses muss gebären.*
> This is the curse of every evil deed, That propagating still it brings forth evil.

The Supreme Court's *Pedicel* judgment significantly influenced the Oslo District Court's reasoning in *Philip Morris*. Instead of conducting the EEA law proportionality test *lege artis*, the District Court based itself on the Supreme Court's *Pedicel* judgment. Focussing on suitability, it found that a ban on the visual display of tobacco products was comparable to an advertising ban. When addressing necessity, the District Court held that different measures may target different groups and that the absence of visible tobacco products in shops could be vital to eliminating the advertising effect, and could play an important role in the de-normalisation of tobacco products. *Philip Morris* pointed to other means, such as a licensing system, stricter enforcement of the age limit, or mass media campaigns. The District Court accepted that such measures might also play a significant role,

[8]See for details Chapter 23.

but it did not analyse those measures as viable alternatives. It concluded in essence that the State had made a reasonable choice when adopting the contested display ban. With this, the State was again given a margin of appreciation that is not in accordance with the EEA proportionality test.

Gaming Machines and Ladbrokes: The State is Always Right In paragraph 51 of the *Gaming Machines* judgment, the EFTA Court held that it was

> reasonable to assume that a monopoly operator in the field of gaming machines subject to effective control by the competent public authorities will tend to accommodate legitimate concerns of fighting gambling addiction better than a commercial operator or organisations whose humanitarian or socially beneficial activities partly rely on revenues from gaming machines. Furthermore, it is plausible to assume that in principle the State can more easily control and direct a wholly State-owned operator than private operators. Through its ownership role, the State has additional ways of influencing the behaviour of the operator besides public law regulations and surveillance. In fact, the effectiveness of public control and enforcement of a genuinely restrictive approach to machine gaming are the focal point of the proportionality assessment in this case. In a situation where the reform of the gaming machine regulation in Norway has not yet taken effect, the Court cannot base itself on the general assumption that public control and policy enforcement will not satisfy these requirements.

These passages obviously meant that as long as the State controlled its own monopoly effectively, the monopoly was deemed to be in compliance with EEA law. But if the State didn't do this, that would be an entirely new ball game.

The Supreme Court nevertheless called the EFTA Court's test intensity moderate and claimed that this was in good harmony with the Norwegian tradition of judicial review of assessments of a distinct political nature ("*Dette viser etter min mening at EFTA-domstolens moderate prøvingsintensitet i denne saken er i god harmoni med den norske tradisjon ved domstolsprøving av vurderinger av utpreget politisk karakter*"). With respect, that was a bit much.

In the Oslo District Court's *Ladbrokes* judgment of 3 October 2008, the EFTA Court's ruling was flatly disregarded. The necessity assessment did not address other, possibly less restrictive means expressly mentioned by the EFTA Court and ignored information provided by *Ladbrokes* with regard to the functioning of a concession system.

STX: Who Cares About the EFTA Court? In its judgment of 5 March 2013, the Supreme Court applied an incorrect proportionality test. The appellants argued that the posting allowance was not proportionate. The Supreme Court simply said that it was its task to assess that and held that the criteria of necessity, suitability and proportionality were fulfilled. Instead of giving reasons, the Supreme Court limited itself to begging the question.

Holship: A Big Step Forward As could be expected after all the turmoil caused by the *STX* case, the Supreme Court held in *Holship* that the notified boycott was unlawful. Justice Skoghøy, writing for the majority, in paragraph 103 underlined that in the case at issue

> the protection of working and payment conditions provided by the right to priority of engagement is relatively indirect [….]. The jobs are protected by effectively shielding the company from outside competition.

In paragraph 118, he added that in his view, it was, from

> a human rights perspective, [….] hard to argue that [the jobs generated within Holship] carry less weight than the jobs at the Administration Office.

As the boycott was already held to be unlawful because it violated the freedom of establishment, Justice Skoghøy did not find it necessary to extensively discuss the possible implications of EEA competition law. However, he did add that also in this regard there were "not sufficient grounds" to depart from the conclusion reached by the EFTA Court in its *Holship* judgment. This is noteworthy since in 1997 its *Port of Sola* judgment, the Supreme Court had found that a boycott profited from the exemption from competition law.

Tor-Inge Harbo argued that Norwegian courts do not completely shy away from employing a test that entails some features of proportionality analysis. Nevertheless, as Supreme Court Justice Arnfinn Bårdsen has observed, there is

> still some way to go [….] to give full effect [to] that principle in the Norwegian Supreme Court,

not to mention the lower courts. I am nevertheless optimistic that in the future, judgments such as the ones rendered in *Pedicel*, *Gaming Machines* or *STX* can be avoided. Certainly, in *Holship* the Supreme Court still preferred a "balancing" over a "means-ends" test. In fact, the judgment refers to the weighing up of "constitutional rights" against "EEA rights" and speaks of the need to strike "a fair balance" between the two. Contrary to previous cases, the differences between the Court's approach and the *modus operandi* of the Supreme Court was, however, minor. From a functional perspective, such disagreement is of little importance. *Holship* is probably the most important ruling the *Høyesterett* has rendered under the EEA Agreement.

5 ESA's Position

On 12 May 2016, I gave a speech at ESA at the invitation of President Sven Erik Svedman. The event was well attended and I put quite some emphasis on the need for ESA to keep an eye on how our judgments were implemented by the national courts of the Member States. Nevertheless, I did not have the impression that the ESA officials present really got the message. As long as they concentrate on the scoreboard, they will not detect what is going on the ground, i.e. in the national courts. The scoreboard is a tool that measures compliance with the EEA Agreement as regards the implementation of directives.[9]

---

[9]See for details Chapter 7.

Chapter 16
Competition Law—A Rare Pleasure

Contents

1 General

According to Article 56 EEA, ESA has only limited competence in the field of competition law; but it does have competence. It is thus amazing that in over 24 years, ESA only took two decisions to impose fines, both for abuse of a dominant position. In the first case, *Norway Post*, the Authority on 16 March 2012 issued a fine of EUR 12.89 million. In the second case, *Color Line*, a sanction of EUR 18.811 million was imposed on 22 September 2010.[1] While the *Color Line* decision went unchallenged, Norway Post elicited an action for annulment. The EFTA Court dismissed the action, but reduced the fine from EUR 12.89 million to EUR 11.112 million because of the length of the administrative proceedings. Importantly, the EFTA Court took this opportunity to render what, according to commentators, is a landmark judgment. After *Norway Post*, the Court dealt with a number of cases concerning access to documents in ESA's possession. These proceedings also resulted in some important rulings. In a State aid case, the question

[1]See for details Chapter 7.

C. Baudenbacher, *Judicial Independence*, Springer Biographies,
https://doi.org/10.1007/978-3-030-02308-9_16

of whether an in-house lawyer may represent his/her own company before the EFTA Court arose. The respective judgment is obviously also relevant in competition law. The number of requests for preliminary rulings was manageable for the well-known reasons that I have already explained. However, some of these references involved fundamental questions of European competition law in the broadest sense of the word.

2 Limits of Collective Bargaining and Industrial Action

2.1 Occupational Pension Insurance Schemes

The question of whether collective agreements concluded between unions and employers' associations are fully sheltered from EEA competition rules was the subject of the *LO* case. The ECJ found in 1999 in *Albany* and related cases that collective agreements aimed to improve the working conditions and therefore were beyond the scope of European competition law. However, the ECJ did not examine the limits of such immunity. In a seminal comparative Opinion AG Francis Jacobs had concluded that in all the systems examined, including US law, collective agreements were to some extent sheltered from competition law, but that such immunity was not unlimited.

The Norwegian Federation of Trade Unions (LO) and other unions instituted proceedings before the Labour Court of Norway against the Norwegian Association of Local and Regional Authorities (KS) and 11 of its member municipalities. The dispute concerned the interpretation and application of provisions of the Basic Collective Agreement for Municipalities. At issue in the national proceedings was whether the defendant municipalities breached certain provisions of that collective agreement when they transferred their occupational pension insurance scheme from one supplier, KLP, a private mutual life insurance company, wholly owned by members of KS, to other insurance companies. The case was registered on 2 October 2000. The oral hearing took place over two days on 30 and 31 October 2001. The municipalities submitted that several provisions in the Basic Collective Agreement were void because they infringed Articles 53 and 54 EEA, the cartel prohibition and the prohibition to abuse a dominant position mirroring Articles 101 and 102 TFEU. The contested provisions of the collective agreement stated, in particular, that a plan to change the pension company should be discussed with union representatives; that before the decision-making body might begin to deal with a possible change of company, relevant offers for a new occupational pension scheme should be put before those members of the pension committee who represented the parties to the collective agreement; that the occupational pension scheme had to be based on a financing system that was gender-neutral and did not have the effect of excluding older employees; that before the matter might be decided upon by the municipality there had to be approval from the Norwegian

Public Service Pension Fund; and that the pension scheme had to be taken note of by the Norwegian Banking, Insurance and Securities Commission.

In its written submissions, Norway urged the Court to stick to the line of argument followed by the ECJ in *Albany*. These observations were drawn up by the Labour Party Government of Jens Stoltenberg, the future NATO Secretary General. At the oral hearing, however, the Norwegian agent, Beate Berglund Ekeberg, withdrew her government's written submissions, sided with the municipalities and asked the Court to follow the Opinion of AG Jacobs in *Albany*. The Stoltenberg cabinet had shortly before been replaced by a Conservative cabinet led by Kjell Magne Bondevik. Berglund Ekeberg stated that according to the Norwegian authorities,

> the occupational pension market should be subject to free competition. Provisions regulating transfer of pension schemes from one company to another company are, in the opinion of the Norwegian Government, not covered by the exemption for social policy objectives.

Per Andreas Bjørgan, now an attorney in private practice, argued the case for ESA. According to him, it seemed that the collective agreement could be applied to secure a monopoly instead of opening up the area concerned for competition. To claim an upfront acceptance from the Banking Insurance Securities Commission for a new product could be contrary to EEA law. If the national court were to find that a refusal to transfer was based on the desire to protect KLP's dominant position, Per Andreas said, we would obviously be outside the scope of immunity. ESA also underlined that the ECJ's case law, which to a great extent excluded the application of the cartel prohibition to collective agreements, made it easier to create monopolies in this field. The Authority finally argued that if a collective agreement was immune from Article 53 EEA, that exception did not extend to prohibition of the abuse of dominance laid down in Article 54 EEA. Since KLP was a dominant firm, but not a party to the collective bargaining agreement, ESA recommended that the national court look into possible connections between KS and KLP and asked the EFTA Court to give guidance on this. It was possible that what was at issue was an example of exclusionary abuse. KS/KLP would enter into an agreement that purported to offer a freedom of choice, but in reality the agreement tied all the municipalities to KLP. Such a situation could also fall within the scope of Article 53 EEA. As regards the crucial question of which test was to be applied, ESA proposed a classical proportionality assessment: if the act in question went beyond what was necessary to attain the social policy objective and could not be justified otherwise, an abuse may well have occurred.

The unions for their part pleaded unlimited immunity. This was in accordance with their belief that everything that concerns collective bargaining or industrial action is part of their core business.[2]

The EFTA Court did not have much experience in competition law. It was thus to be expected that the position of the Commission would carry particular weight.

---

[2]See also infra, II. 2.

The latter was represented by Wouter Wils who was well-known as an excellent man in the European competition law community. I had met him a couple of times at conferences and once he also spoke at the St. Gallen ICF. Wouter did not share ESA's view, but opted for a very limited test. He said at the hearing that the logic of *Albany* was

> precisely to avoid in depth scrutiny under the competition rules of the outcome of the collective negotiations between the social partners.

Wouter went on stating that the ECJ in *Albany* had not followed AG Jacobs' proposal to decompose the agreement into different constituent elements

> and then to look at the necessity and proportionality of these elements.

Instead, Wouter said, the ECJ's approach was a very global and general one. I was flabbergasted at the time and I still am now as I write this book. What the Commission was proposing was that the Court should not look into the clauses of the collective agreement themselves, not look into whether these clauses went beyond a legitimate concept of social goals. At the hearing, I asked Wouter what was wrong with a proportionality test. He answered that instead of a full scrutiny, the Commission recommended

> a marginal control of abuse. Pursuant to such marginal control of abuse, only specific provisions which are manifestly inappropriate or in relation to the social policy objectives pursued by the core of the agreement, or which are applied in a way which shows that they exclusively pursue other objectives, are excluded from immunity and fall within the scope of [the EU and EEA law cartel prohibition].

Under this approach, there would only be a problem

> when it turns out that a clause has no legitimate social purpose at all, has no other purposes than purposes which are not legitimate for social purposes. This is not the same as a proportionality test. Under a proportionality test, even if there is a legitimate social purpose, one would still look further and also look at other effects, other purposes or other effects, in particular the anti-competitive effect, and then one would have some weighing, some balance between the two.

When reflecting on the case, I have the impression that the Commission's agent had not been instructed by Directorate-General (DG) Competition, but by DG Social Policy.

At the time, *LO* was the most complex matter the EFTA Court has had to deal with. For a tribunal of our size, it was a challenge and in fact it took us almost 18 months to do away with the case. Judgment was delivered on 22 March 2002. We reproduced Francis Jacobs' statement from *Albany* almost verbatim and cited the respective paragraph of his Opinion. The ECJ had not even referred to his Opinion. The EFTA Court also held that the good faith of the parties in concluding and implementing a collective agreement had to be taken into account. Francis Jacobs had pointed to this requirement, but the ECJ did not. Finally, the EFTA Court emphasised that the national court must consider the aggregate effect of several elements of a collective agreement. Even if individually they would not lead to any certain resolution of the status of the collective agreement in relation to the applicability of EEA competition law, their aggregate effect could bring the agreement within the scope of those rules. In other words, the Court took a fact-based approach. A few years later, AG Miguel Poiares Maduro referred to us in his Opinion in *Viking Line* where he too argued in favour of a concept of limited antitrust immunity for collective agreements.

The referring Norwegian Labour Court did not follow our ruling, but decided in favour of the unions. ESA whose agent had, in a convincing line of argument, encouraged the EFTA Court to rule against the unions, remained inactive.

2.2 Dockers' Monopoly

Thirteen years later, we had to deal once again with the relationship between collective bargaining and EEA competition law in *Holship*. The facts have been described in Chap. 15.

The EFTA Court held that the exemption of collective agreements from the EEA competition rules did not cover a clause whereby a port user was obliged to give priority to another company's workers over its own employees, or the use of a boycott in order to procure acceptance of the collective agreement containing that clause. A collective agreement falls outside the scope of the EEA competition rules if it has been concluded following collective bargaining between employers and employees, and if it pursues the objective of improving conditions of work and employment. In *Holship*, the first requirement was fulfilled, but the second was not. In that regard, the Court found that the aggregate effect of two clauses of the Framework Agreement, the priority clause and the clause establishing the Administration Office for Dock Work (AO), was to guarantee the AO's workers permanent employment and a certain wage. Their effect was thus to protect only a limited group of workers employed by the AO to the detriment of Holship's workers, who were barred from performing similar work. Moreover, the boycott, notified by the union, was to be attributed to the AO, since it sought to compel Holship to observe the terms of the Framework Agreement. Furthermore, the union participated in the management of the AO and thus had an interest to preserve the AO's market position, thereby combining a business objective with its core tasks as a trade union.

In the light of these considerations, the EFTA Court concluded that the AO's system went beyond the improvement of conditions of work and employment. For an entity such as the AO to be regarded as an undertaking within the meaning of the EEA law competition rules, it had to be engaged in an economic activity. The provision of stevedore services was said to be an economic activity, since it consisted in offering a service on a market where the AO, actually or potentially, competed with other providers. It was for the Supreme Court to assess whether this provision of stevedoring services was attributable to the AO. It was also for the Supreme Court to determine whether the conduct in question had an appreciable effect on trade between EEA States.

As regards the abuse of a dominant position, the Court told the Supreme Court that it had to determine whether the relevant geographic market was limited to the port of Drammen. Should it consider that the AO held a dominant position, it would need to determine whether that position covered a substantial part of the EEA territory. A single port may be regarded as a substantial part of the EEA territory. However, should the referring court find that the port of Drammen could not be regarded as a substantial part of the EEA, it would have to take into account identical or corresponding systems of the AO that might exist in other ports. As for the question of abuse, the referring court was told that it had to assess whether the AO obliged purchasers to obtain all or most of their requirements for stevedoring services from it, charged disproportionate prices, or refrained from the use of modern technology. As regards the cartel prohibition, the Court held that it is was for the Supreme Court to assess whether the thirteen AOs were parties to an agreement or a concerted practice.

Upon a question from the bench, the Commission at the oral hearing put forward arguments on the basis of the judgment of the ECtHR in *Sørensen and Rasmussen* v *Denmark*. In its judgment of 11 January 2006, the Strasbourg Court held that a closed shop arrangement, whereby a specific employment was contingent on the workers joining a trade union with which the employer had a special relationship, infringed Article 11 of the ECHR, the provision that guarantees the negative freedom of association. The EFTA Court affirmatively noted the Commission's argument.

In October 2016, I flew to Oslo for a speech at the Norwegian Bar Association and some meetings. Accompanied by Doris and my Head of Cabinet M-J Clifton, I made a courtesy visit to the leadership of *LO*. The year before, I had given a presentation at *NHO*, the Confederation of Norwegian Enterprise. In view of the fact that the unions had just lost the *Holship* case before the EFTA Court and that I had for years been described as a right-winger in certain circles I Norway, the welcome I received from the employees was a bit frosty. Nevertheless, Gerd Kristiansen, the chairwoman of *LO*, was very friendly. I spoke about our case law, and the *LO* lawyer who had pleaded *Holship* before us said that the system giving unionised dock workers a right of priority in loading and unloading vessels aimed to secure safety and was based "on a one-hundred-year old tradition". He went on to state that the unions could not tolerate that we had interfered with what he called "our core business". I responded that his first assertion was unconvincing and that the two other contentions were not legal arguments. The *LO* officials said that they were confident of winning the *Holship* case in the Norwegian Supreme Court. I did not comment on that, but it was clear to me that if the Supreme Court were to disregard our opinion a second time in a high profile collective labour law case after *STX*,[3] the EEA Agreement would be severely undermined.

On 16 December 2016, the Supreme Court, by 10 against 7 votes, followed our reasoning entirely. The majority emphasised the freedom of establishment, but the court also concurred with our competition law findings. The minority based itself

[3]See for details Chapter 26.

on an alleged factual error on the part of the EFTA Court. The majority considered this irrelevant. The second criticism was that we had said that the AO was pursuing a business objective, whereas in fact their goal was only to protect the workers. The majority found that the AO was in any case engaged in an economic activity.[4]

3 Judicial Review

3.1 Scope

The issue of the standard of review of competition authorities' decisions is one of the most controversial aspects of European competition law. It concerns the fact that not only on the European level, but also in the national legal orders—with the exception of Sweden and Austria—an inquisitorial competition law enforcement system has been established. The investigation is done by a specialised competition authority, which also has the competence to take decisions. In view of the increasing amounts of the fines imposed, more and more attorneys and in-house counsel have started to point to the prosecutorial scheme of the US and claimed that either a fundamental change of the system or, at the very least, a full review of the decisions of the competition authorities by the courts, was required. The ECJ was criticised for performing only a limited ("light") review of fining decisions and for granting the Commission a wide margin of discretion. Even judges of Union courts spoke of a location risk for the EU. The EFTA Court has had two opportunities of dealing with the scope of review in the *Husbanken II* and *Norway Post* cases. I think it's fair to say that it used these opportunities well.

The second *Husbanken* case involved a State guarantee for the publicly owned Norwegian State Housing Bank. ESA concluded that the guarantee constituted State aid, which was, however, justified on the grounds of services of general economic interest. ESA's decision was challenged by the Norwegian Bankers' Association. The Court found in its judgment of 12 June 1998 that the provision on services of general economic interest (Article 59(2) EEA) did in fact apply. In particular, the financial services in question constituted "trade" within the meaning of this provision. The Court noted, however, that ESA "did not go into depth on this condition"; it merely stated in its decision that even if it cannot

> be excluded that the measures under consideration may affect trade between Contracting Parties, in practice such trade effects are likely to be only limited.

Moreover, we held in paragraph 69 that ESA had not considered "to the extent necessary" which market was relevant in this case, whether there were alternative means less distortive to competition than those presently applied, it had not carried out a proper analysis of the costs and benefits of the State aid nor had it made

[4]See for details Chapter 6.

> a proportionality test to assess whether the required balance has been struck between the common interests of the Contracting Parties to the EEA Agreement and the legitimate interests of Norway.

The EFTA Court therefore annulled ESA's decision stating that

> "[t]hese questions call for complex analyses and assessments which the Court cannot carry out but which must be done by the EFTA Surveillance Authority" [....] which "by not carrying out the tests described, [had] wrongly interpreted and applied Article 59(2) EEA."[5]

In *Norway Post*, a case on the abuse of a dominant position, the EFTA Court referenced the *Menarini* judgment of the ECtHR of 27 September 2011 and held in paragraph 100 that

> Article 6(1) ECHR requires that subsequent control of a criminal sanction imposed by an administrative body must be undertaken by a judicial body that has full jurisdiction. Thus, the Court must be able to quash in all respects, on questions of fact and of law, the challenged decision [....]. Therefore, when imposing fines for infringement of the competition rules, ESA cannot be regarded to have any margin of discretion in the assessment of complex economic matters which goes beyond the leeway that necessarily flows from the limitations inherent in the system of legality review.

In paragraph 101, the Court found that although it

> may not replace ESA's assessment by its own and, accordingly, it does not affect the legality of ESA's assessment if the Court merely disagrees with the weighing of individual factors in a complex assessment of economic evidence, the Court must nonetheless be convinced that the conclusions drawn by ESA are supported by the facts.

The EFTA Court's approach to judicial review thus goes beyond a "manifest error" test. Paris lawyer Eric Barbier de La Serre, a former Head of Cabinet of GC President Bo Vesterdorf, observed that

> [in] abandoning the 'margin of appreciation' standard in *Posten Norge* [the EFTA Court] made a very significant contribution to the improvement of the right to a fair trial.

Other eminent competition lawyers such as John Temple Lang and Peter Freeman as well as many others concurred.[6] I may add that my German legal secretary Moritz Am Ende, today an attorney in Vienna, was of great help in the case.

3.2 *Review of Fines*

Under Article 35 SCA, the EFTA Court has unlimited jurisdiction as regards penalties imposed by ESA. For competition fines, this has been specified in Article 31 of 2003 Modernisation Regulation[7] which has, as far as substance is concerned,

[5]See for details Chapter 17.

[6]See for details Chapter 20.

[7]Regulation (EC) No 1/2003.

essentially been incorporated into the EEA Agreement. According to that provision, this unlimited jurisdiction implies that the EFTA Court may cancel, reduce or increase the fine.

In *Norway Post*, the EFTA Court found that the administrative procedure had lasted too long. The initial request for information was sent to Norway Post almost a year after the case was initiated following a complaint. Then it took ESA five years and eight months to conclude its investigation and one year to draft the final decision. The Court considered these periods to be excessive. ESA itself had acknowledged that the duration of the administrative procedure was considerable and had reduced the amount of the fine by EUR 1 million, or 7.2%. On the basis that an infringement of the fundamental right to have one's case adjudicated within a reasonable time requires an effective remedy, the Court decided to reduce the amount of the fine by 20%. The final amount of the fine was therefore reduced from EUR 12.89 million to EUR 11.112 million.

4 Private Plaintiff as Private Attorney General

In a series of follow-on cases to *Norway Post*, the EFTA Court dealt with nullity actions challenging ESA decisions to refuse access to documents it had seized when searching the *Post's* premises. In the first *DB Schenker* case, the Court held that there was a presumption against public access to documents in State aid and merger cases. The system of State aid review would be undermined were interested parties able to access documents to which only the EEA State granting the aid would have access under the applicable procedural provisions. In merger cases, the publication of data concerning the involved undertakings could harm their interest and adversely affect their willingness to cooperate with the authorities. However, when it comes to cases involving cartels and abuse of a dominant position, there is a divergence of opinion between the EFTA Court and the ECJ. The EFTA Court found that not all information concerning a company and its business relations can be deemed to require the protection that must be guaranteed to commercial interests, if the application of the general principle of giving the public the widest possible access to documents held by ESA is not to be frustrated. The

> interest of a company that abused its dominant position on the market to avoid private actions for damages cannot be regarded as a commercial interest

and

> does not constitute a legitimate interest deserving of protection.

It can be assumed that this also applies to cartels, probably with the exception of leniency documents. It was thus logical for the EFTA Court to hold in paragraph 132 of the first *DB Schenker* case:

> [S]pecific policy considerations arise in requests for access to documents as part of follow-on damages cases brought before national courts concerning Articles 53 and 54 EEA. The private enforcement of these provisions ought to be encouraged, as it can make a significant contribution to the maintenance of effective competition in the EEA [….]. ESA's and the Commission's view that follow-on damages claims in competition law cases only serve the purpose of defending the plaintiff's private interests cannot be maintained. While pursuing his private interest, a plaintiff in such proceedings contributes at the same time to the protection of the public interest. This thereby also benefits consumers.

The latter statement points to the concept of a private attorney general as described by Hans Kelsen, Ludwig Raiser, Richard M. Buxbaum and Hannah L. Buxbaum. Kelsen and Raiser have called plaintiffs in this situation functionaries of the general legal order ("*Funktionäre der Gesamtrechtsordnung*").

In the second *DB Schenker* judgment, the Court highlighted the importance of private enforcement of competition law and referred, *inter alia*, to paragraph 132 of DB *Schenker I*. In paragraph 139, it held that ESA's failure to comply with time limits

> was regrettable since it had the potential to undermine private enforcement.

In the fifth *DB Schenker* case, the Court reiterated its statement concerning the role of a private plaintiff and added that AG *Kokott* had signalled her agreement with this approach in paragraph 60 of her Opinion in *Kone and Others*.

5 Right of Audience for In-House Counsel

In *Abelia* v *ESA*, the EFTA Court had to deal with the question of whether in-house attorneys may represent their own company in court. According to Article 17 of the Court's Statute, other parties than the EFTA States, ESA, the EU and the European Commission must be represented before the Court by a "lawyer".

In Joined Cases *Prezes and Republic of Poland* v *Commission*, the ECJ had held that the parallel provision in its Statute precluded employed lawyers from acting on behalf of their employer. The ECJ found in paragraph 24 of that judgment that

> the concept of independence of lawyers is determined not only positively, that is by reference to professional ethical obligations, but also negatively, that is to say, by absence of an employment relationship.

We decided, however, that whether an in-house attorney is sufficiently independent must be assessed in the light of the circumstances. The EFTA Court held in paragraph 46 of *Abelia* that

> the requirement that a party be represented before the Court by an independent third party is not a requirement designed generally to exclude representation by employees of the principal or by those who are financially dependent upon it. The essence of the requirement imposed by EEA law is to prevent private parties from bringing actions in person without recourse to an appropriate intermediary. So far as legal persons are concerned, the requirement of representation by a third party thus seeks to ensure that they are represented by someone who is sufficiently detached from the represented legal person. Whether this is so has to be addressed by the Court on a case by case basis.

In the matter at hand, one lawyer was the head of the Business Legislation Department of the Confederation of Norwegian Enterprise (NHO). Her independence was found not to be affected as the Court had not been provided with information demonstrating that the interests of NHO were largely the same as those of the applicant. The other lawyer was an employee of an independent law firm, from whom she continued to receive her salary, regardless of a contract between NHO and the law firm for the temporary provision of her services. She was also deemed to be sufficiently independent from the applicant. The applicant was thus found to be properly represented before the EFTA Court.

Denying the right of audience to an in-house attorney could amount to a simple restriction of competition and even—as former ECJ President Vassilios Skouris wrote as early as 1975 when he was a university assistant in Germany—a discrimination. It is also essential not to overlook the fact that the exclusion of in-house attorneys from the right of audience was introduced in Germany in 1934 in the light of the fact that a high proportion of them were Jews. Finally, it should be noted that on 14 September 2010, the ECJ in *Akzo Nobel* also denied in-house attorneys the client-attorney privilege. It would therefore only be consequent for the EFTA Court to also apply the case-by-case test in this context in the future.

6 Restriction of Competition by Object

In *Ski Taxi*, the Oslo University Hospital launched two tender procedures for the acquisition of services to transport patients in nine areas in the counties of Oslo and Akershus, including the regions of Southern and Northern Follo, as part of a framework agreement. The first procedure received a single bid for the areas of Southern and Northern Follo, jointly submitted by Ski Taxi and Follo Taxi through Ski Follo Taxidrift AS. The latter was a co-owned management company responsible for the booking system, switchboard operation and communication and IT infrastructure of Ski Taxi and Follo Taxi. The hospital terminated the tender procedure on the grounds of insufficient competition and lodged a complaint with the Norwegian Competition Authority. Later, another tender procedure was launched in which three bids were received. All tenderers were admitted to the framework agreement, including a new joint bid by Ski Taxi and Follo Taxi, through Ski Follo Taxidrift AS.

The Norwegian Competition Authority found that the joint bids had as their object the restriction of competition. There was thus a breach of the cartel prohibition laid down in Section 10 of the Norwegian Competition Act, which is equivalent to Article 53 EEA. This was said to be the case because Ski Taxi and Follo Taxi were competitors and could have submitted separate tenders. Administrative fines were imposed on Ski Taxi SA, Follo Taxi SA and Ski Follo Taxidrift AS. The Follo District Court annulled the decision, but the Borgarting Court of Appeal set this judgment aside holding that the joint bids constituted a restriction of competition by object. The judgment was challenged before the Supreme Court of Norway. On its own motion, the Supreme Court on 24 February

2016 referred the case to the EFTA Court. The reference concerned the legal test and the criteria to be applied when determining whether a form of conduct constitutes a restriction of competition by object.

The EFTA Court held that certain types of coordination between undertakings reveal a sufficient degree of harm to competition that it may be found that there is no need to examine their effects. In order to determine the degree of harm to competition, regard must be had to the content of the agreement's provisions, its objectives and the economic and legal context of which it forms a part. When determining that context, it is also necessary to take into consideration the nature of the goods or services affected, as well as the real conditions of the functioning and structure of the market or markets in question. In addition, although the parties' intention is not a necessary factor in determining whether an agreement between undertakings is restrictive, there is nothing prohibiting the competition authorities, the national courts or the Court from taking that factor into account.

On a crucial point, we did not follow the ECJ's line of argument, but based ourselves on the Opinion of AG Wahl in *CB* v *Commission*. In paragraph 61 of the judgment, we referred to his statement, in point 56 of his Opinion, that only conduct whose harmful nature is easily identifiable, in the light of experience and economics, should be regarded as a restriction of competition by object.

As regards the circumstances of the case, the Court held that since the submission of joint bids involved price-fixing, which is expressly prohibited by Article 53(1) EEA, consideration of the economic and legal context may be limited to what is strictly necessary in order to establish the existence of a restriction of competition by object. However, it still needed to be assessed, albeit in an abridged manner, whether the parties to the agreement were actual or potential competitors, and whether the submission of joint bids was to be regarded as an ancillary restraint.

7 Other Notable Cases

7.1 Protecting Competition Between Airlines

Under the Airport Slot Regulation[8] time slots for the take-off and landing of airplanes are allocated to airlines according to a system of "grandfather rights". If an air carrier is able to show that he operated the slots for at least 80% of the time during the scheduling period for which they have been allocated, he is entitled to the same series of slots in the subsequent equivalent scheduling period. This renders market entry for newcomers rather difficult. In practice, an incumbent airline could keep a slot forever. Attempts to amend the regulation on the allocation of take-off and landing slots remained unsuccessful. A dispute before the Reykjavík District Court concerned the interpretation of the regulation at Keflavík International

[8](EEC) No 95/93.

Airport for the year 2014. On 22 September 2014, that court submitted a request for a preliminary ruling in Case *Wow Air*. The Icelandic court asked for the application of the accelerated procedure under Article 97a of the Court's Rules of Procedure. According to this provision, the President may, at the request of the national court, exceptionally decide to apply such a procedure where the circumstances referred to establish that a ruling on the question put to the Court is a matter of exceptional urgency. I had been to Keflavík many times and I knew about the importance of the airport and about the economic situation. I granted the accelerated procedure on the basis of the economic sensitivity of the case. The potential effects of the judgment on slot allocations in the near future were deemed to be such as to constitute a matter of exceptional urgency. My order stated in that regard:

> To guarantee fair and effective competition is one of the most important goals of the EEA Agreement. Effective competition benefits both consumers and competitors and contributes to the common good. In the case at hand, Iceland's special geographic situation must be taken into account with Keflavík essentially being the only international airport in the country.

Judgment was rendered on 10 December 2014, i.e. within less than three months. Firstly, the Court provided support to the independent coordinator who is competent for the initial allocation of the time slots, holding that

> [i]n order for the system to be effective, the coordinator has to be independent from any vested interests and has to have the necessary financial resources to accomplish the tasks assigned to him by the Regulation. It must be ensured that neither the authorities of the EEA State concerned nor any other party can unduly influence the coordinator before, during and after the allocation process.

This presupposes that there is

> a clear separation of tasks between the coordinator, the coordination committee and the EEA State so as to avoid any conflict of interest at any time in the allocation and monitoring procedure. In other words, the coordinator must have the expertise and the integrity necessary to contribute to the objectivity, transparency and efficiency of time slot allocation.

This was important because coordinators are often former employees of the big flagship carriers. Secondly, the EFTA Court found that the national competition authorities have the right to give direct instructions to the undertakings when it comes to transferring time slots after the initial slot allocation, if this is found to be required under national or EEA competition law. Thereby the system of grandfather rights has, to a certain extent, been opened up to competition.

Some observers wondered why the accelerated procedure had been granted in this case, since, according to traditional understanding, this procedure should normally only be used if the human rights of individuals are at stake. The answer is that the risk that millions of consumers could suffer damage must be deemed to be sufficient to trigger the use of this procedure. Once more, the lack of understanding of many lawyers for economic law becomes manifest in this context. For the sake of order, I add that Article 97a RoP does not specify any grounds for its use.

7.2 *Application of EEA Competition Law to Public Bodies*

In *Sorpa*, the Supreme Court of Iceland referred questions on the interpretation of the prohibition of the abuse of a dominant position laid down in Article 54 EEA. The Icelandic Waste Disposal Act entrusted municipalities with the management of waste produced in their municipal area. Respective centres and sites could not be operated without a licence, which could be issued to private as well as public entities. The entity operating a landfill site was obliged to charge a fee in return for its services, and the entity operating an acceptance centre was allowed to charge a fee. The fee charged for the provision of either waste disposal or waste acceptance services could not exceed the costs incurred. In 1988, the municipalities in the Reykjavík area entered into an agreement whereby Sorpa was established as a municipal cooperative agency and was entrusted with waste management tasks. Two licences were issued to Sorpa for the operation of an acceptance centre and a landfill site. According to the establishment contract, the municipalities in the area of Reykjavík were entitled to receive dividends in proportion to their share in Sorpa's capital. However, the establishment contract provided that, rather than distribute dividends, Sorpa could choose to grant its owners a discount on the fees that it sets for the acceptance and the disposal of waste. Sorpa chose to do so. By a decision of 21 December 2012 the Icelandic Competition Authority found that Sorpa had infringed Article 11 of the Icelandic Competition Act pertaining to the abuse of a dominant position on the market for waste acceptance in the metropolitan area of Reykjavík, where its market share amounted to approximately 70% and it faced competition from only one operator, Gámaþjónustan hf. Moreover, Sorpa enjoyed a dominant position on the market for waste disposal in the same geographic area, where it was the sole operator. Since Gámaþjónustan did not run any landfill sites, it was also a customer of Sorpa. By granting its owners a larger discount than it granted its other customers, in particular Gámaþjónustan, Sorpa had, in the view of the Icelandic Competition Authority, abused its dominant position.

The EFTA Court found an entity of public law to constitute an undertaking within the meaning of Article 54 EEA if it did not act in the exercise of official authority but engaged in an economic activity, which consisted in offering goods or services on a market. I should add here that the Swedish Patent and Market Court in a judgment of 21 December 2016 relied on this finding.

In order to determine whether the provision of waste management services by a municipality or a municipal cooperative agency such as Sorpa was an economic activity, account had to be taken of the existence of competition with private entities and the level of the compensation received. In that regard, the Court noted that under the Waste Disposal Act, licences for the operation of waste disposal centres and landfill sites could be granted to private entities, and one licence was granted to Gámaþjónustan. The fact that Sorpa decided to charge a fee for the provision of waste acceptance services, although it was not obliged to do so, was a further indication of the economic nature of its activity. Under Article 59(2) EEA, undertakings are exempt from the application of EEA competition rules where: (i) they are entrusted with the operation of services of general economic interest; and (ii) the application of such rules would obstruct the performance of their tasks. The Court held that waste management may be regarded as a service of general economic interest. It was left to the referring court to determine whether, as submitted by Sorpa, the application of Article 54 EEA would make it impossible for it to provide the services it has been entrusted with, or to perform them under economically acceptable conditions.

As regards discrimination, we also held that companies belonging to the same group as the dominant undertaking may be regarded as the trading parties of that undertaking. This is because they may contract with that undertaking and either receive goods or services from it or provide it with goods or services. For a trading party of the dominant firm to be placed at a competitive disadvantage, that party must be placed at a disadvantage vis-à-vis its competitors. Since it is a trading partner of the dominant undertaking, that disadvantage must occur on a market either downstream or upstream of the dominated market. The EFTA Court noted that Sorpa granted its owners a larger discount than it granted its other customers, in particular Gámaþjónustan. For the party discriminated against, Gámaþjónustan, to be placed at a competitive disadvantage with the favoured party, in this case Sorpa's owners, that firm would have to compete with Sorpa's owners. Although this was for the Supreme Court to assess, the EFTA Court noted that Gámaþjónustan did not appear to compete against Sorpa's owners on a market upstream or downstream of the market for waste acceptance in the metropolitan area of Reykjavík. Rather, Gámaþjónustan appeared to compete with Sorpa itself on the market for waste acceptance. Therefore, Gámaþjónustan did not appear to be placed at a competitive disadvantage. Finally, the Court held that, should the referring court find that Sorpa did not infringe the prohibition to discriminate laid down in Article 54(2)(c) EEA, Sorpa may, since pursuant to the Waste Disposal Act the amount of the fees charged could not exceed the costs incurred, have engaged in predatory pricing by granting rebates on such fees. The assessment of this question was left to the Supreme Court.

8 Conclusions

In its competition case law, the EFTA Court has emphasised the importance of economic considerations. However, it has always noted that whether there is a restriction of competition or an abuse of dominance is a legal question. The Court has been commended for its approach to competition economics. It was said that it has rejected formalist approaches to competition law. John Temple Lang observed in that regard:

> In general one has the clear impression that the Court deals more readily with economic issues than either the General Court or the European Court of Justice. Economic arguments are set out more clearly and dealt with more concisely than in the judgments of the other two courts. This is partly a result of a less formal judicial style, but it also seems to reveal a more economic approach, which is certainly preferable, in particular in the sphere of competition law.

It would, however, not be permissible to associate the Court with a specific economic school of thought. In a given case, the Court will opt for the solution that it deems to be the most convincing. One must bear in mind in this context that the Court is known for its tradition of revealing the value judgments underlying its decisions.

As demonstrated, the EFTA Court does undertake strict judicial review and thereby has a tight control over ESA's discretion in competition law cases. In the commemorative book marking the EFTA Court's twentieth anniversary, Ian Forrester, now a judge on the GC, expressed the impression

> that the ESA may have a harder job than the Commission in defending its cases in court.

Eric Morgan de Rivery and Alexandre Fall concurred with this assessment.

The EFTA Court put special emphasis on private enforcement. It was the first European court that saw private plaintiffs as actors of the *bonum commune*. In *Wow Air*, its President granted the accelerated preliminary reference procedure in a competition law case, something which was far from self-evident. The Court has also taken a pro-competitive stand on the right of audience of in-house attorneys.

That a court of three with a limited case load had to decide on matters such as *Norway Post*, *LO*, *Holship* or *Ski Taxi*, was a challenge. I have sometimes called this the "boulder situation". Suddenly, a big boulder is thrown into the Court's garden. There wasn't ever a boulder like it before and you don't know whether and when the next one will land. On the one hand, this means that you have no judicial experience of your own on how to tackle the case. On the other hand, you cannot necessarily expect to have another case of this type in the foreseeable future, which means that you must try to score a bull's eye with your first attempt

Photo: © Yaph

Doris at the Luxembourg National Holiday, Photo: © Yaph

Luis Grañena Lopez, Kong Carl av EØS (King Carl of the EEA), © Bergens Tidende

With HSH Hereditary Prince Alois of Liechtenstein and Doris, Photo: © Tatjana Schnalzger

RELAX (chiarenza & hauser & co), ‘is JUSTICE justice?’, 2015, Neon sign, blue light, Commission/permanent work EFTA Court, Luxembourg. Photo: © 2018, Kerstin Schwiesow

With Doris, necklace Gijs Bakker

With EU Commission Vice-President Joaquín Almunia

With Judge Per Christiansen, Andean Court President Luis Diez Canseco and Judge Páll Hreinsson

Welcoming Norwegian Prime Minister Erna Solberg

Chapter 17
State Aid Control—A More Frequent Pleasure

Contents

1 EU Law as a Starting Point

The EEA Agreement reproduces the State aid rules of EU law. The general prohibition of State aid to certain undertakings is deemed to be a major European achievement and State aid control is considered to be the flip side of the "competition coin". In the EU, the Commissioner for Competition has thus traditionally been responsible for both competition policy and State aid control.

In the beginning, EU State aid law lacked bite. The Member States were creative in circumventing the respective provisions, in particular by granting indirect benefits. The Commission reacted by interpreting the Treaty provisions broadly, and step by step developed a rigorous approach. In 1985, when Jacques Delors became President, the Commission wrote in the seminal White Paper *Completing the Internal Market*[1]:

> [I]t will be particularly important that the Community discipline on state aids be rigorously enforced. There are tendencies to spend large amounts of public funds on state aids to uncompetitive industries and enterprises. Often, they not only distort competition but also in the long run undermine efforts to increase European competitiveness. They represent a drain on scarce public resources and they threaten to defeat efforts to build the internal market. As the physical and technical barriers inside the Community are removed, the

[1](COM(85)310 final).

C. Baudenbacher, *Judicial Independence*, Springer Biographies,
https://doi.org/10.1007/978-3-030-02308-9_17

> Commission will see to it that a rigorous policy is pursued in regard to state aids so that public resources are not used to confer artificial advantage to some firms over others.

In recent times, the Commissioner for Competition Joaquín Almunia and his successor, the currently serving Margrethe Vestager, have shown great interest in State aid control, Almunia by trying to modernise the State aid rules and procedures and Vestager by her investigations of tax benefits for undertakings such as Apple, Amazon, IKEA and Starbucks. The latter activities have triggered fundamental controversies.

2 ESA's Approach

In the EFTA pillar, it is ESA's task to monitor State aid. As I have said before, ESA was never keen to apply the EEA competition law rules.[2] In competition matters, there are currently only three ongoing investigations being undertaken by ESA: (1) *DNB, Nordea, Finance Norway* and *BankID;* (2) *Widerøe*; and (3) *Telenor*. On the other hand, State aid control generates significant work for the Authority. This was so from the beginning. In 2017 ESA opened 53 State aid cases and closed 65, even though its Annual Report speaks of a "historical low following the state aid modernisation reform".

Even though there exists a common directorate for both competition and State aid policy within ESA, State aid control was—contrary to the Commission's practice—traditionally split from competition matters within the College. Hannes Hafstein was the first College Member to oversee both dossiers in 2002 and 2003. When Hafstein succeeded Einar M. Bull as ESA President in 2004, Bull received both the State aid and the competition dossiers in return. But otherwise, the division of responsibilities has been rather straightforward: the President has always monitored State aid, while another College Member was responsible for competition matters. The President has almost always been Norwegian, and the College Member in charge of competition has usually been Icelandic.

This division of tasks is interesting because Norway is a champion of State aid not only within but also beyond the EFTA pillar, regularly scoring above the EEA average. Since 2006, Norway has consistently increased its State aid spending. In 2016, the country's State aid expenditure amounted to 0.84% of its GDP, while the average within the EU was 0.65% of a Member State's GDP. This places Norway eighth in the ranking of all EEA Member States. In 2016, the States that handed out more State aid than Norway were: Hungary (1.95% of GDP), Denmark (1.60% of GDP), Latvia (1.46% of GDP), the Czech Republic (1.30% of GDP), Germany (1.27% of GDP), Poland (1.01% of GDP), and Croatia (0.94% of GDP). Compared to Norway, Iceland's State aid expenses were rather modest and amounted to only half of what Norway spent relative to the GDP; Iceland spent 0.42% of its GDP, which ranks it 23rd within the EEA. Liechtenstein spent a mere 0.03% of its GDP on State aid in 2016. Liechtenstein thereby arrives comfortably last in the EEA

[2]See for details Chapter 7.

ranking, with a rather large margin between it and the second to last State, namely Ireland, which spent 0.14% of its GDP on State aid.

The State aid policy of the three EEA/EFTA States differs not only as regards the amount spent on State aid, but also with respect to the objectives pursued. In 2016, Norway's measures focussed on environmental protection (39%) and regional development (31%); Iceland spent most of its money on research and development (59%); and Liechtenstein concentrated on culture and heritage conservation (92%). There is, moreover, a difference in the financing of the aid schemes: Iceland and Liechtenstein prefer grants, whereas Norway hands out 73% of its aid as tax concessions. Here again, Norway scores well above the average, since the EU average use of tax exemptions as an instrument of State aid lies at 32%.

That Norway spends most is reflected in ESA's practice: In 2017, the Authority adopted 18 decisions, 14 regarding Norway, three on Iceland and one on Liechtenstein. Even more interesting is the content of those decisions: in only two of the 14 Norwegian cases did ESA find it necessary to approve the schemes; all other Norwegian cases raised no issues. In the two cases in which approval was deemed to be required, it was given without much difficulty and, in particular, without ESA proposing any amendments to the scheme. As regards the three decisions involving Iceland, ESA found it necessary for one of the schemes to be amended and opened formal investigations into another. The situation was similar in 2016, when none of the 18 Norwegian cases handled by ESA led to amendments of the schemes or formal investigations. However, in relation to Iceland, ESA once again proposed "appropriate measures" in one of the seven cases.

3 Judicial Review

3.1 General

In the majority of its cases, the EFTA Court has dealt with Norwegian aid. It is interesting that in all those cases ESA acted as defendant and never brought a case against Norway. The only two cases brought by ESA against an EEA/EFTA-State in State aid matters concerned the *Icelandic International Trading Companies* and the *Icelandic Investment Incentive Scheme*. Moreover, only a few of the Court's State aid judgments have been rendered at the request of national courts—such as *Íslandsbanki* and *Synnøve Finden*. The relevant case law has thus been developed on the basis of actions brought by States or individuals challenging a decision by ESA. The principle hurdle to bringing such an action lies in Article 36 SCA which states that:

> any natural or legal person may, under the same conditions, institute proceedings before the EFTA Court against a decision of the EFTA Surveillance Authority addressed to that person or against a decision addressed to another person, if it is of direct and individual concern to the former.

On the basis of this, it is rather easy for the EEA/EFTA States concerned to bring a case before the Court, as the decisions are addressed to them. However, problems arise when either a beneficiary of aid or a competitor of a beneficiary intends to challenge a State aid decision. Article 36 SCA corresponds to Article 230 TFEU. That provision is also a high hurdle to jump. The reason for this lies in the *Plaumann* doctrine, which was laid down by the ECJ as early as 1963. Plaumann & Co imported clementines. The German authorities wished to suspend custom duties, but the Commission refused permission. Plaumann sought judicial review of the decision. The ECJ found:

> Persons other than those to whom a decision is addressed may only claim to be individually concerned if that decision affects them by reason of certain attributes which are peculiar to them or by reason of circumstances in which they are differentiated from all other persons and by virtue of these factors distinguishes them individually just as in the case of the person addressed.

The ECJ concluded:

> In the present case the applicant is affected by the disputed decision as an importer of clementines, that is to say, by reason of a commercial activity which may at any time be practised by any person and is not therefore such as to distinguish the applicant in relation to the contested decision as in the case of the addressee.

The action for annulment was thus declared inadmissible. The *Plaumann* doctrine has been applied by the ECJ ever since its creation. In academic literature, the role of the Union courts has been compared to that of Franz Kafka's gatekeeper. In his 1915 parable "Before the Law" ("*Vor dem Gesetz*"), which later became part of the novel "The Trial" ("*Der Prozess*"), Kafka wrote:

> Before the law sits a gatekeeper. To this gatekeeper comes a man from the country who asks to gain entry into the law. But the gatekeeper says that he cannot grant him entry at the moment. The man thinks about it and then asks if he will be allowed to come in later on. 'It is possible', says the gatekeeper, 'but not now.'
>
> *Vor dem Gesetz steht ein Türhüter. Zu diesem Türhüter kommt ein Mann vom Lande und bittet um Eintritt in das Gesetz. Aber der Türhüter sagt, dass er ihm jetzt den Eintritt nicht gewähren könne. Der Mann überlegt und fragt dann, ob er also später werde eintreten dürfen.',,Es ist möglich', sagt der Türhüter, 'jetzt aber nicht.'*

3.2 Locus Standi

Locus standi is a technical term, which means the right to bring an action before a court. Naturally, not everybody can sue anyone for any reason as they please. This is why parties need to establish their standing before the courts. Thus, *locus standi* basically refers to the right to sue, in principle, another person or entity. If a person has such a right, the action is admissible.

The EFTA Court first tackled the issue of admissibility in *Scottish Salmon Growers*. In a complaint to ESA, the applicant, the Scottish Salmon Growers Association, alleged that the Norwegian salmon industry had been granted State aid contrary to the EEA Agreement. ESA declined to investigate the complaint on the grounds that it did not have the competence to assess State aid to fisheries. The applicant asked the EFTA Court to annul ESA's decision. ESA claimed, *inter alia*, that the action should be considered inadmissible as the association did not have *locus standi*. In its judgment of 21 March 1995, the Court noted, however, that the association represented an overwhelming majority of Scottish salmon growers, promoting profitable trade in salmon and pursuing multiple objectives on the growers' behalf. As such, it found that the measures did concern the interests of the association, and "to such an extent" that the action should be considered admissible. That the applicant was not the addressee of ESA's decision did not preclude this finding. The Court did not quote *Plaumann* in this context and the wording of its reasoning does not specifically mirror *Plaumann*.

However, this liberal approach was not sustained. In *Bellona*, a case involving gas extraction from the "*Snøhvit field*" in the Barents Sea, the Norwegian Petroleum Taxation Act had been modified to include very favourable depreciation rates for large-scale liquefied natural gas projects. The Bellona Foundation, a legal entity concerned with environmental degradation and pollution, lodged a complaint with ESA, claiming that the amendments constituted State aid. In the judicial proceedings, Bellona which was represented by the Brussels attorney, and later British judge on the GC, Ian Forrester, invited the Court to adopt a "flexible interpretation of standing", and to set aside the Plaumann formula. Ian argued that doing so would make the test more compatible with the ECHR. ESA, supported by the Commission, submitted that the applicants did not have *locus standi*. At that time, a debate on the extension of the Plaumann formula had arisen with the *UPA* and *Jegó-Queré* cases before the EU Courts. In his Opinion in *UPA* of 21 March 2002, AG Jacobs proposed a more generous interpretation of the element of "individual concern", stating that this would enhance effective judicial protection by making judicial review available to those whose interests are hindered by unlawful acts. In its *Jégo-Quéré* judgment of 2 May 2002, the (then) CFI adopted a teleological approach to establishing individual concern, contrary to the Plaumann test, and stated that there was a need to uphold effective judicial protection. That the CFI criticised the Plaumann formula in *Jégo-Quéré* and based itself on AG Jacobs' Opinion in *UPA* while the *UPA* case was still pending before the ECJ was probably not a smart move. On 25 July 2002, the ECJ rendered judgment in *UPA* confirming the Plaumann approach and stating that any other interpretation of *locus standi* in the light of the Treaties would go beyond its own jurisdiction.

The EFTA Court rendered judgment in *Bellona* on 19 June 2003. It called access to justice "an essential element of the EEA legal framework" and it also acknowledged that the ongoing debate on this issue within the EU Courts, and its "widening [of] the avenues of access to justice" had created some uncertainty. Hence, there existed a need to proceed with caution. The Court then reiterated its findings from *Scottish Salmon Growers*, pointing to the principle of homogeneity, which should also be applied to the understanding of *locus standi*. It went on to examine the expression "party concerned". Article 1(2) of Protocol 3 to the SCA obliges ESA to render a decision only after it has notified the "parties concerned". The provision has been taken over from what is now Article 108(2) TFEU. In *Cook*, the ECJ held that where the Commission, without initiating the procedure that enables the parties concerned to submit their comments finds that an aid is compatible with the common market, the persons intended to benefit from those procedural guarantees may secure compliance therewith only if they are able to challenge that decision by the Commission before the Court. Parties concerned are according to the ECJ the "persons, undertakings or associations whose interests might be affected by the grant of the aid, in particular competing undertakings and trade associations." Through the inclusions of "parties concerned" in the Treaty, the State aid procedure, which, in principle, is a bilateral procedure between the Member State and the authority, is opened up to input from a number of stakeholders, such as the beneficiaries of the aid and the competitors of the beneficiaries. Such stakeholders must be able to safeguard their (procedural) rights before the courts and also be informed of the outcome of the case. In *Bellona*, the EFTA Court referred, *inter alia*, to the ECJ's *Cook* judgment when defining the concept of "party concerned". Based on this, the Court found that not only the undertakings benefitting from the aid could be regarded as concerned. It chose to extend the concept to "persons, undertakings or associations whose interests might be affected by the grant of an aid", particularly those in a competing position. Nevertheless, the Court then proceeded on the basis of *Plaumann* to analyse whether Bellona's competitive position could effectively be hindered by the granting of aid. It started by noting that the measures at issue were of general application, therefore not being able to

> affect Bellona's interests in a manner that would provide a basis for *locus standi*.

The Court held, in addition, that prospective business, or effects which are too indirect or remote, do not suffice to grant legal standing. Unlike the association involved in the *Scottish Salmon Growers* case, the Bellona Foundation was not

> an association with a defined membership on the basis of a community of interests.

It later became clear, that when admissibility is assessed, case law distinguishes between two types of decisions: decisions to close a formal investigation, and decisions not to open a formal investigation after a preliminary examination. For the first type of cases, where usually the merits of a decision are challenged, the EFTA Court applied an even stricter test to assess the applicants' *locus standi*. In order for the challenge to be admissible, the undertaking claiming to be a competitor must show that its market position is "substantially affected"—the mere status as a competitor does not suffice. With regard to decisions not to open a formal investigation, which in essence concern procedural rights, the Court has developed a more relaxed approach on the basis of the notion of "interested party". Both *modi operandi* are also found in ECJ case law.

The distinction between standing to challenge a decision on its merits or to defend procedural rights has been criticised. AG Bot stated in his Opinion in *Kronofrance* that the aim pursued by the applicant is the same, regardless of whether it invokes procedural rights or questions the merits of the decision—in both situations, it seeks to initiate a formal investigation procedure. AG Jääskinen in his Opinion in *Kronoply* and *Kronotex* criticised the legal uncertainty that results from this approach, since it is often impossible to identify, for both parties and the Court, which pleas aim to protect procedural rights and which refer to the substance of the decision.

Nevertheless, the EFTA Court based itself on the notion of "interested party" for the purposes of safeguarding procedural rights for example in *Den norske forleggerforening* v *ESA*, a case involving aid to the Norwegian Digital Learning Arena. The Norwegian Publisher's Association asked the EFTA Court to annul the ESA decision which was rendered without opening a formal investigation. The applicant's *locus standi* to challenge the decision was called into question. In this regard, the Court held that the concept of "interested party" can refer to an "indeterminate group of addressees", in particular competing undertakings of the beneficiary of the said aid. ESA's decision was annulled. The same line of reasoning was followed later in *Míla v ESA*. The Court noted that, even though the applicant had not established that its position on the market could be significantly affected, and hence did not have standing to challenge the merits of the decision, in its capacity as a competitor, it did have a status of "interested party" with regard to the upholding of procedural rights.

The EFTA Court took note of the ECJ's *Kronoply* and *Kronotex* case law, where the latter had stated that even a non-direct competitor of the beneficiary of aid can be an interested party. A direct reference to these cases was made in *Abelia*, where the applicant lodged a complaint with ESA alleging that illegal State aid had been granted to lessors of premises to public schools and other public sector providers. According to the complaint, the Norwegian VAT system had the effect of putting lessors of premises to private schools, as well as private schools themselves, at an economic disadvantage. Essentially the system provided VAT compensation to lessors of premises to public schools and other public sector providers, as well as to the public schools and public sector providers themselves. This compensation was not available to lessors of premises to private schools nor to the private schools themselves. The applicant was a trade and employers' association, which was part of a larger employers' organisation. It represented 1250 companies that provided services in the fields of information technology (IT), telecommunications, research and development, consultancy and education, as well as a number of private schools that offered educational services. ESA concluded, without initiating the formal investigation procedure, that the contested provisions of the Norwegian tax legislation did not constitute State Aid. The Court held, in paragraph 81 of the order in *Abelia* that the possibility is not ruled out

> that an undertaking which is not a direct competitor of the beneficiary of the aid can be categorised as an interested party, provided that that undertaking demonstrates that its interests could be adversely affected by the grant of the aid.

This entails a legitimate interest, such as the protection of the applicant's competitive position. However, in *Abelia*, the applicant failed to

> point to any specific instances where its members, for whom it is substituting itself, find themselves in a relationship of rivalry with the beneficiaries of the alleged aid, that is, lessors of premises to public schools.

As such, the Court stated that it lacked legal standing. Finally, with regard to procedural rights, the Court stated in *Kimek Offshore* that

> an undertaking can be considered an interested party with a view to safeguarding its procedural rights if it shows that its interest might be affected by the granting of aid.

A legitimate interest can stem from the need to protect the competitive position, which would be affected by the State aid measures.

However, the standard is, as mentioned above, stricter when ESA has decided to close a formal investigation. This, too, was derived from ECJ case law. The ECJ had, for example in *Cofaz*, established that *locus standi* could be admitted if: (i) the applicant had been "substantially involved" in the procedure before the authority (in this case the Commission); and (ii) its position on the market was "substantially affected" by the contested aid. The first criterion, however, seems to have progressively lost its importance—albeit it is still used as a tool to assess the effects on the position on the market held by the applicant. The EFTA Court also takes the past procedural involvement into account when determining standing to challenge a decision.

The *Private Barnehagers Landsforbund* case concerned an application for the annulment of an ESA decision on the public financing of municipal day-care institutions in Norway. ESA had concluded that the system did not constitute State aid. The applicant argued that it represented the overwhelming part of the private kindergarten sector in Norway, which it was at the origin of the complaint and was active in the procedure leading to the contested decision. Moreover, it submitted that the alleged distortion of competition at issue was to the detriment of the private kindergartens that its members were exposed to on a daily basis, threatening their very economic survival. The EFTA Court recalled *Bellona*, stating that persons other than the addressees of a decision cannot claim to be individually concerned unless they are affected by the decision by reason of certain attributes peculiar to them, or circumstances in which they are differentiated from all other persons. As such, in State aid, applicants who challenge the merits of a decision are considered individually concerned by it if their market position is substantially affected by the aid to which the decision relates. For an undertaking, it is imperative that it demonstrates that the position on the market of at least one of its members is substantially affected; it cannot rely solely on its status as a competitor of the undertaking receiving aid, but must also show that the circumstances distinguish it in a similar way to the undertaking receiving the aid. The Court added that in determining the *locus standi* of an applicant, the question of whether the aid is new or existing cannot be decisive such that it would safeguard any procedural rights.

This test, i.e. that the position must be substantially affected, was further applied in *Magasin- og Ukepresseforeningen*, a case involving alleged aid to newspapers. The Court restated that, in order to establish *locus standi*, it was not enough that a measure may exercise an influence on the competitive relationships existing on the relevant market. The undertaking at issue must show that its circumstances distinguish it in a similar manner to the undertaking receiving aid, which would be the case particularly where its position on the market is substantially affected by said aid.

The "substantially affected" test was again used in the second *Konkurrenten* case. The EFTA Court noted that some "impact" on the relevant market does not suffice to prove that a competitor's position is substantially affected; indeed, the latter must demonstrate

> the extent of the detriment to its market position.

Thus, *Konkurrenten* should have been able to demonstrate the loss of an opportunity to make a profit or a less favourable development, that is, a definitive link between the measure at issue and the effects on its market position. The mere existence of factors that point to a decline in commercial or financial performance does not suffice.

It should be noted that Konkurrenten implicitly questioned the applicability of a strict *Plaumann* test in the EFTA pillar. The ECJ has dispelled any fundamental rights concerns with regard to the *Plaumann* doctrine. In *UPA* the ECJ stated, for example:

> The Treaty has established a complete system of legal remedies and procedures designed to ensure judicial review of the legality of acts of the institutions, and has entrusted such review to the Community Courts. Under that system, natural or legal persons who are prevented by the conditions for admissibility from directly challenging Community measures of general application can plead the invalidity of such acts: - either indirectly before the Community Courts in an action which challenges the Community measure adopted pursuant to the act at issue, - or before the national courts which, since they have no jurisdiction themselves to declare those measures invalid, can make a reference to the Court of Justice for a preliminary ruling on validity.

Konkurrenten argued that it had standing pursuant to the fundamental right to effective judicial protection under EEA law and Article 6 of the ECHR, because it had no other venue to challenge the validity of the contested decision. It contended that, unlike in the EU pillar, there is no indirect venue for a validity review of ESA's decisions in the EFTA pillar. Advisory opinions are not binding, there is no obligation for national courts of last resort to request such an opinion, and the EFTA Court has not been empowered by the SCA to annul an ESA decision in an advisory opinion. The reasons upon which the ECJ has relied to justify a restrictive test for individual concern would not, therefore, apply to the EFTA pillar. In other words, Konkurrenten asserted that applying the *Plaumann* formula in the EFTA pillar amounted to comparing apples and oranges.

To some extent it seems that it was necessary for the EFTA Court to deviate from the ECJ's mantra on the compliance of the TFEU's admissibility provisions with fundamental rights. The Court stated in paragraph 64 of its Order of 22 December 2017:

> As regards Konkurrenten's submission that it has standing in any event pursuant to its fundamental right to effective judicial protection, the Court notes that the requirements of standing are a recognised part of a judicial procedure. Konkurrenten has not presented any argument that could persuade the Court to conclude that the application of the requirements of Article 36 SCA is in the present case in breach of the fundamental right to effective judicial protection under EEA law, as interpreted in light of the ECHR.

The challenge to *Plaumann* was thus, once again, rejected by a Luxembourg Court. Who knows whether, and if so to what extent, *Plaumann,* which is celebrating its 55th birthday in 2018, will be revisited in the future.

3.3 Substance

Also as regards the substance, EEA State aid law has to a large extent been developed by the EFTA Court in line with ECJ jurisprudence. However, there are certain differences.

The criteria for establishing State aid appear quite straightforward and have been addressed numerous times: in paragraph 39 of *Synnøve Finden* the Court summarised them as follows:

> A finding that a certain measure constitutes State aid within the meaning of Article 61 EEA presupposes that four conditions are met. These are that there is an intervention by the State or through State resources, that the intervention is liable to affect trade between EEA States, that it confers a selective advantage on the beneficiary and that it distorts or threatens to distort competition.

The first case brought before the EFTA Court concerning the substance of State aid was *Husbanken II.* Husbanken was the Norwegian State Housing bank, which provided house-building loans on a large scale. Husbanken did not means-test loan applicants, however, requirements were imposed such as limits on cost and size etc. Its primary capital was contributed by the State. The Norwegian Bankers' Association, which was composed of banks, mortgage institutions and other financial institutions, claimed that the arrangement for publicly-supported housing finance through Husbanken was detrimental to competitive conditions in the Norwegian credit market, making it impossible for its member institutions to compete on equal terms with Husbanken in the area of basic security loans for new dwellings. On this ground, the Association lodged a complaint with ESA. Since ESA's decision was that there was no incompatibility with State aid provisions, the Association brought an action for annulment before the Court. The main question was whether Husbanken's provision of funding constituted State aid within the meaning of Article 61 EEA.

Applying the conditions set by Article 61 EEA, the Court noted that Husbanken, as

> a State institution set up by law, having its own directors and board of directors and board of controllers, its own offices and its own annual accounts

should be considered an undertaking. It then proceeded to assess whether, in procedural terms, the aid at stake was to be considered "existing aid" or "new aid". In this regard, the Court noted that the changes undertaken configured a "decrease in the aid then existing"; as such, the aid at issue should be considered existing aid. The Court then addressed its own powers of judicial review with respect to ESA's discretion. It stated that, according to settled case law

> which involves assessments of an economic and social nature which must be made within an EEA context,

the Court must merely verify whether the facts have been correctly stated by ESA and whether there has been misuse of powers or manifest errors of assessment. Furthermore, the Court established that the assessment of "services of general economic interest" under Article 59(2) EEA cannot depend on the nature of the undertaking,

> but rather [on] the essence of the services deemed to be of general economic interest and the special characteristics of this interest that distinguish it from the general economic interest of other activities.

In the Joined Cases *Liechtenstein* v *ESA* and *VTM Fund Management*, the Court developed the definition of "aid". The two cases concerned an action for annulment of an ESA decision where ESA found that certain favourable rules for the taxation of the assets of investment companies constituted State aid that was incompatible with Article 61(1) EEA. ESA had, moreover, ordered the recovery of the aid from the beneficiaries. There had already been a similar case before the Court a little earlier, which also concerned the Liechtenstein Tax Code: Joined Cases *Liechtenstein, REASSUR AG and Swisscom RE AG* v *ESA*. They concerned a capital tax of so-called "captive insurance companies", which was lower—0.1% or less—than the tax that other companies paid—0.2%. ESA found that this constituted State aid. Thus, on the selectivity of the aid the Court had already established:

> The concept of aid not only includes positive benefits, such as subsidies themselves, but also measures which, in various forms, mitigate the charges which are normally included in the budget of an undertaking and which, thus, without being subsidies in the strict sense of the word, are similar in character and have the same effect.

This was also cited in paragraph 50 of *Liechtenstein* v *ESA* and *VTM Fund Management*. The Court noted in that case that the concept of "aid" must be understood more generally than that of a subsidy. As such, while a measure which favours certain undertakings or the production of certain goods can be classified as State aid, advantages resulting from a general measure applicable without distinction to all economic operators do not constitute State aid. The focus should hence be on the assessment of selectivity, as a condition for State aid. With regard to the difference between existing and new aid, the Court added that this must be resolved without reference to the time that has elapsed since the measure was introduced and independently of any previous administrative practice of ESA. It also cannot depend on a subjective assessment by ESA. With the latter cases, the "shoals" of the EEA Agreement were reached.[3]

In *Asker Brygge*, the Court was called upon to establish the date at which the existence of State aid must be assessed. The case involved an application for annulment of an ESA decision concerning the sale of land. The municipal authority of Asker and the applicant had entered into an "option agreement" granting the applicant the right to purchase property for a fixed price of NOK 8 million. The applicant exercised the option. ESA found that the sale constituted unlawful State aid. Recalling that the concept of aid includes not only positive benefits, such as subsidies, loans or direct investment, the EFTA Court went on to spell out the application of the "private investor test". It stated that the conditions of Article 61 (1) EEA are not fulfilled if the recipient undertaking could, in normal market conditions, obtain the same advantage. When the State is acting as an economic operator, the assessment is made by applying this test. The comparison between the conduct of public and private investors must be made by reference to the attitude that a private investor would have had when concluding the option agreement in question, having regard to the available information and foreseeable developments. If a private investor, operating in normal competitive conditions, would probably have entered into the option agreement on similar terms to those taken by the public authority, the conditions for State aid are not fulfilled. In addition, the question of whether aid has been given must take into account the date when it occurred; as such, conditions are to be assessed having regard to the situation at the time when the measure was actually implemented.

In the KADECO case (*Iceland* v *ESA*), the Court addressed the issue of complex economic assessment with regard to its own powers of judicial review. At issue was an application for partial annulment of an ESA decision concerning municipal tax measures, the sale of real estate and the sale of electricity to a private company. Iceland sought the annulment of ESA's decision insofar as it concerned the sale of real estate. ESA had found that State aid had been granted by the Icelandic State when a real estate purchase agreement was entered into, as the purchase price was below the market value of the property as determined by a central independent authority in Iceland. The EFTA Court noted that "State aid" is a legal concept and, as such, must be interpreted on the basis of objective factors, having regard both to the specific features of the case before it and to the complex nature of ESA's assessments. However, such review must be limited to verifying whether ESA complied with the relevant rules governing the procedure and the statement of reasons, whether the facts on which the contested finding was based have been accurately stated and whether there has been any manifest error of assessment of those facts or a misuse of powers.

---

[3]See for details Chapter 2.

In *Kimek Offshore* ESA's decision on the compatibility with the EEA Agreement of Norway's regionally differentiated social security contributions scheme was at stake. The Court noted that it will perform judicial review that goes beyond the consideration of whether there was a manifest error of assessment in order to establish the existence of serious difficulties. This results from the fact that the notion of doubts or serious difficulties is an objective one.

4 The Court as a Ground Breaker

In several cases, the EFTA Court tackled questions that had not yet been raised before the EU courts. Thereby, it made important contributions to issues such as, for example, the compatibility of social security schemes with State aid provisions, the definition of services of "general economic interest", and the notion of undertaking.

In the *Norwegian Social Security Scheme case (Norway* v *ESA)*, the Court dealt with the question of whether a national social security contribution scheme may constitute State aid. The issue at stake was whether certain reduced rates applicable to some employers in Norway constituted State aid. This was especially important due to the geographic selectivity of the measures. The Court started by noting that, while the tax system of EEA/EFTA States was not covered by the EEA Agreement, it may nonetheless have consequences that would bring it within the scope of application of the State aid prohibition, which covers all aid financed from public resources. With regard to the criterion of the generality of the system, the Court noted that the regional character of the aid at issue could favour certain undertakings in relation to others and create unjustified discriminatory treatment. The system needed to be assessed in relation to the general scheme contemplated—which, in the case at issue, showed that the differentiation was based on regional criteria alone. In fact, the Court stated that for the assessment under Article 61(1) EEA it is not decisive whether the system is based or not on legitimate policy considerations. Moreover, in view of the inexistence of ECJ case law regarding the issue of general measures falling outside the State aid prohibition, with regard to a system such as the one at issue in the case, the Court found that the Norwegian social security contribution scheme constituted State aid. The CFI referenced our judgment in *Salzgitter AG*.

In *Bankers' and Securities Dealers' Association of Iceland*, the Court had to interpret the notion of "general economic interest" in Article 59(2) EEA. The case concerned an application to annul an ESA decision concerning State aid to the publicly operated Icelandic Housing Financing Fund (HFF). ESA had concluded that the HFF system involved State aid within the meaning of Article 61(1) EEA. However, it also found, without initiating the formal investigation procedure, that the aid in question was justified under Article 59(2) EEA. One of the main questions was thus whether the HFF system qualified as a service of general economic interest. The Court noted, with reference to *Husbanken II* that the decisive point was the essence of the services at issue, as well as the special characteristics that distinguished it from the general economic interest of other activities. In addition, the Court stated that national policy may be taken into account when defining the objectives pursued. As regards impact on trade, the Court recalled that the measure adopted need not be the least restrictive possible—the test is rather of a negative nature, that is, whether such measure is not disproportionate. The common EEA interest must thus be balanced with the political goals set nationally.

Private Barnehagers Landsforbund concerned an application for the annulment of an ESA Decision on public financing of municipal day-care institutions in Norway. ESA had concluded that the system of financing did not constitute State aid. The Court was called upon to address the meaning of "doubts" in Article 4(4) in Part II of Protocol 3 to the SCA, when referring to the need to initiate a formal investigation when doubts are raised as to the compatibility with the functioning of the EEA Agreement. It started by stating that this notion was clearly an objective one and, as such, the judicial review of the Court must, in this respect, go beyond the simple consideration of whether or not there was a manifest error of assessment by ESA in not initiating a formal investigation procedure. The first issue raised in this respect was whether municipal kindergartens are undertakings within the meaning of Article 61(1) EEA. The Court noted that, under EEA competition rules, the concept of "undertaking" must be seen as encompassing every entity engaged in economic activity, regardless of their legal status or the way in which they are financed. It added that, when the nature of an activity carried out by a public entity is assessed under the State aid rules, it does not matter whether this activity could be pursued by a private operator; the specific circumstances under which the activity is performed must be taken into account in order to assess whether the service is provided as an economic activity, or rather as an exercise of powers in order to fulfil duties towards the population. Remuneration is here a consideration for the service rendered. AG Kokott recently referred again to this judgment in her Opinion in *Congregación de Escuelas Pías Provincia Betania.*

In *Konkurrenten I*, the EFTA Court debated the difference between existing and new aid. The Norwegian authorities provided compensation to two companies for the provision of scheduled bus services in Oslo. In its decision, ESA concluded that the contested measure, although constituting aid incompatible with the EEA Agreement, was existing aid and, in view of the termination of the aid, no further measures would be required. The Court was thus called upon to interpret Protocol 3 to the SCA in the case of aid granted after the renewal of a concession. It determined that, in order for a renewed concession to qualify as an existing aid measure, it would have to be part of an aid scheme put into effect before the entry into force of the EEA Agreement. This classification must also be made with reference to the provisions providing for the said aid. Moreover, the Court stated that the emergence of new aid or the alteration of existing aid cannot be assessed according to its scale or its amount in financial terms at any moment in the life of the undertaking if the aid is provided under former statutory provisions that are unaltered; what is relevant is whether the aid was granted in accordance with the provisions establishing it. Again this case has recently been picked up by AG Wahl in his Opinion in *Carrefour Hypermarchés.*

5 Aid to Agriculture and Fisheries

From the above, it may seem that the State aid provisions in the two EEA pillars are quite aligned. There are however, two important exceptions. They concern agriculture and fisheries. As is known, such products lie outside the scope of the EEA Agreement. In *Synnøve Finden,* a preliminary reference case, the question arose, *inter alia*, as regards the extent to which the limited product coverage also limits the application of the State aid provisions. The Court acknowledged that national measures that are "inseparably linked" to trade in products not covered by the EEA Agreement must also be seen as falling outside its scope. However, when a subsidy, such as the one at issue in *Synnøve Finden* is not "exclusively linked" to such products, the aid scheme must be assessed under the EEA State aid rules. Thereby, the Court developed something very peculiar within the EEA: State aid schemes, which partially fall within and partially lie outside the scope of the EEA Agreement, but which must, nevertheless, be notified as a whole as State aid.

As regards fisheries, the case law is more straightforward. In *Marine Harvest*, the EFTA Court was called upon to assess ESA's competence to monitor State aid in the fisheries sector. Two decades had passed since the judgment in *Scottish Salmon Growers*, before a case arose to challenge ESA's constant stance that it has no competence on State aid in the fisheries sector. Marine Harvest argued that ESA was to be considered competent to assess such aid in spite of the fact that this area falls outside the scope of the EEA Agreement; the competence to monitor State aid should be interpreted as general, covering all fields covered by the Agreement. ESA, however, refused to extend its own competence, citing not only its long-standing practice, but also the fact that the wording of the EEA Agreement and the SCA were clear. Based on a historical interpretation of the EEA Agreement and the will of the Contracting Parties, the Court decided to dismiss the action, noting that the enforcement of the relevant rules falls, in this case, with the Contracting Parties to the EEA Agreement.[4]

[4]See for details Chapter 7.

Chapter 18
Secondary EEA Law—A Wide Sphere

Contents

1 General

In EU law, the distinction between primary and secondary legislation is of great significance. The main sources of primary law are the treaties. They are the basis for secondary law. The most important acts of EU secondary law are the ones listed in Article 288 TFEU: regulations, directives, decisions, opinions and recommendations. Regulations and directives are the most notable types of secondary legislation.

Whether such a hierarchy also exists in EEA law is not clear. Written sources of EEA law are the Main Agreement, the Protocols and the Annexes. Protocols define, for example, the product coverage of the EEA Agreement. Annexes contain regulatory Single Market provisions. Traditional literature has assumed that there is no hierarchy. The EFTA Court has nevertheless spoken of EEA primary law and academic observers have concluded that it meant the Main EEA Agreement and the general principles of EEA law. Conversely, in particular regulations and directives are, once incorporated in the EEA Agreement, to be regarded as acts of EEA secondary law. The following considerations will be dedicated to some of the most important EFTA Court judgments interpreting directives and regulations.

C. Baudenbacher, *Judicial Independence*, Springer Biographies,
https://doi.org/10.1007/978-3-030-02308-9_18

2 Image of Man in the Internet Age

In *Inconsult*, Judge Wilhelm Ungerank, this time in his capacity as the chairman of the Liechtenstein Appeals Commission of the Financial Market Authority, prompted the reference of the novel legal question to the Court of whether a website may constitute a "durable medium" under the Insurance Mediation Directive[1] and whether it was sufficient that an insurance company had insurance contracts only available on its website without providing customers with a hard copy. The notion of "durable medium" is contained in a number of directives. The EFTA Court affirmed that a website may constitute a durable medium, provided that several criteria were met:

First, the website must enable the customer to store the information in question. Second, it must enable the customer to store the information in an accessible way for as long as it is relevant for the customer in order to protect his interests vis-à-vis the insurance intermediary. This might cover the time during which contractual negotiations were conducted, even if they did not result in the conclusion of a contract, the period during which an insurance contract is in force and, to the extent necessary e.g. for seeking redress, the period after such a contract has lapsed. Third, the website must provide for the unchanged reproduction of the information stored. In this respect, the EFTA Court held that the information must be stored in a way that makes it impossible for the insurance intermediary to change it unilaterally. It is for the intermediary to ensure that the methods of electronic communication he employs permit this kind of reproduction.

With regard to sophisticated websites, the Court distinguished between those acting as a portal for the provision of information on another instrument which can qualify as a durable medium and those that may actually constitute durable media themselves. The first type allows the user to access information, for example in the form of an e-mail with an attachment, which he can copy and store on his own computer. For this method to constitute the communication to the customer of information on a durable medium, the website must contain features that will lead the customer, almost certainly, to either secure the information on paper, or to store it on another durable medium. The second type of sophisticated website contains a secure storage area for individual users, which is accessed by a user code and password. Provided that any possibility of the insurance intermediary changing the information is excluded, this kind of storage can be compared to the user's own hard drive. This type of sophisticated website fulfils the requirement of guaranteeing the unchanged reproduction necessary to qualify as a durable medium.

[1]2002/92/EC.

3 Contractual Model

3.1 Freedom of Contract and Consumer Protection

In *Beatrix Koch*, a case referred by the Princely Court of Liechtenstein, the EFTA Court was asked whether EEA law in life assurance required an assurance undertaking to provide fair advice to a policy holder and also sought clarification regarding the scope of the undertaking's duty to inform the policy holder before the contract is concluded. The Court held that assurance undertakings are not required to provide advice to the policy holder. However, from a consumer protection perspective, it must be emphasised that the Court held that policy holders must be given precise and objective information so that amongst the available products they can choose the one best suited to their requirements and also assess the policy in practical terms. It is not sufficient to only provide the information on the Internet, but the information can be communicated by a third party.

Vienna Life and Swiss Life, two cases referred by the Liechtenstein Supreme Court, concerned the question whether certain consumer protection rules of the 2002 Life Assurance Directive[2] should apply to the purchase of second-hand life assurance policies—. The purchase of second-hand life assurance policies is a specific form of investment. The purchaser has no apparent relation to the insured person(s), meaning he or she is not seeking the insurance aspect of the contracts. This kind of business is motivated by tax considerations and buyers speculate on the lives of people whose drinking and smoking habits they are not aware of. In such a situation, the classical liberal contractual model applies. Negotiating the terms of the contract must be left to the market forces. Since equal partners face each other, the thesis of the "guarantee of fairness" ("*Richtigkeitsgewähr*") of the contract put forward by Walter Schmidt-Rimpler comes to bear. From an economic perspective, contracts concluded between equal partners are a tool for the optimal allocation of resources. In this context it should also be noted that the EFTA Court had already taken a stand against exaggerated paternalism in the prior authorisation cases.[3]

Engilbertsson was referred by the Reykjavík District Court. The EFTA Court held that linking mortgage loans to the Icelandic consumer price index and providing for the review of the interest rate was not categorically prohibited under the Unfair Consumer Contract Terms Directive.[4] One had to assume that the national legislature had excluded unfair terms in consumer contracts since the mandatory rules of contract law strike a fair balance between the rights and obligations of the parties. Mandatory rules are excluded from the scope of the directive. The Court further held that as regards the method for calculating price changes, it was of crucial importance for a consumer to obtain adequate information on a contract's

[2]2002/83/EC.

[3]See for details Chapter 11.

[4]93/13/EEC.

terms and consequences before concluding it. Such information must enable the consumer to make an informed choice before signing the contract. *Sævar Jón Gunnarsson* also involved an assessment of the same questions under the Consumer Credit Directive.[5] Mr. Gunnarrsson had taken out an indexed credit loan. Here too, the main focus was on the correctness of the information provided. The EFTA Court found the term "total cost of the credit" in the directive to comprise all the costs that the consumer was liable to pay under the credit agreement, including both interest charges and charges resulting from the price indexation of the principal. An assumed 0% rate of inflation indicated in a loan agreement, at a time when the actual rate of inflation was considerably higher, did not correctly represent the charges resulting from the price indexation and thus the total cost of credit.

In *Pascal Nobile v DAS Rechtsschutz-Versicherungs AG*, the Court held that the Insurance and Reinsurance ("Solvency II") Directive[6] recognises the free choice of lawyer in any inquiry or proceedings. That rule has general application and is obligatory in nature. There were several factors indicating that DAS' general terms and conditions did not fully recognise the free choice of lawyer. DAS appears to use these terms also in EU Member States and in Switzerland.[7]

3.2 Sanctity of Contracts

In *Matja Kumba*, the EFTA Court was called upon to interpret the Working Time Directive.[8] The Norwegian non-profit foundation Fossumkollektivet offered treatment to young people with alcohol or drug problems. The therapists lived together with the patients in order to create a family-like situation. The working day began at 7 a.m. and ended at 11 p.m. In addition to the time between 11 p.m. and 7 a.m., employees received 2 h of rest per day. Workers slept in apartments in the workplace. They were entitled to 3 months paid leave every three years. At the time in question, there was a "3-7-4-7 rotation system" in place, i.e. the therapists worked for 3 days, had 7 days off and then worked for 4 days followed by 7 days off. The average working time was 56 h per week.

The Working Time Directive provides that Member States must ensure that weekly working time doesn't exceed 48 h, including overtime. However, the directive allows Member States to set a maximum working time of over 48 h, provided that the general principles of the protection of the safety and health of workers are respected. There is more room for exception if the employee agrees. Exceptions can also be made for the prescribed rest periods. Member States may lay down special rules for the reception, treatment and/or care services of hospitals or

---

[5] 87/102/EEC.

[6] 2009/138/EC.

[7] See concerning the aspect of the Court's integrity Chapter 28.

[8] 2003/88/EC.

similar establishments. Norway transposed the directive on the professions in question in a way that the maximum working time was 9 h out of 24 h a day and 40 h in 7 days. Exceptions were provided for, but no more than 13 h were allowed per day and no more than 48 h per week. In special cases, other solutions were possible. According to a decree issued by the Ministry of Labour and Social Affairs, the maximum weekly working time for assisted living was 48 h, but the individual employee could commit to a maximum of 60 h of work in writing. Workers living in the institution were allowed to work for more than 60 h. Employees could only be dismissed if there was an objective reason on the basis of circumstances relating to the company, the employer or the employee. Due to losses in 2009, 2011 and 2012, the Fossumkollektivet Foundation decided to switch from the "3-7-4-7-Rotation" to a "7-7 Rotation". After 7 days of work (i.e. 84 h per week), 7 days of rest followed. This allowed considerable cost savings. The plaintiffs did not accept the proposed change in working time. The employer gave notice of dismissal, combined with an offer of re-engagement on different terms.

The EFTA Court found the "7-7 rotation" to be compatible with the directive in the circumstances, provided that an employee had expressly, freely and individually undertaken to provide 84 h of work per week and that the general principles relating to the protection of workers' health and safety were complied with. If these conditions were fulfilled, the parties could exercise their contractual freedom. Furthermore, the question arose whether an employee could revoke his or her consent to work more than 60 h per week. The EFTA Court stated that the directive did not contain any such provision. The problem had thus to be resolved under national law—within certain limits set by the directive. A provision of national law that did not allow an employee to withdraw his or her consent to work more than 60 h a week in an establishment such as this one—without giving reasons—was therefore considered compatible with the directive, provided that the general principles relating to the protection of workers' health and safety were respected. The Court underlined the importance of a fair balance between the interests of workers and employers.

From an economic law point of view, another important question was whether a notice of dismissal and offer of re-engagement on new terms was a disadvantage for the employee—which would be prohibited under the directive. In the same way as under German law, the EFTA Court distinguished between termination on the basis of urgent operational requirements and termination without the existence of such reasons. Urgent operational requirements exist if there are reasons that are completely independent of the employee's refusal to give his or her consent to the amendment. If this is the case, a notice of dismissal does not constitute a disadvantage within the meaning of the directive.

4 Principle of Liability

4.1 *Liability of a State in a Systemic Crisis*

As set out in Chap. 14 on the economics of a Single Market, the principle of liability is a constituent element of a market economy. Liability means that you have to pay for your debts or to make good the damage you caused. On the other hand, moral hazard, which means a situation in which one party is taking high risks knowing that it is protected because the other party will incur the cost, must be avoided. In its landmark decision in the first *Icesave* case, the Court addressed these principles. *Icesave*, one of the most important cases decided by the EFTA Court in the first 24 years of its existence, will be dealt with in its own Chapter.[9]

4.2 *Award of a Public Contract to the Wrong Bidder*

In *Fosen-Linjen*, the EFTA Court held that a simple breach of public procurement law may in itself be sufficient to trigger the liability of the contracting authority, under the Remedies Directive for the public sector,[10] to compensate the person harmed for the damage incurred, provided that the other conditions for the award of damages were met, such as, in particular, the existence of a causal link.[11] The case will be dealt with in detail in Chap. 21 on the dialogue between the two EEA Courts.

5 Adjustment of Price for a Mandatory Takeover Bid

According to Article 5 of the Takeover Bids Directive,[12] a natural or legal person that acquires control of a company listed on regulated markets in an EEA State is obliged to make a mandatory bid at an equitable price. Norwegian law allowed for adjustment of the bid price if the "market price" was higher than the highest price paid by the offeror during the preceding six-month period. The "highest price paid rule" is the main rule for establishing the bid price for mandatory takeover bids. The Contracting Parties may adopt derogations in certain cases provided that the adjustment is based on circumstances "that are clearly determined". The adjusted price must be calculated in accordance with criteria that are also clearly determined. The purpose of this rule is the protection of minority shareholders according to the

[9]See for details Chapter 25.

[10]89/665/EEC.

[11]See for details Chapter 21.

[12]2004/25/EC.

freedom of establishment. In the *Periscopus* case, Erik Must AS had issued a mandatory bid for the shares of Gyldendal, Norway's largest publishing company. Periscopus AS, the second-largest shareholder of Gyldendal, controlled 30.2% of the shares. The Oslo Stock Exchange (takeover supervisory authority) approved the bid price based on the highest price paid by Erik Must. The market price alternative should be used only in circumvention cases, and due to the low number of trades in Gyldendal shares, it was not possible to determine a sufficiently clear market price. Moreover, Periscopus had been the buyer in virtually all of the trades in question. Periscopus contended that the decision approving the bid was null and brought a damages suit against the Stock Exchange and Erik Must for NOK 37 Million plus interest. Periscopus argued that the market price case should have been chosen. It thereby wanted to achieve an increase of the bid price.

In its judgment of 10 December 2010, the EFTA Court held that a national rule allowing the adjustment of the bid price with reference to the term "market price" without further specification of that term was too vague. Further clarification was needed, in particular, of the time interval relevant for determining the "market price", whether or not the "market price" had to be calculated on the basis of a volume-weighted average, and whether actual trades were necessary or whether standing buy or sell orders sufficed in order to establish a "market price". Later, when I read Knut Hamsun's last novel "On Overgrown Grass" ("*Paa gjengrodde stier*"), I learnt that the Nobel Prize winner in literature owned a considerable number of shares of Gyldendal. In 1947 Hamsun's assets were confiscated by the Norwegian courts for his open support of National Socialism. I assume the Gyldendal stock was among them. "On Overgrown Grass" was, as all of Hamsun's works, published by Gyldendal in 1949.

6 Re-use of Public Sector Information

In *Creditinfo Lánstraust*, the EFTA Court held that where charges are made for the re-use of public sector information under the respective Directive,[13] a substantive examination must have been undertaken at the time when the charge is fixed. The examination must show that the total income from such charges does not exceed the cost of collection, production, reproduction and dissemination of documents, plus a reasonable return on investment. If the factors relevant to performing a calculation are uncertain, an estimate must at least be made. Reference was made to the 1966 US Freedom of Information Act that granted American citizens the right to see the contents of files maintained on them by federal agencies.

---

[13]2003/98/EC.

7 Information About Convictions of Legal Persons

In *Otto Kaufmann AG*, the Princely Court of Liechtenstein wanted to know whether EEA law required that where national law allows for legal persons to be convicted by a criminal court those convictions must also be clearly recorded, for example, in a criminal record. The question could become relevant in public procurement cases. The EFTA Court held that the freedom of establishment and freedom to provide services do not require EEA States to record criminal convictions of legal persons by courts in the criminal record. Nevertheless, provisions of directives concerning public procurement and services in the internal market may require an EEA State to provide information, at the request of another EEA State, on convictions relevant to the competence and professional reliability of legal persons. However, these directives leave the maintenance and handling of the relevant information to national law.

8 Re-monopolisation of Works That Have Fallen into the Public Domain

In *Gustav Vigeland*, the EFTA Court had to interpret the Trade Mark Directive.[14] Gustav Vigeland was a famous Norwegian sculptor whose lifework is displayed in a large park in Oslo bearing his name. He was born in Mandal in southern Norway on 11 April 1869 and died in Oslo on 12 March 1943. Oslo Municipality managed the copyright of Vigeland's sculptures. In view of the actual or imminent lapse of intellectual property protection for copyright protected works by some Norwegian artists, Oslo Municipality applied for trade mark protection for a number of works. The applications were partially refused by the Norwegian Intellectual Property Office. Upon appeal, the Board of Appeal decided to refer questions to the Court concerning, in particular, whether, and if so under what circumstances, registration of a trade mark could be refused on the basis of public policy and accepted principles of morality. I acted as a Judge Rapporteur. The EFTA Court started by saying that in principle, nothing prevents a sign from being protected under both trade mark and copyright law. Trade marks seek to guarantee the identity of the origin of the marked product, their protection ensures market transparency and assumes an essential role in a system of undistorted competition. In order to attain these aims, it is essential that the term of protection for trademarks is, in principle, indefinite. Copyright protection, in turn, provides for an incentive to contribute to the enrichment of the economy and to society at large.

Nevertheless, after this opening, the EFTA Court turned to the specific economic law implications of the case. It held that the lapse of copyright protection serves the

---

[14] 2008/95/EC.

principles of legal certainty and the protection of legitimate expectations, by providing a pre-determined time frame after which anyone can freely draw on the ideas and creative content of others. It followed that a trade mark based entirely on copyright protected work carries a certain risk of monopolisation of the sign for a specific purpose. The interest in safeguarding the public domain, however, speaks in favour of the absence of individual protection for, or exclusive rights to, the artwork on which the mark is based. The Court then held that refusal based on grounds of "public policy" must be based on an assessment of objective criteria whereas an objection based on "accepted principles of morality" concerns an assessment of subjective values. The Court held that the registration as a trade mark of a sign that consists of works for which the copyright protection period has expired, is not in itself contrary to public policy or accepted principles of morality. The words "not in itself" indicate that there are, however, limits.

When dealing with the question of whether a trade mark would be contrary to "accepted principles of morality", the EFTA Court noted that certain pieces of art may enjoy a particular status as prominent parts of a nation's cultural heritage, an emblem of sovereignty or of the nation's foundations and values. Registration as a trade mark may even be considered a misappropriation or a desecration of the artist's work, in particular if it is granted for goods or services that contradict the artist's values or the message communicated through the artwork in question. Consequently, the Court held that whether trade mark registration of a sign that consists of an artwork must be refused on the basis of accepted principles of morality depends, in particular, on the status or perception of the artwork in the EEA State concerned. In that assessment, the risk of misappropriation or desecration of an artwork may also be relevant.

As regards the "public policy" exception, the EFTA Court found that registration of a sign as a trade mark may only be refused on that basis if the sign consists exclusively of a work pertaining to the public domain and the registration of this sign would constitute a genuine and sufficiently serious threat to a fundamental interest of society. Writing extra-judicially, the chairman of the Norwegian Board of Appeal for Industrial Property Rights, Ole-Andreas Rognstad, rightly emphasised that the Court's conclusion that registration of a work whose copyright protection has expired as a trade mark may be refused on public policy grounds, where there is a need to safeguard the public domain, contrasts to a certain extent with the 1996 decision of the German Federal Patent Court in the *Mona Lisa* case.

Vigeland was probably one of the most important judgments of modern times on the notion of public domain after the US Supreme Court's rulings in *Eldred* v *Ashcroft* and in *Golan v. Holder*. In *Eldred v Ashcroft*, the Supreme Court on 15 January 2003 upheld the constitutionality of a 20-year retroactive extension of existing copyright terms by the 'Sonny Bono Copyright Term Extension Act'. In *Golan v. Holder* it found on 18 January 2010 that the expression "limited time" in the Patent and Copyright Clause of the US Constitution did not preclude the extension of copyright protection to works previously in the public domain. This Clause gives Congress the power

> To promote the progress of science and useful arts, by securing for limited times to authors and inventors the exclusive right to their respective writings and discoveries.

Gustav Vigeland has founded a whole dynasty of artists. A grandniece of his, Tone Vigeland, is one of Norway's leading contemporary jewellers. The Design Museum in Munich called her the "Grande Dame of Scandinavian Jewellery". As I have intimated in Chap. 1 of this book, Doris is an avid collector of contemporary jewellery. I knew that she had always wanted to have a piece by Tone Vigeland. However, there aren't many of her works on the market. I was therefore particularly happy when I managed to acquire a fantastic bracelet made by her in an Oslo gallery in October 2014. I found this item strolling through Oslo after the EFTA Court's peace summit with the Norwegian Supreme Court.[15] That made my purchase particularly valuable.

[15]See for details Chapter 26.

Chapter 19
Free Movement of Persons and Social Policy

Contents

1 Introduction

The EU law provisions on free movement of persons have largely been incorporated in the EEA Agreement. The EFTA Court has only on rare occasions dealt with the respective norms. It is, however, safe to assume that the scope of the freedom as well as the notions of "worker", "first time work-seeker" and "worker out of employment" are to be interpreted in accordance with the case law of the ECJ. The EEA/EFTA States were not amused when the EU insisted that the Citizenship Directive[1] had to be incorporated in the EEA Agreement. However, finally, they caved in. On 1 March 2009, the directive entered into force in EEA law. It is not limited to giving EEA nationals the right to reside in another EEA State for any period of time so long as they are workers or self-employed; it goes further and extends the right to stay to EEA nationals who are economically inactive. They may move to another EEA State and stay there for up to three months for any reason. Judge Kjartan Bjarni Björgvinsson from the Reykjavík District Court, a former legal secretary of the EFTA Court, has aptly stated:

[1] 2004/38/EC.

C. Baudenbacher, *Judicial Independence*, Springer Biographies,
https://doi.org/10.1007/978-3-030-02308-9_19

> The inclusion of economically inactive persons arguably transcends the economic integration sought by the EEA Agreement.

There are, however, differences: Political rights of EEA nationals and immigration policy are not part of EEA law. And, importantly, there are no provisions in the EEA Agreement that would mirror the provisions on Union citizenship in the TFEU.

When dealing with the economics of EEA Single Market law,[2] I have pointed to the fact that according to recital 3 in the preamble to the EEA Agreement, the Contracting Parties must strive to achieve a homogeneous and dynamic EEA "on the basis of market economy". In the Norwegian commentary, Professors Finn Arnesen and Halvard Haukeland Fredriksen argued that it is somewhat paradoxical,

> at least for Norwegian lawyers used to a Nordic type of social market economy, [that] the preamble to the EEA Agreement stands out as being more unreservedly free market-oriented than the presentation of the EU internal market that is now to be found in Art. 3(3) TEU. In practice, however, this will in most cases be compensated for by the homogeneity principle. Still, the EFTA Court's president has claimed that the EFTA Court is more free market-oriented and 'business friendly' than the ECJ [....].

Article 3(3) of the Treaty on European Union (TEU) states that the EU must establish an internal market, it must work for the sustainable development of Europe based on balanced economic growth and price stability, a highly competitive social market economy, aimed at full employment and social progress, and a high level of protection and improvement of the quality of the environment. It must, moreover, promote scientific and technological advance, combat social exclusion and discrimination, promote social justice and protection, promote equality between women and men, promote solidarity between generations and protect the rights of children. Finally, it must promote economic, social and territorial cohesion, and solidarity among Member States and it must respect its rich cultural and linguistic diversity and ensure that Europe's cultural heritage is safeguarded and enhanced.

I do not doubt that if the EFTA Court were to face the question of whether the goals listed in this provision are of relevance for the interpretation of EEA law, it would give a sensible answer. All I want to say at this point is that underlining the market-orientation of the EFTA Court does not imply that its case law is anti-social. It means, first and foremost, that the EFTA Court has rejected mercantilist thinking in a number of major cases. The big exception to this is the *L'Oréal* judgment.[3] Nevertheless, the EEA Agreement is not based on the assumption that mercantilist policies are essential to promoting social welfare. Furthermore, to hold that certain limits to collective bargaining and industrial action follow from competition law, the fundamental freedoms and from fundamental rights, as the EFTA Court did in *LO* and in *Holship*, is not anti-social. In *LO*, the Court even had the support of the Norwegian Government.[4]

---

[2]See for details Chapter 14.

[3]See for details Chapter 21.

[4]See for details Chapter 16.

Social policy appears in the EEA Agreement as one of the important flanking policies, which the Contracting Parties undertake to pursue. Recital 11 of the Preamble to the EEA Agreement refers to

> the importance of the development of the social dimension, including equal treatment of men and women, in the European Economic Area and wishing to ensure economic and social progress and to promote conditions for full employment, an improved standard of living and improved working conditions within the European Economic Area

Article 66 EEA states:

> The Contracting Parties agree upon the need to promote improved working conditions and an improved standard of living for workers.

Articles 67–70 EEA detail the specifics with regard to the areas of working environment, especially the health and safety of workers and living conditions, as well as the principle of equal pay for equal work irrespective of gender. These horizontal provisions must be read in the light of Articles 28–45 EEA on the fundamental freedoms.

University of Cambridge Professor Catherine Barnard noted that the EU social *acquis* has largely been adopted by the EEA. Most of the directives on labour law, equality law, health and safety have been incorporated in the EEA Agreement.

2 Transfer of Undertakings

The Transfer of Undertakings Directive is one of the central pieces of legislation around which the social policy case law of the Court has developed. The first four cases, *Eidesund, Langeland, Ulstein and Røiseng* and *Ask* v *ABB and Aker* were dealt with in Chap. 5 of this book. In 2004, in *Rasmussen*, the former and the future employer involved in the transfer were subsidiaries of the same company. The former employer's production and maintenance staff were integrated but, subsequently, only the maintenance functions were transferred to the new employer. Pursuant to the agreement, the former employer's workers would be taken over by the new employer and another affiliated company; however, three of the workers opposed the transfer. The EFTA Court recalled its previous case law on the global assessment of the several factors which compose the transfer, noting, in addition, that the directive does not aim to achieve a uniform level of protection throughout the EEA on the basis of common criteria; rather, it intends to ensure that the employees are protected in their relation to the transferee to the same extent as they were in relation to the transferor. Moreover, the Court held that the purpose of the directive is not to ensure that the employment relationship with the transferor is continued should the employees object to being employed by the transferee—this is to be settled under national law. In *Deveci*, the workers in question were subject to a different collective agreement with a subsequent pay reduction after the expiry of the collective agreement in the transferor's undertaking.

3 Exportability of Helplessness Allowance

The *Liechtenstein Helplessness Allowance* case is of particular interest because the relevant Social Security Coordination Regulation[5] has been dealt with in three different legal contexts, namely under EU law, EEA law and under the bilateral Free Movement of Persons Agreement EU—Switzerland. According to this regulation, all social security benefits, with the exception of social assistance, are coordinated within the EU and the EEA. Such benefits may thus be exported. They must also be provided to beneficiaries residing in another EEA State. The EFTA Court held that a Liechtenstein law that restricted the allowance to residents in Liechtenstein who permanently required a considerable degree of surveillance or help to carry out daily tasks, was incompatible with the regulation. Liechtenstein's argument that the helplessness allowance qualified as a non-exportable "special non-contributory benefit", was rejected. Following ECJ case law, the EFTA Court found that the allowance had to be regarded as a "sickness benefit" that had to be paid independently of the residence of the recipient.

As I have already said, the relevant provisions of EU law are also part of the bilateral agreement on the free movement of persons that was concluded between the EU and Switzerland. In a landmark decision, the Swiss Federal Supreme Court held in 2006 that helplessness allowances was not to be exported to foreign countries under Swiss law. Being a classical public international law treaty, the agreement was interpreted in accordance with the rules of the Vienna Convention on the Law of Treaties. As regards the case law of the ECJ, the Supreme Court found that since the relevant rulings had been rendered after the signature of the Agreement, they were not binding. In 2015, this judgment was confirmed. Article 16 of the Swiss-EU Free Movement of Persons Agreement distinguishes between old and new ECJ case law, as does Article 6 EEA and Article 3(2) SCA.

4 Citizenship Directive

The Citizenship Directive (2004/38/EC) has been applied in four EFTA Court cases: *Clauder*, *Hells Angels*, *Atli Gunnarsson* and *Jabbi*. The two last cases are of particular significance.

In *Atli Gunnarsson*, Mr. Gunnarsson and his wife resided in Denmark from 24 January 2004 to 3 September 2009. During this time, their total income consisted of Ms. Gunnarsson's unemployment benefit, which she received in Iceland up to 1 May 2004, Mr. Gunnarsson's disability pension from the Icelandic Social Insurance Administration, and benefit payments that Mr. Gunnarsson received from two Icelandic pension funds. He paid income tax in Iceland on his income but was precluded from including, for tax purposes, his wife's personal tax credit while they

---

[5](EEC) No 1408/71.

were Danish residents. Under Icelandic tax law, the couple had to reside in Iceland in order to pool their personal tax credits. The Court held that the European law right of residence provisions[6] confer on a pensioner who receives a pension due to a former employment relationship, but who has not carried out any economic activity in another EEA State during his working life, not only a right of residence in relation to the host EEA State, but also a right to move freely from the home EEA State. The latter right prohibits the home State from hindering such a person from moving to another EEA State. A less favourable treatment of persons exercising the right to move than those who remain resident constitutes such a hindrance. The spouse of such a pensioner enjoys similar derived rights.

In *Jabbi*, Mr. Jabbi, a Gambian national, married Ms. Amoh, a Norwegian woman, in Spain in February 2012. Ms. Amoh was not economically active, she did receive welfare benefits. The two stayed together in Spain from September 2011 to October 2012. Ms. Amoh then returned to Norway and in November 2012 Mr. Jabbi applied for residence in Norway as Ms. Amoh's spouse. The immigration authorities dismissed the application. Claiming that he enjoyed a derived right of residence in Norway as a result of this wife's stay in Spain and subsequent return to Norway, Mr. Jabbi instigated proceedings before the Oslo District Court. Dogmatically, the EFTA Court faced the problem that in EU law, derived rights such as the ones in question, may be based on the concept of Union citizenship laid down in Articles 20 and 21 TFEU. However, this concept is without parallel in EEA law. The ECJ had become accustomed to deciding similar cases based on these Treaty articles. In paragraph 62 of its judgment, the EFTA Court noted in all openness

> that a gap between the two EEA pillars has emerged since the signing of the EEA Agreement in 1992. This gap has widened over the years. The EU treaties have been amended four times since then, while the EEA Main Agreement has remained substantially unchanged. This development has created certain discrepancies at the level of primary law. Depending on the circumstances, this fact may have an impact on the interpretation of the EEA Agreement.

In order to close this gap in the interest of homogeneity, the Court interpreted the Citizenship Directive[7] broadly. It held that under the directive, all EEA nationals must have the right of residence on the territory of another EEA State for more than three months if they have: (i) sufficient resources for themselves and their family members not to become a burden on the social assistance system of the host State during the period of residence; and (ii) comprehensive sickness insurance cover in the host State. That right must extend to third-country national family members accompanying or joining the EEA national in the host State. Referring to its judgment in *Atli Gunnarsson*, the Court found that the home EEA State may not deter its nationals from moving to another EEA State in the exercise of the freedom of movement under EEA law. A right to move freely from the home EEA State to

[6]Directive 90/365/EEC and Directive 2004/38/EC.

[7]2004/38/EC.

another EEA State cannot be fully achieved if the EEA national may be deterred from exercising the freedom by obstacles raised by the home State to the right of residence for a third-country national's spouse. Therefore, the provisions of the directive will apply by analogy where the EEA national returns to his home State with a third-country national's family member. EEA States may deny a derived right in cases of abuse of rights or fraud, such as marriages of convenience. In the case at hand, the Norwegian Government, upon a question from the bench in the hearing, stated that there were no factors that pointed to an abuse.

When I gave evidence before the Brexit Committee of the British House of Commons on 7 February 2018,[8] I was asked about the carry-over effect of the *Jabbi* judgment. I answered that in my view, the case had to be seen in the light of its peculiar features. It is common sense that you cannot deny a lawfully married couple the right to live together. One must not overlook in this context that in paragraph 81 of *Jabbi*, the EFTA Court, referring to its *Clauder* judgment, added that

> all the EEA States are parties to the European Convention on Human Rights, which enshrines in Article 8(1) the right to respect for private and family life. According to established case law, provisions of the EEA Agreement are to be interpreted in the light of fundamental rights [....].

The EFTA Court has been walking a fine line when finding in favour of a derived right in this case. However, a case such as *Jabbi* cannot only be decided on legalistic considerations. I concur with Norwegian Supreme Court Justice Ingvald Falch's conclusion in the Norwegian Commentary[9] that in a matter such as *Jabbi*, the assessment must be made on a case-by-case basis.

5 Working Time Directive

The EFTA Court's landmark decision in *Matja Kumba* has been dealt with in Chap. 18 under the title "sanctity of contracts". Judge Tron Løkken Sundet from the Norwegian Labour Court claimed in the Norwegian Commentary[10] that with its findings that: (i) working time amounting to an average of 84 h per week in a cohabitant care arrangement was possibly compatible with the Working Time Directive[11]; (ii) that a national provision, under which an employee's consent to working more than 60 h per week in such an arrangement could not be revoked, could be compatible with the directive in certain circumstances; and (iii) that a notice of dismissal and offer of re-engagement on new terms, following a refusal by a worker to agree to a working time arrangement of more than 48 h over a

[8]For details see Chapter 31.

[9]See Chapter 24.

[10]See Chapter 24.

[11]2003/88/EC.

seven-day period, was not to be considered a "detriment" if the termination of the employment was based upon reasons fully independent of the worker's refusal to agree to perform such additional work, the EFTA Court diverged from the ECJ's approach in that the interest of the employer was given as much weight as the interest of the health and safety of the worker. I should add though that there was a third group involved in the case whose legitimate interest had to be taken into account, namely the patients.

The second Working Time Directive case, *Thue* v *The Norwegian Government*, did not raise any particular legal problems. But it was an important case for other reasons. First, it was the third request for a preliminary ruling from the Norwegian Supreme Court in short succession after the termination of the reference boycott. Second, the normally union-friendly Norwegian Government stood against the Norwegian Police Federation and was supported by the Polish government. The experienced police officer Thorbjørn Selstad Thue had served as a member of a special response unit, whose duties included armed response actions and escort assignments. When carrying out such assignments, the place of attendance could be elsewhere than in the regular police district. In three cases, the driving distance between Mr. Thue's home and the place of attendance varied between one and three hours. The majority of these journeys were approved by the Norwegian government as travel time, but not as working time. The Supreme Court wanted to know whether the time spent on such journeys, when travel took place outside normal working hours, constituted working time within the meaning of the directive. The Court held that the necessary time spent travelling, outside normal working hours, by a worker, such as Mr. Thue, to and/or from a location other than his fixed or habitual place of attendance in order to carry out his activity or duties in that other location, as required by his employer, constituted "working time". *Thue* was my last case as a Judge Rapporteur and President. After having been depicted as a "dark blue President" by certain journalists and after having been suspected of not being sufficiently social by certain academic commentators in Norway, I felt that it was a beautiful coincidence that the Court handed the unions a clear victory against the Norwegian government in this case.

6 Other Cases

6.1 Safety at Work

In *Kolbeinsson*, the Court ruled that it was not compatible with the Directives on Safety at Work[12] to hold a worker liable for all or most of the losses suffered as a result of an accident on the basis of the worker's own contributory negligence when the employer has not complied with safety rules. The main responsibility is that of the employer.

[12]89/391/EEC and 92/57/EEC.

6.2 Social Security Schemes

In *Finnmark supplement*, the Court found that a regional residence requirement for family benefits could be justified as a means of promoting sustainable settlement in an area "where there has been a decline in population, and where living conditions are particularly difficult due to, *inter alia*, harsh climate, vast distances and sparse population".

In *Jonsson*, the Court held that a provision of national law pursuant to which entitlement to unemployment benefits is conditional on actual presence in the EEA State concerned, may not be relied upon against a national of another EEA State. Mr. Jonsson was a Swedish migrant worker who had frequently worked in Norway. After becoming unemployed, he returned to his home in Sweden where he resided at the relevant time.

The *Abuelo Insua Juan Bautista* and *Walter Waller* cases concerned the coordination of social security systems. Both cases were referred by the Liechtenstein Court of Appeal. Abuelo Insua Juan Bautista, a resident of Spain, received an invalidity pension from the Liechtenstein Invalidity Insurance Fund. At the request of the Fund, the Spanish Social Security Institute performed a medical examination of Mr. Bautista. The examining doctor concluded that he was able to perform adapted work full time. On that basis, the Fund decided to terminate the invalidity pension. The EFTA Court held that the debtor institution, when requesting a medical examination by the institution of the place of stay or residence, must be bound by the latter's findings. That binding effect applies to medical findings, not to the legal assessment of whether the claimant is entitled to benefits, which is for the debtor institution to determine under national law. However, a recipient or claimant of benefits is not prevented from challenging the findings of the institution of the place of stay or residence. In the *Walter Waller* case, a resident of Germany received an invalidity pension from the Liechtenstein Invalidity Insurance Fund. A medical examination by a doctor appointed by the German statutory pension scheme found that although Mr. Waller's condition had improved, his ability to work was still reduced. His work capacity was thus deemed to be less than three hours per day. After considering the medical report and information from Mr. Waller's general practitioner stating that he was no longer capable of working, the Fund decided to reduce his invalidity pension from 100 to 50%. The Court held that the debtor institution is precluded from challenging such medical findings. It is implicit in the coordination scheme that requests for medical examinations must be exchanged between competent authorities in the EEA States as a matter of mutual trust. The binding effect of medical findings applies as long as the debtor institution has not invoked its right to have the beneficiary examined by a doctor of its choice. However, the Fund did not invoke this right. The EFTA Court held, moreover, that this binding effect also applies in court proceedings following an administrative proceeding.

6.3 Healthcare

Some of the issues relating to the maintenance of social security systems evoke the freedom to provide services in relation to healthcare. The Court was called to assess situations dealing with medical treatment abroad and their connection with the freedom to provide services. In *Rindal* and *Slinning*, the questions raised concerned the compatibility with the freedom to provide services of the refusal to cover expenses for hospital treatment abroad in cases where either such treatment is experimental and there is no such entitlement in the home State, or adequate medical treatment can be received only within certain time limits in the home State.

Ms. Rindal had received surgical treatment for a whiplash injury in Norway. However, further medical intervention was discouraged, even though she still experienced pain. As a result she sought treatment in a private clinic in Germany. Her application for coverage of the expenses incurred was denied, based on the argument that the medical competence to deal with such issues existed in Norway. Ms. Slinning, on the other hand, had sustained serious brain injury. After having spent time in a nursing home, she sought treatment in Denmark. The rehabilitation arrangement in Denmark was not available in Norway at the time. The coverage of expenses was denied since it was considered that the treatment received was of an experimental nature that was not encompassed by the right to treatment abroad.

With regard to the experimental nature of the treatments, the EFTA Court first acknowledged that medical services fall within the freedom to provide services. The aim to ensure access to high quality hospital treatment and controlling costs are of course aims which may justify restrictions to that freedom, so as to allow for the Member States to organise and keep balanced social security systems. However, these powers must be exercised in compliance with EEA law; thus, the criteria used to assess medical treatment at home and abroad must be objective and non-discriminatory. In particular, since assuming the costs of one isolated case, where treatment was undergone in another EEA State, cannot have a significant financial impact on the system, an overall approach should be taken. The EFTA Court noted that a system of prior authorisation seemed to be a more sensible solution. This was especially the case in relation to experimental treatment; if seeking such treatment were to be discouraged this could also seriously undermine the incentives to medical research.

With regard to situations where treatment at home would be available, we had to assess whether the treatment offered abroad was more advanced, than that offered in the home State. The Court noted that a national rule that made a patient's right to coverage of expenses subject to the condition that the treatment was not available in the home State within a medically justifiable time limit, imposed a burden solely on patients wishing to go abroad. This was by its very own nature a restriction on the free movement of services, only justifiable by the need to attain objectives of overriding public interest. In the light of this, the Court further stated that, when the treatment abroad was not more advanced than the one available in the home State, national authorities could, if necessary, institute a system of waiting lists. Such a solution would prevent putting at risk the planning and rationalisation measures of the home State's social security system, which could be jeopardised if patients could seek treatment abroad in situations where the treatment was available in the home State within a medically justifiable time limit. The Court observed, however, that the mere existence of waiting lists could not lead to a refusal of prior authorisation, without taking into account the specific circumstances of the patient's medical condition.

With respect to situations where the treatment abroad was more advanced than the one offered in the home State, the Court recalled that EEA law does not require the Contracting Parties to extend the range of medical services that are covered by their social security systems. However, when the criteria for a treatment were fulfilled, unless the home State itself can provide treatment that is the same or equally effective for the patient as the treatment abroad within a medically justifiable time limit, there could be no prioritisation of the home treatment.

With this assessment, the Court, while recognising that a heavy financial burden on the social security systems may justify a restriction to the freedom to seek medical treatment in another State, favoured an approach that takes into account not only the specific circumstances of the patient at issue, but also the availability of treatment in a reasonable time within the home State.

In *Norwegian Board for Health Personnel*, a Bulgarian medical doctor had applied for an authorisation to practice as a medical doctor in Norway. Her request was accompanied by a statement from the Bulgarian authorities confirming that she was covered by the recognition of professional qualifications directive,[13] on the basis of her education and professional experience as a medical doctor in Bulgaria. The Norwegian Registration Authority for Health Personnel rejected her application, on the basis of her alleged lack of necessary aptitude. She was only granted a one year licence which would allow her to work as a subordinate medical doctor. *Dr. A*, as she was called in our judgment, challenged this decision before the Norwegian Appeal Board for Health Personnel. We found that an EEA State was not permitted under the directive to make the recognition subject to any further conditions. The system of automatic recognition would be jeopardised if it were open to EEA States at their discretion to question the merits of a decision taken by the competent authorities of another EEA State to award the formal evidence of qualification. Nonetheless, we made the important reservation that an EEA State may make an authorisation to practice medicine conditional upon the applicant having the linguistic knowledge necessary for practising the profession on its territory.

[13]2005/36/EC.

6.4 Equal Treatment for Men and Women

In *University of Oslo*, academic positions were reserved exclusively for women at the University of Oslo. ESA claimed that this was contrary to EEA law.[14] Following the relevant case law of the ECJ, the EFTA Court found in favour of ESA. It held that, as a matter of principle, there must be a possibility for the best-qualified candidate to obtain the position.[15]

[14]76/207/EEC.

[15]See for details Chapter 9.

Chapter 20
Where's the Beef?

Contents

1 The Origin of the Question

On 6 October 2015 I gave a public lecture at the invitation of the Centre of European Law at the University of Oslo. In my past speeches I had, with a few exceptions, conformed to the wishes of my Norwegian hosts and focussed on institutional and constitutional matters. However, this time I felt that I had to address the substance of our Single Market case law—and the way the legal community in both EEA pillars had been dealing with it. Since most academics, in particular in Norway and in Iceland, tend to immerse themselves in issues of sovereignty and the like without showing much interest in the material issues, I decided to give my speech the title "Dealing with the EEA Agreement: Where's the beef?"

"Where is the beef" is an American catchphrase which goes back to a slogan for the fast food chain *Wendy's*. The commercial which was launched in 1984 attacked competitors *Mc Donald's* and *Burger King* for offering big buns and a small beef patty in their sandwiches. In the primaries of the 1984 presidential campaign, Democratic candidate Walter Mondale, a Minnesotan with Norwegian roots, used the phrase to characterise the economic program of Senator Gary Hart as being without substance. Hart replied by saying "Here is the beef!" Meanwhile the question has become a general phrase questioning the substance, the content of an idea.

C. Baudenbacher, *Judicial Independence*, Springer Biographies,
https://doi.org/10.1007/978-3-030-02308-9_20

2 The Diagnosis

In the EEA context, the "beef" is EEA Single Market law, and the Court has been faced with an increasing number of complex cases. Thus, the Court has exercised considerable influence on the development of EU Single Market law. The central point of my lecture was that the legal community in the EFTA pillar, in particular in its largest Member State Norway, had barely dealt with substantive EEA law. As a rule, EEA/EFTA authors tended to limit themselves to addressing institutional and constitutional matters. The usual discourse, as I have said, has from the beginning revolved around issues such as the legal nature of EEA law, legitimisation and the distribution of powers, national sovereignty vs. supranationality, direct effect, primacy and State liability, conform interpretation and the provisional applicability of EEA law, fundamental rights and more recently the respective EU Charter, the independence of the Court vis-à-vis the ECJ, or methods of interpretation including the accusation of judicial activism. A particular centre of interest was the distribution of powers between the EFTA Court and the national supreme courts under the preliminary reference procedure.

I concluded by saying that most of these questions have now been clarified by the Court. After more than 20 years, commentators should not limit themselves any longer to only discussing these issues. The focus must be on what the EEA Agreement means for citizens and market actors (entrepreneurs, workers, investors, dealers, consumers) in both EEA pillars. This is more challenging than the eternal talk about sovereignty and institutions, not least because of the direct relevance of economics.

3 Limited Interest in the Beef in EFTA Circles

The obsession with sovereignty went so far that EFTA authors were virtually unaware of the substantive internal market law, the "beef". At the same time, the interest of EU authors increased continuously. To give a few examples, our *Kellogg's* judgment was amply discussed by EU authors such as Alberto Alemanno, Marco Bronckers, Mirina Grosz, or Nicolas de Sadeleer. In the EFTA pillar, the ruling was basically hushed up. The EFTA Court's second *Husbanken* judgment prompted a number of comments from EU authors such as Leigh Hancher/Tom Ottervanger/Piet Jan Slot and Ian S. Forrester. The only commentator from the EFTA pillar was Michael Sánchez Rydelski, the lawyer who had pleaded the case on behalf of ESA. The same happened with regard to the Court's *LO* judgment. Commentators from the EU competition law community (John Temple Lang, Richard Wish/David Bailey, Femi Alese, Christopher Townley, Constanze Semmelmann) compared *LO* positively with the ECJ's *Albany* approach. ECJ President Vassilios Skouris called *LO* an example of the effective dialogue between the Court and the ECJ in extrajudicial writing. On the other hand, there have barely been any substantial comments by observers from the EFTA pillar. This is all the more remarkable in the light of the fact that that the referring court, the Norwegian Labour Court, appears to have incorrectly implemented the EFTA Court's ruling.[1] Our *Norway Post* judgment was referenced by the GC, by several AG's, and followed by the Swiss Federal Supreme Court in *Publigroupe* and the Federal Administrative Tribunal in *GABA*, *Gebro* and *BMW*. At a conference in Berlin in June 2015, Justice Wolfgang Kirchhoff stated that the German Supreme Court was on the same line. In EU academic literature, *Norway Post* has been qualified as a landmark judgment of Pan-European, if not global significance (Eric Barbier de la Serre, Christopher Bellamy, Marco Bronckers, Ian Forrester, Eric Morgan de Rivery, Alina Kaczorowska, John Temple Lang, Alison Jones/Brenda Sufrin, Laura Brancaccio). Barely any comments were made by authors from the EFTA pillar. The contribution by Siri Teigum in the "Handbook of EEA law" was prompted by my invitation to her. A further example is *Abelia* where we held that whether in-house lawyers have the right to represent their company had to be assessed in in light of the circumstances on a case by case basis. The *Abelia* order caused great interest in the EU and beyond the EU. I immediately received speaking invitations from Germany, Switzerland, Japan, and the US. But there was no reaction from the EFTA pillar. The only publications were written by me and by my Head of Cabinet Philipp Speitler.

The situation was almost the same with regard to the EFTA Court's *Paranova* v *Merck* judgment, which involved modalities for repackaging pharmaceuticals. In *Boehringer Ingelheim II*, AG Sharpston and the ECJ fully endorsed the Court's approach. The German Supreme Court also referred to *Paranova* v *Merck* in a number of cases. In the EU, the judgment was discussed and it was criticised by practising lawyers close to the pharmaceutical industry. In EFTA, arguments against this were put forward by Jonas Myhre who had been the lawyer for Paranova. Otherwise the main focus in EFTA was on the EFTA Court—ECJ relationship.

German authors Marcus Lutter/Walter Bayer/Jessica Schmidt, Heribert Hirte and Hartmut Krause dealt with our *Periscopus* judgment and called it highly relevant also for the EU. The Oxford scholar Thomas Papadopoulos wrote that the clear and precise criteria for the adjustment of the mandatory bid price developed by the Court should in the interest of legal certainty and the protection of minority shareholders be incorporated into the Takeover Bids Directive.[2] As far as I have been able to establish, no EFTA pillar author has discussed the case. The Norwegian database *idunn.no* does not spit out any results in relation to a search for the name *Periscopus*.

Following our *Inconsult* ruling and the judgments of the ECJ in *Content Services* and of the German Supreme Court in *Holzhocker*, the situation was the same. German and Austrian authors immediately started to discuss the differences

[1]See for details Chapter 16.

[2]2004/25/EC.

between the approach taken by the EFTA Court, on the one hand, and the one of the ECJ and the German Supreme Court, on the other. I should also mention authors such as Peter Reiff, Felix Wieser, Arthur Stadler, Jeannine Weissel, Caroline Bovelet, Martin Schirmbacher, Catalina Goantă and David Lewin. In the EFTA pillar, nobody really cared about this groundbreaking judgment except me and my legal secretary Theresa Haas. The last case I want to mention here is *DB Schenker I*. This case was dealt with by EU lawyers Romina Polley and Emanuela Matei. In the EFTA pillar there was once again a resounding silence. Only in relation to tax cases, and to a certain extent for labour law cases, is the situation different. Since large parts of tax regulation is set by global institutions such as the G20 or the OECD, tax lawyers think more globally and there is an international tax law community.

Based on my experience, this lack of curiosity in substantive EEA law is not coincidental. Education in substantive EEA law doesn't seem to be a high priority in the universities of EEA/EFTA. EEA law is often dealt with as part of public international law, and this from the perspective of its (undesired) impact on domestic law. The main focus is on how the subversion of national law can be prevented. Prior to entering the lecture halls both students and professors seem to don a patriotic pair of glasses. EEA law is one-sidedly dealt with from the perspective of national constitutional law and the main interest is safeguarding national sovereignty. Professor Mads Andenaes, who spent many years researching and teaching in the UK, has rightly criticised this approach.

4 Remedial Measures

With my Oslo speech, I launched a debate. Agents appearing before the Court now started to use the expression "the beef" in oral hearings, when speaking about substantive issues. And the subject of the EFTA Court's 2016 Spring Conference which took place on 3 June was "The EFTA Court as a European Single Market Court". In my opening speech, I referred to Single Market law as being "the beef" of EEA law. Further lectures were given on EEA competition law, EEA State aid law, financial market law, and social policy.

The 2017 Spring Conference which was held on 16 June 2017 with a record number of over 170 participants also addressed topics of substantive EEA law including the fundamental freedoms and fundamental rights, the new innovative architecture of financial regulation in the EEA, recent EFTA Court competition law jurisprudence, and the EEA and Brexit. Finally, I should like to underline once more that the *Festschrift* marking the EFTA Court's twentieth anniversary contained numerous contributions concerning Single Market law. The same goes for the "Handbook of EEA law" which I edited in 2016.

I also want to mention that when the Norwegian Government held a competition concerning the incumbent judge's post in 2016, I sent a letter to the (Norwegian) panel in which I underlined that a judge of the EFTA Court must have knowledge and experience as regards substantive EEA Single Market law. I thereby made it clear that general knowledge of international law was not sufficient.[3]

As regards Norway, the reluctance to deal with substantive internal market law inevitably changed with the publication of the Norwegian Commentary. But even there the substantial considerations are overshadowed by the fact that the comments on the principles of homogeneity and reciprocity as well as on dispute settlement are dominated by orthodox dualism. Homogeneity is understood as a mechanical concept. The fact that the reality is characterised by an intensive judicial dialogue between the EFTA Court and the European Courts is basically ignored.[4]

[3]See for details Chapter 28.

[4]See for details Chapter 24.

Chapter 21
Judicial Dialogue Between the ECJ and the EFTA Court

Contents

1 Introduction

As I have already said in Chap. 3 of this book, the one-sided written homogeneity rules have over the years, to a large extent, been replaced by a dialogue between the ECJ, its AGs and the GC, on the one hand, and the EFTA Court, on the other. I have then repeatedly pointed out that the dispute settlement rules of the EEA Agreement are hardly operational in case of a judicial conflict.

Judicial dialogue is a notion that has become fashionable in times of globalisation and regionalisation of the economy. It means that high courts in different jurisdictions talk to each other. This conversation occurs in the form of reference or citation. But there are also increasing opportunities to maintain extrajudicial dialogues, be it at conferences, judges' meetings or through extrajudicial writing. High courts are important players in today's world and international judicial dialogue is a necessity. It works best in the fields of law that are characterised by convergence,

C. Baudenbacher, *Judicial Independence*, Springer Biographies,
https://doi.org/10.1007/978-3-030-02308-9_21

such as human rights law, the law of economic freedoms, energy law, the law concerning the functioning of federal systems, intellectual property law and competition law, to name just a few examples. Certain high courts have a long history of using a comparative approach when faced with novel legal problems. An example is the Federal Supreme Court of Switzerland, which by tradition openly uses and discusses foreign court opinions and foreign academic literature. In its 2002 landmark judgment in *Fairchild* v *Glenhaven Funeral Services Ltd*, an asbestos case in which the claimant, due to insufficient evidence, was unable to identify which of several employers had caused his harm, the House of Lords discussed the legal situation in some 20 jurisdictions and even included Roman law.

For the sake of good order, I want to underline that the modern theory of judicial dialogue is, however, of American origin. This is not without irony since American judges usually have difficulties entering into any kind of dialogue with their colleagues from other jurisdictions. Certainly, they took it for granted that after WWII judges from around the world would orient themselves towards the US Supreme Court. American professors proudly stated that their Supreme Court was an idea-giver for other high courts in the world. Anthony Lester, an attentive European observer, wrote in 1988:

> The Bill of Rights is more than an historical inspiration for the creation of charters and institutions dedicated to the protection of liberty. Currently, there is a vigorous overseas trade in the Bill of Rights, in international and constitutional litigation involving norms derived from American constitutional law. When life or liberty is at stake, the landmark judgments of the Supreme Court of the United States, giving fresh meaning to the principles of the Bill of Rights, are studied with as much attention in New Delhi or Strasbourg as they are in Washington, D.C., or the State of Washington, or Springfield, Illinois.

But when it comes to the reverse question, namely whether American courts should seek inspiration abroad, things are quite different. There is a heated debate whether this can be done, which from a European perspective has some slightly bizarre traits. Be that as it may, outside the US, international inter-court dialogue is a fact of judicial life. The EEA Agreement constitutes a special case because the law in both EEA pillars, EU and EFTA, is largely identical in substance. AG Verica Trstenjak has, in *Marques Almeda*, characterised the dialogue ECJ-EFTA Court as “unique”. On the other hand, Vassilios Skouris, at the time President of the ECJ, stated in 2005:

> Notwithstanding those obvious specificities characterising the relationship between the ECJ and the EFTA Court, I would nevertheless suggest that the ECJ-EFTA Court model of cooperation can serve as a more general paradigm of institutional dialogue between judicial institutions. In my view, the reasons for the successful cooperation between the ECJ and the EFTA Court lie far beyond the similarity of their competences, the pertinent statutory provisions or the geographic proximity of their seat. The success of the ECJ-EFTA Court model of cooperation resulted primarily from the fact that these two institutions have managed, through consistent efforts, to attain a very high level of mutual understanding which allowed them not only to accomplish homogeneity and coherence in their case-law, but also to further develop their jurisprudence.

2 ECJ Going First

2.1 EFTA Court Follows the ECJ

When the EFTA Court took up its functions in January 1994, the ECJ had already created a comprehensive body of relevant case law. In order to secure a smooth integration of the EEA/EFTA States' economies, this jurisprudence was largely taken over by the EFTA Court. Examples from the early years are the ECJ's landmark judgments on free movement of goods in cases such as *Dassonville* and *Cassis de Dijon*. The EFTA Court also built upon the judgment in *Leclerc-Siplec* on television advertisements, the *Spijkers* decision on the concept of the transfer of an undertaking or the ECJ's case law on basic notions of EU competition law. There is hardly a single judgment of the EFTA Court that does not cite ECJ case law. As regards the GC's jurisprudence, the EFTA Court must take the fact into account that the GC is not a court of last instance.

Nevertheless, the EFTA Court has never understood the written homogeneity rules as being absolutely binding, not even in the first years of its existence. It has, for example, occasionally shown a certain uneasiness over embracing the ECJ's *Keck* jurisprudence. The *Keck* judgment was delivered on 24 November 1993 and commentators have dubbed it "the ECJ's November Revolution". In an unusual move, the ECJ complained about the increasing tendency of traders to invoke the provision prohibiting quantitative restrictions on imports between Member States and all measures having equivalent effect (at the time Article 30 of the Treaty)

> as a means of challenging any rules whose effect is to limit their commercial freedom even where such rules are not aimed at products from other Member States.

Departing from its established case law, the ECJ held in a handful of pithy paragraphs that:

> the application to products from other Member States of national provisions restricting or prohibiting certain selling arrangements is not such as to hinder directly or indirectly, actually or potentially, trade between Member States [....] so long as those provisions apply to all relevant traders operating within the national territory and so long as they affect in the same manner, in law and in fact, the marketing of domestic products and of those from other Member States.

Based on this formula, the ECJ concluded that legislation of a Member State imposing a general prohibition on resale at a loss (*in casu* France) fell outside the scope of said prohibition. *Keck* caused considerable legal uncertainty, not least because the ECJ refrained from saying which of its previous cases it deemed to have overruled. In *Ullensaker Kommune*, the Borgarting Court of Appeal asked whether the EEA law provisions on free movement of goods prohibited a municipality from refusing permission for the retail sale of recorded video cassettes (videograms), on the grounds that such permission should only be granted to specialised dealers for videograms and/or that expert knowledge should be built up by established dealers. The EFTA Court, based on *Keck*, answered in the negative, but pointed *obiter dicta* to another thread of the case law. The ECJ held in *Bassano del Grappa* that a national statute that required a trading licence for the opening of shops for the retail sale of certain goods without making a distinction between foreign and domestic goods was not to be regarded as being capable of hindering trade between the Member States. The purpose was not to regulate trade in goods with other Member States, and the potential restrictive effects on the free movement of goods were too uncertain and indirect for the obligation that they imposed to be regarded as being capable of hindering trade between Member States. The too uncertain and indirect formula was also used in *Philip Morris*, the case involving a ban on the visual display of tobacco products at the point of sale. Likewise, in the retail alcohol monopoly case *Wilhelmsen*, the EFTA Court did not specifically deal with *Keck*. As Professor Dr. Gunnar Thor Pétursson, the Internal Market Director of ESA, has observed, the EFTA Court's focus has in all these cases been on market access.

Judging is not an exact science. Even in cases in which the EFTA Court basically follows ECJ case law, it may add its own nuances or clarifications, either in the *ratio decidendi* or in *dicta*.

2.2 *EFTA Court Doesn't Follow the ECJ*

According to Recital 15 in the preamble to the EEA Agreement, the homogeneity goal must be pursued "in full deference to the independence of the courts". It was not until 16 July 2016 that the EFTA Court referred to this in paragraph 70 of its *Jabbi* judgment. Obviously a mature court has more self-confidence than a new court or a court that has just been downsized and lost three important Member States.

For the sake of good order, I want to reiterate what was stated in Chap. 10 regarding the war over constitutional principles; namely that the EFTA Court, as a matter of principle, does not see the ECJ's jurisprudence concerning internal effect and primacy of European law as binding. However, the respective case law is based on a written difference between EU and EEA law, namely Protocol 35 to the EEA Agreement.

As regards substantive Single Market law, the first big case in which the EFTA Court found that ECJ jurisprudence could not be followed was *Kellogg's*. The ECJ had held in *Sandoz* that national rules prohibiting, without prior authorisation, the marketing of foodstuffs fortified with vitamins, which were lawfully marketed in another Member State, were permitted, provided that such marketing was authorised when the addition of vitamins met a real need, especially a technical or nutritional one. The EFTA Court made reference to *Sandoz*, but held that

> [t]he mere finding by a national authority of the absence of a nutritional need will not justify an import ban, a most restrictive measure, on a product which is freely traded in other EEA State.

In *Danish Vitamins*, the ECJ followed us against the advice of AG Mischo. It thereby overruled *Sandoz* in substance.

A case in which the EFTA Court patently refused to follow the ECJ was *Abelia.* Unlike the ECJ in *Prezes*, the EFTA Court held that whether in-house lawyers have the right of audience, must be assessed by the Court on a case by case basis. In other words, the EFTA Court did not rely on a presumption or fiction, but used a fact-based approach.

Important cases in which the EFTA Court forged new paths are *Norway Post* on the scope of judicial review, the *DB Schenker* cases on access to documents, *LO* and *Holship* on the relationship between collective bargaining and industrial action, on the one hand, and competition and free movement law, on the other, *Ski Taxi* on the notion of restriction of competition by object, and *Vigeland* on the re-monopolisation of works of art that had fallen into the public domain.

Our *Norway Post* judgment was cited by AGs Mengozzi in *Fonnship* and in *MasterCard,* Kokott in ECtHR Opinion 2/13 and in *Schindler,* and Wathelet in *Telefonica*. The GC referred to *Norway Post* on countless instances. On the other hand, the ECJ has never referenced the EFTA Court's judgment. It has, however, used language, which in similar terms points to full judicial review. Nevertheless, practitioners are cautious and maintain that the ECJ still leaves the Commission a certain margin of appreciation when dealing with issues of complex economic assessment.

As regards access to documents, the ECJ held in *Energie Baden-Württemberg* that there is a general presumption that the disclosure of documents held by the Commission will, in principle, undermine the protection of the commercial interests of the undertakings involved and the protection of the purpose of the investigations. The interest in obtaining compensation for loss suffered as a result of a violation of the European cartel prohibition cannot constitute an overriding public interest unless it is "necessary" for the private damages claimant to have access to the Commission's case file. The EFTA Court went its own way as regards the presumption against public access to documents. Unlike in EU law, such a presumption only applies in State aid and merger cases. As regards abuse of dominance cases, the interest of the tortfeaser does not constitute a legitimate interest deserving protection. This will, as a matter of principle, also apply to cartels.[1] The statement that a private plaintiff in damages proceedings before a national court is pursuing his private interest, but at the same time contributes to the protection of the public interest, has been cited in an affirmative way by AG Kokott in her Opinion in *KONE and Others*. The EFTA Court referenced that passage in the fifth *Schenker* judgment, it furthermore reiterated its statement concerning the role of a private plaintiff and added that AG Kokott had signalled her agreement with this approach in her Opinion in *Kone*. The GC concurred with this point of

[1]See for details Chapter 18.

view on 28 January 2015 in the two cases *Akzo Nobel* and *Evonik Degussa*, holding in paragraph 84 that

> the right to obtain compensation for loss caused by a contract or conduct liable to restrict or distort competition can make a significant contribution to the maintenance of effective competition in the European Union [....] and thus contribute to the protection of the public interest.

In the joint bidding case *Ski Taxi* we followed AG Wahl and held that only conduct whose harmful nature is easily identifiable in the light of experience and economics should be regarded as a restriction by object.

The EFTA Court's *Holship* judgment was built on its own *LO* precedent. As in *LO*, we used an effects-based approach and relied on an elaborate proportionality test. The referring Norwegian Supreme Court followed our *Holship* ruling. On 15 June 2017, the Norwegian unions decided to bring Norway before the ECtHR for alleged non-compliance with the ECHR. The ECJ has not yet had an opportunity to deal with our case law.

Vigeland was about the attempt to re-monopolise art works that had previously enjoyed copyright protection and had now fallen into the public domain due to the expiry of the copyright protection. The EFTA Court held that copyright provides an incentive to contribute to the enrichment of society. Trade mark registration after expiry is not in itself unlawful, but it could be contrary to "accepted principles of morality" where artworks form part of a nation's cultural heritage or act as an emblem of sovereignty. Trade mark registration may even amount to a misappropriation or a desecration of the artist's work. *Vigeland* is probably the most elaborate judgment of a European court concerning the public domain. University of Amsterdam Professor Martin Senftleben commented:

> The Vigeland decision of the EFTA Court is a milestone in the preservation of the public domain of cultural creations. It paves the way for an important and welcome recalibration of the copyright/trade mark interface. The Court departs from the traditional approach which relies on non-distinctiveness, descriptiveness or genericness to reject trade mark rights. Instead, the Court provides exemplary lines of argument for the application of considerations of public policy and principles of morality as grounds for refusal.

The author found *Vigeland* to be more nuanced than parallel ECJ case law and that the GC has even approached the problem in a schematic way. Önder Erol Ünsal, a trade mark examiner at the Turkish Patent and Trademark Office, wrote that the decisions of the EFTA Court and of the referring Board of Appeal

> will guide us in the evaluation of trademark registration requests of common historical and cultural values encountered in Turkey in recent years.

A significant case, where a straightforward approach was adopted was my Presidential Order in *Wow Air*. This Order granted the application for an accelerated preliminary reference procedure in a case on the allocation of slots at the Keflavík International Airport in Reykjavík. I held that the issue constituted a "matter of exceptional urgency, in particular because of the economic sensitivity of the present case". As far as I can see, the President of the ECJ has rejected applications for accelerated procedure in the context of competition law. The GC has granted such an application in the merger case *Schneider Electric* v *Commission*.

Another example of the EFTA Court using a different approach than the ECJ concerns the obligation of a foreign plaintiff to pay security for costs before domestic courts. We held in *Dr. Kottke* that such a provision entails indirect discrimination of foreigners, but can be justified on the basis of public interest objectives if it is necessary and not excessive in attaining those objectives. The ECJ found in 1993 in a similar case, *Hubbard*, that it was incompatible with the treaties to require a security for costs to be given by someone who brings an action before the courts of another Member State, on the sole ground that he is a national of another Member State. Unlike the ECJ's case law, the *Dr. Kottke* ruling is fact-based.

The EFTA Court's way of proceeding in the abovementioned cases was an emanation of a new understanding of homogeneity. Then ECJ President Vassilios Skouris has aptly written in his contribution to the *Festschrift* marking our twentieth anniversary that the *LO* judgment demonstrates the effective judicial dialogue between the two courts. He noted that the EFTA Court referenced AG Jacobs' Opinion and thus followed an alternative authority to that of the ECJ.

The EEA Agreement does not contain any provisions on procedural homogeneity. However, the EFTA Court held from the beginning that although it is not required to follow the reasoning of the EU courts when interpreting the main part of the SCA, the reasoning, which led the EU courts to their interpretation of expressions in EU law is relevant when those expressions are identical in substance to the ones that must be interpreted by the EFTA Court. Since 2011, the EFTA Court has used the term "procedural homogeneity" when dealing with such issues. The procedural provisions in question refer, in particular, to the question of access to the Court, which may be at issue in all types of procedures. However, the case law shows that procedural homogeneity is a heuristic rule. In particular, aspects of access to justice have played a part. Starting with its very first case, *Restamark*, the Court has consistently held that a national body may constitute a court or tribunal entitled to make a preliminary reference even if its procedure is not *inter partes*. The ECJ followed the same direction in *Dorsch Consult*. In later cases, the EFTA Court has continued to adopt a liberal approach towards the interpretation of the terms "court or tribunal."[2] On the other hand, it did not follow the ECJ's case law concerning the right of audience of in-house counsel.[3]

---

[2]See for details Chapter 24.

[3]See for details Chapter 16.

3 EFTA Court Going First

3.1 ECJ Follows the EFTA Court Explicitly

It soon became clear that the written, one-sided homogeneity rules would at any rate be of limited help since the EFTA Court, in most cases, had to answer novel legal questions. This was so even during the short existence of the five-member Court. I think it was me who coined the phrase the "Going first constellation" for this phenomenon. In the meantime, going first has become a technical term of EEA law. When the respective issues have finally come before the ECJ, the latter in some cases explicitly relied on the EFTA Court's earlier rulings.

In the first ten years of its existence, important cases in which the EFTA Court had to go first were *Mattel and Lego* on TV without frontiers, *Ulstein and Røiseng* on succession of contracts under the Transfer of Undertakings Directive, *Finanger* on the insurance coverage of a passenger accepting a ride from an intoxicated driver, *Kellogg's* on the precautionary principle in food law, and *Fokus Bank* on the taxation of outbound dividends.

The ECJ, advised by AG Francis Jacobs, expressly followed the EFTA Court's *Mattel and Lego* ruling in *de Agostini and TV Shop I Sverige*, a case that had been lodged with the EFTA Court during Sweden's EEA/EFTA membership, and which was withdrawn when Sweden joined the EU. AG Carl Otto Lenz referenced the *Mattel and Lego* judgment in the *Flemish Television* case (*Commission* v *UK*). The GC referred to the EFTA Court's judgments in *Restamark* and *Scottish Salmon Growers* in its seminal *Opel Austria* judgment. In this case the GC dissociated itself from some of the exaggerations in the ECJ's Opinion 1/91.

The ECJ referred to the EFTA Court's judgment in *Ulstein and Røiseng* in *Süzen*. The ECJ's judgment in the *Danish Vitamins* case (*Commission* v *Denmark*) was entirely based on our *Kellogg's* ruling. In *Bellio Fratell*, a case about the cross-contamination of fish flour with bone tissue, the ECJ extensively quoted *Kellogg's*. The ECJ furthermore relied on *Kellogg's* in a case involving the release of GMOs (*Monsanto Agricoltura*) and the GC did the same in two cases concerning the fortification of animal feedingstuffs with antibiotics (*Pfizer Animal Health* and *Alpharma*). *Finanger* was quoted both by AG Geelhoed in case *Candolin* and AG Trstenjak in *Manuel Ferreira*. There are a number of further examples where the EFTA Court's jurisprudence was referenced by the EU judiciary. These examples concern the relationship between the freedom to provide services and the free movement of capital, the concept of homogeneity, EEA State liability, liability for pain and suffering, the question of whether a website can constitute a durable medium.

AG's opinions have from the start been a gateway between our case law and EU case law. Recent examples concern the legal situation of a trust (reference of AG Kokott to *Olsen* in *Panayi*), the qualification of a website as a durable medium (reference of AG Bobek to *Inconsult* in *Bawag*), or the notion of State aid (reference of AG Kokott to *Private Barnehagers Landsforbund* in *Congregación de Escuelas Pías Provincia Betania*).

A particularly illustrative example of dialogue which involved not only the EFTA Court and the ECJ, but also national courts in both pillars and an AG of the ECJ is the second *Boehringer Ingelheim* case. In *Paranova* v *Merck*, Paranova had repackaged pharmaceuticals and moved the colour stripes from the middle of the box to the edges. The Court rejected Merck's argument that the necessity test, as developed by the ECJ, also applied to the change of design and that there was no necessity for the parallel importer to add new design elements in order to gain market access. It held that once the right to repackage and to depict the original trade mark is established, and market access is thereby assured, the necessity test would no longer apply. The interests involved had to be balanced and the function of the parallel importer for the regulation of prices had to be taken into account. We thereby followed a different approach than the Supreme Courts of Germany, Austria and Denmark. This prompted the England and Wales Court of Appeal to refer a fresh case to the ECJ, C-348/04 *Boehringer Ingelheim II*, and to ask, *inter alia*, the following question:

> [D]oes the first condition set out in Bristol-Myers Squibb [….], namely that it must be shown that it is necessary to repackage the product in order that effective market access is not hindered, apply merely to the fact of reboxing (as held by the Court of Justice of the European Free Trade Association in Case E-3/02 *Paranova v. Merck*) or does it also apply to the precise manner and style of the re-boxing carried out by the parallel importer, and if so how?

The English judge in charge of the case indicated that he was sympathetic to the EFTA Court's position. AG Sharpston and the ECJ agreed with the approach taken by the Court and cited *Paranova* v *Merck*. The German Supreme Court for its part overruled its previous case law and based itself on our judgment in cases *STILNOX*, *Micardis* and *Lefax/Lefaxin* without making a request for a preliminary ruling to the ECJ.

To date the EFTA Court has rendered some 200 judgments in contested cases which, have led to 238 references by the ECJ, its AGs and the GC in 151 cases. All things considered, the EFTA Court is the only court of general jurisdiction whose case law is taken into account on a regular basis by the EU judiciary when the latter interprets EU law.

3.2 ECJ Follows the EFTA Court Implicitly

There are cases where the ECJ has taken EFTA Court case law into account without citing it. Here, one could also speak of a silent dialogue. Vassilios Skouris wrote in 2005 that the ECJ has contributed to the fulfilment of the homogeneity objective by taking into consideration EFTA Court case law "although, in most cases, it has not done so expressly". From the EFTA Court's perspective, an explicit dialogue is obviously preferable over an implicit one. A recent example is the judgment in *Panayi* where AG Kokott referenced our *Olsen* ruling. The Opinions of AG Trstenjak in *Menarini and Others* – references to *Federation of Icelandic trade*), AG Geelhoed in *Candolin* (references to *Finanger*), and AG Mischo in *Greenham and Abel* (references to *Kellogg's*) should also be mentioned. Experience shows that whether our case law is explicitly taken into account or not by the ECJ may depend on the individual Judge Rapporteur and the chamber president. The ECJ's Finnish judge Allan Rosas, who advocates an explicit dialogue, wrote in 2008:

> [F]or me the question as to whether judges should be open to the outside world and be aware of discussions taking place in other relevant jurisdictions, is not any longer a question of opinion. It is a question of whether you are competent or incompetent. If you close your eyes, you belong to the latter category.

3.3 No Parallel Case Before the ECJ Yet

There have been many cases where we have rendered judgment without the ECJ having had an opportunity to state its position for years. An important example concerns the question of whether the Norwegian ban on the visual display of tobacco products constituted a measure having equivalent effect to a quantitative restriction if, in fact, the ban affects the marketing of products from other EEA States to a greater degree than that of imported products that were, until recently, produced in Norway (*Philip Morris*).[4] Further examples of such cases are *Vienna Life* and *Swiss Life* concerning trade in second-hand insurance policies, *Creditinfo Lánstraust* concerning access to public sector information or *Otto Kaufmann AG* regarding information on convictions relevant to the competence and professional liability of legal persons.[5]

3.4 ECJ Follows the EFTA Court on a Second Attempt

Experience also shows that in going first cases the ECJ may at first decide not to follow the EFTA Court, but will then align itself with the latter's jurisprudence in later cases. This has happened in the areas of taxation of outbound dividends, State gambling monopolies, and also regarding the interpretation of the concept of a "durable medium" in internet law.

Taxation of Outbound Dividends

As I have explained before, the EFTA Court held in *Fokus Bank* in the context of the taxation of outbound dividends that an EEA State cannot rely on an

---

[4]For details see Chapter 15

[5]For details see Chapter 18.

international double taxation agreement in order to justify an otherwise unlawful restriction on the free movement of capital. To me, *Fokus Bank*, in which I was Judge Rapporteur, did not seem to be a particularly revolutionary step. Both ESA and the European Commission had asked the Court to rule accordingly. After some controversy, the judgment was implemented in Norway. However, in EU countries with a huge budget deficit, our ruling caused greater irritation. In 2005, the German Law Journal *Finanz-Rundschau* published an article bearing the title:

> *Wie drei Richter aus Island, Liechtenstein und Norwegen auszogen, die EU-Staaten das Fürchten zu lehren!* (How three Judges from Iceland, Liechtenstein and Norway set out to teach the EU States a lesson!)

The *Süddeutsche Zeitung*, one of the most prominent German newspapers, wrote on 25 April 2005:

> *Geradezu bizarr erscheint, dass nun auch Richter von ausserhalb der Europäischen Union die Gesetzgebung der nationalen Parlamente eingrenzen wollen.* (It is downright bizarre that meanwhile also judges from outside of the European Union are trying to restrict the law making powers of the national parliaments.)

In November 2005, I gave a presentation at the 6th Colloquium of the European Constitutional Law Network (ECLN) in Berlin. Judges from the European Courts including ECJ President Vassilios Skouris and CFI President Bo Vesterdorf, the highest national courts and experts on European and constitutional law from all over the world spoke and debated about the future EU judicial architecture. A senior bureaucrat from the German Ministry of Finance addressed those present and made it clear that if his Government would have to pay back dividends under the *Fokus Bank* rule, this could put Germany's efforts to balance its budget at risk.

In its first judgment after *Fokus Bank*, *Bouanich*, the ECJ found that international tax treaties could remedy a restriction on the free movement of capital provided that they ensured that non-resident shareholders were not treated less favourably than resident shareholders. In cases *Test Claimants in Class IV* and *Denkavit*, the ECJ, following AG Geelhoed, found that international tax conventions had some relevance. However, in the subsequent cases *Commission* v *Italy* and *Commission* v *Spain*, the ECJ, while maintaining the possibility that a double taxation convention may enable a Member State to comply with its obligations under the Treaty, set the hurdle so high that the likelihood of a Member State ever succeeding on this point is rather remote. By and large, there is hardly any meaningful difference between *Commission* v *Spain* and *Fokus Bank*. Significantly, the ECJ in this case cited the European Commission's pleadings which referred to our *Fokus Bank* judgment. The Commission argued that it was clear from *Fokus Bank*,

> that the State of the source of the income cannot justify discriminatory treatment, even by concluding an agreement which grants a tax advantage in the Member State of residence. A Member State cannot shift its obligation to comply with the obligations imposed on it by the Treaty to another Member State and rely on the other State to make good the discrimination.

Fokus Bank has been referred to in countless books, essays, newsletters and blogs in both EEA pillars and beyond Europe. Tax lawyers and economists as well as tax officers have commented on it, mostly favourably. The ruling itself is even dealt with in the German Wikipedia article on the ECJ. The notion "Fokus Bank claims" has become a technical term for actions where a person is reclaiming a withholding tax in national courts in both EEA pillars, levied in an allegedly discriminatory way.

State Gambling Monopolies

A similar development has taken place regarding the question of whether State gambling monopolies are compatible with the fundamental freedoms. In *Gaming Machines* and in *Ladbrokes* the EFTA Court applied a strict proportionality test when assessing the compatibility of Norway's State gambling monopoly. In its judgment of 8 September 2009 in *Liga Portuguesa*, the ECJ adopted a much more lenient approach to proportionality. But in *Markus Stoß*, the ECJ on 8 September 2010 largely aligned itself with the EFTA Court, although without making any reference to the latter. In later cases, this trend became even clearer, such as when AG Mengozzi cited our *Ladbrokes* judgment in *Markus Stoß*.

Notion of a Durable Medium

The third area where the ECJ has adjusted its case law on a second attempt concerns the interpretation of the notion of a "durable medium" in internet law. In our judgment of 27 January 2010 in *Inconsult*, we held that a sophisticated website that cannot be unilaterally changed may constitute a durable medium. This implied that we expected the consumer to download or print out the respective content. In *Content Services*, the ECJ on 5 July 2012 cited *Inconsult* with regard to the concept of a "durable medium", but concluded, in line with AG Mengozzi, that the consumer may behave completely passively during the transmission of the information. Information found on the seller's website that is only accessible via a link sent to the consumer, was said to be neither "given" to that consumer, nor "received" by him. My good friend Mengozzi had stated at point 33 of his Opinion that

> "even though clicking on a hyperlink is an entirely commonplace action, within the capability of any internet user, not all users are in a position to understand, when the contract is concluded, that they need to click on the link in order to be able, should the need arise, to protect their own rights better in the future." To find otherwise "would risk opening the gates to possible abuses."

The German Supreme Court in its *Holzhocker* judgment of 29 April 2010 also referenced our *Inconsult* ruling. But it took a similar approach to the ECJ, holding that in the light of EU law consumers must receive the instruction concerning the right of withdrawal without needing to take any action themselves.

In *BAWAG*, the ECJ, following AG Bobek, moved in the direction of our *Inconsult* judgment. Both AG Bobek and the ECJ cited *Inconsult*.

3.5 *EFTA Court Adjusting Its Jurisprudence to ECJ Case Law*

State Retail Alcohol Monopolies

As I have explained before, the EFTA Court took a critical approach towards the Norwegian State retail alcohol monopoly in *Wilhelmsen*, basing itself on the ordoliberal theory of "as if competition".[6] However, six months later, on 23 October 1997, the ECJ in *Franzén* used a different kind of reasoning concerning the Swedish State monopoly on the retail of alcoholic beverages, the *Systembolaget*. The Danish AG Michael Elmer, referring, *inter alia*, to the EFTA Court's *Restamark* judgment, took the view that the Swedish system was incompatible with the free movement of goods provisions of the EC Treaty. However, the ECJ did not follow him. It held that the existence and operation of the monopoly was to be considered solely under what is now Article 37 TFEU, the monopoly provision. Restrictions on trade that were inherent in the existence of a monopoly had to be accepted. This included the limitation of the number of points of sale. The ECJ found, in particular, the criteria and methods of selection used by *Systembolaget* to be non-discriminatory since: (i) the monopoly followed a purchase plan that was based on foreseeable changes in consumer demand; (ii) the calls for offers were made irrespective of the origin of traders and types of beverage; and (iii) the offers were selected on purely commercial or qualitative criteria. The ECJ pointed to the fact that blind tasting was used as a selection mechanism and that consumer panels were formed. The fact that the system was able to handicap small producers was accepted. Based on these arguments, the ECJ declared the retail monopoly lawful. It is obvious that the judgment was politically motivated. Swedish Government circles had threatened that a ruling against *Systembolaget* would not be implemented. In *HOB Vín I*, the EFTA Court aligned itself with the ECJ's *Franzén* ruling. Whether this case law is convincing from a legal and economic perspective is doubtful. But in view of the strong feelings of the Scandinavian Governments, it was, at least from a political standpoint, probably reasonable to do so.

International Exhaustion of Trade Mark Rights

The second adjustment was more surprising and more serious. In the *L'Oréal* cases, the EFTA Court on 8 July 2008 overruled its 1997 *Maglite* precedent. In *Maglite*, the Court consisting of Bjørn Haug, Thór Vilhjálmsson and myself had found on 3 December 1997 that under the Trade Mark Directive,[7] the EEA/EFTA States had retained the right to opt for the international exhaustion of trade mark rights. All three EEA/EFTA States had done so. Under the principle of international or world-wide exhaustion, a trade mark owner may not hinder the import of goods bearing the mark if they have been put on the market by the owner himself or by somebody else with his consent somewhere in the world. The *Maglite* flashlights

[6] See for details Chapter 15.

[7] 89/104/EEC.

had been imported into Norway by a non-authorised dealer from California. Since the EEA is a free trade area and not a customs union, it was clear that the flashlights could not be imported into the EU from Norway if the ECJ did not favour international exhaustion. The *Maglite* judgment, in which I (as the junior judge at the time) acted as Judge Rapporteur reflected the traditional approach of all the European States that are committed to the idea of free trade. We knew that the same question was pending before the ECJ in the *Silhouette* case when we gave judgment. That case involved a parallel importer, who had purchased Silhouette spectacle frames in Bulgaria and marketed them in Austria.

In our *Maglite* ruling, we mentioned that the Commission's first proposal for a Trade Mark Directive had provided for international exhaustion. However, this plan was defeated in the European Parliament. The amended proposal limited the exhaustion rule to goods that had been put on the market "within the Community". However, we also pointed to the fact that some Member States, both in the Community and in EFTA, either retained international exhaustion or left the question open for interpretation by the national courts. In substance, we pointed out that: (i) international exhaustion is in the interests of free trade and competition and thus in the interests of consumers; (ii) parallel imports from countries outside the EEA lead to a greater supply of goods bearing a trade mark on the market; and (iii) price levels of products will be lower than in a market where only importers authorised by the trade mark holder distribute their products. Furthermore, the principle of international exhaustion was said to be in line with the main function of a trade mark, which is to allow the consumer to identify with certainty the origin of the products. Finally, the EFTA Court stated that its interpretation of Article 7(1) of the Trade Mark Directive in the EEA context was also in line with the WTO Agreement on Trade-Related Aspects of Intellectual Property Rights (TRIPS), where the issue is left open for the Member States to regulate.

The Governments of France, Germany and the UK, together with the Commission argued against interpreting Article 7 of the directive in favour of international exhaustion. That provision stated:

> Exhaustion of the rights conferred by a trade mark
>
> 1. The trade mark shall not entitle the proprietor to prohibit its use in relation to goods which have been put on the market in the Community under that trade mark by the proprietor or with his consent.
>
> 2. Paragraph 1 shall not apply where there exist legitimate reasons for the proprietor to oppose further commercialization of the goods, especially where the condition of the goods is changed or impaired after they have been put on the market.

The three EU Member State Governments and the Commission claimed that if individual Member States were allowed to determine freely whether holders of rights are able to object to imports from third countries, it could lead to a situation where the same products may be subject to parallel imports into one Member State, but not into another. This could cause internal disparities in the market. Therefore, the principle of free movement of goods had to be the same in all Member States and that principle had also to apply for the EEA.

The EFTA Court rejected this argumentation holding that unlike the EC Treaty, the EEA Agreement has not established a customs union, but a free trade area. According to the rules of origin of the EEA Agreement, the principle of free movement of goods applies only to goods originating in the EEA, while in the Community a product is in free circulation once it has been lawfully placed on the market in a Member State. Since the Maglite flashlights were manufactured in the US and imported into Norway, they were not subject to the principle of the free movement of goods within the EEA.

The Governments of Liechtenstein and of Norway as well as ESA argued that the EEA/EFTA States retained the power to opt for international exhaustion. The Norwegian Government added that more limited exhaustion would allow for price discrimination, stronger segmentation of the markets and reduced price competition, "thereby lessening the efficiency of the economy".

Before we finalised the *Maglite* case, I met with the Judge Rapporteur in the ECJ's *Silhouette* case, the Danish Judge Claus Gulman. We discussed the factual and legal differences of the two cases and Claus told me that we would be foolish not to allow our Member States to retain international exhaustion. It became clear to me that in the light of the legislative history of the directive, the ECJ would find otherwise.

On 29 January 1998, AG Francis Jacobs in his Opinion in *Silhouette* advised the ECJ to rule that in the Community international exhaustion was no longer possible. He cited the abovementioned passages from *Maglite* verbatim and distinguished the two cases in the same way as we had done. Six months after our *Maglite* judgment, on 16 July 1998, the ECJ held in *Silhouette* that the EU Member States were in fact prevented from opting for international exhaustion. The Swedish Government unsuccessfully took the opposite view. The Governments of Austria, France, Germany, Italy and the UK as well as the Commission, argued that such an interpretation was contrary to the wording of Article 7 and to the scheme and purpose of the rules of the directive concerning the rights that a trade mark confers on its proprietor. The ECJ followed this approach and held in paragraph 27 that this was

> the only interpretation which is fully capable of ensuring that the purpose of the Directive is achieved, namely to safeguard the functioning of the internal market. A situation in which some Member States could provide for international exhaustion while others provided for Community exhaustion only would inevitably give rise to barriers to the free movement of goods and the freedom to provide services.

Maglite and *Silhouette* were intensely discussed in academic literature, and free traders from all over the world commended us on the stand we had taken. The EFTA Court was (for the first time) present on the world map. The ECJ, on the other hand, was criticised for its mercantilist approach. The Trade Mark Directive did not aim at complete harmonisation and German Professor Norbert Reich aptly stated that trade mark owners were privileged beyond what was necessary, to the detriment of competition and consumer choice. Other commentators spoke of the "Silhouette of a Trojan horse" when the Opinion of AG Jacobs was published.

Subsequent ECJ case law has made the situation even worse. In autumn 1998, I taught international IP law at the UT, which had a strong IP department. Professors and students took a keen interest in the two cases, not least because on 9 March 1998, i.e. between the delivery of the Opinion of AG Jacobs and the handing down of the judgment in *Silhouette*, the US Supreme Court had signalled its willingness to take a liberal stand on the matter of international exhaustion in its judgment of 9 March 1998 in the copyright law case *Quality King Distributors v. L'anza Research Int'l, Inc.* I was also surprised that in the whole *Maglite-Silhouette* saga the UK, which historically had always been the bastion of unconditional free trade, was suddenly among the pioneers of protectionism.

In October and November 2008, the *L'Oréal* cases were referred to the EFTA Court by the Follo District Court and the Oslo District Court. Both Norwegian courts wanted to know, in essence, whether Article 7(1) of the Trade Mark Directive was be understood to the effect that international exhaustion was permitted in the light of *Maglite*, on the one hand, and of *Silhouette*, on the other. I had published a major essay on *Maglite* and *Silhouette* in the March 1999 edition of the Fordham International Law Journal in which I came to the following conclusions:

> If one assumes that the ECJ will not overrule its Silhouette judgment in the near future, then the ball is now with the competent political authorities. One possibility consists of amending European trademark legislation along lines that would be positive for consumers. Taking this path substantiates the possibility that the old proposal of the Commission to introduce the principle of international exhaustion into the Trade Mark Directive would finally become reality. If all the Member States were bound by this principle, then there would obviously be no distortions of the free movement of goods and services or of competition inside the internal market. In fact, Member States with a long-standing free trade tradition such as Sweden, Denmark, Finland, the United Kingdom, and the Netherlands (with the exception of the Netherlands, all former EFTA States), expressed their concern about the consequences of Silhouette on parallel imports and trademark laws during the Internal Market Council of September 24, 1998. France, Austria, Italy, Ireland, and Germany were on the other hand reticent and concerned about the impact on trademark proprietors. The European Commission is carrying out an inquiry on the consequences of the ruling. It is, however, more likely that the European Union will stick with the reciprocity approach and will try to enter into bilateral talks with its major trading partners. International exhaustion could therefore be an item on the agenda of future trade negotiations. In the meantime, 'many consumers and many retailers' will pay the price.

After some umming and ahing, I recused myself from the cases. The EFTA Court thus consisted of Thorgeir Örlygsson as Acting President, Henrik Bull as Judge Rapporteur, and ad hoc judge Martin Ospelt. The Commission, which originally had favoured international exhaustion as the general standard, asked the EFTA Court to overrule *Maglite* and to align itself with the ECJ's *Silhouette* judgment. ESA, the Norwegian, Icelandic and Liechtenstein Governments invited the EFTA Court to confirm *Maglite*. On 8 July 2008, the Court overruled *Maglite*. Unlike in *Maglite*, where the Court had pointed to the advantages of international exhaustion for competition and consumers, no substantive reasons were given. The EFTA Court simply genuflected before its sister court without addressing the issues. That was difficult to understand, in particular since, similarly to *Maglite*, the goods in question originated from the US. The case could thus easily have been distinguished from *Silhouette*. There is no better witness for this than the long-time President of the ECJ, Vassilios Skouris. In the Court's first *Festschrift*, in 2005, he wrote on the relationship between *Maglite* and *Silhouette* that the ECJ did not follow the EFTA Court's approach and that:

> Advocate General Jacobs explained quite convincingly in his opinion why the differences in scope between the EEA Agreement and the EC Treaty justified that result.

The late Judge Pierre Pescatore, one of the great trade law specialists on the ECJ bench, stated on the occasion of the EFTA Court's Tenth anniversary that he was very much concerned with the protectionist tendencies in the ECJ's jurisprudence and that he considered *Silhouette* "a disgrace in the EC case law". He added in view of a possible future EFTA Court case:

> So, what should the EFTA Court do, in view of this basic difference of principles and approach, if it finds itself either in the situation that it has to cope with a problem which is new and which has, so far, not be tackled by the EU Court, because it is defensive and protective in contradiction to the basic principles of EFTA? What would I do, if I had the privilege of being in President Baudenbacher's place? I would go to the extreme limit of EFTA's own mission by fostering free trade and try my best to dissuade the EC Court from indulging further protectionist tendencies.

As I had expected, the EFTA Court's foes were (and still are) very pleased with the *L'Oréal* judgment. In their eyes, this was proof that the EFTA Court was a largely useless institution, a second class court with no role or function of its own. As one author put it, one could draw the conclusion that in the EFTA Court's own view its decisions only had provisional authority pending a ruling from the ECJ. The logical conclusion of such an assessment was that the only incentive for national courts (and in particular Supreme Courts) to refer cases to us was that in certain circumstances they had the opportunity to initiate a going first case with the prospects of influencing the ECJ. In fact, commentators have with unconcealed malice stated that there was a connection between *L'Oréal* and the unwillingness of the Norwegian Supreme Court to refer cases to the EFTA Court.[8] Some have even used the EFTA Court's U-turn in this case to encourage the national courts to refrain from making references and to keep their cases in the country. All in all, *L'Oréal* is based on a mechanical and thus inaccurate understanding of homogeneity.

With *L'Oréal*, the fortress Europe, which had been built in this field with the ECJ's *Silhouette* ruling, was perfected. That the ECJ in *Silhouette* added that the Community authorities could always extend the exhaustion in question by entering into international reciprocity agreements, is not comforting. This was, at the end of the day, a fig leaf that aimed to conceal the protectionist direction the EU had taken in this field. The US is more liberal. On 30 May 2017, the Supreme Court even held that patent rights are subject to international exhaustion in the case *Impression Products v. Lexmark International*. As everybody knew when *Silhouette* was

[8]For details see Chapter 26.

decided, a reciprocity agreement that could be concluded between the two large Western trading blocs is not in sight. In Europe, the only Supreme Court that sticks to international exhaustion both in trade mark law and in copyright law is the Swiss Federal Supreme Court. In trade mark law, this was decided on 23 October 1996 in *Chanel* and in copyright law on 20 July 1998 in *Nintendo*.

The EFTA Court has also paid a price for *L'Oréal* in Switzerland. Critics of the EEA Agreement henceforth argued that since the Court had not displayed sufficient independence, it was not a suitable option for exercising judicial control over the bilateral agreements concluded between the EU and Switzerland.[9] Having said this, I must add that *L'Oréal* has no precedential value beyond the subject of international exhaustion of trade mark rights; the judgment has never been cited in later cases. It is probably safe to assume that this will remain so in the future. It has even been argued in academic literature that the EFTA Court may subsequently have distanced itself from its position in *L'Oréal*, for example when emphasising, for the first time in paragraphs 70 and 71 of the *Jabbi* judgment, that according to recital 15 in the preamble to the EEA Agreement homogeneity must be achieved "in full deference to the independence of the courts" and that

> [w]ithout independence in its adjudication no court could claim legitimacy.[10]

All in all, *L'Oréal* is the only real blunder in the EFTA Court's history. Such a thing can happen and my criticism is in no way meant to be personal. I am glad to say that my friendly relationship with the judges who decided the case has not been affected by the outcome.

4 Excursus: A Fortress Europe in the Field of Financial Services?

The mercantilist spirit of the *Silhouette* and *L'Oréal* case law has manifested itself in another fundamental ECJ case—*Fidium Finanz*. *Fidium Finanz* was a financial corporation, not a bank, based in St. Gallen, Switzerland. It offered small credits in Germany, mostly over the Internet, at interest rates as high as 14% at a time when normal interests where about 3%. The German Federal Financial Supervisory Authority ("*Bundesanstalt für Finanzdienstleistungsaufsicht*") prohibited this activity and told Fidium Finanz that if it wanted to carry on this business, it had to establish a subsidiary in Germany; a branch alone would not suffice. The Swiss corporation took the case to the Administrative Court in Frankfurt. This court referred the question to the ECJ of whether the relevant activity was covered by the provisions of the EC Treaty on free movement of capital. The provisions of free movement of capital contain a third-country clause, which grants that freedom also

[9] See for details Chapter 30.

[10] See regarding *Jabbi* Chapter 19.

to non-Member States, whereas the provisions on the freedom to provide services do not. It was said that this third-country clause is an outflow of the principle laid down in Article 119 TFEU that the Union shall conduct an economic policy "in accordance with the principle of an open market economy with free competition".

Fidium Finanz is a beautiful case for any class on legal theory. It demonstrates that it is not necessarily dogmatic thought that prompts the ECJ (or any other court) to opt for a certain solution, but that the judges' preunderstanding may play a decisive role. AG Christine Stix-Hackl proposed the ECJ to declare the free movement of capital provisions applicable provided there was no abuse. However, the Grand Chamber of the ECJ did not follow that advice. It held that, in principle, both the freedom to provide services within the meaning of Articles 49 et seq. of the EC Treaty (now: Articles 56 et seq. TFEU) and the free movement of capital within the meaning of Articles 56 et seq. of the EC Treaty (now: Articles 63 et seq. TFEU) were affected. In deciding on which freedom prevailed over the other, the ECJ referred to our judgment in *Íslandsbanki*. In that case, we had applied a centre of gravity test and concluded that the "predominant feature of the case", which involved a national measure leading to a guarantee for loans from foreign lenders being more expensive than for loans from domestic lenders, constituted movement of capital. The ECJ used the same test, but concluded that "the predominant consideration" of the *Fidium Finanz* case was the freedom to provide services. This was not coincidental. Swiss financial market operators have thereby been excluded from doing business on the territory of the EU unless they establish a subsidiary there. Whether they are subject to Swiss banking supervision or not is irrelevant. The ruling was not only directed against Swiss banks, it was also directed against Russian banks, Chinese banks, American banks, Indian banks etc. The ECJ sent a message to all the financial centres in the world: if you want to use our market you will have to conclude a reciprocity agreement with us guaranteeing that our banks can do the same business in your countries. It is the same type of argument as the one underlying the *Silhouette* judgment although financial operators in the EEA/EFTA States are not affected.

5 Contradictory ECJ Case Law

It is not really surprising that a court of the size of the ECJ sometimes has difficulty in maintaining consistency between its many chambers as regards the judgments rendered. If the EFTA Court is faced with inconsistent or even contradictory ECJ case law, its task is a particularly sensitive one. The most important example is the ECJ's jurisprudence concerning the question of whether a public body that has unlawfully awarded a contract to a bidder may be liable for damages under normal tort law or under the State liability rules, which require proof of a sufficiently serious breach. On 30 September 2010, the Third Chamber of the ECJ found in *Strabag* that the normal tort law rules apply. On 9 December 2010, the Second Chamber held in *Combinatie Spijker* that the State liability rules are relevant. In *Fosen-Linjen*, this question was referred to the EFTA Court by the Frostating Court of Appeal which is located in Trondheim. The oral hearing took place on 3 May 2017 and was attended by the Norwegian and the Icelandic Supreme Court *in corpore* and by judges from all three Liechtenstein courts of last resort. It was part of the programme of the first judicial summit of the EFTA pillar in Luxembourg. Since the regular Icelandic judge Páll Hreinsson was ill, the Court sat with the Norwegian judge Per Christiansen, the Icelandic ad hoc judge Benedikt Bogason and myself. Benedikt is an experienced Justice of the Icelandic Supreme Court who has participated in a number of EFTA Court cases. I acted as Judge Rapporteur. The EFTA Court held that a simple breach of public procurement law is, in itself, sufficient to trigger the liability of the contracting authority to compensate the person harmed for the damage incurred, provided that the other conditions for the award of damages are met, such as, in particular, the existence of a causal link. To apply the principle of State liability—and thus to require a sufficiently serious breach—would amount to an unjustifiable privilege for the contracting body. The Court based itself on the finding that a contracting body does not exercise an act of public authority (*actum jure imperii*) when conducting a tender procedure. This is contrary to the situation where a national legislature transposes EEA public procurement law or where national courts render judgments applying the principles set out therein. However, the aim of a tender procedure is rather to conclude a contract *inter partes*, which encompasses a commercial act (*actum juri gestionis*). One must not overlook in this context that the degree of market integration in the area of public procurement is very low. To advantage local bidders is a classical means of mercantilist economic policy. To privilege a state-run contracting authority must also be rejected because it would create a 'moral hazard': the employees of such entities would have an incentive to behave irresponsibly in evaluating the offers because they would hardly be afraid that they would have to assume budgetary responsibility for their actions.[11]

With this, the EFTA Court has not only ruled on issues that have led to conflicts within the ECJ. In substance, it has also objected to the case law of the Supreme Courts of the UK and Norway. In the UK in particular, this has led to comments in the light of the discussion on possible EEA membership of the country on the EFTA side after Brexit. In its judgment of 11 April 2017 in *Nuclear Decommissioning Authority* v *EnergySolutions EU Ltd* case, EnergySolutions had unsuccessfully applied for a contract to provide services in connection with the decommissioning of a nuclear power plant. The Supreme Court interpreted the ECJ rulings in *Strabag* and *Combinatie Spijker* and concurred with the latter. Liability on the part of the contracting authority was therefore only said to occur in the event of serious infringement. The judgment is, untypically for a British higher court, based a formal reasoning. A reference to the ECJ for a preliminary ruling, which would have clarified the relationship between the two decisions, would have been appropriate. The Norwegian Supreme Court will not be able to stick to its 2001 *Nucleus* decision.

---

[11]See regarding moral hazard the EFTA Court's *Icesave I* judgment, Chapter 25.

It can be assumed that if the legal problem in question comes before the ECJ's Grand Chamber, the judgment of the EFTA Court will play a major role; it could even tip the balance.

6 Relevance of ECtHR Case Law

As I have mentioned in Chap. 12 of this book, the EFTA Court has almost from the outset taken into account the ECHR and the case law of the ECtHR and it has made further references to fundamental rights. The ECtHR has, for its part, made it clear that it is aware of a third human rights tribunal on the European level. Thus, one can even speak of a triangle of supranational courts in Europe.

7 Important Judgments on Homogeneity

In its very first case, *Restamark*, the Court broadly elaborated on homogeneity. At the time, the focus was understandably on the EFTA Court following the ECJ. From 2000 onwards, the centre of attention has been the free movement of capital, the reason being that the respective EU law rules had been amended under the 1992 Maastricht Treaty whereas the rules of the EEA Agreement remained unaltered. This gap was closed through judicial dialogue of the two EEA courts. In its 2003 *Ospelt* landmark judgment, the ECJ pointed to the homogeneity rules of the EEA Agreement and held that the provisions concerning free movement of capital of the EEA Agreement are identical to those under Community law. It stated in paragraph 29:

> [O]ne of the principal aims of the EEA Agreement is to provide for the fullest possible realisation of the free movement of goods, persons, services and capital within the whole European Economic Area, so that the internal market established within the European Union is extended to the EFTA States [....]. It is for the Court, in that context, to ensure that the rules of the EEA Agreement which are identical in substance to those of the Treaty are interpreted uniformly within the Member States.

In the following years, the ball was tossed back and forth: we referred to the ECJ and the ECJ referred to us. In 2004, the dialogue reached a climax. The ECJ held in paragraph 34 of *Bellio Fratelli* that both EEA courts have recognised the need to ensure that the rules of the EEA Agreement which are identical in substance to those of the Treaty are interpreted uniformly. The EFTA Court replied eight months later in paragraph 22 of *Fokus Bank* that the objective of homogeneity

> has consistently guided the jurisprudence of the Court as well as of the Court of Justice of the European Communities.

This positive development suffered a setback in the *Rimbaud* judgment of the Third Chamber of the ECJ of 28 October 2010. In the context of a dispute between a company established in Liechtenstein and the French tax authorities, the ECJ held that the case law concerning restrictions on the exercise of the freedoms of movement within the EU could not be transposed in its entirety to capital movements between EU Member States and EEA/EFTA countries. Under French legislation, legal persons owning immovable property in France but having their centre of management in the territory of another Member State were exempt from the 3% tax on the market value of the property, provided that they communicated certain information to the tax authority, such as the market value, the identity of their members and the number of shares held. In the case of legal persons having their centre of management in a "third State", the tax exemption was conditional on the existence, between the respective State and France, either of a convention on administrative assistance in matters of taxation for the purposes of combating tax evasion and tax avoidance, or of a non-discrimination clause prohibiting the legal person from being taxed more heavily in France than in its State of origin. Since no convention of this type had been signed between France and Liechtenstein, companies established in that country were automatically excluded from the tax exemption. The French *Cour de Cassation* asked the ECJ whether this legislation was compatible with Article 40 EEA, the provision guaranteeing the free movement of capital in the European Economic Area.

The Directive concerning mutual assistance by the competent authorities of the Member States in the field of direct and indirect taxation[12] was not made part of EEA law. In the earlier *ELISA* case, in which the facts were almost identical, the Fourth Chamber of the ECJ had ruled that in relations between EU Member States —*in casu* France and Luxembourg—EU law precluded legislation such as the French law at issue. Établissements Rimbaud, ESA, the Commission and the Government of Liechtenstein maintained that Article 40 EEA precluded the French legislation since the latter did not allow a company established in an EEA/EFTA State to provide evidence to establish the identity of the natural persons who were its shareholders. By contrast, the Governments of France, Germany, Estonia, Greece, Spain, Italy, the Netherlands, Sweden and the UK took the view that Article 40 EEA did not preclude such legislation. Both AG Niilo Jääskinen and the Third Chamber of the ECJ followed the position of the EU Member States. The French legislation was found to constitute an unlawful restriction on the free movement of capital. However, this restriction was held to be justified based on overriding reasons of general interest in combating tax evasion and the need to safeguard the effectiveness of fiscal supervision.

I discussed *Rimbaud* with a judge who had participated in the case. In response to my reproach that this was a political judgment, he said, in all frankness, that such a case could not have been decided against the will of nine EU Member States. There are, in particular, two points I want to make in this respect. First, when holding that the *ELISA* case law did not apply to the situation of a company established in Liechtenstein, the ECJ admitted that

[12] 77/799/EEC.

> in the situation which was under consideration in *ELISA*, the Luxembourg authorities were not, by virtue of Article 8(1) of Directive 77/799, under any obligation in principle to provide information (paragraph 46).

The ECJ's further statement in the same paragraph that

> the fact remains that the regulatory framework is quite different

is unsubstantiated. Second, that AG Jääskinen's Opinion was largely based on a value judgment becomes clear in point 53 where he says:

> I have some reservations about extending the scope of *ELISA* to the present case, in that that judgment envisages the possibility of replacing the mechanisms laid down for cooperation between the tax authorities of the various States with documentary evidence provided by the taxpayer.

The German version of the Opinion is even clearer:

> *Es widerstrebt mir, das Urteil ELISA in seiner Bedeutung auf das vorliegende Verfahren zu erstrecken, soweit in diesem Urteil die Möglichkeit vorgesehen wird, die Mechanismen für die Zusammenarbeit der Steuerbehörden der einzelnen Staaten durch die Vorlage von Belegen durch den Steuerpflichtigen zu ersetzen.*

I should add that the EFTA Court has never cited the ECJ's *Rimbaud* judgment and I hope that this will remain so in the future. The problem underlying the case is no longer relevant for Liechtenstein since the country has meanwhile concluded an agreement with France on the exchange of information in tax matters.

8 EFTA Values

I have written before that homogeneity is neither a one way-street nor a mechanical idea. No matter what the written rules state, the ECJ, its AGs and the GC have long made it clear that the EFTA Court is a partner in dialogue. Today, there can be no doubt that homogeneity is a process-oriented concept. Judicial conflicts can only be resolved by way of dialogue and cooperation. The EFTA Court has over the years based itself on specific EFTA values which may have an influence on the outcome and the reasoning of cases. One may also speak of an EFTA DNA. ESA has for its part started to speak of EFTA flavour. The commitment of the EFTA States to free trade and open markets has played a role in this respect. But also issues such as fair taxation, efficiency and a modern image of man have been relevant.

9 Conclusions

Both courts, the ECJ and the EFTA Court, are European courts. Both stand for a European approach on how a Single Market ought to be shaped. And the judges on both courts have proven that they do not wilfully put the homogeneity goal at risk.

Contrary to what some politicians and journalists seem to believe, more than 24 years of experience show that judges are not primarily interested in starting conflicts, but in resolving problems. The mere existence of a second court has changed the game to a significant extent.

Having said this, it is important to be aware of the fact that the arguments of States put forward before a European court must also be seen against the background of internal politics. Cases such as ECJ *Franzén*, *Liga Portuguesa* and *Test Claimants in Class IV* were not only about enforcing certain public policy goals, they were also about securing important sources of revenue for the Member States concerned. As regards the Swedish State retail alcohol monopoly AG Elmer aptly stated in paragraph 108 of his Opinion in *Franzén*:

> Even though the purpose of Systembolaget and, in particular, of the restriction of the number of points of sale is purported to be connected with alcohol policy, there is scarcely no doubt that the system entails a considerable economic advantage for the Swedish State in that all profits from the retail of alcoholic beverages in Sweden go to the Swedish Treasury and these profits are maximized through the reduction of selling costs due to the limitation of the number of shops. However, under the consistent case-law of the Court, no account is to be taken of any loss of resources which the Swedish State would incur if it were required to abolish or adjust the monopoly on the retail of alcoholic beverages in order to render it compatible with the rules of the Treaty.

Let me finally reiterate what I wrote in Chap. 3 of this book:

> [T]he establishment of their own court is probably the biggest accomplishment of the EFTA States.

It not only enables market access, but, importantly, it also provides a possibility for both direct and indirect influence on the ECJ's case law. Direct because the EEA/EFTA States enjoy a privileged standing in Single Market cases, and indirect through their active participation in the case law of the EFTA Court. This is a advantage that no other non-EU State can enjoy. When analysing the case law of both courts, it also becomes clear that the EFTA Court couldn't be further from being a mere "extension" of the ECJ, it is a reliable partner (almost) on a par with the ECJ.

That there are usually a number of ECJ judgments that must be taken into account once a case reaches the EFTA Court, is a natural consequence of the size of the two courts and the number of cases they are dealing with. Whereas the ECJ renders some 700 judgments a year, the EFTA Court's case law remains limited, even if there has been an increase over the past years. In some fields of Single Market law, the EFTA Court has not yet had a chance to express itself at all, for example company law. However, in those areas in which the EFTA Court has had cases, it tends to be faced with important issues. In such situation the balance will not automatically tilt towards the ECJ. It may be that legal thinking on a particular issue is in flux, and that, although the ECJ is of another view, the AGs or the GC side with the EFTA Court. It may also be that the ECJ is divided on a given issue. Even national courts, in particular courts of last resort, have a role in this process. And academic literature may be of significance. As I have always said, the goal must be a coercion-free discourse ("*herrschaftsfreier Diskurs*") as described by Jürgen Habermas—where the most convincing solution prevails.

Chapter 22
The Norwegian Social Model on the Brink of a Downfall?

Contents

1 General

From 2004 to 2007, the EFTA Court dealt with four major Norwegian cases. The first one, *Pedicel*, concerned the advertising ban for alcoholic beverages, the second and third, *Gaming Machines* and *Ladbrokes*, were about the lawfulness of the Norwegian State gambling monopolies, and the fourth one, *Norwegian Waterfalls*, about the compatibility with EEA law of the reversion system for Norwegian waterfalls ("*hjemfall*").[1] In the *hjemfall* case, Thorgeir Örlygsson was Judge

[1]See as regards the details of these four cases Chapter 15.

C. Baudenbacher, *Judicial Independence*, Springer Biographies,
https://doi.org/10.1007/978-3-030-02308-9_22

Rapporteur, in the three other cases, this role fell to me. Norway was in all four cases represented by a lawyer from the Attorney General's Office, Fredrik Sejersted, who would play quite a role in the Court's life. In the two gambling monopoly cases and the *hjemfall* matter, Sejersted played the ball high. His goal was to depict these three cases as being decisive for the survival of the Norwegian social model. And he was determined to pull all the strings that were available. In *Pedicel*, an odd incident helped him out with his game plan.

2 *Pedicel*: If All Else Fails, *Norsk* Will Do It

As already mentioned, in *Pedicel*, the EFTA Court found that the Norwegian advertising prohibition on alcoholic beverages could only be maintained if it was proportionate. It stated that such a prohibition:

> may be justified on grounds of the protection of public health, unless it is apparent that, in the circumstances of law and of fact which characterise the situation in the EEA Contracting Party concerned, the protection of public health against the harmful effects of alcohol can be secured by measures having less effect on intra-EEA trade (Paragraph 61 and operative part).

The ECJ had come to the same conclusion shortly before, with regard to the Swedish ban on the advertisement of alcoholic beverages in the *Gourmet* case. Our judgment was deemed to be along the same lines. In Sweden, the referring Stockholm District Court and the Market Court found that the Swedish advertising ban was unlawful because it was disproportionate. I expected the Norwegian courts to reach the same conclusion.

However, the Supreme Court found in favour of the Norwegian State. The reason for this blatant deviation was detected by two Norwegian authors, Halvard Haukeland Fredriksen and Gjermund Mathisen. While our verdict was deliberated and drafted in English, it was, as all preliminary rulings, also delivered in the language of the referring court, Norwegian. Although the non-English version is only a translation, it is authentic. In *Pedicel*, there was a serious translation error in the Norwegian version both in paragraph 61 and in the operative part. In English, the relevant passage reads:

> A provision against the advertising of alcoholic beverages "may be justified on grounds of the protection of public health, unless it is *apparent*" that the protection of public health against the harmful effects of alcohol can be secured by less restrictive measures.

This was translated into Norwegian as:

> *Et forbud mot reklame for alcoholholdige drikkevarer "kan rettferdiggjøres av hensyn til beskyttelse av folkehelsen, med mindre det er åpenbart" at beskyttelsen av folkehelsen kan sikres ved mindre restriktive foranstaltninger.*

However, *åpenbart* does not mean apparent, it means obvious, *évident*, *offensichtlich*. The English passage in our ruling had been taken from the ECJ's judgment in the parallel Swedish *Gourmet* case. And there, all the language versions were absolutely clear.

„[....] *Sauf s'il apparaît que* [....]"
„[....] Unless it is apparent that [....]"
„[....] *sofern [es] sich nicht [....] erweist*"
„[...] *medmindre [....] fremgår [....]*"

The EFTA Court has no translation service. Translations are done by free lancers and finalised by the cabinet concerned (in this case the Norwegian cabinet). The ultimate responsibility lies with the judge concerned. In the *Pedicel* case, that was Per Tresselt, a man known for his linguistic skills.

In the national proceedings, the Norwegian State pleaded in favour of the Norwegian version and the Supreme Court seemingly attached great weight to the term "obvious" in its decision. Based on a questionable application of the proportionality principle, it found in favour of the State.[2] ESA, which had asked the Court to follow the ECJ's *Gourmet* ruling, remained inactive.

3 *Gaming Machines*: "As Long as" Means Nothing

3.1 The Case

Norway gave the State-owned company Norsk Tipping the exclusive right to operate gaming machines. Private undertakings, which so far had been able to operate gaming machines on behalf of charitable organisations, were thereby excluded from the market. The new statute had not yet entered into force. ESA opened infringement proceedings upon receiving complaints from private operators. The investigation was conducted at the same time as the case was being tried in the Norwegian courts. In October 2004, ESA issued a reasoned opinion rejecting the government's arguments. Some days later, the Oslo District Court found the monopoly to be contrary to EEA law. In August 2005, this judgment was overruled by the Borgarting Court of Appeal, and the matter was brought before the Norwegian Supreme Court. The private operators asked the Supreme Court to make a reference to the EFTA Court, to no avail.

ESA had obviously expected that one of the three national courts involved would bring the matter before the EFTA Court by way of a preliminary reference. In the end, when the Appeals Committee of the Norwegian Supreme Court refused to refer the case, ESA stepped in and brought an infringement action. Before deciding whether the proceedings in the Supreme Court should be stayed until the EFTA Court had given its judgment, the Appeals Committee had a discussion with the other justices of the Supreme Court; opinions were divided. By two votes to one, the Appeals Committee decided to stay the proceedings and to wait for the Court's judgment since the latter would rule "with finality" on the matter. This decision was

[2]The way national courts in the EFTA pillar apply the proportionality principle is addressed in Chapter 15.

absolutely reasonable. According to Article 33 SCA, the EFTA States must take the necessary measures to comply with the EFTA Court's infringement judgments. And yet the decision was criticised by the highest-ranking bureaucrat of the Ministry of Justice's Legislation Department who observed that the Supreme Court "succumbed" to the EFTA Court. In academic literature, "surprise" was expressed.

3.2 Oral Hearing

The oral hearing took place on 8 November 2006 in the Luxembourg *Chambre de Commerce*. The large room was packed. I did not have the impression that ESA was overly keen to win. It seemed that they just could not accept that the Norwegian judiciary refused to seize the EFTA Court on such an important matter. In fact, *Gaming Machines* was the first direct action case on gambling law in the whole EEA. All the eight governments who participated in the case supported the Norwegian State. It was one of those cases in which it becomes apparent that European procedural law is flawed because it does not give standing to those who are affected by a measure such as the one in question, namely the private operators. They are side-lined and have to hope that ESA's agent will handle their case well. After the *Gaming Machines* case, the EFTA Court urged the EEA/EFTA Governments to amend the SCA respectively. They were, however, unwilling to do anything about the situation, which is probably not compatible with the ECHR.

3.3 Judgment

Judgment was rendered on 14 March 2007. The Norwegian Government won the case in that ESA's application for a declaration that Norway had violated the EEA rules on freedom of establishment and on freedom to provide services was dismissed as unfounded. But it was only a half victory. As the reform of the gaming machines regulation in Norway had not yet taken effect, the EFTA Court did not base itself on the general assumption that public control and policy enforcement would not satisfy the new requirements.[3]

3.4 The Supreme Court's Judgment

In its ruling of 6 June 2007, the Supreme Court shared the EFTA Court's view that the nationalisation of the operation of slot machines was lawful. However, it did not address in any way the EFTA Court's reservation that this only applies as long as the activity in question is subject to effective control under the new system.

---

[3] See for details Chapter 15.

4 Ladbrokes: Pick and Choose

4.1 The Case

Ladbrokes, the world's largest bookmaker and gaming company, with headquarters in London, was denied permission to operate and provide different gaming and betting services in Norway and to market these games. The Oslo District Court referred questions to the EFTA Court concerning the compatibility of the national legislation with the freedom to provide services and the right of establishment as guaranteed in the EEA Agreement. Seven EU Member State governments as well as the Icelandic Government participated in the case.

4.2 Oral Hearing

The hearing was held on 31 January 2007. Afterwards, Fredrik Sejersted in an interview with Norwegian media indicated that if the Court did not rule in favour of his government, the judgment would not be implemented and that

> the outcome of this case will be crucial for the legitimacy of the whole EEA Agreement.

His view was that the liberalisation of the gambling market in Europe should not take place through a decision of a Court that only dealt with cases involving Norway, Iceland and Liechtenstein. If the gaming market was to be opened up by means of a judgment, it should be done by the ECJ, which handled matters concerning the EU's (at the time) 27 Member States. Newspapers commented that observers might interpret Sejersted's statement as a threat and that Norway might not want to open up the gaming market, no matter what the EFTA Court had to say. Kjetil Wiedswang, a prominent journalist with *Dagens Næringsliv*, suspected that Sejersted's outburst might have been an expression of frustration that the court under my leadership could make EU (recte: EEA) law in the field of gaming.

4.3 Judgment

In its judgment of 30 May 2007 (E/3/06), the EFTA Court made it clear that the gambling monopoly would be unlikely to pass the proportionality test.[4] The company operating the monopoly had an enormous marketing budget.

---

[4]See for details Chapter 15.

4.4 The Oslo District Court's Judgment

However, the Oslo District Court bought into the arguments of the Attorney General and on 3 October 2008 found in favour of the Norwegian State. It concluded that the Norwegian gaming policy was coherent and consistent as it had sufficiently attractive games to channel players, while keeping the level of gambling and its promotion on a responsible and moderate level. The restriction was deemed to be legitimately motivated, appropriate and necessary, and considered compatible with the EEA fundamental freedoms in question. The District Court's conclusion was that the exclusive rights model, established in pursuance of these acts, contained lawful restrictions.

The ruling was enthusiastically greeted by the Norwegian Government. The Minister in charge Trond Giske called the judgment which was simply based on an incorrect implementation of our preliminary ruling

> a stunning victory for Norwegian gaming policy.

I should mention here that while the *Gaming Machines* and *Ladbrokes* cases were pending before the EFTA Court, Trond Giske paid us a visit. We took him to *Cercle Munster* for dinner. I remember that meal for two reasons: Mr. Giske said he was a total abstainer and drank only water. And he observed without ceremony that his Government attached the utmost importance to winning these cases. I couldn't believe my ears when I heard that.

5 Playing the EFTA Court off Against the ECJ

Ladbrokes appealed the District Court's judgment to the Borgarting Court of Appeal. But then the ECJ's Grand Chamber entered the stage. On 8 September 2009, it handed down its preliminary ruling in *Liga Portuguesa*. This case involved a restriction of the freedom to provide services in the form of offering internet betting on football games. The ECJ first confirmed that according to its established jurisprudence Member States were, in the absence of harmonisation, free to set the objectives of their gaming policy and to define the level of protection sought. Certain overriding reasons in the public interest were recognised, such as the objectives of consumer protection and the prevention of both fraud and incitement to squander money on gambling, as well as the general need to preserve public order. With regard to the suitability of the restrictive measure, the ECJ accepted the argument of the monopoly company, *Santa Casa da Misericórdia de Lisboa*, a Catholic lay brotherhood founded in 1498, and of the Portuguese Government that the main objective pursued by the national legislation was the fight against crime, more specifically the protection of consumers of games of chance against fraud on the part of operators. The ECJ was convinced that the Portuguese system functioned in a secure and controlled way because Santa Casa's long existence and the fact that it operated under the strict control of the Portuguese Government were taken as evidence of its reliability. With regard to the specific facts of the case, the ECJ added that because of the lack of direct contact between consumer and operator, games of chance accessible via the internet involved different and more substantial risks of fraud by operators against consumers compared to the traditional markets for such games. The facts in *Ladbrokes* and *Liga Portuguesa* were different. However, it cannot be denied that the ECJ was quite lenient vis-à-vis the Portuguese monopoly. A Commission lawyer who was present at the hearing told me years later that in order to convince the ECJ of its honourable motives, Santa Casa had even seen to it that one of its agents appeared in a monk's habit.

In Oslo, Minister Giske issued a statement on the government's website in which he called *Liga Portuguesa*

> an important victory for Norway and the other member states within the European Economic Area who wish to protect their citizens against the negative aspects of gambling.

This, he went on, would give Norway a very powerful tool in the ongoing legal dispute with the gaming company Ladbrokes. The ECJ judgment would be a natural part of the legal basis when the Court of Appeal came to consider the *Ladbrokes* case. The trial before the Court of Appeal was scheduled to start on Tuesday 15 September 2009. On 10 September 2009, Ladbrokes withdrew its appeal. The company had obviously come to the conclusion that there was no more hope. What Ladbrokes feared was that the Court of Appeal would do what had seemed to be looming in the first *Finanger* case and what some professors had been recommending for years: namely that in such a situation, a Norwegian court had to mechanically follow the ECJ for reasons of homogeneity.[5] In reality, the national court is thereby given the opportunity to cherry-pick by opting for the solution that best corresponds with what they perceive to be in line with the domestic social model. If the Court of Appeal had kept the case, the only acceptable solution would have been to either distinguish *Ladbrokes* and *Liga Portuguesa* and to follow the EFTA Court or to make a second reference to us.

6 ESA Remains Inactive

Based on the relevant figures, ESA had pleaded in the proceedings before the EFTA Court

> that the extensive marketing and expansion of the national gaming operators entail that the Norwegian State, via its ownership of Norsk Tipping and as regulator of other gaming services, does indeed incite and encourage consumers to participate in lotteries, games of chance and betting to the financial benefit of the public purse.

---

[5]See for details Chapter 11.

Thus, ESA had to consider itself as being among those who had lost the *Ladbrokes* case in the Oslo District Court. In later cases, the ECJ changed its approach concerning the compatibility of State gambling monopolies with the fundamental freedoms and clearly moved in our direction.[6] My former doctoral student Simon Planzer, now an attorney specialising in gambling law, wrote in my 2016 "Handbook of EEA Law", that like the EFTA Court the ECJ has "significantly adjusted its review practice regarding proportionality", "started to review extensive or aggressive marketing practices more critically" and implicitly adopted "some of the wording of its sister court". ESA did not react.

7 The Government's Happiness

The 2012–2013 White Paper of the Norwegian Ministry of Foreign Affairs described the development in the following way:

> The Storting has decided that certain services of particular social significance are only to be provided by the state, i.e. a public agency or a wholly state-owned company. One of the services covered by this decision is gaming and betting services. In Norway, the state lottery (Norsk Tipping) has sole rights to operate the most important money games, such as Lotto and betting on sports competitions, while the horse-betting service Norsk Rikstoto can only offer betting on trotting races and flat-racing. In 2003, the Storting extended this right so that it now also applies to gaming terminals. Gaming and betting services are covered by EEA legislation. Since 2003, two cases have been filed on this issue in the EFTA Court. In the first of these, the gaming machine industry lodged a complaint against the Norwegian state with the EFTA Surveillance Authority, and brought a case before a Norwegian court.
>
> The gaming machine industry argued that the extension of the Norwegian system to prohibit gaming machines run by private operators was a contravention of the EEA Agreement. In the second case, the international bookmakers and gaming company Ladbrokes claimed that the Norwegian state monopolies (Norsk Rikstoto and Norsk Tipping) and the fact that only Norwegian charitable organisations could offer certain kinds of games were a violation of the EEA Agreement. The Norwegian state won both cases outright. The Ladbrokes case continued to be brought before various Norwegian courts for many years, but was eventually withdrawn. In the meantime, the European Court of Justice had passed a judgment in a similar Portuguese case, making clear that national authorities have a good deal of latitude to make use of state monopoly schemes in the gaming industry. Thus, the EEA Agreement allowed for the continuation of the Norwegian monopoly arrangements.

This missed the point completely. Our *Gaming Machines* judgment was an "as long as" ruling and in *Ladbrokes* we essentially found against the Norwegian State. To quote *Liga Portuguesa* and to say nothing about *Markus Stoß* is intellectually dishonest. *Markus Stoß* was rendered on 8 September 2010, which was more than

[6]See Chapter 21.

two years before the White Paper was published. In the meantime, the ECJ has confirmed in several cases that it has become much stricter than it was in *Liga Portuguesa*.

8 *Norwegian Waterfalls - Hjemfall*: The Threat to "Us, Our Children and Grandchildren"

8.1 Pre-litigation Procedure

In June 2001, ESA opened the *Norwegian Waterfalls* case arguing that the Norwegian Industrial Licensing Act was incompatible with the EEA Agreement. Licences of unlimited duration for acquiring property rights to waterfalls could only be issued to Norwegian public undertakings, in all other cases the property rights reverted to the State after a certain period of time. The Norwegian Government took the view that the system of reversion formed part of the national management of natural resources and was therefore outside the scope of the EEA Agreement. Alternatively, the Government invoked Article 125 EEA which states that the Agreement

> shall in no way prejudice the rules of the contracting parties governing the system of property ownership.

8.2 Background

The reversion system has a specific geographical, climatic and historical background. Yearly precipitation in Norway is high which results in an enormous potential for hydroenergy. This prompted foreigners to invest in the country's electricity production, something that led to a complex political struggle shortly after Norway gained independence from Sweden in 1905. In 1983, Tore Tønne, a senior civil servant in the Norwegian Ministry of Petroleum and Energy described the events in the following way:

> According to Norwegian law, rivers, waterfalls and lakes may be privately owned. As a result, it soon became clear that foreign capital could gain control of substantial natural resources. This led to the passage of legislation in 1906 that required anyone, Norwegian or foreign, to obtain a 'concession' from the public authorities before acquiring a waterfall. This Act, which is sometimes referred to as the 'panic act' because of the political circumstances when it was passed, was only temporary, however. Years of legal debates and political struggles resulted in passage of new legislation in 1917—the so-called Concession Act. This Act, with only minor amendments, and the Water Regulations Act passed in the same year have together regulated the development of hydropower in Norway ever since.

> While the immediate objective of the Panic Act had been to avoid foreign takeover of Norwegian waterfalls, the objectives of the Concession Act were broader. It sought to secure public control and the best possible economic utilization of national resources. The Act now provides that no one, except the state, may acquire usufruct or proprietary title of waterfalls of capacities exceeding 1000 natural horse-powers without the King's permission, a 'concession'. The King may grant such a concession to either Norwegian or foreign persons or companies only in accordance with basic rules written into the Act itself and detailed conditions established by the state in each individual case. In addition, Parliament must approve nearly all grants of 'concession'. One of the most important provisions of the Concession Act was a general rule limiting the duration of concessions to private persons or companies. After years of political struggle, it was established that concessions could be granted only for periods not exceeding sixty years. The waterfalls and all power production installations—dams, channels, tunnels, power stations and all their belongings and machinery—were to accrue to the state free of charge at the end of the granted concession. This rule, the *hjemfall*, which was proposed during the political turmoil following passage of the Panic Act, was unique in both the Norwegian and international contexts. Nevertheless, the Supreme Court upheld its constitutionality when it was challenged in 1918 [....].
>
> Some of the powerplants built after the passing of the Concession Act have already accrued to the state, and several others will accrue in the 1980s and 1990s. In many cases, companies that built and operated power stations during a concession period have entered into long-term lease agreements with the state in order to continue operations after the expiration of the concession. Most of those companies have arranged to continue utilizing some of the power for their production of goods, but on revised terms decided by Parliament.

As regards the economic policy context of the *hjemfall* legislation, John Wesley Horrocks wrote in his seminal book on the history of mercantilism that these measures which aimed to bring water power "under State or native control" were a result of neo-mercantilist tendencies. They were not limited to Norway, but also affected Sweden and went hand in hand with attempts

> to protect and conserve the iron ore deposits in the national interest, and in the assistance of shipping by subsidies and in other ways.

Horrocks added that the policy in question

> has not passed without domestic criticism on the ground of its possible effects upon economic relations with other countries, particularly owing the attitude towards foreign capital which it involves, but as yet it would seem to be too early to pronounce upon its results.

Others have confirmed that the right of reversion which was allegedly inspired by similar laws in Switzerland was controversial from the beginning. On the one hand, it aimed at securing that Norway's most important natural resources would not permanently be in the hands of foreigners. On the other hand, there was the expectation that it would barely affect foreign investment, because investors would hardly operate with a time frame of more than half a century.

When the EEA Agreement was concluded, Norway changed the system of reversion so that Norwegian private undertakings and undertakings from other EEA states were treated equally. However, Norwegian public undertakings were still dealt with in a more favourable way since their licences were granted for an unlimited duration and they were exempt from the reversion.

8.3 Judgment

On 26 April 2006, ESA brought the *Norwegian Waterfalls* case. The oral hearing took place on 14 March 2007 following the delivery of judgment in *Gaming Machines*. Iceland intervened in support of Norway. Norway was also assisted by Poland and the Netherlands. On 26 June 2007, the EFTA Court rendered judgment. It held that by maintaining the provisions in question, Norway had infringed the prohibition of restrictions on the freedom of establishment and the prohibition of restrictions on the free movement of capital. The Court found that the national rules in question did not aim at establishing a system of public property within the meaning of Article 125 EEA, but rather at achieving a certain level of public control over the relevant sector of the economy. Furthermore, the objective of collecting a rent was found to be economic in nature and therefore not able to justify the restriction in question. The Court went on to state that ensuring security of energy supply and the protection of the environment are legitimate aims under EEA law. However, the controversial rules were found to go beyond what is necessary in order to attain those aims.

8.4 Consequences

We at the Court thought that the natural consequence of our judgment would be the abolition of the reversion system. However, that turned out not to be the outcome. Members of the Government including Prime Minister Jens Stoltenberg said that they were disappointed and wowed to secure continued public control of Norwegian hydropower. The Ministry of Foreign Affairs' 2012–2013 White Paper describes the Government's reaction in the following way:

> As a result of the EFTA Court's judgment, the Norwegian authorities had to find other ways of safeguarding the system of reversion. But this also provided the key to a new solution: Norway could comply with the judgment by strengthening public ownership. On 10 August 2007, the Government adopted with immediate effect a provisional ordinance under Article 17 of the Norwegian Constitution, to rectify the situation that had arisen following the ruling of the EFTA Court. Its purpose was to ensure that Norway's hydropower resources are under public ownership and that they are managed for the common good. Under the ordinance, private undertakings were no longer to be granted licences for the acquisition of waterfalls and power plants. On the other hand, private undertakings could own up to a third of the capital and votes in public undertakings that had ownership rights to waterfalls. The provisional ordinance was later replaced by amendments to the Industrial Licensing Act adopted in the autumn of 2008 and set out in Proposition No. 61 (2007–2008) to the Odelsting. In the spring of 2009, the Storting adopted additional amendments that allowed the letting of hydropower plants for periods of up to 15 years, as set out in Proposition No. 66 (2008–2009) to the Odelsting.

Chapter 23
The Failed Decapitation of *Kong Carl*

Contents

1 Conflict with the Court's Auditors

The three cases concerning the State gambling monopolies and the reversion system for waterfalls, which according to the Norwegian government's view were decisive for the survival of essential elements of Norway's social model, were all adjudicated in 2007.[1] In the same year, the Norwegian government tried to oust me from the judgeship on the Court. In the summer of 2007, a conflict reached its peak which had been going on for three years.

In 2004, one year after my election as the Court's President, the EFTA Board of Auditors (EBOA), which was largely in the hands of its Norwegian chairman Per A. Engeseth, demanded that the judges had to report how much money they made from occupational activities. Under the Court's Statute, occupational activities had to be approved by the governments and not by the auditors. There is no provision concerning a duty to report the earnings from such activities. Most of the judges of the three-member Court performed such tasks. Bjørn Haug had served as a commercial arbitrator on a regular basis and Thór Vilhjálmsson simultaneously sat on the EFTA Court and on the ECtHR. I had in 1995 made the retention of my professor position at the HSG a condition for accepting the judgeship and this had been accepted. When the Court refused to give the requested information, the chairman of EBOA started a crusade, which culminated in EBOA refusing to issue

[1] For details see Chapter 22.

C. Baudenbacher, *Judicial Independence*, Springer Biographies,
https://doi.org/10.1007/978-3-030-02308-9_23

a certificate for the Court's 2006 accounts, even though they were in perfect order. Distorted information was leaked to journalists, which led to rather aggressive reporting. A development started, which I have seen many times during my tenure as an EFTA Court judge: a legal question was turned into a political issue.

Mr. Engeseth was not willing to stick to EBOA's mandate nor would he contemplate any opposing views. He tried to treat the Court as if it were a Norwegian government entity. During the first years of my presidency, Mr. Engeseth was like a bee in our bonnet, proposing all sorts of initiatives. Legally EBOA was solely responsible for the financial audit. Nevertheless, he wanted to carry out many more controls, performance audits, compliance audits, operational audits. At the end of the day, his attempts to expand EBOA's mandate were fruitless.

Unlike the EU Court of Auditors, EBOA is not a truly independent body. ESA/Court Committee Decision No 5/2002 on the Mandate of EBOA prescribes in Article 6 that EBOA

> shall establish its own annual budget for the audits of the EFTA Surveillance Authority and the EFTA Court,

Nevertheless, I have never seen such a budget. There was no transparency with regard to the origin of the means that were put at EBOA's disposal, nor as regards the costs that EBOA incurred. At one point, EBOA decided to create its own "resource group" consisting of an Icelander and a Norwegian employed by their respective auditing institutions. The legal basis for this initiative was unknown, as were the tasks of the new group and who would bear its costs.

2 Journalists Spice Things Up

Norwegian newspapers covered the three landmark cases before they started. The comments directed at me were at first not unfriendly. But in retrospect it becomes clear that someone was carefully preparing the fight on behalf of the government from the outset. On 16 January 2006, Kjetil Wiedswang published an article on the upcoming *Gaming Machines* case in *Dagens Næringsliv* under the title "Billiongame in Luxembourg" ("*Milliardspill i Luxemburg*"). The journalist wrote that according to the government's lawyer, Fredrik Sejersted, ESA's way of acting against Norway was perceived as a shock and that problems of this importance should not be solved by the small EFTA Court but by the ECJ. These were untenable assertions that served not only to disciple the ESA but—above all—to put pressure on the EFTA Court. In the same issue, Mr. Wiedswang produced a second article with the headline: "Afraid of the Swiss Guy" ("*Frykter sveitser*"). It stated that:

> A Norwegian, an Icelander and a Swiss shall decide on whether national monopolies for gambling machines are compatible with EEA law. The Chief Justice, who is Swiss, is one of the reasons why Norwegian authorities would have preferred to keep the gambling machine case out of the EFTA Court. Norwegian authorities fear the Swiss judge and law professor Baudenbacher. He is President of the Court, and represents Liechtenstein. In

> addition, he is a professor of law at the University of St. Gallen. Baudenbacher is considered 'the number one heavyweight' of the three judges, with an encompassing contact network in the juridical milieu of Luxembourg. He is also considered a supporter of the free market and a liberalist who would be prepared to expand EEA authority by handing down judgments which widen the European markets and thereby to adopt an activist attitude.[2]

The article went on to claim that the ECJ had sometimes taken an activist position by handing down judgments that would widen the European markets. The fear on the part of the Norwegians was that I would keep pushing in the same direction. The Norwegian judge Henrik Bull, who had participated in drafting the EEA Agreement while employed in the Ministry of Justice's Legislation Department during the 1990s, was characterised as very solid in the field of law, a little bit careful, difficult to place politically, but as "a possible support player for the Norwegian side". The case would, according to an observer, be decided by the Icelander Thorgeir Örlygsson.

I spoke with American friends about this "pre-emptive strike", and they told me that even in the US, this would be unusual. I nevertheless thought that I could live very well with being characterised as a believer in a free market because the EEA Agreement is first and foremost about creating and securing such a market and to a much lesser extent about securing State monopolies. Furthermore, qualifying a court or a judge as a judicial activist is a political issue, it is as such an empty formula.[3]

The rendering of the judgment in *Gaming Machines* was scheduled for 14 March 2007 at 10 a.m. Five minutes later, the oral hearing in the second gambling case, *Ladbrokes*, was supposed to start. On the same day, at 00.02 a.m., "E24", a Norwegian online business paper, published an article by journalist Alf Ole Ask with the following sensational lead sentence:

> EFTA judges taking secret second jobs. EFTA judges in Luxembourg refuse to state what assignments and income they have outside of work. This could threaten the Court's independence, according to the Court's auditors.

The article stated that it was unacceptable that the judges of the Court were unwilling to reveal their additional tasks, and what they earned for them. It went on to say that these judges may suspend parliamentary decisions and stand above the Supreme Court, when it comes to assessing whether Norwegian legislation was in line with the EEA Agreement. The essay then spoke of the judgment to be pronounced that day, on the issue of whether Parliament's decision to allow Norsk Tipping to have a monopoly on slot machines was contrary to the EEA Agreement. It mentioned that the EFTA Court would then hold the hearing on the reversion system for power stations in Norway. The article also emphasised the importance of such cases involving strong economic interests that the Court's judges would decide.

Mr. Ask continued that in a letter dated 1 February 2007 to the foreign ministries of the three EEA/EFTA States, EBOA had called the transparency regarding

[2]Unofficial translation from the Norwegian.

[3]See for details Chapter 9.

additional occupational activities an issue of great importance to ensure judges' independence and impartiality and to avoid conflicts of interest of any kind. The matter had been dragging on for more than two years, the journalist added. The situation was so serious that the auditors conditionally approved the Court's accounts for 2005, and then refused to approve the 2006 accounts. Additional work, such as arbitration, had to be approved by the ESA/Court Committee. But this body did not seem to have a full overview of what the judges were doing and how much they earned on the side. At least no such information had been disclosed to the auditors. The article concluded with the remark that in Norway there was a register showing what kind of commitments judges have outside their work, but that such a thing did not exist for EFTA Court judges standing above *Høyesterett*.

The journalist finally made fun of our limited caseload and stated that some believed that the EFTA Court was the only golf club in the world where a doctorate in law was an admission criterion. The following day, the article was reproduced in the Icelandic newspaper *Morgunblaðið*. The joke about the golf club prompted my Icelandic brother on the bench, Thorgeir Örlygsson, to write to *Morgunblaðið* that unfortunately he didn't play golf, but occasionally he would ride one of the two Icelandic ponies he and his wife Iðunn had brought with them when they moved to Luxembourg.

Mr. Ask had called me a week before and I had told him that the occupational activities of judges required the approval of the EEA governments, that such approval had been given and that anything else was none of the auditors' business. There was quite simply no legal basis for any claim that earnings from such activities had to be disclosed.

3 Reappointment Under Unusual Circumstances

It was clear to me that my refusal to comply with the unlawful request from EBOA could jeopardise my reappointment as a judge, which was due in September 2007. Nevertheless, I did not believe that the Norwegian government would go that far. In January 2006 I had been re-elected as the Court's president for a second term, which would last until the end of 2008. Obviously, this position was dependent on me retaining my judgeship. In May 2007, the Liechtenstein government renominated me for a third term of office on the EFTA Court bench. However, on 25 June 2007, one day before the delivery of the judgment in *Norwegian Waterfalls*, the Liechtenstein Ambassador in Brussels, HSH Prince Nikolaus, called and informed me that the Norwegian government was blocking my reappointment because I had not complied with EBOA's unlawful request. According to my knowledge, this was the first and only time that another government acted this way in the entire history of European integration. On 28 June 2007, the EFTA Ministerial meeting took place in Vaduz. The Norwegian delegation was upset because of the Court's *Norwegian Waterfalls* ruling. All three judges participated in the meeting, and Henrik Bull received the information that the minister representing the Norwegian government had been given a speaking note drafted by his entourage that criticised our judgment. I was thus prepared to react to an eventual intervention. However, no remarks were made. I ended my own statement by saying that the EFTA countries were not big countries, but that they were making an important contribution to European integration. However, as a former Belgian King once said, "there are no small countries, there are only small minds". During the Ministerial dinner, I was told that Norwegian delegates had resented this remark, which they believed targeted them. I did not react. As usual, I spent the summer with my family in San Sebastián on the Basque coast. I discussed the situation with them. When I first got to know Doris, she taught me how to draw a decision tree. This is what we did to try and clarify my options.

I also consulted a well-known Paris-based lawyer who specialised in International Labour Organization (ILO) law. The EFTA Court, as the other EFTA bodies, has recognised the jurisdiction of the ILO Administrative Tribunal for cases involving its "workers". Of course, when this was decided, nobody thought that the President of the Court could turn to the tribunal one day. The French gentleman told me that if I wanted to take my case to the ILO Administrative Tribunal, we would rely on the latter's 2003 *Bustani* judgment. José Bustani, a Brazilian diplomat, was appointed the first Director General of the Organisation for the Prohibition of Chemical Weapons (OPCW) in May 1997, with a four-year term. He and his inspectors had to oversee the destruction of two million chemical weapons and two thirds of the world's chemical weapons facilities. He performed to everybody's satisfaction including the United States. One year before the expiry of his term, the Conference of the States Parties unanimously prolonged him for another four years. Bustani's work was highly commended at that time, including by the U.S. government. In 2001, then U.S. Secretary of State Colin Powell sent Bustani a letter thanking him for his "very impressive" work. However, in March 2002, the U.S., alleging mismanagement, demoralization of the Technical Secretariat, and ill-considered initiatives submitted a no-confidence motion at the session of the Executive Council calling for Bustani to resign. Bustani's successful work made him an obstacle to the plans of the government of George W. Bush to invade Iraq. After the motion failed, the U.S. called for a special session in April 2002, where the motion to dismiss narrowly carried. In the OPCW's view, a distinction was to be drawn between the head of an international organisation, whose appointment and role was political in nature, and staff members. The Tribunal rejected this submission holding that "the Director General, as head of the Technical Secretariat, is appointed by decision of the competent authority which establishes his conditions of remuneration and defines the benefits to which he, like other senior-ranking staff members of the Technical Secretariat, is entitled pursuant to the Organisation's Staff Regulations and Interim Staff Rules." On July 16, 2003, the tribunal ruled that José Bustani was unlawfully dismissed from his post in April 2002. Bustani, who did not seek reinstatement, was held to be entitled to compensation in respect of the injury caused by his unlawful dismissal. It was clear to me that my case was different from the Bustani case. But certain aspects of Bustani still seemed interesting. I finally want to mention that the campaign against José Bustani was orchestrated by an American bureaucrat with the name John R. Bolton. On 9 April

2018—the day when my life as an EFTA Court judge ended[4]—Bolton became the 27th National Security Advisor of the United States.

The Liechtenstein government did not nominate another judge. Under the Court's Statute, judges remain in office provided that they want to go on, until the governments have appointed a successor. This meant, on balance, that nothing would change on 6 September 2007. Another factor that played into the hands of the Liechtensteiners was the fact that there was a vacancy in the ESA College because President Grydeland had stepped down in July 2007. Vaduz was therefore able to block the appointment of Per Sanderud, the Norwegian nominee as his successor, until the Norwegians *nolens volens* accepted my reappointment. On 16 August 2007, the respective decision was signed. Mr. Sanderud who, like his predecessor and like all his successors, immediately became ESA President, took the oath before the EFTA Court on 20 August 2007. I presided over the solemn undertaking. After the ceremony, there was a reception for the new ESA President. Everybody complimented him on his (double) appointment and then suddenly a representative from the Norwegian Mission in Brussels said to me:

> I should also congratulate you on your reappointment.

I thanked him politely.

The EFTA Court's accounts were subsequently approved by the EEA/EFTA governments. Those accounts were flawless and as I said, under the Court's Statute, EBOA had no competence whatsoever to audit occupational activities of the Court's judges. Attempts in legal literature to interpret the unlawful actions of EBOA as a consequence of an alleged Nordic understanding of judicial independence were beside the point. As to the rest, the auditors were in no way interested in the extent to which the independence and impartiality of a judge was endangered by the fact that he was kept on a leash by "his" government. Subsequently, the ESA/ Court Committee issued rules on occupational activities and the Court made the respective information public on its website. I did not have the slightest problem with these standards.

The year ended well for me. On 22 September 2007, I was presented with an impressive bilingual *Festschrift* entitled "Economic Law and Justice in Times of Globalisation" ("*Wirtschaftsrecht und Justiz in Zeiten der Globalisierung*"). The ceremony took place during a cruise followed by a dinner and dancing on the Mosel on the boat "*Roude Léif*" (Red Lion). Doris threw a terrific birthday party for me with some 120 guests. Laura Melusine who was a 21 year old law student at Berne University, my alma mater, gave a wonderful speech. The book comprised 60 contributions by national and European judges, AGs, politicians, regulators, lawyers in private practice and academics. The selection of the authors reflected the stations of my professional life so far. The foreword was written by Sir Christopher Bellamy, a former judge of the CFI and President of the UK Competition Appeals Tribunal. John McCarthy, the Roman Catholic Bishop of Austin, Texas, followed

[4]See Epilogue.

with what he called "A paper for a friend". John had over the years become a good friend of ours. The book was edited by former EU Commissioner Mario Monti, Ambassador Nikolaus von und zu Liechtenstein, CFI President Bo Versterdorf, UT Law Professor Jay Westbrook, and the President of the ECtHR, Luzius Wildhaber. My legal secretary Dirk Buschle had been responsible for collecting and formatting the texts and Doris took care of the layout and the cover, which was particularly unique.

4 A Not Entirely Unexpected Sequel

In March 2014, I was invited by the Government of Austria to be part of a five-member expert group whose task it was to investigate the downfall of the *Hypo Alpe Adria Bank*. The Hypo scandal was an affair that involved some of the top politicians of the country and caused a huge damage. In order to be credible, the government chose an independent mind, the former President of the Supreme Court Irmgard Griss, as chair of the expert group. We had got to know each other at conferences at the HSG. In the light of the fact that so many Austrian top bankers and lawyers had, in one way or another, been active in the Hypo saga, she wanted all her co-commissioners to be non-Austrians. In the end, the group consisted of Irmgard Griss together with two Swiss and two German members. The group's task was clearly not occupational, it was a one-off occurrence and thus occasional. This meant that it did not need the approval of the governments of the EEA/EFTA States. The Court did not object to my involvement, because there was no conflict of interest and my position and work as a judge was not affected. For the sake of good order, I also informed the EEA/EFTA governments. Whereas the Icelanders and the Liechtensteiners saw no problem, the Norwegian Mission in Brussels—apparently after having sought instructions from Oslo—took the view that this task required the approval of the governments. They implied that I would obtain this approval, but that I did need to jump through the hoops and apply for it. In the light of the clear legal situation, I refused. It was another attempt to turn a legal question into a political one. It goes without saying that had I applied, they might, after all, have said no.

The Hypo Commission became known as the "Griss Commission" to the Austrian public. On 2 December 2014, the group's 394-page report was presented to the public at a media conference in Vienna.[5] Based on the report, Irmgard Griss became so famous that she decided to run for Federal President in the 2016 election. In the first round of the election, as a political newcomer she finished third and was thus ousted. However, in the autumn of 2017, Irmgard was elected to the Austrian Parliament.

[5]The report is available at: http://www.untersuchungskommission.at/.

5 *Kong Carl av EØS*—A Retrospective

5.1 The Article

If further proof was required that the war against me was politically motivated, this was furnished some years after the 2007 incidents. On 16 April 2011, the Oslo business newspaper *Dagens Næringsliv* published an article by Kjetil Wiedswang, the gentleman who in January 2006 had written the comment "Afraid of the Swiss Guy" (*Frykter sveitser*).[6] Under the headline "King Carl of the EEA" ("*Kong Carl av EØS*"), the lead paragraph read:

> He is politically dark blue and deeply disliked by the Norwegian power elites. Distrust is mutual. Carl Baudenbacher is one of Norway's most powerful men. The government's latest attempt to get rid of the guy was a miserable failure.

The piece was purportedly dedicated to a review of my booklet "The EFTA Court in Action. Five Lectures", but it amounted to a day of reckoning. For those who are not familiar with Norwegian politics: dark blue refers to someone who stands to the right of the political spectrum. I think that it is worthwhile to reproduce the article here. When all is said and done I was a judge and not a politician.

Mr. Wiedswang started by saying that as regards all the laws imported from the EU, the final word was with the EFTA Court in Luxembourg, which was "throned" by a Swiss judge. In the Norwegian Ministry of Foreign Affairs, in Norway's national courts and in the Norwegian administration people were not pleased that Norway's economic future had been, as they perceived it, in the hands of a man they could not stand "for such a long time". When the EFTA Court was created in the 1990s, Norway sent its government lawyer, Bjørn Haug as the Norwegian judge. Little Liechtenstein sent Baudenbacher, who had been an advisor to the microstate during the EEA negotiations. The relationship between the two was explosive right from the start, and things did not greatly improve when Haug eventually went home and was replaced by Per Tresselt from the Ministry of Foreign Affairs' legal department. However, Mr. Wiedswang continued, it was much more than just bad personal chemistry between men with well-developed egos. Baudenbacher, he wrote, was a declared liberal and EU supporter, and he was reading the law accordingly. Baudenbacher had written that the EEA Agreement was first and foremost about creating and ensuring a free market, and to a much lesser extent about ensuring state monopolies. For the Norwegian authorities, who had been fighting to defend their alcohol monopoly, gaming monopoly and the right of reversion for waterfalls, this was simply not good enough. Wiedswang then reiterated the accusation that since I had always been keen to secure the Court's position in relation to the ECJ, the result was a more rigorous and formalistic interpretation of the law than in the ECJ, which sometimes based its judgments on more or less "political" considerations. Wiedswang did concede that I was only one

[6] See supra, II.

of three judges. However, he added that, with the frequent changes in Norwegian judges, I often got what I wanted. In Wiedswang's view, all I had to do was convince the Icelandic judge. He went on to write that, according to researchers who examined the case law, the EFTA Court was "more Catholic than the Pope" in relation to EU law. This, the author claimed, had led to a boycott (sic!) of the EFTA Court by all Norwegian courts right up to the Supreme Court. Norwegian courts preferred to interpret the law themselves and saw "nothing to gain by getting statements from King Carl" in Luxembourg. Baudenbacher, the article went on, responded to such research with salty criticism of how ESA, authorities and judges put politics before the law. I was reported as being of the view that "without me and my interpretation both the EEA and the EFTA Court could go down".

From a political point of view, the following statements are particularly interesting: From 2007 to 2008, the Norwegian authorities attempted to prevent Baudenbacher from being reappointed because he had refused to declare what his side-income was. He came dangerously close to being disqualified, the Norwegians tried to use Baudenbacher's refusal as leverage to prevent his reappointment. Baudenbacher went on the warpath, using the continental legal tradition as ammunition. He claimed that any attempt at "political" interference in the appointment of judges was absolutely impermissible, it amounted to quasi-Soviet methods. He won the battle and was reappointed—and his Norwegian critics had to return home with the tail between their legs ("*og hans norske kritikere måtte reise hjem med halen mellom bena*"). Since then there has been a cold war. The article concluded with the outlook that everything indicated that in view of upcoming cases, in particular *Icesave*, Carl Baudenbacher was looking forward to his time in the limelight and that the Norwegian authorities were deeply concerned about how the dark blue president will lead the processes. However, there was woefully little that they could do about the power of Liechtenstein's Swiss professor in Luxembourg.

Sometime after the publication of the *Kong Carl* article, I gave a lecture in the *Gamle festsal* of the University of Oslo. Mr. Wiedswang, whom I had not met before, was among the attendees. Afterwards he introduced himself and asked me how I had liked his *Kong Carl* piece. I answered that since there was also a world outside Norway, I was quite pleased with my ennoblement. Nevertheless, I said that some aspects merited further exploration. For example, why were all quotes from members of the Norwegian nomenclature anonymous? Furthermore, I noted that my own "alleged" statements had not been verified. It may well be that I had occasionally said that the methods used by EBOA and the Norwegian Ministry of Foreign Affairs reminded me of Soviet times. At the end of the day, I was not the only one who compared certain aspects of Norwegian politics to the former workers' paradise. After the failed merger between Norway's and Sweden's telephone companies, Telenor and Telia, Swedish Industry Minister Bjorn Rosengren, a socialist, had made off-camera remarks in which he called Norway "the last of the Soviet states" and "incredibly nationalistic". As Minister Rosengren spoke, the cameras were still rolling and his comments were broadcast nationwide.

A further significant aspect of the article is that apparently nobody from private practice was interviewed, no attorneys, entrepreneurs or in-house counsel. This sin of omission was, however, compensated for by the commentators on the web; 29 out of 30 comments were in my favour.

5.2 *Össur's Explanation*

After the Ministerial meeting in Schaan, Liechtenstein, in June 2011, Doris and I sat together with the Icelandic Minister for Foreign Affairs Össur Skarphédinsson and former ESA President Knut Almestad and his wife Lydia. Össur represented the Icelandic government and Knut had been invited by the EFTA parliamentarians to give a speech. We had a great time and Össur explained to me the background of the name "*Kong Carl*". When Norway was forced to enter the Union with Sweden after the Napoleonic wars, Carl Johan, Napoleon's former general Jean-Baptiste-Jules Bernadotte, was the King of Sweden. Össur said that the allegation was that the Norwegians suffered under me as they had suffered under him. Henceforth, Össur would refer to me as "*the Kaiser*", also in his memoirs.

When I visited the University of Bergen on 4 March 2014 in order to give several lectures, I was interviewed by a journalist from *Bergens Tidende* on the occasion of the EFTA Court's upcoming twentieth anniversary conference. The conversation took place in a café in a relaxed atmosphere. When the interview was published, I was slightly surprised that it bore the title "King Carl I 20 years on" ("*Kong Carl I 20 år*"). The article started again with the old and somewhat worn-out mantra that I was "deeply disliked by the Norwegian power elites and had the reputation of being a dark blue, liberal fundamentalist". In the meantime, I had become used to the jibes certain newspapers made against me.

6 Postlude

If you are faced with the sort of political warfare I have just described, you sometimes stop to ask yourself who could be behind it all. All the shots against me were fired from the dark. And yet it was not difficult to guess who might have played a leading role. The mantra that the EFTA Court is more Catholic than the Pope is a dead giveaway.

The story of my failed decapitation has not increased my respect for diplomats. However, I will refrain from making inadmissible generalisations. Certainly, the Liechtensteiners always supported me. The behaviour of the Norwegian government was also an insult to them. When dealing with the auditors at that time, I was sometimes reminded of the Roman poet Juvenal's phrase "*Quis custodiet ipsos custodes?*", which could be translated into English as "Who will guard the guards themselves?" My colleague Thorgeir Örlygsson, who from his background knew just how miserable auditors could make your life, advised me to negotiate and to cooperate by giving EBOA some information which would not really hurt. In view of the clear legal situation, I did not follow his proposal. That was probably a mistake.

As regards independence and impartiality, the situation was directly opposed to what the auditors claimed: As I have explained before, given that I am not a Liechtenstein citizen, my chair at St. Gallen was my fallback position.[7] It strengthened my independence from the governments, it enabled me to stay off the leash.

When the whole battle was over, my Registrar Skúli Magnússon worked to ensure that Per Engeseth would pay the EFTA Court a visit. He rightly took the view that since, in one way or another, we all had to get along with each other in the little EFTA pillar, we had to be reconciled. Per accepted our invitation and when he came on 30 June 2009, we took him to Mosconi, the best Italian restaurant in the country. Before we started to enjoy the food, Mr. Engeseth privately asked me whether I felt that I had been treated unfairly. I answered that first of all, there had not been a legal basis for his requests and that in my view leaking information of the kind in question to journalists was unlawful. He then insisted that it was not him who had contacted the press, but somebody at ESA or at the EFTA Secretariat. Even if the latter were true, the question remains as to how Mr. Engeseth could have known that. All in all, those who had started and carried out this war against a sitting judge and President came out of the affair with egg on their faces, and they were isolated. Of course, I wasn't over the moon about the actions taken against me. However, I recalled what I had read in a book about US politics: that one of the qualities you have to have in such a situation is the ability to keep things separate. I have therefore not allowed myself to be discouraged from continuing to travel to Norway, holding lectures and workshops and speaking and socialising with as many people as possible. And Doris was, as always, an important sounding block. On one occasion both Doris and Laura Melusine, who was a law student at the time, accompanied me to Oslo where I gave two lectures. The following day we boarded a plane to Trondheim and took the Hurtigruten boat to Bergen. Although the trip lasted only 24 h, it was an unforgettable event. What I could not have imagined at the time was that a few years later the EFTA Court would have to rule on the lawfulness of State aid to the company operating the respective maritime transport services (*Hurtigruten and Norway* v *ESA*). Norway is certainly one of the most beautiful countries I have ever been to. I have in the course of my years on the EFTA Court bench come across many wonderful Norwegians, in the legal profession and elsewhere. That independent lawyers have not fought for their cause in EEA law with the same doggedness as my opponents in bureaucracy and academia, is to some extent natural. Liberal people are often rather relaxed. I want to conclude this Chapter by thanking my colleagues at the time, Thorgeir Örlygsson and Henrik Bull, who always stood by the Court and therefore indirectly by me. I never took this support for granted.

[7]Prologue.

Chapter 24
"Room for manoeuvre" for Norway!

Contents

1 An EEA/EFTA State Against Its Will

EEA membership on the EFTA side was not what the Norwegian elites had been hoping for. When Norwegian citizens for the second time—following the first rejection in 1973—repudiated EU membership in the referendum of 27 and 28 November 1994 with 52.2% of the votes against, based on a turnout of 88.6%, the ruling circles were shattered. Many of the Yes-people wanted to be part of the European project in an idealistic way and to participate in European cooperation in a more direct way than through the EEA Agreement. Now, they were not only deprived from being part of the EU. From 1995 on they formed the EFTA pillar together with Iceland and Liechtenstein. Although Norway is not a big country, it was now a big fish in a pond with two minnows, one of which was a very small minnow. In particular among Oslo bureaucrats, but also among certain academics, there was, and there continues to be, a widespread feeling that it is beneath Norway's dignity to rub shoulders with such company. The politicians and diplomats who had been looking forward to playing with the big boys and girls of the EU were terribly disappointed.

C. Baudenbacher, *Judicial Independence*, Springer Biographies,
https://doi.org/10.1007/978-3-030-02308-9_24

Let me be clear on this point. I fully understand that that the Yes-people were frustrated after the 1994 referendum. I was also upset when Switzerland rejected participation in the EEA on the EFTA side in 1992, and this would have been a much smaller step. What is incomprehensible, however, is that many of the pro-EU camp believed that they could force EU accession by badmouthing the EEA. And yet, this was what happened. Politicians, government lawyers and certain professors got into the habit of systematically denigrating the EEA Agreement and the two institutions it had created, ESA and the EFTA Court. After the negative outcome of the EU referendum, Norwegian politicians, bureaucrats and certain academics managed to persuade themselves that EEA membership would only be a transitional phase. Even when it became obvious that the EEA was a huge economic success story, they continued to complaining about a myriad of alleged downsides.

In the meantime, the EEA has, according to common parlance, become "the national compromise". The chances that Norway will join the EU in the foreseeable future are basically non-existent. In particular, after the Brexit referendum in the UK, the EEA's approval rate has been higher than ever. However, when it became clear that the French sentence: "it's the temporary ones that last" ("*ce sont les provisoires qui durent*"), also applies to Norwegian EEA membership on the EFTA side, the government stepped up its efforts to defend its interests. The claim was made that when dealing with the EEA Agreement Norwegian Government actors should primarily look for "room for manoeuvre". Government agents, supported by zealous academics, developed a tunnel vision regarding the EEA Agreement. General principles such as reciprocity and loyalty, which undoubtedly bind national governments and courts, were largely absent from the discussion. The basic attitude was always how can we avoid having to adjust our social model to any requirements of EEA law? How can we carve out an area of activity for ourselves? How can we ensure that Norwegian interests are sufficiently taken into account? By "Norwegian", the Government agents didn't mean the national interest in the broad sense of the word. They didn't mean the well-understood interest of the Norwegian nation, which obviously includes those who create wealth, manufacturers, workers, consumers, dealers, financial intermediaries, investors. All they meant were the interests of the government in the narrowest sense, i.e. the executive and the administration, and, as the case may be, the Parliament and the judiciary. Of course, one can argue that each country defends its interests. But what makes the case of Norway a little special is the enormous power of the government.

The first academic entity in Norway that dealt with EEA law in a systematic way was the newly created Centre of European Law at the University of Oslo. During Knut Almestad's presidency, ESA was accused of being more Catholic than the Pope by people from the Centre, meaning that it was tougher on Norway than the Commission was on the EU Member States. After Knut's departure, this charge was dropped. In fact, Knut's successors were less courageous and ESA became a rather toothless tiger. The EFTA Court was at the outset followed with critical eyes by the lawyers from the Centre, but it was not the subject of violent attacks. This changed when I was elected President in 2003 and in particular when we dealt with the three allegedly fateful landmark cases *Gaming Machines*, *Ladbrokes* and *Norwegian*

Waterfalls in 2007.[1] In these cases the revolving door between the University Centre of European Law and the Attorney General's Office played a significant role. The two other Norwegian universities also started to focus on the EEA and the institutions of the EFTA pillar. However, the main resistance continued to come from Oslo. The EEA Agreement and, in particular, the EFTA Court were seen as a threat to Norwegian sovereignty and to the traditional social model. The defenders moved into the mental trenches.

2 The Sejersted Report

2.1 Bombastic Presentation

On 19 January 2012, a 911-page study by a body called the Norwegian EEA Review Committee, which was chaired by Fredrik Sejersted, was presented to the world in the framework of the annual EEA seminar at the Brussels branch of the EFTA Secretariat. The event was hosted by EFTA Secretary General Kåre Bryn, a Norwegian diplomat. As an aside, I would add that the two smaller EEA/EFTA States also issued reports around that time in which they assessed the pros and cons of EEA/EFTA membership from their perspective. However, these reviews were not launched in a comparable setting. The presenters in Brussels were Fredrik Sejersted himself and the committee's secretary Ulf Sverdrup. The committee had been appointed by the Norwegian Government on 7 January 2010 with the mandate "to undertake a thorough, research-based review of the EEA Agreement" and of the other agreements linking Norway to the EU.

2.2 Positivist Approach and Tunnel Vision

The committee gave the report the title "Outside and inside. Norway's agreements with the EU" ("*Utenfor og innenfor. Norges avtaler med EU*"). This title contains a clear message: that Norway has to take over EU law without sitting at the table when it is being adopted. In fact, the most problematic aspect of the EEA Agreement was found to be the fact that Norway is in practice bound to adopt EU policies and rules on a broad range of issues without being a member and without voting rights. The authors nevertheless added that this was not surprising since the democratic deficit was a well-known aspect of the EEA Agreement that had been there from the start. It was said to be the price Norway pays for enjoying the benefits of European integration without being an EU member.

[1] See for details Chapter 23.

The Committee deplored the fact that since the agreement was a compromise nearly all the political parties have been able to live with, there has been little dispute over it:

> Firstly, there are aspects of Norway's form of association with the EU that mask the true nature of our relations, and this has dampened political engagement and public debate. Secondly, the continued disagreement about EU membership has a similar effect.[2]

All things considered, the authors concluded that the agreement had worked far better than many had expected in 1992, that it had created a stable and predictable institutional framework, played a part in the modernisation of the Norwegian economy and society and had safeguarded Norwegian interests and values. The report was written during the time of the Icelandic EU accession negotiations and it quite rightly pointed to the vulnerability of the EEA Agreement.

Generally speaking, the report breathes a rather positivist spirit. Since there has never been an international treaty like the EEA Agreement before, that latter was labelled "unusual". One might also have said "innovative", or one might (and in fact should) have mentioned the characterisation of the agreement by the EFTA Court in the *Sveinbjörnsdóttir* judgment and called it an international law agreement *sui generis*. A statement such as:

> Norway is integrated with a supranational system, but applies traditional international legal instruments to do so. It can be likened to putting on much too tight clothing that bulges out at the buttons and stretches at the seams[3]

reminds me of 19th century German conceptual jurisprudence ("*Begriffsjurisprudenz*").[4] It was also asserted that

> the supervisory and judicial control structures of the EFTA Surveillance Authority and the EFTA Court are rather atypical of international law arrangements.[5]

That this was written at a time when countless scholars around the world spoke and wrote about the ongoing "judicialisation" of international law and European law in particular, is, to say the least, odd.

Everybody knows that the EEA Agreement is a two-pillar treaty whose most important principles are homogeneity and reciprocity. The report is, however, based on a tunnelsight that unfortunately has become the standard in Norwegian Government circles and with patriotic academics. The focus is limited to the EFTA pillar or, even worse, to Norway itself. Reciprocity ("*gjensidighet*") is only mentioned a few times in a very general way. It is said that the EEA Agreement gives rights that can be invoked directly by citizens and businesses, but only after implementation into domestic law. The question of what must happen if secondary law with EEA relevance is not, or is incorrectly, implemented is not addressed in

---

[2]Unofficial translation.

[3]Unofficial translation.

[4]For details, see Chapter 1.

[5]Unofficial translation.

this context. The view to the EU pillar is blocked. When it comes to crucial issues such as internal effect and access to justice, reciprocity is concealed. Instead of taking into account reciprocity and thereby market access, the starting point is the statement that no formal authority is transferred

> to the EU – whether legislative, executive or judicial. In reality though there is massive delegation of legislative power to the EU, a considerable delegation of judicial power to the EU Court and the EFTA Court, and some delegation of executive power to the EFTA Surveillance Authority as well as to the Commission and a number of other EU bodies, such as agencies.[6]

This is inaccurate. The Commission and the ECJ have no authority to directly decide on matters concerning the EEA/EFTA States. Moreover, to mention the Commission and the ECJ, on the one hand, and ESA and the EFTA Court, on the other hand, in the same breath amounts to mixing apples and oranges. In both ESA and the EFTA Court, Norway is present with a Judge and a College Member. To give the impression that these are "foreign institutions" is misleading. Norwegian citizens and economic operators have benefited from the EEA Agreement. On balance, and in particular in view of the committee's mandate, the report was to some extent a shrewd attempt to downgrade the EEA Agreement.

Reciprocity has long been oppressed in most Norwegian academic writing. The claim has always been that national sovereignty is the most important good that needs to be defended against the influx of EEA law into the national legal order and the national legal culture. Reciprocity was thus only dealt with as a programmatic formal matter. Certainly, Icelandic academics have not been much better in that regard. However, as in other matters, they have never acted with the same implacability.

It fits the picture that one of ESA's primary tasks has been described as being an advisor, negotiating party and independent advisory body for the EEA/EFTA States.

2.3 *The New Mantra*

The new magic formula was that Norwegian actors should become more aware of Norway's "room for manoeuvre" within the EEA Agreement and that to create a wider margin of manoeuvrability would become increasingly important. Whereas the concept of reciprocity, which forms a backbone of the EEA Agreement, was largely neglected in the Sejersted report, the notion of "room for manoeuvre" was referred to around 100 times. Once again, the way forward was being paved by sovereigntist academics, who are in no way trade law specialists.

The "room for manoeuvre" paradigm has been fully internalised by the Norwegian administration and people who write studies for the government are told

---

[6]Unofficial translation.

to evaluate this point. To give an example, the authors of the 2016 report "Norway's obligations under the EU Citizenship Directive 2004/38/EC" that was commissioned by the Norwegian Directorate of Immigration (UDI), mention on page 95 that:

> in light of the lack of the concept of Union citizenship referred to in the reservation made in the Joint Declaration, the UDI has asked specifically for an assessment 'on Norway's room for manoeuvre' (as an EFTA state) in the cases falling within the scope of the directive as incorporated into EEA law. Presumably, the UDI has foreseen that any possible differences in the scope of the directive will favour less extensive harmonisation in the EEA legal order as compared to the EU legal order. This seems to be the motivation for the expression in the UDI's invitation to tender, referring to the possibility of 'a wider room for manoeuvre in EEA cases' as the guiding parameter for this analysis.

On page 371, the authors conclude that

> [i]n essence, it has not been possible to identify in existing case law grounds for more 'room for manoeuvre' regarding the interpretation and application of the Citizens Directive as incorporated in the EEA Agreement. On the contrary, there is support for an interpretation of the directive that ensures the same right of freedom of movement for EU member state and EFTA state nationals under the EEA Agreement as for Union citizens in the territory of the EU. Rights for Union citizens going beyond free movement rights are not part of the EEA Agreement.

2.4 *Praising ESA and Bashing the Court*

As I said, ESA had in the early days of the EEA Agreement been accused by Norwegian sovereigntists of being more Catholic than the Pope ("*mer katolsk enn paven*"). In the respective chapter of the report, ESA was generously acquitted. The EFTA Court was not granted that mercy. The observations concerning the Court, which clearly bear the chairman's handwriting, were a logical continuation of the traditional EEA policy of the Norwegian government. They reflected a phenomenon, which I have noted on numerous occasions, namely, that when it comes to defending the "Norwegian model", even against clear international law obligations, certain people from politics, the administration, academia and the courts tend to close ranks. In such a system, mavericks can best survive in private practice and some are tolerated in academia.

Three accusations were in essence made: First, it was alleged that in certain cases, the EFTA Court had rendered stricter judgments than the ECJ. It had thus left the EEA/EFTA states less room for manoeuvre than the ECJ had given the EU states. Second, the Court was belittled because of its size and its low case load. Third, the report complained about the fact that the Norwegian Government had lost seven out of nine infringement cases before the Court, in particular the *Norwegian Waterfalls* case.

2.5 The Norwegian Social Model Safeguarded

With regard to the necessary adaptations of Norwegian law to EEA law, the report concluded:

> During these 20 years, there have been some tensions and conflicts between EU/EEA rules and Norwegian traditions and restrictions, which have been challenged in a number of fields. However, given the large number of adaptations that have had to be made, there have been relatively few conflicts, and many of them were resolved in a way that has made it possible to continue to pursue Norwegian policy aims. In other cases, it has been necessary to make changes in order to harmonise Norwegian law with EU/EEA law. But on the whole, the Norwegian social model has been safeguarded and further developed throughout this period within the framework of the EU agreements in a way that has won the support of a broad majority of the Storting.[7]

There is no mention of why there had been so few conflicts, nor of how these conflicts were resolved without inherited traditions being affected. Essential factors were that: (i) Norway has at all times maintained a degree of control over ESA; (ii) Norwegian courts were told by the Attorney General to keep sensitive cases at home, which they did to a large extent; and (iii) in a number of big reference cases the referring court—again under the influence of the Attorney General—incorrectly implemented our judgment in favour of the State and of the unions.

2.6 Mainly Harmless. The Norwegian Model in Brussels

The Sejersted Committee commissioned a number of sub-reports on specific issues of Norway's relationship with the EU. One of them was written by DN journalist Kjetil Wiedswang and illustrated by DN caricaturist Per Elvestuen. The exposé with the title "*Hovedsakelig harmløs. Den norske modellen i Brussel*" was a humorous description of Norwegians living and Norwegian organisations operating in Brussels. It wasn't a necessary ingredient, but a nice addition which loosened things up a bit. And yet, some people at the Court found it remarkable that the cooperation between Mr. Sejersted and Mr. Wiedswang was continued in this way. Wiedswang had not only played a prominent role in the coverage of our gambling case law. It was also he who had bestowed upon me the title of "King Carl of the EEA" ("*Kong Carl av EØS*").[8]

2.7 Some Are More Equal Than Others

As I have said, the presentation of the Sejersted report took place in the framework of the EFTA Secretariat's EEA seminar on 19 January 2012. It was scheduled for

---

[7]Unofficial translation.

[8]See Chapters 22 and 23.

the afternoon session. In the morning, other presenters dealt with recent developments in legislation, enforcement und judicial control. I gave a talk on the subject of:

> The EFTA Judicial System Reaches the Age of Majority.

We had received a copy of the report just a few days before and the Court's registrar Skúli Magnússon produced a rough translation of the parts dealing with ESA and the EFTA Court. In my speech, I rejected the most inaccurate claims. ESA President Oda Helen Sletnes, who was present, expressed satisfaction that her institution had been "acquitted", an unbelievable statement.[9] After my speech, I told my Head of Cabinet Philipp Speitler and my legal secretary Michael-James ("M-J") Clifton to attend the presentation of Messrs Sejersted and Sverdrup and went for a walk. Kåre Bryn saw to it that the presentation of the Sejersted report was streamed. Since the talk was given in the context of the Secretariat's EEA seminar, one could have imagined that the whole event would have been brought to the attention of the outside world. However, no other speeches were streamed. Henceforth, the Court held its own Spring Conference.[10]

2.8 Striking Back

Among those attending the seminar of the EFTA Secretariat was a freelance journalist I knew who worked for Liechtenstein media, among others. The next day, the newspaper *Liechtensteiner Vaterland* sharply criticised the Sejersted report under the title:

> *Viel Lärm um wenig – enttäuschender Bericht der norwegischen EWR-Evaluationskommission.* (Much ado about little – disappointing report of the Norwegian EEA Evaluation Committee.)

The study was qualified as superficial and unscientific and the article mentioned that I had rejected the accusations against the EFTA Court as unfounded. On 27 January 2012, the Court sent a note on the report to the Norwegian Ministry of Foreign Affairs which was also published on our website.[11] In this paper, the assertions in question were again rebuffed.

The report's observations on the Court are flawed on the following points:

(1) As regards the accusation that the Court has in some cases been "more Catholic than the Pope", it is hard to believe that such a characterisation is time and again used in an official government document of a highly-respected European

[9]See regarding Oda Helen Sletnes in particular Chapter 7.

[10]See for details Chapter 13.

[11]Available at: http://www.eftacourt.int/fileadmin/user_upload/Files/News/2012/2012_A_Note.pdf.

country. As I have said, the metaphor has been employed by cheeky academics before and ESA was the first to have the honour of being suspected of being tougher on Norway than the Commission was on EU Member States. However, in the Sejersted report, ESA was granted absolution. It was said that there was "no empirical basis" ("*noen empirisk grunnlag*") to that effect, but that ESA was, on the contrary, more cautious than the Commission. By speaking of the lack of empirical evidence in ESA's case, the committee implied that its conclusions were research-based. In reality, however, there are no data to support the deduction in question. It is simply a contention based on a gut feeling. The same goes for the assertion that the Court has at times been tougher on Norway than the ECJ is on the EU Member States and that Norway (the State, not the citizens and economic operators!) would have got a better deal before the ECJ on certain occasions. The report speaks of "certain evidence" ("*visst belegg*") without actually mentioning a single case. As Fredrik Sejersted confirmed in the discussion when I gave a talk at the University of Oslo in the spring of 2012, they meant the two gambling law cases, *Gaming Machines* and *Ladbrokes*. He said that although the ECJ had made it clear in previous decisions that it wished to give Member States some leeway in formulating their policy vis-à-vis gambling, we had tried to open up the market. This reproach is untenable for several reasons. First, at that time the ECJ had only dealt with the lawfulness of State gambling monopolies in preliminary ruling cases and some of these cases had a specific Italian background such as that fighting private gambling operators was part of combating the mafia. *Gaming Machines* was the first direct action in the field. In *Ladbrokes*, we applied the proportionality principle *lege artis* whereas the Oslo District Court—under Fredrik Sejersted's influence—misconstrued this maxim and therefore found in favour of the State. It is true that the ECJ was more State friendly in *Liga Portuguesa* than we were in *Ladbrokes*, but one must look at the whole picture. A few years later, the ECJ largely aligned itself with the EFTA Court's *Ladbrokes* approach in *Markus Stoß*.[12] If proof was needed that the whole "more Catholic than the Pope" talk was senseless, it was furnished in the report. But the expression was also inappropriate. When I read that one of those who always used the "more Catholic" slur claimed that the (alleged) Norwegian loyalty to EEA law was a consequence of the country's "Lutheran ethics", I was reminded that the later Nobel Prize winner in literature Sigrid Undset was at the time denigrated in certain circles in Norway because of her conversion to Catholicism.

The idea that the two independent EEA/EFTA institutions will unfailingly march in tandem with their counterparts in the EU is in any case ludicrous. Total homogeneity at any time is excluded by the very existence of two independent surveillance authorities and two independent courts. Homogeneity cannot be understood as a snapshot in time concept, but only as a

[12]See Chapters 21 and 22.

process-oriented notion.[13] The report also deliberately overlooks that in most cases the EFTA Court is faced with legal questions that have not yet been dealt with by the ECJ. In such cases, the Court adopts a cautious approach and gives ample reasons for its conclusions. However, it cannot be excluded that the ECJ will not follow its reasoning. If this happens, it cannot be said that the EFTA Court got it wrong. Nobody on the EU side has ever lost faith in the EEA system because in a later case the ECJ came to a different conclusion. As Knut Almestad has said and written, there are many different things that could cause irritation in EU circles, such as: the lack of direct effect of directives and regulations; delays in incorporating legal acts in the EEA Agreement and subsequently implementing them in the legal orders of the EEA/EFTA States; the fact that ESA has been far too forbearing when negotiating with the Governments; or the tactics that systematically prevent national courts from making preliminary references to the EFTA Court.

(2) To describe one of ESA's primary tasks as being an advisor, negotiator and independent advisory body for the EEA/EFTA States is surprising. Admittedly, unlike the Commission, ESA lacks an open political function. The problem is, however, that its credibility has not been increased by the permanent Norwegian dominance. The statement that ESA is formally independent, but Norway nevertheless has always desired to exert a certain degree of control ("*Selv om ESA er uavhengig, har Norge likevel i hele perioden ønsket å øve en viss kontroll*") by claiming the Presidency and often appointing (sic!) prominent diplomats to that post speaks for itself. That it is a challenge to ensure that the EU does not suspect Norway of letting the wolf guard the sheep, is true. But the Commission seems to take a holistic approach to the EEA, an approach that includes the payments made by Norway not only under the EEA Grants, but also under the Norway Grants programme.[14] On balance, individuals and economic operators have in certain cases been deprived of their rights.

(3) The contention that the EFTA pillar is too small to generate enough cases has in the last years been shown to be false. It was, in any case, hypocritical to hear this from a former employee of the Attorney General, who had been doing everything possible to convince Norwegian judges that they should refrain from making references. As regards the allegation that it was the Court's fault that national courts had been reserved in sending cases because of a lack of trust, Fredrik Sejersted made it clear in the discussion after my 2012 speech at the University of Oslo that in his view the Norwegian courts, in particular the Supreme Court, refrained from making references because we were not prepared to give the "right answers". This argument is simply tautological.

[13]See for details Chapter 19.

[14]See for details Chapter 6.

(4) The accusation that Norway lost so many cases was a blatant attack on the Court's independence. As to the rest, this was just a consequence of ESA having almost only brought cases that they considered to be watertight.

In April 2015, Fredrik Sejersted was appointed Attorney General of Norway. In an interview he said that "fight against slot machines" might very well prove to be the epitaph on his tombstone.

3 The Ministry of Foreign Affairs' White Paper

The 2013 White Paper of the Foreign Ministry was more neutral and avoided the aggressive tone of the Sejersted report towards the Court. However, it was based on the same untenable assumptions and on the same incorrect approach to reciprocity.

4 The Norwegian EEA Commentary

In February 2018, a voluminous Norwegian commentary on the EEA Agreement was published. The book was edited by the four Norwegian Professors Finn Arnesen, Halvard Haukeland Fredriksen, Hans Petter Graver, and Ola Mestad and by Christoph Vedder from the University of Augsburg. The grand old man of Norwegian economic law Erling Selvig called it "a great achievement". The commentary makes frequent reference to my writings. On the whole, I would to some extent concur with Professor Selvig's characterisation of the work. In fact, this opus contains an abundance of thoughts on both EEA law on the books and in practice. Nevertheless, the commentary clearly has a certain political thrust. First, the list of contributors contains none of the leading practising members of the Norwegian bar or in-house counsel. Second—and even more importantly—politically sensitive matters such as homogeneity, reciprocity and judicial conflict have been assigned to three commentators who are known EEA and EFTA Court sceptics or even foes: Professors Finn Arnesen and Halvard Haukeland Fredriksen and Pål Wennerås, a prominent lawyer from the Attorney General's Office. There is a tension, or even a rift, within the book between these three authors who adhere to the orthodox school of national sovereignty and are reluctant to see the EEA, in particular the Agreement's institutional elements, in a positive light, and other authors who discuss legal issues pertaining to the Agreement with a more down-to-earth attitude. The troika is critical of the fact that the EFTA Court recognised fundamental rights under the EEA Agreement and they have a superficial and mechanical understanding of homogeneity as being a one-way street. Pål Wennerås, who commented on the homogeneity rules of the EEA and the SCA, tried to settle the Attorney General's score with the EFTA Court in almost every respect. The mantra is always the same; if a ruling of the EFTA Court displeased the Attorney General's Office, it was either rendered without a proper legal basis or the Court had deviated from ECJ case law. Even the case law on State liability, which was accepted by the Supreme Courts of all three EEA/EFTA States and greeted by the ECJ, was attacked. Wennerås also lambasted the EFTA Court's reliance on opinions rendered by AGs and its references to loyalty, reciprocity and fair trial in the context of the preliminary reference procedure in Cases *Irish Bank* and *Jonsson.*[15] Pål, an outstanding pleader, concurred with an earlier publication by Fredriksen in concluding that "the ECJ is the authoritative interpreter of EEA law". The clear assertion by ECJ President Vassilios Skouris in the EFTA Court's twentieth anniversary *Festschrift* in 2014, that both EEA Courts play an active role in securing homogeneity, was dismissed as a "diplomatic" remark. As regards substantive EEA law, Wennerås criticised basically every ruling that does not slavishly follow the ECJ or that has not been followed by the ECJ, except, of course, for cases concerning effect-related homogeneity. To a large extent, these contentions are no more than a reiteration of the arguments made by the Norwegian Government, which did not succeed in its proceedings before the EFTA Court.

As regards the question of what could happen in the event of a judicial conflict between the EFTA Court and the ECJ, Fredriksen took the view that the EEA Joint Committee may adjust the EFTA Court's interpretation of the main part of the EEA Agreement in order to bring it in line with the view of the ECJ. Here too, the desire to make the EFTA Court look as negligible as possible becomes apparent. As I have explained in detail,[16] this conclusion is incompatible with the very notion of an independent court of law.[17] I may add that serious commentators from the EU never went that far. To give an example, Thinam Jakob and Christian Schultheiß confined themselves to stating that the EEA Joint Committee should seek a solution to the problem.

If further proof was needed that the sections commented by Arnesen, Fredriksen and Wenneras are politically driven, it was delivered at the book presentation in Oslo. According to the report in the lawyer magazine (*Advokatbladet*) of 16 February 2018, Mr. Fredriksen said that the book was intended "for the Norwegian (sic!) academic community and for Norwegian (sic!) practitioners" and stated "that Carl Baudenbacher - President of the EFTA Court - had largely dominated the debate about the EEA". ("*Boken er ment for det norske fagmiljøet og for norske praktikere, selv om den er skrevet på engelsk, fortalte han, og mente at Carl Baudenbacher – EFTA-domstolens president – i for stor grad har fått dominere debatten om EØS.*") The intertitle of the report read "too much Baudenbacher" ("*for mye Baudenbacher*"). I have seen countless book presentations, but it is new to me to play on the man like that on such an occasion. It cannot be an issue if publications and speeches which are critical of the die-hard orthodox dualists fall on open ears in both EEA pillars. When Dr. Stockmann appealed to the public in one

[15]See for details Chapter 8.

[16]See for details Chapter 3.

[17]See for details Chapter 31.

of Norwegian playwrite Henrik Ibsen's most famous dramas, he was shouted down and reviled as "an enemy of the people" ("*en folkefiende*"). On such occasions I wondered whether this is still the attitude of certain EEA lawyers when confronted with other ideas.

Norwegian elites have from the beginning complained about the fact that the EEA Agreement does not give the EEA/EFTA States a full co-decision right, but only a co-determination right in legislation. I always felt this was somewhat exaggerated. If used in a meaningful way, a co-determination right still confers a degree of power. Nevertheless, the critics have a point as regards legislation. Fortunately, at the judicial level, the one-sidedness of the homogeneity concept has to a large extent been avoided because the EFTA Court has over the years been successful in positioning itself as a valid interlocutor of the ECJ. It doesn't make any sense to talk this achievement down and at the same time complain about the lack of reciprocity as regards incorporating EU legislation into the EEA. Self-pity is not something that augurs a bright future. Rather, we should turn the tables and look for ways to increase the influence of the EEA/EFTA countries in legislation. The Brussels-based EU think tank *Bruegel* has developed some interesting ideas, *inter alia*, concerning legislation, in the framework of a possible EU-UK relationship post-Brexit.[18] Together with the UK, and possibly Switzerland, the EEA/EFTA States could perhaps achieve some improvement in this area. Many outstanding Norwegian lawyers have left the trenches of orthodox dualism. It is time for the Attorney General and his academic satellites to do the same.

[18]See for details Chapter 3.

Chapter 25
The *Icesave* Saga

Contents

1 The Rise and Downfall of the Icelandic Banks

In the 2000s, Iceland experienced an unprecedented financial boom. Banks had been privatised and restrictions on free movement of capital had been lifted in the 1990s under the government of Davíð Oddsson. This liberalisation, which was long overdue, was not least a consequence of the country's EEA membership on the EFTA side. The two large State banks Landsbanki Íslands and Búnadarbanki Íslands had been sold. Búnadarbanki Íslands became part of the private Kaupthing Bank, originally established in 1982 as an investment firm. The two banks were disposed of, at a price that was deemed to be modest by the National Audit Office, to persons close to the country's ruling political parties. It was said that the privatisation occurred "*à la russe*". The third player who would become infamous, Glitnir, had always been a private company.

The Icelandic banks were not exposed to foreign competition in Iceland. On the other hand, they invested heavily in Finland, Norway, and Sweden as well as Bulgaria, the Czech Republic, Germany, Luxembourg, the Netherlands, and the UK. Important foreign companies were purchased by Icelandic investors, e.g. the British retailers Debenhams, Woolworths and Hamleys, and the Danish companies

C. Baudenbacher, *Judicial Independence*, Springer Biographies,
https://doi.org/10.1007/978-3-030-02308-9_25

Magasin du Nord and Royal Unibrew. Novator Partners acquired telecoms and other assets around Europe, including České Radiokomunikace, Elisa, Saunalahti, Bulgarian Telecommunications Company, P4 Spółka z o.o., Netia, and Forthnet. Icelandic media called the bankers "the new Vikings". Another term created in this context was "outvasion" meaning that foreign businesses were being acquired by means of a Viking invasion.

The events that led up to the bubble and downfall of the Icelandic banks are described in Chapter seven of the 2010 book "NORDICS IN GLOBAL CRISIS, Vulnerability and resilience", by Thorvaldur Gylfason, Bengt Holmström, Sixten Korkman, Hans Tson Söderström, and Vesa Vihriälä. The chapter is entitled "From boom to bust: The Icelandic story". The book makes it clear that the links with the political parties made the banks basically unassailable. Between 2002 and 2006 the banks paid huge contributions to the political parties. Furthermore, the banks benefited from a special tax regime. Gylfason and his co-authors wrote in that regard:

> You do not tax your friends, especially not when they fund your party directly and indirectly.

The Icelandic Central Bank had also lowered its reserve requirements. The banks offered staff from the Icelandic Financial Market Authority lucrative jobs. They thereby deprived the authority

> of experienced staff and conveying a clear message to those FSA staff members who remained behind, a pattern of behaviour known also from the Securities and Exchange Commission in the United States and elsewhere. If a staff member wanted a big salary increase, he had a clear incentive to do his regulatory job in a manner that won the approval of the banks. The banks were his clients, not the taxpayers.

In the end, the banks went on, what is described by Gylfason et al. as

> an unprecedented borrowing and lending spree that increased the assets of the banking system from 100 percent of GDP at the end of 2000 to more than a baffling 900 percent in mid-2008.

The banks' emphasis was on short-term profits. Customers were induced to borrow at low interest rates in foreign currencies although they only earned Icelandic krónur.

On 8 April 2005, Thorgeir Örlygsson and I spoke at a conference at the University of Bifröst which is located 90 km from Reykjavík. One of the others speakers, a man from the Financial Market Authority, quite openly called the situation a bubble. I also remember this conference for another reason. As I have said before, when traveling to an EFTA State for such occasions, I frequently invited a member of the EU judiciary to come along and to speak.[1] This time it was AG Miguel Poiares Maduro, an outstanding lawyer, who after his time in Luxembourg became a professor at the European University Institute in Florence

[1]See for details Chapter 13.

and later a Government Minister in his native Portugal. Miguel enjoyed his time in Iceland, and the Bifröst students were amazed by his knowledge and understanding of European law. When ESA brought its infringement action against Iceland in the first Icesave case, the Icelanders remembered him and hired him as a member of their team. But let us not jump too far ahead, but relate the saga step by step.

In October 2006 and May 2008 respectively, Landsbanki Íslands hf ("Landsbanki") launched branches in the UK and in the Netherlands, which provided online savings accounts under the brand name "Icesave." The Icesave programme offered market-beating interest rates of 6%. It was said at the time that it sucked in money like a vacuum cleaner. The programme attracted 300,000 depositors in the UK and 100,000 in the Netherlands. It wasn't just the "man on the street" who had an Icesave account. Other heavy investors included: The Universities of Oxford and Cambridge, the Public Auditor's Office, the UK Audit Commission, the Metropolitan Police, the Cats Protection League, 116 local governments and the Scottish chef and former football player Gordon Ramsay, whose restaurants have no less than 15 Michelin stars. Unlike Glitnir and Kaupthing, Landsbanki ran its offices in the UK and the Netherlands as "branches" rather than as subsidiaries.

As part of the worldwide financial crisis, there was a run on Icesave accounts in the UK from February to April 2008. In accordance with the division of responsibility laid down in the Deposit Guarantee Directive,[2] deposits at the British and Netherlands branches of Landsbanki fell under the responsibility of Iceland's Depositors' and Investors' Guarantee Fund ("TIF"), which offered a minimum guarantee of EUR 20,000 per depositor pursuant to Icelandic legislation.

From May 2008, Landsbanki opted to take part in the Netherlands deposit-guarantee scheme to supplement its home scheme. At that time, the minimum amount guaranteed under the Netherlands scheme was EUR 40,000 per depositor, a sum that was later raised to EUR 100,000. The Landsbanki branch in the UK joined the UK deposit-guarantee scheme for additional coverage. Deposits at the British branch of Landsbanki in excess of the minimum amount guaranteed by the Icelandic TIF were later guaranteed by the UK scheme up to a maximum of GBP 50,000 per retail depositor.

On 3 October 2008, the UK's Financial Services Authority (FSA) issued a Supervisory Notice that required Landsbanki to take certain actions with regard to its London branch. The practical effect was to freeze the assets of the Landsbanki branch. On 6 October 2008, Landsbanki's Icesave websites in the Netherlands and in the UK ceased to work and depositors with those branches lost access to their deposits. On the same day, the Icelandic Parliament adopted an Emergency Act that provided for the creation of new banks and the granting of priority status in bankruptcy proceedings to depositors with claims on the TIF. On 7 October 2008, Landsbanki collapsed and the Icelandic Financial Supervisory Authority ("*Fjármálaeftirlitið*" (FME)) assumed power at the meeting of Landsbanki's

[2] 94/19/EC.

shareholders and suspended the bank's board of directors. The FME appointed a winding-up committee which, with immediate effect, assumed the full authority of the board. On the same day, the Netherlands Central Bank submitted a petition to the District Court of Amsterdam asking for a ruling that certain emergency regulations of Netherlands law applied. Between 6 and 9 October 2008, the Icelandic Minister of Finance established new banks under the Emergency Act. On 8 October 2008, the UK government took action under its Anti-Terrorism, Crime and Security Act of 2001 to formally freeze the assets of Landsbanki. Initially, this concerned also funds in the UK relating to Landsbanki owned, held or controlled by the FME and the Central Bank of Iceland. Between 9 and 22 October 2008, domestic deposits in Landsbanki were transferred to the new bank "New Landsbanki", which was established by the Icelandic government. The transfer was based on a decision of the FME of 9 October 2008 that exercised its powers under the Emergency Act to achieve a restructuring of the Icelandic banks. On 13 October 2008, the District Court of Amsterdam declared certain emergency regulations of Dutch law applicable and appointed administrators to handle the affairs of the branch, including all assets and dealings with customers of the branch. On 27 October 2008 and thereafter, the FME made statements that triggered an obligation for the TIF to make payments in accordance with the Icelandic Deposit Guarantee and Investor Compensation Scheme Act to customers of Landsbanki's branches in the UK and the Netherlands. The original three-month time limit for payments was extended to 23 October 2009.

On 19 November 2008, the International Monetary Fund ("IMF") approved a two-year Stand-By Arrangement of USD 2.1 billion to Iceland. Under the Arrangement, USD 827 million was made available immediately, with eight further instalments of USD 155 million to follow. An important feature of the IMF Arrangement was the requirement to introduce stringent capital controls to prevent further devaluation of the Icelandic króna. In late 2008, compensation to depositors was paid under the Netherlands and British deposit-guarantee schemes. All retail account holders in the UK received (or in a very small number of cases, declined) compensation payments from the UK government, to the full value of their deposits. The Dutch government paid all private and wholesale account holders to a maximum of EUR 100,000 per depositor. On 28 November 2008, temporary capital account restrictions were imposed to prevent further depreciation of the Icelandic króna, as an important part of the economic programme Iceland followed during its cooperation with the IMF. All transnational foreign currency movements, except those for the purchase of goods and services, were restricted. On the same day, the Icelandic government presented the EFTA Standing Committee and the EEA Joint Committee with notifications of protective measures under Article 43 EEA. Neither committee reacted unfavourably to the planned protective measures. In December 2008, the Icelandic Parliament ("*Alþingi*") established a Special Investigation Commission to investigate and analyse the processes leading to the collapse of the three main banks in Iceland. The report was delivered to the *Alþingi* on 12 April 2010. By March 2009, 93% of the commercial banking sector in Iceland had failed.

Since October 2008, in total banks representing 99% of the Icelandic banking market became subject to either winding up or financial restructuring.

Following the downfall of the banks, there were weekly protests in front of the *Alþingi*. On 1 February 2009, the coalition government of the Independence Party and the Social Democratic Alliance under Geir Haarde was replaced by a minority coalition of the Social Democratic Alliance and the Left-Green Movement, with the support of the Progressive Party and the Liberal Party. In the parliamentary election of 25 April 2009 the Independence Party, which had been in power for the last 18 years, lost nine seats in the *Alþingi* which consists of 63 members, The Social Democratic Alliance and the Left-Green Movement made gains and formed a new coalition government under Johanna Sigurdardóttir.

On 1 April 2009, the EFTA Standing Committee and the EEA Joint Committee were notified of developments regarding the protective measures. On 9 June 2009, the freezing order in the UK was lifted. On 11 August 2009, the Financial Times wrote in an editorial with the title "In the same boat":

> The £3.3bn Reykjavik agreed to reimburse is a paltry sum for most countries, but it amounts to more than £10,000 for each citizen of the subarctic island. This economic burden – about half a year's economic output – for compensating overseas savers is similar to the cost to the British government of tackling a UK recession less severe than Iceland's.
>
> Some compare the plan to the Versailles treaty's harsh demands of Germany. A better analogy is the 1982 Latin American debt crisis, in which even Chile, poster boy of Chicago School economics, saw the state take over a mountain of private debt. A decade of stagnation followed. The same could be in store for Iceland.
>
> Would that benefit anyone? It would alienate the Icelandic people, already angered by Gordon Brown's use of anti-terror laws to freeze Icelandic assets. Icelanders' support for the recent application to join the European Union is rapidly cooling. The risk is an Iceland geopolitically adrift with its strategic location and important natural resources. Russia is no doubt paying attention: it was the first to offer Iceland economic assistance.
>
> Moreover, there is a joint interest in bringing to light any murky dealings behind the bank collapse. A less confrontational relationship could foster collaboration on investigation – and recovery of assets – which Iceland does not have the resources to carry out alone.
>
> There is plenty of blame to go around, beyond latter-day Viking raiders who built brittle financial empires. Icelandic voters repeatedly elected a government bent on unleashing financial liberalisation while letting regulators sleep on duty. But Dutch and UK authorities could have seen that Icesave's high yields were only as safe as Iceland's ability to cover deposits.
>
> With more even burden-sharing for clearing up the mess, good neighbourliness may prove to bring more than its own reward.

On 4 October 2009, the TIF published a notice in the Icelandic Legal Gazette calling for claims to be submitted within two months. The Netherlands and UK governments submitted claims, as did a small number of other depositors, including four institutional investors. Later, the TIF wrote to all institutional investors to inform them that it was beginning to pay compensation under Act No 98/1999, and seeking an assignment of any claim against the banks themselves. On 23 October 2009, the final deadline for payments expired. In the autumn of 2009, controls on capital inflows in Iceland were removed. Other capital controls remained in place. Meanwhile, a strategy for gradual capital account liberalisation was introduced. These controls were still in force when the facts relevant to the proceedings in the EFTA Court's *Icesave I* case occurred. On 30 October 2009, 16 June 2010, and 1 July 2010, the EFTA Standing Committee and the EEA Joint Committee were further notified of amendments to the protective measures. None of these notifications resulted in any criticism from the committees. In March 2010, the District Court of Amsterdam lifted the restrictions on the Netherlands branch of Landsbanki.

2 Precipitous Application for EU Membership

As already mentioned, Icelandic delegations had repeatedly travelled to Brussels to ask for the possibility of using the euro without becoming an EU Member State. When this was turned down, they realised that EU accession was the only option.[3] On 25 May 2009, a motion to file an immediate application for EU membership was introduced in the *Alþingi* by the Social Democratic Alliance. On 16 July 2009, the *Alþingi* approved the proposal with a narrow majority of 33–28 votes with 2 abstentions. On the same day, the letter of application was signed. Johanna Sigurdardóttir's Government stated that negotiations were to be completed by the end of 2010. At the time, I was frequently asked about the future of the Court once Iceland would have left the EFTA pillar of the EEA. I always answered that in my view the application would most probably fail. The majority of my Icelandic friends were rather sceptical. In addition, from my Swiss experience, I knew that if you want to prevail in a referendum on such an important matter, you need to have a broad majority in Parliament to start with. Right from the outset, the application seemed to me to be a desperate attempt to rescue the Icelandic economy. Johanna's government wanted to throw itself into the arms of an EU that had been far from nice to the country in the Icesave affair.

3 Failed Attempts to Find a Political Solution

The British and Dutch claimed that the Icelandic State had to take responsibility for paying the Icelandic minimum deposit guarantees (up to EUR 20,000 per account holder). This would have amounted to EUR 2.7 billion in the case of the UK and EUR 1.3 billion in the case of the Netherlands. The idea was that the UK and the Netherlands would loan Iceland the respective sums, which ought to be earmarked for payment of the estimated liabilities. The two EU Member States opposed the

[3]See Chapter 6.

granting of the IMF loan unless an agreement was concluded. On 12 November 2008, EU Commission President José Manuel Durão Barroso said that before it could expect any help from the EU, Iceland would have to reach a deal to resolve the dispute. Negotiations were conducted with the involvement of the EU.

Again, language was essential. The British and the Dutch, as a matter of principle, did not say that the sums in question had to be paid, but that they had to be paid back. As far as public opinion was concerned, this semantic manipulation was successful, both in Iceland and abroad. Even Lee Buchheit, an American advisor to the Icelandic government, used the expression "paying back" when describing Iceland's alleged debt to the UK and the Netherlands in a TV interview, which served the purpose of urging Icelandic voters to accept the third Icesave Agreement.

A first agreement was reached in June 2009 and a respective bill was presented to the *Alþingi*. However, since the debate revealed wide opposition, the bill was unilaterally amended with a special ceiling for the state's guaranteed payment, which reduced the risks and liabilities. The amended bill was accepted in Parliament and the President of the Republic, Ólafur Ragnar Grímsson, signed and enacted it on 2 September 2009. However, since the amended bill no longer guaranteed a 100% payment of the almost EUR 4 billion for the minimum deposit guarantees, the Dutch and UK governments rejected it and continued to block the payment of the second tranche of the IMF loan. In a press statement, Prime Minister Johanna Sigurdardóttir said that Iceland could not afford to wait much longer for the second tranche from the IMF and its Nordic neighbours. The first tranches of these loans were activated in late 2009.

In December 2009, the *Alþingi*, voting almost strictly along party lines, passed a new version of the Icesave bill to satisfy the British and Dutch demands. After harsh criticism of the proposal by a Justice of the Icelandic Supreme Court, some 56,000 people, or approximately 23% of Iceland's voters, petitioned the State President not to enact the bill and instead to call for a referendum. On 5 January 2010, President Grímsson acted accordingly. The Finance Ministers of the UK and of the Netherlands made rather awkward statements, with the British Minister even threatening that if the Icelandic people did not accept the second Icesave bill, Iceland would effectively exclude itself from the international financial system. On 19 January 2010, the Norwegian business paper *Dagens Næringsliv* reported that the Dutch Finance Minister Wouter Bos, in a letter to the Dutch Parliament, had pointed out that irrespective of the outcome the Icelandic government had assured the Dutch government that "the debt" would be paid. On 6 March 2010, the referendum took place and the Icesave bill 2 was rejected by 93% of the votes against and less than 2% in favour; the rest of the votes were invalid. Ásgeir Jónsson and Hersir Sigurgeirsson have explained the historic background to the President's action in the following way:

> Iceland's ascendance to a republic in 1944 did not result in many changes to the Danish constitution, and the Icelandic president became the equivalent of the Danish king. European royalty has a mostly ceremonial role in government, and although the monarch's signature is needed for approved legislation to become law, this is usually a formality. The new Icelandic republic considered the presidential office as a kind of safety valve: when a

president refused to sign legislation, it was automatically sent out to a national referendum. Until Grímsson was elected in 1996, the presidential 'veto' had never been exercised. Grímsson's first confrontation with a ruling government came in 2004, when he refused to pass a bill that imposed restrictions on the ownership of newspaper and media corporations. As it turned out, his rejection was no ceremonial flourish; parliament backed down and withdrew the bill. Now, in the wake of the financial crisis, he tested his authority a second time.

On 24 June 2010, the EFTA Ministerial meeting took place in Reykjavík. ESA President Per Sanderud spoke about the activities of his authority and stated in strong language that in the Icesave matter Iceland found itself in breach of its obligations under the EEA Agreement. The Icelandic Minister for Foreign Affairs Össur Skarphéðinsson used his position as the chairman of the meeting for a—as I felt—well-staged outburst. He loudly protested against any form of prejudgment and claimed that he had to defend the honour of his country. Poor Sanderud was somewhat lost and afterwards told a Norwegian newspaper that he had not faced an Icelandic politician, but a volcano.

After new negotiations, the *Alþingi* on 16 February 2011 agreed to a payment deal with more favourable terms and payment conditions by 44 votes to 16. The act that was approved is commonly referred to as the Icesave bill 3. However, President Grímsson saw his chance and on 20 February 2011 he refused to sign the new act. Instead, he called for another referendum. The government had been weakened in the course of the first two Icesave negotiations. The second referendum was held on 9 April 2011, and the improved deal was rejected by 58,9% of voters against and 39,7% in favour; the remaining ballots were invalid. The UK's Chief Secretary to the Treasury, Danny Alexander, stated, *inter alia*, that the matter would now be referred to an international court, which in fact could only be the EFTA Court. In the weeks prior to the second referendum, I had visited Iceland and given speeches on other issues. In a TV interview, I had addressed the question of whether the lack of a written obligation to make a reference to the EFTA Court meant that the courts of last resort of the EFTA States were totally free in their respective decisions. I said that the UK and the Netherlands made it clear that any legal questions arising from the Icesave affair, which arose in an Icelandic court, would be best handled if referred to a tribunal they could trust—namely the EFTA Court. On the grapevine, I heard that the entourage of Prime Minister Sigurdardóttir was not enthusiastic about my statements since they feared that they could strengthen the "no" camp. This had not even occurred to me. My goal was rather to make it clear to my audiences that national courts, and in particular the supreme courts, were not absolutely free to decide whether to make a reference to the Court or not.

On 11 April 2011, ESA issued a statement under the heading "Icesave Referendum" that read as follows:

> The Authority has taken note of the outcome of the Icelandic referendum concerning the Icesave issue. We now expect a swift answer from the Icelandic government to our Letter of Formal Notice of May last year. We will assess the government's reply before we take further steps in the case.
>
> Unless the letter from the government contains arguments that alter our preliminary conclusions in the case, the next formal step would be to send Iceland a final warning, a

> Reasoned Opinion. This final warning will give Iceland two months to rectify their breach of the EEA Agreement. If Iceland continues to be in breach of the agreement, the case will be sent to the EFTA Court.

On 14 December 2011, the EFTA Court held in *Sigmarsson*, a case referred by the Reykjavík District Court that

> a national measure which prevents inbound transfer into Iceland of Icelandic krónur purchased on the offshore market is compatible with Article 43(2) and (4) of the EEA Agreement in circumstances such as those in the case before the referring court.

In paragraph 50 of that judgment, the Court stated that

> [t]he substantive conditions laid down in Article 43(2) and (4) EEA call for a complex assessment of various macroeconomic factors. EFTA States must therefore enjoy a wide margin of discretion, both in determining whether conditions are fulfilled, and the choice of measures taken, as those measures in many cases concern fundamental choices of economic policy.

4 *Icesave I*

4.1 Pre-litigation Procedure

On 26 May 2010, ESA issued a letter of formal notice to Iceland alleging a failure to ensure that Icesave depositors in the Netherlands and the UK received payment of the minimum amount of compensation (EUR 20,000) provided for in the Deposit Guarantee Directive[4] within the time limits laid down in the directive, in breach of the obligations resulting from the directive and/or the general prohibition to discriminate laid down in Article 4 EEA. Iceland was requested to submit its observations within two months. In its reply of 2 May 2011, the Icelandic government maintained that it was not in breach of its obligations under the directive or the prohibition to discriminate. On 10 June 2011, unconvinced by Iceland's reply to the letter of formal notice, ESA delivered its reasoned opinion to Iceland. On 30 September 2011, Iceland replied to the reasoned opinion. On 13 December 2011, Iceland submitted an additional letter, which contained further information on the winding up of the Landsbanki estate including summaries of recent Icelandic Supreme Court judgments concerning the reordering of the priority of creditors in that winding up.

By application lodged at the Court on 15 December 2011, ESA brought an action seeking a declaration, first, that by failing to ensure payment of the minimum amount of compensation (EUR 20,000) to Icesave depositors in the Netherlands and the UK provided for in Article 7(1) of the Deposit Guarantee Directive within the time limits laid down in Article 10 of the irective, Iceland had failed to comply with the obligations resulting from that directive and/or Article 4 EEA the general

---

[4] 94/19 EC.

prohibition to discriminate, and ordering the defendant to bear the costs of the proceedings. In its defence, lodged at the Court on 8 March 2012, and in its rejoinder, submitted on 11 May 2012, Iceland asked the Court to dismiss the application and sought an order that ESA pay its costs.

On 28 March 2012, the European Commission requested leave to intervene in support of ESA. On 10 April 2012, ESA submitted its reply to the defence. On 23 April 2012, following observations submitted by the parties, the European Commission was granted leave to intervene by Order of the President. This was actually a rather sensitive thing because my counterpart in the ECJ had recently in two orders denied ESA and the Norwegian government the right to intervene in direct actions before his court.[5] On 23 May 2012, the Commission submitted its statement in intervention. Written observations were also submitted by the governments of the UK, Liechtenstein, the Netherlands and Norway.

4.2 Composition of the Court

Judge Christiansen who before joining the EFTA Court in newspaper articles had taken the view that Iceland was responsible recused himself from the case and was replaced by University of Oslo Professor Ola Mestad. Ola had already participated in *Nguyen*, a State liability case. It was clear that I had to take the case as a Judge Rapporteur and I did so.

4.3 Oral Hearing

Since our courtroom was too small, the oral hearing was held in the Luxembourg *Chambre de Commerce* on 18 September 2012. The room was packed and there was a lot of Icelandic press in attendance. The Icelandic government marched in with a team of nine lawyers led by the former ESA College Member Kristján Andri Stefánsson, in the meantime a Director General in the Ministry of Foreign Affairs. Iceland's litigator was Tim Ward, an English barrister from London. Former ECJ AG Miguel Poiares Maduro sat with the Icelanders. ESA was supported by the Commission. ESA contended, first, that if all else fails, the State must step in in a case such as the one at hand. There would be an obligation of result, meaning that it was not sufficient for an EEA Contracting Party to simply ensure that a deposit-guarantee scheme was set up and supplied by the banks, but that there was also an obligation of result on the government to ensure that the scheme would effectively pay out money when necessary. By failing to ensure payment of compensation to Icesave depositors holding deposits in other EEA States than Iceland

[5]See for details Chapter 7.

within the time limits laid down in the Deposit Guarantee Directive, Iceland was in breach of its obligations under the directive. Second, ESA argued that should the Court conclude that the provisions of the directive do not impose an obligation of result, Iceland was in breach of Articles 4(1) and 7(1) of the directive and/or Article 4 EEA by treating depositors with domestic accounts differently to depositors with accounts held at Landsbanki branches in other EEA States. The former received full protection while the latter were left without any or any comparable protection.

Iceland submitted that EEA States were obliged to ensure the proper establishment, recognition and a certain supervision of a deposit-guarantee scheme, but that there was no obligation of result. If the Court were to conclude otherwise, Iceland contended that it was prevented from paying out the sums in question by *force majeure*. Iceland also rejected the idea that it had breached the principle of non-discrimination. ESA's application did not in Iceland's view argue for equal treatment, but for different treatment of allegedly comparable situations. If any *prima facie* discrimination occurred, which Iceland disputed, it was none the less justified.

4.4 Judgment

Deliberations went well. My Head of Cabinet Philipp Speitler was, as usual, of great assistance. The fact that ad hoc Judge Mestad was stationed in Oslo could have caused problems, but it did not. The legal secretary in the Norwegian cabinet Thomas Christian Poulsen, who was also the acting registrar when judgment was rendered, did an excellent coordinating job. Thomas was one of the best legal secretaries the Court ever had. He is not only an outstanding lawyer, but also an independent mind who looks at things objectively. After having returned to Norway, he became a part-time judge and then a judge of the country's most important appeals court, the Borgarting Court of Appeal, and this at a very young age.

Delivery of judgment was scheduled for 28 January 2013, a Monday, at 11 a.m. The evening before, I had judges and legal secretaries over to our house where I cooked for them. Since Doris had another obligation, it was a boys' night. In the morning we had to make sure that nobody from the outside world could get into our offices. I did not want anybody to guess from our faces what the outcome of the case would be. One hour before delivery time, I went to the courtroom where the first Icelandic journalists had started to gather. One asked me:

> Is this going to be a good or a bad day for Iceland?

I told him that his question was inappropriate, but he knew this and was just trying to deduce the answer from my expression. By 11 a.m. the courtroom was packed. The delivery of the judgment was filmed by one of the attendees and put on Youtube.[6] When I stated that the Court "dismisses the application", the Icelandic

---

[6]Available at https://www.youtube.com/watch?v=pfAeFANanQI.

Ambassador Thorir Ibsen who was sitting in the first row showed no emotion. Only when I concluded by saying that ESA had to pay the costs incurred by Iceland did he fully realise what had happened. He later told me that being a political scientist by training, he had thought that we had declared a *non liquet*, meaning that the Icelanders would have to return to the negotiating table.

As far as the substance of the judgment is concerned, the starting point with regard to the first plea was the lack of a clear legal basis in the Deposit Guarantee Directive[7] for the State's liability. The methodological question that then arose was thus a rather simple one: would the Court use dynamic interpretation and fill the respective gap so that it could hold the Icelandic State liable if its deposit-guarantee scheme could not pay, and this in a systemic crisis, or would it take the view that without a clear legal basis, it could not make such a step? The Court sided with the Icelandic government, which had argued that

> to underwrite a deposit-guarantee scheme using the resources of the State creates its own problems. These include huge costs for the State, moral hazard on the part of the banks, and a linkage between the liabilities of the banks and the financial exposure of the State. That kind of link can have very serious consequences. A severe financial crisis easily turns to a possible sovereign default.

A systemic banking crisis resulting in the collapse of the entire banking sector could only be addressed with other policy tools. No existing deposit-guarantee scheme, the government went on to assert, would be capable of paying out all depositor claims in a systemic crisis. Liechtenstein and Norway had submitted that the directive deals with the failure of individual banks and not with the downfall of an entire banking system. A general and automatic State responsibility as a last resort would impose an extensive financial burden on EEA States. Such an obligation could not be assumed without a clear and precise legal basis in the directive.

The Court rejected the argument of ESA, the UK, the Netherlands and the Commission, that the TIF was an emanation of the Icelandic State, as being of no significance for the assessment of the first plea. For the sake of good order, we added that, in any event, the evidence presented by ESA to support the claim that the TIF was directly or indirectly operated by public authorities, i.e. under the control of the Icelandic State, was insufficient.

The second and third pleas, alleging that by prioritising payments to domestic savers Iceland had committed a discrimination, were summarily dealt with. The obligation for the TIF to pay was triggered only after the domestic deposits had been transferred to the new Landsbanki. No depositor protection applied to depositors in the new domestic Landsbanki branch. They were, as a result, not in a comparable situation to the depositors in the UK and Dutch branches of Icesave. ESA had asked the Court only to declare whether Iceland engaged in prohibited discrimination by failing to pay the minimum amount of compensation due under the directive, as it had for domestic depositors, to whom no such payment was ever made because the new Landsbanki was a going concern. The court added in

---

[7]94/19/EC.

paragraph 227 in dicta that even if ESA had chosen a wider plea on discrimination, one would have to bear in mind that:

> EEA States enjoy a wide margin of discretion in making fundamental choices of economic policy in the specific event of a systemic crisis.

It noted that in the earlier case of *Sigmarsson*, ESA itself had underlined this point.

The judgment was predominantly based on legal considerations. However, one policy argument played a major role. The Court referred to recital 16 in the preamble to the Deposit Guarantee Directive, where the European legislature stated that deposit insurance "might in certain cases have the effect of encouraging the unsound management of credit institutions". The Court then said:

> 167 This points to the concept of moral hazard. In economic literature the lesson of moral hazard has been described with the words that 'less is more'. Professor Joseph E. Stiglitz has formulated in this respect: '[T]he more and better insurance that is provided against some contingency, the less incentive individuals have to avoid the insured event, because the less they bear the full consequences of their actions' [....].
>
> 168 It is recalled that, in a crisis of a magnitude such as the one experienced in Iceland, an EEA State would have very limited options to ensure compensation to depositors that is, first, it could provide a State guarantee for a loan taken out by the scheme itself, or, second, it could directly fund the scheme or its depositors. Thus, moral hazard would also occur in the case of State funding, serving to immunise a deposit-guarantee scheme from the costs which have, in principle, to be borne by its members.

Speaking about moral hazard, I should mention that in 1986 Doris obtained a Ph.D. degree from Berne University for her thesis "Protection against new investor risks" ("*Schutz vor neuen Anlegerrisiken*"). As she was writing that book she would often speak to me about why it was so important to avoid "moral hazard" in financial matters. When we dealt with *Icesave I*, I remembered what I had learnt from her: that from an economic perspective, a situation in which one party is taking high risks knowing that it is protected because the other party will incur the cost, must be avoided.

4.5 Reactions

Reactions in the British press were mostly favourable. The *Guardian* headline said:

> Icesave ruling raises important moral hazard questions.

And the *Financial Times* wrote:

> This is a victory for law and economic sense. The ruling makes clear that EU law does not require taxpayers to bail out private banks, the mistake that proved so disastrous for Ireland yet still claims pride of place in European banking policy doctrine. It also implicitly shows that if Iceland's deposit insurance scheme was inadequate under EU standards, so is that of every EU country. In practice, the lesson is that if the crisis is big enough, no industry deposit insurance scheme can fend it off, and the state is on the hook until it can no longer

> afford to be. The EU should use its reform of deposit insurance and bank resolution law to shrink the zone of state exposure as much as possible. Reykjavik has been proved right in law; Europe should admit that it had a point in policy as well.

Also the reports in the big American newspapers were either friendly or at least neutral. After our *Icesave* judgment, *Moody's* Investors Service revised its outlook on Iceland from negative to stable. The country's sovereign debt rating was set by Moody's at Baa3, the first step in investment grade.

As regards the academic community, University of Cambridge scholar Michael Weibel wrote:

> Over time, the Court's decision could become an influential authority for the proposition that state and private liabilities are separate, unless a State has expressly assumed such liabilities.

And:

> Whether to provide deposit insurance with a state guarantee in the single market, just like the intensely debated issue of joint deposit insurance in the Eurozone, is a matter for the parliaments to decide, not for the courts.

Benjamin C. Kelsey, the editor in chief of the Boston College International and Comparative Law Review came to the following conclusion:

> In *EFTA Surveillance Authority v. Iceland*, the EFTA Court found that, under the 1994 Directive, Iceland had no obligation to compensate foreign Icesave depositors following its banking crisis. The court focused on the text of the 1994 Directive but also prudently incorporated the policy goals of the 1994 Directive into its analysis. The court's decision was, at its core, driven by concerns of consumer protection and moral hazard. Although the impact of its decision on international banking going forward is unclear, the EFTA Court made the right decision regarding Icesave.

Those who criticised our Icesave judgment argued for the most part politically. On 2 February 2013, the *Economist* deduced from *Icesave* that

> [h]opes that Europe's banking union will include a mutual deposit-guarantee scheme are in any case faint. This week's ruling will only weaken confidence in the willingness of countries to bail out foreign creditors.

The textbook of Chalmers, Davies and Monti criticised the EFTA Court's *Icesave I* judgment claiming that it went against the homogeneity principle. They hazarded a guess that the ECJ would, by relying on teleological reasoning, have concluded that the Member State concerned had to establish a robust deposit-guarantee scheme that would continue to function in a systemic crisis. The authors also called it "bizarre" that

> a supranational court is ruling on the allocation of costs following the effective bankruptcy of a state and financial system.

University of Cambridge scholars Michael Waibel and Fiona Petersen have rightly rejected this position, which is based on an incorrect understanding of the homogeneity principle. They have aptly stated that to describe Iceland's position as a State bankruptcy would be to mischaracterise it.

One of the most experienced Icelandic diplomats later told me that while the Icesave matter was pending, the Icelandic Foreign Service did everything to convince the British and the Dutch to unconditionally accept the EFTA Court's ruling by saying that no matter the outcome Iceland would not contest it. In theory, the British and the Dutch could have called for political dispute settlement proceedings under Article 111 EEA. Again in theory, this could have led to the EU taking safeguard measures or to the provisional suspension of the affected part of the EEA Agreement.[8] The Icelandic diplomats must have been nervous when their State President Ólafur Ragnar Grímsson five days before the delivery of the judgment said in an interview with the BBC, on the fringes of the Davos World Economic Forum, that the judgment would only be a "statement", "an advisory view of the Court", "more a kind of legalistic opinion", which "will not lead to any financial responsibility". I can only assume that President Grímsson had not been briefed properly and was confusing the infringement proceedings initiated by ESA with preliminary reference proceedings. Mr Grímsson ended his interview by cursing Former British Prime Minister Gordon Brown. He said he would never forgive the fact that Brown put Iceland on the list of terrorists, together with organisations like Al Qaeda and ended by stating:

> Gordon Brown will be long remembered in my country for centuries to come long after he has been completely forgotten in Britain.

Once our judgment was handed down, nothing happened. I believe that this was a result of the good standing beyond the EFTA pillar that the EFTA Court had gained over the 19 years, at that time, of its existence. Had the EU initiated dispute settlement proceedings, it would have put the rule of law into question and it would have lost credibility. That means that it is very difficult if not impossible for the EU to go against an infringement judgment of the EFTA Court. I emphasise this because the Swiss Federal Department of Foreign Affairs has misunderstood the role of the EFTA Court in such a case.[9] The issue also plays a role in the post-Brexit debate.[10]

Our *Icesave* ruling had an unintended impact on the outcome of the Icelandic general election of 27 April 2013. The Sigurdardóttir Government was defeated, Össur Skarpedinsson lost his post as Minister for Foreign Affairs and became a simple Member of Parliament. Doris and I paid him a courtesy visit when we were in Reykjavík some three weeks before the vote. He tried to remain optimistic, but the polls were clear.

After the delivery of the *Icesave* judgment, I was invited to give a number of speeches, *inter alia* in Rome at the annual conference of the European Forum of Deposit Insurers (EFDI) in September 2013. During the discussion, the participants, all representatives of national deposit-guarantee schemes, generally remained impassive, although one person did express the view that the Court should have

---

[8]See for details Chapters 21, 30 and 31.

[9]See for details Chapter 30.

[10]See for details Chapter 31.

used a dynamic approach when interpreting the Deposit Guarantee Directive.[11] However, at the dinner many delegates came up to me and complimented me on our "courageous" judgment. I should finally add that AG Mengozzi in *Andrejs Surmačs* and AG Wahl in *Dowling* also referred to the necessity of avoiding moral hazard in the context of the Deposit Guarantee Directive. In both Opinions, reference was made to our *Icesave I* judgment.

5 *Icesave II* and *Icesave III*

In early 2015, the Reykjavík District Court referred questions to the Court in two cases, (*Icesave II* and *Icesave III*) in which the UK's Financial Services and Compensation Scheme (FSCS) and the Dutch national central bank ("*De Nederlandsche Bank*" (DNB)) both sued the TIF. In October 2015, the claims were settled and the cases were removed from the Court's register.

6 Return to the "*Courant Normal*"

6.1 Withdrawal of Iceland's EU Application

In March 2015, Iceland withdrew its application for EU membership. The bid had been suspended after the 2013 election. Negotiations had slowed down because the parties were reluctant to tackle the problem of fishing quotas. At the same time, popular feeling in Iceland had changed after our *Icesave* judgment. When I visited the country while the case was being prepared, I had the feeling that the pro-EU membership camp was in a difficult situation. On the one hand, they hoped that Iceland would win the *Icesave* case. On the other hand, a victory would reduce the chances of the country ever joining the EU.

In an interview with the Brussels-based online paper *POLITICO* in February 2015, Prime Minister Sigmundur Davíð Gunnlaugsson claimed that Iceland wouldn't have rebounded as quickly had it been an EU Member State—"We dodged the EU bullet" he said. If his country's application had succeeded, it might have suffered the fate of Greece or of Ireland. Sigmundur Davíð referred to Greece's long-running economic collapse and Ireland's skyrocketing public debt as a consequence of the government rescuing the banks. He added:

> We might have even gone the other way and become a bankrupt country [....]. If all these debts had been in euros, and we had been forced to do the same as Ireland or Greece, and take responsibility for the debts of the failed banks. That would have been catastrophic for us economically.

[11] 94/19/EC.

Sigmundur Davíð concluded:

> Our relationship with the EU, the model we have with Norway and Liechtenstein, through the EEA agreement, has worked for us.

The article in *POLITICO* made two other points: first, Iceland is a post-crisis success story. Second, unlike most EU countries, as well as the US, Iceland has put the bankers responsible for the crisis behind bars.

The loan from the IMF was repaid and the Icelandic Ministry of Finance has taken the first steps towards ending capital controls. In the spring of 2017, capital was able to move freely again. On 8 June 2018, the rating agency Fitch affirmed Iceland's Long-Term Foreign-Currency Issuer Default Rating at A with a stable outlook.

6.2 Brits and Icelanders Put **Icesave** *Behind Them*

On 29 October 2015, British Prime Minister David Cameron visited Iceland. At a press conference after the Northern Future Forum conference in Reykjavík, he was asked whether he would consider offering Icelanders an apology for Gordon Brown's government's use of anti-terrorist legislation against Iceland in the autumn of 2008. Cameron avoided giving a direct answer, but stated that:

> I think both countries have now put this behind us in our relations and now we can move forward and talk about the other things we should be doing together,

He continued that there was a very strong trading relationship and a very strong tourist relationship "with many British people coming here quite rightly". Cameron then added that there were

> plans collaborating over energy where I know there are great sensitivities and concern but the Prime Minister and I agree to work together on that. So I think, let's look to the future rather than the past.

Chapter 26
Gunfight at the Oslo Corral

Contents

1 The Historic Example

In October 1881, the "Gunfight at the O.K. ('Old Kindersley') Corral," a combat between lawmen and members of a group of outlaws, the so-called "Cowboys", took place in Tombstone, Arizona Territory. Tombstone was a booming mining town near the Mexican border. The gunfight is widely regarded as the most famous shootout in the history of the Wild West. It was the result of a feud between five of the Cowboys and four representatives of the town's authorities, in particular Special Policeman Wyatt Earp and Temporary Policeman Doc Holliday, a gambler, gunfighter and dentist. Countless dramatic and documentary works have been produced about the incident. In movies, Wyatt Earp has been played, *inter alia*, by Randolph Scott, Henry Fonda, Burt Lancaster, James Stewart and Kevin Costner, Doc Holliday by Kirk Douglas and Arthur Kennedy. As a gymnasium student, I had seen some of the films, and during our stays in Texas and trips to other States in the American Southwest, I learnt more about the legendary events. The Gunfight at the O.K. Corral lasted only 30 s, but the conflict between the authorities and the Cowboys had been simmering for a long time. The fight at the Oslo corral lasted from 2013 to 2014, thankfully it did not involve real guns, and the protagonists

C. Baudenbacher, *Judicial Independence*, Springer Biographies,
https://doi.org/10.1007/978-3-030-02308-9_26

were all lawmen (and women). However, it had been boiling for more than a decade.

2 *Høyesterett's* Reference Boycott

2.1 The Facts

I mentioned before that from December 2002 onwards Norway's Supreme Court, the *Høyesterett*, did not refer a single case to the EFTA Court although it dealt with EEA law in plenty of proceedings. If the Supreme Court thought that there was relevant ECJ case law concerning a certain question, it tried to look directly into that case law and deduce the right interpretation from it. If there was no ECJ case law, the Supreme Court felt that it could find the right answer on its own. A third strategy, which contributed to the Supreme Court's poor record, was to pick and choose: the *Høyesterett* was confident of being able to find out whether there was a judicial conflict between the ECJ and the EFTA Court on a legal question. In such a case it would, depending on the desired result (and allegedly in the interests of homogeneity), follow the ECJ. The Supreme Court sometimes even found it appropriate to state that its *modus operandi* was right because the EFTA Court would also have no choice but to follow the ECJ, if it had had to deal with the case. The understanding of homogeneity, which supposedly underpinned this policy, can only be called mechanical.

In earlier days, while Carsten Smith was the Chief Justice of Norway and shortly afterwards, the Supreme Court had made three references.[1] I paid Carsten Smith a courtesy visit when I was the junior judge of the Court on the occasion of my speech at FIDE Norway in December 1997.[2] A number of Norwegians had told me that he was a monist, something that in this strictly dualist country amounted almost to being a Catholic. I remember Carsten as a quiet, self-assured man. He had been appointed Chief Justice in 1991 from his chair at the University of Oslo without having served on the *Høyesterett*. As a result of his international background, Carsten had a very good reputation in all the Nordic countries. In July 2002, he retired and was on 1 August 2002 replaced as Justitiarius by Tore Schei.

From 14–17 October 2003, the Supreme Court *in corpore* paid a visit to the EFTA Court. It was a nice event with good exchanges of view, and the Justices attended the oral hearing in the *Icelandic Air Passengers Tax* case.[3] I hoped that the new Chief Justice Tore Schei would adopt a friendly attitude towards the Court. However, I had heard that in his first public statements, he had not presented himself as an internationalist, to put it mildly. I invited Tore to a breakfast at

[1]See for details Chapter 8.

[2]See for details Chapter 15.

[3]See Chapter 15.

Luxembourg's leading hotel, the "Royal", and asked him what he thought about the preliminary reference procedure. Tore was polite, but he remained uncommitted. What I could not imagine at the time—and nor I think could anybody else—was that the Supreme Court would henceforth, encouraged by the Attorney General and cheered on by certain professors, systematically refuse to make any references.

According to his biography, Tore had never worked abroad. Apparently he had only spent some time at an English university. After his legal studies at the University of Oslo, he was admitted to the bar. For nine years, between 1972 and 1981, he worked for the Government's Attorney General, who for most of that time was Bjørn Haug. During this period, he also served as a deputy judge in a district court with leave of absence from the Attorney General—something that in countries with a clear separation of powers would hardly have been possible—, was promoted to a judge of a court of appeal in 1981 and became a Justice of the Supreme Court in March 1986. On 1 August 2002, he took office as Chief Justice. Tore's father had already been a Supreme Court Justice, and his uncle had served as a Government minister. On 24 December 2002, the Supreme Court referred the *Merck* v *Paranova* case to us. It would be the last reference for 13 years.[4]

In October 2008, I participated in a conference of the Network of the Presidents of the European Supreme Courts in Vienna. Tore Schei who was among the participants greeted me with the statement "we don't have any EEA law cases". I received the same salute from other Supreme Court justices whenever I met them. I knew that it was inaccurate, but I was not yet aware of the magnitude of the problem.

2.2 The Academic Whisperers

The *Høyesterett* had already shown a preference for the mechanical approach to homogeneity in *Finanger*. Between the time we rendered our judgment and the oral hearing in Oslo, the ECJ decided the *Vitor Ferreira* case. The Supreme Court distinguished the cases and followed us. However, academics and government lawyers noted with subdued satisfaction that had the Supreme Court concluded that there was a judicial conflict, it would have followed the ECJ.[5]

This approach culminated in the well-known contention that since the EFTA Court had, in any case, to follow ECJ jurisprudence, its preliminary rulings in going first cases were only "provisional". If the ECJ would not follow the EFTA Court's approach, the latter had no alternative than to overrule the respective judgment. It was thus not worthwhile for Norwegian courts to refer cases to the EFTA Court. Instead, Norwegian courts should look directly to the ECJ and if there was no ECJ

[4]See for details this chapter.

[5]See for details Chapter 11.

case law, the Supreme Court would just be as capable as the EFTA Court of "guessing" what the ECJ would do in a similar situation.[6]

2.3 Untenability of the Mechanical Approach

It is clear that the attitude described above can easily lead to mistakes. First and foremost the special knowledge of the EFTA Court is missing. Furthermore, the Supreme Court also lacks the input of ESA, the Commission and, as the case may be, of EU and EEA/EFTA Member States. At the same time, the Supreme Court is subject to strong pressure from the Attorney General. As I have already said, the justices are something of a pushover for the Attorney General's Office because a high percentage of them have spent their formative time working there, often for ten or more years.[7]

The idea that homogeneity implies mechanical deductions that can be made by any court is equally unconvincing. At this point, I would highlight a strange inclination on the part of certain Norwegian EEA lawyers towards a constructivist approach, which is reminiscent of legal conceptualism and is out of touch with reality.

To assert that since the EFTA Court must follow ECJ jurisprudence in any case, its preliminary rulings in going first cases are only "provisional" is ludicrous. The Court has, in countless cases, rendered the first decision in the EEA on a certain legal question. These "going first" judgments have led to regular citations of the Court by the ECJ, its AGs and the GC. As I have said repeatedly, the EFTA Court has thus been able to uphold specific EFTA values such as the belief in free trade, competition, fair taxation, efficiency, a modern image of man and transparency.[8] A large part of the respective judgments were preliminary rulings. Had the national courts refrained from making a reference, the Court would have been prevented from setting a precedent. Whether it will overrule its previous case law in the light of a later decision of the ECJ in a parallel case, is for the EFTA Court to decide. Regrettably, the Court shot itself in the foot in this regard in the *L'Oréal* case where it overruled *Maglite* in the light of the ECJ's *Silhouette* judgment without going into the substance, even though the cases could and should have been distinguished.[9] However, one cannot conclude from this one isolated incident that there is any kind of automatism. The Court may, based on its experience and/or on input that is not available to a national Supreme Court, come to the conclusion that the case before it must be distinguished from the case decided by the ECJ. Alternatively, the Court may find that in a given case, it should for certain reasons stick to its previous case

[6]See for details Chapter 21.
[7]See Chapter 6.
[8]See for details Chapter 3.
[9]See for details Chapter 21.

law. Homogeneity is not a one-way street and it is certainly not a mechanical concept. It comes as no surprise that the pick and choose approach adopted in Norway has led to untenable results in several cases.

3 Open Conflict

On 23 January 2012, the EFTA Court, upon a reference from the Borgarting Court of Appeal, held in *STX Norway Offshore AS and Others*[10] that terms and conditions regarding maximum normal working hours were covered by the Posted Workers Directive's[11] mandatory rules for minimum protection and that provisions concerning remuneration paid in compensation for working outside normal working hours were compatible with the directive, provided these fell within the notion of "minimum rates of pay". However, entitlement to additional remuneration for work assignments requiring overnight stays away from home was found to be liable to make it less attractive, or more difficult, for undertakings established in other EEA States to perform their services in Norway. Such provisions thus constituted a restriction on the freedom to provide services. The restriction could be justified only if was proportionate. As regards compensation for travel, board and lodging expenses, the EFTA Court stated that such payments cannot fall within the notion of pay within the meaning of the directive.

The Borgarting Court of Appeal didn't follow us and decided in favour of the labour unions. The employers brought the case before the Supreme Court and asked for another reference to the EFTA Court. The Supreme Court refused to do that despite the fact that in our *Irish Bank* landmark judgment, we had restricted the freedom of the courts of last resort to refer.[12] *Irish Bank* had barely been taken note of in Norway. Academic commentators who did look at our considerations concerning the freedom of the courts of last resort to make a reference contented themselves by asserting that the majority of (Norwegian) authors did not share the Court's view, as if this were of any relevance.

On 5 March 2013, a chamber of five including Chief Justice Tore Schei disregarded our *STX* ruling and decided in favour of the unions. New facts had come to light that had not been part of the reference by Borgarting Court of Appeal. Namely, there had been an attempt by the employers to avoid applying the controversial clauses in the collective agreement by establishing an entity in Norway that would allow local recruitment of the same workers. This meant that there was no question of "posting" anymore. The Supreme Court erroneously assumed that whether there is an unlawful circumvention of Norwegian law in an EEA context had to be assessed under Norwegian law. In any case, the clauses in question were

[10]See for details Chapter 15.

[11]96/71/EC.

[12]See for details Chapter 8.

found to be justified on grounds of public policy and of circumvention. The assumption that this was a matter of public policy was, however, incomprehensible.

As regards circumvention, the EFTA Court held in paragraph 87 of *Arcade Drilling*, a case concerning the proportionality of exit taxation of a company,

> that an EEA State is entitled to take measures designed to prevent certain companies established in that State from attempting, under cover of the rights created by the EEA Agreement, from improperly circumventing their national legislation, or to prevent these companies from improperly or fraudulently taking advantage of provisions of EEA law.

However, a national court must assess such conduct in the light of the objectives pursued by EEA law; any restrictions must be proportionate. This jurisprudence was confirmed in *Olsen* and in *Yara*. It largely corresponds to the case law of the ECJ.

No such test was carried out by the Supreme Court. Nevertheless, the Chamber felt prompted to assess the contested clauses in detail. The Justices openly criticised our ruling as if they were looking for trouble. Contrary to us, the Chamber contended that the Posted Workers Directive set out an exhaustive list of the matters in respect of which the Member States may give priority to the rules in force in the host Member State, with the consequence that the EEA Main Agreement, here Article 36 EEA on the freedom to provide services, did not apply. In other words, the Supreme Court held that the directive had fully harmonised national law. They did not understand the difference between harmonisation and coordination.

On that point, the Chamber referred to the ECJ's 1993 judgment in the *Vanacker* case, in which the Disposal of waste oils Directive[13] was interpreted. Paragraph 9 of the ECJ's ruling stated that since the question of the collection of waste oil has been

> regulated in a harmonised manner at Community level by the directive, any national measure relating thereto must be assessed in the light of the provisions of the directive and not of Articles 30 to 36 of the Treaty.

The German version of the relevant passage reads:

> *auf Gemeinschaftsebene eine harmonisierte Regelung,*

The French version refers to:

> *harmonisée au niveau communautaire par la directive,*

The Italian version states:

> *disciplinato a livello comunitario dalla direttiva in base ai criteri di armonizzazione,*

And the Spanish version reads:

> *la cuestion [....] está regulada de forma armonizada a escala comunitaria por la Directiva.*

---

[13]75/439/EEC.

Obviously following the arguments of the Attorney General, the Supreme Court based itself on the Danish version of paragraph 9, which reads:

> *reguleret paa faellesskabsplan ved direktivet.*

The Danish translation is, however, incorrect, it lacks the words for "in a harmonised manner".

On balance, the Supreme Court held that minimum rates of pay under national law must not be reviewed under the provisions of the EEA Agreement on free movement of services and that compensation for travel, board and lodging expenses constituted pay. It further found that minimum remuneration fixed by national rules for work assignments requiring overnight stays away from home constituted pay. Each of these points was contrary to the EFTA Court's ruling. Moreover, the Chamber did not carry out a proper proportionality test and interpreted EEA law in the light of the *travaux preparatoires* for the Norwegian implementing legislation in this case, which was clearly an absurdity.

Criticism was voiced in Norway. On 14 March 2013, the prominent Oslo business lawyer Thomas Nordby in *Dagens Næringsliv* accused the Supreme Court of undermining the EFTA Court and the foundations of the EEA Agreement. On 20 March 2013, only two weeks after the delivery of the *Høyesterett's STX* ruling, the Court handed down its judgment in *Jonsson.* I was replaced by ad hoc Judge Martin Ospelt because I had been hospitalised due to an eye problem. My colleagues used the opportunity to directly respond to the Supreme Court. Paragraph 60 of the *Jonsson* judgment reads:

> [I]t is important, in order to render the EEA Agreement effective, that EEA States apply the margin of appreciation mentioned in paragraph 59 above in respect *inter alia* of the right of EEA workers to move freely and the economic operators to exercise their freedom to provide services, as the case may be. It is equally important that such questions are referred to the Court under the procedure provided for in Article 34 of the Agreement between the EFTA States on the Establishment of a Surveillance Authority if the legal situation lacks clarity (Case E-18/11 *Irish Bank*, judgment of 28 September 2012, not yet reported, paragraphs 57 and 58). Thereby unnecessary mistakes in the interpretation and application of EEA law are avoided and the coherence and reciprocity in relation to rights of EEA citizens, including EFTA nationals, in the EU are ensured [....].

4 Frontal Attack on the Supreme Court—"*Frontalangrep på Høyesterett*"

4.1 First Skirmish in Tromsø

On 19 April 2013, *Hålogaland* Court of Appeal in cooperation with the Law School of Tromsø University hosted a conference on the subject:

> International courts and their importance for the Norwegian legal order.

The driving force behind the event was Arild Eidesen, the President of that court. Arild is a very kind man and a wonderful host. However, his court never referred a case to us. The Court's registrar Skúli Magnússon had paid the *Hålogaland* Court of Appeal a visit some time before and got the impression that Arild did not really care about the EEA Agreement. Be that as it may, the EFTA Court *in corpore*, accompanied by three legal secretaries, flew to Tromsø for the conference. There were some 150 participants from all over Norway including lawyers from the Attorney General's Office. I met people I had not seen for years. Speakers were Arild Eidesen, the Norwegian judge on the ECtHR, Erik Møse, a former Justice of the Norwegian Supreme Court, Norwegian Supreme Court Justice Arnfinn Bårdsen, my Icelandic colleague Páll Hreinsson and myself. Arnfinn, whom I had not met before, turned out to be a bright interlocutor who clearly saw the challenges posed to Norway by international and European law. In the years to come he took a great interest in the EEA and the EFTA Court. It was clear to me that this was a unique opportunity to attack the *Høyesterett's STX* ruling. In my speech with the title:

> The EFTA Court and its Interaction with the Norwegian Courts,

I criticised the numerous errors in the judgment, notably the "beginner's mistake", as I called it, that on the question of whether a directive had fully harmonised national law the Supreme Court relied on a single language version of an ECJ judgment, Danish, which unfortunately contained an error as regards the decisive point. I also voiced my suspicion that the Supreme Court's judgment was politically motivated and ended my speech with the statement that

> it ain't over till the fat lady sings.

Aftenposten had published a critical comment on the *STX* case entitled "The political Supreme Court". The *Høyesterett's* ruling was delivered two months before the Union Congress was to take place and the unions had threatened that if they were to lose, their political support for the EEA Agreement could be at risk because their left wing would gain power. In the discussion, one of the lawyer's from the Attorney General's Office criticised my statement concerning the political background to the Supreme Court's judgment. Once more I noted how thin-skinned some people are, even though they found it normal to criticise the EFTA Court and its judges—as the saying goes they could dish it out but they couldn't take it. I was also flabbergasted that a bureaucrat felt prompted to come to the rescue of the Supreme Court of his country. I answered that it had not been my intention to offend anybody, but that I was also not naïve. Arild Eidesen said that possibly the Supreme Court had felt that the Norwegian social model was at risk. With this remark, he inadvertently described the fundamental Norwegian EEA dilemma. They have signed and ratified an agreement, which imposes certain obligations on them. However, whenever a major feature of their social model is at stake,—be it high taxes, far reaching union power, state monopolies, prior authorisation schemes, State aid or other features—they try to find ways to avoid the application the agreement.

The Tromsø conference was concluded by a panel in which University of Oslo private international law Professor Giuditta Cordero-Moss acted as an *advocata diaboli*, so to speak. I had not met Giuditta before and she turned out to be an asset. Giuditta was the editor in chief of the leading Norwegian law journal "*lov og rett*". She offered to have my speech translated into Norwegian and published in her journal.

The day after the conference, Arild Eidesen invited Arnfinn Bårdsen, Erik Møse and me on a fabulous dog-sled ride in the countryside. Erik was accompanied by his wife and I was with Laura Melusine, who in the meantime had become a legal secretary at the Swiss Federal Administrative Tribunal and a Ph.D. candidate at Zurich University. The relaxed atmosphere and the fun we had together was certainly a first step towards improving the relationship between the Supreme Court and the EFTA Court.

4.2 Aftenposten *Picks up the Issue*

In October of 2013, the issue of "*lov og rett*" with my article came out and, as I had expected, it caused a stir. *Aftenposten* journalist Gunnar Kagge reviewed my article under the headline "Frontal attack on the Supreme Court" ("*Frontalangrep på Høyesterett*"). He correctly reported that I had accused the Norwegian Supreme Court of undermining the EEA Agreement and of not living up to its duty of loyalty. He also stated that this was not only my view, but the view of the whole Court. It turned out to be a blessing that I had been unable to sit in the *Jonsson* case because at least that prevented people from saying that attacking the Norwegian Supreme Court over *STX* was my hobby horse. Most importantly, Mr. Kagge quoted my statement that the Supreme Court was trying to create a "Norwegian EEA law". This charge was one which I had hoped that the Supreme Court of a country that sees itself as morally superior to other countries and as the "best in class" ("*best i klassen*"), would not be able to take without further ado. Chief Justice Schei who was asked to comment by *Aftenposten* did not have much to say. He simply stated that the Supreme Court was fulfilling its obligations and that if I felt that they had it wrong in the *STX* case they would consider my views with interest.

4.3 The Nordic Labour Journal Follows Suit

On 7 November 2013, the EU and labour law editor of the Nordic Labour Journal, Kerstin Ahlberg, published a comment under the title "The Efta court clashes with Norway's Supreme Court". The lead paragraph read:

> Norway's Supreme Court was wrong to rule that companies posting workers to the Norwegian shipbuilding industry must pay their travel, board and lodging expenses, argues the Efta Court's President in a general attack on the Supreme Court. He accuses it of being disloyal to the EEA agreement and indicates the last word may still not be had.

Ms. Ahlberg then wrote that:

> It is not common for judges to criticise each other's decisions in such an open and candid manner as that used by the Efta Court's President Carl Baudenbacher when he attacked Norway's Supreme Court's judgement in the STX Norway case, or the 'shipbuilder case' as it is also known. [….] But these are not only his personal views. Some of them are echoed by an Efta Court judgement which came only weeks after the Supreme Court had passed its judgement. The argument centres on what the EEA agreement actually means – and which of the two courts have the final say.

The story described the clauses in the relevant collective agreement and pointed to the differences between the preliminary ruling procedures in the EU and EFTA pillars. It said that the Norwegian Supreme Court had delivered a judgment that flew in the face of the EFTA Court's clear directions and that:

> The Supreme Court argues that a domestic court must be allowed from time to time to pass a judgement which goes against the Efta Court's opinion as long as the EEA agreement clearly states that they are advisory - although of course there needs to be special reasons for doing so [….]. But Carl Baudenbacher argues this self determination is just a formality; in actual fact the Efta countries' courts are expected to loyally follow the Efta Court's pronouncements in the same way that courts in EU countries must follow the EU Court of Justice. If not, you would end up with a separate Norwegian EEA law, running contrary to the principle of interpreting rules based on EU directives in the same way no matter where you are, he thinks. For that same reason Norwegian courts are for instance obliged to refer cases to the Efta Court even though that is not how it is formulated. The Norwegian courts are not doing well here either, he seems to think.

5 Chief Justices' Teatime

As I have said before,[14] the programme for our twentieth Anniversary Conference on 20 June 2014 included a panel with the title "Chief Justices' teatime." The question to be discussed was a modified version of Hamlet's dilemma: "To refer or not to refer?" At the official reception the evening before the conference, Tore Schei arrived in the company of my Norwegian colleague Per Christiansen. It became clear that Tore feared that I would use the conference to settle old scores, however, I reassured him that nothing was further from my intentions.

Whereas Markús Sigurbjörnsson, the President of the Supreme Court of Iceland, and Andreas Batliner, the President of the Liechtenstein Administrative Court, were proud to point to the records of their respective courts, Tore reiterated the well-known, and by now somewhat stale news regarding the Norwegian Supreme Court's record. The participants, many of them from the Union courts, from continental universities and law firms, were rather astonished by what they felt was an extremist position. When he tried to justify the attitude of his court with the argument that a reference would lead to a loss of time, Andreas Batliner answered

---

[14]See for details Chapter 13.

him "so you prefer to give a wrong judgment over giving a delayed judgment". However, at the end of his presentation, Tore extended an invitation to the EFTA Court to pay a visit to the Supreme Court in order to sort out the problems between us and to improve mutual understanding of our respective procedures. In the EEA/EU section of the *Hoyesterett's* website, the following entry can be found:

> In the summer of 2014, the EFTA Court celebrated 20 years. The Supreme Court then attended a conference in Luxembourg, where there was, inter alia, a panel discussion on advisory opinions entitled 'To refer or not to refer.' Some of the background for the debate was a criticism from the EFTA Court's President against Norway for having asked for advice from the Court in too few cases. Justitiarius Schei explained the practice the Supreme Court had followed and the background for it, but also said that we will review our practice in light of the debate that has been raised. On the EFTA Court's website, the conclusion of the debate is referred to as follows: 'At the end, Chief Justice Schei invited the EFTA Court to a round the table with the Supreme Court of Norway on the matter.' The invitation was followed by a joint seminar in Oslo in October 2014 for all judges and legal staff in the two courts.[15]

6 The Oslo Peace Process

In early October of 2014, the three judges of the EFTA Court accompanied by three legal secretaries flew to Oslo. I had managed to arrange a lunch, before the conference started, with Vidar Helgesen, the Minister of EEA and European Affairs. Mr. Helgesen was accompanied by the Head of Legal Affairs at the Ministry of Foreign Affairs Margit F. Tveiten who three years later would play a rather inglorious role in the context of the reappointment of the incumbent Norwegian Judge Christiansen.[16] The conversation was friendly, but marked by the usual EEA-critical undertone of the EU aficionados. On such occasions, I often wondered why my Norwegian colleagues on the EFTA Court bench did not speak up. I think that in the meantime I have found the answer: they were—at least deep in their hearts—themselves unhappy that their own country hadn't been able to join the EU.

In the afternoon, the first part of the seminar was held in the impressive premises of the Supreme Court of Norway. Talks were given and discussions were conducted in a friendly atmosphere. In the evening, the Supreme Court invited us to a splendid meal at Holmenkollen, the world famous ski area. In my dinner speech I said that well-educated guests usually bring a present, that making presents is, however, a tricky thing so the Court had decided not to make a gift to the Supreme Court, but rather to the Norwegian people. The gift was the Court's recent *FIFA* judgment. As a consequence of that ruling, the Norwegian people had the right to watch all

---

[15]Available at: http://www.domstol.no/no/Enkelt-domstol/-Norges-Hoyesterett/Avgjorelser/EOSEU/.

[16]See for details Chapter 28.

matches of the final stage of the Football World Cup on normal television. At the end of my address I handed Tore Schei a football and concluded with the words:

> Mr. Justitiarius, the ball is now in your field.

The next day at noon, the conference ended in an excellent atmosphere. Group pictures were taken and the EFTA Court's delegation left Oslo full of optimism. The gunfight at the Oslo corral was over. Unlike in Tombstone, Arizona Territory, there were no casualties, just a few scars. In 2015 and 2016, the Supreme Court sent three major cases to the EFTA Court, *Holship* on the relationship between collective bargaining and industrial action, on the one hand, and competition law and the freedom of establishment, on the other, *Ski Taxi* on the notion of restriction of competition by object, and *Thue* on the interpretation of the Working Time Directive.[17] *Holship* was referred while Tore Schei was still in office. I was repeatedly told that the Chief Justice had no say when it came to the question of whether a reference ought to be made because this was for the Appeals Committee to decide. I was never convinced by this argument and in fact I think that Tore didn't want to go down in history as the Chief Justice under whose reign the Supreme Court had carried through a reference boycott. Today, it is fair to characterise the relationship between the two courts as friendly. It definitely goes beyond "peaceful coexistence". Justices of the Supreme Court have attended the Court's Spring Conference on a regular basis. Sometimes, they have also given speeches. When the new Chief Justice, Toril Marie Øie, was appointed in the spring of 2016, I paid her a courtesy visit. And from 2 to 4 May 2017, the Supreme Court *in corpore*, together with their colleagues from Iceland and Liechtenstein, participated in the First Judicial Summit of the EFTA pillar.

7 ESA's Caution

Notwithstanding the fact that the EFTA Court's preliminary rulings are strictly speaking advisory, a national court that does not follow them may bring its country into a violation of its obligations under the EAA Agreement. ESA has been reluctant to become active in such cases. One Icelandic case has been mentioned in the Chapter dedicated to the Authority.[18] Cases where the Norwegian courts deviated from the EFTA Court's ruling had remained without consequences. However, *STX* seemed to be too much even for ESA, not least because of its language and its Pan-European dimension. Certainly, those who defended the Supreme Court's judgment, some of whom were even ESA staff, tried once again to construe a judicial conflict by claiming that the ruling was compatible with ECJ case law. However, this proved to be a hopeless endeavour. On 11 June 2013,

---

[17] 2003/88/EC.

[18] See for details Chapter 7.

Professor Catherine Barnard from Cambridge University gave a lunchtime talk at the EFTA Court on recent developments under the Posted Workers Directive[19] and senior judges from the ECJ who were present made it clear that we were fully aligned with the ECJ.

On 21 October 2013, ESA opened proceedings on the basis of a complaint by the Confederation of European Business ("Business Europe"). Business Europe took the view that the minimum rates of pay should have been assessed by the Supreme Court on the basis of the EEA Agreement, in particular the freedom to provide services, and that the notion of "public policy" should have been interpreted strictly. The matter had been brought to Business Europe's attention by the NHO. ESA invited Business Europe to supplement the complaint asking in particular for specific details of how the Confederation viewed the diverging conclusions of the Court and the Supreme Court on the questions of additional remuneration for work assignments requiring overnight stays away from home and of compensation for travel, board and lodging expenses for work assignments requiring overnight stays away from home in the EFTA Court's *STX* judgment. The Authority must ensure that the Court's judgment is implemented in a way that does not bring the EEA/EFTA State concerned into the situation of a breach of the EEA Agreement. However, it is not an arbiter with the competence to decide who was right and who was wrong. On 21 January 2014, ESA sent a request for information to Norway referring to a complaint from NHO. Norway was asked to clarify how the term "minimum rates of pay" is now interpreted under Norwegian law and about the applicability of the provisions of the EEA Agreement on the freedom to provide services. In its reply, Norway submitted that it did not consider the Supreme Court judgment to undermine the EEA Agreement. This was a typically empty formula.

It was not before 10 July 2015 that ESA sent a letter to Norway setting out the preliminary view that Norway had failed to fulfil its obligations under the EEA Agreement. In September 2015, Oda Helen Sletnes was replaced at the helm of ESA by Sven Erik Svedman. On 28 September 2015 Norway replied justifying its position. The Government also referred to the fact that the Minister of Labour met with NHO and LO in order for them

> to take up dialogue on challenges connected to the Norwegian system of general application of wage agreements.

After numerous discussions, ESA encouraged this dialogue. On 25 October 2016, ESA maintained its preliminary conclusions in a letter of formal notice to Norway. On 20 January 2017, Norway replied, contending that a solution had to be found by the social partners and referring to an ongoing process between NHO and LO. On 25 January 2017, ESA asked for information on the results of the negotiations between the social partners. On 7 April 2017, Norway sent ESA a "Status Report" setting a time frame for "long-term and robust solutions" between the social partners by the spring of 2018.

---

[19] 96/71/EC.

For an independent observer, it may seem that Norway is trying to play for time and that ESA is overly understanding. This may be a consequence of the structure of the EFTA pillar with Norway being the super-power and the paymaster. The mighty Norwegian unions are supportive of the EEA Agreement, but it is an "as long as" support.

Chapter 27
Working Methods and Judicial Style

Contents

1 The EFTA Court's Structure

1.1 Composition

The EFTA Court is a permanent European court that, since September of 1995, consists of three judges and six ad hoc judges. Ad hoc judges are called upon to sit if one of the regular judges is prevented from participating due to bias or illness. The Court's experience with the ad hoc judges is a mixed one, because the governments do not pay enough attention to selecting them carefully. Having said that, I want to emphasise that some of the ad hoc judges were excellent. We don't work with an AG. Since it only consists of three judges the Court always sits in plenum and all judges are involved. This results in some sort of "judicial nationalism", even if this is not intended.

C. Baudenbacher, *Judicial Independence*, Springer Biographies,
https://doi.org/10.1007/978-3-030-02308-9_27

1.2 Cabinet System and Manning Table

The EFTA Court works under a cabinet system as opposed to a pool system. In recent years, the cabinets have consisted of one judge, two legal secretaries, and one personal assistant. In addition to the two legal secretaries, the President has in the last couple of years disposed of a Head of Cabinet, who was also responsible for extrajudicial activities. The cabinet is the judge's little empire. A cabinet system gives the judges more influence on the judgments than a pool system, where judges work with different lawyers depending on the case. The Court also has a registry, which is, however, limited to logistics, finances, human resources and procedural matters. The Court's manning table is small, in 2017 it had a total headcount of 19, which included 3 judges and 7 lawyers dealing with the cases. We had a budget of EUR 5 million.

1.3 Language Regime

The EFTA Court has a different language regime than the ECJ. English is the working language. Our judgments in direct actions are given only in English; preliminary rulings are rendered in English and in the language of the referring court. Both versions are authentic although the non-English version is only a translation of the English version.[1] This may pose problems and in one case, the system was apparently abused.[2]

2 Procedure

2.1 General

At the EFTA Court, as at the ECJ, the judges control the cases. Legal secretaries may provide important input, but they are not decision-makers. Unlike in Swiss courts, they do not sign the judgment even though they may have played a crucial part in drafting it, depending on how the judge in question organises the work in his/her cabinet. In the *Gaming Machines* case, the Norwegian Government wanted one of my legal secretaries to be excluded from the case because he had published an article in a law journal on a previous ECJ judgment that was potentially relevant. The Court rejected this motion holding that legal secretaries are not decision-makers.

[1]See for details Chapter 22.

[2]See for details Chapter 22.

2.2 Assignment of the Case to a Judge Rapporteur

A study by German researcher Jens Frankenreiter carried out on behalf of the Centre for Law and Economics at the Swiss Institute of Technology (*ETH*) in Zurich deals with fundamental questions regarding case assignment to chambers and to Judge Rapporteurs and with the decision to involve an AG in the decision-making process at the ECJ. The author concludes that such decisions are made on the basis of strategic considerations. The main motive seems to be to keep outlier and weak judges under control or to even exclude them from participating in certain cases. It is to be noted that unlike in German or American courts, the President of the ECJ enjoys a wide discretion when making the respective decisions. Together with the rule that both the deliberations and the vote are kept secret, this, according to Frankenreiter, leads to a level of lack of transparency that "is substantially higher as compared to other courts". In the US and in Germany, cases are randomly assigned.

At the EFTA Court, the only problem that arises relates to the assignment of the case to a Judge Rapporteur who in particular has the task of drafting the judgment. He or she has considerable influence over the style and the reasoning, although the other two judges usually take the liberty of interfering with the Judge Rapporteur's draft as they deem fit. Article 8 of the Court's Rules of Procedure states:

> 1. As soon as an application initiating proceedings has been lodged, the President shall designate a Judge to act as Rapporteur.
>
> 2. The Court shall lay down criteria by which, as a rule, cases are to be assigned to Judges.

As regards the second paragraph of this provision, during my 15 years at the helm of the Court I have followed the same unwritten principles as my predecessors. Sensitive cases were, as a rule, not assigned to the judge from the country concerned. The reason for this was twofold: On the one hand, any appearance that the Judge Rapporteur could be biased, in favour of the government that had nominated him or her, had to be avoided. On the other hand, this also helped to protect the judge from the country concerned from political pressure. I don't deny that, in the light of the homogeneity objective, the desire to reduce the influence of orthodox dualism may occasionally have played a role. Moreover, in a court of three, it is indispensable that the special knowledge and experience of individual judges in certain fields of the relevant law is taken into account when cases are assigned. I know that this may sound horrible to German lawyers, for example, and it is clear that it may enable strategic behaviour to a certain extent. But you have to be realistic. Unconditional equal treatment of the judges in a court like the EFTA Court cannot be a solution. What counts, at the end of the day, is not fairness among the judges, but fairness vis-à-vis the parties and the public at large, in particular private operators who are *a priori* in a difficult position when fighting a government or an institution. I add that special knowledge may also play a role in the Union Courts.

At the EFTA Court, as at the ECJ, the Judge Rapporteurs will be engaged in drafting irrespective of whether he/she is in the majority or not. This situation is not unproblematic. I have seen cases in which a minority judge loyally implemented what the majority had decided. A good minority judge will even hinder the majority from making blunders. However, it may also be that somebody who has been overruled will try to undermine the majority decision. In one case, the minority judge had such strong feelings that I was prompted to reassign the case to another judge. Finally, the situation may arise that the minority judge is so offended, allegedly because the two other judges have not really listened to his/her arguments that he/she will throw in the towel and refuse to provide any input.

2.3 Written Procedure

The procedure consists of a written and an oral part, with the written part being the more important one. When the case arrives, and once it has been entered in the Court's registry it is published in the EEA section of the Official Journal of the EU. Written statements may be submitted by the parties, by the EEA/EFTA States, the EU Member States, ESA and the Commission. However, there is a 50-page limit that is strictly enforced. We have had a case in which a lawyer submitted 53 pages instead of 50, and the submission was returned.

2.4 Report for the Hearing

The Judge Rapporteur draws up a preliminary report and then a Report for the Hearing. In preliminary ruling cases, this document is also translated into the language of the applicant. The Report for the Hearing has been abandoned in the ECJ's procedure. In the EFTA Court's setup, it is a means of transparency. However, it does also present certain disadvantages. First, it is often too long and there is too much copy pasting. Furthermore, in a preliminary reference case, the national court may be tempted to pick and choose, selecting from the Report for the Hearing what the Commission, for example, has stated and then saying that the Court's solution does not convince them and that they will therefore follow the Commission and not the Court.

2.5 Applications for Intervention and for Interim Measures

Applications for intervention and interim measures are decided by the President. An intervener is limited to supporting the form of order sought by one of the parties. Intervention is nevertheless deemed to be a stronger way of supporting a certain position than the pure submission of observations.

2.6 *Oral Hearing*

The oral part of the procedure is relatively short. In a pre-hearing meeting, the Court informs the parties and participants that they should focus on points of contention and not repeat what has been stated in the written observations. Many lawyers regularly appear before the Court, These "repeat players" are well aware of how the game is played. Parties and participants are typically granted 15–30 min for their oral argument, in an important case it may be more, and there is a right to reply. Questions are often sent in advance so that those involved can properly prepare for the oral hearing. I have developed a habit of interrupting the agents and asking questions during the hearing. This did not occur in the early years. However, I think that questions should be asked as they arise. To listen to an agent for half an hour and only then to be able to ask questions during a dedicated Q & A session is somewhat artificial. During my stays in Texas, I had attended some court hearings and was impressed by the way American judges conducted the oral procedure.

2.7 *Resolving the Case and Delivery of the Judgment*

Immediately after the hearing, the first deliberation takes place. The Judge Rapporteur may be asked to draft the judgment, or to present a pre-draft before a decision is taken. Following the presentation of the draft, deliberation mainly takes place by written exchange.

Cases are decided by majority vote. In a three-judge panel, that means either 3:0 or 2:1. As Lord Denning, arguably the most celebrated English judge of the 20th century, reportedly said when asked why he moved back from the House of Lords where a panel consisted of five or more judges to the Court of Appeal where cases are normally heard by three judges:

> You only have to convince one.

If at least a majority is satisfied, the case is decided. Further steps are then the external language revision, in preliminary ruling cases the translation, and very importantly, years ago we started reading the judgment out loud to each other. This practice has allowed us to detect mistakes and inconsistencies and to make important final corrections. Sometimes even substantial changes are made at the very last moment. The judgment is handed down in open court and is binding from the date of its delivery. It is then published on the Court's website, in the Official Journal of the EU, and in the Court's Annual Report.

After delivery there may be a need for rectification, in the event of clerical mistakes or errors in calculation, or obvious slips. Finally, an application for interpretation may be made if a party thinks that something is not clear. Decision is given in the form of a judgment.

2.8 Peculiarities of a Three-Member Court

As I said, EEA sceptics tried to use the Court's small size to question the legitimacy of its rulings. That is obviously untenable. First of all, a court of three has advantages when it comes to speed and efficiency. Moreover, Appellate Courts in many countries, including Norway, the UK and the US in most cases, and the WTO AB always, sit in a three-member formation. However, unlike in these courts, no rotation is possible at the EFTA Court. In other words, you always sit with the same colleagues. This means that, after a while, you know your colleagues' approach to law in general and their political preferences. And they know yours. The question then arises as to how you proceed when you want to convince them, or at least one of them.

I have often been described as an influential judge, not least by people who suspected me of wanting to steal their country's sovereignty. It was also said that since the other two EEA/EFTA States changed their judges much more frequently, I was able to build up a power base. I will not comment on these contentions. However, I do want to say something on the question of whether collegiality should be the governing principle when it comes to deciding a case and to drafting the judgment. It is clear that a good working atmosphere is essential in every court, particularly in a small court operating without a dissenting opinion system. Collegiality is also important when it comes to including a judge who finds himself or herself in the minority. A judge of a three-member court must heed former German football world championship coach Sepp Herberger's famous quote that "after the game is before the game". However, I do not subscribe to the contention, which was made by an EFTA Court judge during a meeting with the Federal Supreme Court of Switzerland in July 2017 that maintaining a collegiate ambiance is so important that material concessions should be made in order to accommodate a minority judge. A judge who has been overruled is still required to loyally contribute to a convincing reasoning. He or she must point to weaknesses in the drafts of the majority and make constructive proposals. However, a minority judge cannot expect the majority to compromise the substantive arguments in a way that would weaken the judgment.

3 Reasoning

3.1 Early Considerations

From the very beginning, I took a huge interest in questions of judicial style. In 1997, when I was the junior judge, I published my first major essay on the EFTA Court in the (American) Columbia Journal of European Law. There, I addressed, *inter alia*, the issue of judicial style, starting with the ECJ. As is known, the ECJ cultivates a peculiar way of writing. Originally, it took all its bearings from the

French tradition of wording the entire ruling as one single sentence consisting of a large number of paragraphs. In the French version of the rulings, individual paragraphs started with "*attendu que*" (whereas). This method was abandoned in the late 1970s. The last judgments that use this technique stem from mid-1979. Even so, the ECJ's reasoning still retains elements of this former approach, often leaving the impression that the previous paragraphs have simply been converted into sentences. The fact that French is the working language clearly plays a part in this. The style and language of the ECJ's rulings are not undisputed within the Union itself. A lack of linguistic suppleness is regarded as a particular problem; this results partly from the fact that most rulings are given in translation. The constraints of the multilingual nature of EU law explains, to a certain extent, the habit of repeating sentences or entire passages from case to case. Although this leads to verbal clumsiness, it is also a safeguard against errors in translation. Academic literature has traced the flatness of the ECJ's language back to an effort to make the rulings resemble the outcome of a unanimous decision: Brown and Jacobs have stated with regard to the ECJ's language:

> The tone is measured; there is neither excitement nor humour; [....] the individual voices are muted; they blend in union; there is a single refrain.

Even more important than these formal reservations is the criticism that has been primarily (but not exclusively) voiced by German authors, who argue that the rulings given by the ECJ often lack sufficient reasons. The ECJ does not refer to views put forward in academic literature or exemplified in the case law of national courts. Rather, this task is left to the AGs' opinions. The latter also often contain considerations of comparative law. However, the fact remains that these opinions are written before the judgment is rendered. They are thus only to a limited extent a source for understanding the ECJ's findings. A prominent critic of the ECJ's style is the German Constitutional Court ("*Bundesverfassungsgericht*") which held in its *Gauweiler* judgment of 21 June 2016 when implementing the ECJ's preliminary ruling of 16 June 2015:

> *Die dem Urteil vom 16. Juni 2015 zugrundeliegende Art und Weise richterlicher Rechtskonkretisierung begegnet aus der Sicht des Senats [....] gewichtigen Einwänden mit Blick auf die Erhebung des Sachverhalts (aa), das Prinzip der begrenzten Einzelermächtigung (bb) und die gerichtliche Kontrolle der Europäischen Zentralbank bei der Bestimmung ihres Mandates.*
>
> (The way of judicial legal concretization of the law on which the judgement of 16 June 2015 is based, gives, from the senate's point of view, rise to weighty objections with regard to the collection of the facts (aa), the principle of limited conferral (bb), and the judicial control of the European Central Bank in determining its mandate.)[3]

The Constitutional Court noted further that the ECJ did not deal with other points, that there was a lack of an "overall view", that the ECJ generously accepted alleged objectives of the euro rescue operations of the European System of Central Banks

---

[3]Unofficial translation.

and the European Central Bank and that other issues remained “without an answer”. The Constitutional Court nevertheless followed the ECJ’s ruling.

The ECJ’s manner of reasoning its judgments has also been lambasted in the UK. After my speech at Chatham House on 14 September 2017, a participant came up to me and said that, in an English judgment you could see what the real motives were, whereas in the ECJ’s rulings the rationale would often remain outside the text.

3.2 *What Has Been Achieved?*

Giving Comprehensive, but Succinct Reasons

When I finished my article for the Columbia Journal of European Law in 1997, the EFTA Court’s case law consisted of less than 20 judgments, half of them rendered by the Five-member Court. As regards judicial style, I wrote:

> The EFTA Court’s orientation toward ECJ case law is also evident in its judicial style. Indeed, the degree of similarity is sometimes such that only close reading will reveal which of the two EEA courts has given a certain ruling. One will note, however, that the decisions of the EFTA Court are quite often longer than those of the ECJ.

It was always clear to me that giving comprehensive, albeit succinct, reasons was important for a European court of three that works under rather soft framework conditions. There is, in general, much to be said in favour of dealing with all the arguments put forward by parties and participants and of revealing the real (also policy and economic) reasons underlying a judgment. A further question was whether the case law of national supreme courts should also be cited. I felt that this would contribute towards acceptance and, to a certain degree, reduce the distance between the Court and the citizens, the significance of which should not be underestimated. The same goes *mutatis mutandis* for taking into consideration the leading literature on European law. The practice of referencing academics is, for instance, customary not only in Germany, Austria, Switzerland, but also in the UK and the US.

The question arises as to the extent to which these *desiderata* have been implemented over the past two decades. The answer is: to a considerable extent. The EFTA Court’s judgments are more detailed than the ones of its EEA sister court. There are several reasons for this. First of all, the Court works without AGs. Second, it doesn’t carry the whole French tradition rucksack. Third, a court of three, which has faced open hostility from certain quarters, cannot simply lay down the law, even if it wanted to do so. Fourth, there is no written obligation on courts of last resort in the EFTA pillar to refer cases and preliminary rulings are not formally binding on the referring court. The EFTA Court therefore has to convince, by seeking the acceptance of its audiences, in particular of the branches of government —the legislature, the executive and the judiciary—, but also of academic circles in its Member States. However, it was always clear that other audiences are equally important, the EU institutions and the institutions of the EU Member States as well as academia in the whole of Europe and in some cases beyond Europe. As I have said many times, the Court therefore tried to make a virtue of necessity. And as I have shown, we also tended to be fact-based and effect-based and were reluctant to rely on assumptions, presumptions or fictions. An assumption is something that is accepted as true or as certain to happen, without proof. A presumption is an idea that is taken to be true based on probability; it may be rebutted. A fiction is an unrebuttable presupposition. Obviously, such shortcuts are necessary, but in certain cases, they are at the expense of private operators and may lead to unjust results.

It may have helped us that for quite some time our caseload was limited; this gave us time to reflect. However, between 2011 and 2017, the number of incoming cases increased significantly. Moreover, the fact that the EFTA Court cannot expect to receive another case involving the same, or a similar, problem in the short-term will prompt it to give broad reasons.

Overall, the EFTA Court's approach is closer to the English and German traditions than to the French style. EU lawyers from the practising bar, the judiciary (including the Union courts) and academia have commended us on that. Ian Forrester, now a judge of the EU General Court, wrote in 2014 that the processes the EFTA Court uses

> convey a readiness to listen, to engage in public and to be independent.

Eric Morgan de Rivery and Alexandre Fall, both private practitioners in Paris, underlined in our 20 year anniversary *Festschrift* that

> the EFTA Court has made a soft but significant contribution to the EU legal order by proposing pragmatic and common sense solutions.

John Temple Lang, a practitioner who has also extensive experience in DG Competition and in the Commission's Legal Service, wrote in 2012 that the

> EFTA Court's judgments are more concise, clearer, simpler, more practical and more readable than the judgments of the other European Courts. They are written with confidence and authority, and show less need to recall and repeat extensively the texts of the judgments in previous cases.

At the EFTA Court's Spring Conference in 2017, Peter Freeman, Chairman of the UK Competition Appeal Tribunal and former Chairman of the UK Competition Commission, has pointed to a number of

> examples of a flexible, pragmatic approach which has enabled the EFTA Court to punch above its weight in jurisprudential terms, particularly in the field of competition law.

References to Own Precedents

In the early days of the three-member Court, we had a discussion on whether we should systematically base ourselves on precedent (in the civil law meaning of the term) or not. We knew that the ECJ had only started to reference its own case law after the accession of the common law countries UK and Ireland. I spoke about the problem with WTO AB Chairman Jim Bacchus and he told me that the issue had also been on the table of his institution when it took up its activity. It seems that if a new international or supranational tribunal is established, those who want the institution to keep a low profile oppose the adoption of a precedent system. At the end of the day, we decided to adopt such an approach.

Relying on our own previous case law has several functions. First, it creates predictability and enhances legal certainty. Second, it secures the orderly development of the case law. Third, it also strengthens the position of the Court, in particular vis-à-vis the governments. It does not follow from this that the Court is not prepared to overrule earlier case law. Overruling will or should, however, require careful reasoning.

Those who read our judgments attentively will notice that following the EFTA Court's rendering of its seminal, and controversial, *Sveinbjörnsdóttir* judgment on EEA State liability,[4] there have been ample references to that case. This is not a coincidence, the message had to be got across. We were also quite explicit when exemplifying the proportionality principle in the gambling law cases *Gaming Machines* and *Ladbrokes* or when we held in the first *DB Schenker* case that a private plaintiff seeking damages contributes to the realisation of a market economy. Nevertheless, maintaining a system of precedent constitutes a challenge for a small court. Due to fluctuation, there is a clear risk that the Court will lose its institutional memory. Those who leave do not always pass on what they have learnt, and newcomers sometimes think they know better—or they don't care. In the case of the EFTA Court, there is, in addition, the risk that people will simply look to the ECJ. In the end, this can lead to an institutional amnesia. It is the task of the EFTA Court's judges to ensure that the lawyers working at the Court are conscious of this problem. In addition to participating in the cases, I have tried to contribute through my extrajudicial activities. In October 2013, I chaired an international conference at the HSG in cooperation with the UT on "The Role of Precedent in Dispute Resolution". Speakers were prominent scholars from Europe, the US—*inter alia* Dean Larry Sager from UT law—and Japan as well as judges of international courts. The presentations and discussions are documented in a book.[5]

References to EU Case Law

As regards the dialogue with the EU judiciary, there is hardly a judgment of the EFTA Court that does not cite ECJ case law. This was so from the very beginning and for a new court that wanted to establish itself, it was the right thing to do. I think, however, that in the meantime there is room for improvement. There is, even after all these years, rather too strong a tendency to refer to our sister court. If somebody were to analyse our case law carefully, he or she would easily discover that there are differences in approach between the individual judges.

References to Opinions of AGs

In the early years it would have been unthinkable for the Court to openly take into account the opinions of the ECJ's AGs rendered in parallel cases. However, from

[4]See for details Chapter 10.

[5]See for details Chapter 13.

2001 onwards, the AGs have become the Court's regular dialogue partners. This dialogue is bilateral in nature. On the one hand, we have cited relevant opinions of the AGs and, on the other hand, the AGs have served as a gateway for incorporating our case law into that of the ECJ. I have to say that our relationship with some of the ECJ's AGs has been one of the most positive experiences during my time as an EFTA Court judge.

References to ECtHR Case Law
As I have said before, from 1998 onwards the EFTA Court has taken into account and cited the case law of the ECtHR.[6]

References to National Courts' Case Law
At the Nordic Law Conference 2005 in Reykjavík, I asked the question of whether, from the standpoint of dialogue, but also in reaction to the opposition to the EU Constitutional Treaty, the Luxembourg courts should change their style and try to move closer to the citizens. I said:

> Whether they can go on with their dry legalistic and some say even minimalist style in times of judicial dialogue is an open question. We at the EFTA Court are trying to be more comprehensive, but we have to work without an Advocate General. So I would like to ask in particular two questions: First, should we start to systematically refer to national Supreme Courts or even to academic literature? As far as I can see, the ECJ has once referred to the German Constitutional Court and we once cited the Danish Supreme Court. And the second question is, isn't it time to put all the reasons that have crossed the judges' mind on the table, the real reasons? It could be argued that this is not only a matter of policy, but also of intellectual honesty. And it would enhance the framework conditions for dialogue.

The ECJ does not have a policy of referencing judgments national courts. The close relationship with the ECJ has also prevented the EFTA Court from developing a real policy in this respect. Nevertheless, the Court has cited national courts of both EU and EEA/EFTA countries on a few occasions. A general statement to that effect was already made in 1996. In paragraph 15 of the *Eidesund* judgment of 27 November 1995 and in paragraph 21 of the *Langeland* judgment of the same day, the EFTA Court held that

> in the interpretation of EEA law, it may be a factor of some interest to ascertain how the different Member States have demonstrated, through their implementation into national law of EEA legal provisions, how they perceived and interpreted those EEA legal provisions which the Member States have adopted and which the Court is called upon to interpret. In connection herewith, the interpretation and application by national courts of implementing national legislation may cast light on the contents given to that legislation by the state's legislators. Obviously, how much reliance is to be placed on a national court decision will depend on whether the decision stands out as representative, as does, for instance, an authoritative interpretation given by the highest court of appeals in the country in question.

This apparently caused uproar in the Commission's Legal Service, where it was feared that this (indirectly) could go against the sacred autonomy of Union law. These worries were exaggerated.

---

[6]See for details Chapter 12.

We became more concrete in our *Paranova* v *Merck* judgment of 8 July 2003, a parallel import of pharmaceuticals case. After having described the essential features of the case, we noted that similar cases had been brought before EC Member States' national courts and mentioned three judgments by the Supreme Court of Denmark and one by the English High Court, all delivered in 2002.[7]

In *Beatrix Koch*, the EFTA Court ruled on 13 June 2013 that assurance undertakings must not provide advice to the policy holder, but they must give precise and objective information before the contract is concluded.[8] In paragraph 77, we held that

> without prejudice to other provisions, and as long as their effectiveness is not affected, [....] [the directives concerned] do not prevent the EEA States from applying general principles of national contract law to establish an obligation to provide advice concerning complex financial instruments, such as life assurance, sold to consumers.

On that point, we referred to a judgment of the German Federal Supreme Court (*Bundesgerichtshof*) of 11 July 2012.

In *Creditinfo Lánstraust*, a case concerning the appropriateness of charges made for the re-use of public sector information under the respective Directive,[9] the EFTA Court stated in paragraph 46 of its judgment of 16 December 2013:

> Whether a charge levied in violation of EEA law is passed on, depends on the circumstances of the case, in particular the market structure. For example, a monopoly operator can be expected to pass on the entire charge. If there is competition, an operator may not be able to pass on any part of it (compare with regard to this conclusion the judgment by the Supreme Court of Norway of 28 May 2008 in case 2007/1738, Rt. 2008 p. 738, paragraph 52).

It should be noted that the citations in *Beatrix Koch* and *Creditinfo Lánstraust* were made shortly after the clash with the Norwegian Supreme Court in the *STX* case.[10]

References to Academic Literature

Whether you consult academic literature is a matter of methodology, but whether you cite authors in a judgment is a matter of style. As regards the question of whether "*la doctrine*" should be cited, the EFTA Court has not adopted a real policy. Nevertheless, in three landmark cases, the publications of prominent professors were quoted.

In *Icesave I*, the EFTA Court did not base its decision exclusively on a statutory interpretation of the Deposit Guarantee Directive (94/19/EC) when it held that it did not envisage an obligation of result to ensure payment to depositors in the Landsbanki branches in the Netherlands and the UK by the Icelandic government in a systemic crisis of the magnitude experienced in Iceland. It also held that, from an economic viewpoint, moral hazard had to be avoided and referred to US Nobel laureate Joseph E. Stiglitz. Moreover, it cited a paper by University of Ghent

---

[7]See for details Chapter 21.

[8]See for details Chapter 18.

[9]2003/98/EC.

[10]See with regard to these two cases, Chapter 18.

financial law Professor Michel Tison on another pertinent issue.[11] As regards Professor Stiglitz, some commentators said that quoting an economist in a judgment was inappropriate. I think that is an expression of narrow-mindedness. These people have not understood what economic law is about.

In February 2013, the International Center for Ethics, Justice and Public Life of Brandeis University stated in a blog under the heading "Developments in International Justice" that

> [t]he so-called *Icesave* judgment is notable in being the first in the history of a European court of regional integration to reference academic literature (paragraphs 167 and 176).[12]

This assertion is true although I think, in all modesty, that our *Icesave I* judgment is also notable for other reasons.

Whereas I acted as the Judge Rapporteur in *Icesave I*, I was unable to sit in *Stig Arne Jonsson,* which was decided on 20 March 2013.[13] The EFTA Court confirmed that the Posted Workers Directive

> lays down in its Article 3(1) an exhaustive list of terms and conditions of employment that host EEA States in national law must require undertakings established in other EEA States to observe when they post workers to their territory.

It added that, however, that

> the directive does not harmonise the material content of those terms and conditions. Their content may thus be freely defined by the EEA States, in compliance with the EEA Agreement, in particular the freedom to provide services, and the general principles of EEA law.

On these points, the Court referred to its own case law and to the case law of the ECJ as well as to University of Cambridge Professor Catherine Barnard's seminal book on EU Employment Law.

The third reference to academic literature is contained in my Presidential order of 20 February 2017 concerning the request of the Liechtenstein Princely Court of Appeal for an accelerated procedure to be applied in *Nobile*. The relevant question was whether the Court would still be composed in a lawful way after the decision of the EEA/EFTA Governments to reappoint the incumbent Norwegian judge for a second, non-renewable term of three years of 1 December 2016. Since that decision was replaced by a second decision that granted Christiansen a second term of six years, the request for an accelerated procedure was dismissed. In view of the blatant attack on the Court's integrity and on the independence of its judges, I nevertheless used the opportunity to get a few things straight when stating in paragraph 22 of the order that

> [t]here are indications that the nomination of Judge Christiansen for an abridged term by the Government of Norway was not free of political considerations.

---

[11] See for details Chapter 25.

[12] http://www.brandeis.edu/ethics/internationaljustice/inthenews/2013/Feb2013.html.

[13] See for details Chapters 8 and 26.

I referred to the description of events and the conclusions of University of Oslo Professor Mads Andenæs and University of Bergen Professor Halvard Haukeland Fredriksen in their article "*EFTA-domstolen under press*" (EFTA Court under pressure), which at the time was forthcoming in the Swedish journal *Europarättslig tidskrift* No 1 2017.

Having said this, I admit that citing academic literature is a sensitive thing to do for an international respectively supranational court of our kind that does not dispose of a research department. However, in major cases such citations may, depending on the circumstances, strengthen the judgment.

3.3 Use of dicta

According to English common law tradition, a judgment may contain two elements: *ratio decidendi* and *obiter dicta*. *Ratio decidendi* means the reason or, the foundation on which the judgment rests. *Dicta*, on the other hand, are not necessary for the judgment to be complete. They are said "*en passant*" (in passing) and whether it is appropriate to insert them is often controversial. In the common law, the *ratio decidendi* has precedential value whereas *dicta* are only persuasive.

As I stated when speaking about interpretation, the common law doctrine of precedent does not as such apply in European law. However, there are considerations that are necessary for a judgment to be properly reasoned and other elements, which may or may not be added. As a matter of principle, I have always favoured a liberal approach to the use of *dicta*. A European Court with a limited case load cannot remain silent if it realises that there is an unresolved legal problem it would like to address. This is particularly so if governments try to prevent cases from reaching the Court's table. Obviously there must still be a certain connection to the case at hand. However, the question I have heard all too often "do we really need this?" does not resolve the problem. Even if a decision, strictly speaking, only concerns the parties involved in the case, it will also have effects beyond those parties. Certainly, it is not easy to tell in every case what is the *ratio decidendi* and what are *dicta*. Even the judges may not be unanimous on the issue. There may also be situations where a judge who has strong feelings on the need to address a certain issue may manage to sneak a dictum into the judgment without his or her colleagues realising.

The EFTA Court has included *dicta in its judgments* on a number of occasions. The most serious ones were probably *Irish Bank* and *Jonsson*. *Irish Bank* was referred by the Reykjavík District Court and involved, *inter alia*, the question of whether the EFTA Court should take the questions of the Reykjavík District Court as the basis for its judgment or the amended questions of the Supreme Court. The problem was addressed against the background of the Icelandic appeal system. The EFTA Court responded to the question, but it also used the opportunity to make some fundamental statements on the question of whether national courts of last resort are free to refer a question of EEA law to the EFTA Court or not.

Commentators have seen this in the context of the unwillingness of the Norwegian Supreme Court to make use of the preliminary reference procedure. They were right. *Jonsson*, a reference from the Borgarting Court of Appeal, involved the question of whether a provision of Norwegian law under which entitlement to the payment of unemployment benefits was made conditional on actual presence in Norway was compatible with EEA law. The EFTA Court held that this was not the case. However, it did not leave it at that. Two months before, the Supreme Court of Norway had in its *STX* judgment not only deviated from the EFTA Court's *STX* ruling, but it had also openly criticised the latter. Since the Supreme Court's judgment was flawed in several respects, the EFTA Court used the *Jonsson* case to remind the Supreme Court that if unclear questions of EEA law were not referred to the Court, unnecessary mistakes in the interpretation and application of EEA law could result and coherence and reciprocity in relation to the rights of EEA citizens, including EFTA nationals, in the EU could be jeopardised.[14]

In *Kolbeinsson*, ESA submitted that the principles established by the ECJ in *Köbler* concerning judicial wrongdoing with regard to EU law also applied under EEA law. Accordingly, an EEA State was, in the Authority's view, liable for breach of EEA law by its courts provided that EEA law had been "manifestly infringed". The Norwegian Government disagreed, arguing that there was no basis for State liability for incorrect application of EEA law by national courts. In the EU, State liability for decisions by national courts was a kind of sanction against national courts of last resort breaching their duty to request preliminary rulings on the interpretation of EU law, but there was no such duty under EEA law. The Court noted that the referring court had not posed such a question. But if an EEA/EFTA State were to incur liability for judicial wrongdoing, the breach would have to be manifest under the *Köbler* standard.

A further example is the *Oslo University* case. After having held that earmarking a certain number of university posts for women was unlawful, the EFTA Court in paragraph 57 added a dictum. What counts when you have an application by a man and an application by a woman for a chair at a university? You compare the length of the publication list, the number of courses taught and all other academic activities. The result is that the man's list has one hundred titles whereas the woman's list has only sixty. However, what does not show up on the list is what the woman did in addition to that, namely, gave birth to children, raised children etc. Our judgment acknowledged that female life experience may be relevant to the suitability of a candidate in certain fields of academia.

In *Icesave I*, the Court dismissed ESA's plea that Iceland had acted in a discriminatory way by failing to ensure timely payment of the minimum amount of compensation to Icesave depositors in the Netherlands and in the UK. ESA had not attacked Iceland's decision not to move over the entirety of deposits of foreign Icesave depositors into "new Landsbanki" as it had for domestic Landsbanki depositors. In academic literature, Norwegian Supreme Court Justice Ingvald Falch argued that had ESA not limited the case in the way described,

[14]See for details Chapter 25.

> the Court could hardly have concluded that no discrimination had taken place.

It must, however, be noted that in paragraph 227 of the judgment, the EFTA Court added in *dicta* that even if ESA's respective plea had been formulated differently,

> one would have to bear in mind that the EEA States enjoy a wide margin of discretion in making fundamental choices of economic policy in the specific event of a systemic crisis provided that certain circumstances are duly proven.

ESA itself had made this point in the *Sigmarsson* case.[15]

Another case containing *dicta* is *Hellenic Capital Market Commission*, a reference from the Administrative Court of Liechtenstein. Under Liechtenstein law, a capital market authority of an EEA State that requests information from the competent Liechtenstein authority is obliged to specify the facts giving rise to the suspicion that the prohibition on insider dealing and market manipulation has been infringed. We held that this provision was not compatible with the Market Abuse Directive.[16] In *dicta*, we added, however, that the Administrative Court in its referral raised the question of whether the requested authority may refuse to act if it has reason to believe that the request amounts to a search for incriminating evidence in the absence of reasonable suspicion (i.e. a "fishing expedition"). It was not regarded as necessary to go into this matter because there was no indication whatsoever that this might be the case in the proceedings at hand.

In the *Icelandic Veterinary Checks* case, the EFTA Court held on 14 November 2017 that Iceland had breached the Veterinary Checks Directive[17] by maintaining in force: (i) authorisation systems for the import of fresh meat and meat products, of raw eggs and raw egg products, of unpasteurised milk and dairy products processed from unpasteurised milk (ii) additional requirements concerning certain cheeses; and (iii) an administrative practice requiring importers to make a declaration and obtain an approval for the import of treated egg and dairy products. The Court had in a preliminary ruling already held on 1 February 2016 in *Ferskar kjötvörur* that maintaining rules demanding that an importer of raw meat products applies for a special permit before the products are imported, and requiring the submission of a certificate confirming that the meat has been stored frozen for a certain period prior to customs clearance was not compatible with the directive. In view of the obvious reluctance of the Icelandic Government to take appropriate measures the EFTA Court in the second case in *dicta* drew the attention of private operators to the possibility of suing the Icelandic State for compensation. In paragraph 113, the Court stated, *inter alia*:

> In this context it could be recalled that the proper functioning of the EEA Agreement is dependent on individuals and economic operators being able to rely on the rights intended for their benefit [….]. It is a general principle of EEA law that an EFTA State is obliged to

[15]See for details Chapter 25.

[16]2003/6/EC.

[17]89/662/EEC.

> provide for compensation for damages caused to individuals and economic operators provided that the EEA rule infringed intends to confer rights on them, that the breach is sufficiently serious and that a direct causal link exists between the breach and the damages suffered [….].

The last example I want to give concerns the unlawful reappointment of a judge for an abridged term of only three years. When the first decision in *Nobile* was rendered on 14 February 2017, the composition of the Court was according to the law. The Court nevertheless did not limit itself to stating this, but made it clear in a number of statements that the first decision of the governments' on Christiansen's reappointment was unlawful because it violated the independence of the judges. It also added remarks on the importance of this independence. I did the same, when I decided on whether or not to apply an accelerated procedure in my Presidential Order of 20 February 2017. I felt that the value of judicial independence had to be emphasised even more.[18]

4 Correlation Between Style and Content

There is a correlation between a court's judicial style and the content of its judgments, and in the case of the EFTA Court this connection is quite obvious. In the light of the factors referred to above—size and consequently lack of power, judicial constitution of the EFTA pillar, lack of an AG, limited popularity in our largest Member State,—we knew that we had to foster acceptance by our audiences. The main tools in fostering acceptance are the reasons given in a judgment.

Promoting acceptance is, however, more easily said than done. It does not, in my view, mean that a court should compromise on the merits of a case and, for example, give too much weight to the wishes of governments in order to appease them. Having said that, it is clear that you must always keep a sense of proportion. It may be that the Court was assisted in this by what I sometimes refer to as "Scandinavian-Alemannian pragmatism". The EFTA Court is a down-to-earth court of economic law that resolves the cases brought before it. As I have explained before, this includes, in my view, a functional approach that takes into account the macroeconomic consequences of a certain outcome. However, it has never been our aim to pursue political integration.

Incidentally, the Court's pragmatism and its willingness to question itself also finds expression in its architecture. We were obviously too small to have premises in the style of other European courts. Ours is a rather understated courtroom with plenty of light. However, there is an important piece of art in the courtroom, a blue neon installation, which was made by the artists Chiarenza & Hauser. Marie-Antoinette Chiarenza was born in Tunis and Daniel Hauser in Berne. They are based in Zurich. The installation reads:

---

[18]See for details Chapter 28.

Is JUSTICE justice?

When the Court hears a case, the sign is lit up. I don't know of any other court that would so openly question itself in this way. It makes me proud that my colleagues and I agreed to purchase this piece of art and to place it in the courtroom.

5 Lack of a Dissenting Opinion System

At the EFTA Court, minority judges don't have the right to present a dissenting or a concurring opinion. There exists a secrecy of deliberations and of vote. The judges must take an oath not to break this rule.[19] I have mentioned that in 1999 we have had a critical case in this context when the President at that time, Bjørn Haug, extrajudicially distanced himself publicly from the Court's landmark judgment acknowledging EEA State liability in *Sveinbjörnsdóttir*.[20] The prohibition on making dissent public has been taken over from EU law. In the Union courts, the secrecy has, in general, been preserved. However, there have been some high profile cases in which the vote is believed to be known. Pundits have claimed that the seminal judgment in *van Gend en Loos* from 1963, in which the ECJ acknowledged that provisions of Community law could have a direct effect and could thus be invoked in court, was reached with 4 votes to 3. Some people even claim to know how the individual judges have voted. Another landmark decision is the judgment of the CFI's Grand Chamber of 17 September 2007 in *Microsoft* v *Commission*. In this judgment, the CFI upheld the Commission's decision of March 2004 to order Microsoft to pay EUR 497 million for abuse of a dominant position, at the time this was the largest fine ever imposed by the EU. American journalists claimed that the ruling in favour of the Commission was reached with 7 votes to 6. President Vesterdorf made it clear in later speeches that he was not happy with the outcome of the case.

As I have said before, one of the main reasons for renunciating a dissenting opinion system in what is now the EU was the desire to protect the judges from government pressure. However, this line of argument places the cart before the horse. In reality, the lack of a dissenting opinion system, which is tantamount to a secrecy of vote, has given the ECJ enormous power. At the same time, the protection provided to the judges may not be effective in every case. There are some revolving doors between the ECJ and the capitals of the Member States. News travels fast and rumours even faster. The late German ECJ judge Manfred Zuleeg, who was nominated by the conservative-liberal cabinet of Chancellor Helmut Kohl and appointed in 1988, was suspected of acting against the interests of his government in a number of social policy cases. In other words, the Kohl government resented the fact that Manfred Zuleeg could not be kept on the leash. Zuleeg himself

[19] See for details Chapter 21.

[20] See for details Chapter 10.

said that he felt this pressure keenly. In 1994 he was not renominated by the German government. It seems that at least in one high profile case, Zuleeg had voted in favour of his government's position. However, since he had already gained the reputation of being a leftist, this didn't help him retain his appointment. One could therefore argue that a judge might be better off under an open voting system. It goes without saying that in a three-member court it is even more difficult to ensure that the voting behaviour of the judges does not become known in the capitals.

Occasionally, departing ECJ judges from common law and Nordic countries have criticised this tradition of secrecy in their farewell addresses. Notre Dame University Professor Roger P. Alford, now U.S. Deputy Assistant Attorney General Antitrust, in 2007 lambasted what he called the inferior quality of ECJ decisions when compared with the judgments of other international tribunals and of the US Supreme Court stating:

> The European Court of Justice [....] offers the worst of all worlds: short, deductive judgments rendered by a court with too many members [....] that prohibits concurrences or dissents.

First, this characterisation is exaggerated and it does not do justice to the great achievements of the ECJ. Secondly, it is untenable to claim that without open voting and the possibility for minority judges to dissent it is impossible to draft judgments of a good quality. German courts and, according to many observers, also the EFTA Court have shown that good judgments can be rendered while abstaining from a system of dissenting and concurring opinions. What counts is whether a court is prepared to give comprehensive reasons. Nonetheless, the time has come for the introduction of a dissenting opinion regime both at the ECJ and at the EFTA Court. The current system is not compatible with the need for accountability and the right of minority judges to make their views known to the public. It should be abandoned in favour of an order that allows the appointment of judges and AGs for a single, but longer, term of office. Under such a new system the right to dissent and to concur would have to be introduced. I don't harbour any illusions that this could happen in the near future. That the EEA/EFTA States would establish such a regime on their own is difficult to imagine, both for legal and political reasons. Nevertheless, sometimes things can change faster than one might imagine. If Britain were to join the EFTA pillar after Brexit in one form or another, the system could be altered.[21]

---

[21]See regarding Brexit Chapter 31.

Chapter 28
Attack on the EFTA Court's Integrity

Contents

1 Introduction

The *rubrum* of the EFTA Court's decisions and of the orders of the President always says "Judgment of [....]" or "Order of [...]". On the next line follows the date and below the date keywords are listed that inform readers of the content of the decision. To give an example, in the landmark judgment of 18 April 2012 in *Norway Post*, the following keywords were used:

C. Baudenbacher, *Judicial Independence*, Springer Biographies,
https://doi.org/10.1007/978-3-030-02308-9_28

Action for annulment of a decision of the EFTA Surveillance Authority – Competition – Abuse of a dominant position – Market for business-to-consumer over-the-counter parcel delivery – Distribution network – Exclusivity agreements – Conduct liable to eliminate competition on the market – Justification – Duration of infringement – Fine

This feature has been taken over from the ECJ's style. The keywords are not part of the judgment. They are eye—catching and may, to a certain extent, facilitate the understanding of the ruling by summarising the most important issues involved. I do not think that in the tens of thousands of decisions rendered by the Union courts since 1952 the keywords "Integrity of the Court" have ever been used. That must be because a governmental attack, such as the one experienced by the EFTA Court in 2016, has never been launched against them. For the reasons I will state below, the keyword "Integrity of the Court" has been inserted in the President's Order in *Nobile*.

2 A Second Term for Judge Christiansen?

2.1 Divided Norwegian Administration

As explained in Chap. 3, the EFTA Court judges are, according to Article 30 SCA, appointed for a period of six years by common accord of the governments of the EFTA States Iceland, Liechtenstein and Norway. Every State has the right to nominate one of the three judges. As in the EU, reappointment is possible, and there is no age limit.

I was reappointed three times,[1] and all the judges from Iceland were reappointed once. The first Icelandic judge, Thór Vilhjálmsson, retired after nine years on the EFTA Court bench, the second one, Thorgeir Örlygsson, resigned during his second mandate because he was appointed to his country's Supreme Court and the third one, Páll Hreinsson, is currently sitting. The first Norwegian judge, Bjørn Haug, was 72 when he retired in 1999 at the end of his first term. The second Norwegian Judge, Per Tresselt, was 69 when he also retired at the end of one term in 2005. I do not know whether he had sought a second term, but I do not think so. The third Norwegian Judge, Henrik Bull, stepped down from the Court after five years and became a Justice of his country's Supreme Court. The fourth, Per Christiansen took office on 13 January 2011. The EEA/EFTA Governments appointed him for a term of six years in violation of Article 7 of the Court's Statute which provides that a judge who is to replace a member of the Court whose term of office has not expired

shall be appointed for the remainder of his predecessor's term.

Thus, Per should only have been appointed for the one remaining year of Henrik Bull's term. The Court protested to the governments, to no avail. This breach of the law was not a good omen for the future.

[1]My second reappointment was temporarily blocked by a foreign government; see Chapter 23.

In 2015, Judge Christiansen let his government know that his first mandate would end in January 2017 and that he was seeking a second term. It appears that the Norwegian Ministry of Foreign Affairs was prepared to propose to the other two governments that Per be reappointed for another six-year term. However, apparently the Ministry of Justice and the Attorney General voiced reservations. As time went by, it became clearer and clearer that the refusal to give Per another six-year term was politically motivated. On 6 September 2016, the tabloid newspaper *Verdens Gang* reported that bureaucrats who opposed such a prolongation were arguing that Norway had, as of 2012, lost seven out of nine infringement cases ("*Tapte syv av ni saker*"). When I read this, I was reminded of the Sejersted report where exactly the same charge was made.[2] It became rather obvious that those who had strong feelings in this matter wanted to get rid of Christiansen. In reality, however, Per had nothing to do with the Norwegian Government's big losses. Cases like *Pedicel*, *Gaming Machines*, *Ladbrokes* or *Norwegian Waterfalls* were decided long before he joined the EFTA Court bench. These were the proceedings in which the Court rejected the mercantilist ideas of the government and I was blamed for the outcome in certain press organs. The real reason for the discontent of Per's critics was another. Not all people in the Oslo administration liked the fact that I had been the Court's President since January 2003. In April 2011, Norwegian bureaucrats—who did not want to be named—had expressed their dissatisfaction to the author of the "Kong Carl" article in DN that I had allegedly gained so much power.[3] Since then I had been re-elected as the Court's President a fourth and a fifth time in 2012 and 2015, that means during Per's term of office.

2.2 A Norwegian Panel Dominated by Bureaucrats

A three-member panel was established consisting of the Chair of the Norwegian Advisory Panel on Judicial Appointments, Yngve Svendsen, as President, the former Permanent Under-Secretary of State in the Ministry of Justice and the Police and former Governor of Svalbard, Morten Ruud, and the Director General in the Legal Affairs Department of the Ministry of Foreign Affairs Margit F. Tveiten, the lady we had met when visiting Minister Helgesen in October 2014.[4] In other words, two of the three members were current or former civil servants and there was no representative of the practising bar. In addition, none of the members had any experience whatsoever in EEA law. Yngve Svendsen was the President of a local first instance court, and had a reputation for deferring to the political branch. Morten Ruud had had a central role in judicial appointments while Permanent

[2]See for details Chapter 24.

[3]See Chapter 23.

[4]See for details Chapter 26.

Under-Secretary. He had gained the reputation of being the advocate of the governments interest. After his retirement as a bureaucrat he continued to exercise this function.

The Norwegian government published a vacancy notice. Female candidates were especially encouraged to apply. In addition to the requirements laid down in Article 30 SCA—independence beyond doubt and qualification for the highest judicial office in the Member State or jurisconsult of recognised competence—the notice stated that a law degree, relevant legal experience, very good EEA law expertise, and excellent knowledge of English were required. International experience was only listed as "desirable". The deadline for applications was set as 19 August 2016.

When I read the description of the tasks, I asked myself how on earth a purely Norwegian panel, which only knew the situation in Luxembourg by hearsay, could assess whether a candidate met the needs of a three-member court European court that: had a manning table of 19 and an increasing case load; faced novel legal questions in the majority of its cases; and had to be able to keep pace with its much larger sister court, the ECJ. My fear was that Norway might nominate somebody who would predominantly deal with constitutional and institutional issues und would possibly try to turn back the clock with regard to national sovereignty, but would have difficulties in dealing with the "beef". After some reflection, on 25 July 2016 I sent the panel a letter in which I stated that the important questions relating to: effect; primacy and State liability; the scope of application of the EEA Agreement and its *sui generis* nature; and the consequences of the principle of reciprocity for access to justice, had mostly been settled. The current challenges related to substantive EEA law, i.e. Single Market law. My letter read, *inter alia*:

> EEA Single Market law is economic law. For example, the Court had to deal with the legal consequences of the downfall of the Icelandic banks. This involved questions of financial market law, banking law and bankruptcy law. The Court has furthermore decided cases involving issues of contract law, insurance law, labour law, internet law, capital market law, unfair competition law, IP law, competition law and State aid law, but also all sorts of issues concerning the fundamental freedoms. As regards these freedoms, the principle of proportionality is of utmost significance. Human rights may be addressed in crucial cases concerning matters of economic law. In that respect, issues such as the burden and standard of proof, the scope of judicial review and access to documents may be mentioned as examples.

I ended by emphasising that in the light of the Court's situation, a judge must be able to hit the ground running and handle such cases from the first day. All members of the Court should therefore have a sound background in economic law.

In order to make sure that potential candidates became aware of the letter, I ordered the registry to put it on the Court's website. After the expiration of the application period, I learnt that four people had applied: the incumbent Per Christiansen, University of Oslo Professors Mads Andenæs and Finn Arnesen and Karin Fløistad, a practising attorney and former lawyer with the Attorney General. I had met Finn Arnesen several times and knew Karin Fløistad because she had pleaded before the EFTA Court. Mads Andenæs I had only once briefly seen at dinner after my "beef lecture".[5] But of course I knew him from his publications. Unlike the other Norwegian professors who dealt with EEA law, he had pursued his academic career at top universities in the United Kingdom. Professor Andenæs had already applied for the position of EFTA Court judge in 2010 and Christiansen was preferred to him.

2.3 The Norwegian Public Becomes Aware of the Matter

By inviting the Norwegian Attorney General and the Norwegian Bar Association to comment on the required qualifications, the panel acted in a questionable way. Whereas the Attorney General is a regular player in the proceedings of the EFTA Court and thus has a direct interest in the outcome of the cases, the Norwegian Bar Association is not.

On 6 September 2016, the tabloid *Verdens Gang* wrote that bureaucrats in the Ministry of Justice, with the support of the Attorney General, had seen to it that an open competition was held, instead of renominating Christiansen without further ado. The article said, moreover, that reservations were voiced against Karin Fløistad and Finn Arnesen. However, Fredrik Sejersted who was interviewed did not limit himself to general remarks on the required profile of the candidates, but actively endorsed both Ms Fløistad and Professor Arnesen as being qualified ("*Jeg mener begge er kvalifisert*"). The other two candidates did not get his backing.

Alf-Bjarne Johnson, a journalist from *Verdens Gang*, called me and said that my letter to the Norwegian panel, in which I had written that given the workload and the size of the Court the Norwegian judge must be able to function effectively from day one, was being construed as a plea in favour of the renomination of Per and against the other candidates. I answered that when I sent the letter, I did not know who would seek the position and that it was thus not correct to assume that the letter was directed against any particular candidate. However, the letter was in fact directed against anyone who did not have sufficient knowledge and understanding of EEA Single Market law.

I answered further questions from Mr. Johnson the next day and was correctly quoted in *Verdens Gang* of 7 September 2016 in the following way:

> If an EFTA Court judge is not absolutely independent and impartial, this will not only harm the reputation of the country that has nominated him/her. He/she will also have a bad standing within the court and loose influence on the outcome of the cases.

The newspaper published the article with the title:

> The Court demands impartial judge: warns Norway.

As always in such cases, there was no lack of devious and mischievous people. I will not go into details, but it was obvious that there was a faction in the Oslo

---

[5]Chapter 20.

administration that was hoping for a judge who could not only be kept on a leash, but who would also be capable of convincing at least one of his or her colleagues in sensitive cases to take a government-friendly stand. A change in the office of President would also have been welcome. It seems that the panel even discussed these issues with the candidates.

3 Abridging a Judge's Term at All Costs

3.1 A Cheap Compromise

On 12 October 2016, the applicants were told that the panel had ranked Per Christiansen first. Per was, however, informed that due to the age limit of 70 under Norwegian law, he could only be reappointed for a term of three years. According to an article in *Verdens Gang*, which was not contradicted by the government, the decision to limit his second term to three years was based on a political compromise. When asked by *Verdens Gang* what I thought about this nomination, I said that the three-year term clearly violated Article 30 of the ESA/Court Agreement. In November 2016, the Norwegian Government nominated Christiansen for a second term, which was to last for three years and was non-renewable.

3.2 The Two Other Governments Have Reservations

The governments of the two other EEA/EFTA States Iceland and Liechtenstein indicated that they were not happy with the Norwegian nomination. However, since this had already been made public, the Norwegian bureaucrats who were in charge of the matter felt that they could not change track without losing face.

3.3 The Two Other Governments Cave In

As the super-power of the EFTA pillar, Norway put pressure on the two smaller partner States. After some hesitation, the Icelandic Government concurred. After having prevailed in the *Icesave* saga, they should have known that an independent EFTA Court is of the utmost importance.[6]

As I have said many times to people in the Liechtenstein administration, small countries have no other weapon than the law. Everybody agreed whenever I emphasised this truism. However, it was noted in much the same fashion as a

---

[6]See for details Chapter 25.

Sunday homily. The Liechtenstein Government had already caved in when Christiansen was, in breach of the Statute, given a first mandate of six years in 2011. However, the issue that was now at stake was much more important. The dossier was in the hands of the Minister for Foreign Affairs, Aurelia Frick, a lawyer with a Ph.D. degree. In a first meeting on 22 November 2016, the five-member government did not take a decision. Nevertheless, one week later, on 29 November 2016, the Liechtensteiners threw in the towel. It appears that a former Liechtenstein judge of the ECtHR was asked for his view. Without knowing the EFTA Court's system and probably influenced by the age limit of 70 at his former court, the gentleman said that this was indeed a matter of interpretation. With this, the die was cast and the government gave its consent.

All in all, the attitude of the "two Lilliput States", as a University of Bergen Professor called them in the public controversy over the affair, was shaped by a mixture of incompetence and spinelessness.

3.4 The Unlawful Decision

On 1 December 2016, the three EEA/EFTA Governments adopted a decision to reappoint Judge Christiansen for a non-renewable term of three years. The reason given was that in three years, he would turn 70 and that under Norwegian law, 70 was the mandatory retirement age for Justices of the *Høyesterett*, the Norwegian Supreme Court. The underlying rationale, which was not spelled out in the decision, was that eligibility to the Supreme Court of the nominating country is one of three conditions for becoming an EFTA Court Judge. The governments concluded as follows: since Christiansen will no more fulfil the condition for sitting on the Supreme Court of his country once he reached 70, by analogy he would also be unable to sit on the EFTA Court. This argument was flawed. The condition that a candidate for the EFTA bench must possess the qualifications required for appointment to the highest judicial offices in his or her country relates solely to the competence of the candidates, not to their age. The decision was also dreadful for two other reasons: It stated in a recital that it was

> without prejudice to the term of office of any judge who may be reappointed in the future.

This was blatant discrimination and in direct opposition to the rule of law. Apparently, the two other governments had insisted on a sentence being introduced to ensure that their judge would not be subject to the Norwegian "70-year rule." The decision further stated in Article 6 that

> [b]y assuming office, Mr. Christiansen accepts the conditions of this appointment as stated in Articles 1-5 above.

Christiansen had in fact been forced to accept the three–year term when faced with the threat that if he was unwilling to do so, he would have to go home immediately. Not everybody can be heroic in such circumstances.

The decision of the governments constituted a severe breach of the rule of law. This was already bad enough in itself. However, it was equally worrying that the illegality of the decision was compounded by the fact that the tortfeasors were pretty certain that they would get away with their actions. At this point, I should mention a factor that often contributes to governments daring to proceed in such an unlawful way: namely the mindlessness of other actors. Ignorance and arrogance are the common threads characterising most unlawful government actions.

When I raised concerns, also from the perspective of reciprocity, bureaucrats and diplomats had the delicacy of telling me that ordinary people were not interested in this issue, and if they were, they would probably say, what's wrong with sending a 70-year old chap out to pasture? In the end, they concluded, nobody would even notice what happened if we all kept silent.

4 Courageous Lawyers Stand Up

4.1 Complaints by Norwegian Academics

The EEA/EFTA States classified their decision as "restricted". However, this did not hinder various players from gaining access to the document. On 4 December 2016, seven Norwegian university professors and scholars of European law lodged a complaint with ESA against what they called the irregular appointment of a judge to the EFTA Court. They stated that the appointment for a three-year term contravened Article 30 SCA and that the six-year term was intended to safeguard the independence and efficiency of the EFTA Court. ESA was invited to act by initiating infringement proceedings against Norway, Iceland and Liechtenstein. Since Judge Christiansen's current term was due to expire in January urgent action was needed.

On 6 December 2016, two of the seven complainants, University of Oslo Professor Mads Andenæs, former Director of the British Institute of International and Comparative Law in London and former Director of the Centre of European Law at King's College in London, and Dr Eirik Bjørge, an Oslo-educated junior research fellow at Oxford University's Jesus College and bearer of the King's Gold Medal for his doctoral dissertation, sent a further complaint to ESA. "We are concerned", they wrote:

> that, before the appointment was made, assurances, formal or informal, have been given by ESA, or someone on its behalf, that no action would be taken in the matter. Without commenting here on the appropriateness of such assurances, or the appropriateness of making them known to the decision-makers at the national or EFTA/ESA level, the complaint we have made requires a formal reply.

Referring to the decision of the ESA/Court Committee that had been made available to them by the Norwegian Ministry of Foreign Affairs, Mads and Eirik further stated:

The six-year term is mandatory [....]. It should not be necessary to make the obvious point that, as set out by the International Court of Justice and its predecessor, it is 'a fundamental principle of international law that international law prevails over domestic law'; 'it is a generally accepted principle of international law that in the relations between Powers who are contracting Powers to a treaty, the provisions of municipal law cannot prevail over those of the treaty' (Applicability of the Obligation to Arbitrate under Sections 21 of the United Nations Headquarters Agreement of 26 June 1947, ICJ Reports 1988, p 12, 43; Greco–Bulgarian Communities PCIJ, Series B, No 17, p 32, emphasis added).

Judge Christiansen is not appointed to the Norwegian Supreme Court. 'The statutory retirement age for Norwegian Supreme Court Judges' does not apply to him. There may be an attempt to say that, since he must 'possess the qualifications required for appointment to the highest judicial offices in their respective countries,' he cannot serve after he has reached the Norwegian retirement age. That cannot allow Norway or the other states parties to depart from the clear words of the treaty text. In any event this falls at first hurdle; Judge Christiansen belongs to the category of those 'who are jurisconsults of recognised competence'. There is no Norwegian or other retirement age for 'jurisconsults', or for that matter for 'competence' as the inept procedure and drafting here demonstrates.

In addition comes the fact that the purported agreement would breach the fundamental principle of the equality of judges in international law. The arrangement according to which Judge Christiansen is to sit for only a part of his mandate is in breach of the fundamental principle of the equality of judges in international law. This principle is a principle of international inter-State dispute resolution. As the UN Secretary-General has observed: 'The principle of equality between judges is fundamental'; '[e]quality of judges is a core principle in international inter-State dispute resolution'. It is 'a general principle of law', the UN Secretary General went on to observe, 'that all members of the Court should sit on terms of complete equality' (United Nations, General Assembly, A/62/538, 8 November 2007, paras 35 and 45). This general principle applies with equal strength to the EFTA Court and it has plainly been breached by the purported appointment of Judge Christiansen for only three years.

It has been raised with us that the matter is different if the judge has accepted to serve only a three-year term.

It is not.

There is no less a breach of the clear words of the agreement.

The three year (*recte*: six year) term is mandatory. It is part of the judicial constitution of the EEA. The breach of the mandatory rules of the agreement in the ESA/Court Committee decision of 1 December also affects the position of the other side of the EEA. We understand that there have been no consultations with the European Union over the decision. We have made this complaint known to the European Commission. Urgent action by ESA is important also with a view to restoring confidence in the EEA institutions at the EU side.

The decision or the limitation to three years is invalid also if Judge Christiansen should have accepted three years.

It is inappropriate to put pressure on a judge to attempt to violate fundamental treaty obligations or to attempt to assist in doing so. It may also raise questions about that judge's behaviour in relation to the state in question and the other states parties on the ESA/Court Committee. He will no longer fulfil the requirements to judicial independence. The breach is serious and may disqualify the judge from serving on the EFTA Court. It may be difficult to see how a judge can serve on the Court under such circumstances.

Under the headline "qualified arbitrariness", the two scholars added:

> We are concerned over the statement in the recital that 'said decision is without prejudice to the term of office of any judge who may be reappointed in the future'. The decision is based on a set of individual criteria with no application to other cases. In law, whether international or domestic, words matter. Here the words indicate qualified arbitrariness.

The complaint ended with the words:

> Furthermore, judges elected or appointed in respect of Norway to international courts are usually octogenarian; the arbitrariness of the decision is particularly striking in this light.
>
> Bjørn Haug was Norwegian EFTA Court Judge and President when he retired at 72.
>
> Many further well-known examples could be given.
>
> 76 when he retired: Helge Klæstad (6 December 1885), Norwegian Judge at the International Court of Justice 1946–1961, President 1958–1961; 77 when he retired: Jens Evensen (5 November 1917), Norwegian Judge at the International Court of Justice, retired 1994; 84 when he retired: Rolv Ryssdal (27 October 1914), reappointed several times after 70, and was Norwegian Judge and President of the European Court of Human Rights when he died 8 February 1998.
>
> The age of mandatory/compulsory retirement, 70, has not been reduced since these judges served in international courts.
>
> Current European affairs and recent Norwegian history should make the authorities particularly sensitive not to appear to manipulate retirement ages for judges. See for instance the very different facts in Baka v. Hungary (application no. 20261/12) [....], but with some of the same basic issues and with statements on retirement and the independence of the judiciary. In 1940 the Norwegian Supreme court judges resigned when lower retirement limits opened for packing the court with collaborators.

4.2 ESA Reacts

It was clear, even before the governments took their disastrous decision, where this journey was heading. What was less certain was whether ESA would take action. ESA's legal staff was divided; a senior Norwegian bureaucrat tried to convince the College to remain passive. A Brussels-based EFTA diplomat said to me on 2 December 2016 that the three governments were hoping that ESA would remain inactive and that also in the past, cases had been oppressed (sic!). The important thing, that person went on to say, was that the case did not end up on the EFTA Court's ("your") table. High-level EFTA protagonists even had the nerve to tell me that since Christiansen had accepted the three-year term, everything was fine. Those three years would be the last stage of his professional life, and hence his independence was in no way affected. For these three years, everything was sorted and as regards the future, that was a bridge that could be crossed later. This line of argument was outrageous. Not only was the appointment for three years null and void. One had to take into account the potential consequences of such manipulation. What would this *modus operandi* mean for future judges? Would they not know that they were under strict surveillance by their government? If three years were fine, why would three months not also be all right? All this really amounted to one single fundamental issue: that the judges on the EFTA Court should realise that they were in fact on a leash. Following the complaint from the Norwegian academics, ESA opened proceedings and, departing from its usual practice, it set the governments very short time limits.

4.3 The Liechtenstein Court of Appeal Steps In

On 20 December 2016, the Princely Court of Appeal of Liechtenstein referred the *Nobile* case to the EFTA Court. Two questions were asked concerning the interpretation of the Insurance and Reinsurance ("Solvency II") Directive.[7] A third question, however, related to the Christiansen scandal. The Court of Appeal noted that if the EFTA Court were to decide after 16 January 2017, the day Christiansen's first mandate expired, the question would arise as to whether the judgment would be valid. Article 29 SCA, according to which decisions of the Court are valid only when "all its members" have participated in the deliberations, meant, in the Court of Appeal's view, that the members were appointed in compliance with the requirements laid down in Article 30 SCA. The appointment of judges for short periods was said to constitute a threat to judicial independence. On the latter point, the referring court cited the Universal Charter of the Judge and a leading Norwegian author. The reference caused a flurry in government circles in Vaduz. It was signed by the Presiding Judge Jürgen Nagel who had already made references to us while serving as a judge on the Princely Court. Another member of the three-judge panel was Judge Wilhelm Ungerank.

On 22 December 2016, the Princely Court of Appeal submitted a second request to the EFTA Court, this time for an accelerated procedure to be applied in *Nobile*. On 23 December 2016, the Norwegian newspaper *Verdens Gang* reported on the reference. This created huge interest.

4.4 The Norwegian Judges Association Protests

Also on 20 December 2016, the Norwegian Judges Association, in an open letter to the Minister of EEA and EU Affairs and the Ministry of Foreign Affairs, protested against the three-year appointment. The letter stated that the requirement that Judges of the EFTA Court must be qualified for appointment to the highest judicial offices in their respective countries only deals with the professional qualifications. That there is no age limit under European law also follows from the fact that jurisconsults of recognised competence are eligible. The letter stated that:

[7] 2009/138/EC; see Chapter 18.

> It makes no sense, therefore, to understand the reference to being qualified for appointment to the highest judicial offices to include national age limits.

The letter further deplored the fact that limiting the term of office of a Judge may weaken the EFTA Court's legitimacy and

> can also create a fertile climate for speculation about whether there might in fact be other reasons for reducing the term of office.

The latter remark was a clear reference to the political motives that formed the basis of the Norwegian government's action. The Judges Association added that

> [w]e find ourselves in a situation where the governments of several countries, including in Europe, are endeavouring to undermine the independence of the courts by changing their composition through various formal means. The Norwegian Judges' Association is trying to use its channels to counteract this development, and we know that this is also the Government's policy. We fear, however, that what has happened in connection with the reappointment of Judge Christiansen could undermine Norway's credibility in connection with these efforts.

This was strongly worded stuff and observers noted that one of the undersigned was Supreme Court Justice Henrik Bull, the former Norwegian judge of the EFTA Court. Later, I learned that behind the scenes, President Skúli Magnússon from the Icelandic Judges' Association, the EFTA Court's former registrar, had also been actively involved.

4.5 POLITICO *Accuses Norway of Meddling with Judicial Independence*

On 4 January 2017, the Brussels-based online newspaper *POLITICO* published an article with the title "Norway accused of meddling with judicial independence". Journalist Nicholas Hirst reported the events up to that point in time and wrote that senior Norwegian judges and academics, among them Mads Andenæs, a United Nations special rapporteur,

> accused the government of undermining the court, saying it sets a bad example to authoritarian regimes across Europe. Critics suspect the move is intended as a way of replacing the judge with someone more explicitly pro-Norwegian [....].

The article also mentioned the characterisation of the decision in question as "very unfortunate" by the Norwegian Judges Association as well as the association's allegation that it could be politically motivated. Carsten Zatschler, Director of Legal and Executive Affairs at ESA, said to *POLITICO*:

> Any question mark raised concerning the independence of an EEA institution is a very serious matter, and that makes it all the more important that we give the states a chance to make their point of view known before drawing our own conclusions.

The article finally pointed to the reference of the Liechtenstein Court of Appeal that asked the EFTA Court to clarify whether the abnormal mandate could result in its rulings being invalid. It concluded with references to the statement in the second complaint to ESA by Andenæs and Bjorge that the move was reminiscent of 1940 when

> Norwegian supreme court judges resigned when lower retirement limits opened [the way to pack] the court with collaborators.

On 13 January 2017, the EEA/EFTA States took a new decision repealing their first one and giving Per Christiansen a second mandate of six years with effect from 17 January 2017. On 16 January 2017, *POLITICO* published another article entitled:

> Norway bows to criticism and re-appoints judge for full term. EFTA reverses December decision for a half-term appointment.

5 The Court's Answers

5.1 An Absurd Notion of Bias

That Per Christiansen was biased as regards the question of the lawfulness of his three-year term was clear. I had not commented on the governments' decision of 1 December 2016, but I had in October 2016 publicly stated that the plan to reappoint a judge for a three-year term clearly violated the SCA. I am of the firm view that the President of a court, whose only direct interest in a case was to protect his institution's integrity and functioning, should not be forced to recuse himself. It would have amounted to an abuse of rights for the Norwegian government to first initiate a decision of the ESA/Court Committee that potentially undermined the integrity of the Court, and then to claim that the President of that Court was biased in defending that very integrity. If it were different, it would be very easy for the EFTA State governments to eliminate judicial control of their potentially unlawful actions by the regular Court. After discussions with my colleagues, I nevertheless recused myself from *Nobile* as regards the third question referred.

5.2 The Court's Valentine's Day Decision

On the 13 January 2017, the Court received ESA/Court Committee Decision 2017 No 1 of the same day on the reappointment of a Judge to the EFTA Court and repealing Decision 2016 No 5 of 1 December 2016. Article 1 of the new decision stated that the EFTA States had decided to reappoint Per Christiansen as a Judge of the EFTA Court, under the terms of the SCA, for a period of six years with effect from 17 January 2017.

On 14 February 2017, the EFTA Court, consisting of acting President Páll Hreinsson and ad hoc judges Martin Ospelt from Liechtenstein and Siri Teigum from Norway, issued a "decision" stating that the substantive part of the proceedings, namely the first two questions referred, would be addressed by the

Court's three regular judges. In response to the referring court's third question, the Court found that it was, following the governments' second decision, lawfully composed in a manner ensuring its independence and impartiality. However, the decision also made it clear that the governments' first decision was not compatible with Article 30 SCA. It was the first time the Court sat with two ad hoc judges. I will not comment on the Valentine's Day decision other than to point out that the Court, in violation of its Statute, failed to invite the three governments, ESA and the Commission to submit observations. It would have been particularly beneficial to learn what both surveillance bodies had to say about the Christiansen case, but also about the nomination and appointment process in the EFTA pillar in general.

5.3 The President's Washington's Birthday Order

Despite having recused myself with regard to the substance of the Court of Appeal's question concerning the lawfulness of the decision of the Governments abridging the term of office of a Judge, I retained the competence to rule on the request for accelerated procedure. The respective order was rendered on 20 February 2017, the anniversary of George Washington's Birthday.

In my order, I maintained that the composition of the EFTA Court would, in principle, be a matter of exceptional urgency, since it touched upon its integrity. The six-year term laid down in Article 30 SCA was mandatory and constituted a minimum protection of judicial independence, an essential part of the judicial constitution of the EFTA pillar. Without an independent court, the purpose of the EEA Agreement would be rendered nugatory and the EFTA States would fail to safeguard the protection of the rights of individuals and economic operators. I further emphasised that to maintain the independence of the judiciary was not a privilege for judges, but a guarantee for the respect of these rights and a bulwark of the democratic order. However, the consequences of the Court's findings in its Valentine's Day decision were such that the circumstances that existed when the national court lodged its request for an accelerated procedure ceased to exist. As a result, the request to apply an accelerated procedure was denied.

6 The Governments Show Little Discernment

6.1 The Unheard Call for the Establishment of a Supranational Panel

As I have said before, in 2011 the Court had invited the governments, to no avail, to establish a panel with the task of scrutinising candidates for judgeship nominated by the individual Governments.[8] After the Christiansen scandal, several scholars in Norway and in Sweden concurred that such a panel was necessary. On 3 April 2017, I published an essay in the Norwegian lawyers' journal ("*advokatbladet*"). The editor gave it the following title:

> There are indications that the efforts to get rid of judge Christiansen were politically motivated (*Det er ting som tyder på at anstrengelsene for å bli kvitt dommer Christiansen var politisk motivert*).

The lead read as follows:

> Although this is not the first time the Norwegian executive branch has tried to interfere with the independence of EFTA Court judges, the attempt to pack a court of only three judges is particularly egregious. (*Selv om det ikke er første gang den utøvende makt i Norge har prøvd å legge seg opp i EFTA-dommernes uavhengighet, er forsøket på å fikse en domstol med bare tre dommere spesielt sjokkerende.*)

The article was published in Norwegian, but an English version was made available online. Under the title "Mack the Knife, edition 2017", I stated:

> In the 1931 Threepenny Opera ballad of Mack the Knife, Bertolt Brecht compares the glittering world of the powerful with the dark world of the poor by using the words 'there are some who are in darkness and the others are in light, and you see the ones in brightness, those in darkness drop from sight.' In the Saga of EFTA Court Judge Per Christiansen, it is the other way around: the insignificant and naives are in the spotlight whereas the powerful, the ones who caused the mess that embarrassed the Norwegian Government, still remain hidden in the background.

I then gave a detailed description of the events, from the first decision of the EFTA States party to the EEA Agreement of 1 December 2016, followed by the complaints from Norwegian scholars, the reference of the *Nobile* case by the Liechtenstein Court of Appeal, the open letter of the Norwegian Judges' Association, the article in *POLITICO* and the governments' second decision of 13 January 2017. I explained how the reduction of Christiansen's second term came about, why it was unlawful and why all the attempts to justify the respective decision were futile. I also made it clear that the argument that Christiansen had accepted the three-year term, was irrelevant. On the one hand, the behaviour of the three EEA/EFTA Governments could be classified as mere clumsiness. However, on the other hand, there were indications that the efforts to have the incumbent judge sacked were politically motivated. I pointed to the discussion in the media on whether the incumbent judge had been sufficiently friendly towards the interests of the Norwegian State or not.

Coming back to Bertolt Brecht, I concluded by saying that

> the ones in the dark - in our case the string-pullers – must in the interest of democracy and of the rule of law step forward, come to the light and assume responsibility. These people knew that the three years' limitation would not fly. They wanted something else, namely a safe pair of hands on the Court right now. It is an inherent weakness of international and

---

[8]See for details Chapter 3.

> supranational courts that the right to appoint the judges lies in the hands of the Governments of the Member States who have a direct interest in the outcome of many cases. Although this is not the first time the Norwegian executive branch has tried to interfere with the independence of EFTA Court judges, the attempt to pack a court of only three judges is particularly egregious.

Another striking aspect of the Christiansen affair was the inability of the decision-makers to perceive legal wrong. On 31 May 2017, the State Secretary of EEA and EU Affairs, Elsbeth Sande Tronstad, felt prompted to react to my "Mack the Knife" article. She wrote:

> 13th January this year the three EFTA states in the EEA decided to re-appoint Per Christiansen for a new period of six years. Ahead of the re-appointment, a comprehensive national procedure for nomination of Norwegian judges was performed. The publication of the positon was made through public notice, and a special consultant committee assessed all the candidates thoroughly. In this way one sought to maintain the requirement of the EFTA judges' qualifications and independence, and contribute to an efficient and independent EFTA Court. This is the motivation behind Norway's appointment of the Norwegian judge, both under the re-appointment for six years, and the original appointment for three years.
>
> The decision of 1st December 2016 regarding re-appointment for three years has been set aside. The circumstances between the latter decision and the agreement between the EFTA states regarding the establishment of a supervisory body and a court article 30 is in this matter no longer a legal question as regards the re-appointment of judge Christiansen.
>
> However, I would still like to make a comment regarding the question of the EFTA Courts legitimacy and independence. When the EFTA States made the first decision regarding re-appointment for three years, they referred to the age limit for judges in Norway as a background for this decision. For this reason, the re-appointment decision made it clear that it should not have a precedent effect, i.e. for the other two EFTA states who also stood behind the decision. Ergo, the background was general, and not individual, and linked to Norwegian circumstances.
>
> This has also been referred to in a letter of 23rd January of this year to the Judge Association from the Minister of EEA and EU, Frank Bakke-Jensen, concerning the same matter.[9]

The intervention of the State Secretary shows that at a time when the EU has a functioning supranational panel in place, national committees are no longer sufficient in the EFTA pillar.

6.2 2017 EFTA Ministerial Meeting in Svalbard

At the EFTA Ministerial meeting, which took place on 26 June 2017 in Svalbard, I made the following statement:

> In 2011, the Court proposed to the Governments of the EEA/EFTA States to establish a panel with the task of scrutinizing the candidates for judgeship made by the Governments and to make a non-binding assessment. The Governments did not react. The Court recalls

[9] Unofficial translation.

> the panel set up in the EU under Article 255 TFEU and renews this invitation. There is no any valid reason why the establishment of such a panel – probably in an improved form - should be refused. A panel would contribute to securing the full independence of the Judges. This is not only required in the interest of our own citizens and business operators, but also of their counterparts in the EU pillar of the EEA. It is in other words also a matter of homogeneity and reciprocity.

Before the meeting, I had asked the Supreme Courts of our Member States for their support. The relevant proposal was supported by the Supreme Courts of Iceland and Liechtenstein. At the meeting, the Liechtenstein Government signalled its openness, whereas the Governments of Iceland and Norway remained silent. Nevertheless, when I paid him a visit in October 2017, the Icelandic Minister for Foreign Affairs Guðlaugur Þór Þórðarson pledged that he would support the establishment of such a panel.

6.3 2017 Conference "Norway in Europe"

At the conference in honour of Mads Andenæs, on 18 September 2017, Eirik Bjorge took up the issue. He also raised the suspicion that Christiansen could have entered into a gentleman's agreement with his government according to which he would step down after three years. A number of people from the Norwegian Ministry of Foreign Affairs were present. In the discussion, my old friend Jonas Myhre asked them what the reasons for their attitude of denial were.[10] He received no answer.

6.4 My Last Speech Before the ESA/Court Committee

At my appearance at the annual meeting of the ESA/Court Committee, on 13 December 2017, I recalled the Court's 2011 proposal of creating a judicial appointments panel in the EFTA pillar, which had not been taken up at that time. I observed that with hindsight, it was particularly regrettable that the EEA/EFTA governments, exactly one year earlier, had decided to abridge a judge's term of office from six to three years. I thanked those who had lodged the complaints with ESA, ESA itself for having acted swiftly and the judges in Vaduz who had referred the *Nobile* case to the EFTA Court. I once more called upon the governments to create a panel, also for reasons of homogeneity and reciprocity and concluded with the words that

[10]See for details Chapter 31.

> now is the time to take up this baton, and to see what progress may be made. The strength of the Court reflects well on the EFTA States globally, but its reputation will quickly suffer if outstanding judges are not consistently appointed.

It should be noted, in this context, that the GC has, in its judgment in *FV* v *Council* of 23 January 2018, referred to the EFTA Court's *Nobile* decision. From the point of view of homogeneity and reciprocity, the lack of a panel to examine candidates proposed by governments in the EFTA pillar is untenable. It is incomprehensible that the EU is not taking up this issue in the EEA Joint Committee.

Chapter 29
The Commission—The EFTA Court's Patron Saint?

Contents

1 The Commission's Role

The European Commission is an influential player in the governance structure of the EEA. It represents the Union in the EEA Joint Committee (in most cases). And it would play a part in possible dispute settlement proceedings in the event of a judicial conflict between the EFTA Court and the ECJ. In the meantime, it has, however, become clear that the respective provisions of the EEA Agreement hardly offer an operational solution.[1] Of direct relevance is, however, the fact that the Commission submits written and oral observations in virtually every contested case dealt with by the EFTA Court.[2] In *Icesave I*, the Commission has even, with the permission of the Court's President, made an intervention.[3]

From the outset, the Commission has seen its role in EFTA Court's proceedings as replacing the function of an AG. It is in fact of the utmost importance that the Commission appears in every case. It thereby contributes to securing a homogeneous development of the case law in the EEA and on certain occasions it constitutes a counterweight to EEA/EFTA governments. In the first years after the downsizing of the EFTA Court from five to three judges, this was particularly valuable. However, also today, the Commission's participation is indispensable.

[1]See for details Chapter 21.
[2]See Article 20 of the Court's Statute and Article 97(1) RoP.
[3]See Article 89(2) RoP.

C. Baudenbacher, *Judicial Independence*, Springer Biographies,
https://doi.org/10.1007/978-3-030-02308-9_29

Since it is part of both the EU and the EEA law-making process, the Commission is fully aware of the background to the legislation at issue. Nevertheless, it should not be overlooked that the Commission often has its own agenda. Depending on the situation, it may pursue different strategies when appearing before the EFTA Court.

The Commission is normally represented by one or several lawyers from its Legal Service. In complex cases, there may be an additional pleader from an interested DG. In the past, the Legal Service was led by a Director General who reported directly to the Commission's President and took part in the weekly meetings of the Commissioners (including the luncheon afterwards). In sensitive cases, the Legal Service's Director General will give instructions. Depending on the issues involved, and the form of action, there may also be an exchange of views with individual DGs. The DGs' involvement is stronger in Commission actions against Member States than in preliminary reference cases. In general, the Commission's pleadings were of high quality. The best agents were whose who frequently appeared before the EFTA Court and who thus were familiar both with the peculiarities of the EEA Agreement and the Court's style. In a few cases, Commission representatives based themselves on the incorrect assumption that the law in the two EEA pillars is identical in substance in every respect. And in a major case—*Sveinbjörnsdóttir* on EEA State liability—the Commission's standpoint was hardly compatible with what it had, albeit with a different pleader, argued a few years before.[4]

2 EFTA Court Following the Commission

The EFTA Court has followed the Commission in countless cases. If relevant case law of the ECJ is available, the Commission will usually tell the EFTA Court that in the interest of homogeneity, this case law ought to be followed. From the Court's perspective, this support may be particularly welcome in cases in which governments plead to the contrary, for example because they are defending discriminatory or unjustifiably restrictive national legislation or practice. However, even when the EFTA Court has to break new ground, the support of the Commission may be both important and welcome. Examples are: the Liechtenstein single practice rule cases for medical doctors—*Dr. Brändle*, *Dr. Mangold* and *Dr. Tschannett*; *Norwegian Waterfalls*; *Astra Norge*, where the Commission, together with ESA and other participants, successfully argued that the recognition of a copyright in a summary of product characteristics for pharmaceuticals constituted an unjustifiable restriction of the free movement of goods, and the Icelandic *Fresh Meat* case,[5] in which the respective governments argued politically because from a legal viewpoint they were fighting a lost cause. In such situations, the Commission usually joins forces with

[4]See for details Chapter 10.

[5]See for details Chapters 15, 17 and 27.

ESA. In all of the abovementioned cases, the EFTA Court followed the Commission's and ESA's pleadings.

3 Commission Using the EFTA Court as a Testing Ground

In going first cases, the Commission tends to be inclined to use the EFTA Court as a testing ground for any future litigation involving similar issues before the ECJ. The Commission then operates in a very skilful way. It tells the EFTA Court that it has the opportunity (and the burden) of breaking new ground and appeals to its sense of responsibility.

An early example of such a case is *Finanger* where both the Commission and ESA convinced the EFTA Court to rule that national legislation that excluded those who accepted a ride from an intoxicated driver, if they knew or should have known about the intoxication, from insurance coverage was incompatible with EEA law.[6] The same pattern of behaviour could be seen in *Paranova* v *Merck*. The Commission and ESA submitted that the so-called necessity test, according to which the decisive issue is whether the repackaging of pharmaceuticals was necessary in order for the parallel importer to gain market access in the Member State of importation, applies only to the act of repackaging, not to the presentation of the repackaged product.[7]

In *Olsen*, both authorities took the view that a trust may invoke the fundamental freedoms irrespective of whether it has legal personality or not. The Governments of France, Norway, and the UK opposed that position.

Kellogg's, *Fokus Bank* and *Olsen* are cases in which the function of the EFTA Court for the development of the case law of the ECJ is particularly apparent. In *Kellogg's*, the Commission supported ESA's claim that a national ban on the marketing of foodstuffs could not be justified on grounds of lack of nutritional need in the population. In the *Danish Vitamins* case (*Commission* v *Denmark*), the facts were very similar to *Kellogg's*. The Commission buttressed its infringement action against Denmark with the argument that the EFTA Court's *Kellogg's* judgment ought to be followed because it was "an element in the development of the law" which reflected the considerable changes in the methods used to determine health risks over the past 20 years. The ECJ found in favour of the Commission.[8] In *Fokus Bank* the Commission, with ESA's support, convincingly pleaded that an EEA State that applied a withholding tax on dividends distributed to non-resident shareholders, but refrained from doing this in the case of dividends distributed to residents, violated the rules on free movement of capital. *Fokus Bank* was cited by the

[6]See for details Chapter 11.

[7]See for details Chapter 18.

[8]See for details Chapter 11.

Commission in *Commission* v *Spain* (judgment of 3 June 2010) and in *Commission* v *Netherlands* (judgment of 11 June 2009). In both cases the ECJ moved into our direction. In *Panayi*, the ECJ case parallel to *Olsen*, the Commission stated in paragraphs 30 and 31 of its written observations:

> As the Referring Court points out, this will be the first occasion that this Court will consider the question of whether, and if so how the fundamental freedoms under the Treaty can be applied to a 'settlement or trust'. However, as is apparent from the Order for Reference, the issue has already been raised before the EFTA Court. In Fred Olsen, where the EFTA Court held that a trust may benefit from the freedom of establishment. See paragraphs 93-99 of that judgment. This was the position advocated by the Commission before the EFTA Court.
>
> Several of the considerations now raised by the Referring Court were also at issue before the EFTA Court in the Fred Olsen case. These include the essential features of a trust as they apply in English law such as the lack of legal personality of a trust and the distinct nature of the separate categories of persons within a trust; whether a trust carries on an economic activity and the fact that the Treaty makes no mention of a trust.

ESA argued along the same lines. The ECJ followed these pleadings.

A peculiar case in which the Commission used the existence of a second court interpreting law that is identical in substance to EU law was *Fosen-Linjen.* As I have elaborated,[9] the dispute concerned the question of whether the State should be held liable for a simple breach of the law, just like any other economic operator, when awarding a public contract, or whether the State should benefit from a privileged standard under which it would only be liable for serious violations. As I said, in the *Strabag* and *Combinatie Spijker* cases, two different chambers of the ECJ had given conflicting judgments on this question. The EFTA Court sided with the ECJ's Third Chamber in *Strabag* and held that a simple breach of the EEA public procurement rules could be sufficient to trigger the liability of the authority concerned. It thereby followed the Commission and decided against the Norwegian Government and ESA. In a future case before the ECJ, the Commission would certainly rely on the EFTA Court's *Fosen-Linjen* judgment and ask the ECJ to follow it. For the sake of order, I add that in the judgment of 21 March 2018 in the *Norwegian Public Works Concession* case, ESA pleaded the *Fosen-Linjen* case law. The Commission would undoubtedly have done the same, but surprisingly it did not participate in the case. I didn't take part in the judgment because I was on my way out of the EFTA Court.

---

[9]See for details Chapter 21.

4 EFTA Court Not Following the Commission

In a number of important cases, the EFTA Court has not followed the Commission's suggestions. In *Restamark*, it did not concur with the Commission's proposal to recognise the direct effect of Article 16, the monopoly provision of the EEA Main Agreement.[10] The most important disagreement occurred in *Sveinbjörnsdóttir*. Opposing ESA, the Commission, siding with the Governments of Iceland, Norway and Sweden, maintained that the principle of State liability was not part of EEA law. The EFTA Court acknowledged EEA State liability.[11] Had the Court followed the Commission's recommendation, it would never have won the recognition of the Union judiciary (and at the end of the day also of the Commission) to the extent that it has indeed won it. Again in contrast to ESA, in *LO* the Commission urged the EFTA Court to refrain from scrutinising whether the individual clauses of a collective agreement were exempt from the application of the EEA competition rules. The EFTA Court, following ESA, AG Jacobs in *Albany* and the Norwegian government opted for a comprehensive test.[12] The EFTA Court thereby laid the foundation for its later landmark ruling in *Holship*.[13] Interestingly, the Commission has in no way criticised the EFTA Court's *LO* precedent in *Holship*. The EFTA Court dismissed ESA's infringement action against Iceland in the first *Icesave* case. It thus also rejected the submissions of the Commission, which had supported ESA as an intervener. It is safe to assume that when ESA brought the respective lawsuit it acted in agreement with the Commission.[14] In *Vienna Life* and *Swiss Life*, both ESA and the Commission argued that certain EEA consumer protection rules applied if second-hand life assurance policies were purchased. Since it found the business in question to be a tax motivated form of investment, the EFTA Court came to the opposite conclusion.[15] The EFTA Court did not follow the Commission and ESA as regards the question of whether an in-house lawyer may represent his/her employer in *Abelia*.[16] In *Matja Kumba*, a case involving the interpretation of the Working Time Directive[17] the Commission and ESA argued that: (i) a working plan amounting to an average weekly working time of 84 h in a cohabitant care arrangement offering treatment for young people with drug and/or alcohol problems was incompatible with the directive; and (ii) a provision of Norwegian law under which employees who do have housing in or attached to a cohabitant care institution might not be allowed to revoke their previous consent to a working time of more than 48 h were incompatible with the directive and that a dismissal due to a failure to consent to a working time

---

[10]See for details Chapter 10.

[11]See for details Chapter 10.

[12]See for details Chapter 16.

[13]So for details Chapters 15 and 16.

[14]See for details Chapter 25.

[15]See for details Chapter 18.

[16]See for details Chapter 16.

[17]2003/88/EC.

arrangement of more than 48 h over a seven-day period always constitutes a detriment to the worker. The EFTA Court was not convinced by these contentions.[18]

5 Nullity Actions Against ESA Decisions

In nullity actions against ESA in State aid and competition law cases, the Commission has often supported its sister agency. This is understandable. In State aid cases, ESA and the Commission adamantly stick to the *Plaumann* formula: applicants only have *locus standi* if an act of general application affects

> them by reason of certain attributes peculiar to them, or by reason of a factual situation which differentiates them from all other persons and distinguishes them individually in the same way as the addressee of a decision.[19]

Both authorities have a vested interest in not softening that formula. As regards substantive State aid law, the Commission has, however, occasionally taken a different view to that of its sister watchdog.

In competition law, *Norway Post* is interesting. The EFTA Court barely considered the Commission's arguments in the judgment. When analysing the Report for the Hearing, it becomes clear why: the Commission did not touch upon the substantive core issues of the case in its pleadings, but merely underlined that ESA had applied the correct tests in the contested decision.[20] The question of depth of judicial review, which was at the heart of the judgment, was, for example, disregarded by the Commission. In *DB Schenker I*, the EFTA Court explicitly rejected ESA's and the Commission's view that follow-on damages claims in competition law cases only defend the plaintiff's private interests.[21]

6 Result

The role the Commission has played in the first 24 years of the Court's existence is a positive, albeit a mixed, one. In major cases, both infringement actions and references for preliminary rulings, in which governments often had strong interests, the Commission has indeed acted like a patron saint. In going first constellations, it has quite naturally tried to use the EFTA Court as a testing ground for future cases before the ECJ. This policy has been successful in a number of major proceedings. On other occasions, the EFTA Court, however, did not follow the Commission's arguments. In nullity actions brought by governments or economic operators against ESA decisions, the Commission has, unsurprisingly, pursued its own agenda.

---

[18] See for details Chapter 18.
[19] See for details Chapter 17.
[20] See for details Chapter 16.
[21] See for details Chapter 16.

Chapter 30
Switzerland—From EU-phobia to EU-philia?

Contents

1 The Start: Defensive Attitude vis-à-vis Supranationalism

Switzerland is one of the few European countries that was spared from World War II. Had Switzerland shared the same fate as the Benelux countries, whose neutrality was disregarded by Adolf Hitler's armies, it would most probably have played an active part in European integration. However, since this was not the case,

C. Baudenbacher, *Judicial Independence*, Springer Biographies,
https://doi.org/10.1007/978-3-030-02308-9_30

the Swiss stayed out of this seminal development. Switzerland's attitude towards supranational political integration in Europe was, a defensive one. For all intents and purposes, the country has been in a state of self-chosen spiritual "redoubt". Historically, National Redoubt ("*Réduit Suisse*") was a defensive military strategy whereby the Swiss army would, if an enemy could not be stopped at the border, withdraw to the Alps and defend its mountain stronghold. The concept became famous during World War II, but the construction of diverse fortifications had already started in the 1880s. After World War II, the idea of National Redoubt became part of the Swiss mind-set. As a result, Switzerland remained on the side-lines when the European Communities were established in 1952 and 1957. In 1961, members of the EEC Commission called Switzerland "the blackest of all sheep" among the EFTA neutrals (at the time Austria, Sweden and Switzerland).

Certainly, this attitude did not mean that Switzerland was always on its own. In 1960, the country founded, together with Austria, Denmark, Norway, Portugal, Sweden and the UK, the European Free Trade Association EFTA. Membership of EFTA does not involve supranational integration. When the UK, together with Denmark and Ireland, decided to join the EEC in 1972, Switzerland, like the other remaining EFTA States, entered into a free trade relationship with the EEC. Further bilateral agreements were concluded. Between 1961 and 1963, Switzerland was, together with the two other neutral EFTA States Austria and Sweden, part of a half-hearted attempt to conclude an association agreement with the EEC.[1] In 1963, 14 years after it was founded, Switzerland joined the Council of Europe, an international organisation which aims at upholding human rights, democracy and the rule of law. During the Cold War years, the Swiss were confident that with their cautious approach to European integration they were best prepared for the future. However, in 1987 the Single European Act came into force, the first major revision of the EEC Treaty, which aimed to complete the Single Market by the end of 1992. Together with the other EFTA States, Switzerland decided to enter multilateral negotiations on the conclusion of a comprehensive association agreement with the EEC, the EEA Agreement. This should have prevented any discrimination via-à-vis Swiss industry. In 1989, the Cold War ended with the collapse of the Soviet Union.

2 The Failed EEA Attempt and Its Consequences

2.1 The Federal Council's Blunder

On 2 May 1992, Switzerland signed the EEA Agreement and the SCA in Oporto, together with the other six EFTA States—Austria, Finland, Iceland, Liechtenstein, Norway and Sweden—and the EU. The National Council, the lower house of parliament, gave its approval with 138 votes to 57, the State Council, the upper

[1] See for details Chapter 3.

house, with 38 votes to 2. However, the negotiations had not gone well for Switzerland. Its FDFA was ill-prepared for a multilateral undertaking of this size which acquired increasingly supranational traits. As I said, the Swiss took Commission President Delors' pledge of 17 January 1989 to grant the EFTA States a co-decision right in legislation at face value. Delors withdrew his pledge one year later. However, the Swiss carried on insisting on a co-decision right, whereas the other EFTA States had long since resigned themselves to doing without it.[2] Most of them saw EEA membership as an intermediate step on the road to the EU. That the EFTA States would not only enjoy full access to the EC Single Market, but also retain their sovereignty on foreign trade, agriculture and taxation issues was phased out. Some on the Swiss negotiating team regarded the EEA Agreement as an unworthy agreement and this view still dominates the approach of the FDFA towards the EEA today. At one stage during the negotiations, Switzerland was about to pull out of the project altogether.

Nevertheless, in late 1991 and early 1992 the polls looked quite promising. However, when the Federal Council out of the blue lodged an application for EU membership on 20 May 1992, the EEA's fate was sealed. For the anti-Europeans, it was now easy to argue that the planned referendum was in fact not about EEA membership on the EFTA side, but about accession to the EU. Federal Councillor Adolf Ogi—a former sports official—involuntarily confirmed this by stating that the EEA would be an excellent "training camp" for EU participation.

Two diplomats, Jakob Kellenberger and the late Bruno Spinner had lobbied certain of the Federal Council's members behind the back of the chief negotiator, Franz Blankart, arguing that due to the lack of a co-decision right for the EFTA States when enacting new legislation, the EEA Agreement was fundamentally flawed. The duo claimed that the Agreement could only be submitted to the Swiss people if it was made clear from the beginning that it was merely an intermediary step on the country's path to EU membership. The majority of the Federal Council bought into this argument and decided to lodge such an application with Brussels six months before the EEA referendum. 20 years later, Blankart described the respective events in the following way:

> At the last round of negotiations at ministerial level in Luxembourg there were long waits, during which EC internal consultations and talks among the chief negotiators were held. Finally, it was time. The two competent Federal Councillors held a press conference in front of the assembled Swiss press. Without me as the chief negotiator having been informed or even consulted in advance, the baffled Swiss people were told at 03:00 clock in the morning (!) abroad (!) and yet in the building of the European Commission (!) that in the future joining the EU would be the goal of Swiss European policy. You really have to be out of your mind to commit such a political mistake. From then on, I knew that the EEA was lost. [....] The fact that the chief negotiator learns about this shift of integration policy at the same time as the press did, of course, hurt me; but I have meanwhile learned that it is already an honour if a chief officer is informed no later than the press. [....] Then the formal application for membership followed, which, *inter alia*, was submitted to have an alternative to hand in case of an EEA-No. Theoretically, this consideration was not wrong after

[2]See for details Chapter 5.

> the events in Luxembourg. Today, there is, however, hardly anybody who does not, at least in his heart, admit that it was the biggest political mistake of the Federal Council since Second World War. Moreover, it became known that the decision was politically poorly supported: Four Federal Councillors were in favour: Felber (SP), Cotti (CVP), Delamuraz (FDP) and Ogi (SVP); three were against: Stich (SP), Koller (CVP) and Villiger (FDP). The three major parties in government were thus divided even in the Federal Council, the SVP was divided internally. To take such an important decision on such a weak basis is at least astonishing. The Government parted at 11:30 h, vowing to keep the decision secret and to make it known to the people only two days later after having informed our EFTA partners. An hour later, the decision was reported in the lunchtime news of Radio DRS. There was much wondering about this indiscretion. It probably came from an official close to the Federal Council who wanted to avoid that Ogi would be called to order by his party. For information policy Switzerland does not seem to be particularly gifted.
>
> Federal Councillor Stich recognized the implications of this decision (and as a presumptive EEA opponent he perhaps even welcomed them: 'The fate of the [EEA] proposal was completely sealed [....] on the day after the approval of the Monetary Fund by the people, when after a spontaneous [!] motion the application for membership to the EC was approved.' (*Berner Zeitung* of 15 January 1998, 3).
>
> This step had two serious disadvantages. First, it prompted several respected EEA supporters, such as Former Federal Councillor Chevallaz and National Councillor Allenspach, the Director of the Central Association of Swiss Employers' Organizations, to switch over to the No camp. Second, the EEA enemies were served the strongest argument against the EEA on a silver platter. Whether we like it or not: for most of the EEA opponents the December 6, 1992 vote was an EC membership vote.[3]

In fact, on 6 December 1992, 50,3% of the voters and 16 out of 23 cantons rejected EEA membership. The Federal Council was thus unable to ratify the agreement. After this, the Federal Council was quick to blame the anti-Europeans. Internally, the chief negotiator Blankart was used as a scapegoat. The government did everything to hide the fact that it was responsible for the EEA fiasco.

2.2 *Sectoral Institution-Free Bilateralism as an Intermediate Step on the Road to the EU*

After several years, Switzerland was able to negotiate a set of bilateral agreements ("*Bilaterals I*") with the EU. On 21 June 1999, six and a half years after the rejection of the EEA, seven treaties in the fields of free movement of persons, air transport, land transport, agricultural trade, mutual recognition of conformity assessments, public procurement, and scientific and technological cooperation were signed in Luxembourg. At the time, the Federal Council said quite openly that it was striving to join the EU. In the 1999 Integration Report the government wrote the remarkable sentence:

---

[3]Unofficial translation.

> *Ein Beitritt würde die* Unabhängigkeit *der Schweiz einerseits dadurch stärken, dass sie an den Entscheidungen teilhaben könnte, die sie betreffen (wobei sie sich je nach Umständen und Notwendigkeit mit anderen Mitgliedstaaten zu einem gemeinsamen Vorgehen zusammenschliessen könnte) sowie andererseits dadurch, dass sie bei gegen die Schweiz gerichteten Druckversuchen vom erheblichen Gewicht der EU profitieren könnte.*

> Accession would strengthen Switzerlands *independence* on the one hand by allowing it to participate in the decisions affecting it (joining forces with other Member States as circumstances and needs dictate) and on the other hand by allowing it to benefit from the EU's considerable weight if pressure is exerted against Switzerland.

With the exception of the air transport agreement, where Switzerland accepted the jurisdiction of the ECJ, all these treaties function without a supranational surveillance and court mechanism. Conflicts are dealt with in EEA Joint Committees, i.e. diplomatic bodies that can only decide by unanimity. The agreements on free movement of persons, on air transport and on land transport had, at least officially, not featured on the Swiss wish list. The seven agreements, which constituted the first package, were linked by a guillotine clause, which stipulated that all of the agreements would collectively cease to apply if one of them were to be terminated. Thus, Switzerland is unable to engage in what, from the EU's viewpoint, would amount to cherry-picking. They cannot kill an unpopular agreement by referendum and only keep the ones they like. It is not known who proposed the guillotine clause; there are those who believe that it was a blunder on the part of the Swiss negotiators. I wouldn' t rule that out. The negotiators were on course to join the EU.

Be that as it may, it was in any case extraordinary that Switzerland accepted such a proviso. As one commentator put it, one can only assume that the negotiators had a blackout, as the only alternative explanation is that they wanted to create a "point of no return" for EU membership. From a sovererignty perspective, the guillotine clause is much worse than anything that Switzerland would have had to swallow under the EEA Agreement. However, this time, the Federal Council spoke with one voice in the referendum campaign. One might also wonder why free movement of persons, the most sensitive of the four fundamental freedoms, was fully realised whereas there are no agreements on the freedom to provide services, the freedom of establishment and the free movement of capital. In all these crucial areas, Swiss operators can at any time be discriminated against. In fact, as developments since 2009 have shown, there are discriminations. However, all of these issues were suppressed by the government's propaganda. Obviously, the lack of institutions—a surveillance body and a court—was seen as a success. The fact that their industry had no access to a European court was ignored by the Swiss. The first package of sectoral agreements was presented to the voters as a major achievement. On 21 May 2001, 67,2% of them approved the "*Bilaterals I*". On 1 June 2002, the agreements entered into force. Jakob Kellenberger who had acted as a chief negotiator was beatified, so to speak. His canonisation took place in 2000 when he was appointed President of the International Committee of the Red Cross. Kellenberger owes his popularity not least to his ostensibly modest manner. In the winter semester 1993/1994, he taught a class on European integration together with me at the HSG.

Afterwards, I sometimes took him home for dinner. Laura Melusine was 8 years old and we often played table football.

Jakob Kellenberger's influence on the integration policy of the FDFA was and remains to be high. As a result of his fixation on the EEA co-decision issue and on EU membership, he underestimates the opportunities that EEA membership on the EFTA side offers. The same goes for his unwillingness to recognise the advantages of an own EFTA Surveillance Authority and an own EFTA Court. The Swiss FDFA is full of people who lack a practical legal background. Kellenberger is a philologist who wrote his doctoral thesis on the Spanish playwright Pedro Calderón de la Barca. I am not saying that all diplomats should have a background as practising lawyers, but if you negotiate about a surveillance and court mechanism, you must have at least some relevant experience. None of those who were, or are today, involved in such negotiations with the EU—whether in the EEA context or later in the context of the so-called "renovation of bilateralism"—either had or have the necessary know-how. In my Zurich speech of 20 September 2016,[4] I criticised this situation and said that it would never cross my mind to perform heart surgery without having an education as well as training as a surgeon. Following Kellenberger's departure from the FDFA, others who had also been involved in killing the EEA Agreement continued to promote his ideas. Michael Ambühl, an engineer by training, who was part of Kellenberger's team, later had a meteoric career. From 2001 to 2004, he was the chief negotiator for the second package of bilateral agreements, in 2005 he became State Secretary in the FDFA and in 2010 State Secretary in the Federal Department of Finance.

The aforementioned second package of nine bilateral sectoral agreements ("*Bilaterals II*") was signed on 26 October 2004. They entered into force between 2005 and 2009. These treaties went beyond the pure granting of market access. The second set includes, in particular, agreements on the taxation of savings income and on the accession of Switzerland to the Schengen and Dublin systems concerning cooperation in the areas of justice, police, asylum, and migration. These agreements are also less static than the first ones. Since the Swiss Government had started to see the "bilateral path" as the right Swiss integration model, at least for the time being, it insisted in some instances on being given certain participation rights. Therefore, mechanisms for adopting EU law and for decision–shaping, which are inspired by the EEA Agreement, were introduced. The second package contains no guillotine clause; however, the association agreements concerning Schengen and Dublin state that if Switzerland does not implement a new act and no solution can be found in the EEA Joint Committees, the agreements must be considered terminated, unless the Mixed Committee decides otherwise.

After the conclusion of the "*Bilaterals II*", it became patently clear that large parts of the federal administration had harboured rather lukewarm feelings about the

[4]See for details Chapter 31.

EEA Agreement or had even actively opposed EEA membership on the EFTA side. Now they thought that with the network of institution-free bilateral agreements they had found what they called "the royal road" ("*Königsweg*") to the European Single Market, these people no longer hid their disdain for the EEA. Some of them told me and others that they had voted against the EEA out of fear that Switzerland could be stuck with this—in their eyes—unworthy agreement. Certainly, Switzerland continued to be an EFTA State as regards its relationship with the world outside the EU and it even had and continues to have observer status in the EEA. However, at EFTA Ministerial meetings, the Swiss diplomats would ostentatiously look out of the window when discussions turned to the EEA. The statements they wrote for their Federal Councillors boasted of the allegedly excellent bilateral relations between Switzerland and the EU. For obvious reasons, they did not say that deep in their hearts they were still hoping to join the EU one day. On the occasion of the fiftieth anniversary of the Swiss Mission in Brussels on 17 November 2010, Minister for Foreign Affairs Calmy-Rey contrasted the Swiss model—which in her view was based on direct democracy *and* bilateralism—with the European model. People in the federal administration seemed to take it for granted that Switzerland could walk the royal road of institution-free sectoral bilateralism forever, or at least until it finally joined the EU.

As I have said, the Federal Council was not willing to acknowledge that it was responsible for the No to the EEA. In Berne it was said that the anti-Europeans led by Christoph Blocher had

> forced the country onto the bilateral path.

Many thought that this path was simply a continuation of Switzerland's traditional EU policy. In fact, the first bilateral agreements with the EEC and the ECSC were concluded long before the EEA project was launched. The most important of this first generation of bilateral agreements was the 1972 Free Trade Agreement. However, the new form of bilateralism differed in more than one respect from the old form. Under the old form, Switzerland was in the good company of the other EFTA States. Now the country was on its own. All the other former and actual EFTA States had become Member States of the EEA, either on the EU or on the EFTA side. The Federal Council did not withdraw the application for EU membership and renamed the latter a "strategic goal". This may have helped the Swiss to obtain the approval of the EU to negotiate new bilateral agreements. At the same time, the Commission in a Communication of 1 October 1993 informed Switzerland that such agreements could only constitute transitional measures (COM [93] 486 final 1 October 1993).

The 1990s were the height of open EU enthusiasm, at least in the Federal Council and among the major political parties with the exception of the SVP. Over-enthusiastic supporters of EU accession, however, forced the Federal Council to spell back. On 4 March 2001, the vote on the popular initiative 'Yes to Europe', submitted in 1996, took place. Among other things, the amendment of the transitional provisions of the Federal Constitution by a new Article 23 with the following wording was called for:

> *1. Die Schweiz beteiligt sich am europäischen Integrationsprozess und strebt zu diesem Zweck den Beitritt zur Europäischen Union an.*
>
> *2. Der Bund nimmt ohne Verzug Beitrittsverhandlungen mit der Europäischen Union auf.*
>
> *[....].*
>
> 1. Switzerland is participating in the European integration process and is striving to join the European Union to this end.
>
> 2. The Confederation starts accession negotiations with the European Union without delay.
>
> [....].

The Federal Council wrote that it was striving to join the European Union, but that the initiative required too quick action. Nevertheless, it was hoped in Berne that the initiative would not be rejected with too much more. The National Council rejected it only by 94 votes to 69, the Council of States by 33 votes to 6. In fact, 76,8% of the voters dismissed the initiative. It was clear that there was a great difference between the goals pursued by Berne and what the people wanted.

As a result, a new language regime was introduced. Although the Federal Council still spoke of the goal of accession in 2000, it no longer described it as "strategic". In autumn 2005, EU accession was downgraded to a "long-term option". From now on, the bilateral path was called the Swiss path. Supporters of accession saw this as a tactical measure without abandoning their strategic objective. But there was a growing public belief that EU accession was out of the question.

The downgrading of EU membership to a "long-term option" did not go unnoticed in Brussels. In the eyes of the EU, the basis for sectoral bilateralism without institutions ceased to exist with this policy shift.

3 Towards Institutionalisation?

3.1 2008 Onwards: The EU Pushes for Institutions

In the second half of the 2000s it became clear that the royal road of institution-free bilateralism would lead to a dead end. The Union had not forgotten that in 1993 it had allowed the Swiss to negotiate sectoral bilateral agreements as a transitional measure. With the exception of the Schengen and Dublin agreements, the bilateral treaties are static in nature. New EU law is not dynamically adopted by Switzerland. This is bad for homogeneity and the EU wanted it to be corrected.

What is more, from 2008 on, the EU Council asked Switzerland to accept an institutionalisation of its sectoral agreements in order to secure more effective law enforcement and legal certainty. With institutionalisation, they meant surveillance and judicial control, similar to the EEA Agreement. Observers in the EU and in

Switzerland thought that this could be achieved either by a second attempt at joining the EEA or by sticking to the sectoral approach, but with the additional element of using (so-called "docking" to) the EEA/EFTA institutions, ESA and the EFTA Court. The idea was to conclude a framework agreement ("*Rahmenabkommen*") with the EU. Such an agreement, which had already been discussed in Switzerland in 2005, would serve as a roof for the numerous sectoral treaties. The potential institutional implications of such an agreement were, however, not fully considered at the time.

3.2 2010: A Cautious Opening Towards the EEA?

The immediate reaction of the federal administration to the EU's institutional claims was not to speak of surveillance and judicial control, but of "dispute settlement". This was no coincidence. The Swiss had always wanted conflicts to be resolved politically. This has its roots in history. Professor Leonhard Neidhart, an important political scientist who made his academic career in Germany, in 1970 called Switzerland a negotiated democracy. The federal administration wished the negotiating approach to be extended into the relations with the EU. Speaking of dispute settlement also became common parlance in the media. Nevertheless, from 2010 onwards, the federal administration and even the Federal Council started to seek contact with the EFTA Court, as an institution, and with me personally. In the spring of 2010, Federal Councillor Doris Leuthard who at the time served as Federal President—in Switzerland, the office of Federal President is a rotating job that lasts only one year—invited me to an exchange of views with her and her staff in Berne. I knew Leuthard from the EFTA Ministerial meetings where in her capacity as the Minister of Economic Affairs she had been the leader of the Swiss delegation.

The main point on the agenda was the EU Commission's proposal that Switzerland should use the institutions of the EFTA pillar, ESA and the Court. Under this model, Switzerland could stick to its sectoral approach, whilst subjecting the bilateral agreements with the EU to surveillance by ESA and to the jurisdiction of the EFTA Court. The idea was that Switzerland would be represented in both institutions. Among the President's entourage were a few EEA veterans. It struck me that they assessed the functioning of the EEA Agreement on the basis of their memories of the negotiations from 1989–1991. However, they seemed to have no clue about how the agreement worked in practice. This ivory tower approach still prevails today. Nevertheless, I also sensed that Leuthard had a certain sympathy for a second attempt at joining the EEA.

In the *NZZ* of 22 June 2010, I published an article under the title: "Switzerland should make a second attempt to join the EEA" ("*Die Schweiz sollte einen zweiten EWR-Anlauf nehmen*"). I criticised that under bilateralism Switzerland was living for the day and like Tarzan moved hand over hand from liana to liana. Representatives of the FDFA immediately responded with the usual anti-EEA mantra. On 18 August 2010, I participated, as the only external guest, in a closed convention of the Federal Council *in corpore* on the European question. Federal President Leuthard used her position to bring me on board. The other invitees were State Secretary Michael Ambühl, Ambassador Henri Gétaz, the Head of the Integration Bureau of the Foreign Department/Department of Economic Affairs (IB), and Jacques De Watteville, the Swiss Ambassador to the EU. All three had had a perfect career as bureaucrats. I explained how the EEA and in particular the EFTA Court work in practice, but there was no real discussion. A few days later, the Federal Council announced that it was determined to continue on the "path of bilateralism", with a few adaptations concerning the dynamic adoption of EU law by Switzerland, and the establishment of a horizontal monitoring mechanism and of a court. A working group would develop solutions for the institutional questions together with the EU.

On 17 September 2010, the Federal Council adopted the so-called Markwalder-Report on the evaluation of Switzerland's European policy. National Councillor Christa Markwalder, one of the spokespersons of the Swiss EU membership movement, had requested that the government assess the advantages and disadvantages of the various European policy instruments, and to present a list of priorities containing specific measures relating to Switzerland's future European policy. The report contained surprising mistakes. It was, for example, said that courts of last resort of the EEA/EFTA countries are legally obliged to make references to the EFTA Court. The report stated, in particular, that the institutional issues—including modalities for adapting the agreements to new EU legislation, the interpretation of the agreements, and the settlement of disputes (sic!)—, were to be examined together with the EU in order to find solutions that would facilitate the application of the agreements and at the same time respect the sovereignty of both parties and ensure the smooth functioning of the institutions involved. With regard to surveillance and interpretation (sic!), the report briefly mentioned three models, for example the use ("*Inanspruchnahme*") of ESA and of the EFTA Court by Switzerland, the establishment of an arbitration tribunal and the establishment of a joint Switzerland-EU court. That the second and the third option would be unacceptable to the EU did not concern the drafters. However, with the mentioning of the docking model, the Federal Council had seemingly made a big step forward. As I have said, the idea stemmed from the Commission. Nevertheless, it struck me that the federal administration seemed to assume that after all the downgrading of these institutions the country had the right to use them as and when it deemed necessary.

In the following months, the EFTA Court received a number of visitors from Swiss political and diplomatic circles. I could, however, not shake the impression that some visits were only made so that it could be said afterwards "we have examined the EFTA Court option, it doesn't work for us". Again, the Swiss assessed the EEA Agreement and the institutions of the EFTA pillar in the light of what they remembered from the negotiations during the years 1989–1991. They may also have picked up negative remarks about the EEA from Norwegians who still harboured dreams of EU membership. Swiss lawyers were accustomed to studying EU law, both at their own universities and at EU institutions such as the College of Europe in Bruges or the European University Institute in Fiesole. They were thus familiar with the case law of the ECJ. But they didn't bother to read the judgments of the EFTA Court.

On 17 November 2010, I debated alongside Minister for Foreign Affairs Micheline Calmy-Rey at an evening event in Berne. She said that the EEA was an old-fashioned model and that Switzerland wanted to have something much fancier. I wished her every success.

3.3 2011: Piano Piano

On 7 July 2011, University of Zurich Professor Daniel Thürer in an expert opinion to the Federal Council essentially proposed that the Swiss should either dock to the institutions of the EFTA pillar or set up a Swiss pillar with a Swiss surveillance body and the Federal Supreme Court. Daniel is a scholar with a great reputation in international law, however, he has little experience in European law. It was obvious that the federal administration had implied that the option of EEA membership on the EFTA side was not to be explored. In fact, Berne suppressed everything that had to do with the EEA.

On 29 June 2011, the Administrative Committee of the Swiss Federal Tribunal had in a letter to the Federal Council stated that a preliminary ruling procedure was neither feasible under the current state of the law nor necessary. The Committee refused to be subject to the EFTA Court and—rather surprisingly—proposed the introduction of an informal exchange of views with the ECJ on a reciprocity basis. From the perspective of the ECJ, the proposal looked laughable. At the dinner after the meeting of the Constitutional Courts of the German speaking countries in February 2012 in Luxembourg (the so-called meeting of the six—"*Sechsertreffen*"), I sat next to Supreme Court President Lorenz Meyer and ECJ President Vassilios Skouris. Lorenz presented his "model" to Vassilios who diplomatically responded: "Difficult, difficult!" In this context, the Administrative Committee also completely misunderstood the function of Switzerland's right to submit observations under the new Lugano Convention. In the first case in which the Swiss Government participated, *Folien Fischer and Fofitec*, the Federal Office of Justice submitted its draft observations to the Federal Supreme Court, which then commented on them.

Furthermore, the Administrative Committee welcomed the establishment of an independent surveillance body, which could consist of Swiss or Swiss and EU members. This too was a proposal that had little to do with reality. The Federal Council wanted to keep the opinion and the letter secret, but the weekly newspaper *Weltwoche* which is opposed to any form of institutionalisation made it public on its website. The FDFA only officially published the documents years later.

On 28 October 2011, my institute at HSG hosted a conference on the institutionalisation of the Switzerland-EU relationship. Many of the players were present, *inter alia* the Head of the Swiss desk at the EU Commission (who was also responsible for the EEA), Gianluca Grippa, the EU-Ambassador to Switzerland and Liechtenstein, Michael Reiterer, and Ambassador Henri Gétaz, the Head of the IB. Grippa and Reiterer underlined that a bilateral court or a bilateral arbitration tribunal simply would not fly. Grippa also emphasised that it was unthinkable that a country would be monitored by its own surveillance authority whose decisions would be subject to review by the country's own supreme court.

3.4 2012: The Futile Attempt to Establish a Swiss Pillar

On 3 January 2012, I argued in *NZZ* that a "Swiss solution" with a Swiss surveillance authority and the Federal Supreme Court would simply not be possible ("'*Helvetische Lösung' mit der EU kaum möglich*"). In February 2012, a delegation from the Swiss Federal Supreme Court led by President Lorenz Meyer paid the EFTA Court a visit and I made my view clear again. On 16 May 2012 I gave the keynote speech at a podium organised by the think tank *foraus* at the University of Zurich. Again, I made it plain that a Swiss pillar would never fly. Most of those who intervened shared my view.

Nevertheless, on 15 June 2012, Federal President Eveline Widmer-Schlumpf in a letter to Brussels proposed that Switzerland should establish its own "independent" surveillance authority and that the Swiss Federal Supreme Court should be competent to review the respective decisions. It was perfectly obvious that this would not be acceptable to the EU. I spoke about it with well-informed journalists and they told me that they had no illusions, but that this proposal needed to be put forward for internal political reasons.

On 6 September 2012, the new Minister for Foreign Affairs Didier Burkhalter visited his French counterpart Laurent Fabius in Paris. According to *NZZ*, Burkhalter made "perfectly clear" ("*klipp und klar*") that Switzerland could not renounce an independent (Swiss) surveillance body. Unsurprisingly, at the end of the year, the EU rejected the Swiss proposal. After this, independent experts expected the Federal Council to either declare that for the time being Switzerland would refrain from negotiating further bilateral agreements or to come up with an EFTA solution, be it docking to the EEA/EFTA institutions or EEA membership on the EFTA side. On 4 December 2012, Franz Blankart and I spoke before the parliamentary group of the CVP in Berne. The party's president, Christoph Darbellay, had unashamedly expressed his sympathy for EEA membership on the side of EFTA a couple of days before. However, the spokespersons of the FDFA contended that a second attempt at joining the EEA was out of the question. Nobody could imagine at that time that the leaders of the FDFA would put forward a particularly novel proposal. But let me explain that development step by step.

Didier Burkhalter had succeeded Micheline Calmy-Rey as Minister for Foreign Affairs on 1 January 2012. Under the (outdated) seniority rules of the Federal Council, he basically had the right to choose the FDFA after Calmy-Rey's departure. Burkhalter had been elected to the Federal Council in 2009. An economist by training, he had never exercised a profession. Untypically for a Swiss Federal Councillor, he had forged a political career in the midst of the FDP. Burkhalter had served as a member of the Neuchâtel cantonal parliament from 1990 to 2001, and was also, from 1991 to 2006, a member of the government of Neuchâtel City and its mayor (a rotating post). From 2003 to 2007, Burkhalter was a member of the Swiss National Council and on 11 November 2007, he was elected to the Swiss Council of States. The weekly French-language magazine "*L'Hebdo*" referred to him as an apparatchik.

Under the Swiss constitution, the seven members of the Federal Council are elected by Parliament. The Federal Council, the only directorial government in the world, had from 1959 to 2003 been composed of representatives from Swiss political parties according to the following so-called "magic formula": 2 FDP, 2 CVP, 2 SP and 1 SVP. After the rejection of the EEA in the December 1992 referendum, the SVP rose from its rank as the fourth most popular party to become the strongest political party. In 2003, the SVP managed to break up the magic formula; incumbent CVP Federal Councillor Ruth Metzler was voted out of office and the leader of the SVP, Christoph Blocher, the winner of the EEA battle, was elected in her place. Metzler was the first sitting Federal Councillor since 1872 not to be re-elected. The SVP now had two seats on the Federal Council, but this situation only lasted four years. In 2007, Parliament sacked Blocher because there was a widespread feeling that he had been a government minister and the opposition leader at the same time. Another SVP politician, Eveline Widmer-Schlumpf, was elected in his stead. This move formally honoured the SVP's claim to two seats in the government, however, Mr. Blocher and the SVP were furious. Widmer-Schlumpf accepted her election and after some squabbling founded her own political group, the Bourgeois Democratic Party (BDP). In 2011, Widmer-Schlumpf was re-elected by Parliament even though the BDP had only won 5,4% of the votes. By 2015, the BDP was down to 4,1%, Eveline Widmer-Schlumpf did not stand for re-election and her seat reverted to the SVP.

In 2009, Federal Councillor Pascal Couchepin from the FDP retired. The CVP saw a chance to win back the seat it had lost in 2003 to the SVP, by stealing one seat from the FDP. The CVP nominated State Councillor Urs Schwaller, a lawyer, whilst the FDP's candidate was State Councillor Burkhalter. In 2003, the FDP had supported Mr. Blocher over Ms. Metzler. In 2007, a large part of the CVP parliamentarians had, together with the SP and some smaller parties, contributed Mr. Blocher's fall from power. Therefore, the CVP had good reason for believing that the SP would vote for Mr. Schwaller. In the end Burkhalter won because a high number of social democrats voted for him. The Austrian daily newspaper "*Der Standard*" reported that the SP leadership had supported Burkhalter because he favoured EU membership whereas Schwaller wanted to stick to bilateralism. This is important in view of what would happen after 2013.

On 1 November 2009 Burkhalter took over the Federal Department of Home Affairs, where he operated with rather limited success. When he opted for the Federal Department of Foreign Affairs in 2011, a number of observers felt that

Burkhalter was fleeing his old ministry. Others remarked that he and his spouse liked travelling. Be that as it may, on 1 May 2012, Burkhalter surprised everybody in Berne by choosing Yves Rossier, who had been the Director of the Federal Social Insurance Office as his State Secretary. This choice was also remarkable, because Rossier had no previous experience in European affairs. Rossier too is a member of the FDP. As I will explain, the fact that both men were from FDP would play a fundamental role in the years to come. Burkhalter also filled other important positions in the Ministry of Foreign Affairs with his protégés. What is particularly striking is that there was no seasoned top lawyer with practical experience. His personal advisers were a political scientist and a historian, who also had a degree in international affairs. The head of the Directorate for European Affairs was Henri Gétaz, an economist.

Until the end of 2012, the new leadership of the FDFA seemed to carry out the policy laid down by Micheline Calmy-Rey. Calmy-Rey was in favour of Switzerland joining the EU, but when she realized that the time was not ripe, she pretended to be an intrepid representative of bilateralism. Once it became clear that the EU would not accept the idea of a Swiss pillar, Rossier and Burkhalter were ready to launch another approach. Officially, the EU rejected the Swiss pillar proposal on 21 December 2012. However, a few days before the twentieth anniversary of the EEA vote of 6 December 1992, on 28 November 2012, Burkhalter held a press conference at which he did little more than emphasise that there was no alternative to bilateralism. He also said that the first the signals from Brussels were not as negative as some people thought and ruled out EEA membership on the EFTA side. In the light of what happened in the course of 2013, the following statement is particularly interesting: Burkhalter said that Swiss diplomats had conducted a number of substantial talks both in Brussels and in the EU Member States. This, he claimed, had launched a reflexion process. Ten days earlier, David O'Sullivan, the Irish CEO of the European External Action Service, the EU's foreign ministry and diplomatic corps, had been in Berne to discuss Swiss proposals; a further meeting was planned for January 2013 (*NZZ* of 30 November 2012). With hindsight, it can only be assumed that these talks did not really focus on the Swiss pillar issue, but that they already concerned what would later be dubbed "the ECJ model".

4 From 2013 on: Acquiring Passive EU Membership?

4.1 General

On 1 January 2013, the so-called Integration Bureau ("IB") was renamed as the Directorate for European Affairs and put under the control of the FDFA alone. The IB had been established in 1961 in the context of the association negotiations with the EEC[5] as a joint office of the Federal Department of Economic Affairs and of the FDFA. It was tasked with analysing and assessing European integration and its impact on Switzerland, coordinating integration efforts and communicating Swiss EU policy and European integration. Whether the IB has fulfilled its information task is doubtful. Professor Philipp Zurkinden, a well-informed and courageous Berne lawyer, has called the IB the "Isolation Bureau". Nevertheless, placing the IB solely under the FDFA led to a loss of economic and economic law expertise; political scientists and public international law experts gained the upper hand. These experts have difficulties in assessing an international treaty from an economic law perspective. They have a tendency to turn every question into an institutional or constitutional issue. Their thinking focuses on formalities, sovereignty, and theoretical possibilities. They have little confidence in processes, they stick resolutely to the idea that everything can be regulated in an agreement for eternity and have little understanding of the need for dynamic developments.

In the spring of 2013, senior representatives from the FDFA announced that after many unsuccessful attempts, they had found a solution for the issue of institutionalising the sectoral agreements linking Switzerland to the EU, a solution that had in fact never crossed the mind of any European law specialist. The new approach was essentially described in the following way: If Switzerland and the EU would not agree on a certain question arising from a bilateral agreement in the Joint Committee, each side could *unilaterally* ask the ECJ for an "authoritative" interpretation of the relevant EU law as incorporated into the bilateral law. The decision-making power would, however, remain with the Joint Committee and thus continue to be political. The FDFA people therefore claimed that despite the absence of a Swiss judge, the ECJ would not be a foreign court for Switzerland. It would in fact not be an "adjudicating court" at all, because it would not properly decide. Occasionally, it was even asserted that the ECJ would only be "heard", but would not have the power to decide. Mr. Burkhalter contended that the ECJ would give an "advisory opinion". If the ECJ's answer would be positive for Switzerland, the FDFA argued, the EU would feel bound by it. If it would be negative for Switzerland, the government would retain the freedom to vote against it in the Joint Committee. If it would do so, it would risk the termination of the agreement in question or other compensatory measures. However, the ECJ aficionados said that they had three hopes. First, they started from the premise that the Commission would refrain from unilaterally invoking the ECJ. Second, they assumed that after a negative decision by the ECJ Switzerland would be able to negotiate a compromise solution with the Commission, for instance a partial adoption of the ECJ's ruling, without the ECJ being able to express itself on the outcome. Third, they hypothesised that if ever it should come to a negative ruling for Switzerland, the EU would refrain from actually applying any sanctions.

---

[5]See Chapter 3.

In the Government's view, this model had the further advantage that there would not be any formal monitoring by a surveillance authority and thus there would be no judicial infringement proceedings. Switzerland would monitor itself. There would only be the dispute settlement mechanism which meant that Switzerland could not be "sentenced".

The new policy was marketed under the motto "renovated bilateralism". Rossier and Burkhalter turned everything upside down over night. They shifted up a gear in a way that was new in Swiss EU politics. In the Federal Council, nobody seemed to really care what the new duo in the FDFA were doing. During 2013, when the worst blunders were made, the impression prevailed that Rossier was the "brains" behind the new approach and Burkhalter the "brawn" who would get things done. Burkhalter loved being in the limelight alongside influential and important people, however, he didn't seem to be interested in the substance of the issues. This became particularly clear in 2014, when, according to the rotation schedule, he held the Presidency of the Swiss Confederation. In addition to this post, he also served as OSCE (Organization for Security and Co-operation in Europe) Chairperson-in-Office (CiO), a function without any power and awarded simply by rotation between the OSCE States. Nevertheless, Burkhalter was delighted. He enjoyed flying around the world and being photographed with Russian President Vladimir Putin and other world leaders such as German Chancellor Angela Merkel, French President François Hollande and even with US President Barack Obama. His successes, in particular in the Ukraine crisis, were not nearly as important as his entourage and his court reporters wanted people to believe. In early 2015, his underlings spread all sorts of rumours, for example that he was a serious candidate for the Nobel Peace Prize and for UN Secretary General.

When I first read about the "ECJ model", I was reminded of a well-dressed and self-confident student, who in an exam spouts totally abstruse answers, in a manner that leaves no doubt that he/she is convinced of the truth of these answers. In such a situation, any examiner worth their salt might question whether they are incapable of understanding the student's genial ideas because they cannot, at least not at first, imagine that the answers are simply bogus. I discussed the proposed ECJ model with colleagues from the EU judiciary and from the diplomatic corps in Luxembourg and in Brussels. There was not a single person who warmed to the idea. Many of them just laughed when I mentioned it. On balance, the choice of the "ECJ model" can only be explained as an offshoot of the same thinking that had prompted the FDFA people to undermine the EEA project, in the hope of then persuading the majority of the Federal Council to lodge an application for EU membership and to agree to the guillotine clause in the first package of bilateral agreements. The ECJ model implied that Switzerland should be put on a track that would sooner or later bring it into the EU and on this path, points of no return should be created.

4.2 The ECJ's Rulings: Not Binding—Or Binding, but Not Final?

For its protagonists in the FDFA the so-called "ECJ-model" only presented advantages. They claimed, first and foremost, that the ECJ could not "sentence" Switzerland, but would only "tell us" how EU law was to be understood. Although this verdict would be "authoritative" or even "binding" (in French "*contraignant*"), it would not be the end of the story. Rossier and Burkhalter performed sort of a shell game over the words "binding" and "non-binding". In such games, it is impossible to know under which shell the object actually lies. I sometimes wondered whether the fact that between 2000 and 2004 Mr. Rossier had headed the Secretariat of the Federal Gaming Board, had given him an affinity for such frolics. For a while, it was contended that the judgments would not be binding. When Burkhalter and Rossier had to admit that the ECJ's rulings would be binding, they maintained that Switzerland would, in any case, keep its liberty to reject them or to further negotiate in the EEA Joint Committee. Switzerland could also pass legislation that would block the implementation of the ECJ's ruling. At the same time—and this was said to be the trick of the "ECJ solution"—the EU would feel bound if the ruling was in favour of Switzerland. It was said to be politically unthinkable that the Commission would contemplate turning against the EU's own Court. In other words, the ECJ model was the only model that allowed Switzerland to take the EU to court. That it would be the court of the other side with its own preunderstanding, was deemed to be irrelevant.

The truth of the matter is that, as stated in its first EEA Opinion 1/91 of 14 December 1991, the ECJ is only prepared to adopt decisions whose binding force is guaranteed. The ECJ came to this conclusion in the context of the issue of whether it would be willing to render preliminary rulings at the request of a national court of a non-EU State.[6] However, the ECJ President at that time, Vassilios Skouris, made it clear in a speech at the University of Geneva in October 2013 that this principle would also apply to possible dispute resolution proceedings. It is amazing that the Swiss advocates of the ECJ model did not even take note of this statement, but carried on saying that Switzerland would retain its freedom to say no. The claim that there is a difference between the preliminary ruling procedure and the dispute settlement procedure is without merit in this respect. A judgment in preliminary ruling proceedings must be implemented by the national court, a judgment in dispute resolution proceedings must be effectuated by the EEA Joint Committee. In both cases, compliance may be refused. However, that does not alter the binding force of the judgments. As London School of Economics (LSE) Professor Damien Chalmers once wrote, a main feature of judicial dispute resolution is its "all-or-nothing quality". Once the ECJ has spoken, there is no room for further

[6]For details see Chapter 3.

negotiations. The party that refuses to follow will have to bear the consequences of its actions.

The FDFA's concept was based on a single article of the multilateral EEA Agreement, which was taken out of context and transplanted into a future bilateral institutional agreement between Switzerland and the EU. The relevant provision, Article 111(3) EEA, states under the heading "settlement of disputes" that if the EEA Contracting Parties, the EU on the one hand and the three EFTA States Iceland, Liechtenstein and Norway on the other, cannot settle a dispute, they

> may agree to request the Court of Justice of the European Communities to give a *ruling* on the interpretation of the relevant rules.[7]

In the same vein, the German text speaks of a decision ("*Entscheidung*"), whereas the French and the Italian text state that the ECJ would, if invoked, pronounce on the interpretation of the rules at stake ("*se prononcer*", "*pronunciarsi*"). I leave the question open of whether the fact that the helm of the FDFA consisted of Francophones may have had an impact on the understanding of Article 111(3) EEA.

It should be noted that under the EEA Agreement, the ECJ which, by definition, would lack impartiality in such a case could only be invoked if both sides, EU and EFTA, agree. That the EFTA side would give its consent is hard to imagine. Moreover, as every student of comparative law knows, Article 111(3) EEA must be read in its proper context. It is only *ultima ratio,* which—in theory—could be relevant in case of a judicial conflict between the EFTA Court and the ECJ. This provision has never been put to the test so far. In view of all the serious issues that would accompany the triggering of such a procedure it is quite likely that this provision will remain a dead letter in the EEA Agreement.

4.3 Cabinet Politics: The "Non-paper"

It was not only the substance of Swiss integration policy that changed, but also the method. From now on, cabinet politics was the order of the day. The expression "cabinet politics" harks back to a time of absolutism when rulers conducted their foreign policy without involving the estates and without taking into consideration public opinion. *Mutatis mutandis*, this was what Mr. Rossier—with the acquiescence of his superior, Mr. Burkhalter—did. Yves Rossier, whom I never met in person, is apparently a smart man. He also appears to be a good communicator. In February 2013, the Swiss edition of the big German weekly newspaper "*Die Zeit*" published a portrait of him entitled "A sculptor of foreign policy". He was described as speaking fast with lots of witty anecdotes. *European Voice* called him a "cosmopolitan diplomat". Another title that was bestowed on Rossier was the "high-speed thinker". Rossier's first big announcement was that he had to overcome

[7]Emphasis added.

the deadlock in the negotiations with the EU. Certainly, it would have been child's play to achieve this. All that was required was to acknowledge that the two Commission proposals—EEA II or docking to the EEA/EFTA institutions—were valid options, which merited to be further explored. In this context, one would also have needed to elaborate on the fact that under both options Switzerland would eventually have had the right to nominate a member of the ESA College and a judge of the EFTA Court. But that was not what the FDFA leadership wanted.

In early 2013, Rossier and his counterpart on the EU side, David O'Sullivan, got together at confidential meetings and the two drafted a so-called "non-paper". "The Penguin Companion to European Union" by Anthony Teasdale and Timothy Bainbridge defines a "non-paper" as "an informal document, usually without explicit attribution, put forward in closed negotiations within EU institutions". The older diplomatic language used the term *aide-mémoire*. As it turned out, all the major decisions were already anticipated in this document. At the same time, Rossier warded off criticism by asserting that the document was only a "non-paper". Rossier and O'Sullivan are both alumni of the College of Europe in Bruges. Rossier attended the training ground for civil servants in 1986, ten years after his partner in crime. O'Sullivan had previously held a number of high-level positions in the Commission. FDFA insiders told me that they doubted whether Rossier could cope with such a counter-part. However, Rossier's entourage managed to spread the rumour that since the two chief negotiators had a particularly close relationship, a window of opportunity had opened that needed to be capitalised. The two men, short Rossier and tall O'Sullivan, were seen together at press conferences, where they unfailingly praised and complimented each other. Whenever they appeared in public, I was reminded of the Wilhelm Busch cartoon figures "*Plisch and Plum*", two young dogs that escaped being drowned and then set out on a number of brazen escapades together. *Plisch and Plum* were also the nicknames of Franz Josef Strauss, the conservative Minister for the Treasury and Karl Schiller, the social democratic Minister for Economic Affairs in the first German grand coalition that lasted from 1966 until 1969. Schiller and Strauss developed the famous anticyclical policy and appeared to be inseparable. The new *Plisch and Plum* were less successful. However, at the time, the close relationship between the two chief negotiators hardly provoked any major criticism from the Swiss media.

In a seeming objectivity the "non-paper" set out three options: docking to the EEA/EFTA institutions (option 1); the establishment of joint organs (option 2); and the ECJ solution (option 3). Oddly enough, the ECJ option was called "*coopération juridictionnelle*". The second option was, however, nothing but smoke and mirrors. It was clear *a priori* that the EU would never agree to such a scenario, which would be excluded by both the EEA Agreement and the bilateral "24-hours Agreement" concluded between Switzerland and the EU as regards law that is identical in substance to EU law. The EU chief negotiator must have realised that this option was not meant to be taken seriously. Thus, two options remained: docking to the EEA/EFTA institutions or being subject to the ECJ.

The docking solution would have implied that the bilateral agreements would be subject to monitoring by ESA and the judicial control of the EFTA Court. If ESA was of the opinion that Switzerland was in breach of a bilateral agreement, it could have opened infringement proceedings and ultimately brought an infringement action. If Switzerland won the case, the EFTA Court's judgment would constitute a *res iudicata* and have legal effect for everybody. If Switzerland lost the case, it would be legally obliged to implement the judgment. As I have said before, the docking solution had been proposed to the Swiss by the EU Commission. It was a very generous offer. The EU was prepared to let Switzerland negotiate the right to have its own ESA College Member and its own EFTA Court Judge alongside the three EEA/EFTA States Iceland, Liechtenstein and Norway. The FDFA, which obviously still has the long-term goal of Switzerland joining the EU in mind, rejected the docking model and opted for the ECJ solution. This was in line with the department's traditional policy of avoiding anything that has to do with the EEA as the devil avoids holy water.

After having assessed the Swiss proposal, the External Action Service of the European Commission, rather surprisingly, decided to permit discussions to continue along these lines. This was a mistake, also from an EU perspective. I saw the EU ambassador Richard Jones, a British diplomat, in Berne in March 2013. Richard told me that the ECJ model had not been proposed by the Union, but since the Swiss insisted on it, the Union could not say no. I never felt that Jones really understood the political mechanisms of Switzerland. I was in contact with a lot of senior Swiss politicians at that time and some, in particular in the CVP, realised that the ECJ model would never fly.

The non-paper also mentioned a preliminary reference procedure. According to the respective passage, the parties will assess the possibility of giving Swiss courts of last resort the right to ask the ECJ for a preliminary ruling. Berne civil servants told me that this proposal came from the EU. That Mr. Rossier agreed to it can only be explained by assuming that he did not realise that the ECJ will only give such rulings to a third-country court if their binding force is guaranteed. Had he been aware of this it would be difficult to understand why such a fuss was made about the allegedly non-binding, or at least non-final, character of the ECJ's rulings in dispute settlement proceedings. Under a preliminary ruling procedure, there is no joint committee involved and hence there is *a priori* nothing to negotiate.

4.4 The Six Untenable Contentions About the EFTA Institutions

In order to pave the way for the "ECJ solution," the FDFA made and relentlessly reiterated six incorrect contentions about the functioning of the EFTA Institutions, ESA and the EFTA Court. When I listened to the people from the FDFA and their followers, I was often reminded of the saying of French philosopher Simone de Beauvoir:

> *Le principal fléau de l'humanité n'est pas l'ignorance, car l'ignorant a souvent des excuses, mais le refus de savoir.*
>
> (The main scourge of humanity is not ignorance, because the ignorant often have excuses, but the refusal to know.)

The *first* and most serious wrong assertion was that the judgments of the EFTA Court in infringement proceedings are not binding on the EU. This statement was made, with a regretful tone, to parliamentarians and to representatives of the cantons and of the associations. When I spoke at the New Helvetic Society Aargau on 11 November 2014, I was introduced by the President of the Swiss parent association, Berne State Councillor Hans Stöckli. He said that the parliamentarians had in fact examined whether the EFTA Court could be a feasible solution for Switzerland, but that since its judgments were not binding on the EU, they had had to look for something else. The fact that said addressees believed this assertion is not a good testament of the Swiss militia system. They should have pricked up their ears for at least two reasons: first, they should have questioned whether the Swiss chief negotiator at that time, Franz Blankart, and the Federal Council and the Swiss Parliament would really have agreed to such a bad deal in 1992, when they negotiated the EEA Agreement. Second, they should have asked how the Norwegians, Icelanders and Liechtensteiners had survived for 20 years—seemingly rather well—with such an imbalanced agreement. A simple call to the Liechtenstein embassy in Berne would have sufficed to reveal the falsity of this claim.

The truth is that the judgments of the EFTA Court in infringement proceedings are as binding as the judgments of the ECJ. The most important example is *Icesave I* where the EFTA Court dismissed ESA's action with effect for Iceland, the UK, the Netherlands and the European Commission, who had supported ESA.[8]

One wonders how the FDFA could reach its conclusion irrespective of these facts. At this point, I need to include some additional aspects and go a little further by also referring to the basic understanding of "foreign law" in Switzerland. From the perspective of Switzerland, EU law and EEA law are foreign legal systems. The discipline that deals with foreign law is comparative law. Comparative law cannot be confined to mere textual interpretation. Foreign law can only be understood in the context in which it operates. To do this one must illuminate the political background of the foreign law, and one must explore the economic and social impact. Given the importance of the proposed institutional agreement, one might have expected that an expert group would have been commissioned to deliver a report. Instead, lawyers in the FDFA limited themselves to pondering over the ECJ's second EEA Opinion 1/92. From paragraph 19 of that opinion, which states

> that the EFTA Court [....] will exercise its jurisdiction only within EFTA,

they drew the conclusion that judgments of the EFTA Court could not be binding on the EU and the ECJ. This deduction confuses competence, effect and precedential value. It is a beginner's mistake that undermines the whole ECJ model of the

[8] See for details Chapter 25.

Federal Council. That the EFTA Court is only competent in the EFTA pillar does not mean that its decisions are not binding for the EU. Moreover, as I have already explained, the one-sided written homogeneity rules have in practice been replaced by a largely symbiotic relationship between the ECJ and the EFTA Court.[9] The FDFA's lawyers made a second serious mistake. According to Protocol 48 to the EEA Agreement, decisions of the EEA Joint Committee must not affect the case law of the ECJ. They deduced from this that the EEA Agreement would secure in a binding way that the ECJ will always have the last word. This deduction is also untenable. Not only must the case law of the ECJ remain unaffected by any political decisions; the same also applies to the case law of the EFTA Court. However, this was only expressly laid down with regard to the ECJ in EEA Protocol 48, for political reasons. The EEA-negotiators were keen to appease the ECJ, which in its first EEA Opinion 1/91 had rejected the original idea of establishing a combined EEA Court consisting of judges from the ECJ and from the EFTA countries. By introducing Protocol 48, they wanted to ensure that the ECJ would agree to the establishment of an EFTA Court.[10]

Notre Dame Professor Roger P. Alford has warned of two dangers in comparative law: Selectivity and bricolage. The FDFA made both mistakes.

The *second* wrong contention was that if Switzerland were to prevail in infringement proceedings brought by ESA before the EFTA Court, the EU would most probably open dispute settlement proceedings, in which Switzerland would have a bad hand. The truth is that no such proceedings have yet been triggered in the almost 25 years of the EEA's existence, and that a docking of Switzerland would not change this situation. If the EU had ever wanted to act in such a fashion, it had been given ample opportunity to do so in the context of the first *Icesave* case. In fact, the Dutch had even considered going for dispute settlement proceedings, and there was also considerable discontent in UK government circles and in the Commission. Nevertheless, the EU did not resort to such an action.[11] This is a matter of law. Judgments of an independent court of law can not only be considered from a political perspective. Most people in the FDFA don't have a sufficient understanding of the rule of law because they think that everything is political. The EU might compromise itself if it were to attack a well-reasoned judgment of the EFTA Court in political dispute settlement procedures under Article 111 EEA.

The *third* wrong assertion was that if Switzerland were to dock, it would risk being condemned by the EFTA Court (based on an infringement action brought by ESA), while the EU would remain unchecked. This claim shows a simple lack of understanding, which was probably intentional, of the EEA two pillar model. Under that model, Switzerland would be monitored by ESA and the EU countries would be monitored by the European Commission. The Commission takes its duties rather seriously and is sometimes quicker on its feet than ESA. There have been numerous

---

[9]See for details Chapter 21.

[10]See for details Chapter 21.

[11]See for details Chapter 25.

convictions of EU Member States for breaches of EEA law. I have discussed this with supporters of the ECJ model and they have responded: "Well, if the ECJ will decide in any case on whether the EU Member States are compliant or not, what's then so wrong with our ECJ model?" This answer shows that these people are unwilling or unable to think things through to their logical conclusion. The vast majority of the cases concerning the EEA Agreement are dealt with by the EFTA Court and not by the ECJ.

The *fourth* false contention was that under the docking model Switzerland could be "sentenced" by the EFTA Court. With this, Mr. Rossier said in a nonchalant way, the dice would be cast ("*la messe serait dite*"). The ECJ on the other hand could not "sentence" Switzerland because after the rendering of the judgment Switzerland could continue to negotiate and probably reach a partial implementation of the judgment or refuse implementation altogether. This contention is no more than semantic wordplay—or as we lawyers would call it—sophistry. The truth is that Switzerland could be sentenced under both scenarios. Both ECJ and EFTA Court judgments must be implemented in every case, although the consequences of non-implementation under an ECJ solution would probably be more serious than under an EFTA Court solution. The EFTA Court is not as powerful as the ECJ with its 28 judges and 11 AGs. Due to the unilateral right of action of the European Commission, the alleged dispute settlement proceedings would constitute *de facto* infringement proceedings before the Court of the opposite side. In reality, the freedom of the Federal Council to reject a judgment would only exist on paper. Thus, the only question is, under which model might you be able to nominate your own judge?

The *fifth* false assertion was that under the docking solution, Switzerland would be under ESA's surveillance, which would mean that the country would be flooded by around one hundred new controllers. Under the ECJ model, no new institutions would be created and Switzerland would monitor itself. Any surveillance by a supranational body would be eliminated. The Minister for Foreign Affairs stated this during the debate in August 2013 and reiterated it shortly before his fall in the spring of 2017. However, this contention is already suspect because the Commission has always said that Switzerland's compliance must be monitored. The truth is that, regardless of what might be stated in any agreement, surveillance would in fact lie in the hands of the European Commission, which could at any time unilaterally bring Switzerland before the ECJ. Being subject to the surveillance of the powerful European Commission would probably not be an ideal solution. ESA on the other hand does not have the reputation of being overly aggressive.[12] The image of one hundred new controllers was mere speculation. This assertion also completely overlooked the fact that it is more favourable to have a surveillance organ in which you are represented than to be subject to the opposite party's authority.

---

[12]See for details Chapter 7.

The *sixth* false statement was that since the EFTA Court must follow the ECJ due to the homogeneity rules of EEA law, it has no room to develop its own solutions. Therefore, it is wiser to be directly subject to the ECJ. Here again, it is apparent that people in the FDFA have a tendency to judge the EEA based on the law on the books. Such an assertion is all the more surprising in a country that has always been proud of its pragmatism and its aversion to pure theorising. As I show in Chaps. 3 and 21 of this book, the law on the books is largely characterised by a judicial dialogue between the ECJ and the EFTA Court.

4.5 An Irresponsible Use of the "Foreign Judges" Formula

It is almost unbelievable that the head of the FDFA was not too good to resort to the formula of the foreign judges to discredit the docking solution. Swiss anti-Europeans have played around with the concept of "foreign judges" for quite some time. During the preparatory phase of the accession to the ECHR in 1974, opponents invoked the "Federal Charter" that was agreed in 1291 by the people of the valley of Uri, the democracy of the valley of Schwyz, and the community of the Lower Valley of Unterwalden. This treaty included the obligation to recognise only local judges, and referred to the fighting of the Swiss Confederates to get rid of the jurisdiction of the Imperial Chamber Court of the Holy Roman Empire ("*Reichskammergericht*") at the end of the 15th century. The dispatch of the Federal Council called these references deceptive.

The fear of foreign judges was also fuelled in 1992 during the campaign against the accession to the EEA. University of Zurich legal historian Clausdieter Schott made it clear, however, that the function of modern Swiss judges cannot be compared to the one of medieval judges. Whereas the task of today's judge is to adjudicate, i.e. to hear and decide cases, the medieval judge was excluded from the decision-making. Only the college of jurymen ("*Schöffen*") was empowered to adjudicate. The judge's role was restricted to conducting the procedure. Unlike the judge, the members of the jury always came from the same folk-community ("*Dinggenossenschaft*") as the parties. It follows that a foreign judge could never have been an issue. As regards the tradition of the foreign judges' formula, Schott argues that the passage in question in the 1291 Federal Charter had been totally forgotten for centuries and had been re-discovered for political purposes in 1891 in the context of the 600-year celebration of the Confederation which was marked by nationalist pathos, and then again in the first half of the 20th century. In substance, the foreign judges' formula was not specifically Swiss. It simply set out the plaintiff's obligation to bring its lawsuit before the court of the defendant's domicile and not before a "foreign" court. In other words, the formula described the development of a general rule of jurisdiction. The modern use of the foreign judges' formula in the 1291 Federal Charter is therefore no more than a historical misrepresentation. If one wanted to use the formula today, one could call an international court a foreign court if Switzerland were subject to its jurisdiction without having the right to nominate a judge. The ECtHR is therefore not a foreign court nor would the EFTA Court have been a foreign court had Switzerland ratified the EEA Agreement, because there would have been a judge nominated by Switzerland. Interestingly, the foreign judges' formula was not invoked in the context of Switzerland's accession to the WTO although the chances that Switzerland will ever be in a position to nominate a member to the WTO AB are rather slim.

Highly surprisingly, the "foreign judges" formula was now taken over by the duo at the helm of the FDFA. Thereby, the same lack of earnestness became apparent as when dealing with the question of whether the judgments of the ECJ in dispute settlement proceedings are binding or not. Or, to repeat the analogy I used earlier: those in charge were playing another shell game. The FDFA started to allege that the EFTA Court would be a foreign court for Switzerland even if a Swiss judge were to sit on the bench, because there would still also be a Norwegian, an Icelander and a Liechtensteiner. In the light of the fact that the anti-Europeans contend that a court that does not consist exclusively of Swiss judges is a foreign court, the statement was irresponsible. According to this logic, the ECtHR would also be a foreign court, and that has never been the line of the Federal Council. Minister for Foreign Affairs Burkhalter has defended the ECtHR. This is positive, but it is not compatible with what he has said about the EFTA Court. In addition, if we look at things closely, we see that at the EFTA Court, Switzerland would possibly be able to nominate one out of 4 judges whereas on the ECtHR there is only one Swiss judge out of 47.

4.6 Going Down the Drain Step by Step

The Federal Council was about to take a preliminary decision on the ECJ model in late June 2013. At the EFTA Ministerial meeting in Trondheim, on 24 June 2013, I spoke with the Minister of Economic Affairs, Johann Schneider-Ammann. He belongs to the same political party as Mr. Burkhalter, the FDP. I knew him because I had advised him on the revision of the Swiss Cartel Act. I well remember the Trondheim Ministerial meeting for two particular reasons.

First of all, the trip was memorable because, on the day after the meeting, Doris and I were driven to Stokkoya, an island located 120 km from Trondheim with a marvellous little beach. A lady from the EFTA Secretariat in Geneva had urged us to go there. It was a sunny day; we had lunch on the waterfront and then went for a swim at 13 °C. A local journalist asked for an interview and I was prepared to be pelted with questions about our recent judgment in the first *Icesave* case. However, he simply wanted to know how we found the landscape and the beach and we responded that it was gorgeous.

Second, after my conversation with Federal Councillor Schneider-Ammann, I still had some hope that the Swiss Government would at least postpone a decision on whether to opt for the ECJ model. Therefore, I did not know what had hit me when, two days later, on 26 June 2013, the Federal Council announced its intention of having a negotiation mandate worked out based on the ECJ model. The FDFA was supposed to prepare a draft mandate by August 2013. In the light of what Schneider-Ammann had told me, I was astounded. Apparently party discipline was more important than rational decision-making.

On 27 June 2013, the Zurich-based newspaper *TagesAnzeiger* described the position of Switzerland's political parties. The article demonstrated that the Foreign Ministry had succeeded in causing an incredible confusion. That the president of the anti-European SVP would reject the ECJ model came as no surprise. The SVP leadership refuses to distinguish between a European court with an own judge and a court of the other side. They consider both scenarios to amount to the same thing, since both cases would involve non-Swiss judges. However, the SVP president also rejected the idea that ECJ rulings would not be binding, and on that point he was right. According to the chairman of the CVP, it was unthinkable that the other side's court would decide on issues that impacted on Switzerland. The president of the SP saw the fact that the ECJ would interpret the bilateral treaties as unproblematic. However, he wanted to have a guarantee that the flanking measures, which aim to protect working conditions in Switzerland, would remain untouched. The president of the Green Party babbled on about an arbitration tribunal and reserved the right to assess the ECJ model once the details were known. Her counterpart from the BDP found it acceptable that the ECJ would interpret EU law. It was, however, clear and important, he added, that it must not be a requirement that the ECJ's rulings must be implemented. The head of the Green Liberal Party criticised the consultative recognition of the ECJ. The president of the FDP, Burkhalter's own party, could not be reached for a comment, however, one year later he said that with this model Switzerland would become the least sovereign State of Europe. However, this kind of sentiment did not prevent the FDP from supporting Burkhalter's crazy venture, purely for reasons of internal politics.

I decided to go public and harshly criticised the approach chosen by the Federal Council in an article in the *HandelsZeitung* of 17 July 2013. The weekly business paper published my piece on the front-page under the title "Highest EFTA Justice Attacks Federal Council" ("*Oberster Richter der Efta attackiert Bundesrat*"). Since the Swiss News Agency also took up the story, it was printed in all the major newspapers. I rejected the incorrect contentions on the functioning of ESA and my Court and stated with regard to the intended role of the ECJ that not even at a friendly football tournament ("*Grümpelturnier*") could one team bring its own referee. The FDFA declined to comment.

In August 2013, 15 university professors dealing with European law led by University of Basle Professor Christa Tobler in a letter to the FDFA turned against the ECJ model. They argued that a solution had to be found that would give Switzerland the right to have its own judge on the competent court. Therefore, docking to the EFTA Court would be preferable. Other clear-sighted academics who were not part of the group, such as Daniel Thürer from the University of Zurich and Richard Senti from the Swiss Institute of Technology were also critical of the Federal Council's approach. The Minister for Foreign Affairs rejected the criticism of the professors based on the incorrect argument that if the EFTA Court were to decide in favour of Switzerland, the EU would not be bound. For this reason, the docking solution would not be accepted by the Swiss people. The professors' letter was the only major action taken by a group of academics. Once it seemed that the die was cast in favour of the ECJ model, only a handful of them continued to resist. The majority is indifferent or sitting on the fence. In speeches, I sometimes said that the first damned souls described by Dante Alighieri in his "*Inferno*" (Hell) are "*gli indifferenti alla politica*", the indifferent to politics. And, of course, there are those who get government mandates. On April 1, 2017, Heike Schmoll published an article in *FAZ* with the title

> *Professoren, mischt Euch endlich wieder ein!* (Professors, get finally back in the game!).

The journalist called for a debate on populism. But her sentence is also applicable to one-sided government propaganda. Unfortunately, we live in an age in which such appeals remain unheard.

Since the FDFA refused to reassess the chosen path, I listed the Federal Council's "seven misunderstandings" in the *NZZ* of 16 August 2013 and concluded that no mandate could be given based on inadequate preparatory work. A number of people from Burkhalter's party came to his help and responded by reiterating the wrong contentions on the consultative role of the ECJ, on the one hand, and on the lack of binding force of EFTA Court infringement judgments for the EU, on the other. In the same issue of *NZZ*, an interview with Mr. Rossier appeared in which he repeated all the wrong assertions and concluded that if the docking model was adopted Switzerland would lose more sovereignty than under the "ECJ-solution".

On 23 August 2013, Astrid Epiney, a German Professor teaching public international law at the University of Fribourg, commended the Federal Council, in the *NZZ*, by saying that it had "managed to square the circle". Her article reiterated that the EFTA Court was unable to give judgments that would bind the EU. It ended with an ode to the independence of the ECJ. There was nothing to indicate, she wrote, that the ECJ might have a tendency to decide against Switzerland. On the contrary, its case law was characterised by some sort of "integration logic" that operated independently from any special interest. The issue is, however, that this integration logic is not necessarily the logic of bilateral agreements.

On 11 September 2013, I spoke at a meeting of the foreign policy committee of the FDP in Berne. The party's Secretary General, Stefan Brupbacher, a former student of mine, had insisted that I come, as he put it "out of love for Switzerland" ("*Aus Liebe zur Schweiz*" was an FDP campaign slogan). The Foreign Service had done a good job in preparing the committee. With the exception of a former ambassador, almost everybody in the room had bought into their contentions. The representative of the umbrella association of Swiss industry *economiesuisse* was not really convinced, but—probably for political reasons as *economiesuisse* is close to the FDP—shrugged his shoulders. Rossier was absent, and Gétaz substituted for Burkhalter. After a heated discussion in which the same assertions were endlessly repeated, I felt that I had at least been able to sow some doubts.

On 11 October 2013, the Foreign Policy Committee of the State Council approved the mandate without any amendments by 10 votes to 0 with two abstentions. The matter was not uncontroversial, however as the chairman said afterwards, the committee wanted to back up the Federal Council. Since "the other side was listening", the committee decided to communicate its concerns to the Federal Council in a secret letter. The latter remarks were almost touching. Here it was again, the spirit of the National Redoubt. During World War II, the country was full of posters bearing the motto "The enemy is listening" ("*Feind hört mit*") and "Those who cannot keep quiet, will harm their homeland" ("*Wer nicht schweigen kann schadet der Heimat*"). The committee stated in a press release that Mr. Burkhalter had demonstrated in a credible way that the "ECJ model" was the best way to start the negotiations.

The National Council's Foreign Policy Committee followed suit a few weeks later, but it was more critical. 14 members voted in favour, 6 against and one abstained. Among the 14 members who voted yes, there were some whose only motive was that they didn't want to vote with the anti-European SVP. This was clear evidence of incapacity. On 13 December 2013, the Conference of the Cantons also gave a green light. Only three cantons voted against the mandate, St. Gallen, its neighbour canton Thurgau, and Schwyz which was in the hands of the anti-Europeans. St. Gallen and Thurgau favoured an EFTA solution.

I was astonished that the Canton of Geneva was among those that supported Burkhalter. In September 2012, the Swiss Jurists Day had taken place in Geneva. I was the rapporteur on European and international economic law, and I took the opportunity of visiting Geneva State Councillor David Hiler together with my Head of Cabinet Philipp Speitler. Mr. Hiler told us that his government was contemplating a second attempt at joining the EEA. However, I then learned that Burkhalter had put pressure on the Genevans arguing that as fellow-romands they could not leave him out in the rain. The same obviously goes for the cantons with a strong FDP, the Minister for Foreign Affairs' political party. All in all, it is fair to say that the mandate was obtained surreptitiously. In the end a sentiment of "let's just see what comes out of this" allowed parliamentarians, the cantons and the associations to agree. These actors were briefed by the same people who they are supposed to control. When I told him that the whole "ECJ model" was based on incorrect assumptions, a high representative of Mr. Burkhalter's FDP wrote to me that as a militia man he felt overtaxed in such a situation. It fits the picture that the Swiss mandate is still being kept secret. The same goes for the "non-paper".

Another reason why the Minister for Foreign Affairs got his way so easily was the weakness of *economiesuisse*. Corporate Switzerland had lost a lot of its standing during a contentious referendum on what was called the "Fat Cat Initiative". On 3 March 2013, voters approved tough limits on executives' pay. *Economiesuisse* had heavily campaigned against the initiative, which had been launched by a single citizen who happened to be the head of company that produced herbal toothpaste. In this context it should also be noted that increasingly the CEO's of many large

Swiss corporations are foreigners who, while they may be good at maximising gains, do not participate in the political life of the country. At the same time there is a certain brain drain; people with essential skills leave because they feel too constricted in a country where (sometimes) refined mediocrity is the measure of all things, at least in politics, the judiciary and universities.

5 2014: Mass Immigration Initiative

On 9 February 2014, a slim majority of Swiss voters approved the so-called mass immigration initiative (MII). A new constitutional provision was created that called for the introduction of a quota system for immigrants. The MII had been launched by Mr. Blocher's SVP. The outcome of the vote was not completely unexpected although the general assumption had been that the initiative would be narrowly defeated. In the decisive week prior to the vote, Mr. Burkhalter was conspicuous by his absence from the country. The great traveller was displayed by the media while sipping tea with the Emperor of Japan and hugging Swiss Olympic gold medal winners in Sotschi. Whether the new provision in the Federal Constitution would be compatible with the bilateral Free Movement of Persons Agreement with the EU was an open question. Unsurprisingly, the European Commission declared that it was "disappointed". Vice-President Viviane Reding stated that the vote could jeopardise the access of Swiss operators to the Single Market since the latter was "not Swiss cheese". Nevertheless, State Secretary Rossier observed a few days after the vote that he had something up his sleeve. It became clear that some factions in the FDFA were playing with the thought of asking the people for an "overall vote" on a package comprising the repeal of the new constitutional norm, new bilateral agreements and the "ECJ-model". Clearly, the idea was to blackmail the people by telling them that they either had to swallow the ECJ or—in view of the planned electricity agreement—the lights would go out. I warned against this danger and several parliamentarians shared my concern.

On 13 March 2014, David O'Sullivan gave a talk at the University of Luxembourg. Beforehand he paid me a visit. He told me that the plan was now to terminate the institutional part of the negotiations based on the "ECJ model". Time was of the essence, he said, because in the autumn he was scheduled to become EU ambassador in Washington DC. The institutional agreement would then be put in a deep freezer and only be unfrozen once the free movement of persons' problem would be resolved. His statements smacked of Rossier. In a package referendum, the questions would then have been whether the people were prepared to accept the ECJ, together with the rescission of the mass immigration rules and a few other "sweeteners" such as an electricity agreement or whether they preferred to terminate bilateralism and thereby endanger the access of Swiss industry to the EU Single Market. It became clear that O'Sullivan had no doubt that judgments of the ECJ, under the dispute settlement procedure, would be binding just like any other judgments. Following a negative ECJ judgment the Swiss would be allowed to take some time, according to the standards of courtesy, but then they would have to implement it. What O'Sullivan could not even contemplate was that the Swiss people would never accept this. He did not have much of a clue about Switzerland and the Swiss psyche, and being Irish, he repeatedly compared Switzerland to Ireland. Irish voters had first rejected the Lisbon EU Reform Treaty and in a second referendum approved it bowing to pressure from the other EU Member States. This was obviously where Mr. O'Sullivan had gained his knowledge of direct democracy. What he also underestimated was the effect of Rossier's binding/not binding talk.

At the end of the day, both chambers of Parliament opted for a soft implementation of the new constitutional norm, which was dubbed a "light priority for residents" rule. Whether this is in accordance with the new constitutional norm is questionable. However, the risks involved in launching a new referendum on the same matter were high. For the sake of good order, I should add that in June 2017, the SVP called for a vote to terminate the Swiss-EU agreement on free movement of persons. In January 2018, they started collecting signatures.

On 13 November 2014, I gave the so-called Autumn Lecture at the Swiss German Chamber of Commerce in Zurich, a major event. I criticised the fact that the Federal Council was continuing on its course and was thereby losing valuable time. And I reiterated that the negotiating mandate was based on incorrect assumptions. Reactions were very positive, and the press reported the event widely.

6 2015 Onwards: Treading Water

6.1 Negotiation for the Sake of Negotiation

The years from 2015 to 2017 were lost years. Negotiation round after negotiation round was held and no significant progress was made. That didn't hinder the Minister for Foreign Affairs from claiming on a regular basis that the negotiations were almost finished, that the negotiators were on the final straight and so forth. Journalists started to make fun of these announcements and a major newspaper printed a cartoon of Mr. Burkhalter with a Pinocchio nose. My dictum that the ECJ was the court of the other side and therefore not impartial became accepted among parliamentarians and journalists. In August 2015, State Secretary Rossier was sacked as chief negotiator and replaced by Mr. De Watteville. However, as a major newspaper noted, this was a bluff because the negotiating mandate itself remained unchanged. The Commission started to realise that the ECJ model would not fly in Switzerland, but apparently out of courtesy, it continued to grin and bear the

negotiations. It seems that in their final years, the negotiations mainly revolved around the question of how severe the sanctions might be that the EU could impose on Switzerland if an ECJ ruling was not followed.
In a speech before judges and AG's of the ECJ on 19 October 2015, I said:

> *Dass der EuGH sich mit der Rolle eines mit einer Schreckschusspistole ausgerüsteten Hilfssheriffs abfinden könnte, und das in nicht in einem juristischen, sondern in einem politischen Verfahren, halte ich, ohne der Entscheidung der geschätzten Kolleginnen und Kollegen vorgreifen zu wollen, für ausgeschlossen. Umgekehrt sind die Chancen, dass das Schweizer Volk einer Lösung zustimmen könnte, bei welcher der EuGH – ohne Schweizer Richter - verbindlich entscheidet, ausserordentlich gering. Dass man in Bern augenscheinlich in einem europarechtlichen Elfenbeinturm lebt, ist das eine. Was ich aber nie verstanden habe ist, warum sich die Kommission auf dieses Modell – wenn es denn diesen Namen verdient – eingelassen hat.*
>
> That the ECJ could accept the role of a deputy sheriff equipped with a blank gun, and that it could do so in a political procedure rather than a legal procedure, is, in my view, ruled out, without prejudice to the decision of the honourable colleagues. Conversely, the chances that the Swiss people could agree to a solution in which the ECJ - without a Swiss judge - makes binding decisions are extremely low. The fact that Berne is apparently living in an ivory tower under European law is one thing. But what I have never understood is why the Commission has embraced this 'model', if it deserves its name.

My statement was received with cheerfulness.

Those who had figured out the "ECJ model" either didn't care, because in any event they wanted Switzerland to make an irreversible step towards EU membership, or they thought their solution would be particularly clever and enable them to pull a fast one on the EU. Neither explanation is particularly flattering. Certainly, the EU negotiators saw all this, however, having little experience with the complicated mechanisms of Swiss direct democracy, they obviously thought that this time they would be able to draw recalcitrant Switzerland into the fold.

On 16 and 17 November 2015, members of the EFTA/EU Delegation of the Swiss Parliament visited Luxembourg in order to familiarise themselves with the functioning of the ECJ and of the EFTA Court. ECJ President Koen Lenaerts and I were invited to dinner by the Swiss Ambassador, H.E. Urs Hammer. Koen made it very clear that once the ECJ had rendered a judgment, there would be no room for further negotiations. Although a high representative of the Swiss FDFA was present, the Minister for Foreign Affairs subsequently continued to reiterate his untenable contentions.

In the autumn of 2016, I spoke at the Universities of Zurich and of Basel and repeated my criticism of the failed Swiss integration policy. Interviews were published by *Basler Zeitung* and by the weekly newspaper *HandelsZeitung*. I stated that the Federal Council's foreign policy had run aground. I did the same in March 2017 in a speech in Bregenz, Austria.

6.2 *Mr. Burkhalter's Replacement by Mr. Cassis*

On 14 June 2017, Minister for Foreign Affairs Burkhalter announced his intention of resigning by 31 October 2017. Although he contended that this step had nothing to do with the planned framework agreement with the EU, it was obvious that his resignation was a direct consequence of its failure. It had become increasingly clear that the Federal Council's decision to give a green light to the "ECJ model" in the summer of 2013 was not the result of an in-depth examination of the subject matter. Instead, the seven members had acted according to the maxim "let us try and if the ECJ model flies, we have a solution, otherwise we will look for something else".

On 20 September 2017, National Councillor Ignazio Cassis was elected as Burkhalter's successor by the Federal Assembly and on 2 November 2017, Cassis replaced him as Minister for Foreign Affairs. I had met the new Federal Councillor a couple of times in Luxembourg and Brussels during his tenure as a member of the EFTA/EU delegation of the Swiss Parliament. As I have said, the members of the Federal Council are elected by Parliament. In recent years it has become usus that candidates conduct a kind of election campaign. A key element of Mr. Cassis' programme was his pledge to "hit the reset button" for the European dossier. I wrote in the *NZZ* of 16 November 2017 that hitting the reset button would imply making a fresh start. To this end, it was necessary to take stock. I invited the new Foreign Minister to approach things without blinkers and to consider all options. The Swiss Government had to understand that the ECJ only renders definitive judgments. Once the ECJ has spoken, there is nothing left to negotiate. In early December 2017, Swiss newspapers reported that the FDFA had started looking into the docking solution. However, I immediately got the impression that the usual suspects in the FDFA were trying to undermine any change in approach. This confirmed what I always said in my lectures and speeches: norms matter, but people matter more.

6.3 *The EU Playing Hardball*

In 2016 and 2017, the EU adopted a policy of pinpricks vis-à-vis Switzerland. For a certain period of time, it refused to update existing market access agreements to take into account new developments of EU law. Following complaints from Switzerland, and because the Swiss Parliament largely disregarded the outcome of the mass immigration referendum, this policy was eventually discontinued.

On 23 October 2017, Commission President Jean-Claude Juncker visited the Swiss Federal Council in Berne and was assured that Switzerland would pay the EU a further 1 billion EUR over the course of the next ten years for the benefit of lower income countries in Central and Eastern Europe. In 2007, the Swiss Parliament had approved the payment of the first billion euro. Similarly to the situation for the EEA/EFTA States Iceland, Liechtenstein and Norway, these payments were a *quid pro quo* for access to the Single Market.[13] Juncker seemed to be happy and during a joint press conference with Federal President Doris Leuthard he joked that the planned framework agreement ought to be called "friendship agreement". He indicated that the treaty should be finalised by spring 2018. However, based on his conversation with the Swiss over lunch, Juncker must have got the impression that the Federal Council weren't really serious about the framework agreement. On 21 December 2017, the EU decided to recognise Swiss legislation as being equivalent to the new EU Markets in Financial Instruments rules, but limited the granting of Swiss stock exchanges' access to EU markets to one year. With the exception of the UK, all the EU Member States supported the decision. The US, Hong Kong and Australia had been granted access to EU markets for an unlimited duration. The Commission made it clear that the renewal of the Swiss access would depend on progress in the negotiations between Switzerland and the EU over a framework agreement. President Leuthard accused the EU of wanting to weaken the Swiss financial centre, claiming that there was no reason to "link this technical issue to the institutional question", and that since Switzerland fulfilled the conditions for the recognition of market equivalence, the EU's decision was discriminatory. The Commission for its part claimed that Switzerland's situation differed from that of the three abovementioned countries. The trading of Swiss shares in the EU—and vice versa—was widespread and the limitation of the equivalence to one year was justified because of the

> dissatisfaction that no progress has been made in the institutional negotiations and that no progress will be made in the timeline expected.

6.4 *A Sham Arbitration Mechanism?*

With the inauguration of the new Minister for Foreign Affairs Ignazio Cassis, the ECJ model seemingly receded into the background. However, as I suspected, the EEA phobic circles in the FDFA did not give up the fight so easily. In late December 2017, the *NZZ* wrote that the EU had proposed that the Swiss should adopt the so-called Ukraine model. The association agreements concluded by the EU with the former Sovjet Republics Ukraine, Georgia and Moldova provide for certain disputes being settled by "arbitration". I concur with Dutch trade law specialist Guillaume van der Loo's statement that the EU-Ukraine Agreement is not an appropriate template for the envisaged EU-Switzerland framework agreement because

> [a]s the fourth largest trade partner of the EU in the world with a strong developed economy which is already now closely integrated in the EU Internal Market, Switzerland is too different from Ukraine.

The Ukraine is also not part of the internal market. However, on 5 March 2018, Minister for Foreign Affairs Cassis in a media conference announced that henceforth, Switzerland would favour a dispute resolution mechanism in which an

---

[13]See for details Chapter 6.

"arbitral tribunal" would play a decisive role. With the exception of the SVP, the reactions of the political parties were mostly positive. Amicable dispute resolution is in the blood of the Swiss. This attitude is also manifested in how they want to deal with international treaties. The FDFA favours such a mechanism at least as long as Switzerland is not a member of the EU. Switzerland is an important location for international commercial arbitration. The idea that in all kinds of conflicts an arbitral tribunal is to be established, with each party appointing an arbitrator and the party arbitrators agreeing on an umpire, is widespread. Certain commentators were quick to claim that since a Swiss arbitrator would sit on the panel, the sensitive issue of foreign judges was defused.

To be sure, the arbitral panel proposed by the EU has nothing to do with classical arbitration. Although there is provision for the setting up of an arbitral tribunal in the Ukraine Agreement, Article 322 requires it to refer all important substantive questions to the ECJ that will issue a binding ruling. The EU-Moldova and EU-Georgia Agreements contains the same clause. In an article in the *Basler Zeitung* of 13 March 2018, I called the allegedly new dispute resolution model "The ECJ model in camouflage suits" and stated that the Federal Council risks repeating the mistake of spring 2013 when it pushed for the ECJ model and assuaged critics by arguing that the EU was in agreement. The main difference between the ECJ model and the arbitration model would then be that under the latter, an additional procedure is included. The two most serious disadvantages—decision by the court of the other party and patronizing of the private actors—remain. One cannot overlook that David O'Sullivan, the former EU-partner of the FDFA, played an essential role in the development of the Ukraine strategy. On closer inspection, I tend to conclude that the arbitration mechanisms of the Ukraine and the Moldova agreements may not be compatible with Union law. Although both treaties provide that important substantive issues must be referred to the ECJ for a binding preliminary ruling, the fact remains that the arbitrators may disregard their obligation to refer or may refuse to comply with the ECJ's judgment. In this respect, the Ukraine/Moldova agreements in favour of non-EU states go beyond Article 111 EEA. Under this rule, EEA law, which is identical in substance to EU law, cannot be subject to arbitration. The EU's agreements with Ukraine and Moldova were not submitted to the ECJ for approval. Whether they would have received the blessing of the EU Court is open. A future agreement EU–Switzerland would certainly be brought before the ECJ. Whether it would pass the test of compatibility with EU law can be doubted, especially because the Swiss Foreign Ministry claims that the Ukrainian/Moldovan approach will be changed in favour of Switzerland in that the arbitrators would be free to decide whether and what they wanted to submit to the ECJ.

6.5 Lessons to Be Learned

It may be that when the ECJ model was launched by Rossier and Burkhalter, some people in the FDFA were at least initially of the opinion that after a negative decision from the ECJ, the EU could be engaged in endless discussions in the EEA Joint

Committee. Such hopes were always unrealistic. In the course of the negotiations, it became clear that the ECJ model would not only have been rejected in Switzerland. I am pretty convinced that the ECJ would not have accepted such a court mechanism under Article 218(11) TFEU unless the respective treaty clearly stated that Switzerland would accept the ECJ's rulings as unconditionally binding and final.

On balance, much speaks in favour of the assumption that people in the FDFA tried, and continue to try, to place Switzerland on an EU track, albeit for the time being as a passive member. The applause from the camp of EU accession supporters is striking. The federal administration's training programme for federal officials in European law also suggests that EU membership is the ultimate goal. My Head of Cabinet Philipp Speitler, one of the leading experts in this field, taught for a short time EEA law. Despite (or perhaps because of) an excellent evaluation, his contract was not renewed and lectures on the EEA were deleted from the curriculum, which is financed with taxpayers' money. This kind of censorship is worrying; it is not appropriate in a liberal democracy. Moreover, it is also short-sighted, not to say foolish.

When the EU asked Switzerland to draft proposals for a surveillance and court mechanism for the bilateral treaties, the EEA was immediately ruled out. Newspapers revealed in August 2013 that the federal administration "assessed" the consequences of EEA membership on the side of EFTA in a 9-page document and in a second paper of similar length and depth.[14] No interviews were conducted with the EEA's decision-makers; the Berne bureaucrats apparently did not even make a phone call to the Liechtenstein Ambassador. In the *NZZ* of 23 July 2013, I criticised this approach of suppressing anything that has to do with the EEA. As far as substance is concerned, the points mentioned almost all relate to simple restrictions of competition, which favour special interests. With regard to the institutions of the EFTA pillar, the conclusions were incomprehensible. The authors argued, for example, that a Swiss judge on the EFTA Court "would always be in the minority". This casts a surprising light on their understanding of judicial impartiality and independence. Little wonder then that prominent members of Parliament also adhere to the view that it will eventually be the task of a Swiss judge to represent his country in the EFTA Court. Swiss diplomacy is now paying the price for gazing out of the window at the EFTA Ministerial meetings when the others were discussing the EEA.

The official explanation for this attitude was, and continues to be, that a second attempt at joining the EEA was almost certain to fail. The truth of the matter is, however, that influential people in the FDFA have their own agenda. The EEA haters have never gotten over two features of the EEA Agreement: first, the fact that the EFTA States do not participate in decision-making when it comes to enacting new legislation, but are limited to taking part in the decision-shaping, and second, the fact that in the decision-shaping process the EFTA States must speak with one

[14] Available at: http://www.nzz.ch/schweiz/ewr-beitritt-wuerde-delikate-fragen-provozieren-1.18128173.

voice. They judge the whole EEA Agreement based on these two elements, they refuse to take into account how the EEA functions in practice and form their opinions in the light of their memories from the late 1980s and early 1990s.

In the federal administration, there seems to be, moreover, a surprising lack of knowledge about EU structures, in particular about how the European courts function. To give an example, on 16 August 2013 the *NZZ* conducted an interview with Mr. Rossier. When asked whether the ECJ would accept the role assigned to it in the "non-paper", he replied:

> *Diese Frage muss die EU beantworten. Gäbe es ein Problem, hätte es sie uns das vermutlich gesagt.*
>
> This question must be answered by the EU. If there were a problem, they would presumably have told us.

There is, however, no "EU" that could tell whether the ECJ would agree to taking on the role of a tie-breaker as defined in the "non-paper". The EU comprises the Commission, the Council, the Parliament and—most importantly—the ECJ. An agreement such as the one in question is brokered by the Commission, but it cannot enter into force unless the ECJ has given its OK.[15] It has happened more than once that an agreement negotiated by the Commission was declared incompatible with EU law by the ECJ.

Given the experience from 2013 to 2017, it is, unfortunately, to be expected that the FDFA will continue pushing the so-called arbitration model. History could then repeat itself. Whether the EU will again play ball, remains to be seen. It may also be that Berne is trying to buy time in order to find out what is going to happen on the Brexit front. In any case, it seems that the new Foreign Minister Cassis is less missionary than his predecessor Burkhalter when it comes to connecting Switzerland to the EU.

6.6 The Berne Gracious Lords

Berne bureaucrats have another reason for opposing the EEA or a docking solution. In both cases, private operators would be entitled to defend their rights under the EEA Agreement or under bilateral law on their own motion before the EFTA Court. Under EEA law, they could either lodge a complaint with ESA or ask a Swiss court to make a reference to the EFTA Court. These options would, depending on the concrete drafting, also be available under a docking agreement. On the other hand, the FDFA's approach blocks any access for private operators to a European court. All they can do is to ask the federal administration to take up their case and open talks with the EU. It seems that the FDFA is not be ready to give up its power until

[15]See Article 218(11) TFEU.

Switzerland joins the EU. However, it is unlikely that this will happen in the near future.

The described situation is beneath the dignity of those who create wealth and whose access to the EU Single Market must be guaranteed. For citizens and economic operators to have to resort to begging for diplomatic protection has something paternalistic about it, a whiff of the *ancien régime*. The notion of *ancien régime* goes back to Fench historian Alexis de Tocqueville who gave this name to French society and economy before the French Revolution. After the separation from the German Empire at the end of the Thirty Year's War in 1648, there was no real nobility in Switzerland. But there were patricians, the so-called Gracious Lords. The self-evident way in which the federal administration patronises businesses and citizens is reminiscent of those times. That *economiesuisse* is participating in this game is probably due to the fact that the association representatives have a great influence on the formulation of the Swiss position in the Joint Committees. This would not change if an arbitration tribunal were set up along the lines of the Ukraine Agreement.

6.7 The Crisis of the Swiss Governance System

The question arises as to how the FDFA's bluff vis-à-vis the Federal Council, the Federal Parliament, the Cantons and the associations was possible. As regards the Federal Council, one reason appears to be the loss of significance of the principle of collegiality. At one time, this maxim was deemed to be a crucial element of the Swiss governance system. The idea was that the collegiality of the seven Federal Councillors would keep each other at bay and prevent Councillor(s) from acting independently. In the meantime, the individual Federal Councillors have become lone fighters. Each of them seeks the limelight. If one makes a blunder, the others may smirk because they hope to profit. At the same time, the federal administration is becoming increasingly politicised.

Another cause is the fact that the Swiss "militia" system seems to have reached its limits as regards challenging European integration. Originally, the term "militia" referred to a military force composed of civilians, which was usually deployed in addition to a regular professional army. In fact, the Swiss army has, traditionally, not been an army of professional soldiers, but of militiamen (and later women). The same term is used in a broader sense for the practice of citizens taking on public office on a part-time basis. In other words, the office is not exercised as the main profession. Beyond that, being a militiaman or—woman—is also a question of attitude. The members of the bicameral Federal Assembly (Parliament) are a good example of this. The same holds, for example, true for the members of the Competition Commission (ComCo). Appointments to ComCo are based on political considerations such as party affiliation or regional provenance. Five out of the twelve members of ComCo are effectively appointed by business associations, farmers, consumers and labour unions. Similar systems apply to other commissions. Most political party officials are militiamen. The members of the Federal Council are obviously employed on a full-time basis, however, they have been socialised as militiamen and they are elected by Parliament. To a certain extent, the militia system is a necessity in a small state because, in certain areas, there is insufficient business for professionals. Militiamen are said to have more common sense and be more pragmatic than professionals, however, the lack of professionalism may affect the quality of the work. Since militiamen by definition play multiple roles in politics, society and economy, they may find themselves more frequently embroiled in conflicts of interest than professionals, a situation that can only be mitigated to a limited extent by disclosure requirements. The 1979 St. Gallen doctoral thesis of Reto Hermann Müller listed the following advantages of the militia system: (i) citizens' participation and co-responsibility; (ii) identity of state and people as well as administration by the people; (iii) national integration; (iv) national cohesion; (v) decentralised decision-making; (vi) critique and control of state activities; (vii) expertise and experience; (viii) factual and local proximity; (ix) optimal use of personal resources; (x) objectivity, balance of interests and strengthening of the confidence in public authorities; (xi) assertiveness due to closeness to the people; (xii) low degree of bureaucracy; (xiii) freedom of expression; (xiv) cost-effectiveness; and (xv) idealism and enjoyment of work. As disadvantages Müller mentioned: (a) interconnection of power and undermining of the separation of powers by an accumulation of responsibilities; (b) influence of special interests; (c) lack of transparency; (d) lack of time, minimalism and inadequate performance; (e) irregular presence; (f) political, legal and technical dilettantism; (g) limited capacity; (h) duplication of duties; (i) coordination problems, duplications and slow processing of problems; (j) high personal costs and limited attractiveness of the posts; and (k) endangerment of professional secrecy. Today, the militia system is coming under additional pressure from globalisation and the IT revolution. The system is also jeopardised by the fact that increasingly the CEOs of multinational firms are foreigners who do not actively participate in Swiss political life. Furthermore, militia parliamentarians who exercise their job part-time find it difficult to cope with the increasing complexity of European politics. This gives the federal administration considerable influence. Nowadays it would be fair to speak of a militia system in a crisis.

Chapter 31
Brexit—No to an 'Ever Closer Union'

Contents

C. Baudenbacher, *Judicial Independence*, Springer Biographies,
https://doi.org/10.1007/978-3-030-02308-9_31

1 The Inconceivable Happens

1.1 A Logical Step?

Britain has always had a special relationship with the EEC and later the EU, irrespective of whether it was part of it or not. A first attempt to join the Common Market under the Conservative Prime Minister Harold Macmillan ended badly in 1963 due to the resistance of French President Charles de Gaulle. De Gaulle said "*non*" again in 1967 to the second application that was lodged by Harold Wilson's Labour Government. It was only after Georges Pompidou succeeded de Gaulle in 1969 that the situation changed. Edward Heath, another Conservative, took his country into the EEC in 1973, together with Denmark and Ireland. No referendum was held on that occasion. Norway also tried to accede to the EEC, but this was rejected by the people in a referendum. It seems that Heath and his entourage were conscious of the fact that the UK was joining more than an economic community and they wanted to be able to shape what was developing into a European Union. However, the British public never really took this on board. Once the UK had become a member, it started to cause trouble.

As early as 5 June 1975, Harold Wilson's second Labour Government asked the British people whether the UK should remain in the EEC. Labour's manifesto for the 1974 general election had claimed that the Conservatives had agreed to a bad deal in 1972 and promised a referendum on Britain's ongoing membership. It was the first nationwide referendum in the country's history. Interestingly, the opposition leader at that time, Margaret Thatcher, who later became the EEC's leading critic, fought passionately in favour of Britain remaining in the EEC. Labour was split over the issue. After some concessions were made by the EEC Heads of State and of Government, 67.2% voted in favour of continued EEC membership with 32.8% voting against. In this first stage of EEC membership, one striking feature became apparent that was never overcome: Britain always tended to see EU membership through the lenses of domestic politics. Unlike in Germany or in France, none of the major UK parties has ever unconditionally supported European integration.

After the first referendum, Britain was, as one insider put it, more of a grudging than a leading member. When Margaret Thatcher became Prime Minister, the difficulties reached a peak. I should mention the four-year battle over the UK's financial contributions, which was led by Thatcher under the slogan "I want my money back"! She ultimately succeeded, but not without leaving a bitter taste in the mouths of the other leaders. In her "Bruges speech" of 20 September 1988, Margret Thatcher rejected the idea that the US could be a model for Europe. Whereas European immigrants had created a new unity and pride in being American,

> our pride lies in being British or Belgian or Dutch or German.

Thatcher added that working more closely on matters such as trade, defence or relations with the rest of the world

> does not require power to be centralised in Brussels or decisions to be taken by an appointed bureaucracy.

She didn't even shy away from noting that:

> Indeed, it is ironic that just when those countries such as the Soviet Union, which have tried to run everything from the centre, are learning that success depends on dispersing power and decisions away from the centre, there are some in the Community who seem to want to move in the opposite direction.

Thatcher concluded that she wanted to see Europe more united and with a greater sense of common purpose:

> But it must be in a way which preserves the different traditions, parliamentary powers and sense of national pride in one's own country; for these have been the source of Europe's vitality through the centuries.

In 1990, Thatcher dismissed the idea of Jacques Delors, then President of the European Commission, of turning the European Parliament into the democratic body of the Community, the Commission into the executive and the Council of Ministers into the senate. Later Prime Ministers were more pro-European, but the UK did not adopt the euro and it refused to be part of the EU's open-border Schengen area.

Over the years, what has always struck me when I met British people is that when speaking of the EU, they use the word "Europe" and when referring to themselves, they would say "we". In view of Norway's Schengen membership, ECJ President Koen Lenaerts observed on 2 September 2016 on Dutch radio:

> In a certain way, Norway is more of a Member State without actually being one, than the UK, which formally is one.

1.2 The Vote of 23 June 2016

British judges and AGs of the EU courts in the past occasionally made jokes about the good time they would have if one day Britain were to join the EFTA pillar of the EEA and they would sit on the EFTA Court with its manageable case load. I always replied politely that from my perspective a British judge would be welcome. Nevertheless, no-one ever thought that this eventuality might one day become a reality. Things changed radically when on 23 June 2016 51.9% of British voters said yes to Brexit. I am not good at making prognoses, but I was one of the few who had predicted this outcome. For the first time in the history of European integration, a Member State—an important Member State—decided to leave the EU, and this after more than 40 years of membership. On the one hand, the Brexit decision was the result of internal British politics. But on the other hand, the outcome of the referendum was also a slap in the face to the current EU leadership. It was a protest against the way the former community had changed towards an ever closer union.

In its manifesto for the 2015 general election, the Conservative Party had announced that a referendum would be held on the question of whether Britain should stay in the EU or not. This was intended to unite the Tories, keep the populist UK Independence Party (UKIP) at bay and outmanoeuvre Labour. Prime Minister David Cameron, who was running for re-election, famously said that the

> in-out referendum on EU by 2017 was a cast-iron pledge.

In fact, Mr. Cameron was the first Conservative leader in over two decades to win a majority in the House of Commons. He said later that he

> thought it right to hold the referendum because this issue had been poisoning British politics for years. The referendum had been promised and not held.

In his attempt to renegotiate Britain's EU membership, and in particular, to seek amendments to the free movement of persons, Cameron had failed to obtain substantial concessions. Despite this, he campaigned for Britain to remain in the EU. However, his efforts and communication were largely based on scare tactics. The Remain campaign focussed on economic issues and argued that Britain would be "stronger, safer and better off" in the EU, whereas leaving would be a "leap in the dark". The Leavers, on the other hand, concentrated on migration from the continent. In August 2015, German Chancellor Angela Merkel had unilaterally decided to open German borders to hundreds of thousands of Syrian refugees. This played into the hands of the Leavers. Their mantra was "taking back control". Moreover, two factors appear to have been essential: the tackling of the euro area financial crisis by the EU with London being the most important financial centre, but Britain not being part of the euro area; and the increased power conferred on the European Parliament by the Lisbon Treaty, which played a crucial role in the process that led to the election of Jean-Claude Juncker as President of the European Commission. The UK had particular misgivings with the "frontrunner" ("*Spitzenkandidaten*") model with lead candidates competing for the post of Commission President through campaigns across the EU.

Cameron's relationship with German Chancellor Angela Merkel had been rather cool. The Prime Minister was further weakened by the defection of important allies, in particular former London Mayor Boris Johnson and, most importantly, Labour leader Jeremy Corbyn. Unlike his predecessors Tony Blair and Gordon Brown, Corbyn is a classical socialist and a Eurosceptic. He refused to work with the Tories and preferred to campaign on his own.

The EEA was depicted by the Remainers as not being a viable alternative. On 16 June 2016, Norwegian Prime Minister Erna Solberg visited Cameron at 10 Downing Street and declared that EEA membership on the EFTA side

> is going to be difficult for Britain, because then Brussels will decide without the Brits being able to participate in the decision-making.

She asserted that her country was acting like a "lobbying organisation" in Brussels and concluded that the Brits wouldn't like the "Norwegian model". This couldn't have been difficult for Solberg, because her political party has in its programme that

Norway shall join the EU and because it corresponded to the kind of downgrading of the EEA Agreement that the Norwegian elites had been performing from the outset. Norwegian diplomats and most of the academics acted accordingly. In the Leave campaign, the EEA Agreement was mentioned as a better alternative. Nigel Farage, the leader of UKIP, said in 2015 that the people of Norway, Iceland and Switzerland were happy because they had their own trade deals. However, there were also hard Brexiteers who claimed that Britain should become fully independent by leaving both the customs union and the Single Market.

In the end, the British people voted for Brexit. Within hours of the result, Cameron announced his resignation.

1.3 Hard Brexit—HM Government's First Choice

Theresa May launched her candidacy for David Cameron's job with the slogan "'Brexit means Brexit' and there will be no attempt to remain inside the EU". After becoming Prime Minister, she officially favoured a Hard Brexit solution, i.e. not only leaving the EU, but also the Single Market. This may have been a result of erroneous information that inextricably linked the Single Market with EU membership. In May's opinion, future relations between the UK and the EU had to be regulated by a "bespoke" trade agreement that would not cover free movement of persons. The PM always spoke of a "deep and special partnership agreement" in this context. Under no circumstances would Britain accept the jurisdiction of the ECJ in the future. May placed special emphasis on the latter issue.

Right from the start, the problem for the hard Brexiteers was that if Britain wanted to conclude a "deep and special partnership agreement" with the EU, it would probably have to accept the competence of a non-British surveillance authority and the jurisdiction of a non-British multilateral court of law. Whether you use the term Hard Brexit or Soft Brexit in this context, is irrelevant. The Swiss experience is instructive in this regard. Since 2008, the EU has claimed that Switzerland had to accept such institutions and in the absence of any solution being found, Switzerland has been unable to conclude any new market access agreement.[1]

In the light of this, most of the models of dispute resolution being discussed in the UK's Brexit scenarios are not feasible. This goes, in my view, for arbitration in general. As I have said, arbitration has been proposed by Switzerland to the EU many times and Swiss parliamentarians and business operators find it difficult to understand why it should not be a viable dispute resolution mechanism. However, for the EU, arbitration is not acceptable in a Single Market context because it would mean that the respective arbitration tribunal would rank above the ECJ. The same goes for a bilateral EU-UK court. In the past, there have been similar thoughts, both in Switzerland and in Russia, of having a bilateral court with the EU.[2]

[1]See for details Chapter 30.

[2]See for details Chapter 30.

If the envisaged deep and special partnership agreement were to amount to a market access treaty, it would also not be possible to adopt the dispute settlement mechanism of the EU-Canada Comprehensive Cooperation and Trade Agreement (CETA). The Commission's chief negotiator, Michel Barnier, repeatedly stated this. Furthermore, I have emphasised on many occasions that in Opinion 1/91, the ECJ declared a combined court with judges from the ECJ and from the EFTA States incompatible with EC law. The idea of establishing a "UK pillar" with a British surveillance authority and a British "European" court above the Supreme Court will not fly either. Switzerland proposed this in 2012; it was formally rejected by the EU.[3]

2 A Role for the EFTA Court President?

2.1 Perplexity After the British Leave Vote

Remainers and the EU leadership were devastated by the Brexit vote. Many said that the working class, rural populations and pensioners had defeated the educated, urban and young elite. Being Swiss, I was familiar with that kind of argument; it was the same one as put forward after the negative EEA referendum in December 1992 in Switzerland and I had also used it myself. In the meantime, I recognise that it is a pointless line of reasoning. Either you honour the one man one vote rule or you don't. Some people on the continent breathed a sigh of relief at the prospect that the perpetual troublemakers would now finally leave. This would give the others the chance to deepen political integration. I spoke with some economists from HSG, and at least the Swiss took the view that Brexit could also be a chance because it would quite naturally lead to a certain amount of regulatory competition in Europe. Although I consider myself to be a pro-European, I had similar feelings. In recent years, there was too much that had gone wrong in the EU. The 2007–2008 financial crisis had shown that the decision to create a single currency had been somewhat precipitous, certainly as regards including Member States whose economies suffered from problems. The same goes for the hasty 2004/2007/2013 Eastern enlargement of the EU. Our sister court, the ECJ was, and in my view remains despite its undisputed record, insufficiently grounded, its judicial style does not correspond to the requirements of the times. The European Central Bank and the various European Stability Mechanisms have largely remained unchecked. Finally, the questionable value of the European Parliament became particularly evident when its former President Martin Schulz ran a campaign to become German Chancellor in the summer and autumn of 2017 that can only be called pitiful. The same goes for his attempts to form a new German government.

---

[3]See for details Chapter 30.

2.2 *What Is the EEA?*

During the Brexit campaign, the EEA was in particular denigrated by Remainers. However, the anti-EEA drive only had one focus: Single Market legislation. No adequate description was ever given of the advantages of having an own surveillance authority and an own court. Nor was it pointed out that the EEA/EFTA States had retained their sovereignty in foreign trade and foreign policy, agriculture, fisheries, taxation and currency matters. When I spoke at Edinburgh University on 30 January 2017, a third year student who had travelled to Scotland from Sussex took the floor and said that the EEA Agreement had been trashed during the campaign and afterwards by representatives of the Norwegian government. Being the superpower of the EFTA pillar, the Norwegians didn't even deign to ask their two partners whether they agreed with their approach.

As the Court's long-standing President, I couldn't leave such contentions uncommented. On the contrary, I considered it my duty to explain and, if necessary, to rectify. This was already my *modus operandi* when the Swiss Government started to make untenable claims about the EEA to pave the way for the "ECJ model".[4] I could not see why it should have been different in the case of the UK. By the way, I also thought that if Britain were to turn towards the EEA, this could offer a solution for my home country Switzerland.

2.3 *My Credo*

I was quite well prepared when the inconceivable happened. On 7 May 2014, I gave a lecture at Trinity College Cambridge on "Decentered integration – the case of the European Economic Area". Thereafter, on 26 May 2014, I spoke at the annual meeting of the England and Wales Bar European Group (BEG) in Sorrento on "Life Outside the EU – the EEA and the EFTA Court". The BEG is a specialist association of the English Bar. On 16 February 2016, Doris' birthday, I gave an interview to *Wiener Zeitung* with the title "Europe 2.0 is conceivable" ("*Europa 2.0 ist denkbar*"). What I meant by that was that the Single Market should be the bracket that unites those who want to go for a political union and those who want to limit themselves to economic integration.

In the spring of 2016, my long-time Head of Cabinet Philipp Speitler told me that he would leave the EFTA Court at short notice because he had been offered the opportunity of joining the German judiciary. One month before the referendum, I hired an English barrister as Philipp's successor, Michael-James ("M-J") Clifton. I knew M-J well. He had been working for me for a number of years, both as a

---

[4]See for details Chapter 30.

trainee and a legal secretary. He had left the EFTA Court at the beginning of 2016 and returned to London in order to finish his pupillage, the final stage of training to be a barrister, something he swiftly achieved. After Brexit, M-J became an important comrade in arms on Brexit matters both as my right hand and as a writer, speaker and tweeter. I was determined to speak in the UK about the EFTA Court in general and its relationship with the ECJ in particular.

I have long been convinced that a second structure in Europe is needed. Already in the 1950s there was a divide between two concepts of European integration. After the foundation of the EEC ("the inner six") in 1957, the free trade oriented non-EEC countries established the EFTA ("the outer seven") in 1960, under British leadership. The EFTA was weakened by the accession of Britain and Denmark to the EEC in 1973, of Portugal in 1986 and by the accession of Finland, Austria and Sweden to the EU in 1995. Nevertheless, the EFTA has been preserved as a credible structure. The EFTA pillar of the EEA has played a crucial role in this. After the Brexit decision of the British people, there was an opportunity to involve Britain in EFTA and the EEA.[5]

The need for a non-national judicial mechanism would play an important role. The structures were in place with the ECJ and the EFTA Court. Far-sighted people like the authors of the Bruegel paper recognised this.[6] The European Commission's chief Brexit negotiator, Michel Barnier, also pointed to this need. Influential Labour parliamentarians and a minority of the Tories I met during my London visits thought along the same lines.

Unsurprisingly, certain EFTA politicians and bureaucrats took offence at my actions. However, if you decide to adopt a difficult path, you must be able to withstand pressure. That the Norwegian government was not amused did not come as a surprise. There has always been a fundamental difference between my approach towards the EEA Agreement and the institutions of the EFTA pillar and that of the Oslo administration. They saw the EEA as an unloved intermediary step, a necessary evil on their way to EU membership. Nevertheless, they had managed to adjust themselves rather well to the EFTA pillar, where they naturally played a dominating role. I did everything in my power to secure the independence of the EFTA Court and to establish it as a "valid interlocutor" ("*interlocuteur valable*") for its much larger sister court, the ECJ.

When I accepted the first speaking invitations to the UK and started to give interviews, Norwegian bureaucrats called Vaduz and told their Liechtenstein counterparts that they should stop me from talking and writing about Brexit. This *modus operandi* is yet further proof of the fact that bureaucrats often have no understanding of the concept of the independence of a European judge.[7] In Iceland,

[5]See for details Chapter 32.

[6]See for details Chapters 3 and 18.

[7]See also Chapter 28.

this was different. After my first appearances in the UK, I was contacted by senior Icelandic civil servants who requested copies of my speeches and accompanying slides. Furthermore, when I visited Iceland in early October 2017, both the Prime Minister and the Minister for Foreign Affairs expressed their agreement with my remarks. Certainly, I did not seek out such support, however, it did confirm that the Norwegians' opposition was not related to any alleged inappropriateness of a judge speaking his mind on such matters. It was purely political.

I should finally add that my counterpart at the ECJ, President Koen Lenaerts, on 27 July 2017 referred to the possibility of the UK docking to the EFTA Court. In an interview with Belgian TV, he answered the following questions:

Question: What if there are disputes? Will the ECJ interpret the brexit agreement in the same way as British judges?

Answer: *This can be sorted. A free trade accord exists between the EU Norway, Liechtenstein and Iceland.*

Question: The EU court deals with the EU disputes. A separate court exists for the three other countries.

Answer: *The treaty states that the EFTA Court, which is not at all linked to the ECJ, and our court must come to a homogenous process of law. It has been working for 25 years and it works perfectly.*

Answer: *We don't have to reinvent everything, like the wheel. It exists. The question is, is the wheel is adapted to this new situation? That's the topic of political discussions.*

In my keynote speech at the Annual Dinner of the England and Wales Law Society's competition section on 23 November 2017, I rejected the attacks of bureaucrats with the following words:

> What I will state here tonight are my own personal views. I do not appear here on behalf of my Court, nor do I speak on behalf of the Governments of the EEA/EFTA States.
>
> There is a reason why I emphasise this.
>
> Some, including certain government people, consider that a European Judge's freedom of speech is restricted, or that he or she ought, even, to coordinate his or her speeches and interviews on Brexit and EEA with the respective Government's policy.
>
> I dismiss this contention. Yes, a judge should not do anything that jeopardises his or her independence or his or her competence to sit in any future cases. However, my views on possible Brexit solutions do neither of these. In fact, it is my duty as a Judge and President of the EFTA Court but also as a long-time scholar in European Law, to dispel any misinformation, respond to questions, and provide details that can only be obtained through long experience in the field.
>
> The public in all EEA Contracting Parties, including Britain, is entitled to have an accurate picture of the EEA Agreement and its judicial framework: what it contains, how it works, how it evolves.

3 My First Brexit Activities

3.1 Immediate Reaction

The British referendum took place on Thursday 23 June 2016. On Sunday, 26 June 2016, Doris and I attended the birthday celebration in Brussels of Jacques Bourgeois, one of the grand old men of European economic law and WTO law. A journalist from *NZZ* called and asked whether I would be prepared to give an interview on Brexit and EEA. I answered his questions while watching the UEFA European championship Poland–Switzerland football match. The Swiss lost on penalty kicks, but my interview went well. It was published on Monday, 27 June 2016, and was picked up by a number of other media, also outside Switzerland. I said that the EEA could—in one form or another—be an option for Britain.

3.2 Keidanren

For a number of years Doris and I had spent a week in Tokyo at the end of August and we also did this in 2016. There is a group of Japanese international law professors that is interested in EFTA and the EEA and I always gave a speech to them on recent developments. The Japanese had also visited the EFTA Court, attending hearings and some had even contributed to the *Festschrift* marking the Court's twentieth anniversary. On this trip, my friend Takao Suami, the Chair of European and International Law at *Waseda* University, saw to it that I was invited by *Keidanren*, the Federation of Japanese Industry, to give a talk on Brexit. Japanese business leaders and politicians were, and still are, deeply concerned about Brexit because of the huge Japanese investment in the UK. My lecture was scheduled on my birthday, 1 September 2016. With the exception of Takao Suami, nobody had even heard of the EEA. I said that in my view, the UK would not be able to secure access to the EU Single Market post-Brexit if it did not accept a non-British court. The Swiss experience proved that. At the same time, the Brussels-based think tank *Bruegel* published a paper addressing the most important issues of a future EU-UK relationship.[8] I met one of the authors, the Chairman of the Foreign Committee of the Bundestag Norbert Röttgen in December 2016 in Berlin.

3.3 October 2016 in London

Kings College invited me to give the 42nd Annual Lecture of its Centre of European Law on 13 October 2016. Doris and M-J accompanied me and Laura

---

[8]See for details Chapter 3.

Melusine who was practicing law with a Brussels firm came as a surprise guest with the Eurostar. My speech "After Brexit: Is the EEA an Option for the United Kingdom?" was widely publicised and accompanied by many tweets. Some 500 people attended. I said that from a legal standpoint, both EEA membership on the EFTA side and docking to the EEA/EFTA institutions—ESA and the EFTA Court—could be options. I also pointed to the fact that although the EFTA Court took homogeneity very seriously, it had a mind of its own and had gone its own way on important issues. And it had quite an influence on its sister court, the ECJ. The EFTA Court's language was English and its judicial style was closer to the English than to the French tradition. I finally expressed my concern that with Britain gone, mercantilist tendencies in the economic policy of the EU, which were already present, could gain the upper hand.

During my London stay, I visited the Brexit Secretary David Davis at 9 Downing Street and met influential members from both Houses of Parliament. Mr. Davis had a team of four around him. He was friendly and rather well-prepared. However, he was very critical of the EU and the ECJ in particular. I started to get a real sense of what bothered many Brits, not just the extreme Brexiteers, about the EU and the ECJ specifically. It was, in short: free movement of persons; the Brussels centralism; the principles of direct effect and the primacy of EU law; and the fact that EU law was essentially an offspring of civil law, in particular French law. Having taught comparative law for some time in Germany, the US and Switzerland, I understood their concern.

The overall impression I gained from this first London visit was that the Conservative Party was firmly in the hands of its anti-European wing, which was determined to not only leave the EU, but also the Single Market. The Tories also had the anti-European UKIP breathing down their necks. Nevertheless, there were influential conservative MP's who listened carefully when I spoke about the "docking model" that had been proposed to Switzerland by the EU in 2013. The dominant theme was free movement of persons. Since this fundamental freedom is, as a matter of principle, also part of the EEA Agreement, albeit with some differences compared to the EU, full EEA membership on the EFTA side was deemed to be a problem.

3.4 German-Speaking Countries

In the autumn of 2016 and in the spring of 2017, I spoke at large gatherings in Zurich, Basel, St. Gallen, Bonn and Bregenz. In my lectures in Zurich and Basel, I discussed the possible opportunities offered by Brexit for Switzerland. The Swiss Government lacked any imagination in that regard. The only consequence they drew from the Brexit decision was that they wanted to conclude a free trade agreement with Britain. This Swiss Government policy was apparently driven by the fear that a more pro-active approach might annoy the EU. And the FDFA did not want to be dissuaded by Brexit from his conviction that Switzerland would one day have to join the EU.

On 2 November 2016, I spoke on Brexit at the opening of the academic semester of the German University of Administrative Sciences in Speyer. Doris and I spent the following night in Deidesheim, a picturesque little town in the heart of one of Germany's most important wine-growing regions, the Palatinate. The place we stayed in had become well-known when former German Chancellor Helmut Kohl hosted heads of government and of state and foreign ministers from all over globe there. In the morning we went for a walk, I stumbled and broke the femoral neck in my left leg. I underwent emergency surgery in a small denominational hospital in Speyer the same afternoon. I still have fond memories of both the surgeon and the nursing staff who did an excellent job. After a week, I was released. I didn't take any time off, but worked in bed and walked on crutches.

3.5 Scotland and Wales on Crutches

My accident didn't stop me from continuing to do my job at the EFTA Court and from pursuing my activities in the UK and elsewhere. For six weeks, I was on crutches and after that, I relied on a silver-handled cane, which I had last used in my student fraternity days. It finally served a real purpose. In late January 2017, I flew to Edinburgh, accompanied by Doris and M-J, and gave lectures at the Universities of Edinburgh and Glasgow. In Edinburgh, my group had an extensive exchange of views with the Rt. Hon. Nicola Sturgeon MSP, First Minister of Scotland and we met the Lord Advocate, the Rt. Hon. James Wolffe, QC. My hosts wanted to discuss whether it would be possible for Scotland (as for Wales and Northern Ireland) to remain in the British Union and at the same time become Contracting Parties to the EEA Agreement in the EFTA pillar. I answered in the negative; only sovereign States can do that. On our way back to Luxembourg, we got together with some Labour MPs, *inter alia* with the Brexit Shadow Minister Sir Keir Starmer in London. I kept in touch with Sir Keir and in the autumn of 2017, he paid the EFTA Court a visit. In March 2017, I spoke in London and Cardiff. In late May of that year, I was invited to lecture at Trinity College Dublin and at Queen's University Belfast. On all of these trips, I not only saw academics and judges, but also members of government and parliamentarians. In Cardiff, I had a meeting with the Rt. Hon Carwyn Jones AM, First Minister of Wales, in Dublin with John Callinan, Second Secretary General in the Department of the Taoiseach (Brexit Sherpa). In Belfast, M-J, Doris and I were invited to Stormont Castle where a roundtable, chaired by Sir Malcolm McKibbin, Head of the Northern Ireland Civil Service, was held. Afterwards, we were given an impressive tour of the Belfast peace walls. The talks in Dublin and Belfast were particularly enlightening. When I heard about the possible future problems at the border between the Republic of Ireland and Northern Ireland, I told my hosts that they should look into the concept of "parallel marketability", which has allowed Liechtenstein to be simultaneously part of the EEA free trade area and to maintain a customs union treaty with Switzerland. I also pointed to the mechanisms facilitating the free movement of goods and persons at the Norwegian-Swedish border.

One of the most welcome add-on benefits to my appearances was that they were frequently chaired by old friends, Sir Francis Jacobs, the former AG of the ECJ, in London, Sir David Edward, the former British ECJ Judge in Edinburgh, John Cooke, the former Irish Judge of the GC and John Temple Lang, the former Director at DG Competition in Dublin.

4 Things Heat Up

4.1 Summer 2017

In June 2017, a journalist from the Daily Express called and I agreed to give an interview. It was published on 24 June 2017 under the title

> 'I fear for EU when it loses Britain' – Top European judge on Brexit warning for bloc.

I reiterated what I had said before. I did the same in an interview with The Times on 21 August 2017. That conversation was published under the heading

> Leading European judge promotes plan for UK access to single market after Brexit.

In the same edition, The Times published a leading article with the heading "Control and Compromise". It stated that isolation was not a price worth paying for absolute control over Britain's laws and that "a Swiss judge" offered a solution to the thorniest Brexit challenge, dispute resolution:

> For a man whose job is technically to rule on European trade disputes, Judge Carl Baudenbacher is not shy about plunging into international geopolitics. As it turns out this is a good thing. Theresa May and David Davis should welcome his input on Brexit, which could help them to deliver a sensible compromise on judicial sovereignty instead of an acrimonious and costly divorce.

The editorial went on to state that the idea of using the EFTA Court post-Brexit had three obvious selling points. First, if the UK wanted to conclude a trade deal with the EU, a mutually agreed forum for dispute resolution would be necessary. Second, unlike the ECJ, the EFTA Court's rulings do not trump those of national courts. Third, the EFTA Court was tried and tested. Brexit Secretary David Davis was asked to look into the possibility of Britain using the EFTA Court without necessarily being a full EFTA Member. The article ended with the statement:

> Judge Baudenbacher appears to be an enterprising and practical figure, and an anglophile to boot. He makes little secret of his preference for common law over the Napoleonic variety and will visit Westminster next month. He deserves a hearing.

Apparently, this piece had been written in view of the imminent publication of a new Department for Exiting the EU (DExEU) paper on how the planned new deep and special partnership between the EU and the UK could be monitored and implemented to the satisfaction of both sides, and how disputes could be resolved. On 23 August 2017, the report was published under the title: "Enforcement and dispute resolution - a future partnership paper". In a contribution to the LSE's Brexit blog entitled:

> Could the U.K. use the EFTA Court to resolve disputes following Brexit?

I briefly addressed that paper. I wrote that both when dealing with the homogeneity principle underlying the EEA Agreement and when addressing the issue of how to resolve a judicial conflict between the ECJ and the EFTA Court, the paper was curiously limited to the law on the books. It didn't address the law in action. In that respect, I was reminded of my Swiss compatriots.

In late August 2017, I was in Tokyo again and gave a talk on Brexit and EEA at the Research Institute of Economy, Trade and Industry (RIETI), the think tank of the Japanese Ministry of Economy, Trade and Industry (METI). I was also interviewed by Nikkei Asian Review on the docking model.

4.2 My September 2017 Trip to London

Journalists learned that I had been invited to give lectures in the House of Commons and at Chatham House in the second week of September 2017. On 3 September 2017, the Guardian published an article under the sensational title: "Efta court chief visits UK to push merits of 'Norway model'" The text started with the sentence:

> An unusual judge-led drive to persuade the UK government to resolve the Brexit crisis by joining the European Free Trade Association (Efta), the so-called Norway model, is to be promoted by the head of the Efta court himself in a series of speeches in London this month.

Not everyone was happy about this. I was seriously told that there was a line between law and politics that I could not cross as a judge and president. Significantly, I did not receive an answer to my question as to where this line was running. I had never claimed to express the view of the Court. However, from now on, I expressly stated that I was speaking on my own behalf. I also started to add that I was not speaking on behalf of the Governments of the EEA/EFTA States. Obviously, those who listened to the latter statement understood the background.

Subsequently, the leading Italian business paper "*Il Sole 24 Ore*" brought an article and even the Vietnamese press reported on my planned visit to London. On 11 September 2017, Gazette, the publication of the Law Society of England and Wales published:

> A warm welcome to Carl Baudenbacher, who is visiting the U.K. this week to offer a solution to one of the apparently intractable problems posed by Brexit. This is the question

> of dispute resolution forum [....]. Baudenbacher has been touring the world (in a personal capacity, he stresses) promoting an off-the-shelf alternative.

On 13 September 2017, I spoke at a meeting of *UKLegalFuture*, a group of lawyers that was formed after the Brexit vote, which aims to inform parliamentarians and others about issues related to the UK leaving the EU. My subject was "Beyond Brexit: The UK and the EFTA Court". The event took place in the House of Commons, and there were also a number of judges present. The day after, on 14 September 2017, I gave a talk at Chatham House on "The EFTA Court: A Way to Resolve Brexit's Jurisdiction Conundrum?" The ambassadors of Iceland and Switzerland and a Counsellor from the Norwegian Embassy were among the participants. I was asked what the EEA/EFTA States were thinking about Britain docking to ESA and the EFTA Court and I passed the question on to the diplomats. The gentleman from Iceland straightforwardly stated that his government would welcome a docking solution. The Norwegian representative was less outspoken, but at least he indicated that Norway would be open-minded if the UK were to consider that option. Afterwards, the Icelander whom I had met once in Brussels said to me that this was a new tone for Norway. Apparently, the Conservative Norwegian government was more relaxed after having won the general election three days before. The Swiss ambassador limited himself to explaining his Government's official position, but added that it would take years before a solution could be expected. That was in marked contrast to what his Minister for Foreign Affairs had been stating for years.[9]

M-J had received more than ten requests from news agencies and newspapers that wanted to interview me. He therefore set up a media briefing, which took place at Chatham House on 14 September 2017. Both Reuters and Bloomberg reported my statements and I was particularly pleased that the concept of "docking" to the institutions of the EFTA pillar was becoming known further afield. The Reuters piece was picked up by the New York Times. During my stay in London, I also gave interviews to the BBC radio's Today programme, ITV News and I went on CNN's "QUEST MEANS BUSINESS" show where I was queried by their British news anchor Zain Asher. The latter was quite an experience with the host putting the questions from New York over an ear plug and me answering from a small dark chamber in London.

4.3 An Unexpected, Yet Easily Comprehensible Attack

On 17 September 2017, Doris and I flew from London to Oslo and the following day, I gave the opening speech at a large conference at the University with some 300 participants. My subject was:

[9]See for details Chapter 30.

The EFTA Court's Contribution to the Realisation of a Single Market in Europe.

The title of the programme, which featured illustrious Norwegian and foreign speakers from academia, the judiciary, the administration and private practice was "Norway in Europe". In reality, it was a colloquium in honour of Professor Dr. Dr. Mads Andenæs, who had celebrated his 60th birthday two months before. Some odd internal rules prevented Mads' name from being mentioned in the title of the event. My lecture had nothing to do with Brexit. But two Norwegian newspapers had on 4 September 2017 picked up the article from the Guardian on the purpose of my London trip. They called my Brexit activities my "one-man campaign to lure the United Kingdom into the EEA". Some people simply could not miss this opportunity of taking a shot at me. After my speech, Ulf Sverdrup, the former secretary of the Sejersted Committee, took the floor and asked me in a well-prepared statement whether I found it appropriate, in my position as the President of the EFTA Court, to travel to the UK and to actively sell the EEA Agreement to the Brits. I answered that I had received many speaking invitations, that I was presenting my personal views, that there was no conflict of interest and that there was a lot of misinformation about how the EFTA Court functioned in practice. I finally added that if others did not react, I felt duty-bound to rectify any humbug so that people could decide based on the facts.

I had forgotten the incident when on 2 October 2017 a friend emailed me an article by Mr. Sverdrup from *Dagens Næringsliv*, the business paper that amusingly had bestowed the title "King Carl of the EEA" on me some six years previously.[10] The article started with innocuous considerations on why the Brexit negotiations were making no headway and on the need for a dispute resolution mechanism in order to avoid a Hard Brexit. The author went on by stating that the President of the EFTA Court was now promoting "another solution" (as if this was something out of the blue), namely the EFTA Court. According to Baudenbacher, he wrote, the EFTA Court may and should play a role: either because the UK becomes a member of EFTA and the EEA, or because the UK "docks" to the EFTA Court. The article truthfully stated that I had been on a tour of the UK to promote this solution. Mr. Sverdrup then doubted whether my proposal was realistic, possible and desirable, as he had every right to do. Finally, he criticised me for actively promoting the EFTA Court in the UK. He recognised my efforts to ensure the independence and recognition of the EFTA Court, however, he contended that my message to the Brits that the EEA would be less burdensome than EU membership did not correspond with the EFTA Court's record. Rather than creating more room for manoeuvre ("*handlingrom*"), the EFTA Court was not only on an integration-friendly line, but had been more integration-friendly than the ECJ.

When I read this, I realised that Sverdrup must have had friendly helpers. His focus on "room for manoeuvre", as well as the claim that the EFTA Court had been more integration-friendly than the ECJ (another expression for "more Catholic than the Pope") clearly pointed to a protagonist who, as so often, preferred to remain in

[10]See for details Chapter 23.

the dark. As for his other remarks, the accusation that it was illogical to claim that the EFTA Court was going its own way when it had refused to take into account the special wishes of the Norwegian government in the past, is based on a fundamental misunderstanding. Going its own way means living up to EFTA values, deciding in a fact–based manner, giving comprehensive reasons and being transparent. It doesn't mean giving special leeway to governments beyond what is stated in the EEA Agreement and in the SCA.

Norwegian friends advised me to strike back, but I did not want to do that. I just reflected on the fact that when ECJ President Koen Lenaerts proposed that the UK dock to the institutions of the EFTA pillar, the only guy who attacked him was Nigel Farage, the former leader of UKIP. However, on 3 October 2017, Professor Mads Andenæs and Dr. Eirik Bjorge, the two scholars who had played a crucial role in the Christiansen affair, published a letter to the editor of *Dagens Næringsliv* under the title "Pikant from Nupi." They wrote that Ulf Sverdrup had launched a violent and personal attack on me, which had

> probably circulated in draft among like-minded people. Sverdrup was the secretary of the EEA Review Committee led by Fredrik Sejersted.

The authors concurred with Sverdrup's statement that I had made a lot of effort to ensure the independence and recognition of the EFTA Court. They added that I was

> the rescue man of the EEA Agreement.[11]

Without me and my credibility, it could not be taken for given that the EU would have let the system survive. Mads and Eirik concluded that Sverdrup's article illustrated the need for me to continue explaining the legal questions and the relationship between the EFTA Court's and the ECJ's practice.

4.4 My November and December 2017 Trips to London

On 15 November 2017, I announced that I would resign from the EFTA Court by the end of March 2018. One week later, I was in London again. Professor Panos Koutrakos had long before invited me to give a talk at the City University of London, whose alumni and alumnae include names such as Mahatma Ghandi, Clement Attlee, Margaret Thatcher and Tony Blair. On 23 November 2017, I spoke on the subject "Without the ECJ, but within the Single Market?" The event was well attended, and there were both senior civil servants and media people present. The night before, I had the honour of giving the keynote address at the annual black tie dinner of the competition section of the Law Society of England and Wales. My

[11]Unofficial translation.

group of three got together again with Sir Keir Starmer and we met Stephen Kinnock, a Labour MP who is favourable towards an EEA solution for the UK. Importantly, we were also received by the Lord Chancellor and Secretary of State for Justice, the Rt Hon David Lidington MP.

During my November stay in London, a Norwegian friend sent me an essay written by a scholar from the Oslo-based research center *ARENA* which seemed to indicate that Norway was slowly changing its position on the question of British EEA membership. I also met Marc Jones again, the Reuters journalist who was in charge of covering foreign guests coming to the UK. On 29 November 2017, Reuters ran a story under the title

> UK could get outsized power if it joins EFTA Court after Brexit - Court head.

The article stated that I had made a fresh attempt to convince Britain to join the EEA after Brexit, that London might be allowed two judges rather than the one given to the existing members Norway, Liechtenstein and Iceland, and that in my view, three options were available: Britain could become a full-fledged EEA/EFTA member; it could "dock" to the Court on a long-term basis; or it could dock for a shorter period, during the post-Brexit transition. The text finally pointed to the reservations of the Norwegian government and to the determination of HM Government to leave the Single Market. It was immediately picked up by the New York Times.

On 5 December 2017, I was back in London in order to give a keynote speech on the EFTA Court option at the Institute for Government. I was also interviewed by Robert Peston, the Political Editor of ITV News. My message remained the same. I started to understand what every politician knows; namely, that if you want to convince people, you have to reiterate your statements again and again. On 15 December 2017, Swiss TV broadcast a nice portrait of me that focussed on my Brexit activities. They had filmed both in London and Luxembourg and Doris and M-J, my two most important supporters, were part of the piece.

4.5 The Joint Report of 8 December 2017

On 8 December 2017, Britain and the EU struck a last-minute deal in the form of a joint report from the negotiators of the EU and the UK Government on progress during phase one of the Brexit negotiations. It was agreed that there would be no hard border between the Republic of Ireland and Northern Ireland, that the constitutional and economic integrity of the UK would be maintained and that EU citizens living in the UK and vice versa would have their rights to live, work and study protected. For eight years after Brexit, UK courts would have the right to refer questions involving the rights of EU nationals to the ECJ. Some sort of understanding was also reached regarding a financial settlement including budget contributions during a two-year transition period after March 2019. However, the whole deal was more of a memorandum of understanding than a real agreement. Its purpose was to allow the two sides to move Brexit talks on to the next phase.

4.6 Early 2018: Giving Evidence to Both Houses of Parliament

On 31 December 2017, my presidency of the EFTA Court ended after 15 years. On 16 January 2018, I gave evidence on dispute resolution before the EU Justice Sub-Committee of the House of Lords. At the end of the session, Lord Polak stated:

> What you have said is refreshing and interesting. The one thing that I would say is that, over here, we believe very little of what we read in the newspapers, with reference to your last comment. I have found this extremely practical. I note that you are finishing on 31 March. If anyone is listening, I think that from 1 April you should advise our Government on what is practical and possible.

The Chairman added:

> A consultancy job awaits you, Judge Baudenbacher. I want to say thank you. It was very illuminating having you here. It has been invaluable, so thank you so much. I think that the EFTA Court has been hugely lucky to have had you leading it for 15 years. We wish you well into the future, because you have clearly have been a very distinguished judge and leader of that court. We feel honoured that you have come to testify before us.[12]

The day after, I spoke at a Brexit Series Briefing at Asia House.

On 6 February 2018, I delivered a keynote speech on Brexit at the "Institute for Public Policy Research". On 7 February 2018, I gave evidence to the Exiting the European Union Committee of the House of Commons. I had met the Chair, the Rt Hon Hilary Benn MP, before and I knew some other members of the committee who greeted me like an old friend. I had been told that the Commons would be somewhat harsher than the Lords on such an occasion, but that turned out not to be true. The press covered my appearance before the Commons in a sensational way. In the evening, I spoke on "Brexit in Context: What Does 'Docking' Mean?" at UCL. The event was chaired by the Europe Director at the Foreign and Commonwealth Office, Caroline Wilson CMG. At dinner, I sat next to another interesting lady, Marina Wheeler, QC, the wife of Foreign Secretary Boris Johnson. I had met Marina before. On 28 March 2018 she gave written evidence before the EU Justice Sub-Committee of the House of Lord. In her paper, she expressed a very balanced view on docking to the EFTA Court. On 11 February 2018, Bloomberg ran a big story about my UCL speech. I had the impression that HM Government's determination to leave the Single Market was faltering.

---

[12]Available at: http://data.parliament.uk/writtenevidence/committeeevidence.svc/evidencedocument/eu-justice-subcommittee/brexit-enforcement-and-dispute-resolution/oral/77242.html.

4.7 March 2018: Cross Party Event and Lecture at Queen Mary University

On 19 March 2018, it was reported that the UK and EU had agreed on a large part of the agreement that would lead to the orderly withdrawal of the UK from the EU. I was scheduled to speak at Queen Mary University on 21 March 2018 and planned to fly to London in the evening of 20 March 2018. However, M-J got notice that in the afternoon of that day, the first cross party Brexit event would take place in Westminster under the title:

> Brexit, no more nonsense: the EEA EFTA option.

Panellists were the five MPs Stephen Kinnock and Heidi Alexander from the Labour Party, Stephen Hammond and Antoinette Sandbach from the Conservatives and Norman Lamb from the Liberal Democrats. When the organisers heard that I was on my way to London, they invited me to participate as a foreign expert. We changed our flight schedule and at 3 p.m. I was sitting on that panel. I had met the two Stephen's before, but not the other MPs. All of them made it clear that they were determined to fight the government, that the result of the referendum did not justify a hard Brexit and that major economic damage to the UK's economy had to be avoided.

The event was well attended and, to my surprise, there were a handful of Icelandic and Norwegian parliamentarians in the room. The head of the EFTA group of the *Storting*, the Norwegian Parliament, Svein Roald Hansen, whom I knew from numerous EFTA Ministerial meetings, tried to take the traditional hard line of his government against British EEA membership on the side of EFTA. He was, however, told by British participants that other Norwegian protagonists, not least Prime Minister Erna Solberg, had long since taken a much more pragmatic position.

The next day, I spoke at Queen Mary University and met members of the House of Lords and journalists.

5 A Largely Domestic Problem?

5.1 The Start: PM May in the Hands of the Brexiteers

Based on my experience, it had become clear to me that in the British Brexit debate, the number one issue was immigration. When Theresa May, who as a Home Secretary had half-heartedly supported the remain camp, became Prime Minister, pro-European Tories were side-lined. It is important to remember that the right of the party had already been delighted by Maggie Thatcher's anti-EU aggressiveness. The Brexiteers' battle cry of "taking back control" relates first and foremost to the free movement of persons. This means that since this fundamental freedom has largely been made part of the EEA Agreement, EEA membership on the EFTA side is a hard option to sell. When asked about this, I usually said that it was a political question and pointed to the Bruegel paper and the situation in Switzerland and in certain Eastern European countries. It is also possible that in the future, the EU will become more flexible on this point. As regards, the demonisation of the ECJ, which included talk about "foreign judges", I was vividly reminded of the situation in Switzerland. However, in this context it is important to remember that the ECJ undeniably stands in the tradition of civil law and not common law.

5.2 *The Failed Snap Election*

In April 2017, PM May announced that a snap election would be held on 8 June 2017. Her goal was to get a stronger mandate for the Brexit talks. May was overconfident and refused to take part in televised debates between party leaders. However, she lost the election and the Tories fell below the 326 seats needed to form a majority government. May was thus forced to form a minority government, which is reliant on the 10 MPs of the Northern Irish Democratic Unionist Party (DUP) in a confidence and supply arrangement. UKIP, which was essentially established as a platform for the single issue of Britain leaving the EU almost disappeared. However, its Hard Brexit views became the predominate attitude of the majority of the Tories.

5.3 *Labour's Dilemma*

In the Brexit campaign, important Labour protagonists had argued in favour of remain. However, as I said, Labour's own campaign was separated from the remain actions of the conservatives. Moreover, large sections of the Labour vote were in favour of Brexit. After the Brexit referendum, the pro-Europeans in the Labour leadership found themselves on the defensive. As a result of the snap election, they became stronger, but their handicap is that large parts of their electoral basis are pro Brexit. That is why also for Labour, continued free movement of persons seems to be a no-go.

5.4 *The Usual Mantras*

Those who publicly oppose a docking solution put forward the same contentions that have already been used in the Swiss debate. As regards legislation, they point to the complaint of the Norwegian elites that the EEA Agreement does not give the EEA/EFTA States a full co-decision right when it comes to new legislation.[13] The EFTA Court's role has been downgraded by a group called "Lawyers for Britain", which in fact consists of just three jurists. They have relentlessly claimed that if Britain wants to escape from the clutches of the ECJ, it should not accept the jurisdiction of the EFTA Court because the latter was a slave, a mere vassal of the ECJ. The former Director-General of the EU Council's Legal Service, Jean-Claude Piris, even claimed that in the event of a divergence between the EFTA Court and the ECJ on internal market law, "the EU Court would prevail" (FT of 16 November 2017). Mr. Piris, a graduate of the French *écoles nationales* (a so-called *énarque*), is personally a very kind man who is married to an Icelander. I always wondered where his knowledge of the functioning of the judicial system of the EEA comes from. It was surprising that Mr. Piris allowed himself to be provoked by a Temporary Officer of the Icelandic Embassy in Brussels, Oddur Valsson, who in a letter to the editor of the FT on 20 November 2017 claimed that the EFTA Court was not bound to make use of ECJ rulings. Two days later, Piris replied that in the event of a judicial conflict, the EEA Joint Committee, a diplomatic body, could overrule the judgment of the EFTA Court. He thereby took the same position as Halvard Haukeland Fredriksen in the Norwegian Commentary.[14] As I have explained elsewhere in this book, this conclusion is neither compatible with Western culture (in German: "*Abendländische Kultur*") in general nor with the principle of the independence of the judiciary.[15] I fully concur with what ESA's Director of Legal and Executive Affairs, Carsten Zatschler, wrote on 24 November 2017 in another letter to the editor of the FT, namely that

> the question of which side 'prevails' should ultimately come down to the quality of the reasoning underpinning the respective courts' judgments.

5.5 Parliament Speaks up

On 8 April 2018, the Brexit Committee of the House of Commons called on the Government to consider negotiating for either a continued EEA membership or to join EFTA after Brexit. In a report on the future UK-EU relationship, the Committee recommended that if negotiations on a "deep and special partnership agreement" would prove unsuccessful, EEA/EFTA membership should "remain an alternative". Chairman Hilary Benn said:

> It is vital that UK businesses are able to continue to trade freely and sell services into our largest market after we leave, without additional costs or burdens or a hard border in

[13]See for details Chapter 3.

[14]See for details Chapters 3 and 24.

[15]See Chapter 3.

> Northern Ireland and that we maintain close co-operation on defence, security, data and information sharing and consumer safety.

He added that:

> Should negotiations on a 'deep and special partnership' not prove successful, we consider that EFTA/EEA membership remains an alternative which would have the advantage of continuity of access for UK services and could also be negotiated relatively quickly.

On 8 May 2018, the House of Lords even went one better. After having dealt a dozen defeats to the Government on the EU withdrawal bill, the Peers voted for an amendment to the bill saying that remaining in the EEA should be a negotiating objective. 83 Labour MPs disregarded orders that they should abstain during the division. It became clear that HM Government could in the end be forced to switch to a Soft Brexit.

6 The Position of the 27

Immediately after the Brexit vote of the British people, the remaining 27 EU Member States were scared. Certainly, there were those who felt that getting rid of the UK was preferable to the endless fights. Former Commission Vice-President Viviane Reding tweeted:

> "A successful divorce is better than a failed marriage. Good luck to this new and future third country! #Brexit."

But with the presidential election looming in France on 23 April and 7 May 2017 and the parliamentary elections scheduled for 15 March 2017 in the Netherlands and for 24 September 2017 in Germany, there was a great deal of insecurity. In all three countries, anti-European parties seemed to be destined to perform well. In Austria, a politician from the far-right anti-European Freedom Party appeared to be on the verge of becoming Federal President. He had promised a ballot if the EU were to become more centralised following Brexit. A few days before the final round of the Austrian election, in late November 2016, EU Commission President Jean-Claude Juncker urged EU leaders not to hold referenda on the membership of their countries in the bloc because he feared their voters might also choose to leave.

However, in all four countries, the anti-Europeans were defeated. In the meantime, the remaining 27 EU Member States have recovered, at least politically, from the Brexit after-shock and the old arrogance seems largely to have reinstated itself. The official line is that the Brits have made a huge mistake, that they will pay dearly for it and that they will regret it. I am not so sure that this will in fact occur. My impression is that there were several favourable circumstances that glued the 27 together, not least US President Trump's erratic behaviour. However, the fact remains that the EU is not sufficiently free trade oriented, that it is too centralised and bureaucratic and that its institutions are not popular with EU citizens. Not to speak of the unresolved crisis concerning the euro, the distribution of refugees, the rift between Western and Eastern EU Member States, the antagonism between Northern and Southern Member States, and the democratic deficit.

That the EU leadership could not resist the temptation of using Brexit as leverage to put pressure on Switzerland in the negotiations concerning the "ECJ model", is a further example of the kind of behaviour that has caused resentment. On 23 March 2017, the EU Ambassador to Switzerland said in an interview with *NZZ* that the institutional question should be clarified as soon as possible because once the British letter to formally leave the EU reached Brussels, Brussels might not have the capacities and the flexibility to negotiate a solution with Switzerland. The process should be slightly accelerated.

7 A Unique Chance for EFTA

7.1 General

The attitude of the EFTA States towards Brexit has, overall, been marked by an appalling lack of courage and imagination. The EFTA States too tend so see Brexit and its implications through national lenses. With the exception of the Icelanders, the EFTA politicians perceived Brexit as a phenomenon that would primarily affect the EU and accession to the British market after Brexit. Consequently, their main goal was to find solutions that would secure their respective bilateral interests to enjoy the benefits of unhindered trade with the UK. Again with the exception of Iceland, the EFTA States found it difficult to develop a multilateral approach that would take into account the possibility of the UK joining EFTA and/or—in one form or another—the EEA.

The EFTA Ministerial meeting of 27 June 2016 in Berne provided an opportunity for the four EFTA Governments to take a stand on the new situation. The statements made by the ministers were, however, inconsistent. The Swiss Minister of Economic Affairs who hosted the event, tried to spread some optimism about a possible EFTA membership for Britain. This would have meant the possibility of Britain entering existing FTA's between EFTA and numerous non-European countries and negotiating new agreements. There is the utmost flexibility on this aspect. If the EFTA States cannot agree to march together, each EFTA States has the right to go it alone. The Swiss apparently negotiated their FTA's with Japan and China on their own and they also administer those treaties without involving the EFTA Secretariat. The Icelanders may have had some informal help from the EFTA Secretariat when negotiating their FTA with China. However, influential Norwegian parliamentarians immediately objected stating that British EFTA membership was not in Norway's interest.

The EEA Council held its 48th Meeting on 14 November 2017. Discussions were held as to the implications of Brexit upon the EEA Agreement. The conclusions adopted at this meeting do not reveal anything of significance.

7.2 Norway

Norway has found it particularly difficult to adopt a clear stance. Its official position has long been that the UK should not join EFTA in any capacity. High-ranking Norwegian bureaucrats made several statements to that effect. The newly appointed Minister of EEA and EU Affairs, Marit Berger Røsland, gave a speech in Dublin on 9 November 2017, entitled "Norway's relationship with the EU in light of Brexit". Ms Røsland did not outline any specific position. She was, however, reported as saying with regard to the EEA: "It is hard to see that it will be a model that fits the needs of the UK after Brexit". The statement seemed to echo PM Erna Solberg's views, who told the Norwegian newspaper *Verdens Gang* on 4 September 2017, one week before the Norwegian general election, that the UK joining EFTA

> would weaken EFTA as an instrument for small countries.

Former Norwegian Europe ministers Elisabeth Vik Aspaker and Frank Bakke-Jensen also said that it was doubtful whether it was in Norway's interests to let the British in because they would supposedly want to dominate EFTA and the EEA. Al in all, the Norwegians feared for their position as a super-power within the EFTA pillar. However, after having won the election in September 2017, the Norwegian government softened its stance. At a conference in Oslo in 28 November 2017, State Secretary Elsbeth Tronstad said:

> Prime Minister Theresa May made it clear that the EEA is not an alternative and she is seeking a bespoke agreement with the EU [....]. If this should change, we will keep an open mind on the question of possible UK membership of the EEA. The interests of the EEA/ Efta countries will be our key concern when considering this issue.

This followed off-the-record statements made by Norwegian officials in September 2017 stating that if the UK were to knock at the door, they would be flexible. It should also be noted that the leader of the Centre Party, Trygve Slagsvold Vedum, said immediately prior to the September general election:

> If the British want, they should enter EFTA.

This statement appeared to be directed towards the UK joining the EFTA pillar of the EEA rather than just EFTA alone.

Norway has not outlined a position as regards the possibility of the UK "docking" to ESA and the EFTA Court. Unlike in Switzerland and in the UK, docking has not really been a topic of discussion in Norway.

On 23 January 2018, Prime Minister Erna Solberg gave an interview to the BBC's economics editor, Kamal Ahmed, at the World Economic Forum in Davos. Ahmed reported on Twitter that:

> She says UK and EU should push for a soft Brexit. Argues membership of EEA is best option but doubts UK agrees as it comes with EU 4 freedoms obligations including freedom of movement.

Such a TV interview could not have been more prominent, yet many in the UK continued to be fearful that Norway may hinder a Soft Brexit. Prime Minister Solberg was, however, clear: Norway would ultimately not be an obstacle. On 13 May 2018, Solberg openly supported British EEA membership in an interview with the Financial Times stating, *inter alia*, that this would add bargaining power on the EFTA side.

7.3 Iceland

Iceland was from the beginning more enthusiastic about the UK joining EFTA, either just the free trade association alone or the EEA on the EFTA side. The Minister for Foreign Affairs, Godhlaugur Thór Thórdharson, repeatedly called for the UK to either join EFTA alone, or as part of an EEA membership. On 5 September 2017, Mr. Thórdharson gave an interview on the BBC’s Today programme in the UK. He said that cooperating with Britain would strengthen EFTA. Godhlaugur Thór further suggested that the UK could join EFTA along the lines of the “Norway model”, which means EFTA/EEA membership. This is consistent with what he had said earlier on 2 August 2017 during a meeting with the UK Secretary of State for Environment, Food and Rural Affairs, Michael Gove, in Reykjavík. There, Godhlaugur Thór declared:

> For Britain, Iceland is a prime example of a country that chooses to stay outside of the European Union while still maintaining a strong relationship with both the EU and its member states, not least when it comes to free trade. We can therefore share our various experiences and at the same time strengthen our relations with the United Kingdom.

The Minister for Foreign Affairs confirmed this view when I paid him a visit in Reykjavík in early October 2017.

Apart from Mr. Thordharson, the Icelandic Cabinet’s website has a page dedicated to Brexit. There, it is stated that

> it is too early to rule out any option when it comes to arrangements for future relations with the United Kingdom. Although Britain has rejected membership of the single market and thereby given the EEA solution the kick, it is not ruled out that it may suit British interests to pursue EFTA membership [….].[16]

I am not aware of whether Iceland has outlined a position with respect to the UK “docking” to ESA and the EFTA Court. However, in the light of Iceland’s positive attitude and of my talks with influential members of government, I assume that they would view this option positively.

[16]Unofficial translation.

7.4 Liechtenstein

Liechtenstein has barely outlined a clear position on the issue in question. On 19 May 2017, Prime Minister Adrian Hasler said:

> The UK mustn't get a better deal with the EU than non-members who went through the effort of obtaining access to the single market.

On the other hand, Liechtenstein has alleged on a number of occasions that it is not against the UK joining the EFTA pillar of the EEA Agreement. The Government has signalled openness, but it has remained cautious.

7.5 Switzerland

Switzerland is in a different position to the other three EEA/EFTA States. It has its own network of bilateral sectoral agreements with the EU, but the latter has refused to conclude new agreements since 2008 unless Switzerland would accept a surveillance and court mechanism. Negotiations on a so-called "framework agreement", which ought to put an institutional umbrella over existing and future sectoral agreements, started in 2014, but were not concluded.[17] Federal Councillors have focussed on the country's bilateral relationship with the UK and on possible UK EFTA membership.

The Federal Council regretted the outcome of the Brexit vote, not because it felt that this was bad for European integration, but because the alleged "window of opportunity" for the conclusion of the framework agreement would now close since the EU would soon be totally preoccupied dealing with the UK. Then Minister for Foreign Affairs Didier Burkhalter, the main proponent of the "ECJ model",[18] tried to seize the day by stating that Switzerland was prepared to accelerate things to find a bilateral solution as soon as possible. Unsurprisingly, he didn't think of joining forces with the UK. His colleague Schneider-Ammann from the Department of Economic Affairs spoke of a solution within the next one or two years. As to the rest, Schneider-Ammann pursued what the Germans would call a "*Schaukelpolitik*" (seesaw policy). Occasionally he indicated that the UK would be welcome to re-join EFTA, but he also voiced doubts as to whether the huge UK would fit into EFTA. Federal President Doris Leuthard was at least clear when she stated on 29 March 2017 that Switzerland would need some kind of free trade agreement with Britain.

But nobody in the Berne administration tried to understand that with Brexit looming, a new multilateral approach could become an option. Swiss foreign policy remained fixated on bilateralism (and EU membership as the ultimate goal) as if the only thing that had happened was that the path had now become even stonier. The

---

[17]See Chapter 30.

[18]See for details Chapter 30.

leading bureaucrats didn't have enough imagination to think what Britain docking to ESA and the EFTA Court could mean as regards resolving its own institutional problem. In a document entitled, "Switzerland-UK relations post-Brexit", which was published in July 2017, the Swiss Government stated:

> Switzerland wishes to ensure that the existing mutual rights and obligations in its relationship with the UK will continue to apply after the UK leaves the EU and to develop these rights and obligations where necessary. (Mind the Gap Strategy)

Frankly, I do not believe it is appropriate to use the term strategy for such an unimaginative attitude. Friends in the Berne federal administration sent out emails in which they made fun of this by using the words "mind the nap" and "mind the slap".

7.6 Conclusions

To allow the UK into the institutions of the EFTA pillar wouldn't be a grant of grace; it would be in the EEA/EFTA's best interests. As Former ESA President Sven Erik Svedman said in December 2017, the institutions of the the EFTA pillar are not weak, but they are vulnerable.[19] Britain joining the EEA on the EFTA side or docking to ESA and the EFTA Court could, moreover, offer the EEA/EFTA countries the opportunity to negotiate and finally obtain what they were promised by Jacques Delors in 1989: namely, to essentially be put on an equal footing with the EU Member States when it comes to the enactment of new secondary legislation. Conversely, the EU would benefit from the fact that Britain would stay in the Single Market as well as from the moderate systemic competition that would quite naturally come from a strengthened EFTA pillar.

---

[19]See Chapter 13.

Chapter 32
"Two Souls in Europe's Breast"

Contents

1 Jacques Delors' Desire

In 1992, EU Commission President Jacques Delors said at a meeting of the Conference of European Churches that if, over the next ten years, Europe was not imbued with a soul, meaning that it would acquire a spirituality and a deeper sense of the reason for its existence, the game would be over. He added that he would therefore like to revive the intellectual and spiritual debate on Europe. In 2018, the EU is further away from having found that soul than ever before. That, however, doesn't necessarily mean that European integration should grind to a halt.

C. Baudenbacher, *Judicial Independence*, Springer Biographies,
https://doi.org/10.1007/978-3-030-02308-9_32

2 Political Integration Versus Economic Integration

2.1 Status quo

As I have mentioned several times in this book, Europe appears to be characterised by a duality of souls, one that is, at least officially, striving for political unification, for an "ever closer Union", and a second one that wants to limit integration to economic aspects and leave the pursuit of political objectives to intergovernmental action. The three EEA/EFTA States, Iceland, Liechtenstein and Norway, prosper outside the EU; their ambition is limited to economic objectives, namely to being part of the Single Market and securing their operators unhindered access to that market. To that end, they have largely adopted the EU internal market *acquis*. Within the framework of this economic objective, they maintain their own common surveillance and court system, which is closely linked to the respective mechanisms in the EU. At the same time, the three EEA/EFTA States have safeguarded their sovereignty in crucial areas, which in the EU have been communitised, such as agriculture, fisheries, foreign trade or foreign policy.

Switzerland is linked to the EU by a series of bilateral agreements that do not, however, cover the whole internal market *acquis*. Instead, the country pursues a sectoral approach; it has concluded agreements in the fields of free movement of goods and of persons, but not regarding free movement of services and of capital nor the freedom of establishment. The goal is to secure Swiss industry access to the Single Markets in the sectors covered by the agreements. Conflicts between Switzerland and the EU are essentially dealt with in EEA Joint Committees. There is, for the time being, no supranational surveillance and court mechanism. Like the three EEA/EFTA States, Switzerland does not participate in the EU common policies concerning agriculture, foreign trade and foreign policy.

After the Brexit vote, the UK is on the verge of becoming a third State from the EU's perspective. HM Government has so far interpreted the outcome of the Brexit referendum in June 2016 as a mandate to leave both the EU customs union and the Single Market. As regards the EU's common policies, the debate has initially been dominated by Britain's wish to regain sovereignty of its foreign trade. In recent times, however, the prospect of regaining control over agriculture and fisheries has come to the fore. When I was in Westminster in March 2018, I was told that, for a traditionally seafaring island nation, re-establishing control over its fisheries was also emotionally important. As regards judicial control, HM Government wants to terminate the jurisdiction of the ECJ. Post-Brexit, the government intends to conclude a "bespoke" deep and special partnership agreement with the EU. It is, however, unclear how disputes under this new agreement would be settled. In any case, at the time of writing the last word on Brexit has not yet been spoken.

If anyone refers to two souls in the German-speaking world, it involuntarily brings to mind Johann Wolfgang von Goethe, whose Faust famously exclaimed:

Zwei Seelen wohnen, ach! in meiner Brust.

(Two souls, alas, dwell in my breast.)

In his lament, Faust describes one soul as clinging to the world with love's robust desires and the other as rising from the dust to reach sublime ancestral regions.

2.2 A Look Back into History

Looking back, we learn that there were always two approaches to integration in Europe after World War II. The American European Recovery Plan ("Marshall Plan") was launched in 1947 and in 1948 the Organization for European Economic Co-operation (OEEC) was established. The OEEC was an intergovernmental organisation without supranational structures. Its first objective was to prepare the recovery of the European economy using the aid available under the Marshall Plan.

In 1951, the ECSC Treaty was concluded by the States that would later become the "founding six"—France, Germany, Italy and the three Benelux States. Although the treaty had only a limited material scope, it represented a revolutionary step by implementing, for the first time, the concept of supranationality. From 1956 onwards, Switzerland, together with the UK, tried to avoid a division of Western Europe by promoting the idea of a wide free trade zone within the OEEC. These efforts were reinforced following the conclusion of the EEC Treaty with supranational institutions on 25 March 1957. The EEC Treaty aimed to create a customs union and a common market. However, the negotiations on the establishment of a large free trade zone broke down due to French resistance.

On 4 January 1960, the multilateral EFTA Convention was signed in Stockholm by Austria, Denmark, Norway, Portugal, Sweden, Switzerland and the UK. EFTA's goals were far more modest than those of the EEC. EFTA was (and remains) a free trade area that has eliminated customs duties on industrial products among its members. However, each EFTA State retains its foreign trade sovereignty and therefore has its own customs duty regime vis-à-vis third countries. EFTA has no competence to enact legislation, there is no common surveillance and no common court and membership can easily be terminated. The dispatch of the Swiss Federal Council of 5 February 1960 particularly emphasised the lack of supranationality.

EFTA was an immediate economic success. Its members were referred to as the "Outer Seven" as opposed to the "Inner Six" EEC States. However, the EFTA States suffered from the "tariff wall" erected by the EEC and EFTA had limited political appeal, in particular for the UK. The attractiveness of the EEC, later the EC and the EU, became too strong and from 1973 onwards, when the UK and Denmark left EFTA for the EEC, most EFTA States were determined to switch sides and in fact succeeded in doing so at the end of the Cold War.

A fundamental realignment became necessary after 1995 when EFTA was downsized to four Member States. From now on, three of them—Iceland, Liechtenstein and Norway—would be linked to the EU via the comprehensive multilateral EEA Agreement, whereas Switzerland had concluded its own sectoral bilateral agreements with the EU. An updated EFTA Convention was signed on 21 June 2001 in Vaduz and entered into force on 1 June 2002. The most important novelty was the integration of the rules and principles of the EEA Agreement and of the bilateral agreements between the EU and Switzerland into the EFTA Convention. The benefits of the privileged relationship that the three EEA/EFTA States, on the one hand, and Switzerland, on the other, obtained vis-à-vis the EU were thereby transposed to the EFTA States' own internal relations. At the same time, the revised Convention provides for an enhanced platform for EFTA to develop their trade relations with non-EU States. EFTA has in many cases been able to conclude such bilateral agreements before the EU. On certain occasions, when the four EFTA States found that they had diverging interests, an individual EFTA State might conclude such an agreement outside EFTA.

In recent years, with the EU gradually transforming from an economic to a political undertaking, its attractiveness for the four EFTA States has declined once again. This disenchantment is reinforced by the fact that the UK, an important EU Member State, is determined to leave the Union.

3 Common Law and Civil Law

3.1 *General*

The descriptions of the two most important legal systems in the world—common law and civil law—are legion. To give an example, on University of California's website at the Berkeley School of Law, the following text can be found under the title "The Common Law and Civil Law Traditions":

> Most nations today follow one of two major legal traditions: common law or civil law. The common law tradition emerged in England during the Middle Ages and was applied within British colonies across continents. The civil law tradition developed in continental Europe at the same time and was applied in the colonies of European imperial powers such as Spain and Portugal. Civil law was also adopted in the nineteenth and twentieth centuries by countries formerly possessing distinctive legal traditions, such as Russia and Japan, that sought to reform their legal systems in order to gain economic and political power comparable to that of Western European nation-states.

In the civil law tradition, the focus is on legislation whereas in the common law tradition it is on court jurisprudence.

3.2 *Legal Origins Theory*

The comparative law theory of legal origins argues that institutions depend on political factors, in particular: the dominant beliefs in France, on the one hand, and in England, on the other; on the roles of the King/Queen/Government, the Parliament, the judiciary and individuals in society. The theory's basic finding has been described by Professor Paul G. Mahoney from the University of Virginia, in the following words:

> English common law developed as it did because landed aristocrats and merchants wanted a system of law that would provide strong protection for property and contract rights, and limit the Crown's ability to interfere in markets. French civil law, by contrast, developed as it did because the revolutionary generation, and Napoleon after it, wished to disable judges from thwarting government economic policies. Thus, quite apart from the substance of legal rules, there is a sharp difference between the ideologies underlying common and civil law, with the latter notably more comfortable with a centralised and activist government.

This does not mean that common law states will always act according to common law tradition and civil law states always according to civil law tradition. After World War II, there was a certain degree of osmosis in that civil law countries began to rely increasingly on case law and common law countries started to regulate more and more areas by statutory law. Nevertheless, it seems that the core differences are still in place.

3.3 Stare decisis: *The Most Important Common Law Doctrine*

In order to achieve certainty, uniformity and consistency, the common law relies on judicial precedent. Precedent roughly means that previous judicial decisions on an issue are regarded as being binding general rules. The Latin expression *stare decisis* means "to stand by what has been decided". When a court engages in vertical *stare decisis*, it follows a precedent from a higher court. A court adhering to its own precedent or a precedent by another court on same judicial level engages in horizontal *stare decisis*. The precedent system was exported from Britain to the whole Anglo-Saxon world. The US Supreme Court stated on 27 June 1991 in *Payne v. Tennessee*, that *stare decisis*

> promotes the evenhanded, predictable, and consistent development of legal principles, fosters reliance on judicial decisions, and contributes to the actual and perceived integrity of the judicial process.

However, the doctrine also allows for a certain degree of flexibility given the need to interpret precedents, which may result in either applying or distinguishing one set of facts over/from another. Under specific conditions, courts may also overrule, reverse or disapprove of previous decisions. As a result of the precedent system, judges have enormous power to shape the law and, unlike the case of the civil law judge who is only to apply the written law, "judge-made law" is generally accepted as important part of the legal system.

Civil law systems place a stronger emphasis on codes of law or acts of law. Courts rule on the law by interpreting codes and other statutes enacted by the legislature. The lower courts are not bound by judgments made by higher courts under an accepted rule of *stare decisis*. Nevertheless, in practice they will follow the case law of the higher court.

Whether a court in a common law system is prepared to overrule previous case law, depends on value judgment. In *Planned Parenthood of Southeastern Pennsylvania v. Casey*, the US Supreme Court on 29 June 1992 laid out the factors to be considered when the question arises. Overruling important precedent was said to be appropriate only: where a doctrine has become unworkable and irrelevant, or has become unclear; if society has not built upon the precedent; where facts have changed. A court also disposes of a certain discretion when deciding whether a case should be distinguished from a previous case. If a later case is distinguished because the facts are different, the holding of a precedent does not apply. A court may use a restrictive or a non-restrictive approach when distinguishing the facts.

3.4 Von Hayek's Spontaneous Order Theory Applied to the Law

According to the Austrian-British Nobel Prize winner in economics Friedrich August Von Hayek, it is not only market economies that constitute spontaneous orders in that they secure a more efficient allocation of resources than any design could achieve.[1] Von Hayek maintained that the same applies to the common law, which creates knowledge over time by trial and error. Von Hayek thus extended his spontaneous order theory to the development of law. The common law, like the market, is in his view not the result of human design, but of human—in this case judges'—action. This is in direct contrast to the legislative decrees that characterise the civil law.

4 Commonalities of the Five Non-EU States

4.1 Belief in Free Trade and Open Markets

All five countries at issue are characterised by their belief in free trade and open markets. As regards the four current EFTA States Iceland, Liechtenstein, Norway and Switzerland, this proposition requires no justification. The UK has since 1973 been part of the EU customs union and has as such been prevented from pursuing its own foreign trade policy. The very idea that unconditional free trade is beneficial for the economy is, however, of British origin. And the desire to reclaim sovereignty of its foreign trade matters has been one of the driving forces behind the Brexit decision.

---

[1]See for details Chapter 14.

Efficient financial markets seem to arise and flourish better under common law than under civil law. Massimiliano Vatiero, an Italian economist teaching at the *Università della Svizzera Italiana*, discovered that there seems to be a correlation between a flexible labour market, diffuse ownership in corporations and radical innovation, as opposed to incremental innovation. The distinction between radical and incremental innovation goes back to the Austrian economist Joseph Schumpeter who famously wrote:

> Radical innovations create major disruptive changes and incremental innovations continuously advance the process of change.

Interestingly, the correlation between a flexible labour market, diffuse ownership in corporations and radical innovation has not only been found in common law countries such as the US and the UK, but also in Switzerland.

4.2 Notion of the State

As regards the notion of the State, it seems that the UK and Switzerland, in particular, have much in common. Unlike other continental countries, the Hegelian concept of state has never been influential in Switzerland. The glorification of the state as "the reality of the moral idea" and similar theories have barely found any followers. Nor has the French idea of "*la Nation*" as being not one force among others, but the only legitimate power, been adopted. In Switzerland, the State is seen as a useful institution, nothing more. In that respect, the Swiss concept of state is much closer to English and American thinking than to German or French. In Switzerland, as in the US, there is a civil society that takes responsibility for important areas of social life. The Swiss are less likely to expect the State to ensure their well-being than, say, the Germans. The same goes, to a large extent, for Liechtenstein. Norway is, on the other hand, characterised by a strong state. This is, however, not the case in Iceland, at least not to the same extent as in Norway.

4.3 Religious Foundations of Capitalism

Calvin's doctrine of wealth, the basis of the Protestant work ethic, has spread from Geneva via what is now the UK to the US. This doctrine which essentially says that financial well-being is considered pleasing to God, was further developed by the Puritans. In his seminal and highly influential 1905 book "The Protestant Ethic and the Spirit of Capitalism" ("*Die protestantische Ethik und der Geist des Kapitalismus*"), the German sociologist and economist Max Weber searched for the foundations and prerequisites of modern capitalism. His initial question was what the peculiarity of Western modernity consists of. Weber singled out the specific, Protestant ethic as one of the decisive roots of the typically occidental form of economic activity, which offered capitalism an idealistic basis and came closest to it. In his view, capitalism developed in Northern Europe where Protestant, in particular Calvinist, ethics prompted people to develop their own businesses and to engage in trade and accumulating wealth for investment. Protestant work ethics was thus deemed to be an important force behind the unplanned and uncoordinated emergence of modern capitalism. Weber's findings still seem to be relevant today. Petrus L. Steenkamp from the University of Pretoria concluded in 2013:

> The Protestant (work) ethic is more than a cultural norm that places a positive moral value on doing a good job. It is based on a belief that work has intrinsic value for its own sake.

This attitude to money and wealth appears to be reflected in both the UK and Switzerland. Napoleon is said to have referred to the English as a nation of shopkeepers. The remark was meant disparagingly. However, in reality it is a backhanded compliment. In his World War I book "*Händler und Helden*" (merchants and heroes), German economist Werner Sombart who later became a national socialist described the Germans as a nation of heroes animated by primordial motives and the English as calculating merchants. If we were to transpose this (in)famous juxtaposition to the Swiss, they would certainly appear among the merchants. In fact, the money-mindedness of the Swiss has been described on many occasions throughout their history. The saying "*point d'argent—point de Suisse*", which literally means that where there is no money you will find no Swiss, dates back to French 17th century dramatist Jean Racine. But it seems to be of enduring timeliness. It alludes to a time when many Swiss were much sought after and consequently rather greedy mercenaries. Peter von Matt, Professor of Literature at the University of Zurich, aptly remarked that, unlike Austria, France or Italy, Switzerland does not define itself outwardly by its culture. It rather behaves as a utilitarian enterprise and defines and presents itself from a market perspective.

4.4 Legal Systems

The UK is the birthplace of the common law, whereas the current EFTA members Iceland, Liechtenstein, Norway and Switzerland are labelled as civil law countries. As regards the role of the judge, however, the Swiss system comes the closest to the common law approach. I have already mentioned that Article 1 of the Swiss Civil Code gives the judge the power and the duty to act like a legislature in certain situations.[2] The late University of Fribourg Professor Alfred E. Von Overbeck wrote in 1977 that:

> "[a]lthough Switzerland certainly is not a 'mixed civil law and common law jurisdiction,' its legal system attributes to judges a measure of freedom which seems greater than they have in other civil law jurisdictions and might be of some interest, especially for American

[2] See for details Chapter 9.

> lawyers," and that "there is a large field where the judge is sufficiently free to adapt the law to the needs of the everchanging situations of life. Common lawyers may discover some similarities with the reasoning of their own judges."

Benjamin N. Cardozo, who in 1932 became a Justice of the US Supreme Court concluded in 1920:

> I think the tone and temper in which the modern judge should set about his task are well expressed in the first article of the Swiss Civil Code of 1907.

Whether this open approach also applies in Liechtenstein, which has adopted the Austrian General Civil Code rather than the Swiss Civil Code, is controversial. The Austrian Code does not contain a provision such as Article 1 of the Swiss Code. However, there is a certain Swiss influence due to the fact that in Liechtenstein courts—in addition to Liechtensteiners and Austrians—there are also Swiss judges.

Iceland and Norway do not have concise civil codes. The courts have thus been given a significant role in developing judge-made law. Combined with their Germanic legal roots, this makes these systems into exotic hybrids whose approach lies somewhere between common and civil law.

The Swiss Civil Code including its Article 1 was adopted by Post-Ottoman Turkey in 1926 during Mustafa Kemal Atatürk's presidency. The current political situation in Turkey makes it difficult to consider its further integration into Europe. Nevertheless, in the late 1990s Madeleine Albright, who was then US Secretary of State, repeatedly advocated Turkey's accession to the EEA in the EFTA pillar.

There are further similarities between the common law and the legal orders of the EFTA States. In international company law, Switzerland, like the common law countries (and the Netherlands) has traditionally adhered to the incorporation theory. A company is thus subject to the legal order according to which it was established by its founders. The incorporation theory has also been adopted in Liechtenstein and in Iceland. On the other hand, the real seat theory, which applies in Germany, Austria, France, Belgium and Luxembourg, links the applicable law to the administrative seat of the company. This is the place where the fundamental decisions of the management are made and implemented. The real seat theory has traditionally also been applied in Norway, although the situation currently appears to be in flux.

According to the case law of the ECJ, the incorporation theory applies throughout the EU. The EFTA Court has not yet ruled on the issue. However, it can be safely assumed that, in view of the homogeneity objective underlying the EEA Agreement and the fact that the incorporation theory allows for more flexibility than the real seat theory, the EFTA Court would follow the ECJ's approach in the future.

As regards Liechtenstein, it should be added that it is the only civil *law* jurisdiction to have largely adopted Anglo-Saxon *trust* legislation.

4.5 Image of Man

Both in the UK and in Switzerland, courts base themselves on the assumption that human beings are reasonable in the sense of "normal". They are not stupid or careless, nor are they overly cautious. In 1933, Lord Justice Greer in *Hall* v *Brooklands Auto-Racing Club* ([1933] 1 KB 205) famously referred to the reasonable man as "the man on the Clapham omnibus". Clapham is a district of south west London. The case involved the owners of a racing track for motor cars. Spectators paid a fee and were allowed to view the races; stands were provided from which they could do this in safety. Nevertheless, many of them preferred to stand along and outside the railing. Two cars hit each other and one shot into the air and crashed into the railing, killing two spectators and injuring others. No accident of this kind had ever happened before. Lord Justice Greer held that if he attended such a motor race he

> would know quite well that no barrier would be provided which would be sufficient to protect him in the possible but highly improbable event of a car charging the barrier and getting through to the spectators.

The man on the Clapham omnibus would therefore deny compensation to the victims injured by the car. In Switzerland, the same liberal image of man has been used by the courts in unfair competition law cases. Likewise, in cases such as *Inconsult* or *Vienna Life* and *Swiss Life*, the EFTA Court has based itself on a similar idea of man.[3]

The man on the Clapham Omnibus contrasts above all with the German idea that average people are dumb and naive and therefore in need of protection. In Germany the relevant hypothetical figure is called "*Lieschen Müller*" (Lizzie Miller).

5 Conclusions

5.1 The Five EU Outsiders Ought to Join Forces

Those who have decided to remain outside the EU or to leave it, namely the Icelanders, Liechtensteiners, Norwegians, Swiss and British, take a rather sober approach to integration. They want to limit themselves to the economic and social aspects—free trade, open markets, efficiency, fair taxation and social justice. In my view, there is room for two structures in Europe: one camp comprising the countries that are determined to create a European Federal State; and a second camp consisting of States that wish to cooperate multilaterally towards economic integration. The bracket holding these two groups together could be the Single Market. This

[3]See for details Chapter 18.

would enable a limited form of systemic competition that would benefit both camps.

In view of the history of the EU and the EEA and in particular of the important role played by citizens and economic operators in enforcing the law, each of the two structures would need to have its own surveillance body and its own court of justice. The experience of the EEA Agreement and of its institutions, ESA and the EFTA Court, could play a role in this. In order for the two courts, the ECJ and the second tribunal, to function, they would, as a matter of principle, have to consist of independent and impartial judges. Given its size, London could be granted two seats in the Court.

The States belonging to the second camp haven't found common cause with each other yet. Following my speech of 7 February 2018 at UCL, Professor Piet Eeckhout rightly said that they would be well-advised to join forces. Otherwise the EU would take them on individually.

5.2 *What About the Orphaned Insiders?*

The UK's closest partners in Northern Europe—the Netherlands, Denmark, Ireland, Sweden, Finland and the Baltic states—appear to feel orphaned by Brexit. These countries were used to looking to Britain when it came to issues such as free trade, liberal economic policies or safeguarding national sovereignty in tax matters. Recently, there has been talk of a "Northern Alliance" and of a "21st century Hanseatic League" or a "Hanseatic League 2.0". The original Hanseatic League was a merchant and defensive organisation of Northern European powers that aimed to protect their mutual trading interests. The group dominated commercial activity in Northern Europe from the 13th to the 15th century.

The Northern EU Member States are reluctant to accept French President Macron's proposals for strengthening the monetary union. Their approach to trade and economic policy is basically the same as that of the five EU outsiders. It might, therefore, be safe to assume that the Northern EU Member States have a vested interest in supporting the two European integration structures outlined above.

The concerns of the Northern EU Member States are all the more justified since President François Hollande stated, just a few days after the Brexit vote, that the EU27 should consider "adapting" EU competition law to focus more on growth, employment and investment.[4] Such a shift in competition policy could easily go hand in hand with an (even) more protectionist trade policy.

---

[4]See for details Chapter 31.

Epilogue

1. Announcement of My Resignation

As I have said above, on 15 November 2017, I announced that I would resign from the EFTA Court by the end of March 2018. My fourth term of office as a judge would have lasted almost two additional years. However, the assault on the Court's integrity and its consequences had changed the situation fundamentally. After having spoken with Doris and with Laura Melusine who, as I said, in the meantime was a lawyer in a major law firm in Brussels, I came to the conclusion that I needed a new challenge.

The Swiss News Agency DPA distributed the Court's press release; *MLex*, a leading European antitrust news provider, and *POLITICO*, the Brussels-based publication, announced my stepping down. *Euractiv* even ran a story under the title "EFTA court boss quits, reducing UK's post-Brexit chances". Most commentators reacted with surprise. I received countless emails and text messages from judges, politicians, civil servants, lawyers, academics and friends who expressed their disappointment. Discussions began on social media and there seemed to be a unanimous feeling that an era was coming to the end. "*Nationen*", the Norwegian farmers' newspaper, whose journalists are very fair, indicated that Norwegian diplomats were relieved because I had failed to "synchronise" my Brexit activities with them. There it was again, this incredible lack of understanding that judges of a European Court are not supposed to be on the leash of their governments. Instead, there is an implicit desire to keep them reined in. European judges are frequently restricted as regards their publications, speeches and interviews, essentially forcing them to act as if they were government agents.

C. Baudenbacher, *Judicial Independence*, Springer Biographies,
https://doi.org/10.1007/978-3-030-02308-9

2. The EFTA Court Is Firmly Established

When the EEA negotiations were concluded, the Norwegian news agency *NTB* wrote that the life span of the agreement might be shorter than the length of the negotiations. This prognosis turned out to be wrong. Today, the EEA Agreement is the basis for a singular model of integration in Europe. This model does not aim to create "an ever closer union", but is limited to facilitating sophisticated economic cooperation. In spite of the fundamental principles of homogeneity and reciprocity, the EFTA Court has been able to uphold specific EFTA values such as the belief in free trade and open markets, fair taxation, efficiency and a modern image of man. At the same time, it has rejected mercantilist claims in major cases.

Both in Switzerland and Norway, EEA sceptics complained from the very beginning that the EEA Agreement does not give the EEA/EFTA States a full co-decision right, but only a co-determination right in Single Market legislation. The Swiss Foreign Ministry's fixation on this issue ultimately led to the rejection of the EEA Agreement by the people and the cantons in the referendum of 6 December 1992. However, if used in a meaningful way, a co-determination right can provide considerable influence. It is furthermore crucial to bear in mind that the EEA/EFTA States have retained their sovereignty with regard to the common policies. Nevertheless, these critics have a valid point.

As regards the judicial level, however, this one-sidedness has largely been avoided. The EFTA Court has over the years successfully positioned itself as a valid interlocutor of the ECJ. Self-pity is not something that augurs a bright future. We should rather turn the tables and look for ways to increase the influence of the EEA–EFTA countries in the legislative process. In late August 2016, the Brussels-based think tank *Bruegel* put forward some new ideas, *inter alia* concerning legislation, in the framework of a possible EU–UK relationship post Brexit. Together with the UK, and possibly Switzerland, the EEA/EFTA States could well achieve improvements in this respect.

3. A Partial Victory of Independence

Lord Judge said in his last speech as the Lord Chief Justice of England and Wales on 3 July 2013 when talking about the domestic judiciary:

> It is inconceivable that a judge might lose office or be demoted because he or she gave judgment against the wishes of the government of the day. It is inconceivable that any minister might write to a judge, or get a secretary to telephone a judge, and let it be known that a particular result was expected.

That such or similar incidents are also inconceivable in a European court such as the EFTA Court, is less certain.

Indeed, my years on the EFTA Court bench were marked by a struggle for the institution's recognition in both EEA pillars and beyond the EEA as a whole. Oddly enough, it was easier to earn that appreciation in the EU pillar than in the EFTA pillar. When I became President in 2003, my influence both on the case law and on the Court's extrajudicial functions increased. However, opposition from those whose goal it was to keep the Court down also grew.

My dual activity as a judge and professor was a good thing. My St. Gallen chair facilitated the building up of a network with Union judges and AG's as well as with EU Commissioners, EU senior civil servants and domestic actors. Furthermore, due to my teaching and research at St. Gallen, I was able to stay abreast of recent developments in economic law in general, not only in Europe, but also in the Americas and in Asia. I profited in particular from my exchanges with economists and those in the field of business administration. As I have explained, my professorship was also my fallback position should things not work out in Luxembourg.

Right from the very beginning, the EFTA Court had the support of the political branch and of important judges in Liechtenstein. In Iceland, the situation was, and still is to a certain extent, mixed. The relationship with the courts was always marked by respect and has steadily improved over the last ten years. However, certain politicians had, and continue to have, difficulties in complying with the country's obligations under the EEA Agreement. The strongest resistance against the Court, and against me personally, came from Norwegian bureaucrats, certain judges and from Norway's many government-oriented academics. Whereas the EFTA pillar superpower tends to pat itself on the back for being the best pupil in class when it comes to implementing directives and regulations, its ruling class, including large parts of academia, has been less positive in its dealings with the EFTA Court. By its own admission, the Norwegian Government has always sought a degree of control over ESA. That such control over the Court was not possible disturbed certain bureaucrats. Norwegian courts were thus told to keep cases for themselves and the Norwegian Supreme Court refrained from referring a single case to us for more than 12 years. I am, however, proud to say that the EFTA Court's relationship with the Supreme Court has improved enormously over the past three years. And thankfully, a number of free spirits have come to the fore in the Norwegian academic world in recent times. The problems arising from the fact that governments have too much influence on the nomination of "their" judge remain, however, unresolved.

On 1 January 2018, Páll Hreinsson became President of the Court. In March, the governments appointed Bernd Hammermann to succeed me as a judge. After his time as an ESA College Member, Bernd had served in the Liechtenstein administration, first as head of the then Land and Public Registry Office and since 2013 as head of the Office of Justice.

On 9 May 2018, the Norwegian Government published a paper entitled "Norway in Europe. The Norwegian Government's strategy for cooperation with the EU 2018–2021". It is the most positive official report on the EEA from Oslo I have seen in my twenty-two and a half years on the EFTA Court bench. Whether this will also change the attitude towards the institutions of the EFTA pillar remains to be seen. Nevertheless, this first step is remarkable.

On 13 May 2018, Norwegian PM Erna Solberg declared in the Financial Times that Norway was prepared to see the UK join the EEA. "I think we will cope very well if the Brits come in. It will give bargaining power on our side too. And it would ease Norway's access to the UK" she added.

4. Parting from the Court

On 9 April 2018, I left the EFTA Court bench. A solemn undertaking was held in *Cercle Cité*, in the historic hall where a little more than 15 years ago my presidency had begun and where the Court had held its tenth and twentieth anniversary conferences. Swiss national TV reported on the event in the evening news. ECJ President Koen Lenaerts was interviewed and said that with my contribution to securing EEA homogeneity I had gained the respect of all the members of the ECJ and that in a way I had been part of the ECJ. For me this was a gratifying confirmation of my approach to homogeneity. Of course, the ECJ had noticed that in recent years we had taken our own line on a number of important issues. However, it was also understood that we had not done this thoughtlessly. In my farewell speech, I said, among other things, that a trade court cannot fulfil its task without taking economics into account and that this is not limited to competition and State aid law. In all Single Market law, the question inevitably arises of whether the proposed solution to a case is efficient. At the same time, considerations of justice and equity remain relevant. I pointed to the fact that the father of classical free market economics, Adam Smith, had written two seminal books. Before he published "An Inquiry into the Nature and Causes of the Wealth of Nations", he brought out a volume entitled "The Theory of Moral Sentiments".

After more than 22 years, I am now free to spread my wings and fly to wherever I wish. I am grateful that I, a non-EEA citizen, have been given the opportunity to play an active part in European integration. Living in a European capital has changed my and my family's way of thinking. We have discovered the Nordic countries, an area of the world with its own character and an incredibly beautiful nature. I am confident that I will succeed in maintaining the global network I have built up over the past two decades. The unrelenting fighting for the Court's independence was sometimes tiring, but I didn't dodge the bullets and yet they didn't really hurt me. Sometimes I was reminded of Friedrich Nietzsche's saying: "What does not kill me makes me stronger." ("*Was mich nicht umbringt macht mich stärker.*") Having said that, I want to emphasise that all the fights were fought by peaceful means. When you see what is happening in other parts of the world, this is particularly important. All in all, my time on the EFTA Court bench was rewarding. In June 2018, Norwegian Supreme Court Justice Ingvald Falch commented on my resignation in *Lov og Rett* with the words that I should be acknowledged for my substantial contribution to the fact that the EEA Agreement works as it was supposed to do.

Although Ingvald has, due to his background as a business lawyer, more understanding for market orientation and a critical attitude towards protectionism than other Justices, I believe that this is not just a minority opinion. During all these years, through all the ups and downs, I always tried to remain true to myself. And I think that I have succeeded in being what I always wanted to be: An independent European judge, a judge off the leash.

Bibliography

(The electronic sources were checked on 26 June 2018.).

Abbott Frederick M./Verkade Feer D. W., The Silhouette of a Trojan Horse: Reflections on Advocate General Jacobs' Opinion in Silhouette v. Hartlauer, Bijblad Bij De Industriële Eigendom, Vol. 66, p. 111, 1998, https://papers.ssrn.com/sol3/papers.cfm?abstract_id=1921869&rec=1&srcabs=1921856&alg=1&pos=6.

Ahlberg Kerstin, The Efta court clashes with Norway's Supreme Court, Nordic Labour Journal, 7 November 2013, http://www.nordiclabourjournal.org/nyheter/news-2013/article.2013-11-06.7982273279.

Alemanno Alberto, The Precautionary Principle, in: Baudenbacher, Ed., The Handbook of EEA Law, Springer, 2016, 839 ff.

Alemanno Alberto, The HOB–vín Judgment: A Failed Attempt to Standardise the Visual Imagery, Packaging and Appeal of Alcohol Products, European Journal of Risk Regulation Vol. 4, 2013, 101 ff.

Alemanno Alberto, The Philip Morris Norway Judgment: The First International Challenge to Point of Sale Tobacco Display Bans, 2012, https://www.transnational-dispute-management.com/article.asp?key=1875.

Alemanno Alberto, The Legality, Rationale and Science of Tobacco Display Bans after the Philip Morris Judgment, European Journal of Risk Regulation, Vol. 4, 2011, https://papers.ssrn.com/sol3/papers.cfm?abstract_id=1948507.

Alemanno Alberto, Trade in Food. Regulatory and Judicial Approaches in the EC and the WTO, London 2007.

Alford, Roger P., The Inferior Quality of ECJ Decisions, Opinio Juris, 2007, http://opiniojuris.org/2007/10/31/the-inferior-quality-of-ecj-decisions/.

Alford, Roger P., Misusing International Sources to Interpret the Constitution, 98 American Journal of International Law, 57 ff. (2004).

Alighieri Dante, The Divine Comedy ("La Divina Commedia"), John Ciardi, translator, 2007 (first published 1320).

Almestad, Knut, Natural Resources, in: Baudenbacher, Ed., The Handbook of EEA Law, Springer, 2016, 763 ff.

Almestad, Knut, The Notion of 'Opting Out', in: Baudenbacher, Ed., The Handbook of EEA Law, Springer, 2016, 85 ff.

Almestad, Knut, The Essentials, in: EFTA Court, Ed., The EEA and the EFTA Court: Decentered Integration, Hart, Oxford/Portland Oregon 2015, 299 ff.

Almestad, Knut, Reflections on the Postal Services Directive and the EEA Review, in: EFTA Court, Ed., Judicial Protection in the European Economic Area, Stuttgart 2012, 77. ff.

C. Baudenbacher, *Judicial Independence*, Springer Biographies,
https://doi.org/10.1007/978-3-030-02308-9

Almestad, Knut, The Squaring of the Circle—The Internal Market and the EEA, in: Martin Johansson/Nils Wahl/Ulf Bernitz, Eds., A European for all seasons: Liber Amicorum in Honour of Sven Norberg, Brussels 2006, 1 ff.

Almestad, Knut, The duties of co-operation of national authorities and the Community institutions under Article 10 (ex Article 5) of the Treaty of Rome: the EEA variant, FIDE: XIX congress. Vol. I, 2000, 427.

Amerasinghe Chittharanjan F., Judges of the International Court of Justice—Election and Qualifications, 14 Leiden Journal of International Law, 335 ff. (2001).

Andenæs Mads, Contribution to the farewell symposium of the President of the Oberlandesgericht Düsseldorf, Anne-José Paulsen, 1 February 2018, file with the author.

Andenæs Mads, Sovereignty, in: Baudenbacher, Ed., The Fundamental Principles of EEA Law: EEA-ities, Springer, 2017, 91 ff.

Andenæs Mads/Fredriksen Halvard Haukeland, EFTA-domstolen under press, Europarättslig tidskrift, No. 1 2017.

Angell Svein Ivar, Den historiske bakgrunnen for heimfallsinstituttet ("The historical background of the reversion institute"), 2006 MAGMA Econas Tidsskrift for Økonomi og Ledelse ("Econas Journal of Economics and Management"), Bergen.

Anstey Roger, King Leopold's Legacy, London 1966.

Armengod Héctor/Baudenbacher Laura Melusine, The Repackaging of Pharmaceutical Products and Parallel Trade in the EU, RAJ Pharma December 2009, 783 ff.

Areeda Philip E., Antitrust Law, Little, Brown 1978.

Arnesen Finn/Fredriksen Halvard Haukeland/Graver, Hans Petter/Mestad, Ola/Vedder, Christoph, Agreement on the European Economic Area, A Commmentary, C.H. Beck/Hart/Nomos 2018.

Arnesen Finn/Fredriksen Halvard Haukeland, Preamble, Art. 1 Object and purpose, in: Arnesen/Fredriksen/Graver/Mestad/Vedder, Agreement on the European Economic Area. A Commentary, 2018.

Aznar-Gómez Mariano J., Article 2, in: Zimmermann/Tomuschat/Oellers-Frahm, Eds., The Statute of the International Court of Justice. A Commentary, Oxford 2006.

Bain Joe S., Industrial Organization, New York 1959.

Barbier de La Serre, Eric, Standard of Review in Competition Law Cases: *Posten Norge* and Beyond, Morgan de Rivery, Eric/Fall Alexandre, The EFTA Court—A Court of Business Law? in: EFTA Court., Ed., The EEA and the EFTA Court: Decentered Integration, Hart, Oxford/Portland Oregon 2015, 417 ff.

Barnard Catherine, Social Policy Law, in: Baudenbacher, Ed., The Handbook of EEA Law, Springer, 2016, 809 ff.

Barnard Catherine, Reciprocity, Homogeneity and Loyal Cooperation: Dealing with Recalcitrant National Courts? in: EFTA Court., Ed., The EEA and the EFTA Court: Decentered Integration, Hart, Oxford/Portland Oregon 2015, 151 ff.

Barnard Catherine, European Union Law, Oxford University Press, Second Edition, 2014.

Barnard Catherine, EU Employment Law, Oxford University Press, Fourth Edition, 2012.

Bartie Susan/Gava John, Some Problems with Extrajudicial Writing, Sydney Law Review 34, 637 ff.

Batliner Andreas, Practical Issues Regarding the Application of EEA Law through the Eyes of a National Judge, in: EFTA Court, Ed., The EEA and the EFTA Court: Decentered Integration, Hart, Oxford/Portland Oregon 2015, 95 ff.

Batliner Andreas, Die Anwendung des EWR-Rechts durch liechtensteinische Gerichte – Erfahrungen eines Richters, LJZ 2004, 139 ff.

Baudenbacher Carl, Reciprocity, in: Baudenbacher, Ed., The Fundamental Principles of EEA Law: EEA-ities, Springer, 2017, 35 ff.

Baudenbacher Carl, Brexit, EFTA und EWR ("Brexit, EFTA and EEA"), Schweizerisches Institut für Auslandsforschung ("Swiss Institute of International Studies"), Zurich 2017, 87 ff.

Baudenbacher Carl, Ed., The Fundamental Principles of EEA Law - EEA-ities, Springer 2017.

Baudenbacher Carl, "[M]ust be interpreted in the light of economic considerations': some reflections on the case law of the EFTA Court", in: David/MacLennan/Komninos, Eds., Ian S. Forrester QC LLD, A Scot without Borders, Liber Amicorum, Volume II (Institute of Competition Law 2015), 90 ff.

Baudenbacher Carl, Ed., The Handbook of EEA Law, Springer, 2015.

Baudenbacher Carl, EFTA-domstolen og dens samhandling med de norske domstolene, 2013 *Lov og Rett*, 515 ff.

Baudenbacher Carl, Das Vorabentscheidungsverfahren im EFTA-Pfeiler des EWR ("The preliminary ruling procedure in the EFTA pillar of the EEA"), in: Schumacher/Zimmermann, Eds., 90 Jahre Fürstlicher Oberster Gerichtshof, Festschrift für Gert Delle Karth, Jan Sramek Verlag, 2013.

Baudenbacher Carl, Some Thoughts on the EFTA Courts Phases of Life, in: Judicial Protection in the European Economic Area, EFTA Court (Ed.), Stuttgart 2012, 2 ff.

Baudenbacher Carl, Swiss Economic Law Facing the Challenges of International and European Law. Report to the Swiss Jurists Day 2012, ZSR 2012 II, 419-673.

Baudenbacher Carl, The EFTA Court in Action. Five Lectures, Frankfurt, 2010.

Baudenbacher Carl, If Not State Liability, Then What? Reflections Ten Years After the EFTA Court's Sveinbjörnsdóttir Ruling, 10 Chicago Journal of International Law, 333 ff. (2009).

Baudenbacher Carl, Some Considerations on the Dialogue Between High Courts, in: Baudenbacher, Ed., Dispute Resolution, Stuttgart 2009, 175 ff.

Baudenbacher Carl, Der Finanzplatz Schweiz im Angesicht der Reziprozitätspolitik der EU, ELR 2006, 398 ff.

Baudenbacher Carl, Governments before the EFTA Court, in: Festskrift til Claus Gulmann, Copenhagen 2006, 23 ff.

Baudenbacher Carl, Der EFTA-Gerichtshof, das EWR-Abkommen und die Fortentwicklung des EG-Vertrags, Festschrift für Herbert Batliner, Vaduz 2004, 97 ff.

Baudenbacher Carl, Judicial Globalization: New Development or Old Wine in New Bottles? 38 Texas International Law Journal, 505 ff. (2003).

Baudenbacher Carl, Between Homogeneity and Independence: The Legal Position of the EFTA Court in the European Economic Area, 3 Columbia Journal of European Law, 169 ff. (1997).

Baudenbacher Carl, Wirtschafts-, schuld- und verfahrensrechtliche Grundprobleme der Allgemeinen Geschäftsbedingungen ("Basic economic law, contract law and procedural law problems of general terms and conditions of contract"), Zurich 1983.

Baudenbacher Carl, Suggestivwerbung und Lauterkeitsrecht ("Suggestive advertising and unfair competition law"), Zurich 1978.

Baudenbacher Carl/Clifton Michael-James, Courts of Regional Economic and Political Integration Agreements, in: Romano/Alter/Shany, Eds., The Oxford Handbook of International Adjudication, Oxford University Press, 2015.

Baudenbacher Carl/Haas Theresa, Webseiten als dauerhafte Datenträger ("websites as durable media"), GRUR Int, 6-2015, 519 ff.

Baudenbacher Carl/Haas Theresa, Proportionality as a Fundamental Principle of EEA Law, in: Baudenbacher, Ed., The Fundamental Principles of EEA Law: EEA-ities, Springer, 2017, 169 ff.

Baudenbacher, Carl/Speitler, Philipp, Der Syndikus der Gegenwart – Interessensvertreter oder Anwalt des Rechts? NJW 2015, 2011 ff.

Baudenbacher Carl/Tresselt Per/Örlygsson Thorgeir, Eds., The EFTA Court Ten Years On, Hart, Oxford/Portland Oregon 2005.

Baudenbacher Laura Melusine, Aspects of Competition Law Enforcement in Selected European Jurisdictions, 37 European Competition Law Review 2016, 343 ff.

Baudenbacher Laura Melusine, Vom gemeineuropäischen zum europäischen Rechtsmissbrauchsverbot, Baden-Baden 2016.

Baudenbacher-Tandler Doris, Schutz vor neuen Anlegerrisiken, Berlin/St. Gallen 1988.

Baumol William J./Panzar John C./Wilig R Robert D., Contestable Markets and the Theory of Industry Structure, 1982.
Baur Georges, Decision-Making Procedure and Implementation of New Law, in: Baudenbacher, Ed., The Handbook of EEA Law, Springer, 2016, 45 ff.
Baur Georges, Suspension of Parts of the EEA Agreement: Disputes About Incorporation, Consequences of Failure to Reach Agreement and Safeguard Measures, in: Baudenbacher, Ed., The Handbook of EEA Law, Springer, 2016, 69 ff.
Baur Georges, Preliminary Rulings in the EEA – Bridging (Institutional) Homogeneity and Procedural Autonomy by Exchange of Information, in: EFTA Court., Ed., The EEA and the EFTA Court: Decentered Integration, Hart, Oxford/Portland Oregon 2015, 169 ff.
Bayard Olivier, EUROPÄISCHE INTEGRATION IM NEUTRALEN VERBUND? Der schweizerische Assoziationsversuch mit der EWG 1961–1963, in: Schweizerisches Bundesarchiv BAR, Gouvernementale Aussenpolitik (EUROPEAN INTEGRATION IN A NEUTRAL ALLIANCE? The Swiss association attempt with the EEC 1961–1963, in: Swiss Federal Archives BAR, Governmental Foreign Policy), Berne 1999, 87 ff.
Bellamy Christopher, ECHR and competition law post Menarini: An overview of EU and national case law, Christopher Bellamy, e-Competitions, N°47946, 5 July 2012.
Benvenisti Eyal, Reclaiming Democracy: The Strategic Uses of Foreign and International Law by National Courts, 102 American Journal of International Law, 241 ff. (2008).
Bergsteinsdóttir Guðrún, Positive action within the field of sex-equality in the context of EEA law, European Journal of Law Reform, Vol. 5 (2003), Issue 3–4, 447 ff.
Bernitz Ulf, The Application of EEA Law in Sweden, in: Monti/von und zu Liechtenstein/Vesterdorf/Westbrook/Wildhaber, Eds., Economic Law and Justice in Times of Globalisation, Festschrift for Carl Baudenbacher, Baden-Baden/Berne/Vienna 2007, 29 ff.
Bernitz Ulf, European Law in Sweden, Stockholm 2002.
Bernitz Ulf, The EEC-EFTA Free Trade Agreements with Special Reference to the Position of Sweden and the other Scandinavian EFTA Countries, 1986 CMLRev. 567.
Björgvinsson Davíð Þór, Application of article 34 of the ESA/Court Agreement by the Icelandic courts; in Monti/von und zu Liechtenstein/Versterdorf/Westbrook/Wildhaber, Economic Law and Justice in Times of Globalisation, Festschrift for Carl Baudenbacher, Nomos Publishers, 2007.
Björgvinsson Davíð Þór, EES-réttur og landsréttur, Reykjavík, Bókaútgáfan Codex, 2006.
Björgvinsson Kjartan Bjarni, Free Movement of Persons, in: Baudenbacher, Ed., The Handbook of EEA Law, Springer, 2016, 473 ff.
Boettke Peter J., Which Enlightenment, Whose Liberalism?: Hayek's Research Program for Understanding the Liberal Society, http://ebooks.bharathuniv.ac.in/gdlc1/gdlc4/Arts_and_Science_Books/commerce/economics/Economics/Boettke/Boettke%20-%20Which%20Enlightenment,%20Whose%20Liberalism%20 ~ %20Hayek%27s%20Re.pdf.
Bork Robert, The Antitrust Paradox: A Policy at War with Itself, New York 1978.
Bornkamm Joachim, The German Supreme Court: An Actor in the Global Conversation of High Courts, 39 Texas International Law Journal, 415 ff. (2004).
Botschaft zu einem Bundesgesetz über Kartelle und andere Wettbewerbsbeschränkungen (Kartellgesetz, KG) of 23 November 1994, BBl 1995 I 468, 502 ff. ("Dispatch on a Federal Act on Cartels and Other Restraints of Competition (Cartel Act, KG) of 23 November 1994, Federal Gazette 1995 I 468, 502 ff.").
Bourgeois, Jacques, Ne bis in idem and Enforcement of EEA Competition Rules, in: Monti/von und zu Liechtenstein/Vesterdorf/Westbrook/Wildhaber, Eds., Economic Law and Justice in Times of Globalisation, Festschrift for Carl Baudenbacher, Baden-Baden/Berne/Vienna 2007, 313 ff.
Brancaccio Laura, The Standard of Judicial Review of the ICA's Decisions: The Italian Supreme Court Rules on the ACEA Case, Rivista Italiana di Antitrust/Italian Antitrust Review N. 3 (2014), 241 ff.

Bronckers Marco, Exceptions to Liberal Trade in Foodstuffs: The Precautionary Approach and Collective Preferences, in: Baudenbacher/Tresselt/Örlygsson, Eds., The EFTA Court Ten Years On, Oxford and Portland, Oregon 2005, 105.

Bronckers Marco/Vallery Anne, Norway Post: The EFTA Court advances the debate on human rights and administrative competition law enforcement, 2012 ELR, 108 ff.

Brown L. Neville/Jacobs Francis G., The Court of Justice of the European Communities, London, 1977.

Brown L. Neville/Kennedy Tom, The Court of Justice of the European Communities, 5th ed., London 2000.

Bull Henrik, 'Shall be Made Part of the Internal Legal Order': The Legislative Approaches, in: EFTA Court., Ed., The EEA and the EFTA Court: Decentered Integration, Hart, Oxford/Portland Oregon 2015, 203 ff.

Bull Henrik, European Law and Norwegian Courts, in: Mueller-Graff/Selvig, Eds., The Approach to European Law in Germany and Norway, Berlin 2004, 95 ff.

Bull Henrik, The EEA Agreement and Norwegian Law, E.B.L.Rev. 1994, 291.

Buschle Dirk, The Free Movement of Capital in the EEA – A Lehrstück in Homogeneity, in: Monti/von und zu Liechtenstein/Vesterdorf/Westbrook/Wildhaber, Eds., Economic Law and Justice in Times of Globalisation, Festschrift for Carl Baudenbacher, Baden-Baden/Berne/Vienna 2007, 75 ff.

Buschle, Dirk/Jourdan-Andersen, Brigitte, Energy Law, in: Baudenbacher, Ed., The Handbook of EEA Law, Springer, 2016, 773 ff.

Buxbaum Hannah L., The Private Attorney General in a Global Age: Public Interests in Private International Antitrust Litigation (2001). Articles by Maurer Faculty. Paper 387, http://www.repository.law.indiana.edu/facpub/387.

Buxbaum Richard M., Die private Klage als Mittel zur Durchsetzung wirtschaftspolitischer Rechtsnormen, Karlsruhe 1972.

Calabresi Guido, Some Thoughts on Risk Distribution and the Law of Torts, 70 Yale Law Journal 499 (1961).

Cardozo Benjamin N., The Nature of the Judicial Process, Quid Pro, LLC, 2010.

Cashin Ritaine Eleonor/Lein Eva, La notion de proportionnalité appliquée au droit des jeux de hasard - Les cas Placanica et Autorité de surveillance de l'AELE/Royaume de Norvège, Schweizerisches Jahrbuch für Europarecht = Annuaire suisse de droit européen 2006/2007, 355 ff.

Chalmers Damian, *Icesave* – Limited Homogeneity and Unlimited Judicial Interpretation, in: EFTA Court., Ed., The EEA and the EFTA Court: Decentered Integration, Hart, Oxford/Portland Oregon 2015, 407 ff.

Chalmers Damian/Davies Gareth/Monti Giorgio, European Union Law, Cambridge University Press, 3rd ed., 2014.

Clark John Maurice, Competition as a Dynamic Process, Washington 1961.

Coase Ronald H., The Problem of Social Cost, The Journal of Law & Economics, Vol. 3 (Oct 1960), 1 ff.

Cohen-Eliya Moshe/Porat Iddo, Proportionality and the Culture of Justification, 59 American Journal of Comparative Law 463 ff. (2011).

Cordewener Axel, Wie drei Richter aus Island, Liechtenstein und Norwegen auszogen, die EU-Staaten das Fürchten zu lehren! ("How three Judges from Iceland, Liechtenstein and Norway went out to teach the EU States a lesson!"), Finanz-Rundschau, 8 April 2005.

Easterbrook Frank, The Limits of Antitrust, University of Chicago Law Occasional Paper, No. 21 (1985). University of Chicago Law Occasional Paper, No. 21 (1985).

EFTA Court, Ed., Judicial Protection in the European Economic Area, Stuttgart 2012.

EFTA Court, Ed., The EEA and the EFTA Court. Decentered Integration, Hart, Oxford/Portland Oregon 2015.

EFTA, EFTA 1960–2010: Elements of 50 Years of European History, 2010.

EFTA, European Economic Area 1994–2009, 2009.

Einarsson Ólafur Jóhannes, Articles 30–33 EEA, Recognition of diplomas, certificates, Freedom of establishment, Exemptions for exercise of official authority, Exemptions, in: Arnesen/Fredriksen/Graver/Mestad/Vedder, Agreement on the European Economic Area. A Commentary, 2018.

Eliantonio Mariolina/Stratieva Nelly, From Plaumann, Through UPA and Jégo-Quéré, to the Lisbon Treaty: The Locus Standi of Private Applicants Under Article 230(4) EC Through a Political Lens, https://www.researchgate.net/publication/228220333_From_Plaumann_Through_UPA_and_Jego-Quere_to_the_Lisbon_Treaty_The_Locus_Standi_of_Private_Applicants_Under_Article_2304_EC_Through_a_Political_Lens.

Entner-Koch Andrea/Bischof Thomas, Liechtenstein EEA Coordination Unit, in: Baudenbacher, Ed., The Handbook of EEA Law, Springer, 2016, 241 ff.

Eucken Walter, Grundsätze der Wirtschaftspolitik ("Principles of Economic Policy"), UTB, Stuttgart, 7th Edition, 2004 (1st edition 1952).

Falch, Ingvald, Carl Baudenbacher trer av ("Carl Baudenbacher steps down"), Lov og Rett 2018, 320 f.

Falch, Ingvald, Art. 4 EEA, in: Arnesen/Fredriksen/Graver/Mestad/Vedder, Agreement on the European Economic Area. A Commentary, 2018.

Femi Alese, Federal Antitrust and EC Competition Law Analysis, New York (NY) 2008.

Fløistad Karin, Arts. 28, 29 EEA, Free movement of workers and Social security for workers and self-emplyed persons, in: Arnesen/Fredriksen/Graver/Mestad/Vedder, Agreement on the European Economic Area. A Commentary, 2018.

Fløistad Karin, Fundamental Rights and the EEA Agreement, ARENA Report No 1/2004, January 2004.

Forhandlingene ved Det 35 nordiske juristmøtet ("Proceedings of the 35th Nordic Law Conference"), Oslo 1999, 977 ff.

Forrester Ian, The Style of the EFTA Court, in: EFTA Court., Ed., The EEA and the EFTA Court: Decentered Integration, Hart, Oxford/Portland Oregon 2015, 21 ff.

Forman John, The EEA Agreement Five Years On: Dynamic Homogeneity in Practice and Its Implementation by the Two EEA Courts, 1999 CMLRev. 751 ff.

Fossum John Erik/Graver Hans Petter, Squaring the Circle on Brexit. Could the Norway model work? Bristol 2018.

Franklin Christian, Art. 3, Principle of loyalty, in: Arnesen/Fredriksen/Graver/Mestad/Vedder, Agreement on the European Economic Area. A Commentary, 2018.

Fredriksen Halvard Haukeland, Art. 105, Homogeneous interpretation of EU and EEA law, Art. 111, Dispute resolution in the EEA Joint Committee, Art. 112, Safeguard measures, Article 114, Rebalancing measures, in: Arnesen/Fredriksen/Graver/Mestad/Vedder, Agreement on the European Economic Area. A Commentary, 2018.

Fredriksen Halvard Haukeland, The Troubled Relationship between the Supreme Court of Norway and the EFTA Court—Recent Developments, 2014, 2, http://dspace.uib.no/bitstream/handle/1956/7861/The%20Troubled%20Relationship%20between%20the%20Supreme%20Court%20of%20Norway%20and%20the%20EFTA%20Court%20-%20Recent%20Developments.pdf?sequence=1&isAllowed=y.

Fredriksen Halvard Haukeland, EU/EØS rett in norske domstoler, Sub-Report to the Sejersted Report, 2011, http://www.europautredningen.no/wp-content/uploads/2011/04/Rap3-domstoler.pdf.

Fredriksen Halvard Haukeland, Watching the Rendezvous from the Sidelines—Norway, the EEA Agreement and the EFTA Court, in: Jørn Øyrehagen Sunde/Knut Einar Skodvin, eds., Rendezvous of European Legal Cultures, 2010, 97 ff.

Fredriksen Halvard Haukeland, Er EFTA-domstolen mer katolsk enn paven? Noen betraktninger om EFTA-domstolens dynamiske utvikling av EØS-retten og streben etter dialog med EF-domstolen ("Is the EFTA Court more Catholic than the Pope? Some considerations about the EFTA Court's dynamic development of EEA law and strive for dialogue with the European Court of Justice"), Tidsskrift for Rettsvitenskap 2009, 597 ff.

Fredriksen Halvard Haukeland/Mathisen Gjermund, EØS-rett, 3. Utgave, 2018.
Frick Mario, Liechtenstein Chamber of Lawyers, in: Baudenbacher, Ed., The Handbook of EEA Law, Springer, 2016, 331 ff.
Gadamer Hans Georg, Wahrheit und Methode ("Truth and Method"), De Gruyter, 2nd Ed., 2011.
van Gerven Walter, The Genesis of EEA Law and the Principles of Primacy and Direct Effect, 16 Fordham International Law Journal, 955 ff. (1992–93).
Goantă Catalina, Information Duties in the Internet Era: Case Note on Content Services Ltd v. Bundesarbeitskammer, European Review of Private Law/Revue européenne de droit privé/ Europäische Zeitschrift für Privatrecht 2013, 643 ff.
Goldoni Carlo, The Servant of Two Masters, Hall Lee, Ed., 1999 (written 1746).
Gorton Georg, Bestätigung der Staatshaftungsrechtsprechung des EFTA-Gerichtshofs, 2002 ELR, 260 ff.
Graver Hans Petter, The Effects of EFTA Court Jurisprudence on the Legal Orders of the EFTA States, ARENA Working Papers 04/18, 2004, http://www.sv.uio.no/arena/english/research/publications/arena-working-papers/2001-2010/2004/wp04_18.pdf.
Graver Hans Petter, Supranationality and National Legal Autonomy in the EEA-agreement, ARENA Working Papers 00/23, 2000, http://www.arena.uio.no/publications/wp00_23.htm.
Grendstad Gunnar/Shaffer William R./Waltenburg Eric N., When Justices Disagree. The Influence of Ideology and Geography on Economic Voting on the Norwegian Supreme Court, Retfærd (Nordic Journal of Law and Justice) 34(2), 2011, https://www.uib.no/filearchive/grendstadshafferwaltenburg-fc2011-retfaerd.pdf.
Grimm Dieter, Europa ja - aber welches? Zur Verfassung der europäischen Demokratie, München 2016.
Griswold Erwin, Law Schools and Human Relations, Washington University Law Quarterly, No 3, 1955, 217 ff.
Grosz Mirina, Sustainable Waste Trade Under WTO Law: Chances and Risks of the Legal Frameworks' Regulation of Transboundary Movements of Wastes, Zurich 2010.
Gylfason Thorvaldur/Holmström Bengt/Korkman Sixten/Söderström Hans Tson/Vihriälä Vesa, Nordics in Global Crisis, Vulnerability and resilience, Helsinki 2010.
Habermas Jürgen, Theory of Communicative Action, Volume One: Reason and the Rationalization of Society, 1981. Translated by Thomas A. McCarthy, Boston, Mass., 1984.
Haltern Ulrich, Europarecht. Dogmatik im Kontext ("European law. Legal doctrine in context"), 2nd ed., Tübingen 2007.
Hallvarðsson Einar Karl, Attorney General of Iceland, in: Baudenbacher, Ed., The Handbook of EEA Law, Springer, 2016, 225 ff.
Hamsun Knut, On Overgrown Paths, København/Los Angeles 1999, first published 1949.
Hancher Leigh/Ottervanger, Tom/Slot, Piet Jan, EU State Aids, 5th ed., 2016.
Harbo Tor-Inge, The Function of Proportionality Analysis in European Law, Boston/Leiden 2015.
Haucap Justus/Schwalbe Ulrich, Economic Principles of State Aid Control, 2011, http://www.dice.hhu.de/fileadmin/redaktion/Fakultaeten/Wirtschaftswissenschaftliche_Fakultaet/DICE/Discussion_Paper/017_Haucap_Schwalbe.pdf.
Von Hayek Friedrich August, Der Wettbewerb als Entdeckungsverfahren ("Competition as A Discovery Procedure"), Kiel 1968.
Hegel Georg Wilhelm Friedrich, Grundlinien der Philosophie des Rechts oder Naturrecht und Staatswissenschaft im Grundrisse (1821), Suhrkamp Werkausgabe, Bd. 7, Frankfurt am Main 1970.
Helfer Laurence R./Slaughter Anne-Marie, Why States Create International Tribunals: A Response to Professors Posner and Yoo, 93 California Law Review, ff. (2005).
Herndl Kurt, Der EFTA-Gerichtshof und Österreich – ein Beispiel für nützliche Zusammenarbeit? ("The EFTA Court and Austria - an example of useful cooperation?"), Afmælisrit ("Festschrift") Thór Vilhjálmsson, Reykjavík 2000, 247 ff.
L'Heureux-Dubé Claire, The Importance of Dialogue: Globalization and the International Impact of the Rehnquist Court, 34 Tulsa Law Journal, 15 ff. (1998).

Hirsbrunner Simon/Seidl Simone, Ein Urteil für eine Festung Europa im Dienstleistungsbereich? Besprechung des EuGH-Urteils Fidium Finanz ("A verdict for a Fortress Europe in the service sector? Discussion of the ECJ judgement Fidium Finanz"), Europarecht 2007, 503 ff.

Hirte Heribert, Anmerkung zu EFTA-Gerichtshof, Urteil v. 10.12.2010 Rs. E-1/10, EWiR Art. 5 RL 2004/25/EG 1/11, S. 133-134 (Periscopus) (keine Erhöhung des Pflichtangebotspreises allein aufgrund allgemeiner gesetzlicher Bestimmung zur Berücksichtigung des „Marktpreises") (no increase of the mandatory offer price based on a statutory provision to take "market pice" into account).

Hofstötter Bernhard, Rechtsfehlerhafte Abweisung einer EWR-Staatshaftungsklage als judikatives Unrecht? (Erroneous dismissal of a state liability action as judicial injustice?): (Urteil des Obersten Gerichtshofs [Judgment of the Supreme Court], 7. Dezember 2006 [CO.2004.2-25]), Jus & News 2007, 33 ff.

Holmes Oliver Wendell, The Common Law, Holmes Press, 2012.

Holter Dag Wernø, Legislative Homogeneity, in: Baudenbacher, Ed., The Fundamental Principles of EEA Law: EEA-ities, Springer, 2017, 1 ff.

Hoppmann Erich, Workable Competition als wettbewerbspolitisches Konzept, in: Besters, Ed., Theoretische und institutionelle Grundlagen der Wirtschaftspolitik, ("Workable Competition as a competition policy concept, in: Besters, Ed., Theoretical and institutional foundations of economic policy"), Berlin 1967, 145 ff.

Hoppmann Erich, Die Funktionsfähigkeit des Wettbewerbs, in: Jahrbücher für Nationalökonomie und Statistik ("Workable competition, in: Yearbooks for Economics and Statistics,"), Vol. 181, 251 ff.

Hoppmann Erich, Fusionskontrolle ("Merger control"), Tübingen 1972.

Horrocks John Wesley, A short history of mercantilism, 1925.

Hreinsson Páll, General Principles, in: Baudenbacher, Ed., The Handbook of EEA Law, Springer, 2016, 349 ff.

International Center for Ethics, Justice and Public Life of Brandeis University, Developments in International Justice, February 2013, http://www.brandeis.edu/ethics/internationaljustice/inthenews/2013/Feb2013.html.

Jakob Thinam/Schultheiß Christian, Das EWR-Abkommen ("The EEA Agreement"), in: Schröter/Jakob/Klotz/Mederer, Europäisches Wettbewerbsrecht, 2. Auflage, Baden-Baden 2014.

Jennar Raul Marc, Europe: d'étranges «pères fondateurs», https://blogs.mediapart.fr/raoul-marc-jennar/blog/141012/europe-d-etranges-peres-fondateurs.

Jóhannesson Jón, A History of the Old Icelandic Commonwealth, Íslendiga Saga, translated by Haraldur Bessason, The University of Manitoba Press 1974.

Johansson Martin, Judicial Protection in the EEA EFTA States – Direct Effect of EEA Law Revisited, in: EFTA Court., Ed., The EEA and the EFTA Court: Decentered Integration, Hart, Oxford/Portland Oregon 2015, 311 ff.

Jones Alison/Sufrin Brenda, EU Competition Law, 6th ed., Oxford 2016.

Jónsson Ásgeir, Why Iceland?: How One of the World's Smallest Countries Became the Meltdown's Biggest Casualty, McGraw-Hill Education 2009.

Jónsson Ásgeir/Sigurgeirsson Hersir, The Icelandic Financial Crisis. A Study into the World's Smallest Currency Area and its Recovery from Total Banking Collapse, London 2016.

Judge Lord, Our Independent Judiciary, in: The Safest Shield. Lectures, Speeches and Essays, Oxford/Portland Oregon 2015, 366 ff.

Kaczorowska-Ireland Alina, European Union Law, 4th ed., Routledge 2016.

Kafka Franz, The Trial, Parable of the Law, http://www.kafka-online.info/before-the-law.html (Original 1915).

Kälin Walter, The EEA Agreement and the European Convention for the Protection of Human Rights, 3 EJIL (1992), 341 ff.

Kantorowicz Hermann U., Der Kampf um die Rechtswissenschaft (The fight concerning legal science), Heidelberg 1906 (published under the pseudonym 'Gnaeus Flavius').

Kantzenbach Erhard, Die Funktionsfähigkeit des Wettbewerbs (Workable Competition), Göttingen 1966.

Keif Echo Marie, Logrolling in the Supreme Court, Thesis Harriet L. Wilkes Honors College of Florida Atlantic University, Jupiter FL, May 2008.

Kelsen Hans, Reine Rechtslehre (Pure Theory of Law), Tübingen 1960 (first published 1934).

Kelsey Benjamin C., Crisis in Iceland: Deposit-Guarantee Scheme Failure and State Liability, 38 Boston College International and Comparative Law Review, Electronic Supplement, 30 ff. (2015).

Keynes John Maynard, A Tract on Monetary Reform, 1923.

Kmiec Keenan D., The Origin and Current Meanings of "Judicial Activism", 92 California Law Review, 1441 (2004).

Kohler Christian, Dialog der Gerichte im europäischen Justizraum. Zur Rolle des EuGH bei der Auslegung des neuen Übereinkommens von Lugano, in: Monti/von und zu Liechtenstein/Vesterdorf/Westbrook/Wildhaber, Eds., Economic Law and Justice in Times of Globalisation, Festschrift for Carl Baudenbacher, Baden-Baden/Berne/Vienna 2007, 141 ff.

Kokott Juliane/Dittert Daniel, European Courts in Dialogue, in: EFTA Court., Ed., The EEA and the EFTA Court: Decentered Integration, Hart, Oxford/Portland Oregon 2015, 43 ff.

Konow Berte-Elen R., Art. 72 EEA, Provisions on consumer protection, in: Arnesen/Fredriksen/Graver/Mestad/Vedder, Agreement on the European Economic Area. A Commentary, 2018.

Kjønstad Asbjørn, Er Høyesterett statsvennlig? ("Is the Suprem Court state-friendly?"), 1999 *Lov og Rett*, 97 ff.

Kötz Hein/Schäfer Hans-Bernd, Judex economicus, Tübingen 2003.

Kraus Karl, Half-Truths and One-And-A-Half Truths: Selected Aphorisms, The University of Chicago Press, 1990.

Krause Hartmut, Periscopus and Clear Criteria in European Public Takeover Legislation. Comments on Periscopus AS vs Oslo Børs ASA and Erik Must AS (EFTA Court), ECFR, Volume 8 Issue 1 (2011), 70 ff.

Kuijper Pieter Jan/Bronckers Marco, WTO Law in the European Court of Justice, 2005 CMLRev. 1313 ff.

Lagrange Maurice, Address given by Advocate General Maurice Lagrange at the formal sitting of the Court on 8 October 1964, http://www.cvce.eu/obj/address_given_by_maurice_lagrange_8_october_1964-en-f2f00c1c-2587-497f-ace0-6890bf0cb85f.html, 1964.

Legal Realism - The Persuasion And Characteristics Of Individual Judges - Law, Cardozo, Court, and Courts - JRank Articles, http://law.jrank.org/pages/8160/Legal-Realism-Persuasion-Characteristics-Individual-Judges.html#ixzz5Ifkt3dIn.

Leitner Brian, American Legal Realism, The University of Texas School of Law, Public Law and Legal Theory Research Paper No. 042, October 2002.

Lenaerts Koen, The Free Movement of Goods in EEA Law: The *Philip Morris Norway*, *Commission v Italy* and *Mickelsson and Roos* Cases, in: EFTA Court., Ed., The EEA and the EFTA Court: Decentered Integration, Hart, Oxford/Portland Oregon 2015, 371 ff.

Lester Anthony, The Overseas Trade in the American Bill of Rights, 88 Columbia Law Review 537 ff. (1988).

Lewin David, Continental European Legislative and Judicial Trends: European Free Trade Association Court Defines "Durable Media" in Directive on Insurance Mediation, http://www.gccapitalideas.com/2011/06/01/continental-european-legislative-and-judicial-trends-european-free-trade-association-court-defines-%e2%80%9cdurable-media%e2%80%9d-in-directive-on-insurance-mediation/.

von Liechtenstein Nikolaus, The EEA Joint Committee – A Political Assessment? in: EFTA Court., Ed., The EEA and the EFTA Court: Decentered Integration, Hart, Oxford/Portland Oregon 2015, 475 ff.

Llewellyn, Karl, The Bramble Bush: On Our Law and Its Study, New York 1930.

Lutter Marcus/Bayer Walter/Schmidt Jessica, Europäisches Unternehmens- und Kapitalmarktrecht (European Company and Capital Market Law), 6. Ed., Berlin/Boston 2017.

Lyal Richard, Tax Law, in: Baudenbacher, Ed., The Handbook of EEA Law, Springer, 2016, 721 ff.

Mackenzie Ruth/Romano Cesare P.R./Shany Yuval/Sands Philippe, Manual on International Courts and Tribunals, Oxford University Press, 2nd Ed., 2010.

Magnússon, Skúli, The Authority of the EFTA Court, in: Baudenbacher, Ed., The Fundamental Principles of EEA Law: EEA-ities, Springer, 2017, 139 ff.

Magnússon, Skúli, Icelandic Courts, in: Baudenbacher, Ed., The Handbook of EEA Law, Springer, 2016, 277 ff.

Magnússon, Skúli, Efficient Judicial Protection of EEA Rights in the EFTA Pillar – Different Role for the National Judge? in: EFTA Court., Ed., The EEA and the EFTA Court: Decentered Integration, Hart, Oxford/Portland Oregon 2015, 117 ff.

Mahoney Paul, From Strasbourg and Back: Speculating about Human Rights Protection in the European Union, 32 Human Rights Law Journal, 73 ff. (2011).

Mahoney Paul G., The Common Law and Economic Growth: Hayek Might Be Right, The Journal of Legal Studies, Vol. 30, No. 2 (June 2001), 503 ff.

Mason Edward S., Market Power and Business Conduct: Some Comments, The American Economic Review, Vol. 46, No. 2, Papers and Proceedings of the Sixty-eighth Annual Meeting of the American Economic Association (May 1956), 471 ff.

Matei Emanuela, Fifty shades of fair exit taxation of corporations, Kluwer International Tax Blog, 27 November 2015, http://kluwertaxblog.com/2015/11/27/fifty-shades-of-fair-exit-taxation-of-corporations/.

von Matt Peter, Das Kalb vor der Gotthardpost. Zur Literatur und Politik der Schweiz (The Calf in the Path of the Gotthatd Mail Post), Munich 2012.

Mayer Michael, Staaten als Täter. Ministerialbürokratie und "Judenpolitik" in NS-Deutschland und Vichy-Frankreich. Ein Vergleich ("States as offenders. Ministerial bureaucracy and 'Jewish policies' in NS-Germany and Vichy-France. A comparison"), München 2010.

Mengozzi Paolo, The Advocates General and the EFTA Court, in: EFTA Court., Ed., The EEA and the EFTA Court: Decentered Integration, Hart, Oxford/Portland Oregon 2015, 53 ff.

Molinari Laura, The Effect of the Kalanke Decision on the European Union: A Decision With Teeth, But Little Bite, 71 St. John's L. Rev. 591.

Montesquieu (in full Charles-Louis de Secondat, baron de La Brède et de Montesquieu), De l'esprit des lois (1758), electronic edition, http://classiques.uqac.ca/classiques/montesquieu/de_esprit_des_lois/de_esprit_des_lois_tdm.html.

Morgan de Rivery Eric/Fall Alexandre, The EFTA Court – A Court of Business Law? in: EFTA Court., Ed., The EEA and the EFTA Court: Decentered Integration, Hart, Oxford/Portland Oregon 2015, 387 ff.

Müller Reto Hermann, Das Milizsystem unter besonderer Berücksichtigung der Organisation für wirtschaftliche Landesvorsorge (The militia system with special consideration of the Organisation for National Economic Provision), Diss. St. Gall 1979.

Müller-Graff Peter-Christian, The Impact of Climate, Geography and Other Non-Legal Factors on EC law and EEA law, in: Baudenbacher/Tresselt/ Örlygsson, Eds., The EFTA Court Ten Years On, Oxford and Portland, Oregon, 55 ff.

Myhre Jonas W., Parallel imports and "co-branding" of pharmaceuticals – analysis and comments, 2008 Nordiskt Immateriellt Rättsskydd, 388 ff.

Myhre Jonas W., The Icesave Judgment: Iceland did not fail to comply with the obligations in the Iceland Act No. 98/1999, implementing Directive 94/19/EC of 30 May 1994 on deposit-guarantee schemes, 2013 ELR, 38 ff.

Nietzsche Friedrich, Götzen-Dämmerung, Sprüche und Pfeile, 8., 1888, electronic edition, http://www.gutenberg.org/cache/epub/7203/pg7203-images.html.

Norberg Sven, Disputes in Intergovernmental Economic Relations of a Traditional Character and in those with Supranational Mechanisms, Respectively, in: Baudenbacher, Ed., Dispute Resolution, Stuttgart 2009, 43 ff.
Norberg Sven, Perspectives on the Future Development of the EEA Agreement, in: Afmaelisrit (Festschrift) Thór Vilhjálmsson, Reykjavik 2000, 367 ff.
Norberg Sven/Hökborg Karin/Johansson Martin/Eliasson Dan/Dedichen Lucien, The European Economic Area, EEA Law. A Commentary on the EEA Agreement, Stockholm 1993.
Norberg Sven/Johansson Martin, The History of the EEA Agreement and the First Twenty Years of Its Existence, in: Baudenbacher, Ed., The Handbook of EEA Law, Springer, 2016, 3 ff.
Nordby Thomas, The Role of Individual Lawyers in EEA Law, in: EFTA Court., Ed., The EEA and the EFTA Court: Decentered Integration, Hart, Oxford/Portland Oregon 2015, 141 ff.
Nordby Thomas/Nerland Kristoffer, Norwegian Bar, in: Baudenbacher, Ed., The Handbook of EEA Law, Springer, 2016, 309 ff.
Norwegian Ministry of Foreign Affairs, The EEA Agreement and Norway's other agreements with the EU, Meld. St. 5 (2012–2013) Report to the Storting (White Paper), https://www.regjeringen.no/contentassets/fc5aa7428fd04f23af2a251d1c8c6710/en-gb/pdfs/stm201220130005000engpdfs.pdf.
OECD 2017 Global Forum on Competition, http://www.oecd.org/competition/globalforum/.
Örlygsson Thorgeir, Iceland and the EFTA Court, Twelve Years of Experience, in: Monti/von und zu Liechtenstein/Vesterdorf/Westbrook/Wildhaber, Eds., Economic Law and Justice in Times of Globalisation, Festschrift for Carl Baudenbacher, Baden-Baden/Berne/Vienna 2007, 225 ff.
von Overbeck Alfred E., Some Observations on the Role of the Judge Under the Swiss Civil Code, 37 Louisiana Law Review, 681 ff. (1977).
Papadopoulos Thomas, Acquisition of Corporate Control and Clear Criteria in the Adjustment of the Mandatory Bid Price, March 2013, https://www.researchgate.net/publication/256054591_Acquisition_of_Corporate_Control_and_Clear_Criteria_in_the_Adjustment_of_the_Mandatory_Bid_Price.
Perju Vlad, Reason and Authority in the European Court of Justice, 49 Virginia Journal of International Law, 307 ff. (2009).
Pescatore Pierre, Discussion statement, in: Baudenbacher/Tresselt/Örlygsson, Eds., The EFTA Court Ten Years On, Oxford and Portland, Oregon, 143.
Pettiti Louis-Edmond, Independence of International Judges, in: Shetreet/Dechênes, Eds., Judicial Independence, Dordrecht/Boston/Lancaster 1985, 496 ff.
Pétursson Gunnar Thor, Article 11 EEA, Quantitative restrictions on imports, in: Arnesen/Fredriksen/Graver/Mestad/Vedder, Agreement on the European Economic Area. A Commentary, 2018.
Pfirter Didier, Diplomatic Conflict Resolution, in: Baudenbacher, Ed., Dispute Resolution, Stuttgart 2009, 21 ff.
Pisani-Ferry Jean/Röttgen Nobert/Sapir André/Tucker Paul/Wolff Guntram B., Europe after Brexit: A proposal for a continental partnership, Brussels 2016, http://bruegel.org/2016/08/europe-after-brexit-a-proposal-for-a-continental-partnership/.
Planzer Simon, Liga Portuguesa – the CJEU and its Mysterious Ways of Reasoning, 2009 ELR, 368 ff.
Planzer Simon, Gambling Law; in Baudenbacher, Ed., The Handbook of EEA Law, Springer, 2016, 687 ff.
Polley Romina, Third Party Access to File in Competition Cases, Morgan de Rivery, Eric/Fall Alexandre, The EFTA Court – A Court of Business Law? in: EFTA Court., Ed., The EEA and the EFTA Court: Decentered Integration, Hart, Oxford/Portland Oregon 2015, 435 ff.
Polley Romina/Clifton, Micheal-James, The Principles of Transparency and Openness, and Access to Documents, in: Baudenbacher, Ed., The Handbook of EEA Law, Springer, 2016, 625 ff.
Posner Eric A./Yoo John C., Reply to Helfer and Slaughter, 93 California Law Review, 957 ff. (2005).

Posner Eric A./Yoo John C., A Theory of International Adjudication, University of Chicago, Law & Economics Olin Working Paper No. 206; UC Berkeley Public Law Research Paper No. 146, 2004.
Posner Richard, Should a Judge Rely on the Law or His Own Common Sense? Slate, 18 September 2017, http://www.slate.com/articles/news_and_politics/jurisprudence/2017/09/should_a_judge_rely_on_the_law_or_his_own_common_sense.html?via=gdpr-consent.
Posner Richard A., Antitrust Law: An Economic Perspective, Chicago 1976.
Poulsen Thomas Christian, Norwegian Courts, in Baudenbacher, Ed., The Handbook of EEA Law, Springer, 2016, 257 ff.
Pound Roscoe, A Survey of Social Interests, 57 Harvard Law Review 1 (1943).
Pritchett Herman, The Development of Judicial Research, in: Joel Grossmann/Joseph Tanenhaus, Eds., Frontiers of Judicial Research, New York 1969, 42.
Pritchett Herman, The Roosevelt Court: A Study in Judicial Politics and Values, 1937–1947, New York 1948.
Raiser Ludwig, Rechtsschutz und Institutionenschutz im Privatrecht (Legal protection and institutional protection in private law), in: Summum ius summa iniuria, Tübingen 1963, 145 ff.
Rasmussen Hjalte, On Law and Policy in the European Court of Justice, Dordrecht 1986.
Ravarani Georges, To Refer or Not to Refer? Confession of a National Judge, in: EFTA Court, Ed., The EEA and the EFTA Court: Decentered Integration, Hart, Oxford/Portland Oregon 2015, 107 ff.
Reich Norbert, Understanding EU Law, Antwerpen/Oxford 2005.
Reiff Peter, Zusammenfassung von „Anmerkung zum EFTA-Gerichtshof vom 27.01.2010, E-4/09 (Anforderungen an Website eines Vermittlers als ‚dauerhafter Datenträger')", („Summary of Comment on the EFTA Court of 27.01.2010, E-4/09 [Requirements for an intermediary's website as ‚durable medium'"], VersR 2010, 793 ff.
Rognstad Ole-Andreas, Intellectual Property Law, in: Baudenbacher, Ed., The Handbook of EEA Law, Springer, 2016, 703 ff.
Romano, Cesare P., The Proliferation of International Judicial Bodies: The Pieces of the Puzzle, 31 New York University Journal of International Law and Politics, 709 ff. (1999).
Rosas Allan, Methods of Interpretation – Judicial Dialogue, in: Baudenbacher/Busek, Eds., The Role of International Courts, Heidelberg 2008, 185 ff.
Rosas Allan, The Content of Requests for Preliminary Rulings to the European Court of Justice and the EFTA Court – What are the Minimum Requirements? in: EFTA Court., Ed., The EEA and the EFTA Court: Decentered Integration, Hart, Oxford/Portland Oregon 2015, 83 ff.
Rust Alexander, To Tax or Not to Tax: Reflections on the Case Law of the EFTA Court, Morgan de Rivery, Eric/Fall Alexandre, The EFTA Court – A Court of Business Law? in: EFTA Court., Ed., The EEA and the EFTA Court: Decentered Integration, Hart, Oxford/Portland Oregon 2015, 459 ff.
de Sadeleer Nicolas, EU Environmental Law and the Internal Market, Oxford 2014.
Sandemose Aksel, En flyktning krysser sitt spor (Ein Flüchtling kreuzt seine Spur), 1933.
Sanders Andreas R. Dugstad/Sandvik Pål, Avoiding the resource curse? Democracy and natural resources in Norway since 1900, in: Badia-Miró/Pinilla/Willebald, Eds., Natural resources and economic growth, Routledge 2015, 313 ff.
Sánchez Rydelski Michael, State Aid, in: Baudenbacher, Ed., The Handbook of EEA Law, Springer, 2016, 575 ff.
Scalia Antonin, A Matter of Interpretation, Princeton University Press, 1998.
Schermers Henry G., The International Court of Justice in Relation to Other Courts, in: Muller/Raič/Thuránszky, Eds., The International Court of Justice: its Future Role After Fifty Years, Editorial Introduction, The Hague Boston London 1997, 261 ff.
Schermers Henry G., The Direct Application of Treaties with Third States: Note Concerning the Polydor and Pabst Cases, [1982] CMLRev. 563 ff.
Schiller Friedrich, The Death of Wallenstein, 2006, http://www.gutenberg.org/files/6787/6787-h/6787-h.htm (first published 1799).

Schirmbacher Martin, Kurznachricht zu „Anmerkung zum Urteil des EFTA-Gerichtshofs vom 27.01.2010, Az.: E-4/09 (Website als ‚dauerhafter Datenträger') (Short note on ‚Comment on the judgment of the EFTA Court of 27.01.2010, Ref.: E-4/09 [website as a ‚durable medium')", CR 2010, 262 ff.
Schmidt-Rimpler Walter, Grundfragen einer Erneuerung des Vertragsrechts („Basic Issues of a Renewal of Contract Law"), AcP 147 ff.
Skåre Jan, Betydningen av Høyesteretts sammensetning („The significance of the Supreme Court's composition"), 1999 *Lov og Rett*, 67 ff.
Schluep Walter R., Was ist Wirtschaftsrecht? ("What is economic law?"), Festschrift für Walther Hug, Berne 1968, 25 ff.
Schmauch Magnus, Equality, in: Baudenbacher, Ed., The Fundamental Principles of EEA Law: EEA-ities, Springer, 2017, 215 ff.
Schumpeter Joseph, Theorie der wirtschaftlichen Entwicklung ("The Theory of Economic Development"), 1912.
Schweizer, Rainer J., Die schweizerischen Gerichte und das europäische Recht ("The Swiss courts and European law"), ZSR 1993 II, 570 ff.
Sejersted Fredrik, Between Sovereignty and Supranationalism in the EEA Context, in: Müller-Graff/Selvig, Eds., The European Economic Area: Norways Basic Status in the Legal Construction of Europe, Berlin 1997, 43 ff.
Semmelmann Constanze, Staatshaftung in Liechtenstein – ein Sonderweg im EWR?: (Fürstlicher Oberster Gerichtshof Liechtenstein, Urteil vom 7. Dezember 2006, CO.2004.2 – 25.) (State liability in Liechtenstein – a special path in the EEA?: [Princely Supreme Court Liechtenstein, judgment of 7 December 2006, CO.2004.2]), 1997 ELR, 131 ff.
Semmelmann Constanze, The future role of the non-competition goals in the interpretation of Article 81 EC, Global Antitrust Review 1, 15 ff. (2008).
Sevón Leif, Primacy and Direct Effect in the EEA. Some Reflections, in: Liber Amicorum Ole Due, Copenhagen 1994, 339 ff.
Sevón Leif/Johansson Martin, The protection of the rights of individuals under the EEA Agreement, [1999] 24 European Law Review, 380 ff.
Sigurbjörnsson Markús, To Refer or Not to Refer? in: EFTA Court., Ed., The EEA and the EFTA Court: Decentered Integration, Hart, Oxford/Portland Oregon 2015, 101 ff.
Skoghøy Jens Edvin A., Dommeratferd og dommerbakgrun ("Judges' behaviour and judges' background"), Fetstskrift till Torgny Håstad, 2010, 711 ff.
Skouris Vassilios, The Role of the Court of Justice of the European Union in the Development of the EEA Single Market: Advancement through Collaboration between the EFTA Court and the CJEU; in EFTA Court., Ed., The EEA and the EFTA Court: Decentred Integration, Oxford/Portland Oregon 2014, 3 ff.
Skouris Vassilios, The CJEU and the EFTA Court under the EEA Agreement: A Paradigm for International Cooperation between Judicial Institutions, in: Baudenbacher/Tresselt/Örlygsson, Eds., The EFTA Court Ten Years On, Oxford and Portland, Oregon, 2005, 123 ff.
Slaughter Anne-Marie, Judicial Globalization, 40 Va. J. Int'l L. 1103 ff. (2000).
Slotboom Marco M., Do public health measures receive similar treatment in European Community and World Trade Organization law? 37 Journal of World Trade, 553 ff. (2003).
Smith Adam, An Inquiry into the Nature and Causes of the Wealth of Nations, University of Chicago Press, 1977 (first published 1776).
Smith Adam, The Theory of Moral Sentiments, Gutenberg Publishers, 2011 (first published 1759).
Sombart Werner, Händler und Helden ("Merchants and Heroes"), Munich 1915.
de Sousa Pedro Caro, The European Fundamental Freedoms: A Contextual Approach, Oxford University Press, 2015.
Róbert R. Spanó, The EFTA Court and Fundamental Rights, European Constitutional Law Review 2017, 475 ff.
Speitler Philipp, Judicial Homogeneity as a Fundamental Principle of the EEA, in: Baudenbacher, Ed., The Fundamental Principles of EEA Law: EEA-ities, Springer, 2017, 19 ff.

Speitler Philipp, Right of Establishment and Freedom to Provide and Receive Services, in: Baudenbacher, Ed., The Handbook of EEA Law, Springer, 2016, 437 ff.

Stadler Arthur/Bovelet Caroline, Fortgeschrittene Internet-Websites als dauerhafte Datenträger: (Inconsult Anstalt vs. Finanzmarktaufsicht, EFTA-Gerichtshof, Urteil vom 27.01.2010, E-4/09) (Sophisticated websites as durable mediums: [Inconsult Anstalt vs. Financial Market Authority, EFTA Court, judgment of 27 January 2010, E-4/09], 2010 ELR, 177 ff.

Stadler Arthur/Weissel Jeannine, Fernabsatz-Richtlinie: Hyperlink kein 'dauerhafter Datenträger' ("Distance Selling Directive: Hyperlink not a 'durable medium'"), ELR 2012, 116 ff.

Steenkamp Petrus L., Protestant ethic: Contributing towards a meaningful workplace, HTS Teologiese Studies/Theological Studies, Vol. 69, No. 1, 2013, https://hts.org.za/index.php/hts/article/view/1315/3447.

Stefánsson Stefán Már, State Liability in Community Law and EEA Law, in: Baudenbacher/Tresselt/Örlygsson, Eds., The EFTA Court Ten Years On, Oxford and Portland, Oregon, 2005, 145 ff.

Steindorff Ernst, Politik des Gesetzes als Auslegungsmassstab im Wirtschaftsrecht ("The Policy of a Statute as an Interpretative Standard in Economic Law"), Festschrift Karl Larenz, Munich 1973, 217 ff.

Stiglitz Joseph E., Risk, Incentives and Insurance: The Pure Theory of Moral Hazard, The Geneva Papers on Risk and Insurance, 8 (No 26, January 1983), 4 ff.

Sundet Tron Løkken, Art. 68 Labour Law, in: Arnesen/Fredriksen/Graver/Mestad/Vedder, Agreement on the European Economic Area. A Commentary, 2018.

Svedman Sven Erik, Prosperity in the EEA, in: Baudenbacher, Ed., The Fundamental Principles of EEA Law: EEA-ities, Springer, 2017, 109 ff.

Sverdrup Ulf, Review of Baudenbacher/Tresselt/Örlygsson, Eds., The EFTA Court Ten Years On, European Law Books 2005.

Tamanaha Brian Z., Beyond the FORMALIST-REALIST Divide. The Role of Politics in Judging, Princeton and Oxford 2010.

Tamm Ditlev, The History of the European Court of Justice Since its Origin; in Rosas/Levits/Bot, Eds., The Court of Justice and the Construction of Europe: Analyses and Perspectives on Sixty Years of Case-law, Springer, 2013, 9 ff.

Tatham Allan Francis, Book Review: The EEA and the EFTA Court. Decentred Integration, 53 CMLRev. 1487 ff. (2016).

Teasdale Anthony/Bainbridge Timothy, The Penguin Companion to European Union, 2012, https://penguincompaniontoeu.com/.

Teigum Siri, Competition Law: A National Perspective, in: Baudenbacher, Ed., The Handbook of EEA Law, Springer, 2016, 547 ff.

Tellesbø Ola, Hvorfor Høyesterett er statsvennlig ("Why is the Supreme Court State-friendly"), Retfærd (Nordic Journal of Law and Justice) Årgang 29, 2006, 65 ff.

Temple Lang, John, The Principle of Sincere Cooperation in EEA Law, in: Baudenbacher, Ed., The Fundamental Principles of EEA Law: EEA-ities, Springer, 2017, 73 ff.

Temple Lang, John, Competition Law: The Brussels Perspective, in: Baudenbacher, Ed., The Handbook of EEA Law, Springer, 2016, 523 ff.

Temple Lang, John, Judicial Review of Competition Decisions under the European Convention on Human Rights and the Importance of the EFTA Court: The Norway Post Judgment, 2012 European Law Review, 464 ff.

Temple Lang, John, The Duties of National Courts Under Community Constitutional Law, 22 European Law Review, 3 ff. (1997).

Terris Daniel/Romano Cesare P.R./Swigart Leigh, The International Judge: An Introduction to the Men and Women Who Decide the World's Cases, Oxford University Press, 2nd Ed., Oxford 2007.

Timmermans Christiaan, Creative Homogeneity, in: Johansson/Wahl/Bernitz, Eds., A European for all seasons: Liber Amicorum in Honour of Sven Norberg, Brussels 2006, 471 ff.

Tison Michel, Do not attack the watchdog! Banking supervisor's liability after Peter Paul, Working Paper Series, Financial Law Institute, Universiteit Gent 2005.

Tobler Christa, Case note on Case E-1/02, EFTA Surveillance Authority v Norway, CMLRev, 41, 2004, 245 ff.

Tobler Christa, Die Fidium Finanz-Entscheidung des EuGH: ein Vorbote der Luxemburger Rechtsprechung zum bilateralen Recht? ("The Fidium Finanz judgment of the ECJ: a harbinger of Luxembourg jurisprudence on bilateral law?"), Schweizerische Zeitschrift für internationales und europäisches Recht 2006 397 ff.

Tønne Tore, Energy Policy: A Norwegian Perspective, 5 Northwestern Journal of International Law & Business, 722 ff. (1983–1984).

Þórisson Stefán Geir, Icelandic Bar, in: Baudenbacher, Ed., The Handbook of EEA Law, Springer, 2016, 319 ff.

Townley Christopher, Article 81 EC and Public Policy, Oxford/Portland Oregon 2009.

Tschütscher Klaus/Baudenbacher Carl «20 Jahre Unterzeichnung des EWR-Abkommens Ein Vierakter mit Original-Darstellern» ("'20th anniversary of the signature of the EEA Agreement' A four act play with original actors 2 May 2012 at Gasthof Löwen"), ed. by the Government of the Principality of Liechtenstein (Prime Minister Klaus Tschütscher) und the EFTA Court (President Carl Baudenbacher). With contributions of Klaus Tschütscher, Hans Brunhart, S.D. Prinz Nikolaus von und zu Liechtenstein, Claus-Dieter Ehlermann, Franz Blankart, Knut Almestad, Sven Norberg, Roland Marxer, Mario Frick, Carl Baudenbacher, Kurt Jäger, Andreas Batliner, Marino Baldi, Schaan 2012.

Twining, William, Karl Llewellyn and the Realist Movement, London 1973.

Ünsal Önder Erol, Is it possible to register the Vigeland Park statues as trademarks? Grupofis Marka/Patent 2017, https://www.grupofis.com/detay/is-it-possible-to-register-the-vigeland-park-statues-as-trademarks.

Ungerank Wilhelm, Liechtenstein Courts, in: Baudenbacher, Ed., The Handbook of EEA Law, Springer, 2016, 293 ff.

University of California at Berkeley School of Law, The Common Law and Civil Law Traditions, https://www.law.berkeley.edu/library/robbins/CommonLawCivilLawTraditions.html.

Utenfor og innenfor - Norges avtaler med EU, NOU 2012: 2, Utredning fra utvalg oppnevnt av Utenriksdepartementet 7. januar 2010 (Europautredningen) Avgitt til Utenriksdepartementet 17. januar (Outside and Inside: Norway's agreement's with the EU, 2012, Report from the committee appointed by the State Department 7. January 2010 [Europautredningen], delivered to the Foreign Ministry 17. January 2012), https://www.regjeringen.no/no/dokumenter/nou-2012-2/id669368/sec1.

Van der Loo Guillaume, The EU-Ukraine Association Agreement and Deep and Comprehensive Free Trade Area, 2016.

Vesterdorf Bo, EFTA Court 10th Anniversary, in: Baudenbacher/Tresselt/Örlygsson, Eds., The EFTA Court Ten Years On, Oxford/Portland, Oregon 2005, 187.

Viehweg Theodor, Topik und Jurisprudenz ("Topics and Law"), C.H. Beck Verlag, 5th ed, München 1974.

Viol Marion, Die Anwendbarkeit des Europäischen Kartellrechts auf Tarifverträge – unter rechtsvergleichender Betrachtung der Rechtsordnungen der Schweiz, der USA und Deutschlands ("The applicability of European antitrust law to collective agreements - from a comparative perspective of the legal systems of Switzerland, the USA and Germany"), St. Gallen 2004.

Voeten Eric, The Politics of International Judicial Appointments, 9 Chicago Journal of International Law, 387 ff. (2009).

Wahl Nils, Uncharted Waters: Reflections on the Legal Significance of the Charter under EEA law and Judicial Cross-Fertilisation in the field of Fundamental rights, in EFTA Court, Ed., The EEA and the EFTA Court: Decentred Integration, Hart Oxford/Portland Oregon 2014, 281 ff.

Waibel Michael, Iceland not responsible for the liabilities of its deposit insurance scheme, 28 January 2013, https://www.ejiltalk.org/iceland-not-responsible-for-the-liabilities-of-its-deposit-insurance-scheme/.

Waibel, Micheal/Petersen, Fiona, State Liability in the EEA, in: Baudenbacher, Ed., The Fundamental Principles of EEA Law: EEA-ities, Springer, 2017, 231 ff.

Weber Max, Die protestantische Ethik und der Geist des Kapitalismus ("The Protestant Ethic and the Spirit of Capitalism"), AREA Verlag ein Imprint der TANDEM VERLAG GmbH, 2005.

Wennerås, Pål, Art. 6 EEA, Homogeneity, Art. 3 SCA, Relevance of ECJ case law, in: Arnesen/Fredriksen/Graver/Mestad/Vedder, Agreement on the European Economic Area. A Commentary, 2018.

Wennerås, Pål, Attorney General of Norway, in: Baudenbacher, Ed., The Handbook of EEA Law, Springer, 2016, 211 ff.

Werner Philipp/Verouden Vincent, Eds., EU State Aid Control. Law and Economics, Kluwer 2016.

Wiedswang Kjetil/Elvestuen Per, Hovedsakelig harmløs. Den norske modellen i Brussel ("Mostly harmless. The Norwegian model in Brussels"), http://www.europautredningen.no/wp-content/uploads/2011/04/Rap_plux2.pdf.

Wieser Felix, Zu den Rechtsbegriffen "dauerhafter Datenträger" und "Textform" im Fernabsatz, ÖJZ 2010/18, 797 ff.

Wish Richard/Bailey David, Competition Law, 8th ed., Oxford 2015.

van der Woude Marc, The Friday Slot (13), Chillin'Competition, 2012, https://chillingcompetition.com/2012/11/16/the-friday-slot-13-marc-van-der-woude/.

Wren-Lewis Simon, The return of schools of thought in macroeconomics, 2012, https://voxeu.org/article/return-schools-thought-macroeconomics.

Zatschler Carsten, Priority, in: Baudenbacher, Ed., The Fundamental Principles of EEA Law: EEA-ities, Springer, 2017, 123 ff.

Zbinden Martin, Der Assoziationsversuch der Schweiz mit der EWG 1961–1963. Ein Lehrstück schweizerischer Europapolitik (Switzerland's attempt to associate itself with the EEC 1961–1963. A lesson in Swiss European politics), Berne 2006.

Zhang Angela Huyue, The Faceless Court, 38 University of Pennsylvania Journal of International Law, 71 ff. (2016).

Zurkinden Philipp/Baudenbacher Laura Melusine, Freihandelsabkommen und weitere Abkommen, ("Free trade agrements and other agreements"), in: Schröter/Jakob/Klotz/Mederer, Europäisches Wettbewerbsrecht, 2. Auflage, Baden-Baden 2014.

Newspaper Articles and Interviews

Andenæs Mads/Bjørge Eirik, Pikant fra Nupi ("Piquant from Nupi"), DN, 3 October 2017.

Ask Alf Ole, Oda Sletnes blir ny EU-ambassadør. Presidenten i EFTAs overvåkingsorgan Oda Helen Sletnes vil i sommerta over som Norges ambassadør til EU. ("Oda Sletnes to become the new EU ambassador. The President of the EFTA Surveillance Authority Oda Helen Sletnes will in the summer take over as Norway's ambassador to the EU"), Aftenposten, 7 May 2015, https://www.aftenposten.no/verden/i/jJBe/Oda-Sletnes-blir-ny-EU-ambassador.

Ask Alf Ole, EFTA-dommere tar hemmelige bijobber. ("EFTA judges take secret side activities."), E24, 14 March 2007, https://e24.no/utenriks/efta-dommere-tar-hemmelige-bijobber/1688307.

Baudenbacher Carl, Das EuGH-Modell im Tarnanzug. ("The ECJ model in camouflage suits. The Federal Council's proposals on framework agreements are an optical illusion."), BAZ, 13 March 2018, https://bazonline.ch/schweiz/standard/das-eughmodell-im-tarnanzug/story/11640108.

Baudenbacher Carl, Zur "Reset-Taste" in der Europapolitik ("On the 'Reset button' in European policy"), NZZ, 17 November 2017, https://www.nzz.ch/meinung/zur-reset-taste-in-der-europapolitik-ld.1329382.

Baudenbacher Carl (interview), 'I fear for EU when it loses Britain' – Top European judge on Brexit warning for bloc, Daily Express, 24 June 2017, https://www.express.co.uk/news/politics/819162/Brexit-news-Efta-court-head-judge-Carl-Baudenbacher-Britain-EU.

Baudenbacher Carl (interview), Leading European judge promotes plan for UK access to single market after Brexit, The Times, 21 August 2017, https://www.thetimes.co.uk/article/top-european-judge-reveals-plan-for-british-access-to-single-market-after-brexit-r7j637q5g.

Baudenbacher Carl, Die Schweiz sollte einen zweiten EWR-Anlauf nehmen ("Switzerland should make a second attempt to join the EEA"), NZZ, 22. Juni 2010, https://www.nzz.ch/die_schweiz_sollte_einen_zweiten_ewr-anlauf_nehmen-1.6201781.

Baudenbacher Carl (interview), Europa 2.0 ist denkbar ("Europe 2.0 is conceivable"), Wiener Zeitung, 16 February 2016, https://www.wienerzeitung.at/nachrichten/europa/europaeische_union/801311_Europa-2.0-ist-denkbar.html.

Baudenbacher Carl, EØS-avtalen: Sterkere enn noen gang? Etter 25 år må man stille spørsmålet om det var verdt innsatsen ("EEA agreement: Stronger than ever? After 25 years one has to ask whether it was worth the effort"). Bergens Tidende, 2 May 2017, https://www.bt.no/btmeninger/debatt/i/lP9Qk/EOS-avtalen-Sterkere-enn-noen-gang.

Baudenbacher Carl, Could the U.K. use the EFTA Court to resolve disputes following Brexit? 31 August 2017, LSE's Brexit Blog, http://blogs.lse.ac.uk/europpblog/2017/08/31/could-the-uk-use-the-efta-court-to-resolve-disputes-following-brexit/.

Baudenbacher Carl, Det er ting som tyder på at anstrengelsene for å bli kvitt dommer Christiansen var politisk motivert ("There are indications that the efforts to get rid of judge Christiansen were politically motivated"), advokatbladet, 3 April 2017, http://www.advokatbladet.no/2017/04/det-er-ting-som-tyder-pa-at-anstrengelsene-for-a-bli-kvitt-dommer-christiansen-var-politisk-motivert/.

Baudenbacher Carl, (interview) «Die EU müsste mehr Mitbestimmung anbieten als 1992» ("The EU would need to offer more co-decision than in 1992"), NZZ, 27 June 2016, https://www.nzz.ch/schweiz/aktuelle-themen/grossbritannien-im-ewr-20-die-eu-muesste-mehr-mitbestimmung-anbieten-als-1992-ld.91741.

Baudenbacher Carl, Obituary of Former EFTA Court President Thór Vilhjálmsson, 21 October 2015, http://www.eftacourt.int/fileadmin/user_upload/Files/News/Former_President_Thor_Vilhjalmsson.pdf.

Baudenbacher Carl, Europarechtliche Missverständnisse ("Misunderstandings regarding European law"), NZZ, 16 August 2013, https://www.nzz.ch/meinung/debatte/europarechtliche-missverstaendnisse-berns-1.18133727.

Baudenbacher Carl, Verzicht auf eigene Richter. Bern unterdrückt, was mit dem EWR zu tun hat ("Waiver of own judges. Berne suppresses what has to do with the EEA"), NZZ, 23 July 2013, https://www.nzz.ch/meinung/debatte/der-efta-gerichtshof-hat-gewicht-1.18121257.

Baudenbacher Carl, «Helvetische Lösung» mit der EU kaum möglich («Helvetic solution» hardly possible with the EU), NZZ, 3 January 2012, https://www.nzz.ch/helvetische_loesung_mit_der_eu_kaum_moeglich-1.14038189.

Bergens Tidende, Juridisk strid om EØS. EFTA-domstolens president mener norsk Høyesterett undergraver EØS-avtalen. Dette spørsmålet bør få en avklaring, ("Legal dispute about the EEA. The President of the EFTA Court believes the Norwegian Supreme Court undermines the EEA agreement. This question should be clarified"), 22 October 2013, https://www.bt.no/btmeninger/leder/i/EJ9Ol/Juridisk-strid-om-EOS.

Bodoni Stephanie, If Brexit Means Brexit, Little-Known Court Offers Non-ECJ Option, Bloomberg, 11 February 2018, https://www.bloomberg.com/news/articles/2018-02-11/if-brexit-means-brexit-little-known-court-offers-non-ecj-option.

Bowers Simon, Icesave ruling raises important moral hazard questions, The Guardian, 28 January 2013, https://www.theguardian.com/business/blog/2013/jan/28/icesave-ruling-moral-hazard-questions.

Brexit problem solved? The Law Society Gazette, 11 September 2017, http://directories.lawgazette.co.uk/news/obiter/brexit-problem-solved/5062786.fullarticle.

Carswell Simon, Norway facing 'hard Brexit' without transitional deal. Politician questions aptness of Norway/Sweden border as model for EU/UK, The Irish Times, 8 November 2017.

Control and Compromise. Isolation is not a price worth paying for absolute control over Britain's laws. A Swiss judge offers a solution to the thorniest Brexit challenge of all, Leading article, The Times, 21 August 2017, https://www.thetimes.co.uk/article/control-and-compromise-79hzr7k58.

CVP-Regierungskandidat auf SP-Stimmen angewiesen ("CVP government candidate depends on SP votes"), Der Standard, 6 September 2009, https://derstandard.at/1252036723680/CVP-Regierungskandidat-auf-SP-Stimmen-angewiesen.

Daum Matthias/Teuwsen Peer, Yves Rossier. Ein Bildhauer der Aussenpolitik ("Yves Rossier. A sculptor of foreign policy"), Die Zeit, 7 February 2013, https://www.zeit.de/2013/07/Yves-Rossier-Schweiz.

Epiney Astrid, Quadratur des Kreises gelungen ("Squaring of the circle successful"), NZZ, 23 August 2013, https://www.nzz.ch/meinung/quadratur-des-kreises-gelungen-1.18137608.

Falnes Johan, Solberg: Vi må lære oss å slåss for EØS ("Solberg: We must learn to fight for the EEA"), Nationen 31 March 2018, https://www.dn.no/nyheter/2018/03/30/1119/EUs-energibyra-Acer/erna-solberg-vi-ma-laere-oss-a-slass-for-eos.

Freisinniger Didier Burkhalter neuer Bundesrat ("Liberal Didier Burkhalter new Federal Councillor"), Der Standard, 16 September 2009, https://derstandard.at/1252771492832/Freisinniger-Didier-Burkhalter-neuer-Bundesrat.

Hirst Nicholas, Norway accused of meddling with judicial independence, POLITICO, 4 January 2017, https://www.politico.eu/article/norway-accused-of-meddling-with-judicial-independence-per-christiansen-efta/.

Hirst Nicholas, Norway bows to criticism and re-appoints judge for full term. EFTA reverses December decision for a half-term appointment, POLITICO, 16 January 2017, https://www.politico.eu/article/norway-bows-to-criticism-and-re-appoints-judge-for-full-term/.

Johansen Signe, Brunost: the Norwegian cheese that's a hot topic, The Guardian, 24 January 2013, https://www.theguardian.com/lifeandstyle/wordofmouth/2013/jan/24/brunost-norwegian-cheese-hot-topic.

Johnsen Alf Bjarne, Norsk toppdommer kan bli byttet ut ("Norwegian top judge may be replaced"), Verdens Gang, 6 September 2016, https://www.vg.no/nyheter/innenriks/i/227al/norsk-toppdommer-kan-bli-byttet-ut.

Johnsen Alf Bjarne, EFTA-domstolen forlanger upartisk dommer: Advarer Norge ("The EFTA Court demands impartial judge: warns Norway"), Verdens Gang, 7 September 2016, https://www.vg.no/nyheter/innenriks/i/Kwgly/efta-domstolen-forlanger-upartisk-dommer-advarer-norge.

Jones Marc, Britain might be able to use EFTA court after Brexit, court head says, Reuters, 14 September 2017, https://www.reuters.com/article/britain-eu-efta/britain-might-be-able-to-use-efta-court-after-brexit-court-head-says-idUSL5N1LV45O.

Jones Marc, UK could get outsized power if it joins EFTA Court after Brexit - Court head, Reuters, 29 November 2017, https://www.reuters.com/article/uk-britain-eu-eftacourt/uk-could-get-outsized-power-if-it-joins-efta-court-after-brexit-court-head-idUSKBN1DT21R.

Kagge Gunnar, Frontalangrep på Høyesterett ("Frontal attack on the Supreme Court"), Aftenposten of 21 October 2013, https://www.aftenposten.no/norge/i/9mylp/Frontalangrep-pa-Hoyesterett.

Kong Carl I 20 år, ("King Carl 20 years on"), Bergens Tidende, 16 June 2014.

Lawsky David, A small dog with a big bite. How did the EFTA court acquire an influence out of all proportion to its tiny size? Review of "Baudenbacher, The EFTA Court in Action: Five lectures", European Voice, 11 October 2010, https://www.politico.eu/article/a-small-dog-with-a-big-bite/.

Martyn-Hemphill Richard, Iceland PM: We dodged the EU bullet. Gunnlaugsson claims the country wouldn't have rebounded as quickly had it been in the bloc, POLITICO, 11 February 2015, https://www.politico.eu/article/iceland-pm-eu-bullet-membership-assession/.

Milne Richard, Oslo thaws on UK joining EEA after Brexit, FT, 13 May 2018, https://www.ft.com/content/fda3fa32-538a-11e8-b3ee-41e0209208ec-.

Morgan Sam, EFTA court boss quits, reducing UK's post-Brexit chances, Euractiv, 16 November 2017, https://www.euractiv.com/section/uk-europe/news/efta-court-boss-quits-reducing-uks-post-brexit-chances/.

Müller Reinhard, Zigaretten als Bückware? ("Cigarettes as under the counter goods?"), FAZ, 7 September 2011, http://www.faz.net/aktuell/politik/staat-und-recht/rechtspersonen/carl-baudenbacher-zigaretten-als-bueckware-11133143.html.

Nytt storverk om EØS-avtalen (New major work on the EEA Agreement), http://www.advokatbladet.no/2018/02/nytt-storverk-om-eos-avtalen.

Nordby Thomas, EFTA-domstolen undergraves ("EFTA Court undermined"), DN of 14 March 2013.

Oberster Richter der Efta attackiert Bundesrat ("Highest EFTA Justice Attacks Federal Council"), HandelsZeitung, 17 July 2013, https://www.handelszeitung.ch/politik/oberster-richter-der-efta-attackiert-bundesrat-470201.

Piris Jean-Claude, Britain is deluding itself over single market access, Financial Times, 16 November 2017, https://www.ft.com/content/7a3d13ee-cabf-11e7-8536-d321d0d897a3.

Risch Manfred, Kreative Denkpausen zwischen Bern und Paris (Creative Breaks between Berne and Paris), NZZ of 7 September 2012.

Romei Valentina/Murphy Hannah, Boom, bust and boom again: Iceland's economy in charts, Financial Times, 17 March 2017, https://www.ft.com/content/26270ef4-0a35-11e7-97d1-5e720a26771b.

Rossier Yves (interview), Es gibt keine fremden Richter ("There are no foreign judges"), Blick, 18 October 2013, https://www.blick.ch/news/politik/staatssekretaer-yves-rossier-ueber-den-konfliktfall-mit-der-eu-es-gibt-keine-fremden-richter-id2481020.html.

Rossier Yves, Souveränitätsverlust beim EWR-Andocken ist grösser ("Loss of sovereignty in case of EEA docking is greater"), NZZ, 16 August 2013, https://www.nzz.ch/schweiz/souveraenitaetsverlust-beim-ewr-andocken-ist-groesser-1.18133645.

Saga Ends with Icesave Redemption, FT, 29 January 2013, https://www.ft.com/content/78b96684-6a21-11e2-a80c-00144feab49a.

Schmoll Heike, "Professoren, mischt Euch endlich wieder ein!" (professors, get finally back in the game!), FAZ of 1 April 2017.

Schott Clausdieter, "Fremde Richter – fremde Gerichte". Tradition oder Missverständnis? ("Foreign judges - foreign courts". Tradition or misunderstanding,), NZZ, 26/27 September 1992, 25.

Spalinger Andrea, Stilles Arbeiten im Schatten des grossen Bruders ("Quiet work in the shadow of the big brother"), NZZ, 11 February 2004.

Sverdrup Ulf, Når dommer blir advokat ("When a judge becomes an advocate"), DN, 2 October 2017, https://www.dn.no/avisen/DN_2017-10-02/4.

The Icesave ruling, In the cooler. A court ruling over an Icelandic bank is a blow to global banking, The Economist, 2 February 2013, https://www.economist.com/finance-and-economics/2013/02/02/in-the-cooler.

Viel Lärm um wenig – enttäuschender Bericht der norwegischen EWR-Evaluationskommission ("Much ado about little – disappointing report of the Norwegian EEA Evaluation Committee"), Liechtensteiner Vaterland of 20 January 2012.

Vermes Thomas, EFTA-domstolens president håner norske Europa-politikere ("The President of the EFTA Court is scorning Norwegian politicians"), ABC Nyheter, 13 May 2017, https://www.abcnyheter.no/nyheter/politikk/2017/05/13/195302230/efta-domstolens-president-haner-norske-europa-politikere.

Vermes Thomas, Oda Sletnes blir ny ESA-president ("Oda Sletnes to become the new ESA president"), ABC Nyheter, 17 June 2011, https://www.abcnyheter.no/nyheter/2011/06/17/132636/oda-sletnes-blir-ny-esa-president.

Vogel Toby, Yves Rossier – cosmopolitan diplomat. Profile of the secretary of state at the Swiss foreign ministry, European Voice of 26 June 2014, (https://www.politico.eu/article/yves-rossier-cosmopolitan-diplomat).

Vuichard Florence, Der Schnelldenker Yves Rossier ("The high-speed thinker Yves Rossier"), Bilanz, 18 March 2014, https://www.bilanz.ch/machtnetz/der-schnelldenker-yves-rossier-362788.

Wiedswang Kjetil, Kong Carl av EØS ("King Carl of the EEA"), Dagens Næringsliv, 16 April 2011, https://www.dn.no/meninger/kommentarer/2011/04/16/kong-carl-av-eos.

Wiedswang Kjetil, Makt i Brussel ("Power in Brussels), DN 2 February 2007, http://www.dn.no/meninger/kommentarer/2007/02/07/makt-i-brussel.

Wiedswang Kjetil, Frykter sveitser ("Afraid of the Swiss guy"), DN 16 January 2006.

Wiedswang Kjetil, Milliardspill i Luxemburg ("Billiongame in Luxembourg"). DN 16 January 2006.

Wintour Patrick, Efta court chief visits UK to push merits of 'Norway model', *The Guardian*, 3 September 2017, https://www.theguardian.com/world/2017/sep/03/efta-court-president-suggests-uk-should-join-efta-to-end-brexit-crisis.

Zuwanderung: Unterhändler Rossier hat eine kleine Idee ("Immigration: Negotiator Rossier has a small idea"), TagesAnzeiger of 20 February 2014, (https://www.tagesanzeiger.ch/schweiz/Zuwanderung-Unterhaendler-Rossier-hat-eine-kleine-Idee/story/22965924).

MIX
Papier aus verantwortungsvollen Quellen
Paper from responsible sources
FSC® C105338

If you have any concerns about our products,
you can contact us on
ProductSafety@springernature.com

In case Publisher is established outside the EU,
the EU authorized representative is:
Springer Nature Customer Service Center GmbH
Europaplatz 3, 69115 Heidelberg, Germany

Printed by Libri Plureos GmbH
in Hamburg, Germany